Foundations of Education

FOUNDATIONS

Third Edition

By the same author

The Educational Philosophy of National Socialism (Yale)
The Education of the Mexican Nation (Columbia)
Higher Learning in Britain (California)
Existentialism and Education (Wiley, 1964)
Introduction to the Philosophy of Education (Wiley, 1964)
The Art and Science of Creativity (Holt)
Educational Anthropology (Wiley, 1965)
Logic and Language of Education (Wiley, 1966)
Education and Economic Thought (Wiley, 1968)
Education and the Scientific Mind (Wiley, Fall, 1971)

OF EDUCATION

George F. Kneller, Editor

Professor of Education
University of California
Los Angeles

John Wiley & Sons, Inc.

New York · London · Sydney · Toronto

Copyright © 1963, 1967, 1971 by John Wiley & Sons, Inc.

All rights reserved. Published simultaneously in Canada.

No part of this book may be reproduced by any means, nor transmitted, nor translated into a machine language without the written permission of the publisher.

Library of Congress Catalogue Card Number: 78-138913
ISBN 0-471-49505-0

Printed in the United States of America

10 9 8 7 6 5 4 3 2 1

Preface

This book is designed to introduce the student to the principal ideas and findings of the discipline of education. This discipline includes all branches of inquiry—from history and philosophy through the social sciences to theories of testing—that concern themselves with educational institutions and their sociocultural setting. The leading ideas that guide inquiry in these fields, and the facts that they have helped to establish, together constitute the foundations of education. They are what any person needs to know if he wishes to make wise decisions about education or to pursue the study of it.

This book is also a symposium. Its contributors are among the foremost authorities on American education today. At my request each of them has written from his own point of view. Each has made his own suggestions for the improvement of education.

Although a collection of essays of this kind may lack unity of theme and tone, it has the merit of giving specialist views on many aspects of education. Moreover, as Professor Cohen shows in Chapters 1 and 2, the diversity of American educational thought and practice reflects the diversity of American culture. It is fitting, therefore, that there should be diversity in educational expression. Nevertheless, a greater effort has been made to give coherence to the work as a whole and to provide continuity from chapter to chapter than is the rule with most symposia.

In this third edition, all previous chapters have been completely revised. In response to dramatic developments during the past five years chapters have been added on minorities, aesthetics, existentialism, logic and analysis, technology, political socialization, and educational research.

The history of education has been reinterpreted and expanded to two chapters. Finally, the chapters have been reordered, so that social foundations now precede philosophic foundations. These revisions have been made as a result of a careful study of recent trends in conceiving and teaching courses in the foundations of education.

Since the parts of this text are relatively independent, the instructor may alter the sequence to suit his taste. He may begin with history and proceed to philosophy or vice versa. He may begin with structural foundations and continue with social foundations, or again the reverse. In any case it is not expected that all instructors will assign every chapter in the book.

Finally, let me say a word about the study of education as a discipline. Many teachers prefer to present the subject matter in terms of certain issues and problems that confront the educator today. One might call this a pragmatic, *ad hoc,* or problem-oriented approach to the study of education. Now I entirely agree that the ideas and findings that make up the discipline of education are of little value unless they can be used to improve the actual process of education or, if you like, to resolve particular educational problems. But this implies only that the knowledge gained should be usable or seen to be usable, not that the first principles of this knowledge need to be acquired in the context of problems to which they may be applied. The first task of a general study of education is to produce an understanding of education rather than a practical competence in teaching or administration. To this end, a general study of education should be organized around the concepts and facts by means of which education can be understood rather than around the problems that make such understanding necessary. A course cast in terms of certain problems is not likely to pass beyond those problems, whereas a course organized around principles will produce the general understanding of education that is applicable to *all* educational problems.

George F. Kneller

University of California
Los Angeles

Contents

❖❖

Part Three

PHILOSOPHIC FOUNDATIONS

Part Four

SCIENTIFIC FOUNDATIONS

Part Five

STRUCTURAL FOUNDATIONS

Foundations of Education

PART ONE

HISTORICAL FOUNDATIONS

1

The Forming of the Common School

Sol Cohen

❖❖

> Wee shall be as a Citty Upon a Hill, the eies of all people are uppon us; soe that if wee shall deale falsely with our god in this work wee have undertaken and soe cause him to withdrawe his present help from us, wee shall be made a story and a by-word through the world.
>
> *John Winthrop*

I. The Colonial Experience

The colonies established along the Atlantic seaboard during the early decades of the 17th century were essentially a new frontier of Western European civilization. The early colonists assumed that their culture would be transmitted through old and familiar means. But European culture endured a severe shock upon contact with the American environment. The first and second generations of settlers made a desperate effort to fight the powers of darkness and maintain the civilization they knew. The critical point was the transmission of culture to the young. All the colonies turned to this with the gravest concern. It is thus as part of the

3

story of the threat of barbarism and of a severe disorganization of the social mechanisms that had supported culture that the history of education in the colonial period may best be understood. In the course of adjustment to a new environment the familiar pattern of education was largely destroyed. By the late 18th century, education in America was a very different process from what anyone in the early 17th century would have expected. On almost every point the expectations of the first generation of settlers had been frustrated. These expectations form the necessary background for understanding the history of education in colonial America. The Puritans will be discussed more intensively than any other group of colonists. For nearly 100 years Puritans dominated New England and until quite recently, New England dominated American culture.

Religion was the heart of the matter, the most pervasive influence in colonial New England. "That which is our greatest comfort, and means of defense above all others," Francis Higginson wrote in *New England's Plantation*, "is, that we have here the true Religion and holy Ordinances of Almighty God taught among us . . . Thus we doubt not but God will be with us, and if God be with us, who can be against us?" Theirs was to be a society dedicated to the glory of God. To the 17th century Puritan, the ideal society was the society of believers governed by a hierarchy of the elect. From its inception, the Massachusetts Bay Colony joined Church and State into a unified theocracy that accepted the idea that education was a public responsibility whose chief aim was to produce pious and learned Christians. The search for sanctity, the quest for salvation, was uppermost. But salvation required learning, in pursuit of which all were supposed to join regardless of natural ability or worldly circumstance. When the colonists came to America, the study of the classical languages of Greek and Latin had become the staple of higher education. Many of the earliest Puritan leaders had been grounded in the classics in the grammar schools or universities of England and they moved promptly to establish similar institutions in America.

However, the society the early settlers had left in England had long depended on forms of education that were "largely instinctive and traditional, little articulated and little formalized." The family, the patrilinial group of extended kinship gathered into a single household—not the school—served as the central agency for education and the socialization of the child. Within these kinship groupings, skills that provided at least the first step in vocational training were taught and practiced. The family's role in vocational training was extended and formalized in a most important institution of education, apprenticeship, the typical English method of bringing up male children to be useful. Nor was apprenticeship limited to training in a craft. A master was expected to see to the literacy of his charges, and was required by law to bring them up in good Christian cultivation, and to see to their proper deportment. Most of the learned professions too, rested upon apprenticeship rather than formal training. Traditionally, the role of the State in the education of the young was passive and indirect. Schools were provided by private endowments, and by religious and charitable organizations. The exception to this policy of *laissez-faire* was a series of "Poor Laws" passed by Parliament in the late 16th century, which concerned the problem of poor relief. On the American frontier, the English heritage was drastically altered. Formal institutions of education were assigned new responsibilities. By the end of the colonial period, education had become controversial, deliberate, and formal; had become an agency of social change and a means of shaping the American character.

Nothing so clearly illustrates the Puritan determination to create their New Zion as their zeal for education. By 1636 it was time that education was seen to. Without it, the way of life could not be maintained. That year Harvard was founded, and at about the same time, the Boston Latin Grammar School was established. Harvard was based on Emmanuel College, Cambridge; the classical curriculum of the Boston Latin Grammar School followed English precedent. (And the dame schools, in which housewives taught children to read in their homes, resembled those in countless villages in England.) Before 1647, eleven of the sixty towns in New England had voluntarily established, and were supporting by various means—subscription, land rentals, tuition, endowment—grammar schools. Still, the family was expected to carry the greatest educational burden. Within a short time, however, it became clear that parents would not or could not be depended on to do their duty; they would have to be forced to by law. The famous Massachusetts Law of 1642 was one of a series of expediencies aimed at shoring up the weak structure of family discipline. Parents and masters were to be compelled to see to it that children and apprentices were taught to read and understand the principles of religion and the laws of the country, and also taught some definite calling or trade.

The Statute of 1642 required compulsory education of children, while placing the entire responsibility for their education upon masters and parents. It soon became apparent that schools would have to be maintained if children and youth were to receive the amount and kind of education deemed essential. Five years later, in 1647, the Massachusetts Bay Colony enacted the famous "Old Deluder Satan" Law. The Law of 1647 stipulated that all towns of fifty or more families would be required to provide a master to teach "all such children as shall resort to him to read and write." Towns of 100 or more families were to set up a grammar school, the master thereof to prepare children for the college. Such an enactment was without precedent in England, and testifies to the exigencies of the time. The traditional educational responsibilities of family, community, and church were breaking down in the wilderness environment of the New World. Formal institutions of learning would have to take up the slack. The Law of 1647 is a remarkable statute in several respects. The assumption of a determinative role in education was a daring move by the State; passing the burden of management and finance on to the towns was a shrewd one. In its periodic meetings, the town handled the school in just the same manner that it did any public business. Thus the school could not escape the impact of ordinary town politics and financial pressures. Dependent for support on "gifts" or general taxation, education everywhere in the colonial period came under the direct control, not of those responsible for instruction, but of those who created and maintained educational institutions; American education would always be sensitive to community pressure, to the pressure of funding and sustaining groups.

That many New England towns were taxing themselves to provide a suitable part of the cost of maintaining schools is clear from the record. It is equally clear that the picture so often drawn of every New England town, with its public school free and open to all, is without foundation in fact. To be sure, the Massachusetts schools were, in some key respects, public. The initiative was taken by citizens in town meetings. The towns in their corporate character voted to have schools, chose the teachers, fixed the compensation, and supervised the schools. But public support was not compulsory; few schools in the 17th century were completely free. Furthermore, religious piety permeated the teachings of the schools. The *New England Primer*, the "Little Bible of New England," with its alphabetical rhymes—"In Adam's Fall We Sinned All"—was the chief staple of instruction in the lower schools. The Latin grammar schools stressed religious indoctrination as well as classical studies. Evangelical religion permeated Puritan education; it even led the Puritans into a vain and tragic effort to educate the Indians.

The Puritans spoke of the New World as "a wilderness." But to the Indians it was home, history, country. To the Puritan the Indian was a savage, and it was the Puritan's divine duty to convert him. But it was apparently also his divine duty to take the Indian's lands and even destroy him. Save the Indian, and you saved one of Satan's victims; destroy the Indian and you destroyed one of Satan's partisans. Concern for the education of the Indian appeared early in the history of the English colonies in the New World. Money was sent to New England as early as the 1630s for missionary work. In 1646 John Eliot, having learned an Indian dialect, began systematically to preach to the Indians in their own language. In 1651 Eliot founded Natick, a Christian-Indian town where he conducted a summer school, "setting up a lecture among them in logick and theology once every fortnight." Eliot's school was hardly more fanciful than the Indian College at Harvard set up by President Dunster, or the college at Dartmouth founded for the education of youth of Indian tribes as well as of English youth. The Puritans who were setting out to create their dream society could find a place in it for the Indian only if he would become what they were—white, Anglo-Saxon, Christian.

Englishmen, Puritans, and Indians were not the only ones who participated in colonial enterprise. The Dutch came to New Netherlands, Swedes to settlements along the Delaware, Scots-Irish and Germans to Pennsylvania, Swiss to North Carolina, French-Huguenots to South Carolina, and Negroes eventually to all the colonies; in the building of America, people were drawn from many lands. Nor did Massachusetts have any monopoly on the fear that children would grow up wild and illiterate. All the colonies were concerned with the threat of barbarism. The Dutch, English Quakers, Scots-Irish Presbyterians and German Pietists quickly set up denominational schools. In the Southern colonies, too, there was persistent concern among Anglicans lest the children grow up wild. But facts of geography, environment and economics militated against the establishment of town school systems. Thus, in the South, tobacco was king. Tobacco cultivation required large tracts of land, enforcing ruralness and militating against urban development, then the *Sine quo non* of an effective school system. Education remained the province of parents, endowed schools, and religious charities. Almost the only general educational legislation of the Virginia colony, for example, dealt with paupers and orphans, applying and extending precedents established in the English Poor Laws. A racial element, present in the South almost from the beginning, complicated the situation. The first Negroes who landed in Jamestown in 1617 were neither slaves nor free men; they were indentured servants. By 1715, however, one-fourth of Virginia's population were Negro slaves; five-eighths of South Carolina's population were slaves. Little argument was needed to convince masters that slaves who had some conception of modern civilization and understanding of the language of their owners would be more valuable than ignorant men with whom one couldn't communicate. On the other hand, weren't slaves easier to exploit, and more docile, if they were uneducated?

The majority of Southerners finally saw it this way. But in the beginning many masters encouraged the enlightenment of their slaves. Especially active in the education of the Negro in the South were the clergymen of the Society for the Propagation of the Gospel, and Anglican missionary society that was mainly interested in the conversion of the heathens (though acquiescing in colonial laws that permitted baptized Negroes to be held in slavery), but also taught them the three R's. It may be said, by way of conclusion, that education took on regional characteristics as colonial society matured.

The cities of America have always fascinated European visitors. In the mid-18th century astonishment and approval animated most of them at their first sight of any of the five metropolises of the English colonies: Boston, Philadelphia, Newport, New York, and Charlestown. What they saw, as they sailed into any of the five harbors, was not a wilderness of tall trees and fierce animals, but rather, rising centers of civilization, cities as busy, as large, and as sightly as any but the great capitals of Europe. The steady stream of immigration, improved transportation and communication, physical expansion, and economic prosperity, taken in conjunction with the maturing effect of a century of urban life, presaged rapid and profound changes in the cultural and intellectual life of the colonies. In no place was the change more dramatic than in New England. It was only natural that certain modifications should have taken place with respect to both the purpose of education and the means of its diffusion.

The 18th century was a period of very swift economic and social change, change at a pace with which the established educational system could not keep up. New England needed navigators to chart courses for its ships, surveyors to lay out lands bought by prosperous merchants, and bookkeepers and scribes to keep the records of its countinghouses and shops. In search of training for these occupations, no one turned to the town Latin grammar schools, circumscribed in content and aim by the humanistic tradition and college entrance requirements. Their limited functions were well known and approved. Youth who wanted to secure a technical, business, or commercial education, or who desired a certain refinement of taste, had to seek it elsewhere. Eighteenth century colonials did, in the private-venture or English schools, so well described by Seyboldt, and then later in the academy. The appearance of the private-venture or English school marked the transfer of vocational training from the family and apprenticeship, where a trade, a skill, or a craft, could retain its "mystery," into a world of publicly available schools, and marked the early end in America of certain restrictive practices by which control of education and apprenticeship, and hence recruitment into the trades of an orderly society, had been maintained. It was an early indiction that America was going to be an open, fluid, mobile society, in which the lines of social stratification would be soft and penetrable; the schools would provide an opportunity for careers.

In the 18th century, then, the rising merchant and trading classes began to press for an education more appropriate to their interest, an education more useful and utilitarian than that of the Christian scholar and gentlemen. If the gap left by the town schools was to be filled, however, what was needed was no fly-by-night institution, but one able to command private or public support and to survive the death or departure of masters. In the latter half of the 18th century, the private English schools gave way to the academies, which were usually incorporated and founded on a more permanent basis. The father of the academy movement was Benjamin Franklin, the apostle of practicality. But Franklin's influence has been much more pervasive. His lifelong efforts at gaining an education have come to symbolize a characteristic American commitment to self-improvement through self-culture; "The doors of wisdom are never shut," Poor Richard once remarked. Franklin has become the American archetype of the immigrant arriving in a new world of opportunity, seeking his fortune in a society where talent and industry were rewarded more than birth and privilege. Possessed of a consistently positive attitude toward life, ready to learn from experience, able to improvise and adapt, Franklin epitomized much that became the American ethos of self-help, rugged individualism, and inevitable success.

With apparent casualness, Franklin cast aside two traditional guides to education—academic custom and religious orthodoxy. In his "Proposals Relating to the Education of Youth in Pennsylvania" (1749), Franklin put forward his plan for the establishment of an academy. He spoke for the awakening middle class. The academy's character was to be utilitarian and secular in tone and content. Franklin had no quarrel with cultural subjects as such, only their monopoly on education. In a sense the curriculum of the academy was an effort to combine the values and content of the Latin schools and English schools into one institution; the academy was to have a Latin department and an English department. It has been said, disparagingly, that Franklin's "Proposals" were the most elaborate plan for a utilitarian education in the colonial period. Of course the Proposals were utilitarian. Indeed, who did not expect education to be useful? Franklin's innovation consisted of the kind of utility he had in mind. He wanted subjects and instruction that trained not for limited goals, not for close-bound predetermined careers, but for the broadest possible range of enterprise. What lay behind his interest in libraries, Junto, self-improvement, and the academy, was the hope that America would be a mobile, fluid society where one's life was not fully cast at birth, where opportunities beyond the expectations of birth could be reached by effort and education.

Franklin's Philadelphia Academy was founded in 1751. By 1757 it had fallen into the hands of the classicists, a conservative elite whose cultural ties were closer to London than to Philadelphia. Franklin then severed his relations with the academy, asserting that it "was no longer concerned with education for such a country as ours." Regardless of how well Franklin anticipated colonial needs, the almost conditioned response of his associates to look back over the Atlantic for guidance precluded the establishment of a strictly American kind of school. Yet, the academy marked the begining of a significant new movement in American secondary education, by helping to introduce English literature, modern languages, social studies, and technical and business subjects, none of which were being studied in the Latin schools. Many academies were truly comprehensive. Some had a four-year "classical" course to prepare for the university, a three-year course to prepare for business and commerce, and a one-year teacher-training course to provide teachers for the lower schools. A few of the early academies accepted girls; some were open to girls only. The academy became the dominant form of secondary education until after the Civil War. Despite its adaptability, it in turn would fail to meet the needs of the 19th century. In 1827, Massachusetts enacted legislation requiring "high schools" to be established in every town of 500 or more families, publicly supported, publicly controlled, and open to the public. By the late 19th century, the academy had gone the way of the private-venture schools.

American schools thus very early responded to American needs. These schools were children not so much of theory as of necessity, reflecting immediate concerns and the political, economic, social, and cultural conditions of the New World; American education was pragmatic in origins. This was the case even in higher education. In England, a "liberal education," which would supposedly liberate a man from the narrow bounds of his time and place, was the property of an exclusive few. The traditional hallmark of a liberal education in 18th century England, the Bachelor of Arts degree, could, under Parliamentary authority, be awarded only by Oxford and Cambridge. Efforts to found additional degree-granting institutions were repeatedly defeated. The monopoly of Oxford and Cambridge was complete until London University was founded in 1827. In America there was to be no such monopoly in higher education. Religious denominationalism was the most important factor behind the diffusion of collegiate education in America. The motives in establishing the first three colonial colleges, Harvard in 1636, William and Mary in 1698, and Yale in 1701, were distinctly religious and these were the only colleges until 1745. Not until the mid-18th century, and the outburst of religious enthusiasm known as "The Great Awakening," did the rash of colonial colleges appear. The Great Awakening led to splits in the Congregational, Presbyterian, Anglican, Methodist, Lutheran and Baptist groups. By the time of the Revolution, nearly every major Christian sect had a college of its own. Each college founded by one sect was another good reason for every other sect to found a college in order to save more Americans from the untruths of its competitors. Here was an accelerating movement that does not seem to have stopped yet. Before the outbreak of the Revolution, nine colleges were already granting degrees. In all England at the time, there were still only two degree-granting institutions of higher learning. One obvious effect of the dispersion and proliferation of colleges was to diffuse learning widely in the terms of place and class, and to increase the number of college degrees. Whether the colonial colleges were simply distributing to the many what in England was reserved for the privileged few, or whether they were issuing an inflated currency, is another question.

By 1776, then, education in America was a radically different process from what anyone in the early 17th century would have expected. On almost every major point the expectations of the first generations of settlers had been frustrated. As the country passed out of the colonial into the early national period, schools receded in character from English or European models, and emphasized more and more distinctively American characteristics. Education had been cast loose from its old moorings, and its functions had become problematical and controversial; schools and formal schooling had acquired new importance. Many kinds of schools were educating the American people; town schools, endowed schools, denominational schools, and private schools. By the end of the colonial period, education was no longer dedicated exclusively to the classics and religion. The layman with his interests in the more practical pursuits of life was beginning to charge the schools with a great variety of responsibilities. Education had become an instrument to achieve social and economic as well as religious goals. Education was all things to all men. It was for individual self-improvement, economic development, social betterment, and moral and ethical training. The picture is one of tremendous fragmentation, diversity, and variety—in goals, in support, in sponsorship, and in state participation, as well as in the forms instruction assumed. On almost every major point the original inheritance had been called into question, challenged, altered, and discarded. By 1776 the homogeneous, integrated education of a homogeneous, integrated society had been shattered into multiplicity.

II. Education in the Early Republic

The American revolution had a disastrous effect on all colonial educational institutions. But Americans of the revolutionary generation were only distracted by their military exertions. When the war was ended and they assumed the role of Founding Fathers, they returned with new zeal to the education of the people. In the postwar period, the new nation was faced with the uncertainties of peace and independence. Gradually, as Americans began to assess the implication of their Revolution, the euphoria of triumph receded before a wave of doubts about the future. The ebullient new Republic had neither reigning house nor landed aristocracy and a bad record of mob violence and political instability. Just as the Puritans feared failure in their errand into the wilderness, so many leaders of the infant nation feared failure in their experiment in Republicanism. What could unify such a widely scattered and diverse people? The answer seemed to lie in the diffusion of learning, and in the deliberate construction of a distinctive "American way of life." High priority was accorded the role of the schools. Even the Continental Congress, through grants of land under the Land Ordinance of 1785 and the Northwest Ordinance of 1787, endeavored to further education.

In the early national era, many plans for the development of a system of education "best adapted to the genius of the Government of the United States" were formulated. The traditional education was to be discarded in favor of an education that would be universal, utilitarian, and "republican." Perhaps the most significant feature of the various plans was their concern that popular education have a predominantly political aim. Benjamin Rush, for example, urged the establishment of one general and uniform national system of education that would "render the mass of the people more homogeneous, and thereby fit them more easily for uniform and peaceable government." The new nation, Rush stressed, required schools to produce "Republican machines." Schoolbooks, strongly colored by religion in the colonial period, were, at the beginning of the national period, rededicated to patriotic virtues. Noah Webster wished to inculcate patriotism through uniformity in spelling and pronunciation and all textbooks of instruction. "Begin with the infant in his cradle," he admonished in the preface of his *Reader*; "let the first word he lisps be 'Washington.' "

One of the earliest plans for a new American education was Thomas Jefferson's "Bill For The More General Diffusion of Knowledge," presented to the Virginia Assembly in 1779. Jefferson, like Rush and others, proclaimed that the key to Republican government lay in the diffusion of knowledge among the people. In the bill, Jefferson proposed the establishment of a system of elementary and grammar schools, wholly under the auspices of the civil authority, and wholly supported by public funds. Free children were to be entitled to free education for at least three years and as much longer at private expense as their parents wished and could afford. Annually there would be a competition to select a few poor boys for further education at the grammar school, and then at William and Mary College, to be made into a public institution. By this means, Jefferson asserted, "twenty of the best geniuses will be raked from the rubbish annually." No doubt Jefferson wished to broaden the base of recruitment from the aristocracy of birth to the "natural aristocracy of talents and virtues." But one suspects that he believed that the aristocracy of talents and virtues was a small one, and could be found for the most part among families of means. Jefferson departed from announced democratic principles in one other regard. Every teacher, said the author of the Declaration of Independence, must "give assurance of fidelity to the Commonwealth." And as founder of the University of Virginia, Jefferson would use political tests in the hiring of faculty and prescribe the textbooks to be used in the classroom—students would have to be protected from Federalist doctrine.

The various educational plans set forth in the early national period are on the whole informed by a generous view of mankind. Human capabilities, the possibilities of human improvement, the great power of nurture over nature—these articles of 18th century Enlightenment faith directed the founders to think expansively. But their commitment to enlightened public opinion was hedged with apprehension that the Republic might founder on too much liberty and freedom. To help make this experiment work, political indoctrination was required. Thus the Founding Fathers raised a problem still inherent in American education. Can one train a citizen to think critically, but be patriotic above all?

Jefferson's "Bill" was never enacted. Indeed, none of the proposals of the Founding Fathers became operational. The Constitution was silent on education; the responsibility for the establishment of schools remained vested in each of the individual states of the Union. The states delegated substantial educational powers to local school districts. In the early national period, schools in all regions of the country fared badly. The country was poor and debt-ridden, still overwhelmingly agricultural and sparsely settled. In 1800, the population of the country was only about 4 million. As late as 1820, only thirteen cities had populations of over 8000; only about 5 percent of the population lived in these "cities." The overwhelming majority of Americans lived in isolated villages and farms, learning what they had to know in the family, in the field, and in the church. By the early national period, free education had become closely associated with pauperism. The Continental system of education—private schools for the well-to-do, and charity and catechetical schools for the poor—was much in evidence. The wild enthusiasm with which Englishman Joseph Lancaster's monitorial system of education was received in the early 19th century can be explained in a large part in terms of the widespread interest in establishing a philanthropic system of education. The monitorial system, it was hoped, would be efficient and cheap, staving off taxation for free schools. It would be the last effort to establish a charity system of mass education in the United States.

III. The College-Founding Movement

The structural characteristics of American education took concrete form during the 19th century. At the beginning of the century, no state could boast of having a statewide system of public elementary schools, just as no state could lay claim to a system of public high schools or a state university. Everywhere, the European two-track system of education was much in evidence. The "ladder system" so typical of modern American education, whereby elementary schools, high schools, and colleges and universities were so coordinated that a child could proceed naturally from the elementary school to the high school to the college or university did not exist at the opening of the century. By the end of the century, most states had developed such a system.

It is paradoxical but true that colleges came before the common schools in America. The American tendency to have a great number and variety of colleges has already been referred to. These tendencies were exaggerated in the era of the common man; the 1820s and 1830s were witness to a veritable college-founding mania. The American people went into the Revolution with nine colleges. They went into the Civil War with 250, of which 182 still survive. And this figure is trifling compared to the number of colleges founded in the same period that failed to survive. Many factors go into explaining the college-founding mania—

the temper of the time, for example. It was the Age of Jackson. America was a busy, restless, speculating, optimistic, mobile country that required colleges as scattered and mobile as the people themselves. The sheer continental dimensions of the United States and the difficulties of travel tended to encourage localism and regional pride, thus augmenting the number of colleges. Another element behind the seemingly reckless competition for colleges was the grass-roots conviction that the average citizen was entitled to a chance for higher education and that this could be best achieved by regional and decentralized institutions of learning. Most important, however, was religious rivalry. After the Great Awakening of the 1730s and 1740s, religion was in temporary eclipse, overshadowed by the concerns of business and politics. At the turn of the century, the fires of religious zeal flared up again, swept the country from the Atlantic to the Mississippi, and set the evangelical churches off on a crusade of reform and expansion with profound effects on higher education. As the population moved West, so did the revitalized denominations. The denominations would not let religion (or culture) die on the frontier. The Dartmouth College case, decided by the United States Supreme Court in 1819, cleared the way by guaranteeing private and denominational colleges the right to exist free from fear of expropriation and popular pressures.

Higher education in pre-Civil War America was fragmented, particularistic, and decentralized. Still, there were unifying forces at work that counteracted the absence of central direction: the influence of organized religion as reflected in denominational sponsorship; the inherited intellectual tradition, as reflected in the classical curriculum; the collegiate way of life as reflected in the country setting, the dormitory, the dining commons, and the kindly paternalism and discipline and guidance of the president and faculty; and finally the extracurriculum. Even to those most familiar with the major developments of American higher education, the importance of students in molding and changing American higher education may come as something of a surprise. But fraternities and sororities, athletics, literary and debating societies, musical and dramatic organizations, student publications, student government—the impact of all these parts of the extracurriculum have also altered American higher education in significant ways.

The college responded only very slowly to social change. Although a college education was an advantage, it was not so necessary in the pre-Civil War period to go to college to become a doctor or a lawyer or a politician. Higher education was more a luxury, less a utility than it is today. In a society so mobile, so rich, so expansive, and yet so unspecialized, opportunities beckoned to young men directly out of grammar schools or academies. But American society was too democratic to accept completely the idea of a gentlemanly education, too practical to accept complacently the college's classical content, and too competitive to accept the old-time college's monopoly of higher education. If the old-time college wouldn't or couldn't adjust, America would create new institutions to serve its purpose. When the changes did make their way, it would be through the state university and land-grant college movement. The state universities, publicly controlled, publicly supported, free, closely articulated with and the capstone of the common-school system, grew up in the Midwest as a consequence of the government practice, beginning in 1787, of granting federal lands to new states to support colleges. The rise of the state university served to democratize the college by offering practical education as well as publicly supported, publicly controlled, free higher education, and also introduced the service function into higher education. Federal aid supplied by the landmark Morrill Act of 1862, called by one historian the most important piece of agricultural legislation ever passed by the U.S. Congress, encouraged the further broadening of curriculum and constituency already underway.

IV. The Era of Common-School Reform

The common school, the basic unit of the American school system, emerged as a response to the conditions of American life during the period 1825-1860. What were these conditions? Some were economic. Commerce and industry were expanding. Improvement in transportation and communications were bringing communities closer together and stimulating the exchange of goods and services. The thirteen cities of 1820 increased to 44 by 1840 and to 141 by 1860. The new order required higher levels of education among more people. As the taxable wealth of American communities increased, it became more feasible to provide free tax-supported schools. Some of the causes were political. In the Jacksonian era, not only did more and more voters take part in elections, but also more and more offices were thrown open to popular election. The idea grew that if the mass of people were to govern, then the mass of people must be educated. Some of the causes were in the growing heterogeneity of the population. In the 1830s to 1850s came the great tide of German and Irish immigration. The influx of hundreds of thousands of Catholics stirred a variety of feelings (most of them unfriendly) in the hearts of America's "native" population, now predominantly home-born or home-bred, and of a distinctively Anglo-Saxon, Protestant hue. As the forces of xenophobia and nationalism gathered strength, so did the argument that the public schools offered the best hope of transforming foreign children into Americans. Some of the cause lay in the emergence of a workingman's movement. It was virtually inevitable in the period of unrest that characterized Jackson's administration, that workingmen should turn to political action. The programs of the early unions and their affiliated political parties were far more concerned with social protest than with economic protest. Labor turned to public education, supported by public taxation, free to all, as a means of preserving the open society in America for their children. Finally, in the Age of Jackson, the Enlightenment doctrine of progress shed its glow on the common man. The 1830s and 1840s witnessed a veritable farrago of reform and uplift movements. The common schools were caught up in the enthusiasm. Such was the cradle of the common-school movement. Out of decades of agitation emerged a basic democratic institution—the free, publicly supported, publicly controlled, nonsectarian common-school system.

The fight for free schools was a hard one. The full story, largely hidden in state and local records, has yet to be told. The common-school crusade began in the settled older regions of the East, where new social conditions were most visible and painful, and spread West, frequently carried by transplanted New Englanders. The movement was led by an inspired group of proselytizers: Horace Mann and James Carter of Massachusetts, Henry Barnard of Connecticut, John Pierce of Michigan, John Swett of California, Samuel Lewis and Calvin Stowe of Ohio, Caleb Mills of Indiana, Charles Mercer of Virginia, Robert Breckenridge of Kentucky, and Calvin Wiley of North Carolina, among others. The acknowledged leader was Mann. It was Mann who, better than anyone else, articulated the 19th-century American faith in public education, epitomized the type of reformer active in the common school movement, and provided the program and rhetoric of common school reformers.

In 1837, Mann, then president of the Massachusetts Senate, signed an act that was to decide his future. By this act, a state board of education was finally established in Massachusetts. Mann became its first secretary. Although Mann was raised a Puritan, he rejected the stern Calvinist predestinarianism of his youth in favor of the gentle, more liberal Unitarianism that attracted other New England intellectuals during the first half of the 19th century. As a Unitarian, Mann was predisposed to visualize the education of children hopefully. His acceptance of phrenology as the true science of the human mind reinforced his confident assurance that education, if widely dispersed, could speedily effect an individual and social reformation. Mann was a dedicated spirit, setting forth on behalf of a sacred cause. This is an important key to full understanding of educational thought in 19th-century America. "I have long been accustomed to look at this great movement of education as part of the Providence of God," explained Mann, "by which the human race is to be redeemed." His twelve years in office were a successful crusade, but one that raises many important questions about the nature of reformers and the rhetoric and substance of school reform.

Mann waged a remarkable campaign of propaganda and persuasion. In it he appealed to all classes and all interests. Universal, free public education was the basis of Republican government. An educated people was a more industrious and productive people. Education was "the great equalizer of the conditions of men . . . the balance wheel of the social machinery." Vice and crime would be extirpated by education. As Mann argued, education became the panacea for every social ill and the highway to Utopia. All of this became the public school ideology, its faith. It aroused enthusiasts, made converts, and worked wonders. But it has also bequeathed enormous problems. The public school system has been nourished on false and inflated promises. By promising too much, the system has been afflicted with an endemic frustration, a perpetual irritation. There are other unfortunate consequences of making excessive claims for the redemptive powers of education. By failing to state clearly what the school can and cannot be expected to do, by contributing to the popular myth that education is the panacea for every social and personal shortcoming, educators have greatly oversimplified social problems and obscured the relationship between schools and social problems.

The common schools were to teach more than the three R's and facts about geography and history; Mann and his contemporaries firmly believed that schools should shape morality and character and patriotism as well as intellect. The schools would also teach the common elements of Republicanism and Christianity. The common-elements curriculum raises the vital problem of how to build a common-school system for a heterogeneous people. Mann was convinced that to make Republican government work, the schools must teach something about politics and government. But the Constitution is subject to different readings. The policy of different administrations is subject to party strife. There is the danger of the classroom becoming a political battleground to the ruin of the common schools. Mann's urgent advice to teachers was to avoid controversy and teach the elements of Republicanism common to all political factions. The dictum "when in doubt leave it out" certainly avoids controversy, but whether it also avoids some of the most valuable things that might be taught is another question. To criticize Mann, is not to argue away the problem—how to build a common school curriculum for a people of various political convictions.

The immediate challenge, however, that confronted the common-school reformer was the religious problem—the place of religion in the common school. Protestant religious instruction had been an integral part of the elementary school curriculum throughout the entire colonial period. Following the Revolution, interest in religion declined somewhat; interest in patriotism rose. Yet the interest in religion was still intense. Mann, with his contemporaries, believed that a community could not be moral without religion, and that no community would be religious without a religious education. But there were many religious sects: Congregational, Baptist, Episcopalian, Unitarian, Methodist. Whose creed should be taught? Mann believed that the common school would founder if any sectarian creed were taught in the schools. His solution was to teach nonsectarian religion, the common elements of Christianity as found in the Bible, without commentary on the part of the teacher.

"Nonsectarian" for Mann, it must be stressed, did not mean nonreligious, it meant nondenominational religion, that is, the Biblical truths common to all Protestant sects. Mann apparently did not consider the possibility that Catholics and non-Christians attending the public schools would object to his kind of nonsectarian liberal Protestantism. But by mid-century, Roman Catholic church leaders began to urge with increasing vigor that Catholic parents educate their children in Roman Catholic parochial schools. Jews, and some Protestant groups that rejected the interdenominational consensus, were also impelled to institute separate systems of parochial schools. Still, without some such compromise as Mann's, it is doubtful whether common schools could have been established, much less prospered. Mann's solution became the general Protestant position. It was never assumed by Protestants that one day the Bible itself might be considered sectarian. If this point is not understood, then one cannot explain the bewildered and angry outcry when the U.S. Supreme Court outlawed Bible reading and prayers in the public schools in 1962 and 1963.

By 1860 the following conception of the common school had emerged. The common school was not to be a "private" school affected with a public interest, nor a "public" school supported in part by private donations, but a school controlled by publicly appointed officials, financed from the public treasury. The common school was to be free, paid for by the taxpayers at large. It would teach the three R's and also promote a nonsectarian Christian morality and a nonpartisan Republicanism. And, ideally, the common school would be so excellent that no one would wish to send their children to private schools. But schools could be no better than the teachers who taught in them. It was time to look to teacher training.

In the earliest days of our history, American communities found it hard to secure good teachers. They settled for what they could get—a high proportion of misfits and incompetents. They tended to conclude that teaching was a trade that attracted rascals, and, having so concluded, were reluctant to pay the rascals more than they were worth. What helped American education break out of the vicious cycle was the development of the graded primary school, the emergence of the woman teacher, and the development of the normal school. It is difficult to fully comprehend the serious obstacles that surrounded school teachers of early America: the total absence of training facilities, the dearth of suitable textbooks, the primitive condition of the schoolhouse, and the ungraded school. Gradually, however, in urban common schools, younger children were separated from older children, and then children were divided into classes and grades depending on age and achievement. By 1860, almost all city schools were organized on a grade basis. The graded school made possible smaller classes of more or less homogeneous groups of pupils, increased the need for teachers, and opened up the trade for women. Until the 1830s, most teachers were men. The notion prevailed that women were inadequate for the disciplinary problems of the classroom, especially in large classes and with older age groups. The emergence of the graded school provided a partial answer to these objections. Opponents of women teachers were still to be heard, but they could be silenced when it was pointed out the women teachers could be paid one-third to one-half as much as men. Since it was possible to find a fair supply of admirable young girls to work at low pay, and to keep them at work only so long as their personal conduct met the most rigid standards, the acceptance of the woman teacher solved the problem of character as well as cost; the normal school helped solve the problem of competence.

Before the 1830s there was little interest in popular education and no interest in teacher education as such. As a rule, teachers in the grammar schools received their preparation in an American college or European university. The completion of the elementary course itself was a sufficient preparation for an elementary school teacher. At the beginning of the national period, the only qualifications generally required of a teacher were that he be a professed Christian, have some knowledge of the three R's, and have the ability to keep order. In practice, the chief requirement was the ability (or strength) to keep order. Inspired by reports of teacher-training seminaries in Prussia and France, and fearful that the common schools, unless competent teachers could be secured, would come to be regarded as pauper schools, first James Carter and then Mann began to urge that the Massachusetts legislature establish normal schools. On July 3, 1839, Mann had the pleasure to preside over the establishment of the first public normal school in the United States, at Lexington, Massachusetts. The experiment was successful. Other states followed the lead of Massachusetts. By 1865, there were at least 15 state normal schools, and more municipal normal schools. The normal schools were a tremendous improvement over what had gone before, but the decision to train teachers in separate institutions created a grave problem for the future of the teaching profession. The normal school imbued ill-paid, put-upon teachers with a sense of mission, a sense of calling, a unique *esprit de corps*. But the price was paid in isolation from the larger community of scholars. The effect of Mann's position on teacher education was to hasten the development of the teacher as a technician, but to retard his development as a professional.

It is worthy of note that Mann's conception of universal education fell short in the area of further education. At the very time that Mann was arguing that the state's responsibility ended at the secondary level, Michigan's John Pierce was working out an educational system including public high schools and capped by a state university! On the whole, however, the public high school movement did not really get under way until after 1865. The 1870s saw a series of judicial decisions in the state courts of Illinois, Wisconsin, Kansas, Missouri, and Michigan, the most influential of which was the Kalamazoo decision, handed down by the Michigan Supreme Court in 1874, which finally laid a sound legal basis for the public high school. With the legal basis thus clarified, local school boards began to feel free to establish high schools as the demand arose. State legislatures were also encouraged to pass laws permitting local boards to establish high schools, to offer aid to those districts that did so, and finally to actually compel high schools to be established in larger and more populous districts. By the end of the century the high school, supported and controlled by the public, had come of age.

Mann affirmed the belief that democracy could not exist without an educated public, and that universal education was the great equalizer of the conditions of men, and he saw further benefits in the school common to all children; the ideal of social harmony to be achieved by mixing children of all backgrounds in the "common" school was an important end in itself. And it has been accepted that the common-school ideal triumphed by the time of the Civil War. But more careful examination of the real availability of common-school education is necessary. Many children were educationally disenfranchised because of race or poverty. The South in general, and certain minority groups in particular, did not share the benefits of the common school. In the South academies existed for the upper and middle classes until the late 19th century; the poor went largely without schools or were dependent on church and charity schools. Not until the very end of the century did the South begin to move in the direction in which the rest of the nation had already made great strides. Insofar as the Negro was concerned, education, instead of being the palladium of the Republic that Jefferson made it, became the shield and buckler of the slavocracy. There were no common schools for Negroes in the South. Legal prohibition of Negro education began in South Carolina and Georgia in the 1740s. After Nat Turner's insurrection (1831) it was against the law to teach a slave to read or write in most Southern states.

Although slavery eventually confined itself to the region below the Mason-Dixon Line, discrimination against the Negro and a firmly held belief in the superiority of the white race were not restricted to one section, but were shared by an overwhelming majority of white Americans. The Negro's quest for educational opportunities prompted strong and frequently violent protests in the North. The common schools of most Northern states excluded Negroes or separate schools were established for them. Negroes protested repeatedly against segregated schools. But in 1849, in the famous *Roberts v. City of Boston* case, won by the city, the court's defense of the "separate but equal" doctrine established a precedent in American law. By 1860 most Northern states had provided for separate Negro schools. Separate schools were also the rule for minority children on the West coast. A law enacted by the California legislature in 1860 required that Negroes, Indians, and "Mongolians" (referring to Chinese at first, and after the turn of the century to Japanese), be excluded from attending public schools with caucasian children. Sometimes separate schools were established for Negro and Chinese children. The Indian didn't receive this much. Indians were carefully excluded from the privileges of citizenship. Numerous treaties promising schools and teachers had been concluded before the Civil War, but in only a few instances were such pledges even partially fulfilled. Adequate schooling was so rare that as late as 1880, few Indians could speak English.

There is a dearth of monographs describing American education in the 19th century. One important but overlooked source of information are the commentaries of European observers. Europeans invariably called attention first to the American belief in education; education was America's religion. The willingness of Americans to extend the benefits of free public education to the level of secondary schools and in some states to the university, and the widespread diffusion of educational opportunity, were tangible evidence of this belief. Europeans offered several reasons for the American commitment to education. Some maintained that America was dependent on the common schools to bring the foreign born into the folds of democracy. Others maintained that education for citizenship, for all children, was the overriding aim of American education. There was one other element of the American faith in the common schools to which Europeans called attention—the ideal of equality of opportunity. To Sir Michael Sadler, perhaps the most perspicacious of all European observers of American education, this was the supreme objective animating American education from the beginning: the "intense and indeed religious belief in the rightness of giving to every boy and girl in the community, as far as possible, an equal chance to make the most of his or her natural powers." This explained much, the faith in education, the widespread accessibility of schools, the provision of free high schools, and the "ladder" system of organization characteristic of American education. Europeans were generous in acknowledging the strength of the ideal and the sincerity of America's efforts to reach the ideal in practice. Praise for the "noble educational spirit" of the American people did not deter Europeans from commenting on certain problems in American education—certain inequities, a certain distance between the ideal and the reality. Europeans observed that the American ideal of the classless common school was just that: an ideal. In practice, social distinctions did tell with marked effect in American schools. Visitors also called attention to the fact that the American ideal of equal educational opportunity was still far from being achieved in practice. The inequalities in the educational provisions in the South in general, and for the Negro in particular, came in for comment. But Europeans had no doubt that eventually the ideal must be triumphant. This was the unfinished task of American education.

References

Bailyn, Bernard, *Education in the Forming of American Society: Needs and Opportunities for Study*, University of North Carolina Press, Chapel Hill, North Carolina, 1960. Viewing education as acculturation, Bailyn presents a new approach to the history of American education, as well as an invaluable bibliographical essay.

Bullock, Henry Allen, *A History of Negro Education in the South: From 1619 to the Present*, Harvard University Press, Cambridge, Mass., 1967. Winner of the 1967 Bancroft Prize. A unique study of the role of education in determining the Negro's place in American society.

Cremin, Lawrence A., *The American Common School: An Historic Conception*, Teachers College, Columbia University, New York, 1951. The standard history of the common school movement.

Fenton, William N., *American Indian and White Relations to 1830*, University of North Carolina Press, Chapel Hill, North Carolina, 1957. Points up a continuing racial problem of yesterday and today.

Fraser, Stewart E. and William W. Brickman, eds., *A History of International and Comparative Education: Nineteenth Century Documents*, Scott, Foresman & Co., 1968, Glenview, Ill. A transatlantic exchange of educational views, valuable as literature and history.

Katz, Michael B., *The Irony of Early School Reform: Educational Innovation in Mid-Nineteenth Century Massachusetts*, Harvard University Press, Cambridge, Mass., 1968. A major reinterpretation of the common-school movement.

Middlekauff, Robert, *Ancients and Axioms: Secondary Education in Eighteenth-Century New England*. Makes a persuasive case for the longevity of the classical curriculum and thus qualifies Bailyn's thesis.

Rudolph, Frederick, *The American College and University: A History*, Alfred A. Knopf, New York, 1962. The history of higher education in the U.S. from the beginning becomes social and intellectual history.

2

The Transformation of the School

Sol Cohen

"I have long been accustomed to look at this great movement of education as part of the Providence of God by which the human race is to be redeemed"

Horace Mann

❖❖

I. Progressivism in Education

The years following the Civil War witnessed a phenomenal expansion of the American educational system. By 1918 the vast majority of American children attended elementary school for some shorter or longer period of their youth. High schools, in 1865 confined largely to the cities and more affluent rural areas, were by 1918 a recognized part of American education. Much the same thing might be said for colleges and universities and professional schools. New institutions such as the kindergarten, the junior high school, and the junior college were fashioned to meet the needs of specific groups. By 1918 more than 22.5 million students were enrolled at all levels. Classroom and supervisory staff numbered over 650,000. Total school expenditures were $763 million. In 1918, one author remarks, American education had become "big business." But in 1970, the public schools enrolled some 58.6 million students. Classroom teaching and supervisory staff numbered more than 3,000,000. School expenditures for all purposes amounted to almost $65 billion! By 1970 the American school system was different not only quantitatively but also qualitatively. The functions of the schools, at all levels, had been redefined. The key role in the transformation of American education, as Lawrence A. Cremin has brilliantly demonstrated in *The Transformation of the*

25

School, was played by a complex of educational reform movements that can be subsumed under the rubric "progressive education."

Contrary to the widespread misconception that progressive education was an isolated educational creed foisted on a beguiled American public by John Dewey and some of his lieutenants at Columbia University's Teachers College, or that it dated from the advent of the Progressive Education Association in 1919, it was the educational phase of the broader progressive movement in American life and thought. Progressive education actually began in the late 19th century as part of that broader effort to cope with the often baffling and urgent problems created by the rise of the city, the rise of the factory, and the massive influx of immigrants from South and East Europe. Progressive education meant at least this much—that the functions of the public schools were to be extended far beyond their traditional, formal, intellectual concerns, extended in any direction in order to "meet the needs of the city," as contemporaries frequently expressed it. But first, what was it that the progressives transformed?

Twentieth-century American educational theory and practice to a great extent might be characterized as a reaction against the 19th-century cluster of ideals on secondary and elementary education epitomized in several National Education Association reports—the Report of the Committee of Ten on Secondary School Studies (1893) and the Report of the Committee of Fifteen on Elementary Education (1895). In classic language, the Committee of Ten affirmed that the high school's main purpose was to prepare boys and girls "for the duties of life," and that this could best be accomplished by "strong and effective mental training"—the development of the minds of the students—through the study of academic subject matter. The Report, largely composed by Charles W. Eliot, Chairman of the Committee, became the gospel for policy makers in the burgeoning high schools for a generation. The high schools in turn set the standard for the elementary schools. As William Torrey Harris, speaking for the Committee of Fifteen, declared: "The first and most important thing . . . is to make everybody a reader." Though discipline and character development were not neglected, the emphasis was clearly on linguistic training. The child was to be provided with the "tools of learning," with which he could appropriate the "experience of the race," digested for him in textbooks.

The Committee of Ten, the Committee of Fifteen, Eliot, Harris, and the rest, thought that they were ushering in a new age. In retrospect, they were ushering out the old. By 1910, certainly by 1915, the Reports of the Committee of Ten and the Committee of Fifteen had taken on the charm of period pieces, for they marked the end of an era, not the beginning of one. Eliot and Harris had failed to reckon with the reality of life about them—the cities and their problems. Progressives would rectify their failure. In the 1880s, a new world was coming into being; America was being transformed by the forces of industrialism, urbanization, and immigration. So would American education be transformed. On the heels of the transformation of American society would come a point-by-point rejection or repudiation of the cluster of educational ideals and practices represented by the Committee of Ten, the Committee of Fifteen, and the rest of the Old Guard. Since the changing social context looms so important, it is well to begin with a brief description of this context.

With dramatic suddenness, America emerged, by the last years of the 19th century, as the world's foremost industrial nation and a powerful rival to England and Germany in world trade. The impact on America was profoundly shocking. In the last decades of the 19th century, the whole face of the land was made over. Almost overnight, the Industrial Revolution converted a peaceful agricultural country into a nation of bustling factories. Made over too were millions of men and women from rural America and Europe who poured into the new industrial centers and were subjected to the discipline of factory labor. How could Americans adjust to, if not wholly to master, the techniques of industrial society? Could the rural and native-born, and the foreign-born of all degrees of ethnic and religious diversity, learn to accept the imposed discipline of industrial labor? What role would the public schools play in the new industrial society?

Urbanization posed greater problems for the schools. By the turn of the century we had become a nation of cities. As late as 1860 less than 16 percent of Americans lived in cities; in 1890, 33 percent; and in 1900, 40 percent. Between 1880 and 1900, the population of Chicago grew from 500,000 to 1.5 million; that of New York, from 1.9 million to 3.5 million; and that of Philadelphia, from 850,000 to 1 million. By 1900 St. Louis, Boston, Baltimore, and Washington, D.C. each had about a million residents. Cincinnati, Buffalo, and Pittsburgh each had about 850,000. The cities grew up unplanned. Housing was scarce and land expensive. Owners piled floor atop floor and pushed buildings back to back and side to side, and the infamous tenement slums made their appearance—unsanitary, unattractive, overcrowded firetraps that spread "like a scab" to Boston, Chicago, Pittsburgh, New York, and other large cities. If the tenements were morbific for adults, what did they do to children? Perhaps no factor affected child life more than the growth of cities. Instead of the traditional experiences of childhood celebrated in song and literature—field, countryside, and open lots—now there was the shabby tenement or the alley or the street or the saloon. A group of investigators from Albany sent down to investigate New York's tenement districts expressed the widely shared sentiment:

> They are centres of disease, poverty, vice and crime, where it is a marvel, not that children grow up to be thieves, drunkards, and prostitutes, but that so many should ever grow up to be decent and self-respecting.

When the stability of home and family and neighborhood is shaken, what happens to the school? Could it go along in its old ways?

The growth of the city was fed from two sources—one internal and the other external. Lured by the lights, the noise, the gaiety, the variety, and the jobs, the rural population moved to the city in droves. And for the great majority of immigrants pouring into the land beginning in the 1880s, the city was their destination. Between 1880 and 1914 by far the greatest and presumably the last of the great waves of European immigrants flooded to America; some 22 million of them. By 1900 the immigrants constituted about 40 percent of the population of the twelve largest cities in the country and another 20 percent of the second generation. Contemporaries began to make invidious distinctions between the "old" immigration—the pre-1880 immigration, when 95 percent of the immigrants came from the Western and Northern parts of Europe, largely English-speaking, and with the exception of the Irish, of Protestant religious background, and the "new" immigrants—Italians, Greeks, Slavs, Russians, and Poles from South and Eastern Europe, largely non-English speaking, and largely non-Protestant (mostly Italian and Central European Catholics, and Russian and Polish Jews). Many Americans began to urge an end to unrestricted immigration; by 1924 they were successful. In the meantime, what about the immigrants who were already here? They were unprepared for the cities, and the cities were unprepared for them. And they were prolific breeders of children. By 1910, in the public schools of 37 of our largest cities, 57.5 percent of the children were of foreign parentage. What happens to the schools when they fill with immigrant children? Can they go along their old ways?

The picture of the urban-industrial city with its myriads of impoverished immigrants, its squalor, and its wretchedness, was brought home to the American public with brilliant clarity by many journalists and muckrakers of the 1890s, led by Jacob Riis' *How the Other Half Lives* (1890). The schools would not be able to escape the challenge of the city. "It is all a matter of education," said Riis. In the 1890s, against a background of mounting social crisis, Americans seized on education and the public schools as the Great Panacea. The public schools would have to help solve the problems of health, hygiene, recreation, vocation, congestion of population, assimilation of the immigrant, and more. But first they would have to be transformed. Public schools still emphasized formal training in intellectual skills. Progressives would force the schools to meet the challenge of the city. The social-settlement movement acted as the spearhead for reform.

Social settlements originated in England, in the slums of late 19th-century London, soon spread rapidly through England and West Europe, and within a few years came over to the United States. By 1910 there were over 400 settlements, including the Henry Street Settlement, New York City; South End House, Boston; and the country's most famous settlement, Hull House, Chicago, founded by Jane Addams and Ellen Gates Starr in 1889. Settlement activities knew no boundaries. Opportunism and expediency governed their practices. Settlement leaders fought for housing and sanitation reform, for the elimination of sweatshops and child labor, for parks and playgrounds, for more schools, and for a different kind of school. Any effort to improve the lot of the slum dweller was assiduously pursued. Always, settlement residents took their cues directly from neighborhood needs. Settlements founded antifilth societies and junior street-cleaning brigades and provided baths, showers, drinking fountains, and social and recreational facilities of all sorts. Settlements taught health and hygiene and became first-aid centers and headquarters for visiting nurses. They also provided libraries and study rooms, and experimented with vocational education and vocational guidance and with classes for the physically and mentally handicapped. Settlements introduced kindergartens and day nurseries and noon lunches for children. More and more the settlements found themselves in the business of education. By the mid-1890s they found themselves with a sprawling educational program on their hands and turned to the public schools for relief. The schools would have to be less formal; they would have to become, in Cremin's felicitious phrase, "legatee institutions." At first untheoretical and pragmatic, the whole movement of school expansion arose from the social and humanitarian needs of the city. It added up to a concept of the school going far beyond its formal, intellectual concerns to an active concern with all aspects of child welfare and neighborhood improvement; a concept of the school as an industrial-training agency, a social or neighborhood center, and a child-welfare center.

The movement to redirect the school was not just an urban phenomenon. In the country, rural spokesmen, out of a concern for the abandonment of the farm for the city, turned to the school as the only possible agency to inculcate rural values, improve farming and, hopefully, stop the drift to the city. Thus, from Cornell University in the late 1890s, horticulturist Liberty Hyde Bailey, chairman of the Country Life Commission (1908), called for a new kind of rural education: "I want to see our country schools," Bailey urged, "without screwed-down seats and to see children put to work with tools and soils and plants and problems." The public schools of Menomonie, Wisconsin, perhaps best illustrated this ideal in practice. Everywhere, in the country and in the city, the schools were to be agents of individual and social change. Nor was the university immune to pressures to be relevant. However much Progressivism has come to be associated almost exclusively with the reform of elementary and secondary education, the fact remains that it deeply affected the universities as well. Particularly in the Midwest, public higher education quickened during the Progressive Era in response to many of the same influences that were transforming the lower schools. The leading example is Wisconsin University during the La Follette period. There, under the vigorous presidency of Charles Van Hise, the university became the pivotal element in that larger program of statewide reform commonly referred to as "the Wisconsin Idea."

In the early decades of the 20th century, the public schools gradually, often reluctantly, began to accept the progressive's program of school reform, largely as the result of pressure from social workers, muckrakers, social reformers, and political-reform movements. Although most of the pressure was from outside the educational establishment, there were some students of education who gave philosophical sanction to the longstanding contention of progressives that public education had to be rethought in terms fitted to meet the needs of the new urban-industrial world, some thinkers who made the new education palatable to the teaching force of the country: Francis W. Parker, G. Stanley Hall, Edward L. Thorndike, and in the vanguard, towering above the rest, was John Dewey, the most commanding figure in the history of American education. Progressive education can be plotted along two coordinates: a new conception of society, cooperative, collectivistic, group-centered, is at one, and a new conception of the child-romantic and primitivist is at the other. The rise of a native, child-centered pedagogy was essentially the work of Parker and Hall. With Dewey, as we shall see, progressive education enters a collective phase. As early as the 1870s, Parker made the Quincy, Massachusetts, public schools world-renowned. Here Parker successfully introduced an activity-oriented curriculum based on the needs and interests of the children, later described in his *Talks on Pedagogics* (1894), a fascinating potpourri of Rousseau, Froebel, Pestalozzi, and Transcendentalism. But Parker's work was suffused by an intense and increasingly old-fashioned religiosity. If child-centered pedagogy were to appeal to a younger generation of teachers, it had to be verified by science. This is where Hall came in. So different from Parker in background and education, he ended up in the same camp, making a gospel of childhood. But because he was a psychologist, a "scientific" student of the mind and the founder of the child-study movement, his thoughts had the stamp of approval of science. Applying the theory of evolution to child study, Hall concluded that the development of the child followed laws of its own—laws with which teachers had best not interfere. Now science gave the child-centered school the importance that Parker had preached in the name of God. America believes as does no other country that education must be based on a study of psychology. That this is so may be due in no small degree to the influence of Hall. But few psychologists have had the prodigious impact of Thorndike. In a brilliant career spanning forty years, Thorndike instructed a whole generation in the doctrines of connectionism. With his S→R bond psychology, Thorndike, operating from a base of power at Teachers College, Columbia University, was to deliver the decisive blow against the concept of formal discipline of the mind. By the turn of the century, advocates of a mind possessed by faculties that could be trained by mental discipline were fighting a losing battle. As against a faculty of memory or imagination or reason that man was taught to employ, it was now concluded that man engages only in specific acts of memory, imagination, or reason; habit rather than intelligence ruled man's behavior. With the successful assault on faculty psychology, what subject would prove most immediately useful to children became a more frequent question than what subject would provide the best intellectual training. That this came about was due in no small measure to the work of Thorndike.

Nevertheless, in the history of American education, Dewey has no serious rival. He is to American education what Aristotle was to medieval education, not *a* philosopher, but *the* philosopher. Dewey was born in 1859 and died in 1952. In the intervening nine decades, America was transformed from a country of farms and small towns and open frontier into a nation of factories, sprawling metropolises, and continental super-highways. Upon graduating from the University of Vermont, John Dewey took his Ph.D. at Johns Hopkins. He subsequently secured a teaching appointment at the University of Michigan. After a ten-year career at Michigan, Dewey moved, in 1894, to the University of Chicago as chairman of its new department of philosophy, psychology, and pedagogy. In the 1890s, all the evils and vices of American urban life seemed to be exaggerated in Chicago, but reform was also stirring there, and the center for reform activities was Hull House. Dewey soon became a habitué of Hull House, a friend of Jane Addams, active in settlement affairs, much influenced by the settlement ideal of education. In 1896, Dewey established an experimental elementary school at the University, "The Laboratory School," one of the earliest experiments in progressive education.

In 1899, Dewey delivered a series of three lectures to parents and patrons of the Laboratory School in which he tried to explain the New Education to them, especially the introduction of manual training, shopwork, sewing, and cooking into elementary education. The talks were published as a little tract, *School and Society,* which became an immediate best seller. Dewey's main thesis was that the traditional curriculum no longer met the needs of the new society that had been created by the forces of industrialism. Dewey reminded his readers of the time when the farm household was practically the center around which was carried on, or about which was clustered, all the typical forms of industrial occupation, the time when children were gradually initiated into occupations through direct participation, and when they learned by doing. Now these days were over. The city and factory had changed everything. The influences of home and community had ceased to be educative as they had been in the old agrarian society. The necessary disciplinary and character-building forces were no longer at work in the daily life of the child. The question Dewey posed was how to preserve the values of this earlier society in the urban-industrial world of the 20th century. Dewey's answer was that the schools would have to take up the slack. How? Each school must assume the character "of an embryonic community life, active with occupations that reflect the life of the larger society." Central to this objective was the incorporation of "occupations," manual training, shop work, sewing, and cooking, into the elementary school program. Indeed, they were to *be* the school program.

The publication of *Schools of To-Morrow* in 1915 provided Dewey with an opportunity to amplify and expand the pedagogical doctrines he first set forth in *School and Society.* Everywhere Dewey and his daughter went in their tour of the *Schools of To-Morrow* they saw healthy, happy children playing and working in school shops and kitchens, studying nature first hand, and thereby presumably learning the fundamentals of the three R's, history, geography, science, and mathematics. But it was William Wirt's experiment in Gary, Indiana that most nearly exemplified Dewey's ideal school, and to it Dewey accords the most comprehensive treatment. The boldly innovative Wirt had devised a radical plan of industrial education that started in the fourth grade, employed skilled laborers as instructors, used workshops as classrooms, employed children as apprentices in all the maintenance and repair and construction work needed in the school, and correlated all the subjects of instruction around "occupations." Further, the children's health and recreational needs were looked after. And the schools were used as community centers. As the *New Republic*'s Randolph Bourne explained, the Gary school plan represented the most complete application yet attempted of Dewey's educational philosophy.

Dewey is difficult to read. His prose style is ambiguous and frequently opaque. It is interesting to speculate how fundamentally Dewey's thought would have influenced education in this country and abroad had he not found in Professor William Heard Kilpatrick of Teachers College, Columbia, a remarkably persuasive interpreter of his philosophy, especially its application in the form of the "project method" of teaching.

Between 1893 and 1918 a revolution occurred in American secondary education also. At the heart of this revolution lay a shift in the conception of the high school, of what should be its primary goals and responsibilities, its organization, its curriculum. In 1893, the secondary school was viewed as an institution designed to prepare that small proportion of the youth of the country attending high school for the duties of life by disciplining and developing their minds through the study of academic subject matter. The most memorable document expressing this view was the NEA's Report of the Committee of Ten. By 1918, the high school was viewed as an institution that should hold *all* youth to the age of 18 and prepare them for the duties of life in a manner in which intellectual ability and academic subjects were scarcely mentioned. The most memorable document expressing this view is another NEA report—the Report of the Commission on the Reorganization of Secondary Education, a document that would set the tone and provide the terminology for all quasi-official educational statements concerning the high school until the 1950s.

Compulsory school attendance marked a new era in the history of American education. Between 1890 and 1920 high school enrollment rose from 360,000 to 2.5 million. The creation of a system of mass secondary education for the New America would not simply be an extension of the old system. It would be different in function. It would have its own books, its own teacher-training institutions, and its own ideology. It was increasingly apparent by 1910 that the Committee of Ten and all it stood for was losing ground. In 1913, the NEA appointed a 27-member commission significantly called the "Commission on the Re-organization of Secondary Education." The Commission was led by Clarence Kingsley, an official of the Massachusetts State Department of Education. Five years in the making, the Commission's report finally appeared in 1918. The Report, which was given a quasi-official endorsement by the U.S. Bureau of Education, marked a complete break with the world of the Committee of Ten.

The Report was a masterful summary of progressive doctrine current at the time. Its opening sentence proclaimed that secondary education should be determined by the needs of society, the character of the students to be educated, and the knowledge of the best educational theory and practice available at the time. The Report pointed to the changes taking place in these three areas of concern—all of which called for extreme modification of the curriculum and organization of secondary education. Noting that the theories of mental discipline and transfer of training had been repudiated, the Commission rejected mastery of academic subject matter as a goal for American secondary education. In the latter's place it substituted the seven "Cardinal Principles of Education"—Health, Command of Fundamental Processes, Worthy Home Membership, Vocation, Citizenship, Worthy Use of Leisure, and Ethical Character. Thus, the Commission drew up a set of educational objectives in which neither the development of intellectual capacity nor the mastery of secondary-level academic subject matter was ever mentioned. Now all subjects in the high school curriculum were to be reorganized in order to contribute to the achievement of the Cardinal Principles. That such a change should have taken place in just twenty years is staggering until one remembers the context. The Cardinal Principles testify to the exigencies of American society: the decline of the patriarchal, stable, agrarian home, the weakening of religion, the appearance of an industrial proletariat, the changing character of immigration, and the changing character of the secondary school population—immigrant children with their lacks and needs. To Kingsley and the others the high school had to assume responsibility for "nothing less than complete and worthy living for all youth . . . ." This sort of rhetoric, and the pedagogical principles it represented offended tradition-minded college and university professors. Increasingly, the latter turned away from the problems of public education, which they now saw as the preoccupation of some new and strange breed of academician. Educationists were happy to see them withdraw; the field was now left to them with little authoritative criticism or opposition. The mental world of the professional educationist became increasingly separated from that of the academic scholar, a separation to be rectified only in the mid-1950s.

II. Progressive's Progress

Progressive education may be summed up in one word, "more." From the beginning, progressives had conceptualized a public school whose functions were vastly expanded beyond formal instruction to encompass responsibilities formerly left to other agencies, a conception of the school as a legatee institution. By 1917, public schools had begun to assume the responsibility for the physical, social, recreational and vocational needs of children. In the 1920s progressives went the rest of the way—to demand that the schools assume responsibility for the emotional and personality development of children.

World War I marks a great divide in the history of progressive education. The war with its carnage, and then the lost peace afterwards, were taken as the final manifestations of a depraved and bankrupt civilization. The younger generation especially, lost faith in the prewar political and social solutions. They turned their backs on social salvation to search for personal salvation. Now the enemy was convention, not capitalism. The restraints and shackles of Puritanism and Victorianism were to be overthrown. America was to be redeemed by art and Freud, by creative self-expression and psychoanalysis. It all added up to a post-war revolution in manners and morals. Progressive education, as it crystallizes in the 1920s, is a faithful reflection of this mood. The child, too, was to be freed—freed from the restraints of the traditional teacher and the shackles of the authoritarian school, freed by art and Freud. If a new educational system could be introduced, one in which children are encouraged to develop their personalities, then the world would be saved by this new, free, generation. So progressives believed.

Freud himself wrote little on education. His work was applied to education by a group of disciples in psychology, in social work, and especially, in the mental hygiene movement. As revealed in the writings of the latter, the pattern for the new education can be found. In this pattern the following are key strands. Maladjustment, antisocial behavior, and mental illness could be prevented or ameliorated. The emotional life of the individual was the key to behavior. The emotions could be molded or trained or controlled if the right environment were supplied in childhood. Finally, the public school was the strategic agency for the training of the emotions. Certain consequences follow from these assumptions. In the etiology of maladjustment and neurosis, failure and retardation in schools ranked high. Failure and retardation would be eliminated by abandoning or minimizing formal courses of instruction, abandoning or minimizing academic subjects, and abandoning or minimizing competition and achievement. In their place would be substituted projects and other group activities, play, and especially creative self-expression through art and other aesthetic activities. For the ethic of psychoanalysis and that of creative self-expression were joined in the mental hygiene movement. Among the foremost values of mental health, creativity is prominent. For some the absence of creativity is not just a symptom of neurosis, but the very essence of it. Conversely the release of creativity becomes close to being identical with mental health. The concern of many progressives for "creative activities"—art, music, theatre, and dance—was not so much to make education as rich and rounded as possible, but as a form of therapy. Progressives, armed with theory, now set about reconstructing the public school system of the country.

Even before World War I there were many progressive schools in existence, such as City and Country School, Walden School, Park School, and Shady Hill School. The schools differed among themselves, but they shared several characteristics: they were overwhelmingly upper middle class in terms of sponsorship, support, and clientele. And they subscribed to the list of basic principles, the "New Articles of Faith," catalogued in Harold Rugg and Ann Shumaker, *The Child-Centered School*—Freedom, Child-Initiative, Child Interest, Creative Self-Expression, and Personality and Social Adjustment. After the war, it was easier than ever to secure a hearing for new educational principles. In the spring of 1919 a small coterie of wealthy Washington matrons, private school teachers, and a sprinkling of public school people, under the leadership of Stanwood Cobb, organized the Progressive Education Association. What had formerly been a rather loosely joined revolt against pedagogical formalism now gained vigorous organizational voice. Only few people were involved, but the PEA was launched as no modest venture. It aimed at nothing short of reforming the entire public school system of America. From the beginning something of a religious fervor suffused the Association's activities. Progressive education, as Cobb put it, was "a great humanitarian movement for the benefit of the world's children." Progressives hoped to secure the final abolition of unhappiness, the final extirpation of all social problems. Through progressive education, every child could become a happy, creative, well-adjusted child.

The PEA developed slowly. For about five years informal news letters and bulletins were its chief means of publicity. For money it depended on individual contributions and even tried a chain-letter system. Then in 1924, a wealthy donor made it possible for the PEA to publish *Progressive Education*, a handsome, high-quality journal that soon established a national reputation, and the Association was on its way. In 1926 Dewey consented to assume the post of honorary president. Between 1926 and 1928 membership jumped from about 3500 to 6600 and the PEA was busy cementing ties, abroad with the New Education Fellowship, the European wing of progressive education, and at home with progressive organizations like the American Association of University Women. By 1928, one school reformer could assert, "anything less than progressive education is quite out of date in America." The boast was a bit premature. The PEA's growth had been impressive, but much work remained to be done. The 1930s were the progressives' decade.

Progressive education scored its biggest successes during the Depression. Nor should this be surprising. Metaphorically speaking, progressive education had been waiting for just such a moment. Now, more than ever, in the confusion and demoralization bound to follow in the wake of a crisis such as a world-wide depression was the time to turn to the schools and the education of the "whole child." The progressive's concern with the emotional and personality adjustment of children appealed to both militant humanitarians, and those concerned with domestic security. In the late 1930s, the PEA reached its peak membership of over 10,000. And by the late 1930s, thanks to grants from the foundations, the Association was more affluent and active than ever. On October 31, 1938, *Time* magazine featured Frederick L. Redefer, Executive Secretary of the PEA on its cover; the story was entitled, "Progressive's Progress." *Time* quoted Redefer as saying "We are no longer a rebel group." Twenty years ago, he said, progressive education was mainly a private school affair. Now it was predominantly a public school affair with strongholds in the elementary schools of New York City, Chicago, Los Angeles, Cleveland, Detroit, San Francisco, and elsewhere. Here was progress. Paradoxically, however, the zenith was not far from the nadir.

By the late 1930s the PEA was under fire from assorted intellectuals and scholars as the quintessence of anti-intellectualism, and from a ragtag of critics as sentimental or subversive or both. Internecine quarrels further weakened the Association. In the 1930s, a Columbia University Teachers College group, including George Counts, Harold Rugg, Kilpatrick, and Dewey tried to move the PEA in the direction of a radical politics. The social frontiersmen, or the social reconstructionists, as they were variously called, helped dissipate the strength of the PEA and helped discredit it in the eyes of the public. In the early 1940s the foundations withdrew their support and membership plummeted. The very words "progressive education," in the 1920s a talisman of success, had by now become tainted. In 1944 the PEA changed its name to American Education Fellowship (in 1953 the group shifted back to its former name). But now it was all downhill. The Association folded in 1955, one of the casualties of the lacerating attacks on progressive education that broke out in the early 1950s.

While the PEA went into decline, well-trained cadres were waiting in the wings to take up the torch of progressive education. In the 1940s leadership in American public education passed from the PEA to more orthodox centers of power—the NEA and its satellite, the U.S. Office of Education. Progressives had established a secure foothold in the elementary schools. It was time to turn attention to the high schools. In the late 1930s and early 1940s, a series of books and pamphlets, all reaffirming the Cardinal Principles of Education, issued forth from the NEA, culminating finally in the "life-adjustment movement," to this date the last progressive foray into the public schools.

The problem of youth came to the attention of the American public during the Depression. By the 1930s there was an army of youth in the high school. Indeed, one of the main educational achievements of the 1920s and 1930s was to make high school education almost as universal as the preceding 100 years had made elementary education. Between 1920 and 1940, high school enrollment climbed from 4.8 million to 7.1 million. But youth were then lost in the hustle and bustle of World War II. In the postwar period, youth were brought into the limelight again. In 1945, there was a meeting of the Division of Vocational Education of the U.S. Office of Education in Washington, D.C. At the close of the session, Charles A. Prosser, a former lobbyist of the National Society for the Promotion of Industrial Education, rose to speak. The high schools, he declared, were not meeting the needs of the great majority of youth. The high schools were preparing 20 percent of youth for college. They were preparing another 20 percent for "desirable skilled occupations." The needs of the remaining 60 percent were not being met. What they needed, in Prosser's fateful words, was an education for "life adjustment." With breathtaking certainty then, the majority of the nation's high school youth were written off as being more or less uneducable, unfit not just for academic studies, but even for programs of vocational education leading to desirable skilled occupations. What kind of education did they need? Practical training in being family members, workers, consumers, and citizens. Here, as the authors of *Life Adjustment Education for Every Youth* put it, was "a philosophy of education which places life values above acquisition of knowledge." The conception implicit above that knowledge has little or nothing to do with "life values" was an essential premise of the whole movement. Repeatedly, life-adjustment spokesmen were to intimate that intellectual training is of no use in solving the "real-life problems of ordinary youth." Thus the life-adjustment movement stated, in extreme form, the proposition toward which progressive education had been moving for over four decades—that in a system of mass education, an academically serious training is an impossibility for more than a modest fraction of the student population. After the Prosser resolution was passed, a tremendous drive was launched on national, regional, state and local levels to translate life-adjustment principles into curricula practice.

III. Crisis in Education

Only in the early 1950s did Americans become aware of vast changes in the public schools. Only after the post-World War II adjustment did any large numbers of Americans wake up to what had happened. The life-adjustment movement was the last straw. Then, against a background of deepening public concern over national security, the voracious demands of an "expert society" for trained manpower and skilled technicians, and the emergence of a new generation of parents who possessed both the competence and the motivation to be concerned with the quality of the education their children were receiving, the dam of criticism burst. It was this new generation of well-educated parents who provided the audience in the 1950's and 1960's for books like *Quackery in the Public Schools, The Diminished Mind, Schools Without Scholars, The Mis-Education of American Teachers*, and the writings of Arthur Bestor, Admiral Hyman Rickover, and James B. Conant, and who provide the support for organizations like The Council for Basic Education and for schools like those that follow the Montessori method.

In the 1950s a new educational line, a hard line or "counterprogressive" line made its appearance. Whereas the central thrust of progressive education had been expansionist and had sought to extend the functions of the school, the central effort of the 1950s and 1960s was rather to define more precisely the school's responsibility, to delineate those things the school needed to do because if the school didn't do them they would not get done—namely, intellectual development. The Federal Government, through the National Defense Education Act and the National Science Foundation, began to expend millions of dollars to upgrade the teaching of science, mathematics, and foreign languages. Largely on the initiative of university scholars, and with the support of the Ford Foundation for the Advancement of Education as well as of other foundations, new high school curricula began to appear in physics, biology, chemistry, mathematics, English, social studies, and foreign languages. There were new developments in the elementary school, too, as a new generation of educational psychologists like Jerome Bruner of Harvard downgraded "learning readiness" theory. Bruner, in 1960, made the startling assertion that any subject matter can be taught to anybody at any age in some form that is intellectually honest. Much of today's curriculum reform is based on this hypothesis. This is not to suggest, however, that the pressures for the reform of education emanated only from academics or foundations or parents of college-bound children. In the past decade the demands for the strengthening of education have been reinforced by a revolution in race relations.

Gunnar Myrdal, in his classic 1944 study of the Negro, *An American Dilemma: The Negro Problem and Modern Democracy*, states that in America, education has always been the great hope for both the individual and society. In the "American Creed" it has been the main ground upon which equality of opportunity has been based. American Negroes took over this faith in education. After the Civil War, ex-slaves, young and old, men and women, flocked to study the alphabet and spelling book and Bible in old plantation sheds or at town street corners. The first generation of emancipated Negroes trusted that education would lead them to the promised land. A hope soon shattered for a people disenfranchised, economically suppressed, socially barred by rigid rules of caste, and subjected to humiliation and terror.

The last decades of the 19th century saw the waning of genuine antagonism between the North and the South. The Negro was a victim of the reconciliation. More than twenty years of post-Reconstruction "progress" had made the United States a less promising place for Negroes than it had been just after the Civil War. By 1900 the civil rights of Negroes were overwhelmed in a rising tide of white supremacy, legally enforced in the Southern states (but unofficially endorsed by the entire nation) and left intact by the Supreme Court. The Supreme Court's *Plessy v. Ferguson* decision (1896) took the constitutionality of separate schools for granted. Even so, the formula "equal but separate" (usually recalled as "separate but equal") was ignored by politicians and educational administrators who participated in the new era of Southern public school development that opened at the turn of the century. In 1895, South Carolina spent $3.11 for each white student and $1.05 for each Negro student. In 1911, the figures were, respectively, $13.02 and $1.71. Emancipation was unreal. So, too, was the Negro's drive for education.

During the nadir of Negro rights in the United States, an ex-slave,

Booker T. Washington, became the chief spokesman for his people. Thwarted on every hand, their early hopes to rise through education dashed, Southern Negroes learned from Washington a gospel of industrial education, thrift, and acceptance of segregation. In a speech to white Southerners in 1895, later labeled "the Atlanta Compromise," Washington declared that agitation over questions of social equality was extreme folly. "In all things that are purely social we can be as separate as the five fingers," he said, "yet one as the hand in all things essential to mutual progress." As a compromiser, Washington brought down upon himself the wrath of Negro integrationists like W. E. Burghardt du Bois, one of the founders of the National Association for the Advancement of Colored People. In the context of the times, however, of opposition by Southern whites to *any* kind of education for freedmen, Washington's position deserves sympathetic hearing.

The last to be hired, the first to be fired, the Negro suffered harshly during the Depression. During World War II, economic opportunities for the Negro improved. Yet school segregation continued to belie the premises of the common school. As late as 1951, twenty-one states and the District of Columbia either compelled or permitted by law the separate education of the races. In 1954, after a long, carefully planned legal campaign led by the NAACP, the Supreme Court in *Brown v. Board of Education* (of Topeka, Ka.), concluded that separate but equal is inherently unequal, and that "segregation is a denial of the equal protection of the laws." The Court subsequently left with district courts the duty of enforcing compliance "with all deliberate speed." With the *Brown v. Board of Education* decision, the "Second American Revolution" began. At first—inspired by a new national leader, the Reverend Martin Luther King—nonviolent and restrained, by 1964 it had become more aggressive and violent, and more and more turned attention to the inequality of the treatment of Negroes (and other nonwhites) in the North.

The civil rights movement had three major lines of development in relation to the schools. At first, civil rights advocates concentrated on fighting racial segregation in the Old South and border states. The second line of development concerned the fight against segregated schools of the Northern states, especially in the large cities, where there had been a tremendous influx of Negro migration from the South. In these Northern metropolitan areas, racial segregation came to be referred to as *de facto*, having its basis typically in residential patterns rather than in actual legislation. The third major area of concern was in improving the quality of public school education in all the urban centers of the nation, especially for culturally disadvantaged children. The position of civil rights advocates was that schools must provide the kind of education that would overcome or compensate for the effects of racial discrimination and cultural deprivation.

In response to the thrust of the civil rights movement, as well as other developments in American life referred to earlier, the infusion of quality into American education now came to be one of the prime concerns of the Federal Government. Since 1954, the Government has responded with an extraordinary series of laws and a massive influx of funds. First came the passage of the 1958 National Defense Education Act under which the U.S. Office of Education sponsored efforts to upgrade the teaching of foreign languages, mathematics, and science. During the next seven years the Federal Government was to expand this initial narrow outlook into an unprecedented concern for the total quality of American education. This landslide of educational legislation culminated in the Elementary and Secondary Education Act of 1965, which committed the Government to expenditures of $1.3 billion for 1965 alone, with most of the authorization for programs designed to meet the needs of culturally disadvantaged children. President Lyndon B. Johnson put it well: "The first session of the Eighty-ninth Congress will go down in history as 'The Education Congress.'" Yet, the massive influx of funds has apparently had little effect. The National Advisory Commission on Civil Disorders (1968) has documented the bleak performance of the public schools: "In critical skills—verbal and reading ability—Negro students are falling further behind whites with each year of school completed." The failure of our inner-city schools is so great that some thoughtful observers like Kenneth Clark are beginning to think the unthinkable. They argue that the urban public schools have failed on so grand a scale they might well be replaced or radically altered by contracting out education to nonpublic organizations, to private industry or the foundations, for example. Nor has the drive to desegregate schools, North or South, fared better. Some Negroes have given up on integration as the panacea for Negro education, and have begun, ironically, to call for segregated school systems—black schools for black children, taught by black teachers, controlled by black parents, responsible to the black community, a position that receives some support in the Coleman Report, *Equality of Educational Opportunity* (1966), a study sponsored by the U.S. Office of Education.

Community participation was an original plank of the common-school movement. Long in eclipse as an educational desideratum, community participation took a new and dramatic turn in the 1960s as inner-city leaders and parents increasingly demanded a role in determining policy for the schools that were failing to educate their children. Appearing originally as part of the black civil rights movement, the demand was taken up by other urban minority groups—Puerto Ricans in New York City; American Indians in the West; and Mexican-Americans in the Southwest, the "forgotten Americans" of whom Professor González writes so eloquently in Chapter 5. Segregation of Mexican-American children in the public schools of the Southwest was never rigidly fixed by statute and ordinance as was done with the Negro in the South. Nevertheless, the unwritten laws of many communities in the Southwest established a system of segregated schools that ensured inadequate education. In California, it was only as late as 1947 that school segregation of Mexican-American children was declared illegal. Yet most of the Mexican-American children in the Southwest in fact still attend segregated schools. Minimal or no attention is given to the Mexican-American heritage or to contemporary issues in Mexican-American life. It is usual for the public schools to ignore the cultural heritage and the language of the Spanish-speaking children as if it didn't exist, or worse, as if it required eradication.

The predicament of the Mexican-American child brings up again questions of unity and diversity that have troubled American education from the beginning—questions that have involved Indians and Negroes and immigrant ethnic groups in turn. From the time of the Revolution, substantial numbers of Americans have supposed that the free citizen was the uniform man, and that diversity somehow endangered the promise of American life since it threatened cohesiveness. Others saw a free society as a place where it was comfortable to be different. Diversity, said these pluralists, was a blessing, not a curse. The education of the Indian, the Negro, and the immigrant from the south and east of Europe earlier posed the problem of diversity within unity; the education of the Mexican American opens the question once more. White, middle-class America has long paid lip service to a pluralistic American way of life, while rejecting the culturally different in practice. Too often, the attempt has been to use the schools as instruments for the forced assimilation of minority groups into the Anglo-Saxon world. We shall see whether the time has finally come to accept in practice as well as in theory the values of diversity; whether the time has finally come to provide an environment in which many cultures can flourish; in which an un-common school system can flourish.

IV. Which Way American Education?

It would not be accurate to say that progressive education is dead. The Progressive Education Association may be dead, but progressive education is a very lively cadaver, strongly entrenched in the schools. Progressive education had all the characteristics of a mass movement. No mass movement can die a sudden death. Most important, progressive education enjoys enormous support from the culture. The old middle-class values of thrift, work, achievement, and competition have in the past eighty years been assaulted all along the line. The work ethic is being challenged by a play ethic, competition by cooperation, character by personality, the individualistic ethic by the social ethic. This is the message of books like William Whyte, *The Organization Man,* and David Riesman, *The Lonely Crowd.* The schools are oriented to such considerations. Today schools are called upon to supply the psychological supports and social skills no longer provided children by the stable family and neighborhood. It's no wonder they emphasize sociability, personality development, and leisure-time activities. The concern for mental hygiene has certainly not receded; books under the heading of mental hygiene or social adjustment and education are legion. The tremendous instability of marriage and the early age at which many marriages occur keeps the pressure on schools to educate the "whole child." The general anti-intellectual tone of progressive education finds wide support in the culture. Marshall McLuhan has announced that we are moving into the post-literate era. The cult of art and creative self-expression still reigns. The education editor of *Look Magazine* tells us that today children must learn how to "sing and dance and interact." There is a large audience of flower children of all ages for neo-progressives like Paul Goodman; A. S. Neill and Summerhill have been rediscovered. The progressive movement in the universities is alive—heading towards its uncertain denouement. Youthful radicals, seizing on the service function of the university, have insisted that the university serve the causes that *they* hold dear. Education does not proceed in a vacuum. Its character is determined by the group culture. Plato once wrote: "What is honored in a country will be cultivated there." Was the era of progressive education a short-term phenomenon or part of a basic trend? Is the new "hard line" a passing thing, temporarily excited by the shocks and strains of international and domestic tension? It is very difficult to say. The schools are made of our flesh and bones, of our thoughts and emotions and values. Our public schools supply training for life in America. But Americans are not very sure of the kind of life they want. Little wonder public education is an arena of strife and conflict.

America's is surely the most remarkable education system. No other school system in the world deals with students in such great numbers and with so much liberality and persistence. Yet there has never been a time when there has been more dissatisfaction with the schools. Of course the schools have contributed to the power, the affluence, and the fantastic technological achievements of the nation. Yet one aspect of the democratic revolution in the United States was that America was to be the land of the fresh start. The school was to be one of the chief agents of social mobility and self-improvement. Within the past few decades there is increasing evidence that the American public school system, more elaborate and more efficient than ever before, has paradoxically become less effective as an instrument of social mobility, let alone of individual self-fulfillment. Indeed, there is increasing evidence, as a spate of recent books by Paul Goodman, John Holt, Jonathan Kozol, Herbert Kohl, Edgar Friedenburg, and others vigorously point out, that the educational practices of our public schools have resulted in consolidating or intensifying the distinctions among the classes, and stifling or deflecting into mean channels the potential of many who pass through its doors.

There is a constant of American history; the belief in America's unique mission in the world; America, the City Upon a Hill. Another constant has been the ubiquitous sense of mission that has shaped the thinking and rhetoric of American educational theorists. This pietistic-perfectionist streak in the American temper contains within it a repugnant strain of authoritarianism, self-righteousness, and naiveté. It has also inspired much generosity, self-awareness, and social concern. For better or worse, America is, and always has been, a nation of pietists. If this has led to a noxious feeling of superiority, it has also led to indomitable efforts to close the gap between reality and aspiration. It is both the despair and the promise of America, and of American education.

References

Bowers, Claude A., *The Progressive Educator and the Depression: The Radical Years*, Random House, N.Y., 1969. An important study of a neglected era in American education.

Callahan, Raymond E., *Education and the Cult of Efficiency*, University of Chicago Press, Chicago, 1962. A study of the social forces that helped shape the educational bureaucracy, from 1900 to 1930.

Cremin, Lawrence A., *The Transformation of the School: Progressivism in American Education, 1876-1957*, Random House, New York, 1961. The path-breaking history of Progressive Education and much more besides. A Bancroft Prize winner.

Harlan, Louis R., *Separate and Unequal: Public School Campaigns and Racism in the Southern Seaboard States, 1901-1915*, University of North Carolina Press, Chapel Hill, North Carolina, 1958. A richly detailed and convincing exposition of the subject.

Krug, Edward A., *The Shaping of the American High School*, Harper and Row, New York, 1964. A comprehensive and illuminating history of the high school in the period 1880-1920.

Grebler, Leo, Joan W. Moore, Ralph C. Guzman, *et al.*, *The Mexican-American People*, The Free Press, New York, 1970. The best study available on all aspects of the nation's second largest minority.

Veysey, Laurence R., *The Emergence of the American University*, University of Chicago Press, Chicago Illinois, 1965. Developments from 1865 to 1910. The authoritative history of the subject.

Welter, Rush, *Popular Education and Democratic Thought In America*, Columbia University Press, New York, 1962. An intriguing study of the influence of educational thought on political attitudes and vice-versa.

PART TWO

SOCIAL
FOUNDATIONS

3

The Impact of Culture

George F. Kneller

❖❖

In the first two chapters Professor Cohen presented several dramatic examples of the diverse interplay between education and the surrounding culture. These examples enable us to consider more intimately three important aspects: cultural values, cultural discontinuity, and cultural change. Let us begin by reviewing the meanings of some fundamental terms.

Culture, Society, Community. First, what is "culture" and how does it differ from "society" and "community"? Culture in general is the totality of ways of life that have evolved through history. A particular culture is the total shared life of a given people—their modes of thinking, acting, and feeling, as expressed in religion, law, language, art, technology, child-rearing, and, of course, education. Society in general is the totality of peoples that have existed in history. A particular society is a given population living in a certain region whose members cooperate over a period of time for the attainment of certain ends. Putting the contrast in a sentence, we may say that a culture is the way of life of a people, whereas a society is a people with a way of life. A "community" may be defined as a subsociety whose members (1) are in personal contact, (2) are concerned for one another's welfare, (3) are committed to common purposes and procedures, (4) share responsibility for joint actions, and (5) value membership in the community as an end in itself.

In any large society there are usually a number of communities or subsocieties that feel themselves to be distinct. These groups will have developed certain values and practices and so will possess their own subcultures. There are probably more subcultures in the United States than in any other society. They include racial and ethnic subcultures, such as Indian, Mexican, Negro, Puerto Rican, and Jewish ones, together with a host of subcultures deriving from age and occupation, such as those of the armed forces, the police, labor unions, rock musicians, teenagers, and college students. These subcultures intermingle. A Negro with deep loyalties to his people may nevertheless identify strongly with rock and college subcultures. But each group defends its culture against groups it regards as hostile. Thus we find Negroes and college students demanding the right to their own life styles as against those of the "establishment" and the police. Indeed, as later chapters will show, America is in turmoil today because many groups are insisting that society at large recognize the dignity and value of their ways of life and the contribution they make or can make to American culture as a whole.

Education, Enculturation, Acculturation. Education is the means by which society provides for the transmission or advancement of its culture, for without a viable culture there is no common life by which men are associated. Education may further be defined as the inculcation of knowledge, values, skills, and attitudes by means of institutions that have been created for this end. For many young people education is a part of "enculturation," or the process by which they are initiated into a way of life they feel is their own. For youngsters from a strong subculture, however, especially an ethnic or racial one, education becomes a process of "acculturation," in which they are confronted with a way of life they do not feel to be theirs. A youngster from a ghetto area normally is enculturated by his family, his peers, and other institutions of the ghetto. He is acculturated by the school and other formal institutions of the dominant culture. When these two processes conflict, they may leave the youngster desperately unsure of himself. Usually he settles for the values of his peers and identifies with the subculture of the ghetto. Later he may join the larger society. In doing so, however, he may abandon those values on which his selfhood has been founded and as a result become deeply and painfully "alienated," for he has chosen a way of life determined by others rather than one founded on his own experience.[1]

[1] For a moving account of alienation, see Clark E. Moustakas, "Alienation, Educa-

The problem that educators must resolve is how to acculturate and enculturate at the same time. One way is to employ capable teachers who themselves were raised in ghetto areas, teachers who are acceptable to ghetto members, know the customs, speak the language, share the feelings of minority students, and at the same time appreciate the values of the dominant culture. Another is to enable schools in ethnic communities to adapt their curricula to the local culture, even if this means dropping content that is regarded as important elsewhere. Both these proposals aid the development of local minority cultures and so promote cultural diversity. Two other proposals seek to make the prevailing culture easier for the minority child to assimilate. One of them is to enroll ghetto pupils in largely white schools and in this way avoid the split that occurs in ghetto schools between the white acculturating curriculum and the non-white enculturating subculture of the student body. Another proposal is for middle-class teachers to teach in ghetto schools. These teachers will naturally have to be dedicated, able, and sensitive to ghetto values. They will also have to be acceptable to ghetto members and hopefully will live in ghetto areas. There are not likely to be many of them.

Ultimately, however, the general public must support integrated schooling. Only in an integrated school can the young person develop a natural respect for his fellow man, regardless of color, creed, cultural heritage, or economic status. We are a multiracial, culturally diverse, politically pluralist, democratic society. We are also one nation. And the true purpose of integrated education should be to equip the student to fulfill himself in the larger society, where greater opportunity prevails, rather than to perpetuate old inequalities and disparities. This, however, is a larger order than most people think, and I shall have more to say about it later.

---

tion, and Existential Life," MS., Merrell-Palmer Institute, Detroit, n.d., p. 3: "The alienated person . . . learns mechanically or automatically to make the proper gestures or facial expressions, to denote the appropriate feeling; a smile is not a smile, joy is not joy, and sadness is not sadness; the movements of the face and body are properly placed to take on the appearance of the appropriate emotions . . . . He is anesthetic; he is embedded in a world without color, without excitement, without risk or danger, without mystery; in a word, without meaning." Worst of all, says Moustakas, alienation is taken in some schools to be "a sign of healthy adjustment." Those in power "defeat a genuine existence through conditioning, use of external symbols of status and reward, authoritarian persuasiveness, and numerous [other means] to crush rebellion and resistance and overwhelm and defeat the stubborn person. The child in school very soon becomes separated and detached . . . ."

Cultural Values

I have said that every culture and every subculture will fight to defend its values and sometimes to propagate them. The values of a culture are the things its members believe to be worth striving for. Some values are easy to define—keeping one's word, for example, or maintaining integrity. Others, such as individual freedom or social responsibility, are notoriously vague. Some values, like justice and equality, receive a lot of lip service. Others, like that of private property, are less often acknowledged.

Cultural values are amazingly diverse.[2] What is sacrosanct to one culture may be of no importance to another, while being utterly abhorrent to a third. That competition is morally good and practically beneficial is taken for granted in virtually all walks of American life. We are always urging our friends and our children to get ahead. We want to win, to be on top, to forge forever ahead. Yet in some cultures competition is regarded as vulgar and brutalizing. The Hopi believe that people should cooperate with one another and with nature. A Hopi child is taught never to win a game or excel his classmates.[3] Among the Mixtecans of Mexico envy and competitiveness are regarded as vices. A Mixtecan in authority will suggest a course of action rather than give orders. Collective decisions are reached by consensus rather than by a bare majority.[4]

The average man, however, finds it difficult to view his values with detachment. In his childhood he learned to regard them as universal and absolute and so not to be compromised, for the child cannot understand that something is good unless he also believes that it is good for all men everywhere. The idea that certain acts, such as lying, may be wrong in general but justified on occasion is too sophisticated for a ten-year-old to grasp. Moreover, having been absorbed for the most part unconsciously in the process of enculturation, these values have entered into the personality of the mature man and have done much to mold it.

Let us now consider two aspects of the relation between cultural values and education: (1) The discrepancy between a culture's values and its actual practices—the discrepancy, that is, between "ideal" and "manifest" values, and (2) the disparity between the dominant values of the culture and the values of minority groups within the culture.

2 For an account of how different cultures interpret "equality," for example, see Dorothy Lee, "Equality of Opportunity as a Cultural Value," in *Freedom and Culture*, Prentice-Hall, Englewood Cliffs, New Jersey, 1959, pp. 39-52.

3 Wayne Dennis, *The Hopi Child*, Appleton-Century, New York, 1940.

4 Kimball and Romaine Romey, "The Mixtecans of Mexico," in Beatrice B. Whiting, Ed., *Six Cultures: Studies of Child Rearing*, Wiley, New York, 1963, p. 565.

1. *Values—Ideal and Manifest*

Every culture legitimizes certain goals together with certain norms of behavior for attaining them. These norms need not be efficient, but they are compatible as a rule with the existing values and institutions of the culture. Although the goals are sought, the norms are not always followed. In fact, the less efficient the norms become as means of reaching the culture's goals, the less they tend to be observed. A culture whose norms are widely flouted begins to break down. Eventually it may reach the condition that Emile Durkheim called *anomie,* or normlessness, when the official norms no longer answer to the realities of life in the culture.[5]

Let us look close at hand for a contrast between norm and reality. In America certain success goals, especially those connected with wealth and its symbols (the summer home, the winter cruise, the private airplane), are advertised much more broadly than the institutionalized means for attaining them. Our culture insists that, if a man works long and hard, he will succeed in life—that is, he will make a lot of money. Yet only a few men can get rich by working long and hard, for "rich" is a relative term and the rich by definition must necessarily be few. (In a country of millionaires, only billionaires are wealthy.) This is not to mention other barriers to success, such as social class or ethnic origin, which may not make hard work futile but may considerably limit the benefits to be gained by it. Thus, despite the fact that the culturally sanctioned norm of hard work rarely leads to the wealth it is supposed to, all men are urged to strive for success as the culture defines it. The result may be not only anxiety and frustration but also antisocial behavior, as men seek more effective ways than the official norms to gratify the success drives implanted in them.

Of itself lack of opportunity does not cause deviant behavior; it is the combination of lack of opportunity with the advertisement of success goals for all members of a culture. The culture, in short, arouses expectations that cannot always be fulfilled in the ways it provides.

Let me mention a few more discrepancies between the ideal and the manifest in American culture. On the one hand, we extol free enterprise; on the other, a few large firms dominate the economy. Broad sectors of this

---

[5] Robert K. Merton, "Social Structure and Anomie," *Social Theory and Social Structure,* The Free Press of Glencoe, New York, 1957, p. 135: "With such differential emphasis upon goals and institutional procedures, the latter may be so vitiated by the stress on goals as to have the behavior of many individuals limited only by considerations of technical experience. In this context, the sole significant question becomes: Which of the available procedures is most efficient in netting the culturally approved value?"

economy, such as defense and aviation, are financed by the Federal Government. The small, independent businessman, praised by chambers of commerce, is crushed by the economics of mass production. Again, individualism is prized but togetherness is practiced. Youngsters are encouraged to date early and marry late, yet premarital intercourse is frowned upon. Teachers are mocked as "theoretical" and "impractical," yet they are criticized when they combine their profession with business or political activity.

In a thousand and one ways American schools transmit and reinforce the values of their culture. Since most teachers come from the middle class, much educational practice reflects, however covertly, middle-class values.[6] Although schoolmen differ in many respects, all nevertheless embrace certain values, such as the importance of adult authority, the need for order and discipline, the worth of educational achievement, and such middle-class virtues as cleanliness, punctuality, neatness, politeness, and correct speech. The culture's values also are manifested in the school curriculum. Courses in civics and government convey the values of an open democracy, majority decision, and the permanent possibility of improving the human lot through collective action. Courses in history tend to set one's own nation above others. One's soldiers have always been brave, one's leaders honorable. The enemy, on the other hand, has generally proved cowardly in battle and, what is worse, devious in defeat. (Perhaps this is to be expected. If the enemy had not deserved to be taught a lesson, we would not have fought him, would we?)

A school's organization and activities also reflect accepted values. In the classroom the child learns to respect authority, be industrious, write legibly, use paper sparingly, and so forth. Raising his hand to make suggestions and answer questions reinforces the drive to compete and excel. In games the child learns to play fair and to take his turn with others. In clubs he enjoys the experience of holding a position. From school festivities he acquires loyalty to his school and solidarity with his fellows. Of course he may not absorb all these values or absorb them equally. Other factors may counteract them, such as the special norms of the peer group, the unpopularity of certain teachers, or perhaps lack of parental interest in his education.

---

6 Robert J. Havighurst, "Social Class and the American School System," in George Z. F. Bereday and Luigi Volpicelli, Eds., *Public Education in America: A New Interpretation of Purpose and Practice*, Harper, New York, 1958, p. 86: "Teachers attempt to serve as trustees of the educational system in the interests of the entire society *as they understand these interests.* This means that they tend to favor the teaching of middle class skills and attitudes in the schools, and they favor types of education which promote social mobility."

Inevitably the school finds itself caught in the conflict between ideal and manifest values. Should the school educate the child to strive for certain theoretically desirable objectives or should it condition him to the existing realities of the culture? According to the democratic ethos, people should cooperate to get things done, but in much of our society they compete. Hence, the school oscillates between encouraging children to cooperate and encouraging them to compete; it does not take a firm stand for either value. We extol the idea that everyone should have an equal opportunity to pursue the career most suited to his talents; yet in most careers it is disproportionately difficult for women to succeed. As a result, the school wavers between encouraging girls to become career women and training them to be housewives.

Perhaps the greatest gulf lies between the ideal of equality and the fact of segregation. Not only are many schools and social institutions still segregated, but even in the greater part of the country where segregation officially does not exist, it is difficult for a Negro student to get as good an education as a white student, partly because schools in Negro neighborhoods tend to be poorly staffed and partly because the predominantly white schools are pervaded by white attitudes to which the Negro student is unaccustomed. Other ethnic minorities, such as Indians, Mexicans, and Puetro Ricans, are in a similar plight, as will be revealed in the chapter on minorities.

2. *Dominant versus Minority Values*

The Disadvantaged. The world long has been divided into the "haves" and the "have-nots," the "advantaged" and the "disadvantaged." In the United States the disadvantaged are made up mostly of minority people who have not succeeded in making their way in the dominant society. But there are others as well: those who (1) live in impoverished rural or isolated areas (including millions of whites); (2) belong to strange or unpopular religious groups; (3) are of unusual ethnic origin, national background, or language; (4) lack adequate physical, mental, or spiritual health, no matter from what walk of life; and (5) happen to be girls, for in many parts of the country the education of young women is more restrictive than that of young men. In short, the disadvantaged may be said to be those who live mostly outside the dominant culture and who, by race, religion, sex, or other characteristic, find themselves handicapped in an educational system controlled by the values of the dominant culture.[7]

---

[7] Since my concern in this book is with cultural rather than physical anthropology,

Now, of course, many members of these groups have no taste for the dominant culture and do not aspire to join it. They reject dominant values, or at least see no reason to substitute them for their own. Although sound reasons can be given in support of their attitude, much of it has to be understood as a consequence of, or a reaction against, inadequate and inappropriate education. For these groups, the acculturation process has been both deficient and unproductive.

Who, then, are the culturally disadvantaged pupils? They come usually from the lower classes and are academically backward, the second characteristic being generally a consequence of the first. Although their parents are eager to have them go to school, they are unable to help them with their studies. Since these parents often do work that requires little education, their children frequently do not appreciate the importance of education for their own lives. Coming often from slums or from broken homes, they have little feeling that society as a whole cares about them. Consequently they are more aggressive or intractable than other children; they are also more prone to neuroses and breakdowns; and they turn more readily to delinquency. Many of them cannot cope with the normal academic curriculum (another blow to their already faltering self-esteem); many drop out of school; and very few aspire to a college education. They are further handicapped by their tendency to move from one neighborhood to another, disturbing their own education as well as that of their less mobile fellows.[8]

A child of an advantaged home tends to bring to his school a very different outlook. From infancy he has been more carefully fed, clothed, and

I consider race here as a cultural, not a genetic phenomenon. Whether cultural deficiencies are genetically as well as environmentally conditioned is an area of controversy I do not enter. In their book, *The Disadvantaged: Challenge to Education*, Harper and Row, New York, 1968, pp. 4-5, Mario D. Fantini and Gerald Weinstein broaden the definition of "disadvantaged" to include "all those who are blocked in any way from fulfilling their human potential. . . . Anyone deprived of the means . . . of reaching any basic human goal . . . is disadvantaged, for it is the purpose of our democratic social institutions to advance the development of these human goals for all people."

8 The National Commission on the Causes and Prevention of Violence, chaired by Milton Eisenhower, concluded in 1969 that a combination of environmental factors is responsible for present unrest in ghetto areas and consequent violence. Home, family, neighborhood, school, and job have ceased to stabilize. Corroborating what I have said above, the Commission adds that the father of the typical child of the black slums is "sometimes or frequently intoxicated, or replaced by another man." He is often unemployed, unfair in his treatment of the child, or himself treated disrespectfully by others. No wonder, the Commission remarks, that a slum child grows up resenting such authority figures as policemen and teachers.

protected by parents who have the time and money to spend on him. Tenderness and understanding, pride and affection, have been shown him from the beginning. He usually is at ease in a world in which he assumes that he will succeed as a matter of course. Having absorbed the drive and directedness of his parents, he is purposeful and self-confident.

The typical American school expects children to be polite, to follow the conventions, and to respect other people's property. It encourages hard work, efficiency, and, above all, ambition. To all these values the middle-class child is already accustomed. His teachers, members of the middle class themselves, respond to him with understanding and appreciation. But to the disadvantaged child many of these values are foreign. Because the values of school are not his, he feels he does not belong. Hence, disadvantaged children rarely do as well in school as middle-class children of equal and even lesser ability, and some of them drop out even when they are intellectually capable of continuing.[9]

The school's middle-class culture hinders the disadvantaged child in many ways. The language of the school is unfamiliar to him. Most textbooks appeal to middle-class values, their illustrations depicting middle-class situations. He is not at ease with his teachers, who dress, talk, and think differently. The subjects that he studies—grammar, history, and science—seem to him to have little or no bearing on the sordid and sometimes desperate circumstances with which he must cope when he returns home. The very procedures of the school may violate the values he has learned to hold dear.[10]

Educating the Culturally Disadvantaged. Educating the culturally disadvantaged, long a problem in this country, has now become a matter of extreme urgency. The problem has been aggravated by the exodus of the white middle class to the suburbs and the inflow of the rural poor, many of them Negro and Spanish-speaking.[11] Every year some 50,000

[9] Robert J. Havighurst found that for every high school dropout from the upper and upper-middle classes there were about 32 from the upper-lower and lower-lower classes. Moreover, fifteen students entered college from the two top social classes for every one from the two lower classes. Havighurst also found that, when the proportion of middle-class children in a school approached or fell below 40 percent, their parents began either to leave the neighborhood or to enroll their children in private schools. (Robert J. Havighurst et al., *Growing Up in River City*, Wiley, New York, 1962, pp. 50-53.)

[10] Note that some children of the Plains Indians fail because they will not behave competitively. Although each child is expected to recite publicly and be praised for his display of knowledge, few do so because this is felt to be boastful and a public shaming of one's kinsmen.

[11] Clemmont E. Vontress, "Our Demoralizing Slum Schools," *Phi Delta Kappan,* **XLV,** 2 (November 1963), 77.

whites leave New York City, and some 20,000 leave Chicago and Los Angeles. In the meantime, Negroes and Puerto Ricans pour into New York, Negroes and Mexicans into Los Angeles, and Negroes and Appalachian whites into the big cities of the North and Midwest. In the hearts of these cities housing is generally bad, population density high, and privacy minimal. Many of the inhabitants are on public relief. Most have scanty education and little vocational competence. Families are disorganized and crime flourishes, especially among the young. In most of our large cities the number of disadvantaged children, incredibly enough, will soon equal or exceed the number of advantaged children.

The purposes of programs for the disadvantaged are (1) to surmount cultural differences without sacrificing their special values, and (2) to raise the culturally disadvantaged child to middle-class standards of achievement.[12] How are teachers to accomplish these purposes? First, to understand the attitudes that children bring to school, they must study the subcultures in which the children are reared. They must use this knowledge to develop appropriate techniques for all aspects of instruction. They will find that many classroom problems arise not because the pupil or his parents are hostile but because they are unaccustomed to the language, values, and customs of the school.[13]

Second, teachers should run a critical eye over prevailing typologies of student characteristics, many of which ignore the subcultural determinants of student behavior. A child from a Mexican home may be an "underachiever"; more likely he is being badly acculturated. A Negro child may have "deficient motivation"; more likely he is being subjected to Anglo-American standards of academic success. Children from subcultures may express themselves physically and emotionally rather than verbally. When asked to speak out in class, an Indian hesitates, gets stage fright, and is unable to express what he feels. He is then assigned to a class of "remedials" or, worse, to a school for the "mentally retarded." Teachers should bear in mind that the terms I have quoted have been invented and

12 Publications on the education of the disadvantaged are now legion. A good anthology is Staten W. Webster, Ed., *The Disadvantaged Learner*, Chandler, San Francisco, 1966. *School and Society* devoted an entire issue to the problem (96, 2, March 30, 1968).

13 The story is told of an intelligent but unruly Korean-American boy who was nearly expelled from his school because the school authorities did not comprehend the cultural traditions of his Korean father. Unaware of the veneration accorded by Koreans to the head of the household, school representatives tried persistently to reach the mother. Finally, when the father was approached in the manner to which he was accustomed, he cooperated with the school in controlling the child.

applied by social scientists who come from the dominant culture and may be biased by its assumptions.[14]

Third, teachers should encourage bilingualism.[15] One's ability to speak English is not hindered by the ability to use a foreign language. Teachers of Mexican and Puerto Rican children especially should learn Spanish. Clearly, these children must master English, but they should not be penalized for reverting to their own language, particularly in conversation among themselves. If they are to retain the pride in self to which they are entitled and which is necessary for effective learning, their language must be treated with the respect it deserves and not as an inferior argot used to deceive or exclude teachers. A command of Spanish can win for a teacher the affection and trust of pupils with whom other teachers have little influence.

Fourth, the teacher should examine the influence of culture on his own conduct. He should scrutinize his own values and try to trace their origins. What are values for him might be biases in the eyes of his pupils. Unless the teacher knows the cultural signals he himself is sending out, he gains little from perceiving the signals of his pupils. Likewise he should learn to distinguish between significant and insignificant values. A child's manner of eating, drinking, dressing, and playing is certainly less important than such basic values as integrity, honesty, loyalty, kindness, and consideration. A teacher who chides a pupil for his style of dress, grooming, or eating, or for some other relatively inconsequential way of behaving, can hardly expect to win confidence and trust when dealing with really important values.

Finally, school counselors should foster vocational ambitions receiving

14 In February, 1969, a federal judge ordered California public schools to revise testing procedures so as to prevent shunting children from non-English-speaking homes into "mentally retarded" classes. The order required (among other things) that (a) all such children be tested both in their primary language and in English, (b) they be tested in ways that do not require a middle-class background to succeed, (c) state psychologists devise a new IQ test for Mexican-American children that will reflect their culture.

15 Encouraging here is the Yarborough Bill, August, 1967, S.428, authorizing the expenditure of federal funds to help schools build on the cultural strengths a pupil brings to the classroom, including bilingualism. The object of the bill is to (a) cultivate ancestral pride in the child, (b) give him a sense of personal identity essential to social maturation, (c) reinforce the language he speaks natively, (d) impart a knowledge of the history and ideals of his subculture, (e) provide teachers, equipment, etc. to do the job, and (f) engage in relevant research and experimentation. The program began modestly in the school year 1969-1970.

little or no encouragement from parents, community, or peers.[16] They should provide examples of successful adulthood that lower-class youngsters can imitate and in so doing develop long-term ambitions of their own as well as the personality traits needed to attain them. They should also acquaint students with examples of successful professional persons from their own racial, ethnic, or class background, and they should encourage parents to sympathize with the newly awakened ambitions of their children.[17]

However, special programs for the culturally disadvantaged raise some ethical questions that we must answer here. First, will these programs, beginning as they do at an intellectually less demanding level, simply provide the disadvantaged pupil with an inferior education? No, for their purpose is to ground the pupil thoroughly in fundamentals so that he may then study more sophisticated subjects. Unless the culturally disadvantaged pupil receives special attention early in school, the deficiencies in his environment, which have slowed his intellectual development, will cause him to experience increasing difficulty with a curriculum designed for middle-class children.[18]

Next, are these programs fair to other children? I think so. The principle that special educational problems merit special programs at extra cost already has been accepted in the case of physically handicapped, mentally retarded, academically gifted, and emotionally disturbed children. If culturally deprived children are to have the same educational opportunity as other children, the only way to compensate for their deficiencies is to give them more attention in the school. Moreover, these programs save the community money in the long run by producing more competent citizens and so cutting expenditures on welfare and rehabilitation.

Finally, do these programs perpetuate segregation in fact if not in

16 Cf. David P. Ausubel, "A Teaching Strategy for Culturally Deprived Pupils: Cognitive and Motivational Considerations," *The School Review*, Winter 1963, 462-463.

17 I lack space here to list or evaluate the programs that the Government has sponsored for the disadvantaged child. Suffice to say that in general these programs succeed when teachers take a personal interest in the pupil. Also, many agencies report that general behavior is improved before acadmic behavior; better speech, better dress, and better grooming generally precede greater interest in studies.

18 Cf. David P. Ausubel, op. cit., p. 465: "[Beginning at the pupil's actual state of readiness] . . . is merely a necessary first step in preparing him to cope with more advanced subject matter, and hence in eventually reducing existing social-class differentials in academic achievement. To set the same initial standards and expectations for the academically retarded culturally deprived child as for the nonretarded middle-or-lower class child is automatically to insure the former's failure and to widen prevailing discrepancies between social class groups."

name? No, they counteract segregation because they enable disadvantaged students to take part in activities with children from all over the school district and because they qualify some disadvantaged students for college-preparatory courses, where they can interact socially with white middle-class children.[19] These programs also enable children to gain competencies that eventually will facilitate their moving to white middle-class neighborhoods.

The ultimate challenge, of course, is to eliminate the need for compensatory education for the disadvantaged, but this is a task to which the nation as a whole must be committed. The school cannot do it alone. The ultimate goal is the truly "open" society in which *all* children will have access to quality education.[20]

Cultural Discontinuity

Let us now turn to an experience that is shared by young Americans of all backgrounds, the experience of crossing the gap that separates the world of the child from that of the adult. All young people everywhere must cross into maturity, but an American youngster faces a particularly rough passage. Contrary to the custom in many primitive societies, where the growing child is introduced to adult roles little by little from his earliest years, in the United States, as in other industrial societies, the youngster is kept a child until adolescence and is then expected to suddenly become an adult. So to the biological stress of adolescence is added

[19] Virgil A. Clift, "Factors Relating to the Education of Culturally Deprived Negro Youth," *Educational Theory*, **XIV**, 2 (April 1964), 77-78. In answering these ethical questions I am assuming that integration is desirable. Not all are convinced of this. See, for example, Robert V. Dumont and Murray L. Wax, "Cherokee School Society and the Intercultural Classroom," *Applied Anthropology*, **XXVIII**, 3 (Fall 1969), 217-226. "Ethnic integration," they maintain, "is not an essential precondition for satisfactory education of groups from a low socio-economic background." What is needed is "consolidation of rural schools into larger, better-staffed, better equipped schools" for the Indians themselves. Even when Indian children were "incarcerated in boarding establishments . . . to shape them in the molds of the conquering society . . . the Indians developed their own norms and values, which were neither those of their Indian elders nor those of their non-Indian instructors."

[20] For an excellent clinical study, see Deborah Elkins, "Instructional Guidelines for Teachers of the Disadvantaged," *Teachers College Record*, **LXX**, 7 (April, 1969), 593-607. On the nation's obligation to provide for *all* its varied peoples, I cannot refrain from quoting Lord Acton, who as early as 1862 proclaimed: "A state which is incompetent to satisfy different races condemns itself; a state which labors to neutralize, to absorb, or to expel them, destroys its own vitality; a state which does not include them is destitute of the chief basis of self-government."

the shock of sudden enculturation into a way of life for which he has been little prepared.[21]

In America childhood and adulthood are discontinuous in many ways. The American family is fairly self-contained, and until he goes to school, the child lives almost wholly within his family. When he meets adults other than his parents, it is in this setting. Thus early in life his expectations of older people are shaped almost entirely by his parents and older siblings.[22] What is more, he is brought up almost entirely by one person, his mother. It is mainly she who disciplines, rewards, and loves him. His father, who is absent most of the day, is both less real to him and less influential. After five or six years of close dependence on his mother the child naturally has difficulty in adjusting to other people.

Today the American child is free of any significant social or economic responsibility.[23] In cities especially his play does not prepare him for an occupation. As American society becomes more and more industrialized, it requires a greater social competence of the young adult. At the same time it makes this competence more difficult for the child to achieve, for as education grows longer and more abstract, and as work becomes more technical, the world of the child has less and less in common with the world in which men actually earn their living. Except among the lowest income groups, the money that the child earns as a paper boy or golf caddy is either of marginal importance to his family or else goes into his own pocket. In fact his parents may well pay him to do chores that in

[21] Some primitive societies allow the child to mature at his own pace, permitting him to be initiated into adulthood when he is ready for it and not necessarily when he has reached a certain age. Many primitive societies, it is true, provide a protracted and often painful initiation into adulthood; but the ordeal is nearly always deliberately devised and carefully controlled to reorient the adolescent from one way of life to another, whereas the ordeal of the modern adolescent confuses rather than reorients him. See Ina Corinne Brown, *Understanding Other Cultures*, Prentice-Hall, Englewood Cliffs, New Jersey, 1962, p. 50; Kimball and Romaine Romney, "The Mixtecans of Mexico," in Beatrice B. Whiting, Ed., *Six Cultures: Studies of Child Rearing*, Wiley, New York, 1963. p. 630; William F. and Corinne Nydegger, "Tarong: An Ilcos Barrio in the Philippines," ibid., p. 280; and George D. Spindler, "Personality, Sociocultural System, and Education among the Menomini," in George D. Spindler, Ed., *Education and Culture: Anthropological Approaches*, Holt, Rinehart and Winston, New York, 1963, p. 381. According to Spindler, by the age of five a child of the Menomini Indians is "at least dimly aware" of all the roles and statuses of his tribe.

[22] Cf. Grace Graham, *The Public School in the American Community*, Harper and Row, New York, 1963, pp. 159-160; and John L. and Ann Fischer, "The New Englanders of Orchard Town, U.S.A.," in Whiting, op cit., p. 967.

[23] Ruth Benedict, "Continuities and Discontinuities in Cultural Conditioning," in W. Martin and C. Stendler, Eds., *Readings in Child Development*, Harcourt, Brace, New York, 1954, pp. 142-148.

previous ages he would have performed as a matter of course. Hence he contributes nothing significant to society by working. Indeed, the law forbids him to work full time. Yet as soon as he reaches maturity he is expected to compete on equal terms with adults.

Again, in America children are expected to be submissive and adults dominant. As a result the adolescent is caught between his old habit of submitting to adults and his new need to be self-assertive.[24] The conflict is particularly acute for a young married couple who must make a family of their own only shortly after leaving their parental homes. The girl, accustomed to being looked after by her parents, must suddenly take responsibility for the health and welfare of a husband and children. The young husband, used to being indulged, must now take care of an entire household.

There is a disparity also between the relative freedom of the adult to release his impulses and the self-control expected of the child. Adults may smoke, drink, tell racy stories, and engage in sexual intercourse. The child with a taste for these pleasures must satisfy it on the sly. Our culture is particularly severe in its repression of youthful sexuality. It teaches the child that sex is wrong, and then, having informed him in his teens about the facts of reproduction, it forbids him to experiment with what he has learned. Pregnancy is often camouflaged, breast-feeding is hidden, and many girls experience menstruation for the first time in ignorance of its meaning. Virginity and continence are extolled, but on the wedding night the woman is expected to be sexually intelligent and responsive and the man skilled enough to reassure her.[25]

I am not arguing that we should allow our children to smoke, drink, and be promiscuous. Far from it. Our culture requires a level of behavior much more sophisticated than that needed in primitive cultures, and consequently the techniques of competent adult behavior are here less easily and less quickly acquired. With good reason we teach our children to restrain impulses that we permit adults to express, for children lack experience to count the consequences of emotional release. On the other hand, there is nothing sacrosanct about many of the curbs now placed on children's behavior. The child is aware that his parents freely express impulses that he is supposed to restrain, and this awareness not only taxes his self-control but also leads to deceit and feelings of guilt. How much

[24] Ruth Benedict, op. cit., pp. 142-148.

[25] Cf. Jules Henry, *Culture Against Man*, Random House, New York, 1963, p. 237. Among the Pilagá Indians of Argentina children may enjoy sexual intercourse, listen to and tell sexual stories, and smoke when tobacco is available. They drink little, not because drinking is held to be immoral but because it is reserved for older men.

of this strain is necessary and indeed salutary and how much can be avoided is matter for debate. What cannot be doubted is that in an increasingly hedonistic culture parents and teachers cannot expect children and young people to obey the stringent standards of an earlier day.

Yet suppose these discontinuities did not exist. Living as he does in a complex and swiftly changing culture, the modern youth would still be subject to greater strains than youth in primitive societies, since he has more, and also more complicated, choices to make and so runs more risk of choosing inappropriately. The anxieties of decision are multiplied not only by the existence of conflicting moral and social standards but also by our belief in the importance of choice and in the individual's responsibility for the consequences of his behavior. Youngsters also mature physically earlier than they used to and so take up such activities as dating and going steady, for which they are psychologically less prepared than an earlier generation.[26]

As young people mature earlier physically and remain at school longer, the period of social adolescence is prolonged and a mass adolescent subculture arises marked by conformity to the peer group and hostility or indifference to parental values. Centering on the high school, this separate culture, whose members rely on one another for psychological support and social reward, "maintains only a few threads of connection with the outside adult society."[27]

Other factors may also alienate the adolescent from his parents. The pace of social and cultural change outmodes the knowledge and attitudes of parents more quickly than it used to. The modern adolescent is all the more aware that his parents' standards are dated because the mass media daily provide him with the latest styles of teen behavior, with evanescent customs and a special argot. Again, economic specialization has helped to alienate father from son, partly because the son need no longer follow

---

[26] Cf. Margaret Mead, "The Young Adult," in E. Ginzberg. Ed., *Values and Ideals of American Youth*, Columbia University Press, New York, 1961. Mead writes that the importance of dating in American culture adds to the anxieties of the adolescent, who as often as not lacks firm values of his own and so feels unable to resist peer group pressure to engage in sexual activities that he may not really desire. Boys in particular, who mature more slowly than girls, often are forced into female company for which they are ready neither physiologically nor psychologically. Instead of making deep friendships with members of their own sex, they come to distrust other males as competitors for girls. According to Mead, this premature heterosexual association leads to antagonism between the sexes, to "hostility to females on the boys' part and, on the girls' part pressure toward marriage combined with contempt for males" (p. 79).

[27] J. S. Coleman, *The Adolescent Society*, The Free Press of Glencoe, New York, 1961, p. 3. See also C. Wayne Gordon, *Social System of the High School*, Free Press of Glencoe, New York, 1957.

his father's career, and partly because, if he does, the knowledge and skills that he must learn will probably be too complex for his father to have time to teach him. Moreover, family cohesion is weakened because the adolescent contributes nothing substantial to the family's economy and because the family rarely teaches him any specific knowledge or skills that fit him for a role in the adult community. Finally, in a swiftly changing and pluralist society he is exposed to the conflicting values of a range of religious and secular systems, an experience that undermines still further whatever convictions he may have acquired as a child. Feeling that the standards of his elders are irrelevant to his world, he turns for reassurance to his peers, not thereby attaining real independence, but choosing another kind of conformity.

What attitude should the teacher take toward culturally induced discontinuities in the pupil's development? That will depend on the philosophy or values of the teacher. Some teachers will accept discontinuity as inevitable and indeed desirable in life. They will therefore teach their students to understand it and to cope with it successfully.[28]

It can also be argued that discontinuity is a necessary condition of growing up. By shattering the mold of childhood, the cultural shock of adolescence gives the young person a chance to find values of his own instead of reinforcing those that have been instilled in him. In order to grow up, he must continually reshape his attitudes and behavior in the light of fresh experiences. A modern society requires its members to advance much further from their early experiences than does a primitive society.[29] Hence a modern society must necessarily increase the discontinuity between childhood and adulthood.

Other teachers will wish to mitigate this discontinuity as much as possible. They will gradually give the pupil more freedom and responsibility. They will treat him as a potential adult, cooperating with him rather than commanding him. Does this conflict with the principle that

---

[28] Those taking this point of view have a powerful ally in the anthropologist Bronislaw Malinowski, who writes ". . . at any stage of culture the chances of spiritual freedom . . . depend, first and foremost, upon the existence of a number of mutually independent institutions, which, though related, enjoy a considerable degree of autonomy. Indeed, in several educational devices of the primitives, we see that joining a new institution or passing through initiation ceremonies entails a definite attempt to break down the loyalties and interests acquired in earlier life and to introduce new values. The institutions thus each exercise an autonomous spiritual influence on the growing mind." (Bronislaw Malinowski, *Freedom and Civilization*, Allen and Unwin, London, 1947, pp. 143-144.)

[29] Richard Church, *Language and the Discovery of Reality*, Random House, New York, 1961, pp. 138-139.

the child should be treated according to the needs and desires of his age? No, it conforms to this principle. The pupil may be allowed more freedom if only because he cannot be expected to manifest the consistency and self-control of the adult, which are the fruit of greater experience. Now, if we deal in this way with the childlike nature of the pupil instead of imposing on him the discipline we expect of an adult, we in fact make his growth more continuous, for we do not require him to shift suddenly in adolescence from control by others to self-direction.

I close this section by suggesting a few other ways of narrowing the generation gap that discontinuous enculturation entails. (1) Let the student study some urgent problems of our society, such as unemployment, crime, poverty, discrimination, and urban renewal, not as academic exercises but as problems vitally affecting the environment in which he lives. (2) Let the teacher take his students into the community to examine these problems at first hand and to talk with labor leaders, policemen, city planners, social welfare workers, and others whose job it is to handle them. (3) Let students have a genuine voice in school government. Let them share in some of the decisions affecting their own education. (4) Let students increasingly enroll in extracurricular activities that will put them in touch with the life of the adult community.

Cultural Change

Culture is constant yet always changing—constant in that certain of its elements, such as language and law, persist without major alteration for long periods of time; changing in that all its elements, however gradually and subtly, are undergoing a continuous metamorphosis. Cultural change can take place in at least three ways. (1) New practices may be invented within the culture itself. Progressive education, for instance, developed within the United States. (2) Practices may be borrowed from other cultures, as in the adoption by American educators of the Italian Montessori method. (3) Existing practices may be modified to meet fresh circumstances, as in the extension of federal aid to education.

Unless it is very highly integrated, a culture does not react as a whole to any single change, however important. The mutation of some major aspect of culture will sooner or later affect almost every other aspect, but it need not affect them all equally or immediately. For example, the invention of nuclear weapons soon influenced the popular attitude toward war, but the peaceful uses of nuclear energy have barely begun to be exploited.

When some areas of a culture change more slowly than others, we are faced with what is called "cultural lag." One of the most striking cases of cultural lag in this country is the discrepancy between technology and values.[30] Technology often seems to be the most dramatic pacemaker of modern culture because it changes by accumulation rather than by replacement. As a rule, one technical device or process leads to another, and the rewards and penalties of change are fairly tangible, whereas a change in values or beliefs generally involves a complete substitution. Technology itself, however, is pervaded by values, for new technological devices and processes are linked through their functions to the forms of conduct that a culture approves. The automobile exemplifies the values of mobility, private property, and speed. The thermometer and the clock testify to the conviction that nature can and should be measured, that all such units of measurement are of equal worth, that life is governed by knowable and invariable laws, and that what can be observed and repeated is important.

We may therefore envision two orders of cultural values, which may or may not coincide. One is fed by innovations in technology; the other is the sum of established values. If the values expressed in technological change are compatible with established values, then the culture will adjust to the changes easily enough. It is not so much the rate of technological change that causes cultural disorganization as the emergence in this change of new and conflicting values.

The more integrated the culture, the more its technology and values are likely to interpenetrate. It is mainly in less integrated cultures like the United States that technology can unmoor itself from the order of established values. In earlier times and in primitive societies cultural values were expressed through the technology by which a society maintained itself. Among the Maya Indians of southeast Yucatán, agriculture is not only a means of securing food but also a way of worshipping the gods. Before planting seedlings, an Indian builds an altar in the field and prays by it. The field becomes a kind of temple that he is forbidden to profane by speaking boisterously. Planting forms part of a perpetual contract between gods and men, in which the gods grant men the fruits of the earth in return for piety and sacrifice.[31] The modern assembly line, in contrast,

---

[30] John J. Honigmann, *The World of Man,* Harper, New York, 1959, p. 252: "A novelty in social organization or ideology rarely builds on previous areas of behavior but rather will encourage their replacement through substitution. In the case of techniques and their accompanying artifacts, secondary inventions are frequently added to a basic invention." The pace of cultural change may be set by other factors, however, such as ideology, as in modern Russia and China.

[31] Robert Redfield and Lloyd W. Warner, "Cultural Anthropology and Modern

implicitly rejects many traditional values of the culture, notably the belief that the individual is an end in himself. On the floor of a modern plant each worker is an interchangeable part and a means to the end of production.

As a culture changes—from, say, agrarianism to industrialism—either some or all of its values will change or become reinterpreted, although not necessarily together or immediately. Of late in America, the values of the Puritan ethic have yielded to those of an industrial society geared to abundance. In order to provide for its own growth, industry must constantly persuade people to consume ever larger quantities of non-essentials. Thus abstinence is overcome by consumption and thrift by installment buying.[32] Sexuality, once the prime example of abstinence, is being stimulated more and more by dress, advertising, and mass entertainment. Saving for the future seems less attractive than "living it up" today.[33]

The conflict between traditional and emergent values naturally affects education. It often appears in a discrepancy between the intent and the actual effect of teaching, between the effect the teacher wishes to have and probably thinks he has and the effect he actually does have.[34] On the

Agriculture," *Farmers in a Changing World: 1949 Yearbook of Agriculture,* United States Government Printing Office, Washington, D.C. Quoted by Dorothy Lee, *Freedom and Culture,* op. cit., p. 166.

[32] George Dearborn Spindler, *The Transmission of American Culture,* The Burton Lecture, 1957, Harvard University Press, 1959, p. 6; and "Education in a Transforming American Culture," in George D. Spindler, Ed., *Education and Culture: Anthropological Approaches,* op. cit., pp. 136-137.

[33] Some critics deny that the nucleus of the American value system has changed at all. See Talcott Parsons and Winston White, "The Link Between Character and Society," in Seymour Martin Lipset and Leo Lowenthal, Eds., *Culture and Social Character: The Work of David Riesman Reviewed,* The Free Press of Glencoe, New York, 1961, pp. 89-133. This nucleus, say Parsons and White, is the concept of "instrumental individualism," or the belief that a person should aim at the kinds of success that benefit his society. Today, they maintain, a person is still expected to work hard and not relax until he has achieved success. What has changed are the specific ends to be achieved and the means for achieving them. At one time the goal was monetary profit by means of investment, and the type was the entrepreneur. Now the goal is high competence in a specialized role within a large organization, a goal attained by performing the role responsibly in order to meet approval. The type is the flexible, other-directed executive. Nevertheless, whether the values emerging from the social and economic changes of the twentieth century are replacing fundamental American values or merely reinterpreting them, the fact remains that these values exist and are at odds with the values—or interpretations—formerly emphasized.

[34] Of course, not all such discrepancies are the result of a conflict in cultural values. The pupil may simply not respond in the way the teacher anticipates. Cf. Jules Henry's

whole, educators tend to be less traditional in their values than the general public.[35] Young teachers especially are likely to hold emergent or radical values, older teachers rather less so. Administrators are usually a little more conservative. School boards tend to be the most conservative of all, since they generally consist of people who have succeeded in the established order. Children from traditionally minded families will tend to hold traditional values less firmly than their parents, and children of liberal parents will tend to embrace liberal or radical values more whole-heartedly. On the other hand, children may also take up extreme traditional or emergent positions as part of a rebellion against their parents or adults in general.

Teachers are the official transmitters of the cultural heritage. They are also unconscious reflectors of cultural conflict. Having experienced and internalized the conflicts of the culture, teachers tend to pass them on to their students, thereby frustrating many intended goals of education. These conflicts permeate the subculture of formal education. They appear in the design of curricula, in methods of teaching, in textbooks and teaching aids, in student-teacher relations, and in teacher training.

Let us consider some examples. Social studies are designed to acquaint the student with the theory and practice of American democracy, yet in the name of doing things democratically and by consensus in the classroom they often fail to train the capacity for independent, abstract thought, which democracy also needs.

Textbooks often communicate unintended meanings. A textbook in home economics declares that it seeks to help the student "share meaningful experiences in the home." Although it provides a host of details on various household activities, such as choosing recipes, finishing seams, and doing laundry, it says nothing about the people who share these activities or who are being helped. Another textbook states that its goal is to help the student enjoy the home "creatively" and to "appreciate" family living, yet it treats housework as something to be done as efficiently as possible so that one can have more time away from it. Still another text states that it seeks to develop a mature personality (which one would suppose called for some attention to the life of the intellect and the imagination), yet it emphasizes the external traits, congenial to the other-directed personality, of grooming, manners, popularity, making friends, and using one's time

discussion of three kinds of attitudes: "indeterminate," "antithetical," and "pseudo-complementary," which the teacher may arouse unconsciously: "A Cross-Cultural Survey of Education," *Current Anthropology,* I, 4 (July 1960), 301-302.

[35] George D. Spindler, "Education in a Transforming American Culture," in George D. Spindler, Ed., *Education and Culture: Anthropological Approaches,* op. cit., pp. 139-141.

efficiently. All these textbooks, then, contain matter that is at odds with their declared goals.[36]

Take the teacher himself. Inheriting as a rule the traditional values of the middle or lower-middle class, the prospective teacher enters the subculture of a training institution whose values are generally emergent. This institution tends to regard the prime end of education as enabling the child to work and play harmoniously with the other members of his group, often to the detriment of individual growth. Thus the future teacher is in a sense being acculturated, and yet somehow must handle the conflict between the values of his own culture and those of the new culture with which he is in contact.

The teacher may react in a number of ways. If he feels threatened by the new values, he may reaffirm his old values all the more emphatically and project them uncompromisingly in the classroom. He may also over-compensate the other way by accepting the new values uncritically and seeking group harmony at all costs. If he is not given to introspection, he may internalize both sides of the conflict unconsciously without synthesizing them into a consistent value pattern of his own. He will then oscillate between different methods of handling groups and individuals and, through his inconsistencies, make trouble for himself and his pupils. Finally, if he is thoughtful and stable, he may acknowledge the conflict but not feel threatened by it, in which case he will synthesize elements of both patterns into a coherent system of his own. In the classroom he will follow a *via media* between extreme individualism and extreme groupism.[37]

There is no easy way of avoiding the transmission of cultural conflicts. A principal or counselor can study the teacher's practice in the classroom and then, by showing the teacher how inconsistency or rigidity make him communicate less effectively, he can help him to deepen and broaden his

[36] Dorothy Lee, "Discrepancies in Teaching of American Culture," in George D. Spindler, Ed., *Education and Culture: Anthropological Approaches*, op. cit., pp. 173-191.

[37] George Dearborn Spindler, *The Transmission of American Culture*, op. cit., pp. 27-28. In Spindler's view, the first two types of teacher transmit too narrowly; the former because, contrary to his declared knowledge and intentions, he communicates effectively only with middle-class children who share his values; the latter because he aims at a group harmony that pays little attention to individuals. Both teachers may stimulate a few children, but they will fail to influence the majority. The third type communicates to many children in many ways, but is too weak and too inconsistent to transmit the culture effectively. The fourth teacher, on the other hand, having consciously synthesized the best elements of both value patterns, is able to reach more children in more ways; hence, he "transmits along many channels."

approach. But should this be done? Cultural conflicts transmitted to children may well be beneficial, for they may contribute to variations in personality types and so to cultural innovation. One solution might be for the teacher to acknowledge these conflicts explicitly, even in the act of transmitting them or perhaps to transmit only selected conflicts. But this too may be dangerous, for if we can control the conflicts we transmit, we may transmit the culture too narrowly and so induce conformity. Suppose, then, the teacher seeks to be eclectic and to stimulate as many children as possible. Can he at the same time transmit the cultural heritage effectively to each of these children? It is hard so say. We are left with a problem that each teacher must seek to resolve as best he may: in order to encourage individual differences without creating unconscious conflicts in his students, he must seek to know and control the conflicts he himself transmits; at the same time, he must avoid creating the undesirable conformity that this self-knowledge and self-control may give him the power to produce.

An educational system responsive to the needs of the culture is bound to be affected by the conflicts from which these needs arise. But it need not be crippled by them, for the process of education is, or should be, one of intellectual emancipation. In the classroom both teacher and student can examine and evaluate some of the changes that are occurring in the culture. They can study the trends of the times and form some opinion as to which should be encouraged and which opposed.

Can the Schools Change the Culture?

I am often asked by students whether schools can change the culture. True, recent federal court rulings on integration are based on a conviction that social interaction among children of various racial and ethnic backgrounds is beneficial for all and that the society will benefit ultimately from this interaction. The school is viewed, therefore, as an institution that can indeed change the social order. My own answer would be a bit more circumspect. In my view, all depends on who controls the schools and who has power in society. As I point out in Chapter 6 on "Political Ideologies," in a society ruled by a single leader or by a single party, the schools may well be used to create a "new man" with the beliefs and sensibilities needed to build or perpetuate a "new order." In such a case, political decision makes education an instrument to transform a culture; but it is only one instrument among many that are being used for the same end. The school contributes to what already is being done by economic planning, propaganda, direction of labor, censorship, legal reform, and other means. Today in Russia, China, and Cuba the schools are being used to consolidate a social and cultural transformation set in motion by a political revolution (not by schools).

Cultural change entails a transformation of the thoughts and acts of individuals—a transformation, in short, of private life. When the culture is transformed by the state, private life is transformed into public life. The individual participates in a culture that is inspired or directed by the state (that is, by the group or party that controls the state), and this culture in turn is internalized so that the individual acts and thinks in harmony with the goals of the state. Private life is not abolished but rather changed, so that the individual ceases to be at variance with the new order and instead carries it within him during his most intimate transactions. He makes love, marries, writes, and teaches, not for himself alone but for the order of which he is now a part.

Only a party seizing and holding absolute power can hope to plan and carry out the transformation of an entire culture. In a democracy any such planned transformation seems impossible. A democracy implies a legal functioning opposition, and so long as this opposition exists, no government will be able to carry through a profound cultural revolution. In a democracy culture may be reformed by government but hardly transformed. Transformation may come perhaps through the working of forces much greater than those that a democratic government can hope to command, forces such as those we call the Industrial Revolution. But transformation through political or educational decision seems out of the question.

In a democracy, too, a system of public education will normally reinforce those values and practices that society as a whole finds desirable. This will include inculcating certain attitudes that seem desirable at certain times, just as patriotism and national service seemed desirable during the Second World War and respect for the environment will seem desirable during the 1970s. Here education reflects, rather than affects, the attitude of society as a whole.

Even to speak here of "education" or "the schools" as agencies of change is misleading, for to whom do these words refer but to teachers themselves? When we realize that the question is whether *public school teachers* can serve as catalysts of specific cultural changes opposed by the government and by the mass of society, the answer is clearly negative. For teachers do not control public education; the government and the people do. Even if *per impossibile* teachers were to agree as a body on a program of cultural reform, they could bring very little influence to bear on the government or on public opinion, for they neither form nor represent a social class and they do not possess adequate social, political, or economic power. It may be said that a prolonged general strike of teachers across the nation would be a very effective weapon against any government. So it might, if the strike were for higher salaries and improved working conditions, for teachers would be then identifying their interests with those of organized labor (which is not of course to say that organized labor would necessarily support them). But a strike for the right of the teaching profession to teach reform or revolution would be a strike by teachers acting pretty much on their own independently of social classes. Since the class loyalties of most teachers would probably be stronger than their professional loyalties, few teachers would be likely to join a strike to which the middle and working classes were opposed. Even if such a strike were backed by the majority of teachers, it would soon collapse from lack of public support and from a failure to damage the economy.

Does this mean that the teacher can do nothing but reflect the cultural attitudes of his day? Not at all. I have argued only that teachers as a body can hardly expect to bring about particular cultural changes to which the government and public opinion are opposed. But the individual teacher can do much to open the minds of his students, so that they may enter the adult world as thinking people capable of appraising their culture and society. By persuasion and example a good teacher can also lead his students to adopt attitudes more enlightened than those of many people in today's society. Indeed, it is a teacher's duty to liberate his students from prejudice as much as he can. Since any society is far from perfect even by the standards that its statesmen acknowledge, it is a responsibility of the teacher to set before his students those humane ideals that the great thinkers and artists of the culture have expressed in the past and in accordance with which the human condition today may be criticized and improved. A century ago, as the industrial age got under way, Matthew Arnold urged the schools to teach the young "the best that has been thought and said in the world." Any teacher today who teaches wisdom that has been achieved as wisdom for use will indeed provide his students with the high ideals they need to both judge and improve the world around them.

References

❖❖

The study of the relation between culture and education is known formally as educational anthropology. Aside from my own book, *Educational Anthropology: An Introduction* (Wiley, 1965, 171 pp.), I know of only one comprehensive work (in English) in this field: Ruth Landes, *Culture in American Education* (Wiley, 1965, 330 pp.), which has a rich collection of case studies. Unfortunately neither Rachel Reese Sady, *Perspectives from Anthropology* (Teachers College Press, 1969, 98 pp.), nor Clara K. Nicholson, *Anthropology and Education* (Merrill, 1968, 92 pp.), deals at all with American education. Henry G. Burger's *Ethno-Pedagogy* (Southwestern Cooperative Educational Laboratory, Albuquerque, 1968, 318 pp.) is a rambling "Manual in Cultural Sensitivity" for those who wish to acquire what Burger calls "Techniques for Improving Cross-Cultural Teaching by Fitting Ethnic Patterns."

In a class of its own is Jules Henry's *Culture against Man* (Random House, 1963, 495 pp.), a deeply felt and forcefully written account of the damage done to contemporary youth by cultural "disorientation." The book is a "passionate ethnography" describing what American culture could be if only we would learn from the example of other cultures.

The only relevant anthology available is George D. Spindler, Ed., *Education and Culture* (Holt, Rinehart and Winston, 1963, 571 pp.). With his wife, Louise, Spindler also edits a series of case studies on education in other cultures, published by Holt, Rinehart and Winston.

Alan R. Beals's *Culture in Process* (Holt, Rinehart and Winston, 1967) pays more attention to education than do most texts in general cultural anthropology.

4

Social Change

Carl Weinberg

❖❖

The notion of "social change" is, among other things, a perspective of analysis. It provides those who wish to study the phenomena of education a framework within which to place relevant components. As a perspective it is closely linked to two other perspectives that have already been considered, the historical and the cultural. The historical presents us with the events that illustrate the process of change. The cultural describes the values at the core of change. That is, any change in the structure of a phenomenon such as education must involve a change in the value system that supports it.

A description of the difference between the historical and the social-science perspectives for viewing educational change should provide a sound basis for understanding the approach that this chapter takes.

The historian is interested in events, their meaning, and the relationship between these events. For example, how did event A, let us say the common-school movement, influence event B, let us say progressive educational techniques.

The social scientist who is interested in describing the process of change is also concerned with events, but only insofar as these illuminate or represent that process. He would not be primarily interested in the events themselves. His major question is "what are the dynamics of the process of social change and what events exemplify such a process?"

The historian is interested in actual events, as these reveal the past. The social scientist is interested in the structure of events, how they were produced, the kinds of value changes that accompany them, and patterns of interaction that emerge or disappear concomitant with them. He is asking the question "what is society, how does it work?" He seeks the answer to this question in change, and he looks for change in actual events.

In this way we can try to understand education, to know what it is by focusing on the way it changes. By doing this we discover the structure of education, the fundamental social patterns that distinguish the school from other social institutions. The school may change the form of its interaction patterns—for example, evolve a very democratic rather than an authoritarian pupil-teacher relationship—but nonetheless, it is an institution that runs on role relationships that are differentiated, stratified, patterned, and maintained. This is what is meant by an institutional structure.

We will begin our analysis of the school in society from the perspective of social change, keeping in mind that we are looking for structure in change, not history. Whatever that structure is, and it should begin to be revealed as the chapter proceeds, is that which would tell a Puritan schoolmaster, thrust into 1970, that he was standing in a schoolroom rather than any place else regardless of 250 years of substantive changes.

Society and Education

Society is organized around several institutions that have evolved to serve the collective need. The need to care for and socialize the young is assumed by the family; the need to regulate and protect is serviced by the political legal institution; the need to develop participants in the social and economic enterprise is serviced by education. These institutions take their form and change along lines prescribed by the nature of the society that they serve. A complex industrial society such as our own requires a division of labor, a separation of functions such as producing, caring for children, and educating. The notion of social change and its relationship to education can be illustrated by focusing briefly on one point in the evolution of the school. As our population increased and became concentrated in a few areas called cities, the demands on the school changed from what they had been in a rural society. We moved from family-based general education to society-based occupational education. Changes in educational patterns are intrinsically linked to shifts in the larger social context, and we will deal with these shifts and the educational responses they produced in the next section.

Education is a functional part of a total society, and we can fully expect that a reciprocal change relationship will always be observed between the several parts. Any strain on the human organism affects some adaptation of its organic parts, and any problem with any of the organic parts will make its presence felt on the total system. We want to discuss, in the sections that follow, those social patterns that produced important educational changes. At the same time we want to consider the way in which educational processes have or could make significant changes within the larger society. We also want to look at the structure and functions of education in such a way as to explain the kinds of effects that the school does and does not have on the total social body.

Sources of Social Change

The source for any single change, for an individual as well as a society, is found in the condition of that society or person at a given point in its development. A person changes because his needs at one stage of his development cannot be met by the behaviors that were adequate at an earlier stage.[1] At the point where society attaches certain values and attitudes to specific developmental stages, change becomes a matter of developing new strategies to meet new demands and expectations. The child, until he enters school, learns the expectations of one role, that of a child within the family. As he extends his institutional affiliation he adopts new roles as student, friend, choir boy, boyfriend, etc. Industrial society evolves and changes in a similar fashion. As population grows, as international trade and interaction increase and diversify, as resources appear or are developed, as persons increase their capacity to buy and sell, as human needs expand and change in response to economic and social opportunities, and as values change to accommodate the whole spectrum of social possibilities, institutional life adjusts accordingly. Patterns of economic, educational, religious, political, and family life emerge and become attached to normative values where they exist and influence value changes, when

---

[1] For example, his hunger needs may be met at the age of six months by his screaming at the top of his lungs. The same behavior 20 years later in a restaurant would produce a very different result.

the values are out of balance with the new styles. This process will be illustrated as we begin to trace the development of educational innovations.

Institutional life, and the changes we wish to consider as these affect educational policy, cannot be explained adequately by any kind of linear history. That is, we cannot consider the evolution of political or family patterns without reference to a set of interdependent developments. What happens in national or international politics influences economic development, changes in family patterns, and educational structures. We can attempt to keep the lines of cause and effect as direct as possible, but we should always keep in mind that any complete explanation of the present state of social life can only be managed with a comprehensive description of all of social history. We cannot, nor would we wish to, attempt to explain the presence of equal-opportunity programs within the schools as the end product of a hundred years of Negro history, or a thousand years of an evolving humanitarian ethic. We will attempt to link specific educational change to the limited social forces that appear to bear most directly on these changes. These forces will be treated in five separate categories, although each category bears an undeniable relationship to each other category. For our purposes the following categories are designated as the major sources of educational change: (1) population shifts, (2) shifts in status characteristics, (3) interinstitutional interaction, (4) the scientific revolution, and (5) social movements.

Population Shifts

Where people live, the number of them that live there, and the kinds of persons they are, can be directly associated with the kind of education that they receive. Low population density, such as in rural areas, may mean multigrade classrooms, limited facilities, poorly paid and often weakly trained teachers, limited course offerings, and a curriculum slanted to the needs of a rural society. High population density will usually mean economic and racial homogeneity, a complex bureaucratic structure, close ties to training programs within colleges and universities, and a depersonalized mass-production kind of relationship between students and teachers.

The highly personalized quality of rural society, where persons were intimately familiar with other members of the community, had its counterpart adaptation within the school. Favoritism was reflected in the patterns of mobility that were provided for some students and not for others.[2] Although families were differentiated on the basis of their status within the community, the pattern of interaction was highly personal. Persons were known by names and family ties. As population centers emerged, a different form of interaction was necessitated. In order to reduce the anxiety of relating to many unfamiliar others, people found it necessary to classify others according to salient characteristics. Occupation, language, dress, and qualities of nationality and race were utilized to reduce the complexity to manageable dimensions. In the schools, ability grouping based on test scores, and curriculum allocation based on occupational interest, duplicated the pattern. Students were what their intelligence scores and interests defined them as being. Beyond this, definitions of student qualities arose out of associations with dress, manner, language, and ethnic characteristics. To this day the urban adaptation to education remains highly non-individualized. In the same manner in which persons would utilize labels or uniforms, schools manage their own complexity by creating their own labels, by typing students.

Urbanization

Urbanization, a product of changes in industrial capacity, produced significant changes in all forms of institutional life. The family ceased servicing the total needs of its members. A division of labor emerged wherein human and social needs were allocated to separate institutional structures. Education, which earlier had dealt only with limited basic skills, began to service the whole child, to mold him in an image suitable for functioning in an industrial society. The school found it necessary to be responsive to most of the disruptions produced by urban living. It was required to make persons employable, committed to functioning within an industrial capacity, and socialized to act responsibly and morally despite the temptation of urban vice.

As the schools made their adjustments to new demands prompted by industrial needs, a number of problems emerged in the communities that they serviced. Increasing population led to a degeneration of living conditions, crime, delinquency, prostitution, family disorganization, widespread aggression between ethnic groups, and a number of other

---

2 See A. B. Hollingshead, *Elmtown's Youth,* for a description of the social-class basis of educational differentiation in a small-town high school.

disruptive patterns began to characterize urban life. Novelists like Theodore Dreiser and Frank Norris wove their topical tales of a society founded on competitive instrumental values. The prominent ethic of the time was competition, and to this day the schools have paralleled such a development. The new educational structures built upon, rather than reduced, the competitive nature of urban social interaction.

Specifically, the schools' adaptation to urbanization was the development of patterns to efficiently allocate, through a process of competitive differentiation, students to the industrial enterprise. Occupational training was emphasized; differentiation along career lines required vocational advisors and eventually an elaborate pattern of testing. The curriculum was reorganized along career-linked lines, and specialists within career-training categories evolved. Education developed on a community basis and facilities were acquired that would meet the presumed needs of community types. Teachers were trained for specific kinds of tasks and educational administrators began to develop capacities to help them run a community school within the framework of community characteristics. Public-relations skills became a necessary part of an administrator's training.

The pattern of change produced by ecological organization and reorganization is operating today. As urban complexes become graphically differentiated along socioeconomic and racial lines, the school responds with a greater differentiation of its own offering, its training patterns, its development of specialists, its capacity to support innovation, both economically and psychologically, and its receptiveness to governmentally supported programs.

At the turn of this last century the acceleration of immigration imposed a specific task on the schools. The ideology of education, and the American ethic, was one of equal opportunity, and the requirement of the time was to cohere this extensive urban ethnic heterogeneity into an American type. No other institution could facilitate this goal but the school. The pattern is being repeated today in Israel, where persons from different national backgrounds have come together hoping for a better life. The problem for the schools today is the same. Educational change is a product of an unavoidable challenge to the schools to make one nation out of a society badly divided along racial lines. The American city today is a pattern of black and white tension and conflict, and the urban pattern is typically a black inside and a white outside. This is the latest stage of the effect of industrialization and urbanization on social interaction. The schools are beginning to be aware that the old structures of competitive differentiation have not been able to solve this problem. New problems require new structures and these should be forthcoming in this decade.

Shifts in Status Characteristics

Education is always responsive to changing expectations within the larger society. They are responsive in the same way, because they are forced to be, to the community. However, since community composition changes more quickly than does the total society, there is often a lag within the schools. If new skills are required to meet new demands there will be a period of transition in which the offerings of the school will be out of line with the needs of particular types of students. In time the school will make an adjustment but often, by then, the community demands may have shifted again. Actually, many of the disruptions that affect educational systems today are produced by this kind of disequilibrium.

A person's status within a society such as ours is determined by his relationship to the economic order. Persons who occupy highly valued social and economic positions develop a set of attitudes that are often different from the attitudes and values of persons who occupy less esteemed positions. As persons become upwardly mobile within the economic order they adopt many components of the value system of those above them. Due to the efforts of labor unions and the general affluence produced by the Second World War, a large segment of the society was able to take a giant step upwards on the socioeconomic ladder. With this economic achievement came a vested interest in the status quo. The new middle class wanted to hold on to what it had and stabilize its position through the efforts of its children. To this end the place of education came to assume a prominent role. Not only were the better jobs available to those with a higher education, but also, a style of life that was congruent with middle-class values could be assured through extensive education. The school was now required to service a large segment of the population that was college bound. To this end a greater number of specialists were required. Good teachers were a critical necessity in the preparation of students who needed to enter and succeed in college. Vocational advisors gave way to career advisors in secondary schools, and a major emphasis was placed on guiding students through to the college campus.

On the community level the patterns of mobility were more complex. The emergence of new communities in the process of suburbanization required a specific kind of educational emphasis that differed sharply from the emphasis observed in schools where average community income dropped considerably. Students in suburban schools received a better education than students in the communities in transition. Transition has meant, typically, a shift from one economic level to a lower one, and a better education has come to be equated with providing students with the skills and opportunities necessary to go on to college.

The interaction of community and school can be conceptualized in two important ways: first, persons within communities translate their status into political influence, and second, the qualities of persons of different status characteristics provide cues to educators regarding the type and quality of education they need to provide. Schools in communities with heavy migration, family instability, poverty, and tendencies towards association with deviant activities, begin to conceive its function as stabilization, control, and ethical socialization, and only minimally as providing cognitive skills, that is, learning. In the affluent communities, educators accept the family's responsibility for control and socialization and focus on the cognitive factors necessary for educational mobility.

Neighborhoods that change their status composition are usually those that have been abandoned by the upwardly mobile to either the lower classes or to nonwhite minority groups. Rarely is the direction the other way. Urban renewal is not an unfamiliar concept, but it is not a common pattern. In an age of high socioeconomic homogeneity in schools, urban-renewal communities have the greatest apparent problem in terms of building a patterned program. High-status members of these communities, however, usually resolve the schools' dilemma by sending their children to private schools.

The changing neighborhoods of the 1950s have settled into the ghettos of the present. The adaptation (specifically the discrepancies in personnel and facilities) that the school has made to the configuration of community characteristics, central of which is race, is evident.[3] But the problems of the ghetto, like problems of war, have influenced innovations, and for the same reason, survival. When being poor and being black evolves into a threat to the survival of institutional life as many wish to preserve it, then innovation and change become politic. Whereas, at one time, a high concentration of poor people meant that schools could avoid political pressure, the tables have turned considerably. Pressure is exerted from the bottom (the community) and from the top in the form of an administrative challenge at the highest levels, to make things "right." The

[3] James Coleman, *Equality of Educational Opportunity*, National Center for Educational Statistics, U.S. Government Printing Office, Washington, D.C., 1966.

restructuring of ghetto schools, with extensive local and national support, is inevitable in the near future.

Interinstitutional Interaction

Segments of the society change their value composition and corresponding patterns at different rates. Changes in one segment usually require an adaptation on the part of other segments, since these segments interact in all forms of institutional life. What happens in the school is, in part, a function of what happens in the family, in age-based peer groups such as adolescents, in the world of politics and government, in the church, and in the economic system. Let us look at some representative interactions.

The Family

Patterns of family life have changed considerably over the past fifty years. The preindustrial family assumed the responsibility for managing its own affairs in training and educating younger members, producing for its needs, entertaining itself, and ministering to its physical and spiritual needs. Cohesiveness and a high degree of dependency were necessary and therefore highly valued. Children were trained to assume the roles of their parents. The succession of roles passed from parents to children. A father would be hurt, and often find the idea intolerable, if his son should choose a vocation or craft other than his own.

Urban life made it almost impossible to hold strongly to the value of this kind of succession. The diversity of occupational possibilities and the fact that parents were required to leave the home to seek employment meant that training and occupational allocation had to be assumed by another institution. The school, of course, began to expand its function. The role of women is another useful example. With the onset of affluence and the availability of labor saving devices in the home, the preparation of daughters for domestic careers has become an almost obsolete phenomena. Again, the schools had to adapt to a new set of family expectations regarding the future of females. Coeducational higher education is a normal condition of American life. Women have been freed not only because they sought equality, but because there is no longer an economic basis that would support inequality. Women would not go into the pasture because their old roles were obsolete. The schools had to make room for the new aspirations of women, and an elitist education based on both sex and economics became highly unrealistic.

As women increased their marketability and began to enter the labor force, the phenomena of the working mother had its effect on the school, which was required to assume a greater share of the responsibility for the development of the child. Nursery school education has experienced a phenomenal growth rate, partly because parents have become sensitive to the need for a transition between home and school, but to a large extent because mothers want to resume careers delayed or interrupted by child bearing and raising.

The family, as an agency of child socialization, is finding it increasingly more difficult to provide children with the kind of knowledge and guidance that are required in a complex and rapidly changing society. As standards and values become more flexible and generally more permissive, the school will assume an even greater share of the responsibility for child socialization. The consistently expanding awareness of the need for sex education in the schools is a graphic case in point. The success or failure of such programs, as educators must realize, will depend on evolving new structures within which new goals and responsibilities can be facilitated.

The Peer Group

The strength of peer-group loyalties as determinants of attitudes and behavior has never been greater. The reasons are simple. The rapidity of social and cultural change has forged almost unbridgeable gaps between the generations. Adults are busy with their own activities, and institutions like the church and the school find it difficult to reorganize their structures to accommodate the every-day needs, fears, and interests of young people. Adolescents in particular have formed their own society with a network of values, norms, and patterns that distinguish them from other age groups. The purposes of this cohesion of age mates are several. One purpose is identification, the sense of belonging, and with this comes a feeling of being protected and supported in expressing needs or independent commitments that might vary from the expectation of the adult society. A second purpose is exposure to a number of new roles such as friend, leader, or even member of a group where participation in productive cooperation can be viewed as a useful educational experience. Probably the most important function of the adolescent peer group is that it socializes young people to the expectations of the adolescent society in ways that no other group or institution can. It provides information about others that aids people in making comfortable adaptations to new and heretofore fearful experiences.

The ways in which peer groups have interacted with the institution of education are both subtle and dramatic. Schools are sometimes responsive to the expressed interests of students when these do not constitute part of the formal educational program. The organization of extracurricular activities, athletic events, dances, and the like, as part of the school program is such a response. Many administrators and teachers who are sensitive to the student society have found ways to make educational activities congruent with student values. Some schools and school districts have held the line in opposition to changing patterns of student interests, dress, and personal grooming, but other schools have revised their codes to permit the student society considerably more freedom than in the past. Some school districts are currently wrestling with possibilities of incorporating into the formal program educational experiences associated with changing values, such as sex education and courses dealing with drugs and family relationships.

The power of the peer group, to affect educational programs, is currently being observed on many college and some high school campuses. The confrontation of students with their masters, often peaceable but sometimes not, has influenced administrators and faculties to reconsider their responsibility to students. Any college or university not involved in this kind of self-inspection is out of the mainstream of contemporary university life where there is some attempt to develop programs in line with the conceptions of young people about how they learn and what is relevant to learn.

The Scientific Revolution

The ethos of the twentieth century is efficiency. Poets, existentialists, and humanists in all fields may provide our times with an image of what it all could be like should we rediscover our humanness. But the forces of productive efficiency have taken hold of our culture with a grip that individuals appear unable to break. Inherent in the culture of efficiency is change. The search goes on for a better way. We cannot even comprehend the best way. We live with the belief that the machines we have created and will create will show us the way to a better machine and then a better one.

In order to do things in a better way we need to discover more about the world we wish to manipulate. Industry discovered that in order to ensure its growth and success it had to know more about what people wanted. Later it discovered ways to make people want what it had to offer.[4] To maximize gains and minimize losses, the vast industrial complex began to roll on wheels of technology, a technology that made old tasks and thereby jobs obsolete, and created new skills and tasks for which people had to be trained. The school was required to be responsive to the way in which industry was moving, since skill training and career allocation has always been a central responsibility of the school.

The tools and methods of science accumulate and have been doing so for many hundreds of years. Inquiry is more systematic, knowledge more complete, and scientists more plentiful. The success of the scientific enterprise in the 20th century, the age of discovery and of revolution in all facets of human life, has established science as far more than an activity or a method. Science has become, in our time, a value. It is, in all its forms—discovery, fact, invention, inquiry, career, or labor-saving device— an esteemed concept. We are willing to put our lives into its hands, to undergo mystifying medical treatments, fly in giant fortresses, subject our dishes and laundry to its mechanisms, pay our computerized bills, and so on and on. We trust science to the point that we are willing to change our way of life in short spaces of time, and so our way of life does change. In the same way, educational change is produced.

The trait that best characterizes contemporary cultural attitudes towards change is not the acceptance of doing new things but of doing old things in new ways. We do not, for example, approve of new sexual standards, but have little objection to scientific innovations in birth-control techniques. In education, new mental-health curricula would stir resistance from the community that would not protest the teaching of foreign languages with dozens of new contraptions.

In the process of producing new ways to handle old matters, an attitude of positive regard for invention made a significant dent in the old patterns. The society, growing up with technological advances, began to live comfortably with change and even to expect it. New consumer products, from TV to foods to cigarettes, made their pitch on the basis of containing some new element, even if that new element, such as XG70 in toothpaste, had no real meaning to the consumer.

Adolescents, growing up and facing the world of occupational identi-

---

[4] See J. K. Galbraith, *The Affluent Society*, Boston, Haughton Mifflin, 1958, for a discussion of the power of contemporary industrial structures in influencing consumer tastes.

fication, were faced with several difficult possibilities. First, the skills that they would learn could become quickly obsolete; second, many new and challenging careers were opening regularly; and third, the kind of training necessary to survive in a highly specialized occupational structure, required greater and greater amounts of education. When the future becomes, as it has for a generation growing up under the threat of nuclear holocaust and incredible technological advances, highly problematic persons often turn to other resources. Students have turned to dropping out, drugs, confrontations with the "establishment," a generalized hedonism, or a retreat to the verities of the past found in new forms such as religious cults, humanistic organizations, or new schools where degrees become irrelevant. These general attitudinal and behavioral changes within the society are beginning to effect changes within the school. New curricula to treat problems of personal disorganization, innovations in the way large masses of students are taught, and a searching for relevance in the traditional content areas are emerging themes.

In the more formal sense, the culture of efficiency, with increasing demands to do old things in a better, more efficient way, has led to the transformation of educational systems into a monolithic bureaucracy. The many roles within education, from student to superintendent, have undergone a reformulation in terms of responsibility and task. Teachers were forced not only to specialize in content areas but also in age-grade levels. The teacher-generalist and the student-person form an interaction pattern in the process of being replaced by the specialist plying his trade on the product. The self-contained classroom is at the edge of obsolescence, and the quarter system in higher education is making it possible for students to intensify their already overtaxed efforts to get somewhere faster. This may be the greatest irony of contemporary education—persons running themselves into the ground to prepare for a society that will be changing a little faster than they.

The specific components of the scientific revolution and its impact on education are taken up in a later chapter.

Social Movements

The movement that has had the most significant impact on educational change, and is likely to continue in that influence, is the civil rights movement. The Supreme Court's desegregation decision in 1954, culminating many years of Negro striving for equal educational opportunities, marked an end of the informal and a beginning of the formal stage of racial confrontation. When our major cities burst into summer flames, white society became poignantly aware that the black man's problems, of which he was cognizant and often in sympathy, had suddenly become the white man's problems. With a burst of confidence the black society emerged as a cohesive political force in the second half of the twentieth century. The goal was freedom, equality, and in the most general and relevant political sense, power. Sixteen years after the desegregation decision, segregation is still a monumental reality, in the North as well as the South. The effect of racial isolation continues to have severe educational repercussions for nonwhite minorities.[5] In order to reduce the invidious consequences of segregation, specific educational changes have been recommended and many implemented. The most prominent innovation, in terms of widespread implementation, has been a set of programs designated as compensatory education. New programs such as Head Start, and many variations on the early-childhood theme, Upward Bound, tutorials, and generally improved standard programs have been effected with government support. Attempts are being made and have been made to involve parents and other community representatives in the task of improving the education of low-income communities.

Confrontation with the schools over the issue of an inferior education for nonwhite children is steadily increasing, and school administrators are seeking ways to preserve the viability of education in Negro, Mexican-American and Puerto Rican communities. In some places teachers have been frozen into their jobs to stem the tide of teacher migration to suburban schools. In other places white teachers have been removed from their jobs because of blatant racist attitudes and behavior. Many schools have, overnight, switched from white to black administrators, instituted courses in black history and culture, reduced class sizes, and added paid helpers from the community, often out-of-work adolescents. There is much talk about school decentralization, and this has been tried in some places. Should decentralization become a reality it will signify the most dramatic educational change since schools broke from their church affiliation. Nonwhite minorities see decentralization as community control, the function of which will be to assure that education in the ghetto does not maintain the invidious distinctions between the races nor guarantee the perpetuation of unequal opportunities.

The struggle for equal opportunities and justice is far from over. The civil rights movement, even in its most militant posture, has forced con-

---

[5] *Racial Isolation In The Public Schools,* A report of the Commission on Civil Rights, U.S. Government Printing Office, Washington, D.C., 1967.

scientious white supporters to call for an end of a totally white-dominated educational system. Higher education has been forced to accede, time and again, to the demands of indignant and angry students, to bring more nonwhite students on the campus through a system of support, and to maintain them there through a system of tutorials, even though such students do not meet the requirements of entrance. College faculties are being better integrated, and black studies programs are being instituted on campuses across the country. From peaceful sit-ins in the South to angry protests in the North, the civil rights movement advances with different faces, all conspiring to produce a profound effect on American institutional life. The school is passing through a difficult stage in its emergence as an agency of social change, but it appears that there are sufficient forces available to insure a safe passage to that destiny.

The second most significant social movement affecting educational innovation, probably to emerge as the most prominent in the next twenty years, is what we might call the *humanistic movement*. This involves the organized, and also often disorganized, attempts of persons to live a less depersonalized existence. The force is vigorously alive in adolescents who are struggling for their identity in a society that offers them no real place in their mobility from childhood to adulthood. It is alive in college students across the country who will no longer be manipulated in computerized fashion, and who stand ready to put their academic careers on the line, if need be, to ensure some participation in the decisions that profoundly affect them. It is alive in adults who are responding to their desperation by a vigorous search for involvement rather than guaranteed affluent detachment. The fever for participation in sensitivity or encounter groups is one clear symptom. Together, these persons constitute a force for, if not change, than at least inspection of our major institutions.

There has been such change. Personnel-management policies in major industrial complexes have responded to the communication gap with ongoing sensitivity programs. Medical schools are permitting their criteria for admission to expand beyond the scientific emphasis. The church is becoming increasingly involved in political and social areas, and particularly in movements for civil liberties where detachment reigned earlier. The school has also changed its structure in areas where the personal needs of youth are perceived. Dress codes have become more flexible to permit adolescents to express their individuality, and in scattered places courses directly tied to the personal concerns of youth have been implemented. At the college level, students have earned participation in matters ranging from curriculum to recruitment of faculty. It is becoming more difficult to dismiss a faculty member of whom students approve, and harder to retain those of whom they don't. Experimental courses are ballooning and in many major universities students are permitted a wider range of acceptable courses, including independent study. Grade structures are beginning to change to reduce pressures, and students are being offered extensive opportunities to participate in meaningful informal activities such as colloquiums, discussion groups, and interest-based organizations. The dictates from students are clear. Education must be more than a rite of passage, more than books and lectures and laboratories. Education must be a complete human experience, cognitive and affective, something to help a student discover himself as a person rather than an occupational type. As college and high school students protest the indignities of formal education, and as parents begin to raise similar questions about the education of the elementary school child, the school will be forced to move to the left, to liberalize its structures, and to extend its conception of function to incorporate humanistic goals.

The School as an Agent of Social Change

The school has been most accurately described as an agency of social stability, whose main function is to maintain the status quo by socializing youth to the values that uphold the present order of social life. Institutions are organized and maintained by the general society in order to ensure the viability of that society. What is required is a guaranteed flow of persons committed to participation in the society that inherits them. When institutions change, it is ordinarily because the society has changed its expectations and requirements, and institutional structures are reorganized to accommodate the new demands. The role of the school in the period of high immigration or accelerating industrialization is representative of that process.

The guarantee that the school will play its appointed role is embedded in what we have come to call the public trust. This trust assumes structural presence in the form of boards of education, state and local legislatures, and community groups. These pose as guardians of the public welfare, attempting to insure that schools meet their obligation to the general public. Within this framework change is indeed difficult to bring about, and if there is to be change at all it must occur gradually. Otherwise the guardians will worry and a conservative reaction will ensue. This is not to say that public schools cannot be innovative. They can, but only if educational leaders can discover ways of effecting change within the structure as it presently exists.

Higher education, on the other hand, can and does play an important role in promoting social and cultural change. It does so in several areas. Universities are places where large-scale research operations are conducted. This research contributes knowledge and technology, which influences changes in industry, urban organization, methods of farming, food production and distribution, medicine, and mental health. Discoveries in atomic physics and oceanography open vistas for the future utilization of resources. Higher education, with its emphasis on scientific inquiry, cultural relativism, and self-exploration, leads to a questioning of traditional belief systems. The exposure of students to persons of diverse cultural backgrounds, and to ideas considered too "controversial" for elementary or high school, leads people to a more liberal position socially, and often into action activities intended to reconstruct patterns of institutional life that are incongruent with these belief systems. Higher education has helped to produce a specialized society, and can reverse this trend as it moves to make education more relevant to the personal needs and commitments of students.[6]

Higher education has become the only viable channel for status mobility in our society. Since the end of World War II, when the GI Bill made education feasible for millions who could not have otherwise afforded it, college has become increasingly accessible to more and more people. With special grants-in-aid and even flexible admissions criteria, the university is attempting to increase the possibilities of attracting low-income nonwhites to the campus. These nonwhites have made and are making a difference, both in the organized activities of the campus itself, and in the nonwhite communities where leadership is emerging in such a way as to improve vastly the power base of these communities.

The Context for Change

Why is it that higher education can play an active role in producing social and cultural change, whereas lower education plays only a passive role? What are the conditions that differentiate these contexts and make for a more productive environment for change? There are many factors, and some of them are quite obvious. The age of the students is one. The older people become, the more willing society is to permit them to be exposed to controversy. As in the family, children are given more free-

6 Burton Clark, *Educating the Expert Society*, Chandler Publishing Co., San Francisco, 1962, pp. 28-39.

dom to explore their interests, as they grow. By the time children have reached college age, we expect them to have the capacity to differentiate between right and wrong. It is not that they couldn't before; we are simply more willing to trust them at this age, or rather to trust that we have done our socializing adequately.

A second important factor is the relationship between the type of educational institution and the source of control. Lower education is community based. Fulfilling the expectations of local parents is essential to maintaining a working relationship with the community. Teachers are highly sensitive to the administration's concern that students do not go home after school and report "irregularities," disruptions in the traditional format. Higher education, if private, is controlled by a board of trustees whose authority is usually independent of the requirements of parents of students. If public, the control is in the hands of the state and a board of regents who, while watchful of what might be considered dramatic departures of program, permit extensive autonomy to university administrators.

A third important factor is that education after high school is voluntary rather than compulsory, as at the lower levels. This means that if parents do not like the style or programs of the college they can easily withdraw their children.

A fourth factor is the differential power that faculties have over what they teach and how they teach it. Public school teachers do not have the kind of organization or influence that would permit them to determine the kind of freedom they have in the conduct of their professional lives. University faculties, through the American Association of University Professors nationwide and a system of faculty senates on each campus, have created and maintained a system of academic freedom that is critical to the process of free and open inquiry.

A fifth and a final factor is the substance of university instruction. Organized around disciplines, such as history and chemistry, subject matter content rather than socialization to civic responsibility structures the curriculum. If discipline of students becomes an issue, it is someone other than the academic staff who must assume the responsibility. Within the classroom students are free to work for understanding or grades in whatever way they choose, or to choose not to work for either. The ethos of the university and college is knowledge, productivity, and inquiry. These ideas in themselves are supportive of innovation and change. The ethos of the public schools is stability, morality, tradition, and conformity. It is not surprising that the schools resist innovation and experimentation as they do.

It has not been the intention in this section to communicate the notion that higher education is a potent force in social change. Many of the structural conditions that retard the ability of lower education to actively support innovation are present at the higher levels. The bureaucratic organization of education is itself a deterrent to performing a change function. And the way in which the college is tied to the requirements of the larger society, in terms of career preparation and allocation, makes it difficult to stray from the established patterns. This is not to say, however, at any level of education, that schools cannot envision a future different from the present and facilitate that conception. It is possible, that in the near future, educational planning will involve, as it does in industry, the organization of tasks around some prediction of where society is, or even should be, heading.

Change and Values

Ultimately the critical factor that makes change possible or impossible, viable or temporary, is the value system of those who will experience that change. A person's social behavior can be explained in terms of the beliefs he holds about what he may or may not do—not what he is physically capable of doing, but also what he is psychologically capable of doing. Our psychic disposition to behave in certain ways is largely a matter of our values, the ideas about human behavior we respect and those we do not respect, in others or in ourselves. We value life, stability, loyalty, honesty, wealth, status, education, knowledge, beauty, and so on and on. Our culture has offered us, and we have accepted, a legion of verities. Our society has refined these verities to fit our social and personal needs. We can qualify, within standard limits, the quality and intensity of our loyalties to these values. We may value wealth, but devalue dishonest ways of accumulating it. If honest ways become rare, we may be forced to qualify our conception of dishonest ways. As value systems interact we experience a process of this kind of qualification. We may value life, but taking the lives of those who we see as threatening our way of life is acceptable. We engage in war. We respect knowledge but we respect degrees more. When our values are incompatible we make adjustments, and then we rationalize these adjustments. In this way certain values lose their power over us and others gain ascendency. In the process society changes.

Institutions make similar adjustments. When the task of institutions like the political structure and the school becomes unmanageably complex, we evolve principles that assume preeminence over isolated values. We come to value the principle. The paramount value-principles that guide institutional life are efficiency, stability, cohesion, and goal attainment.[7] Efficiency is a matter of organizing resources quickly and reliably to "do the job"; stability is a matter of infusing in the participants the belief that the institution, its purposes and methods, are worthy; cohesion is a matter of finding one's place, and the relationship between the several places in the life of the institution; goal attainment is a matter of accomplishing something, achieving the goals that the members value.

It is within this kind of value system that change occurs. Visible change must, in some way, come to grips with each of the principles. Those who wish to produce change can only do so with an understanding of the value basis of the established forms of institutional life. The value system of the larger society, and its specific application in the school, provides us with the structure within which we must work in order to produce change. If we are to work for change in the school we must learn the values that schools support, and that support schools. Controlled social change is only possible within the limits of social and personal values. We cannot, for example, do away with vacations, which both teachers and students value, unless we can replace them with something that is valued as much, perhaps money.

Conclusion

Social Change and Educational Alienation

We have looked at some of the processes within the society and within the school that help to explain the phenomena of change. We noted the kinds of forces that account for the organization of goals and structures within educational systems. We also discussed the contribution that schools make in facilitating change within the larger society. And finally, we have briefly considered the way that value systems are critical to the process of change.

We have not, however, made any assessment of those changes as they are related to some important considerations of the human condition. Change for what? Institutions are changing, patterns of social life are changing, and education, as a body of knowledge about how people learn and what they need to learn, has grown in substance and in precision.

---

[7] See T. Parsons, *The Social System*, Free Press, New York, 1951.

If we take the view of social evolution that sees social forms differentiated and arranged, and then rearranged towards some perfection of the human condition, then what sense can we make of the symptoms of human alienation that we observe everywhere in our schools and in our society? If predictive efficiency, technological advance, and increased specialization and expertise are good for education, then why do we witness crisis and disorder? How do we explain poverty, racial strife, wholesale drug taking, the disaffection of prime students, widespread neurosis, campus disorder, and generalized alienation?

Alienation is a popular concept today. It has been used in social-science literature to refer to a range of disruptions in personal and social life. Marx utilized the concept to refer to the consequences, for man, of surrendering an important part of himself, his capacity to produce, to the industrial machine. Since that time the notion of alienation has been applied to any condition wherein man is removed from activities or decisions that affect his life. He is alienated if he cannot influence decisions, if he does not comprehend the meaning of his involvement in social institutions, if he cannot achieve his ends by legitimate means, if he is isolated from others because his conception of the meaning of events differs from theirs, or if he finds himself engaged in activities that are incongruent with his sense of his abilities or needs.[8]

Most people fall within one of these categories. Perhaps they always have done so. But now, it appears, they are becoming aware of it. The kinds of changes that we have observed within our society, as these affect the state of alienation, have either been to intensify the forces that produce alienation, or to remove some of the barriers to recognizing that it exists. Certainly increased specialization and machine technology have removed man even further from his products, sometimes out of the picture entirely, and isolated him from others. Whereas the two cultures signified a rift between scientists and humanists, the divisions within each of the "cultures" has been widening. The cry on college campuses for relevance, is in part a reaction to this trend. Man is not only becoming estranged from his products, he is isolated from his kind, and often from himself. Is this not what education, in its drive for efficiency, has produced? Have not educational systems evolved into impersonal monoliths finely tuned to the task of turning humans into bureaucratic role-players, unprepared to deal with interpersonal and intrapersonal demands in other than mechanistic ways?

[8] M. Seeman, "On the Meaning of Alienation," *American Sociological Review*, **24** (Dec. 1959), pp. 783-91.

Education today is in the process of conceiving new functions dedicated to the eradication of many of the symptoms of alienation. The goals are usually worthy, but the mechanisms for facilitating these functions are slow to emerge. But they must emerge, not because it is morally necessary, but also because society looks to the schools for help in what appears to be a critical time. Society, and thereby its officials, are charging educational systems with a responsibility to reduce the conflicts inherent in a society in rapid transition. Out of this kind of social demand will emerge experimental programs, a restructuring of traditional forms of educational process, and the development within educational roles of a new commitment to improve the quality of instruction and interpersonal relations. Change is impersonal, and any objective analysis of social and educational change such as is contained in this chapter, must also be impersonal. But we must recognize, unless we support the view that social evolution is above human intervention, that human intelligence is the only mechanism that will permit us to guide and control change processes. The only version of education that can solve the problems of alienation and conflict is one that sees the responsibility of the school as an ethical rather than an occupational one. If we can produce men who can take us to the moon and beyond, we surely can produce some who can take us out of the age of alienation.

References

❖❖

Clark, B., *Educating the Expert Society*, San Francisco, Chandler Publishing Co., 1962. A basic presentation of the school's function in American society. Focuses on the role of the school as an agent of cultural change.

Etzioni, A., *Social Change*, New York, Basic Books, 1964. Presents writings from major sociological thinkers, dealing with the subject of social change. The editors interpret the significance of the selections.

Miller, H. L. and R. R. Woock, *Social Foundations of Urban Education*, Hinsdale, Illinois, The Dryden Press, 1970. An elementary survey of the social condition of education in the urban world.

Reiss, Jr., A. J., *Schools in a Changing Society*, New York, Free Press, 1965. A collection of readings that look at the effects on school administrators of changing community patterns.

Weinberg, C., *Education and Social Problems*, New York, The Free Press, 1971. Looks at social and educational change in the light of critical problems facing the school.

5

Education for Minorities

❖❖

EDITOR'S INTRODUCTION. Within American society a number of racial minorities deserve special forms of education. The two largest minorities, Negroes and Mexican-Americans, are considered here in separate sections. Other minorities include Indians, Puerto Ricans, and Orientals. I regret that there is not space in this chapter for a third section, which would have been devoted to the American Indian, for his plight is perhaps worse than that of any other minority. Of the 150,000 young Indians in this country less than half reach high school and less than a quarter complete it. Most Indians live in extreme poverty and many have serious health problems. Today they are America's "prisoners of war," shut away in surroundings that degrade and destroy them. It is high time we restored to the former masters of this land the dignity and freedom to which they are entitled.

Simón González and Wendell P. Jones recommend ways of improving the education of the Mexican-Americans and the black Americans. Their recommendations hold, with slight changes, for American Indians and other minorities. Let us see what these educators propose.

A. The Mexican-American
Simón González

In the bright Texas sun, two high school football teams battle for the afternoon's honors. From the bleachers stretched along the field, hundreds of students watch eagerly, absorbed in the athletic drama. On the dusty track before the stands, a small group of girls—the cheerleaders in jerseys, pleated skirts, and white boots—sing, scream, and twirl to the brassy tunes of the school band. But the girls are all Anglo-Americans from a school enrolling more than eighty-five percent Mexican-American stu-

98

dents. What has been the basis for the girls' selection? Their mothers, recognizing the importance of extracurricular activities in personality development, have seen to it that the criteria include a requirement that the cheerleaders' parents be high school graduates, a rule that automatically disqualifies Mexican-American girls, most of whose parents have not attended school beyond the fourth or fifth grade.

In a California class for mentally retarded children, a group of eight- and nine-year-olds are watching two boys playing checkers. All except one of the children are Mexican-American. The one Anglo boy, a hydrocephalic, steps toward the group and picks up some checkers, disrupting the game. The participants and observers are angry, but they tolerate the boy, whose abnormally large head, poor speech, and antisocial behavior are indicative of abnormality. They do not know that his mother, aware of her child's need for socializing influences, has arranged for his placement here. The Mexican-American children have been classified as mentally retarded by English-speaking psychologists using culturally biased tests written in the English language. Some of the more alert youngsters have been wondering why they are not in the regular classroom. They also wonder if being in the "Special Class" makes them like the boy with the large head.

Myriad incidents and practices that damage the self-image of Mexican-American children contrast today with numerous national, state, and local programs to equalize educational opportunities for the second largest ethnic minority in the United States. The changes needed to counter decades of insensitive and discriminatory treatment by the public schools and by the dominant society, however, have not been sufficiently extensive because those in responsible positions in government, business, and education have a limited understanding of the Mexican-American and the social, economic, and educational barriers that impede his upward mobility. In addition, most institutional leaders possess little knowledge of how society's pervasive racism causes the Mexican-American to view the Anglo and his culture with fear and suspicion and to cluster in the *barrios* and *colonias*, the less desirable areas of the community.

Notwithstanding the lofty pronouncements of professional organizations and leading educators proposing equality of educational opportunity for all American children and youth, the public school has failed to provide the instruction needed by a large sector of the Mexican-American population. The school has not only been dysfunctional for the Mexican-American child, it has also negatively affected the social position of this ethnic minority within the larger society.

Who Are the Mexican-Americans?

Some Mexican-Americans are the descendants of the Spaniards who settled in the Southwest more than 370 years ago. Others may be first-generation offspring born in the United States of Mexican parents who only recently arrived here. Various terms of identification provide a precise description of this ethnic group and also delineate the wide chasm that has prevented the unity essential to obtain social, political, and economic change.

Until the early 1920s, Spanish-speaking people in New Mexico, Colorado, and California, although American citizens by birth, called themselves Mexicans. As the great waves of rural migrants began arriving from Mexico during that period, prejudice and discrimination increased, and the earlier residents, wishing to disassociate themselves from the new arrivals in the eyes of the Anglo, adopted the names "Spanish Americans" and "Hispanos." The myth has persisted, particularly in New Mexico and Colorado, where many Spanish-surname people today continue to consider themselves to be white Americans of Spanish, not Mexican, ancestry.[1] In Texas, too, some felt a need to disavow any relationship with the waves of destitute rural immigrants continually arriving from Mexico. The early settlers, who by hard work, education, or exploitation of their own people attained a certain amount of affluence, chose to be identified as "Latin Americans," an ambiguous phrase since the name is applicable to any person born between the Rio Grande and Tierra del Fuego.

People of Mexican descent in the United States are perhaps 95 percent *mestizo* and use the term *La Raza* extensively in referring to themselves as a group apart from other citizens. As in all Latin America, they celebrate October 12 not as Columbus Day but as *El Dia de la Raza*, The Day of the Race. From that day in 1492 Europeans began to blend with Indians to form the *mestizos*, who today constitute the majority of the population of Mexico, Central America, and South America.

Largely unskilled rural residents from Mexico, most migrants came north seeking a better way of life for their families in the rural areas and small communities of the Southwest. With Indian blood predominating, the *mestizos'* physical characteristics—brown pigmentation, short stature, high cheekbones, brown eyes, and black hair—have given them a visibility that sets them apart as a distinct racial group. Generalizations,

---

[1] Nancie L. Gonzales, *The Spanish Americans of New Mexico: A Distinctive Heritage*, Mexican-American Study Project, Division of Research, Graduate School of Business Administration, University of California, Los Angeles, 1967, pp. 125-129.

however, must be made with caution, as the Mexican migration has included individuals from a wide spectrum in social class, racial composition, education, and personal goals.[2]

In recent years the term *Chicano* has been gaining wide popularity,
particularly among the young and the working-class sector, those who
have borne the brunt of racism. *Chicano* is a diminutive of Mexicano;
the *ch* sound substitutes for *x* in the language of the Nahua Indian tribe
of Mexico. Widely employed in Southern California, where the largest
concentration of Mexican-Americans is found, the usage is spreading
rapidly throughout the Southwest. It can be compared with the use of
the term "black" in place of Negro. Charged with emotion, the word
Chicano has been extremely valuable in promoting unity and in convey-
ing a feeling of pride, identity, and self-respect.

Comparing the European Immigrant
and the Mexican-American

One often hears references concerning the experience of the European
immigrant of the last century, and the inquiry invariably arises, "Why
haven't the Mexicans risen socially and economically as did the Italians,
Irish, Polish, and other immigrants?" Although it is true that American
ethnocentrism has been the basis of economic exploitation of, and social
discrimination toward, all immigrants, six reasons may be found to explain why this particular ethnic group has remained in a cycle of poverty.

First, when the European immigrant was arriving, the United States
was developing as an urban-industrial complex, and laborers were in
heavy demand to build its major cities and industries. The immigrants
provided the unskilled labor, gained a foothold in the economy, and
enabled their children and grandchildren to move up to skilled, white-
collar, and professional employment.[3] Urban employment needs for laborers without skills, however, diminished markedly during the time the
Mexican-American population has been shifting from the rural to the
urban environment.

Second, the flagrant racism prevalent in American society has impeded
the acculturation of this group to an even greater degree than the Amer-

---

[2] Octavio Romano V., "The Historical and Intellectual Presence of Mexican
Americans," *El Grito*, **II**, 2 (Winter 1969), p. 32.

[3] *Report of The National Advisory Commission on Civil Disorders*, U.S. Government Printing Office, Washington, D.C., 1968, p. 143.

ican Negro. Like the blacks, the *Chicanos* can be quickly identified and have been the target of prejudicial attitudes and racial persecution. Unlike most European immigrants, they cannot lose themselves in the "mainstream of middle-class America." Possibly because of their strong democratic ideology, many Americans have consistently refused to realize that Mexican-Americans have been members of a caste system that the dominant society has consistently exploited and from which escape is difficult. In many communities in the Southwest as late as World War II, employment as bus drivers, postmen, or even clerical helpers was denied to this group. Prejudice on the part of the dominant population toward this and all other minorities has had a detrimental effect on the total society.

Third, geographic proximity to Mexico also makes the *Chicano* experience different from that of the European immigrants. The latter crossed a vast ocean intent upon becoming Americans. They had a keen interest in acquiring the language and behavior patterns that would enable them to enjoy the economic and social benefits this land of plenty had to offer. The Mexican who was here as an early settler became the conquered and humiliated foreigner, stripped of his rights, his property, and, in many cases, even his women. Further, the waves of migrants from Mexico came primarily to perform the stoop labor that was in demand in the fields and the unskilled labor needed by the railroads and the mines of the Southwest. Most migrants continued to think of returning to the homeland. They retained the Spanish language, their values, and their culture and transmitted these to their children. Proximity to Mexico also facilitated visits back and forth. Radio programs from Mexico brought favorite soap operas and famous Mexican artists into the homes of millions residing along the border. The dream that some day, in some way, Mexico might regain its lost territory persisted until World War II.

Fourth, unlike the Europeans and Asians, whose entry into this country was drastically curtailed or eliminated by congressional quotas and exclusion acts, Mexicans entered legally and illegally as the need in the Southwest for cheap farm labor kept the border open. This across-the-border migration not only helped to perpetuate the stereotype of the illiterate Mexican but also prevented the already settled residents from organizing to demand higher wages for their labor.

A fifth important difference is that many Europeans settled in rapidly growing cities having powerful political machines that provided employment for their constituents in the construction of public buildings and in municipal services. In contrast, the Mexicans settled primarily in rural areas and small towns where voting restrictions effectively disenfranchised

them. Without a political base, the *Chicano* has been powerless economically and socially.

Sixth, since most European immigrants could assimilate socially, movement into heterogeneous neighborhoods prevented their segregation in
the public schools. Separation of children into a "Mexican school" or
"Mexican room" has been made under the pretense of providing better
opportunity for learning English. This is evidence of either lack of understanding of the learning process or misguided planning on the part of
administrators and school boards. Some school districts test Mexican-
American children with culturally biased tests of mental maturity and
then place them in classes for the mentally retarded to separate them
from Anglo children. Gerrymandering of school boundaries has also been
used extensively. Numerous lawsuits have been filed to require school
officials to cease the practice of segregating Spanish-speaking children
solely on the basis of their ethnic origin.[4]

Acculturation and Assimilation

Throughout the history of the United States, Americans have believed
that the good citizen is the person who pledges unquestioned loyalty to
his country, and historians have praised the rapidity with which Europeans have divested themselves of their language and their heritage to
become Americans. Max Lerner refers to this practice as the slaying of
the European father, with each new group, feeling its Americanism challenged, blatantly claiming to be more American than the others.[5] It has
been popular to imagine the United States as a "melting pot," a crucible
into which immigrants jumped eagerly to become transformed into Americans. Assimilation and acculturation both imply the necessity of rejection
of one's native culture as the price to be paid for acceptance as an American citizen. The schools have been given the direct responsibility to
"Americanize" ethnic groups, and they have assumed the task with avid
determination. The goal, however, has not been attained with many
Mexican-Americans. After more than a century of contact with the Anglo
culture, this minority continues its struggle to retain its identity, a practice viewed as a problem by the dominant culture because its institutions

[4] Lawrence B. Glick, "The Right to Equal Opportunity," in Julian Samora, Ed.,
La Raza: Forgotten Americans, University of Notre Dame Press, Notre Dame, Indiana,
1966, pp. 96-97.

[5] Max Lerner, *America As a Civilization,* Volume II, Simon and Schuster, New
York, 1957, pp. 23-28.

then function improperly. The rationale for assimilation is that social expenditures are conserved; when people are standardized, one system works for everyone. When a sector of the society refuses to fit standard molds, the system is dysfunctional and conflicts arise.[6] It must be recognized, however, that nonassimilation has resulted only in part from the refusal of Mexican-Americans to reject their heritage. As stated previously, racism and economic exploitation have also been major factors that have prevented this group from sharing in the "American dream."

A great change has begun to take place among Mexican-Americans in recent years. They are no longer content simply with retaining their language and their heritage at the expense of economic and social discrimination. Supported by Federal and state legislation on civil rights and encouraged by the progress of the blacks, the young *Chicano* activists are insisting that the concept of cultural pluralism be adopted by American society and that the schools be made responsible for building upon, rather than destroying, ethnic traditions. High school demonstrations and walkouts clearly show that Mexican-American students are very aware of the failure of the schools to educate them. When acknowledged student attrition in schools with a predominantly Mexican-American student body exceeds fifty percent, as so commonly occurs, complacent administrators must be forced to correct inequities.

At the same time that students in high schools, colleges, and universities are organizing as United Mexican-American Students (UMAS), *Movimiento Estudiantil Chicano de Aztlan* (MECHA), and Brown Berets to develop pride in the Mexican-Indian heritage and to demand changes in the schools, the adult community organizations are gaining strength. The United Farm Workers Organizing Committee, the Association of Mexican-American Educators, the Community Service Organization, the Mexican-American Political Association, and other organizations are demonstrating the sophistication and the ability to cooperate and to work toward common goals. Their activities range from conferences and meetings to power-producing community organization efforts, nonpartisan voter registration, get-out-the-vote campaigns, picketing, and nonviolent social protests.[7] The common objective that unites the various organiza-

---

[6] Deluvina Hernandez, *Mexican American Challenge to a Sacred Cow.* Monograph No. I. Mexican-American Cultural Center, University of California, Los Angeles, April 1970.

[7] John R. Martinez, "Leadership and Politics," in Julian Samora, Ed., *La Raza: Forgotten Americans,* University of Notre Dame Press, Notre Dame, Indiana, 1966, pp. 47-61.

tions is the attainment of cultural pluralism through an education that will permit Mexican-Americans to maintain their own culture and at the same time participate as equal members of American society.

Role Models and Self-Image

Many disadvantaged Mexican-American children entering kindergarten and first grade meet Anglo youngsters for the first time. Others have never been left with an English-speaking adult. They are bewildered and frightened by this strange new world that at times demands rigorous conformity. Without the broad range of experiences and opportunities that provides the readiness the school expects, they soon conclude that many aspects of this new world simply cannot be understood. Comments from parents and siblings about discrimination and ridicule, coupled with their own negative experiences at school, cause many to begin to doubt their sense of personal worth.

As the children continue in the elementary and junior high grades, scholastic failure and an increasing awareness of social and institutional prejudice further develop a poor self-image, denigrating their potential as individuals and as learners. Since this ethnic group carries the burden of obviously inferior economic and social position in the United States, many *Chicano* children accept the statements of teachers, school books, and the mass media implying that their socioeconomic status results from lack of initiative, indifference, and cultural limitations.

Robert Rosenthal and Lenore Jacobsen have conducted research studies that demonstrate the powerful influence of the teacher on children's achievement. They informed a group of teachers that certain of their pupils, including those from low-income Mexican-American families, could be expected to show considerable improvement during the school year. The teachers thought the predictions were based on tests that had been administered the preceding school year. In reality, the potential "spurters" were randomly selected. The performance of these children on achievement tests given during the year indicated remarkable progress. Children who were not designated as having a high potential were not rated favorably by their teachers. This "self-fulfilling prophecy" shows that the teacher's expectation of a child's behavior is communicated, perhaps in subtle ways, to the child and influences his behavior. The teacher's tone of voice, facial expression, touch, and posture all communicate her expectations to the children. One might conclude that perhaps the Mexican-American child's shortcomings may originate, not in his different ethnic background, but in his teacher's attitude toward that background.[8]

A child's self-image is enhanced when he identifies psychologically with people he admires. An Anglo-American child can select a role model from a variety of people who look, speak, and act in ways that are familiar to him. He then adopts his model's behavior and the attitudes he believes the model possesses. A boy may identify with a male teacher, a television star, a hero in a novel, or a neighborhood gang leader.[9] Three major problems complicate this process for the Mexican-American child. First, in his ethnic group he can seldom find role models who represent the values and attitudes or "success image" stressed by the school. Most of the limited few who have attained status in the dominant society move out of the Mexican-American community. Second, it is difficult, and in most cases impossible, for him to identify psychologically with an Anglo-American. Third, school books, television, and movies seldom present Mexicans or Mexican-Americans in positive roles.

School administrators must be alert to new instructional materials presenting Mexican-Americans in a favorable light and their heritage in true perspective. In-service education programs can help teachers learn more about this minority. The knowledge gained may assist in changing teachers' attitudes and can in turn be used by the teachers to influence attitude change in Anglo children. When selecting subject matter for class discussions, teachers should be constantly on the alert for news articles containing names and pictures of Spanish-surname people who have excelled in sports, fine arts, business, politics, or the professions. Additionally, young *Chicano* student leaders might be invited to speak to classes or to the student body about the goals of their organizations as these relate to the needs of Mexican-Americans. Principals should encourage student contact with individuals who have been successful in the world of the Anglo-American without rejecting their cultural heritage and who are assisting others in attaining their right to biculturalism. School boards should consider naming some schools after prominent Mexican-American leaders who have contributed to the development of *La Raza,* or after *Chicano* heroes. These approaches, undertaken at the same time the school is strengthening the basic skills indispensable for scholastic success,

[8] Robert Rosenthal and Lenore Jacobsen, "Teacher Expectations for the Disadvantaged," *Scientific American,* **CCXVIII** (April 1968), 19-23.

[9] Frederick J. McDonald, *Educational Psychology,* Wadsworth Publishing Co., Belmont, California, 1965, pp. 319-326.

may well provide the role models desperately needed by Mexican-American children to aid them in developing wholesome self-images.

Innovative Programs and Practices

If the schools are to function properly for Mexican-Americans, educators must accept the role of change agents. They must widen their range of information about this minority and develop meaningful policies with appropriate methods for implementation. As innovators and creative educational activists, they must take risks in trying out new ways of teaching and in creating instructional materials aimed toward a more relevant education for minorities. While a large segment of the general student population is prepared at home to meet the demands of the school, the disadvantaged Mexican-American child requires special attention to compensate for some specific needs.

Bilingual-Bicultural Education

Thousands of children of Mexican descent enter school unable to speak or to understand English; their personalities and experiences have been influenced by the Spanish language. Some develop a limited Spanish vocabulary and an equally limited English vocabulary to express themselves. Others speak English using Spanish pronunciation and syntax. Since it is not possible to assume that the home will reinforce the school's efforts in English instruction, the school must necessarily accept full responsibility for the development of English proficiency. To accomplish this goal many schools prohibit the use of Spanish in class or on the playground, and some punish those who disobey the rule.[10] Although the intent is to force the child to use English, thereby increasing practice and developing proficiency, often the child concludes that his mother tongue, and indeed his entire culture, is being suppressed because it is inferior.

On the other hand, the school may succeed so well that the children reject the Spanish language and even renounce their parent's customs and traditions in an effort to please their teachers, only to be thwarted in their acculturation attempts outside the classroom. The majority, however, are unable to cope with the traumatic exhortation to speak English

[10] Stan Steiner, *La Raza: The Mexican Americans,* Harper and Row, New York, 1970, p. 209.

and simply withdraw, sitting quietly in classes until eventually they leave the school.

A high student attrition rate forecasts serious consequences for the next generation. Many parents of Mexican-American children have received very limited educations themselves; they are not prepared to assist their children at home with formal school subjects requiring verbal fluency in English. Table 1 shows the appalling differences in the educational levels of Anglo, Spanish-surname, and non-white adults.[11]

Some educators are, at last, beginning to give increased attention to the advantages of using the Spanish language along with English for instructional purposes. They are encouraging children to express themselves in their native tongue, and bilingual teachers offer instruction in Spanish to facilitate the learning of concepts in all areas of the curriculum. Simultaneously, the children receive instruction in Mexican history, the influence of Mexico on the culture of the United States, contemporary Mexico, and other relevant topics that will contribute to the development of pride in their heritage. The use of Spanish also encourages chil-

Table 1

Median Years of School Completed by Spanish-Surname Persons of 25 Years and Over Compared with Other Population Groups

Standard Metropolitan Statistical Area	Anglo	Spanish Surname	Non-white
Abilene	12.0	4.0	8.8
Albuquerque	12.5	8.7	10.9
Austin	12.3	4.4	8.6
Corpus Christi	12.2	4.5	8.0
Dallas	12.1	6.4	8.6
Denver	12.3	8.8	11.4
El Paso	12.4	6.6	11.7
Fresno	10.7	6.1	8.8
Los Angeles-Long Beach	12.3	8.9	11.1
Lubbock	12.1	3.1	8.3
Phoenix	12.1	6.1	8.5
San Antonio	12.1	5.7	9.4
San Diego	12.2	8.9	10.7
Waco	11.0	5.5	8.2

[11] Adapted from Leo Grebler, *The Schooling Gap: Signs of Progress*, Mexican-American Study Project, Division of Research, Graduate School of Business Administration, University of California, Los Angeles, 1967, p. 18.

dren to participate actively in classroom discussions and provides the transition needed for learning English.

Research evidence may be found to support the effectiveness of these bilingual-bicultural programs. Theodore Anderson considers the development of the child's verbal ability in his mother tongue to be the most important new advance in language instruction and cites research to urge that Spanish-speaking children and their parents be oriented to school by native speakers.[12] Elizabeth Ott and T. D. Horn have conducted studies in San Antonio and McAllen, Texas, and in New York City on language and reading from kindergarten through fourth grade; they have subsequently designed a program to equip Spanish-speaking children with communication skills in English and Spanish to enable them to participate successfully in the academic setting.[13]

The major difficulty in implementing bilingual programs is that few Spanish-speaking teachers are available.[14] Some school districts have initiated Spanish-language classes to prepare their faculties for this new thrust. However, to require already overworked teachers to become proficient in a second language may be an unreasonable demand that might result in further increasing the flight of otherwise competent teachers from disadvantaged Mexican-American communities. Nevertheless, all teachers can be expected to acquire a sound understanding of cross-cultural values and social issues affecting this minority. Such knowledge is indispensable if teachers are to gain a more positive attitude toward the Mexican-American and are simultaneously to influence Anglo children to acquire new perspectives and to eliminate stereotypes and prejudices.

Bilingual aides are being used effectively in the instructional program. As integral components of an educational team, they add significantly to the growth and development of children.[15] Aides not only work with children in both English and Spanish but also do much to improve home and school relations by explaining the school program to parents, by visiting parents at home, and by planning and organizing parents' meet-

[12] Theodore Anderson, "A New Focus on the Bilingual Child," *Modern Language Journal,* **II** (March 1965), 156-160.

[13] Charles B. Brussell, *Disadvantaged Mexican American Children and Early Educational Experience,* Southwest Educational Development Laboratory, Austin, Texas, 1968, p. 80.

[14] Armando M. Rodriguez, "Speak Up, Chicano," *American Education,* **IV** (May 1968), p. 27.

[15] Gordon J. Klopf, Garda W. Bowman, and Adena Joy, *A Learning Team: Teacher and Auxiliary,* Bank Street College of Education for the United States Office of Education, U.S. Government Printing Office, Washington, D.C., 1969, p. 119.

ings. As resource persons aware of the needs of the students and the community, aides may encourage students in developing higher aspirations and assist them in overcoming peer-group pressures against scholastic achievement.[16]

Mexican-American Teachers and Administrators

Factors such as a low level of aspiration, lack of encouragement by teachers, and few financial resources have limited sharply the number of teachers, counselors, and administrators of Mexican descent. While it is true that similarity of ethnic background does not in itself insure the empathy required for effective teaching, carefully selected Mexican-Americans can play a vital role in the school. Their intimate acquaintance with the problems confronting the child in the school and their ability to establish rapport with parents can contribute signficantly to the improvement of the teaching-learning process.

Slowly, colleges and universities have begun to recruit *Chicano* students. Funds for scholarships, counseling services, tutoring, and special-entry programs are encouraging many who ordinarily would not consider preparing for teaching as a career. The validity of traditional admissions criteria, particularly grade-point average and aptitude tests, is being questioned as institutions of higher education begin to place more emphasis on leadership qualities, commitment to the *Chicano* movement, and motivation to succeed academically.

Federally Supported Programs

The United States Office of Education has in recent years begun to provide financial support to school districts to promote innovative programs specifically designed to improve instruction for disadvantaged children. The Head Start programs offer learning experiences that enable ethnic minority and Anglo children from low-income families to close the gap that exists between them and middle-class children before they enter first grade. Follow Through programs have as their purpose the prevention of regression after the children enter school. Both programs offer intensive learning experiences and involve the parents in the education of their children. Youth Tutoring Youth programs pay disadvantaged children to teach their peers on a one-to-one basis, thus motivating the

[16] Gertrude Noar, *Teacher Aides at Work*, National Education Association, Washington, D.C., 1967, pp. 19-21.

tutor to learn because of a teaching responsibility. Upward Bound offers Saturday and summer instruction for high school students in preparation for college. Teacher Corps and Urban Teacher Corps are designed to prepare teachers for schools in the *barrio* and the *ghetto* as well as to promote curricular changes in teacher preparation and in the schools.

The Elementary and Secondary Act of 1965 has provided funds for a wide range of programs directly affecting many Mexican-American children. Title I supports the establishment, expansion, and improvement of special programs, including the construction of school facilities to meet the special needs of educationally deprived children of low-income families. Title III provides funds to develop exemplary and innovative elementary and secondary programs to serve as models. Special personnel, equipment, and educational services are made available in centers for the use of the entire community. Title IV allocates resources for reasearch, authorizes the training of research personnel, and encourages dissemination of information derived from educational research and development.[17] Title VII, recently added to ESEA, provides funds for the Bilingual Education Program previously described, and Title VIII has as its purpose the reduction of the number of high school dropouts through improved counseling and curricular change. These and numerous other federally supported programs can facilitate educational innovations of considerable benefit to the Mexican-American community; however, the programs do require educators who have a sound understanding of the psychological and social factors affecting learning as well as a thorough knowledge of this minority group.

Conclusion

Most Mexican-American children come to school from low socioeconomic homes. They are taught by middle-class Anglo teachers, few of whom have acquired an understanding of cultural and social-class differences that impede the attainment of educational goals. Educators have failed to take advantage of the Spanish language and cultural characteristics—such as respect for others, humility, respect for authority, and familial relationships—to facilitate instruction and learning. They have failed to communicate with the children's parents and have neglected to enlist their cooperation in effecting desired behavioral changes, thus

[17] Francis Keppel, *The Necessary Revolution in American Education,* Harper and Row, New York, 1966, p. 192.

alienating both children and parents so that few have seen the school as an agency that can help in the attainment of a better way of life.

A rapidly changing society requires dynamic and imaginative teachers who can motivate children, teach them the basic intellectual skills, and guide them in acquiring the problem-solving techniques needed for critical thinking. Unfortunately, far too few schools have implemented research findings concerning concept formation, the changing of attitudes, motivation, problem-solving, transfer, social-class influence, and other factors that directly affect learning. Many schools have rigidly adhered to the philosophy that education consists of a body of knowledge to be covered, that it is the teacher's responsibility to transmit this knowledge, and that some children, through no fault of the school, will fail to master the required material. Damaging as an overemphasis on memorization may be for all children, this practice inevitably results in failure for a disproportionate number of children from racial and ethnic minorities and from low-income Anglo families. In previous decades school dropouts could find jobs as manual laborers; today's urban society demands that its workers possess greater competencies and skills. Inappropriate education has meant that innumerable families have remained trapped in a cycle of poverty—a cycle of failure—from one generation to the next.

Mexican-Americans are beginning to unite, stating that the schools cannot continue to blame their children for failure and insisting that teachers and administrators must be held accountable for the results of the instructional program. They have been joined in their concern by a few dedicated Anglo-Americans at the local, state, and national levels. Working cooperatively, they are developing an educational philosophy and undertaking research on techniques and materials that will enable all Mexican-American children to learn at school the skills, attitudes, values, and understandings necessary to become active participants in American society without rejecting their language and heritage. Concurrently, vigorous efforts must continue to be made to protect the rights of this minority to complete suffrage, adequate housing, good health, and fair employment. When these goals are reached, the United States can truly claim that it provides equality of opportunity for its Mexican-Americans.

References

Brussell, Charles B., *Disadvantaged Mexican American Children and Early Educational Experience*, Southwest Educational Development Laboratory, Austin, Texas, 1968. A synthesis of the literature on Mexican-Americans including a brief history, social characteristics, a rationale for educational programs, and a description of a variety of projects sponsored by the Laboratory.

"Equal Educational Opportunity," *Harvard Educational Review*, 38, 1 (Winter 1968). A special issue dealing with the concept of equality of educational opportunity. Factors of race and social class are discussed and research and policy issues considered in depth.

Grebler, Leo, et al., *The Mexican-American People: The Nation's Second Largest Minority*, Free Press, New York, New York, 1970. A comprehensive study covering historical, cutural, religious and political perspectives of this ethnic group. Excellent resource book for educators.

Manuel, Herschel T., *Spanish-Speaking Children of the Southwest: Their Education and Public Welfare*, University of Texas Press, Austin, 1965. A psychologist with long experience working with Spanish-speaking children, Manuel provides insight into the causes of school failure and suggests educational programs to correct inequities.

Samora, Julian, *La Raza: Forgotten Americans*, University of Notre Dame Press, 1967. A compilation of essays concerning history, religion, politics, the plight of the migrant workers, demographic characteristics, and the emerging middle class.

Steiner, Stan, *La Raza: The Mexican Americans*, Harper and Row, New York, New York, 1969. A vivid account of the contemporary leaders of Mexican ancestry in the Southwest and the problems, goals, and resistance they encounter as they struggle to obtain justice and equality of opportunity for Mexican-Americans.

Vasquez, Richard, *Chicano*, Doubleday & Co., Garden City, New York, 1970. A novel about a Mexican family that migrates to Los Angeles, California. Describes, in a dynamic way, the unique life style of the family and acculturation efforts of the young.

B. The Black Man

Wendell P. Jones

The quest for equality has been, in one form or another, the dominant activity of black men throughout their history in America. Black men have always been seeking full participation in all aspects of American life. The goal has not been achieved, for through means sometimes subtle and sometimes direct the majority racial group in America has managed to deny the black man full citizenship. Especially has this been true in the area of education, which the black man has through the years perceived as the gateway to a better life, even in a racist society. The denial of equal educational opportunity has led to feelings of frustration and hopelessness; it has also led to contests in the courts, challenges to authorities, and the rise of a general militancy demanding better education—and equal education—for America's black population.

No attempt is made here to review the sweep of history that has led to the sense of frustration and hopelessness of many black people and is reflected in the current militancy. It should be noted, however, that the search for education has, for the black man, always been a struggle won by comparatively few. A historical overview, although too brief, may indicate some of the roots of the contemporary situation.

Historical Overview

In the eighteenth and early nineteenth centuries, there was practically no education of slaves. Records do indicate that in a few communities along the Eastern seaboard, schools with one or two teachers were opened by church groups to provide religious and reading instruction. In addition, some slave owners provided basic education for favored slaves, often their own descendants. Several freed blacks had received limited education from their former owners; some of these taught in schools that they themselves established. As slaves increased in number and revolts became more frequent, many states made it illegal to teach slaves to read and write.

The Civil War made a difference. Many fugitive slaves reported to camps of the Union Army, which began the establishment of schools for them. Throughout the North, organizations were formed to assist the fleeing slaves, and send teachers, books, and resources to support schools

114

for both adults and children. It has been estimated that by the end of the war some 20,000 had been taught to read.

The post-Civil War period produced the first significant organized program for the education of the black man in this country. The Bureau for Freedmen, Refugees, and Abandoned Lands, commonly known as the "Freedmen's Bureau," was created by an act of Congress in March 1865. In the five years of its operation, it was responsible for the establishment of more than 4000 separate schools providing for the education of 250,000 pupils. It appointed state superintendents of schools to coordinate the efforts of missionary and philanthropic agencies, and contributed to the construction of schools for both the freed blacks and the poor whites. It cooperated with religious groups in the establishment of "colleges" that were then good secondary schools but now are the leading private higher institutions in the Southern states with predominantly black enrollment.

Following the Civil War, state constitutional conventions and legislatures enacted statutes that provided equally for the education of whites and blacks; the voting power of the black man during reconstruction was strongly felt on the education issue. In all states, a great increase occurred in the enrollment of black and white children in public schools. To maintain equality, more revenue than was readily available was needed if the increasing enrollments were to be maintained. The upper classes, who held the positions of leadership and power, were challenged on this and other issues by the power of the white small farmer. The Southern rich had traditionally not been enthusiastic about public education at the expense of taxpayers. However, the lower economic classes looked to public education as the basis of a better life for their children, and before 1900 they were in control of Southern political affairs. Inequities in the expenditures on education for white children and for black children rapidly became the common practice in these states, with the blacks being the ones to suffer.

It has been said that the best education (although a limited one), available to blacks in the South immediately after the Civil War was paid for through the philanthropy of the average citizen of the North. Many missionary enterprises provided teachers and financial support; individuals sent gifts to individual schools. Gradually much of this role was assumed by large foundations. The Peabody Fund (1867) contributed heavily to the training of teachers, the Anna T. Jeanes Fund (1905) to the supervision of teachers in small rural schools, the Rockefeller-supported General Education Board (1903) to the improvement of higher education, the Julius Rosenwald Fund (1910) to the building of elementary schools, and the Carnegie Corporation (1902) to the establishment of college libraries. Many smaller philanthrophies made important contributions.

In general, it can be said that the education of blacks in the Southern states has been at an undesirably low level. Admittedly, there are many who have nevertheless achieved unquestioned academic and professional success. However, in terms of the numbers of blacks who have embarked on the education ladder, the "successful" ones represent no more than five percent. While economic, social, and psychological factors are part of the mosaic, the nature of the educational enterprise available to the black student militated against an achievement comparable to that of white students in the same geographic area.

As indicated earlier, appropriations for the education of blacks tended to be lower, per student enrolled, than for whites, whether at the school district, county, or state level. A few illustrations will indicate the disadvantaged position of the black school child.[1] In 1910 the average length of the school term for the white child in the southern states was 128 days and for the black child 101 days; in 1929 the average length of the school term for the white pupil was 164 days and for the black pupil 144 days. State expenditures for the education of white and black children showed a similar disparity. In 1915 the average per capita annual expenditure for the education of the white child in the southern states was $10.82 and for the black child only $4.01. By 1930 the expenditures had increased markedly, but the black child had become an even greater loser. Average per capita annual expenditure for the white child was $42.39 and for the black child $15.86. The average monthly salary paid white public school teachers in eleven southern states rose from $60.60 in 1909-10 to $118.01 in 1928-29. During the same period the average monthly salary paid black teachers rose from $32.67 to $72.78. The gap between salaries paid white teachers and black teachers did not close until after the second World War. School facilities for black children were just as unequal. In fact, in 1915 the average black child was attending school in a structure whose per capita investment value was only $7.34, while the average white child was receiving instruction in a building with a per capita investment value of $29.84.

Outside of the South similar, although not identical, problems existed. With the migration of large numbers of blacks to the great urban areas beginning with World War I, the black ghetto was born, always pressing

[1] See Henry Allen Bullock, *A History of Negro Education in the South,* Harvard University Press, Cambridge, Massachusetts, 1967, Chapter VII, "The Failure of an Experiment," pp. 167-193.

outward but always contained. As schools became predominantly black, learning materials became less available, and school buildings and grounds received less care and repair. Moreover, the better teachers (usually white) sought other assignments, leaving many schools heavily staffed with beginning teachers. Black teachers were rarely appointed to regular positions, but could take temporary assignments that did not command the salary of a regularly appointed teacher. Black supervisory and administrative personnel were practically unknown. In fact, during the school year 1946-47 there was only one black school principal in the city of Los Angeles and only one in the city of Chicago. Other large metropolitan areas such as New York City had none.

Conditions such as those described have been constant irritants to most black people, and pressures of various kinds brought some changes. The blacks in the South began a series of legal appeals to the courts in the early thirties and added the nonviolent demonstration in the early sixties. The blacks outside the South began their attacks—a combination of the violent and nonviolent tactics—in the mid-sixties.

The Legal Struggle

It was in 1896, in the case of *Plessy v. Ferguson*, that the United States Supreme Court gave sanction to both the theory and practice of segregation if accommodations were equal. This decision was used to justify *de jure* separation of the races in public schools, elementary and secondary, until 1954. (At various times, segregation was required by law in such non-Southern states as Arizona, California, Indiana, Missouri, New Mexico, New York, Ohio, West Virginia, and Wyoming.)

The twentieth-century legal fight for equality of educational opportunity began in 1933 when Thomas R. Hocutt secured a mandamus to compel the University of North Carolina to admit him to its School of Pharmacy, there being no institution in the state offering such training to blacks. The case was lost on a technicality. During 1935 and 1936, however, Donald Murray waged a successful court fight for admission to the law school of the University of Maryland. Whereas the Murray case was decided in the state courts, similar lawsuits filed in other states were lost. Lloyd Gaines's suit for admission to the law school of the University of Missouri was approved by the Supreme Court. These cases primarily sought the provision, for blacks, of educational facilities within the borders of a state equal to those provided there for whites.

In 1950 the Supreme Court handed down two decisions ending the concept of "separate but equal" higher education. G. W. McLaurin, a black enrollee in the University of Missouri graduate school who had been segregated from other students, sued for treatment equal to that of other students. Herman Sweatt in his suit for admission to the University of Texas Law School contended that a segregated institution, by its very nature, was inferior; he wished admission to the law school of the University of Texas regardless of the existence or nonexistence of a law school for blacks. In both cases, the rulings favored the plaintiffs, removing the last legal barriers to equal higher-education opportunity.

Perhaps the most important and far-reaching decision of the Supreme Court regarding the education of blacks was that handed down on May 17, 1954 in the case of *Brown v. Board of Education of Topeka, Kansas.* The Court concluded that the doctrine of "separate but equal" has no place in the field of education. It affirmed that the segregation of children in public schools solely on the basis of race deprives the children of the minority group of equal educational opportunities and so denies them the equal protection of the laws that is guaranteed by the Federal Constitution. A year later the Court established rules for putting the principles into practice, placing the responsibility for implementation in the hands of United States district courts. State and local districts were required to devise desegregation plans with all deliberate speed and in good faith. The stage was now clear for the prompt and reasonable start toward an integrated equal public school system in the seventeen states affected by the decision and in the District of Columbia.

Reactions

These landmark decisions were not unexpected and were received with relative calm in the states affected, by both whites and blacks. As regards the 1950 higher-education decision, it should be noted that several states and the District of Columbia had already begun the limited desegration of some of their professional and graduate schools. After the 1954 decision, all the states, with the exceptions of Alabama, Mississippi, and South Carolina, opened their undergraduate colleges to black students without serious incidents. In these states, students were admitted but faced demonstrations and near riots led by state and school executives, townspeople, and some students.

Black students are now enrolled in nearly all of the Southern state-supported colleges and in most of the Southern private institutions that were traditionally all white. Some formerly all-black institutions enroll a few whites and a few of these institutions in border states have a heavy enrollment of white students. Among these are West Virginia State College and Lincoln University (Missouri), with enrollments approximately 40 percent white, and Delaware State College and Kentucky State College, with enrollments approximately 30 percent white. Enrollments of blacks in predominantly white institutions in the South is estimated at 3 percent of total enrollment; enrollments of whites in predominantly black institutions is estimated at 2 percent of total enrollment. With the barriers down and enrollment patterns changing, it is predicted that the racial mix of these institutions will increase rapidly.[2]

The public school situation was quite different. Only five states—Kentucky, Maryland, Missouri, Oklahoma, and West Virginia—and the District of Columbia readily adopted desegregation plans. Five states—Arkansas, Delaware, Tennessee, North Carolina, and Texas—had no state plans but had several cities and districts that submitted satisfactory plans. Florida and Virginia resisted strongly. South Carolina, Georgia, Alabama, Mississippi, and Louisiana became known as the "hard-core" states because of their long refusal to submit plans for desegregation. In only one or two districts in each state were plans submitted that were acceptable to the Courts—until the Department of Health, Education, and Welfare began withholding federal funds from noncomplying districts in 1966. Perhaps the most extreme negative response to the integration order was the closing of all public schools in Prince Edward County, Virginia, for five years. White pupils continued their education in hastily established private schools, but black pupils whose parents were financially unable to support private schools suffered irreparable educational deprivation.[3]

During the first ten years following the public school desegregation ruling, despite the state plans mentioned, only one percent of the black pupils in the seventeen southern states were enrolled in integrated schools. By 1970, with federal funding pressure being applied, the percentage rose to 40. Many districts still practice token integration, enrolling one or two blacks in white schools and no whites in black schools. Other school districts have accepted the mandate of the courts and of the Department of Health, Education, and Welfare fully, providing for changes in patterns of teacher and pupil assignment to make school integration a real-

[2] See John Egerton, "Almost All-White," *Southern Education Report*, 4, No. 9 (May 1969), pp. 2-17.

[3] Benjamin Muse, "The South's Troubled Years," *Southern Education Report*, 4, No. 10 (June 1969), p. 16.

ity. However, both subtle and direct resistance to integration remains in some areas of the South and in most cities of the North and West. The concept of racial balance in the schools, legally sanctioned, is viewed as a threat to the "neighborhood" school pattern. To develop racial balance in many public schools, officials must devise school-integration plans requiring schools in totally white residential areas to enroll black pupils and schools in totally black areas to enroll white pupils, a possibility not welcomed by the general white population and resisted by some blacks.

The post-1954 period has been a bitter one and has left scars. Many communities have accepted desegregation without apparent discomfiture. In hundreds of communities throughout the South there have been racial confrontations, and conflicts over the mixing of pupils in classes, violent enough to require the services of the state guard and even the National Guard. White parents have preferred to open private schools at their own expense. Black parents have resisted the closing of the school attended by their children, especially if closing it meant the transporting of their children to a distant school. Proponents of desegregation, chiefly black, have had their property destroyed, have been intimidated, and have been fired from nonschool jobs. Black teachers have been released at the end of the school year and some black administrators have been demoted. In other situations black teachers have been assigned to formerly white schools and white teachers have been assigned to formerly black schools; black and white principals have interracial staffs.

The New Black Awareness

A dissatisfaction with the status of the black man in American society has been growing for many years, but it gained most of its momentum during the fifties. The movement may be a general product of the times in which we live and its roots may be many and varied, all entertwined. Indeed, the American black has been inspired by the emergence of black Africa into the world community of nations. As a returnee from several wars, the American black has new perspectives based on broader experiences. As a more literate man, he is much more aware of the restrictions placed on him, in every aspect of American life, by a dominant group. He has faith and belief in the principles of American democracy, but sees that principles and practices do not agree. He feels oppressed, frustrated, and subjected to a control over himself that is not his own. He believes that the only way he can control his destiny is through the exercise of the kind of power that the dominant race now has, treasures, and does not wish to relinquish. Without this power, however, he can never be a free and equal participant in the mainstream of American life. Under domination, he has lost the image of himself that he once had and has reached out to the image of another. He must find his own image, define his goals, and become unified. The black man will then have sufficient black power to enable him to participate in the social, economic, and political activities of the country. In the process he will strengthen the country, for he will have freed the white man of domination and institutional racism. He will have enabled the country to practice its ideals and redeem its conscience.

There has been no leader of black Americans with the following of Martin Luther King since his assassination on April 4, 1968. Rather, many persons are playing roles of leadership in different organizations and activities. All the leaders, each with a significant following, appear to have accepted the position that there is an urgent need for building the black image, setting goals, achieving unity. There is no agreement, however, as to what the procedures should be or what methods should be followed. The leaders do agree that education is an essential ingredient. But the question is, *what* education?

Some Current Developments

Black Studies

Since 1965 a major concern of black school and college students has been the "relevance" of education programs to the needs of blacks in American society. A major outgrowth of this concern has been the introduction into school and college curriculums of "Black Studies."[4] In the forefront with demands for this curriculum change have been the Black Student Unions. These Unions, sometimes known by other names, are an outgrowth of the sudden increase in the number of black students on the campuses of predominantly white colleges and universities. At most institutions the Union has waged an ongoing campaign for the admission of more black students on scholarships, arguing that traditional admission requirements are not the only criteria by which students should be admitted. It has insisted on the addition of blacks to the academic

[4] Charles V. Hamilton, "The Question of Black Studies," *Phi Delta Kappan,* **LI,** No. 7 (March 1970), p. 362.

faculties, often identifying persons who should be employed. The Union has often alone and sometimes with faculty members developed new courses or groups of courses to comprise black studies programs. It has been successful in achieving these goals and on many campuses now special centers become involved in minority communities through service and research.

In pursuit of Union programs (and often without much experience), a few members have had to devote a disproportionate amount of time to the endeavor. In other cases, Unions have been involved in violent activity (as have many other groups). It appears, however, that theirs has been a major contribution in awakening colleges and universities to blackness in a meaningful way. The Unions persist, despite the feeling of some blacks that their time should be used in the more traditional manner.

Black Student Unions have spread from the white institutions to the predominantly black institutions. Here, they are most often in direct conflict with black administrators and professors. Their object is to spur the "establishment" to make the curriculum more relevant to black needs and to render better service to campus and town. They feel that these institutions have lost contact with the black concept and, having copied the patterns of white prestige colleges, are not preparing the students through relevant programs for service in and to the black community. The demands are primarily directed toward more historical and cutural studies as well as toward courses and field work dealing with the variety of contemporary problems that beset blacks in this country.

The movement has moved into secondary schools with similar purposes and has been responsible for curriculum additions such as black history and Afro-American literature. In elementary schools the emphasis has been on improving the self-image of the black child and on motivating him to succeed. Textbooks and other instructional materials are increasingly multi-ethnic in content and illustrations, more black males are being placed in positions of authority, and more resource material is being drawn from the black experience the child has known.

The concept of black studies is emotionally loaded. It has generated considerable rhetoric as well as confusion over definiton, objectives, and program patterns.[5] The speed with which institutions have sought to meet the demands is an admission that American education has been "white" education and has failed to attune itself to the total population. In so doing it has contributed to the development of the idea that the

---

[5] John W. Blassingame, "Black Studies: An Intellectual Crisis," *The American Scholar*, **38**, No. 4 (Autumn 1969), p. 548.

nation's development was the work of the white population only, thus building and strengthening attitudes of superiority in whites and inferiority in blacks and other minority groups. Ideally, except for the specialist, black studies should not be necessary. The black man's role in all aspects of the nation's development, culture, and problems should be studied as an integral part of the whole. Only this procedure can lead to the mutual understandings and appreciations essential to the elimination of racism and the survival of the democracy.

Compensatory Education Programs

It is well established that the child of poverty has not achieved as well in the regular public school as has the child from more advantaged homes and communities. Economic deprivation, cultural isolation, and ethnic segregation have not fostered the motivation and background needed for normal success in the general school system. During the last decade massive programs, chiefly federally financed, have been instituted to overcome the effects of the environment of the poor and to bring the children of the poor up to the level at which they can be served effectively by existing school patterns. This effort has been termed "compensatory education" and has embraced a large proportion of the black children throughout the country.[6]

The most widely known of the compensatory education programs is "Head Start," designed to take preschool children from disadvantaged homes and prepare them for entry into regular primary schools. More than one million black children have been enrolled in the program. Evaluations have shown that the enrollees do make significant gains during the training period and that these gains carry over into the first year of school. Head Start enrollees, however, appear to do no better after the first year in regular school than do non-Head Start pupils from the same neighborhoods. It is recognized that the Head Start programs were hastily developed and that many of the teachers were not especially equipped to work with the poverty children. As a result of evaluations, the programs are being improved, and it is very likely that in the future they will contribute significantly to the school readiness of black children.

"Upward Bound" is a successful compensatory education program. Primarily concerned with developing an interest in higher education

6 Doxey A. Wilkerson, "Compensatory Education?", *Southern Education Report*, **4**, No. 4 (November 1968), pp. 2-9.

among high school students from poor families, it offers at nearby higher institutions programs to remedy academic deficiencies and to develop an interest in college life. The programs consist of summer campus residential experiences followed by evening and Saturday enrichment activities during the regular school year. Data from the first programs indicate that approximately 80 percent of program enrollees entered college, in contrast to the 8 percent who would normally have gone to college from this group.

Community Control

For the twenty years preceding the now-famous 1954 Supreme Court decision outlawing segregation in education, the black leadership worked for integrated schools as the means of providing equal educational opportunity for blacks. In the Brown case, the Court concluded that the separation of blacks from others of similar age and qualifications solely on the basis of their race would generate feelings of inferiority not likely to be undone. The slow and painful process of desegregation then began.

More recently, particularly in urban areas of the North and West, new voices are expressing strong dissatisfaction with integration as the answer to the black's educational needs.[7] Integration plans in these areas tend to rely heavily on the busing of black pupils from their ghetto residences to predominantly white schools, a practice viewed as another form of white paternalism and racism. Further, in the remaining predominantly black schools to which white pupils are seldom transferred, increased funding has produced no marked improvement in pupil achievement. Perhaps most important, some black citizens question the ability or the desire of the predominantly white school to develop and strengthen the self-image of the black child and to help him in his search for identity, functions that black parents consider to be of primary importance in the education of the black child.

Anti-integrationists, therefore, advocate the extension of the principle of community control of schools to the population of ghetto areas rather than leaving the decision-making power in the hands of white majorities removed from the realities of black ghetto life. The principle of community control is well established in the United States, and many ghetto areas exceed in population most urban communities that do control their schools.

Proponents of black community control of schools contend that blacks

[7] Alex Poinsett, "Battle to Control Black Schools," *Ebony,* **XXIV**, No. 7 (May 1969), pp. 44-54.

should determine policies and practices of schools attended by black children. They should, for example, have the major responsibility for the selection and retention of teachers, supervisors, and administrators in order to eliminate the negative influence of racist white teachers on young black children and to expose the black children to black authority figures as positive models of capability and success, who are inspirational and worthy of emulation. Likewise, the curriculum should be determined by the community through its representatives, insuring adequate treatment of black history and culture and, through recognition of black heroes and notable movements as well as general atmosphere, fostering group solidarity and pride. It is not proposed that the teaching of skills and knowledges essential to full participation in the mainstream of American life be abandoned. Rather, the aim is to permeate school life with experiences specifically designed to eliminate feelings of inferiority, heighten the black self-image, and motivate for and encourage success. These are tasks that community-control advocates do not believe will be accomplished in white-controlled schools, whether predominantly white or predominantly black in enrollment.

In Summation

Whither black education? The rank discrimination and segregation of the past is a great tragedy in the history of America, standing in stark contrast to principles upon which the country was founded and which it still expounds. The efforts of the recent years to remedy the situation, while laudable, can be viewed as primarily expanded tokenism. The problem is not just one of equal educational opportunity; it is a problem of the lack of commitment on the part of American society in all of its sectors to support, foster, and practice the concept of human equality. The failure of white America to accept blacks as equal human beings in matters economic, social, and political is quite clear. Blacks know that the history of deprivation and denial at the hands of the majority group has—for the black masses—stifled creativity and enterprise and eroded expectations of success and recognition in the total society, leaving little incentive for success in school. This knowledge spurs black leaders and increasing numbers of their followers to agitate more and more militantly for the eradication of inequality. The problem will remain, however, until white America, if only in the interest of national unity and internal peace, elects to support, foster, and practice the concept of human equality. White education aimed at the elimination of white racism may yet solve the difficulties of black education!

References

❖❖

Ashmore, Harry S., *The Negro and the Schools,* The University of North Carolina Press, Chapel Hill, 1954. Facts and figures on biracial education in the South to 1954.

"Black Leaders Speak Out on Black Education," *Today's Education* **58**, No. 7, 25-32 (October 1969). Special feature article in which ten black educators and leaders answer specific questions regarding black education.

Bond, Horace Mann, *The Education of the Negro in the American Social Order,* Octagon Books, Inc., New York, 1966. A detailed account of the education of the Negro in America with special reference to historical roots, the impact of economics and finance, and current problems.

Bullock, Henry Allen, *A History of Negro Education in the South: From 1619 to the Present,* Harvard University Press, Cambridge, Massachusetts, 1967. While describing education of blacks in the Southern states, the author depicts how much of what happened was historical accident.

Carmichael, Stokely and Charles V. Hamilton, *Black Power: The Politics of Liberation,* Vintage Books, New York, 1967. Presentation of a political framework and ideology for American society with special reference to power, black and white.

Clift, Virgil A., Archibald W. Anderson, and H. Gordon Hullfish (Eds.), *Negro Education in America: Its Adequacy, Problems, and Needs.* Sixteenth Yearbook of the John Dewey Society, Harper and Row, New York, 1962. An excellent general background to present problems, with focus on anthropological and sociological factors and the changing situation.

Franklin, John Hope, *From Slavery to Freedom: A History of Negro Americans,* Alfred A. Knopf, New York, 1967. The best and most comprehensive history of Negro Americans. Beginning with African backgrounds, the account ends with the beginnings of the current Negro revolution in America.

126

Harding, Vincent, "Black Students and the Impossible Revolution," *Ebony*, **XXIV**, No. 10, 141-148 (August 1969). A discussion of the motivations and goals of protesting black students on white and black campuses.

Harvard Educational Reveiw, *Equal Educational Opportunity*, Harvard University Press, Cambridge, Massachusetts, 1969. An examination of the concept of equal educational opportunity in the context of recent research findings and the current school crisis.

"Race and Equality in American Education," *The Journal of Negro Education*, **XXXVII**, No. 3, 185-358 (Summer 1968). Collection of articles dealing with the assessment of Negro capacity and achievement and programs for improvement.

"The Higher Education of Negro Americans: Prospects and Programs," *The Journal of Negro Education*, **XXXVI**, No. 3, 187-347 (Summer 1967). Papers on the definition and evaluation of the role of the predominantly Negro college and means of improving the provision of higher education for Negroes.

6

Political Ideologies

George F. Kneller

❖❖

"Keep politics out of the school; keep the school out of politics!" How often we hear this slogan. What is meant, however, is not really politics but *partisanship*; for politics is the art and science of structuring social arrangements, and the school is one of these arrangements.

A nation's political and educational systems are mutually reinforcing. Any political system not only regulates the activities of citizens but also provides, through education, the means by which individuals may fulfill themselves within limits sanctioned by the system itself. Likewise, education contributes to politics. The university, for example, may claim to be nonpolitical, but the people within it cannot avoid political involvement. Professors and students frequently become party activists, commentators on political events, advisers, consultants, and researchers on matters of public policy. University representatives lobby continuously in legislatures to get their programs approved and adequately financed.

The term "politics" springs indirectly from the Greek noun *polis*, meaning "city-state," and directly from the Greek adjective *politikos*, meaning whatever concerns the member of a *polis* as a citizen rather than as a private person. Voting in an election is a political matter because

128

it involves the individual as a citizen; an argument with his wife is not, because it concerns him only as a private person. The study of politics, then, examines critically the principles and institutions that men create in order to live together as citizens, which is to say as social beings with common interests.

Historically the study of politics has consisted largely of moral and social philosophy. About a hundred years ago it was extended to include constitutional law and governmental institutions. After World War II it became "political science," having taken on a behavioral orientation in the manner of sociology and psychology. Contemporary political science thus seeks to establish generalizations about actual political practices and institutions without necessarily considering which of them are most suited to the needs and aspirations of men as social beings. Today, however, there is a growing concern to expose the ideological commitments made by supposedly objective studies of political behavior. As the hidden value judgments of political scientists are made manifest, there is a return to political philosophy. In this chapter I will consider political philosophy rather than political science, and I will limit myself to philosophic conceptions of government in relation to matters educational.

State and Government

A *state* is the supreme political authority regulating the affairs of the inhabitants of a certain territory. Its powers may be embodied in a written constitution, as in the United States, or they may be unwritten but sanctified by tradition, as in Great Britain. To study the nature and extent of state power has become a major task of modern political philosophy. Rightly or wrongly, the state exercises an ever-growing influence in our daily lives with respect to education, health, welfare, transportation, and housing. Consequently, any teacher of future citizens has an obligation to consider such questions as these: By what right do some men govern others? What are the limits of that right? How far should the state intervene in matters of education and public welfare?

Government is the machinery through which the power of the state is maintained. It differs from other social institutions such as the family, the church, and the school in being able to enforce its policies through police action. How much force is used and when depends on the nature of the state. In a Western democratic state, force is generally used only as a last resort. Nevertheless, *ubi societas, ibi ius*—where there is society, there must be law. And, we might add, law enforcement!

Theories of the State

Today all nations are concerned with such fundamental problems as the limits of political power, the relation of church and state, community autonomy, and the training of leaders. These concerns have a long history. Aristotle (384-322 B.C.) held that the state should steer a middle course between government by an elite, which is liable to become corrupt, and government by the masses, who are prone to prefer mediocre leaders to able ones. He urged that the franchise be limited to the upper and middle classes, who would be most likely, he thought, to govern the nation in its best interests. St. Thomas Aquinas (1225-1274) maintained that the state should care for man's natural needs and the church for his supernatural ones. The state, he said, should also protect the church so that it can save men's souls in safety. Niccolo Machiavelli (1469-1527) asserted that if the state is to survive it must put its needs before abstract moral principles. In the interest of national unity he urged that absolute power be vested in a single ruler. His most celebrated work, *The Prince*, describes the qualities of the ideal ruler as well as the techniques that he should use to achieve his ends. Because of his insistence on *Realpolitik*— politics based on power—and his belief in a benevolent dictatorship, Machiavelli has been much admired by those who favor strong personal rule.

American political thought has been influenced notably by the theory of the "social contract," expounded with different emphases by Thomas Hobbes (1588-1679), John Locke (1632-1704), and Jean-Jacques Rousseau (1712-1778). Although these three thinkers differed in many respects, they all maintained that government should be founded on the consent of the governed. They believed that the true end of the state is to guarantee to each individual a greater amount of freedom than he could achieve under conditions of anarchy. The state is therefore created by men to serve human ends, and its power is limited and revocable.

Hobbes used the social contract to justify a near-absolutist political system. Men create states, he said, because the alternative is chaos. Since all men are potential lawbreakers, the only way they can live in peace is by creating a power they dare not disobey. Therefore they transfer their rights to one man, the sovereign, who agrees in return to protect his subjects against the violence they would otherwise inflict on one another. As Hobbes pointed out,

> . . . the laws of nature, as justice, equity, modesty, mercy, and, in sum,
> *doing to others as we would be done to,* of themselves, without the
> terror of some power to cause them to be observed, are contrary to our

natural passions, that carry us to partiality, pride, revenge, and the like. And covenants, without the sword, are but words, and of no strength to secure a man at all.[1]

For Locke the state's function is to protect the life, liberty, and property of its individual members. In his own words,

> Men being . . . by nature all free, equal, and independent, no one can be put out of this estate and subjected to the political power of another without his own consent, which is done by agreeing with other men, to join and unite into a community for their comfortable, safe, and peaceable living, one amongst another, in a secure enjoyment of their properties, and a greater security against any that are not of it.[2]

Admittedly, Locke had little confidence in the political intelligence of the masses and maintained that the power to govern should remain in the hands of an aristocracy based on birth and property. However, he introduced the notion of the separation of powers, according to which legislation, justice, and administration are carried out by different agencies.

Rousseau insisted that man could become moral only if he were the citizen of a state. We are free, he declared, only when we accept voluntarily the decisions of a government in which we all participate:

> The passage from the state of nature to the civil state produces in man a very remarkable change, by substituting in his conduct justice for instinct, and by giving his actions the moral quality that they previously lacked . . . for the impulse of mere appetite is slavery, while obedience to a self-prescribed law is liberty.[3]

Is the majority ever entitled to impose its decisions on the minority? Rousseau replied that the individual has two wills, one "real," the other "apparent." The first is what a man desires as a moral being and hence is identical with the wills of all other moral beings. The second is what a man thinks he desires but really does not, since it fails to spring from his moral nature. To the extent that the majority represents the "real" will of the people, it is entitled to coerce the minority in the name of their own true will.

[1] Thomas Hobbes, "Of Commonwealth," *The World's Great Thinkers, Man and the State: the Political Philosophers,* Saxe Commins and Robert N. Linscott, Eds., Random House, New York, 1947, pp. 3-4.

[2] John Locke, "The Second Treatise on Civil Government," *John Locke on Politics and Education,* Howard R. Penniman, Ed., Van Nostrand, New York, 1947, p. 123.

[3] Jean Jacques Rousseau, *The Social Contract,* Henry J. Tozer, trans., Allen and Unwin, London, 1920, p. 114.

Unfortunately there is no sure means of telling whether on a particular occasion the majority does in fact represent the real will of the community, or whether it has equated its own interests with those of society as a whole. Ironically, Rousseau's democracy raises the possibility that the people themselves as a community may not realize where their true interests lie. From this point it is not too great a step to the theory put forward by Hegel and later modified by fascism that the real will of the community cannot safely be interpreted by the mass of its members but should be decided by a *corps d'élite*.

The social contract is no longer accepted as an accurate account of the way in which states were actually formed, since many states arose from civil strife or external intervention. Nevertheless the theory remains significant as an attempt to explain the moral basis of government in terms of the consent of the governed. Especially important is the difference between Rousseau's belief that the purpose of government is to create a particular kind of free, moral human being and Locke's view that the state's task is to protect existing rights rather than to create new ones. The state guarantees individual freedom, said Locke, by interfering as little as possible in the lives of its citizens. This outlook still persists in Western political thought, although we recognize that the state today must regulate the life of the community to an extent never envisaged by the early apologists of liberal democracy.

Contemporary Political Systems

In order better to understand the interrelation of politics and education, we must examine pertinent aspects of the political systems of fascism, communism, and socialism. Some may object that fascism is no longer important. This is not true. For many, fascism still constitutes a solution to the urgent problems of life, as is shown by the existence of quasi-fascist ideologies and governments in many parts of the world today.

Fascism and National Socialism

Fascism declares that the good of the individual is inseparable from that of the nation. The individual can develop as a person only to the extent that he dedicates himself to an end greater than himself, the national will. Fascism also rejects the notion of equality. Men, it declares, are inherently unequal. The nation must select its leaders from the natural aristocracy of the race (for National Socialism, the Aryan race and its elite, the German people) or the culture (for Italian fascism, the Italian culture descending from the Roman Empire). Despising the weakness of "bourgeois democracies" committed to abstract rights, fascism extols the values of courage, discipline, devotion to duty, and respect for tradition.

In the early 1930s the leading theorist of Italian fascism, Giovanni Gentile, maintained that the will of the state represents the will of God embodied in history. Debate over the relation of the individual to the state is pointless, he said, for we are all born citizens of a state, to which we owe our moral nature and from which no amount of ratiocination can separate us. The state derives its authority from the fact that it represents the collective will of the people. It can, therefore, coerce dissident parties or individuals on the grounds that the will of the whole is superior to that of the parts.[4]

Fascist leaders revived the spirit of nationalism, urging their countrymen to imitate the wisdom and courage of their ancestors. Mussolini contrasted the past glory of Italy with its insignificance in his own time and called on his countrymen ultimately to prepare for war:

> The more fascism considers . . . the future development of humanity . . . the more it believes neither in the possibility nor the utility of perpetual peace. It thus repudiates the doctrine of pacifism—born of a renunciation of the struggle and an act of cowardice in the face of sacrifice. War alone brings up to its highest tension all human energy and puts the stamp of nobility upon the peoples who have the courage to meet it. All other

---

[4] Here, Gentile spoke in the tradition of national idealism founded by the great German philosopher, Georg W. F. Hegel (1770-1831). The state, said Hegel, is the concrete manifestation of the ultimate reality of Mind or Spirit. The state is thus more "real" than any of its members because it is closer to ultimate reality than they are. "Society and the state," declared Hegel, "are the very conditions in which freedom is realized." The obligations of citizenship do not restrict freedom but rather make freedom possible. In the Hegelian idiom: "The perpetually recurring misapprehension of freedom consists in regarding that term only in its . . . subjective sense, abstracted from its essential objects and aims; thus a constraint put upon impulse, desire, passion—a limitation of caprice and self-will is regarded as a fettering of freedom. We should on the contrary look upon such limitations as the indispensable proviso of emancipation." (J. Loewenberg, Ed., *Hegel: Selections*, Scribner, New York, N.Y., 1929, p. 391.) Let me point out, however, that Gentile soon disassociated himself from Mussolini's regime, claiming rightly that Il Duce had violated the moral responsibilities that, according to Hegel, the state should take upon itself. Gentile realized what many liberal critics are prone to overlook, that not all who speak in Hegel's name speak in his spirit.

trials are substitutes, which never really put men into the position where they have to make the great decision—the alternative of life or death.[5]

In Germany the loss of the First World War, the indignity of the Versailles Treaty, mounting inflation, and the weakness of the Weimar Republic combined to spread resentment and dissatisfaction, especially among the middle classes, who finally became convinced of the need for decisive action to save their nation from a proletarian revolution backed by Soviet Russia. They turned to Adolf Hitler's astutely named "National Socialist Workers' Party," which became a government allegedly supported by all classes.

Rejecting the liberal democratic view that art, literature, and education should be international in their appeal, fascism insists that these should express the special qualities of particular races and peoples and should be made to serve national ends. The writer, the artist, and the teacher should articulate the highest aspirations of the nation. In particular, they should praise the virtues of honor, self-sacrifice, and courage rather than love, pity, and individualism.

Part of the appeal of fascism lies in its seeming solution of the problem of rootless individualism, which besets most Western democracies.[6] In my view, however, no Western democracy can accept a solution that denies individualism itself. A truly humanitarian society must balance the claims of the individual against the claims of the state without negating either. Better a rootless individualism than an individualism rooted permanently in an absolutist, all-consuming ideology.[7]

Fascist Education

In the sixteenth century Machiavelli called education an instrument used by the ruler to further the interests of the state. Higher education, he said, should provide the state with the ruling elite that it needs for its wise administration.

---

[5] Benito Mussolini, "The Political and Social Doctrine of Fascism," in Albert R. Chandler, Ed., *The Clash of Political Ideals*, Appleton-Century-Crofts, New York, 1949, p. 208.

[6] Cf. Giovanni Gentile, *The Reform of Education*, Harcourt, Brace, and World, New York, 1922, p. 29.

[7] For a recent, fairly objective treatment of fascism, see A. James Gregor, *The Ideology of Fascism: The Rationale of Totalitarianism*, The Free Press, New York, 1969.

Adolf Hitler put his own interpretation on this thesis. The schools, he declared in *Mein Kampf*, should cultivate in the young an emotional and intellectual commitment to the ideal of racial purity. This ideal gave the National Socialist school its three main goals—to develop the body, to train the character, and to educate the intellect, in that order. All children received an extended elementary and technical schooling, while the elite were prepared for leadership in special boarding schools run by the National Socialist party.

The National Socialists gave priority to physical education because they believed that the spiritual qualities of the race sprang ultimately from its genetic constitution. "As a certain racial quality," wrote Hitler, ". . . is the presupposition of intellectual efficiency, so must all education first of all develop physical health. For generally speaking a healthy and strong mind will be found only in a healthy and strong body." By training the growing body, and by convincing the young that marriage with the physically unfit or racially inferior was a crime against the nation, the school prepared each generation for its role as vanguard of the Aryan people.

The school sought to form a German character marked by patriotism, courage, and discipline. It therefore emphasized the study of German history and the great men who made it. It also sought to develop the finest traits of the German intellect, regarded as an instrument of the race's will to power.

Fascist education simplified the relation of student and teacher and obviated some of the disciplinary problems that arise in the democratic West. The individual student became one among a well-defined community of students sharing the same racial ideals as the teacher himself. The teacher had to be carefully trained, since he was not only the guide of the student but also the servant of the state. It was not enough for him to be a scholar. He had to be a natural leader able to arouse the admiration of his pupils and to inspire them with the belief that the greatest honor was to serve the nation. The teacher had to illuminate subject matter with ideology. Content and methods of teaching were uniform. Although, inevitably, each student would read a book or listen to a lecture in a different way, differences nevertheless were to be limited. Allowing students to interpret knowledge as they chose would encourage self-deception rather than true freedom.[8]

[8] See George F. Kneller, *The Educational Philosophy of National Socialism,* Yale University Press, New Haven, Connecticut, 1941, p. 154.

Communism

The three main architects of communist theory were Karl Marx, Friedrich Engels, and Nikolai Lenin. What they wrote has become the official ideology of the Soviet Union, China, Cuba, and most of Eastern Europe. It has also proved attractive to many people, especially intellectuals and students, in the developing nations.

Karl Marx. For Western liberalism the basis of society is the individual. For Marx the basis is the class. The individual, he declared, is a product of his class, which forms his morality, his tastes, and his conduct. To understand individuals we first must understand classes. Normally there is a ruling class, which controls the economy of the society (the means of production), and a subservient class, which provides the labor for the economy.

Class interests by their very nature are irreconcilable. The formal institutions of a class society—such as the civil service, the schools, and the police—are not a means for promoting the general welfare but an instrument of class oppression. During the Industrial Revolution, control over these institutions passed from the aristocracy to the new middle class—the "bourgeoisie"—which uses them to exploit the increasingly impoverished working class—the "proletariat." In Marx's words, "The executive of the modern state is but a committee for managing the common affairs of the whole bourgeoisie."[9]

In Marx's view, the bourgeoisie dominates the industrialized nations through its ownership of the means of production and through manipulation of the parliamentary system. The proletariat cannot better its condition through democratic means because the bourgeoisie will not permit the institutions of democracy to be used against its interests as a class. Since there can be no cooperation between the classes, revolution is unavoidable; the class war must be fought to a finish.

The overthrow of the bourgeoisie will be followed by a transitional period known as the "dictatorship of the proletariat," during which the vestiges of bourgeois rule and bourgeois thinking will be eliminated. Then the "classless society" will be created.[10] The forces of production

[9] Karl Marx, "Communist Manifesto," in Saxe Commins and Robert N. Linscott, Eds., *The World's Great Thinkers, Man and the State: the Political Philosophers,* Random House, New York, 1947, p. 490.

[10] *Ibid.*, p. 511: "In place of the old bourgeois society with its classes and class antagonisms, we shall have an association in which the free development of each is the condition for free development of all." For a reliable treatment, see Shlomo

and distribution will be publicly owned, men will work together for the common good, and the individual will realize himself in the service of the whole.

Communists maintain that, when the bourgeois philosopher says that limited government is necessary for individual freedom, he is really expressing the desire of the middle class to maximize profits and exploit labor. Communists also reject the charge that they themselves deny individual freedom. On the contrary, they say, the individual is really free only when he works with his fellows for the good of all, when the means of production and distribution are owned by all, and when there is no more class exploitation.

Nikolai Lenin. Fifty years later, Lenin revised Marxism in three important ways. First, in developing the conception of imperialism, he admitted that the capitalist nations of Western Europe had to some extent alleviated the condition of the proletariat. He pointed out that this was because the bourgeoisie could not further depress the wages of the workers without cutting the purchasing power that produced their own profits. In addition they had begun to exploit the labor and resources of the colonies. But the rivalry of the imperialist powers in search of markets would shortly lead to war among nations. Then the workers, conscripted for military service, would see that the war was being fought for the interests of the ruling classes, and would turn their weapons on those who had armed them. In this way the Revolution would be fulfilled. (However, when the First World War failed to lead to the general uprising he had expected, Lenin stated that this was not the imperialist war he had in mind.)

Second, Lenin revised Marx's assertion that the Revolution would have to wait until the capitalist system was exploded by its internal contradictions. According to Lenin, the Revolution could and should be established first of all in the semifeudal society of Russia, where the oppressors were not the middle class but the aristocracy, and the oppressed were not an urban proletariat but the peasants.

Third, he redefined the role of the Communist Party. Where Marx had assumed that the proletariat would rise spontaneously, Lenin asserted that their activities had to be planned, executed, and consolidated by a hard core of dedicated revolutionaries. This group was to retain power during the dictatorship of the proletariat in order to stifle counterrevolu-

Averini, *The Social and Political Thought of Karl Marx*, Cambridge University Press, 1968.

tion or outside intervention. Thus the framework of the new society would be created not by the whole people, who lacked the necessary revolutionary consciousness, but by the Communist Party, which truly understood the laws of historical and social development.

Post-Lenin. Lenin had expected the Russian Revolution of 1917 to touch off a chain of similar revolutions throughout Europe. Instead the new Soviet government, beset by strife within and intervention without, discovered itself alone in a hostile world. Lenin's successor, Joseph Stalin, decided that Russia had to develop its military and industrial capacity to equal or eventually surpass that of the capitalist powers. To this end the nation's entire life was regulated by the Party, and the Party in turn was dominated by Stalin. Under the leadership of Nikita Khrushchev, a certain amount of decentralization took place and some individual rights were restored. Nevertheless, the Party today remains the chief driving and organizing force of national life.

In the Communist view, all institutions and activities must play their part in building the classless society. The trade unions, the media of communications, and the arts and sciences must all function within limits laid down by the Party. Communists criticize the free press of the Western democracies for being no more than the mouthpiece of dominant financial interests. Press, radio, and television, they say, should speak for the whole community and not simply for the ruling class.

Differences of opinion exist within the Communist Party, and so freedom of expression is said to prevail. Nevertheless, this freedom is kept within limits defined by the leadership. Party members may disagree on an issue before the leadership has decided on a policy, but once the policy has been laid down, it cannot be violated.[11]

Soviet Education

In the Soviet Union, education ranks next in importance to defense and public health, and is treated as part of the overall program of national growth. All major decisions on policy and practice are made either by Party congresses or by the Party's Central Executive Committee. Educational standards apply throughout the nation; they do not, as in the U.S.A., vary from state to state. Curricula are drawn up according to national specifications, so that pupils everywhere study the same required subjects. Since there must be no waste of human resources, students are

[11] For a sympathetic account, see Jessica Smith, *Soviet Democracy and How It Works*, National Council of American-Soviet Friendship, New York, 1969.

educated to assume tasks that society assigns to them. The nation's needs for various skills are assessed, and young people are educated in appropriate numbers to possess these skills.

A classless society requires a classless education. The opportunity to learn is open to everyone regardless of income or social status. Schooling is free at all levels, with higher education dependent on political reliability. Private schools are forbidden, lest they weaken the contribution of public education to the national effort and permit the reemergence of a privileged class.

Although fascism and communism both train a political, managerial, and technological elite, communism nevertheless affirms man's fundamental equality. The Soviet Union seeks to attain both objectives by raising the level of popular education and by sending the most capable students to special schools, higher technical institutes, and universities. Until the age of fifteen, children are educated alike, for as adults they are expected to enjoy equal rights no matter what their occupation. There is considerable emphasis on group study and mutual criticism. The individual learns that only the shared life is truly satisfying and that no achievement is worthwhile unless it benefits society as a whole. Even after the age of fifteen, students are expected to follow the same general course of study, specializing only at higher levels.

Soviet education also seeks to preserve traditional Russian culture within the communist world view. It extols the classless society not as an alien import but as the fulfillment of aspirations long present in the Russian soul. Devotion to the Party is synonymous with devotion to Mother Russia herself. In order to inculcate this point of view and to promote pride in the nation and its achievements, the schools devote much time to traditional singing, dancing, and folklore. They also describe how the great heroes of Russian history envisaged the very society that the Revolution finally has brought into existence. Always conscious of themselves as a chosen people, the Russians have assumed a new mission, the conversion of the world to communism.

Polytechnization. The communist respect for work is seen in the Soviet program of "polytechnization." This is a form of training, compulsory since 1952, that endeavors to educate hand and brain together by combining technical instruction with physical labor. Young people study such subjects as electricity, crop cultivation, and transportation. At the same time they put their knowledge into practice by working in factories and laboratories, and on farms and industrial projects. Polytechnization is fundamental to all further education. It is an important part of general education, along with such subjects as the natural and social sciences, mathematics, history, and Russian culture, language and literature. Combining formal study with socially useful labor, it teaches respect for, and skill in, work itself, and seeks to remove all trace of class distinction between mental and manual workers. It treats technical education with a seriousness unmatched elsewhere in the world.

Reform. However, new school programs, launched since 1965, recognize the aversion of students to combining too much manual work with their studies. Polytechnization has therefore been diluted and more electives provided, especially in science, technology, and mathematics. There are courses specially designed for gifted students.

The pupil now may receive three years of elementary education and five years of secondary education. After the age of fifteen, the student leaves school unless he has shown clearly that his abilities justify spending another two years in the secondary school. A growing number of children go to boarding schools, which the state encourages on the grounds that they can provide a more thoroughly communist upbringing than can regular schools. In fact, the state hopes that by 1975 over three quarters of Russia's youth will be in boarding schools.

Those who leave school at fifteen may continue their education in the same curriculum as that given in the last two years of secondary education by attending special schools after work or by taking correspondence courses. These schools are favored by the state because, by actually working for society, students prove their right to further education. Secondary education is also provided in *technicums*—secondary specialized schools—which train students for management in industry, agriculture, education, culture, and health.

The two main institutions of higher education are the universities and the higher technological institutes. During their first two years students normally work during the day and either attend evening classes or take correspondence courses. They may then take up residence for an additional three years. Since as graduates they are supposed to devote themselves primarily to the building of a communist society, students are selected with due consideration for their political as well as their academic attributes. As much weight is given to the recommendations of Party, trade union, and educational officials as to the judgments of teachers.[12]

---

[12] For a comprehensive treatment of education in fourteen communist countries, see Wasyl Shimoniak, *Communist Education: Its History, Philosophy, and Politics,* Rand McNally, Chicago, 1970, 506 pp.

Comparison of Communism and Fascism

Communism and fascism frequently are classed together on the grounds that both entrust the role of government to a single political party. Here, however, the similarity ends. Communism sees man as a rational, tool-making animal who will attain his true stature as a human being only when the irrationalities in his social institutions have been removed. Hence he must be educated to play his part in the creation of a society free from all class distinctions. For fascism, it is *will* rather than reason that rules men's lives. The task of education is to teach the individual to fulfill himself by merging his partial will into the total will of the nation. Because communism regards reality as ultimately material, it considers science to be an end in itself and gives it prominence in the curriculum. Fascism, however, extolling will over matter, insists that science is primarily an instrument of the will to power of the nation. Although Soviet schools instill a devotion to Mother Russia, communism itself theoretically is committed to the idea of the universal brotherhood of man. It aims to liberate all people everywhere from their capitalist and imperialist oppressors. Fascism, on the other hand, upholds the "natural" inequality of men and races. Under National Socialism, education sought to convince every German of the superiority of his own nation. Under Mussolini's fascism, education inculcated a belief in the cultural supremacy of the Italians. Finally, fascism, unlike communism, embraces a modified capitalism and accepts religion as a way to truth.

Socialism and Socialist Education

Like communism, modern socialism is an attempt to create a new kind of society in which the alleged injustices of capitalism have been abolished and men are genuinely equal. Although both movements were inspired by Marx, there are profound differences between them. Whereas communism is dogmatic, ideological, and antireligious, socialism is moderate, pragmatic, and liberal. Denying the Marxist contention that society in its present form must be overthrown by force, socialism advocates the use of democratic means to reform capitalism from within.

Unlike communism, socialism does not advocate a political oligarchy, self-appointed to control all phases of national life until the classless society is attained. Rather, it is a broadly based ideology that seeks to achieve the aspirations of the working class through winning a majority at the polls. Socialism repudiates the communist view that private property as such must be abolished, advocating instead a mixed economy of both public and private sectors. It also says that the state should provide services, especially in education, health, and housing.

Contemporary socialists assert that too many people still belong to privileged groups. Education must be reformed so that it no longer perpetuates class distinction. Every student should be educated according to his ability, not according to his social position or his capacity to pay. Children from lower-income groups should be taught not only to ply a trade but also to realize themselves as people. To this end, educational opportunities should be markedly increased, and schooling should be free and life long. Teen-agers must not be sent into the world half-educated.

Socialism respects the parent's right to educate his children at private schools, but insists that private schools should not perpetuate social privilege. Indeed, in a truly socialist society private education will perform two main services: it will undertake experiments of a kind not possible for the public school, and it will provide for religious instruction. Finally, socialism expects governments to direct and finance education to a degree that conservative thinkers criticize as inhibiting private initiative.

It should be noted that no fully developed socialist society yet exists. Most nations have embraced a large measure of state planning, but problems of equality and social justice remain to be solved. Socialist parties exist in almost every democratic society, but they generally are content to advocate and enact meliorative social and educational reforms.

The New Left and Herbert Marcuse. Today's younger, more radical socialists are often called "The New Left." One of their favorite thinkers is Herbert Marcuse. In his book *One Dimensional Man,* published in 1964, Marcuse could see little chance of revolutionizing society. Now, in *An Essay on Liberation* (Beacon, 1969), he maintains that a socialist utopia is a real possibility because modern technology is capable of providing a life of abundance for all, provided it is redirected. Most people are unaware of this possibility because they have been conditioned to accept the present consumer society as a sufficient horizon for human aspirations. Only those who are not incorporated in this society, notably students and blacks, perceive how it trivializes men and stunts their capacities. These outsiders, says Marcuse, form "the advanced consciousness of man," and it is they, rather than the working class, who are now the potential agents of revolutionary change. Marcuse himself has not suggested any steps for hastening the revolution. Indeed, he has emphasized the enormous counterrevolutionary powers at the disposal of fully developed capitalist societies, including, one might add, the markedly unrevolutionary mood of most of their members.

Marcuse also maintains that so-called freedom of speech is really the freedom of the ruling class to monopolize the mass media and to prevent radical critics of the status quo from getting a fair hearing. Moreover, those who defend society as it stands are objectively wrong and should therefore be prevented from advocating their views.

Marcuse's illiberal attitude towards the right of free speech has been heavily criticized on the grounds that, while free speech does not guarantee that truth or justice will prevail, it at least guarantees that people will be heard, which is more than any dictatorship can boast. It is also pointed out that not only are right and wrong often difficult to distinguish but that most men are objectively "right" on some occasions and objectively "wrong" on others. Are they then to open up when they are right and to hold their peace when wrong? And how are they to know when they are which, since as a rule what one advocates one believes to be right anyway? Many people sympathize with Marcuse's criticism of the misuses of technology and the trivialities of a consumer society. But his analysis of free speech has been widely, and I think rightly, criticized. It is alien to the liberal democratic tradition, to which we shall shortly turn.

The more radical students, such as the members of the Students for a Democratic Society (SDS), would start the revolution with the university. They would replace the traditional university, dedicated to scholarship, with an institution serving the community and run exclusively by students and teachers. Courses of study would be made "relevant to student and community needs." Boards of regents, trustees, and overseers would give way to student-teacher boards of control. Administrators would be appointed only by those to whom they "relate," namely students, teachers, and the rank and file of the people. Faculty appointments, promotions, dismissals, and tenure would be determined jointly by teachers and students. Taxpayers (especially corporate taxpayers) would not only contribute more money to education but would also pay salaries to students. Today's students, it is said, are tomorrow's artists, executives, and professional men. Their brains and their creativity are society's greatest resource. If people will contribute money to corporations, museums, and hospitals, why not also to those who will run these places? Thirty-five dollars per week per student will do for a start.

How much success have the radicals had? The more that such groups as the SDS have resorted to violence, the more they have alienated themselves from the body politic—and indeed the body educational, for many universities have expelled them altogether. Nevertheless, they have made their presence felt everywhere. They are, as they want the universities to be, in the streets. When they are apprehended, they are defended vigorously, as they should be, in the courts. Most importantly, they have forced the universities, and society as a whole, to reexamine values and practices that have prevailed uncritically for too long. There is no doubt that radical socialism is part of America's liberal political tradition, and valuable reforms have emerged as a result. On the other hand, this tradition will not tolerate the use of physical violence or any unlawful usurpation of power.

Democracy—Ideal and Manifest

We owe both the term and the initial conception of democracy to the ancient Greeks. To them it meant "government by the people" under a constitution. But since the franchise was granted only to "free-born" male citizens, not even the constitution of Athens under Pericles, during the most creative era in Greek history, would qualify today as being truly democratic. It is really to certain political writers of the nineteenth century that we owe our present conception of democracy as government of, by, and for the people. In his book *Representative Government,* John Stuart Mill (1806-1873) called for universal manhood suffrage, an ideal that took many decades to fulfill. Like the Greeks, America's founding fathers preferred to restrict the vote to certain classes. Not until after the enfranchisement of slaves and women did the provisions of the Constitution become fully democratic. Today, too, civil rights bills, enacted in 1964 and 1965, are slowly converting the principle of universal suffrage from an ideal to a reality.

But simply defining democracy does not tell us very much about it. Let us, therefore, examine its central principles as they are generally understood in America today.

1. *The state is not an end in itself but a means for the attainment of human ends.* The basic function of the state is to secure "the greatest happiness of the greatest number." It is to enable every citizen to make the fullest use of his own capacities *without restricting the right of his fellow citizens to do the same.* The state is then not, as fascism maintains, an embodiment of the true will of an entire people, superior to the wills of all individuals, but rather a set of institutions that men have established over the course of time in order to govern themselves in their own interests.

2. *All men possess certain inalienable rights.* These rights, which the Constitution calls "life, liberty, and the pursuit of happiness," are uni-

versal. They belong to all men irrespective of race, class, or creed. They spring not from society but from human nature itself.

"Democracy," wrote Chesterfield, "is a dangerous business." There cannot be human rights without human responsibilities. The more freedom we enjoy, the more responsibility we must assume. This responsibility presumes not only the intellectual equipment to vote and to assess policy, but also the willingness to take part in politics. Thus, it is not merely as a *quid pro quo* that we balance duties against rights; more important, it is in order to maintain these rights that we must commit ourselves to active participation in political life.

3. *Democracy preserves and enhances individual freedom.* Traditionally, democratic theory has identified individual freedom with the absence of external control. But to be free is not simply to be uncoerced. It is to have the *power of effective choice.* True democracy rejects the authoritarian tenet that the individual becomes free only by accepting social responsibilities. It insists instead that men are freest when they are allowed rationally to pursue their own worthy goals and when they possess the means (education, income, etc.) to do so.[13]

4. *All men are to be regarded as equal in certain respects.* At first glance the idea that all men are equal appears absurd. Look at a class of children. How *un*equal they are in character, intelligence, and physique! Nature, it would seem, is no democrat, and her children face the world very differently endowed. What, then, do we mean by human equality? We mean that, however widely men may differ in their attributes, they are the same in their common humanity, which differentiates them from other living things. All are bound by the same human condition. As individuals we cannot hope for the same income, the same house, or the same intelligence. But we have the right to expect fair and just treatment in certain very important respects. We are entitled, for instance, to equality before the law, to equality of political rights and of educational opportunity, and, some say, to equality in matters of physical and economic well-being. The conviction that all men should be treated equally in matters of health has found practical expression in the nationalization

---

[13] At first it was assumed that the greatest good proceeded only from healthy competition among individual citizens with a minimum of government interference. However, we now realize that, when all men are free to follow their own interests without restraint, the strong and the aggressive may win their freedom at the expense of the weak and the less self-seeking. We also know that men are capable of cooperation and self-sacrifice. They have interests in common; they desire human fellowship; and they need to belong to a more organic community than that founded on a policy of rugged individualism.

of medical services in Great Britain, and, in the United States, in the Medicare program for the elderly.

5. *Democracy implies faith in human intelligence.* If we believe in democracy, we also must believe that men are capable of conducting their common affairs rationally. No society is infallible. Nevertheless, when the correctives that mark a flexible democracy—the ballot, the amendment, and judicial review—are used by an informed electorate, that electorate can be trusted to solve its own problems intelligently. To the extent that men are allowed as a result of poor education to remain ignorant or irresponsible, democracy itself is in danger.

6. *Democracy grants the right of peaceful dissent.* By restricting government intervention in the spheres of religion, speech, press, and assembly, the First Amendment to the American Constitution recognizes that the state must not obstruct men in their quest for truth. It also recognizes that no one person, party, or organization has a monopoly on truth. The right to be wrong warrants the same protection, if not always as much respect, as the right to be right. Indeed, the right to be wrong can be defended on grounds of expediency as well as principle, if only for the fact that it is not always possible to know in advance which views are right and which wrong. In order to participate realistically in the politics of a democracy, we must either maintain some element of doubt about the rightness of our own views or accept the fact that, when all views have been allowed to compete, the resulting compromise, although not acceptable to all, will be satisfactory to most.

7. *Democracy requires a party system.* Unless men can organize into groups to express their views, freedom of speech remains politically ineffective. Whether a two-party system, as in the United States, is more democratic than a multiparty system, as in France or Italy, is open to debate. The latter permits parliamentary representation of a wider range of political attitudes, but it tends to prevent the emergence of any party strong enough to form a government on its own. The result is that coalitions are formed in which the cooperating parties abandon or modify their policies so as to attain a mutually acceptable compromise. Two-party systems lead to greater governmental stability at the cost of expressing fewer shades of opinion.

8. *Modern democracy is widely representative.* In the city-states of ancient Greece, it was common for citizens to participate directly in the processes of government—so, too, in republican Rome. But political communities now have grown so large that direct participation is no longer practical save in the kind of town meeting that characterizes local American politics. Today the principle of representation is common to every

democracy, although it is implemented in different ways. In the United States candidates must be nominated by the people before they can run for election. In Britain the parties nominate their own candidates. France and Germany have adopted proportional representation, whereas most English-speaking countries have not.

9. *Democracy involves separation of powers.* The Constitution was drawn up to protect individual liberties from an all-powerful executive and an all-powerful assembly. The founding fathers foresaw the corruptive influence of power on those in office and feared the potential extremism of the masses under the influence of a demagogue. They therefore separated the legislative, executive, and judicial functions and set up the Supreme Court as the "watchdog of the Constitution" to guard both the national interest and the rights of individuals and minorities. They also divided the responsibilities of government between the central authority and the federating states, leaving such functions as education to local control.

Individuals are also protected against arbitrary government action by the concept of "due process," as expressed in the Bill of Rights and other Constitutional amendments, and as extended through court decisions. This concept states that no person may be deprived of life, liberty, or property unless certain legal procedures are followed.

This division of power, it must be admitted, has two weaknesses: (1) The doctrine of states' rights can be used to hinder the necessary centralization of power in a highly organized society; and (2) not only can Congress and the President easily frustrate one another, but the Supreme Court may advance or obstruct social reforms through its power to affirm, nullify, or otherwise interpret legislation. This aspect of our system has been criticized as a "more ingenious way of moderating, delaying, sidestepping, and hamstringing the will of the majority than any other nation has thought it necessary or desirable to submit to."[14] However, its net effect has been to force the majority to legislate moderately and to seek minority support wherever possible. Our governmental organization may be slower to act than more centralized systems, but we may be sure that its actions are more widely approved by the people they affect.

Democracy and Education

The conduct of education in a democracy is guided by a number of accepted principles, the most important of which I will now discuss.

---

[14] Carl L. Becker, *Freedom and Responsibility in the American Way of Life,* Vintage Books, New York, 1958, p. 75.

1. *Since the people themselves elect their government, they should be educated to do so responsibly.* Not only must they be trained to think clearly and to distinguish truth from falsehood, but they must also acquire a knowledge of the issues on which they are called to vote. They must deal in school with such matters as management and labor, freedom of the press, racial strife, corruption and crime, and the influence of the mass media. Unless men are taught to think clearly and critically about political problems, the governments they elect are likely to be no more enlightened than they are themselves, and, which, may become a sight more unscrupulous.

What political knowledge should the school teach? If we expect young people to be committed to democracy, they must know what it is worth. They should understand how the nation is governed at all levels, who gets what and why, and the part they themselves should play in politics. Since we live in a world of many different political systems, among which the United States is called upon to exercise a decisive leadership, students also should be acquainted with the ideologies and systems of other countries. The student's understanding of democracy should be based on a realistic, clear-headed assessment of the strengths and weaknesses of his own system as it develops out of our cultural heritage and as it compares with other systems.

2. *Through education every individual is expected to develop his own talents to the full.* To achieve this end, education fosters higher interests—esthetic, intellectual, professional—which, in the uneducated man, remain largely untapped or dormant.

3. *Men must be educated to be free.* In a democracy, education does not, or should not, mold us to a rigid pattern imposed from without. It prizes, or should prize, not uniformity but uniqueness, seeking to draw out and develop the special blend of talents that each of us possesses. Freedom, however, entails the acceptance of restraints. If the school permits unrestricted self-expression, it develops not freedom but license. Self-realization requires self-discipline. In school the maturity and wisdom of the teacher guide the development of the child who, left to himself, might dissipate his energies in trivial pursuits. The teacher knows that the individual is free as an adult only if he learns certain things as a child. The freedom and fulfillment of the mature man presuppose the guidance and discipline of the young.[15]

[15] Individual freedom admittedly is difficult to handle. In every classroom, teachers discover unique talent, whose healthy growth must be nourished. "Taste," says Picasso, "is the enemy of creativity." Any acceptance of restraints, any capitulation

4. *Education should train the open mind.* Democracy is open and experimental. Its citizens should not be fixed uncritically in their ways, but should be intelligently flexible and prepared for change. The school should encourage the child to look at a problem from all sides, to suspend final judgment until all the evidence is in and, even when he has made a decision, to be prepared to change it should later events prove him wrong. The open mind is not the empty one, but the balanced one, which respects and understands the views of others. In a democracy policies are formulated through consensus and majority vote. A man may disagree with the actions of his government, but he accepts the right of the government to act, because he knows that the government has been elected by majority vote and that it aims to respond to public opinion and remain open to persuasion. He knows, too, that it can be defeated in the legislature, and that it must submit itself at the appointed time to the vote of the electorate. Indeed, public debate is the method of democracy. Policies are argued pro and con in the open. That is why the United States is called an "open" society.

5. *Education should develop the habit of productive cooperation as well as healthy competition.* A democracy attempts to achieve through voluntary cooperation what an authoritarian society tends to attain by coercion or cajolery. In the United States the tradition of voluntary association is strong. Every school sponsors student associations, and the child should be encouraged to join those that interest him. There he acquires the knack of give and take and the habit of working with others. As an adult he is then able, hopefully, to contribute to the many voluntary associations—churches, political parties, unions, and professional groups—that give democracy its vitality.

6. *Wherever feasible, we should adopt democratic practices in school behavior.* The legitimate place of democracy in school behavior is a problem of some complexity. I have inserted "wherever feasible" advisedly, for I certainly do not mean that democratic rule should be applied indiscriminately to all sorts of school organizations and activities. For one thing, a school is not a political unit. It is a special kind of society whose aims and practices differ from those of the larger society. For another, the rights of students in an educational setting differ from the rights of

to accepted custom must be accompanied by provision for individual creativity, even if such creativity appears unorthodox. One of the most important but also one of the most difficult things for a teacher to do is to discover and nurture individual uniqueness. On the one hand, uniqueness is indispensable and priceless; on the other, it can be elusive, rebellious, and disruptive of class organization.

teachers and administrators; and the rights of all of these differ from the rights of citizens.

This means that student self-government, although highly desirable, is necessarily limited by the responsibilities it can assume. Student governments are free to institute disciplinary and other measures only to the extent that they can be held accountable for their decisions. Furthermore, effective self-government demands the cooperative action of mature, intelligent, experienced citizens who can make judgments and execute policy on a broad scale. While students must obey decisions that have been made by the majority of the electorate, the distinction between obeying the rule of the majority and agreeing to it needs to be more clearly drawn. Students should not feel intimidated by majority rule but rather should be given every reasonable right to express dissident views. They may have freedom where they do not have democracy.

7. *Political control over education must be kept to a minimum.* Four principles guide the extent of political control of American education. First, under the general principle of academic freedom, instruction by qualified teaching personnel must remain as independent as possible of governmental influence. It is largely for this reason that nonpartisan school boards are usually elected. Second, educational policy must be relatively stable and not suffer from political upheaval. Third, educational policy must respond to the needs of home and community. Thus we tend to elect laymen rather than professional educators to boards of education because we feel that the former best represent the community's opinions. Fourth, we insist that our educational system be easily accessible to the people. Not only do local school boards insure that educational policy responds to community need and feeling, but also their nonpartisan character enables them to change policy without having to depend on political party platforms. In short, the prohibition of party interference with educational programs supports academic freedom and stability, while the existence of nonpartisan local school boards insures an educational system that is responsible to the wishes of the community.[16]

What, then, may American democracy expect of its educational system? It may expect, first of all, that the youth of the nation will be equipped to assume a responsible place in the body politic. This means that democracy's history, institutions, and present practices must be discussed openly and realistically in the schoolroom. In order to benefit

---

[16] Cf. Samuel W. Brownell, "Education and Government," *Harvard Educational Review*, **XXV**, 3 (Summer 1955), 133-144.

from our political system, we must be aware of its weaknesses as well as its strengths. The teacher must not conceal the ugly facts of political corruption, moral turpitude, and hypocrisy in high places. At the same time, he must make clear how much the system contributes to the realization of the good life. He must inspire a faith in the long-term worth and effectiveness of democracy as opposed to monolithic systems elsewhere in the world. In the chapter on political socialization we shall take a closer look at what the American student is actually learning about the politics of democracy today. Other chapters deal with different concepts and different aspects of the interplay of politics and education. In the chapter on school organization and administration, for example, we shall see the principle of checks and balances at work in educational systems. All three levels of government—local, state, and federal—are concerned with education, each exercising a degree of power appropriate to its special responsibilities. And as federal interest in education increases, the whole system of checks and balances moves into play to prevent undue centralization.

To study the role of the teacher is to consider him a leader on the political as well as the educational scene. His professional responsibilities entail a commitment to community leadership, whose execution requires a mature and responsible understanding of political ideas and practices.

References

On comparative politics, see Robert G. Neumann, *European and Comparative Government* (McGraw-Hill, 1966, 818 pp.); and G. A. Almond and G. Bingham Powell, Jr., *Comparative Politics: A Developmental Approach* (Little, Brown, Boston, 1966, 348 pp.). The best and most comprehensive basic text I know is Karl W. Deutsch, *Politics and Government: How People Decide Their Fate* (Houghton Mifflin, 1970). For the analysis of political concepts, see T. D. Weldon, *The Vocabulary of Politics* (Pelican, 1960, 199 pp.); Richard Peters, *Authority, Responsibility, and Education* (Atherton, 1966, 137 pp.); and David Easton, *A Framework for Political Analysis* (Prentice-Hall, 1965, 143 pp.). For a straightforward statement of democratic principles, see *The Power of the Democratic Idea*, Report #6 of the Rockefeller Brothers Fund (Doubleday, 1960, 74 pp.). Written from the Roman Catholic point of view, Thomas Dubay's *Philosophy of the State as Educator* (Bruce, Milwaukee, 1959, 237 pp.) has much relevance. James S. Coleman has edited a wide-ranging anthology, *Education and Political Development* (Princeton University Press, 1965, 620 pp.).

7

The Role of Religion

Philip H. Phenix

❖❖

The Nature of Religion

One of the issues causing great concern today is the place of religion in the public schools. This concern starts with the very meaning of religion, on which people do not agree. Immanuel Kant regarded religion as "the recognition of all duties as divine commands," Salomon Reinach as "a sum of scruples which impede the free exercise of our faculties," Alfred North Whitehead as "what the individual does with his own solitariness," Erich Fromm as "any system of thought and action shaped by a group which gives the individual a frame of orientation and an object of devotion," and John Dewey as "whatever introduces genuine perspective."[1]

Perhaps the most useful way to get at the meaning of religion is to distinguish between its experiential basis and its objective expressions. On the experiential side, religion is concerned with such aspects of the universal human predicament as the following: (1) the recognition that

[1] The classic treatment of the nature of religion is Rudolph Otto, *The Idea of the Holy*, Oxford, New York, N.Y., 1958. See also the excellent analysis in Thomas F. O'Dea, *The Sociology of Religion*, Prentice-Hall, Englewood Cliffs, N.J., 1966.

one must die, the fear that stems from that recognition, and the search for a hope that will conquer the fear, (2) the threat of meaninglessness in the face of the bewildering contradictions in the struggle for existence, and the need for assurance to overcome that threat, (3) the consciousness of guilt in having chosen evil rather than good, and the need for acceptance and forgiveness, (4) conflict and confusion about one's goals, and the hunger for guidance in directing one's life towards worthwhile ends, (5) besetting doubts in the presence of the mysteries and paradoxes of the world, and the longing for a faith that gives assurance, (6) a feeling of weakness in the face of the multiple demands of life, and a reaching out for a power that transcends one's limitations, and (7) awareness of the fragmentation of existence, and a search for an all-embracing reality that will lend ordered wholeness to the scattered pieces.

On the expressive side, these basic concerns are objectified in the following four ways: (1) in intellectual formulations of faith, including mythologies, philosophies, and creedal statements, (2) in ritual practices that formulate the faith in symbolic acts rather than in words, (3) in codes of moral conduct that provide norms for the daily life of the believer, and (4) in institutional structures that represent the social formulations of the life of faith. Any comprehensive view of religion must include all of these components. Different religions emphasize the various factors in different degrees. Thus, there are religions, like Buddhism, that put major emphasis on the experiential side, for example, on the problem of suffering due to inordinate desire. Others, like orthodox Lutheranism, are more concerned with right belief, or, like some forms of Judaism, with correctness of ritual practice. Ethical Culture, on the other hand, stresses moral conduct, and Roman Catholics and Mormons are strongly committed to specific forms of ecclesiastical institutions.

Religion and Education: General Relationships

We are now in a position to consider in a preliminary way the relation of religion to education. On the experiential side, as we have seen, religion has to do with what Paul Tillich called "ultimate concerns," that is, with matters that are of supreme importance to the person, such as his final destiny, his purpose in life as a whole, his conscience, and the integrity of his existence, in contrast with what may be called the "penultimate concerns" of everyday, such as particular items of knowledge, specific limited goals, and their means of realization. Education ordinarily is designed to prepare people to manage the penultimate concerns—to pursue a vocation effectively, to understand the nature of the world about them, and to act intelligently in the context in which they happen to live. But since these penultimates are influenced by a framework of ultimate concerns, education is necessarily affected by religious factors. Teaching and learning are never directed solely to immediate goals. Consciously or unconsciously, in the background, every limited aim is part of a total life-orientation that acts as a selective and directive agency in relation to the particulars.

Education, then, like every other human activity, has a faith basis, in the sense that its meaning and direction are set within the context of certain fundamental persuasions about the ultimate purpose and worth of human life. It follows that one of the tasks of the intelligent educator is to examine the faith presuppositions—the deepest commitments—that constitute the large framework for his decisions. This is the most general form of the relationship of religion to education.

A second and more obvious relationship stems from the fact that the experiences and the various expressive forms of religion comprise a significant sector of human life and culture with which it is important that every person be acquainted. Since religious phenomena are universal to human society, one cannot claim basic knowledge about the life of man without an understanding of religious faith and practices. Thus, regardless of what his own faith may be, and regardless of his opinions about the value and truth of any or all religions, an educator dedicated to fostering inclusiveness and depth of understanding of the life of man will include the study of religion.

A third type of relation between religion and education arises from the efforts of religious communities to educate. An important task of every religious group is to communicate its faith to the coming generations, to instruct the faithful so that they may better understand what they have committed themselves to, and to win new adherents. These several ways of propagating religion through education constitute what is customarily called "religious education."

Religion and Education in Historical Perspective

Of the three modes of relating religion and education indicated in the preceding section, historically the third—"religious education"—has been the predominant one. Not until recently have the other two modes—that of conscious concern for the faith presuppositions in education and that of religion as a subject of objective study in the curriculum—come to the fore.

In the past, for the most part, education in religion has been regarded as a means of inculcating the faith, or of indoctrination. All the religions of mankind have possessed teaching institutions, personnel, and materials to propagate what the leaders of the religious community considered right belief and practice. In all primitive societies, the ability to practice various rituals is an important part of the skill to be acquired by the young, and instruction in them and initiation as participants are central parts of education—at least as important as the teaching of the "penultimate" arts of hunting, warfare, agriculture, cooking, weaving, and the like.[2]

In the polytheistic cultures of the ancients, such as those of Egypt, Greece, Mesopotamia, and Rome, religion became an important tool of statecraft, and the hierarchy of deities largely reflected the political position of subgroups in the population made up by consolidation of tribes subdued by conquest. Religion thus played a central role in civic governance, and the appropriate forms of devotion became a basic element in civic education.

Each of the great world religions possesses an elaborate system for self-propagation and for instructing new adherents. The complex rules of caste in classical Hinduism prescribe precisely what the devotee has to know and do in his particular station in life. Buddhism essentially comprises a system of teaching how to achieve freedom from suffering through following the "Noble Eightfold Path" of detachment from inordinate desire. At the core of the Confucian system is instruction in correct relationships to various classes of persons in the social order and the provision of a curriculum for examinations to assign positions in the civil service. Judaism is fundamentally a teaching religion, its chief religious functionaries being rabbis, or teachers, the course of study centering on the Torah, or Law of God, in which are prescribed the rules of conduct, both ethical and ritual, that characterize the faithful Jew. Christianity and Islam likewise depend, for their conservation and extension, on the proclamation of the central message of judgment and salvation, and on instruction by approved interpreters of the divine plan as the respective communities of faith conceive the revelation.

The primary instruments of instruction in religious education are the Sacred Books that contain accounts of the beginnings of the community's faith and record the most significant elements in its developed belief and practice. A second basic component in religious education is instruction

---

2 See the illuminating treatment of the relationship of religion in primitive cultures to practical knowledge, in Bronislaw Malinowski, *Magic, Science, and Religion*, Doubleday, Garden City, N.Y., 1954.

in the distinctive sacred acts or rituals of the community, and the method of learning these is mainly through participation in the corporate rites. A third element is comprised of the standards of moral conduct that are expected by the faithful and that are sustained by a variety of sanctions. Finally, some communities of faith possess and teach the creeds and theologies that have been elaborated to conceptualize the beliefs to which the adherent is expected to subscribe.

In consequence of the essentially indoctrinative character and purpose of what I have here called religious education, instruction by religious communities historically has had an exclusive tone and a divisive effect. If religion has to do with one's comprehensive and ultimate loyalties, then (since one cannot serve two masters at the same time) adherence to one faith entails the exclusion of all others. It is not surprising, therefore, that the story of religion is filled with conflicts and rivalries among the various contending faith groups. These divisions are among the most bitter and sustained of all that set group against group, precisely because the commitments that define the respective group memberships are not provisional and partial, but unconditional and total. Furthermore, religious education designed to strengthen the visible community of believers thereby becomes a political enterprise, and hence is subject to all the relativities and compromises inherent in the interplay of political forces, as revealed particularly in the longstanding and complex problem of church-state relationships.

Religion and Education in the United States

The history of the relationships between religion and education in the United States is particularly instructive in showing the changes effected by democratization, modernization, and secularization. In the colonial period, religion and education were still related according to the essentially political patterns inherited from the European scene. In the beginning, the colonies accepted the system of religious establishment—the Congregational and Presbyterian establishments in New England, the Reform establishment in the New Netherlands, and the Anglican establishment in Virginia and the Carolinas—under which ecclesiastical and political powers were effectively joined in mutual support. All educational efforts, by whatever agency, had to conform to the patterns of belief and practice accepted within the official religious orthodoxy.

During the 18th century the system of a single established church came increasingly under attack by those—like the Baptists and Quakers—who sought freedom to worship in other than the officially sanctioned forms. The first consequence of this struggle was a shift from a single establishment to a multiple establishment, under which, though political authority was still linked to ecclesiastical organization, provision was made for state support of more than one church.[3] The growing diversity of religious organization during the colonial period resulted in a shift from governmentally sponsored education to privately controlled schools, many of which were founded by local churches or particular denominations dedicated to the task of rearing the young in the faith of the fathers.

The principle of religious toleration carried with it a logic that went beyond multiple establishment to the secularization of the state, that is, to the complete separation of political and ecclesiastical powers. This movement toward separation, beginning before the Revolution in a number of the original thirteen colonies and not completed in all the states until well into the 19th century, received its historic expression in the First Amendment to the Federal Constitution, adopted in 1789 and ratified by the states two years later:

> Congress shall make no law respecting an establishment of religion, or prohibiting the free exercise thereof. . . .

With respect to education in the public domain, this provision, in principle, abolished religious instruction in the sense of sectarian indoctrination. It proclaimed that the state and its agencies have no authority to direct the life of faith or to limit freedom of belief and worship according to the dictates of conscience.

The full significance of this landmark principle was not immediately evident in American educational practice. Indeed, after more than a century and a half, its implications for American schools are still being worked out. Part of the difficulty stemmed from the fact that public education was one of the matters left by the Federal Constitution to management by the states, and the several state constitutions differed both on educational matters and on questions of the relationship of church and state. The Fourteenth Amendment, which requires that rights guaranteed by the Federal Constitution and its amendments not be abridged by any state laws, resulted in the eventual realignment of state regulations to accord with the First Amendment.

Despite the official secularization inherent in the First Amendment,

---

[3] The shift from a single to a multiple establishment is well documented in R. Freeman Butts, *The American Tradition in Religion and Education*, Beacon Press, Boston, 1950.

much American public education during the 19th century and more than half of the 20th century continued to reflect the Protestant Christian ethos that was dominant in the nation. Thus, for example, Horace Mann in his celebrated Twelfth Report wrote:

> That our Public Schools are not theological seminaries is admitted. . . . But our system earnestly inculcates all Christian morals; it founds its morals on the basis of religion; it welcomes the religion of the Bible; and, in receiving the Bible, it allows it to do what it is allowed to do in no other system—*to speak for itself.*[4]

Although Mann's intent was to promote morality through education of a nonsectarian type, in fact his schools were inculcating a broadly Protestant Christian outlook—a fact of which Roman Catholics and some Protestants more orthodox than Mann were evidently well aware, as their vigorous opposition to Bible reading in the schools showed.

It should not be surprising that notwithstanding constitutional prohibitions, American public education through most of the nation's history has tended to promote the religious outlook of the majority. Given the American tradition of local control, the citizens have regarded the public schools as their own, to be used to implant the values that are dominant in the local community, including those of faith and morals. For this reason, through most of America's national history, the public schools in many places have complemented the religious instruction of home and church by prayers, Bible readings, hymn singing, and instructional activities with a clear sectarian religious bias.[5]

This persistence of religious education in public schools indicates how slowly the ideas have matured concerning what it means to be a secular state and a truly pluralistic society with genuine freedom of religion. The full significance of these ideas began to become clear as a consequence of the massive immigration into the United States that took place during the 19th and 20th centuries, bringing people with an increasingly wide range of differing beliefs, customs, and traditional loyalties. Particularly important in this regard were the Roman Catholics, who established a large system of parochial schools to educate their young in a total con-

[4] *Twelfth Annual Report of the Board of Education, Together with the Twelfth Annual Report of the Secretary of the Board,* Dutton and Wentworth, Boston, Mass., 1849, pp. 116-117.

[5] An excellent summary of the variety of religious practices in the public schools and of the state laws governing them, prevailing up to the mid-20th century may be found in *The State and Sectarian Education,* the 1956 Research Bulletin, Volume XXXIV, No. 4, of the National Education Association, Washington, D.C.

text of faith, and the Jews, who presented a vital and persistent contrast to the dominant Christian ethos.

Religion and Education in Supreme Court Decisions

The most influential means of hammering out the import of American pluralism and national secularization in education was a series of decisions by the United States Supreme Court, in which was set forth the precise bearing of the First Amendment on educational practice. These decisions will be discussed in detail in the next chapter, to which the student is referred for fuller treatment of the subject. At this point it will suffice to summarize the major principles and trends established by these decisions.

One landmark principle was laid down in the celebrated Oregon decision,[6] to the effect that the state may not require a child to attend public school, but that parents have a right to educate their children in competent private schools if they so elect. In particular, parents may have their children taught within the context of the religious community and thereby receive religiously oriented education. This principle sets a clear limit to the powers of the state and sustains the religious freedom of parents who as a matter of conscience elect to educate their children under religious auspices. It presupposes that the state is not the ultimate authority in the lives of citizens, its competence being limited to certain defined activities of a temporal and political character.

A second area in which the highest court ruled concerns the nature of permissible public school activities related to religion. The fundamental principle established was that the First Amendment forbids any activities that promote any or all religions in the sense of persuasion, indoctrination, or inculcation. Thus, *McCollum v. Board of Education* (1948)[7] ruled out sectarian religious instruction in public schools, even on "released time," i.e., outside regular school classes, though *Zorach v. Clauson* (1952)[8] upheld released-time religious education where public school buildings were not employed for the instruction. *Engle v. Vitale* (1952)[9] held unconstitutional the use in public schools of a nonsectarian prayer supplied by the state Board of Regents, and *Abington v. Schempp*

6 See p. 184.
7 See p. 182.
8 See p. 182.
9 See p. 182.

(1963)[10] and *Murray v. Curlett* (1963)[11] forbade Bible readings without comment in public schools and the use of the Lord's Prayer in school devotional exercises.

The crux of these decisions is that public schools may not act in any way that presupposes acceptance or advocacy of a certain religious faith, but must remain strictly neutral. This does not mean, however, that all reference to religion must be excised from the curriculum. Indeed, in the Abington case on Bible reading, Justice Tom Clark wrote:

> It might well be said that one's education is not complete without a study of comparative religion or the history of religion and its relation to the advancement of civilization. It certainly may be said that the Bible is worthy of study for its literary and historic qualities. Nothing we have said here indicates that such study of the Bible or of religion, when presented objectively, as part of a secular program of education, may not be effected consistent with the First Amendment.[12]

These decisions make clear that the political secularization affirmed in the First Amendment does not carry with it a complete divorce of public education and religion. They do forbid the use of public education to perpetuate or extend the interests of a community of believers. What is allowed, and in fact encouraged, is the objective study of religion as part of the secular program of education.

A third fundamental principle laid down by the Supreme Court in relation to religion in education is that while the agencies of government may not aid religion, they may assist persons as citizens, including children in nonpublic schools. Thus, *Cochran v. Louisiana State Board of Education* (1930)[13] confirmed the right of a state to provide for free textbooks, on secular subjects, in parochial as well as in public schools, *Everson v. Board of Education* (1947)[14] upheld the right of a school board to provide the same bus fare for parochial school and public school pupils, and *Board of Education v. Allen* (1968) upheld a statute in New York requiring local school boards to buy secular textbooks and loan them without charge to nonpublic school children. The basic argument in these cases is that in making the various grants to nonpublic education, the state is not aiding the nonpublic schools, but is providing benefits to the children indirectly through the schools.

[10] See p. 182.
[11] See p. 182.
[12] *School District of Abington Township v. Schempp,* 374 U.S. 203 (1963).
[13] See p. 180.
[14] See p. 180.

As the more extended discussion of the legal questions in the next chapter indicates, the ultimate effect of the child-benefit theory of state aid to nonpublic schools has yet to be determined. In the cases cited above, the benefits permitted have been of a somewhat marginal character, involving bus transportation and textbooks. The issue is increasingly being joined as state legislatures consider bills authorizing the use of funds from the public treasury for the payment of, for example, salaries of teachers of secular subjects. The logical conclusion of the child-benefit principle would be to introduce a fundamentally different conception of fund allocation by granting payments directly to students or their parents and guardians, to be used for educational purposes in whatever institutions they might choose, provided only that certain general standards of quality and appropriateness be observed. There is ample precedent for such a procedure in the federal support granted discharged military personnel under the so-called "G.I. Bill of Rights" (under which the beneficiaries receive tuition and subsistence allowances to enable them to pursue their education at institutions of their choice, public or nonpublic, and in whatever field of study they elect—not excluding religion).

Financial Aid, Public Interest, and Religious Freedom

The issues involved in the question of public financial support for nonpublic schools require a consideration of just what makes a school "public" or "nonpublic." The obvious answer is that a public school is owned and controlled by the people, through the appropriate agencies of government, and a nonpublic school has nongovernmental ownership and control. On the other hand, one can consider the matter from the standpoint of public interest, and maintain that a school not owned and governed by state agencies still serves a public function in the preparation of citizens. This has been one of the basic contentions of some spokesmen for religious schools, who urge that since their schools prepare students to be citizens, they should receive their due share of public financial support. Such proponents do not claim that public funds ought to be provided for religious education, but they do make the claim for those aspects of the school program that are secular in nature, as, for example, in science, mathematics, and languages. In fact, considerable federal funds have been allocated to parochial schools since 1958 under the National Defense Education Act to aid instruction in such subjects.

This argument in terms of the public interest, like that based on child benefit, depends on the possibility of identifying a separable secular function served by the nonpublic schools. It also underlines the difficulty of making a sharp division between the public and the nonpublic spheres. In publicly owned and controlled institutions, there are clear limits to what can be demanded by the public authority. In particular, the public school must respect the student's privacy in matters of faith and conscience. Thus, he cannot be required to salute the flag, contrary to his religious belief.[16] Hence the public schools are affected by private interests and must operate accordingly. On the other hand, nonpublic schools are affected by public interests, both in the service they render to the formation of an educated public, and administratively by virtue of compulsory-attendance laws and standards of health and safety required by public authorities.

An interesting attempt to define more clearly the distinction between the public and the nonpublic domains in regard to the religious issue is in the concept of "shared time," under which the child's school time is divided between public schools and religious schools, the former being devoted to secular studies such as physical science, languages, and industrial arts, and the latter to religious studies and other subjects, such as history and literature, that may be affected by sectarian interests.[17] A major aim of the shared-time proposal is to diminish the financial burden on religious schools in a period of rapidly mounting school costs, especially since relatively fewer members of religious orders are available to teach in the religious schools, at considerably lower pay than lay teachers. Shared-time arrangements amount to a system of cooperation and partnership between public and nonpublic educational agencies that still preserves the distinction between religious inculcation and secular instruction. Perhaps the fundamental issue concerning shared time is whether it is really possible or desirable, educationally and religiously, to make a sharp division in terms of subject matter between the secular and the religious. Is it desirable for instruction in the humanities, for example, including religious studies, to be conducted with a sectarian bias and for the purpose of indoctrination? Also, is it desirable to foster the assumption, as the shared-time arrangement tends to do, that the public schools in their secular teaching can or should be purged of all religious elements?

Another facet of the public-interest question concerns the role of the schools, both public and nonpublic, in a pluralistic society. One of the main functions of the public schools in the United States has been to

16 *West Virginia v. Barnette.* See p. 183.

17 A symposium on the shared time plan may be found in *Religious Education,* **57** (January-February 1962), pp. 5-35.

create a common ethos in a nation nourished from many diverse cultural sources. A multiform immigrant population had to be welded into a single people—*"e pluribus, unum"*—and the common school was one of the most powerful instruments for achieving this goal. But the question may now be raised as to whether the public school has not become a means of homogenizing the young and thus of deterring the cultural pluralism that is one of the sources of richness and variety in a democratic society. At the present stage of American history, is it in the public interest to encourage uniformity or diversity, and if diversity, may it not be desirable to use public funds to support culturally diversified schools, by granting educational subsidies to a variety of nonpublic agencies, or perhaps, as suggested earlier in this chapter, by making educational grants to families for use in schools of their choice?[18]

The argument most commonly advanced by proponents of public financial support for education in nonpublic schools is based on the two ideas of religious freedom and distributive justice. According to this argument, the fundamental principle in the American tradition is religious freedom. This entails the liberty of the parents to educate their children according to the dictates of conscience, including, in particular, the freedom to send them to schools under religious auspices. In order to do this, many if not most parents need a fair share of financial resources comparable to those available to parents who send their children to public schools. If no such share of public funds is available, so that tuition must be charged, and if no relief is given the parents from the burdens of ordinary taxation, then those families will be forced, by financial pressure and contrary to conscience, to send their children to public schools or pay tuition in nonpublic schools and thus suffer the injustice of what amounts to double taxation. The proponents of this view claim, then, that justice in the distribution of public funds contributed by all the people for the education of all dictates that equitable public grants be made in support of the education of all children, including those who in accordance with their right to religious liberty receive their education in religious schools.

There are two fundamental arguments against any and all grants for education under religious auspices. The first is that religious institutions must be kept strictly free of all political connections in order that the

---

[18] For an excellent discussion of this issue by a group of educators and social scientists, see the monograph *Subsidized Pluralism in American Education* (William W. Brickman, Ed.), The Society for the Advancement of Education, New York, N.Y., 1959. See also Seymour W. Itzkoff, *Cultural Pluralism and American Education*, International Textbook Co., Scranton, Pa., 1969.

principle of religious freedom may be maintained in full purity. The other is that public financial support of nonpublic schools would undermine the common school and increase divisiveness and intergroup hostilities and rivalries that would weaken the life of the commonwealth. It is one of the continuing tasks of the American people to resolve the question as to whether the interests of religious freedom and civic democracy are better served by maintaining a sharp distinction between public and nonpublic schools or by giving various forms of public financial support to nonpublic schools to the extent that they can be shown to serve the public interest.

Religious Practices in the Schools

In our earlier analysis of the meaning of religion, it was pointed out that among the important elements in any complete description of religious phenomena are the practices that characterize the religious community. Religion is not only or even primarily a matter of intellectual belief. Since religion ideally has to do with the ultimate life commitments of people, it is natural that faith should find expression in acts that engage the senses and the emotions as well as the rational mind—hence the centrality of cult and ritual in the life of the worshipping community.

Rituals, of course, do not belong exclusively to religious communities. Every group has its characteristic symbolic acts that express the meaning of its common life. In particular, schools have rituals, including songs, cheers, and a variety of ceremonial occasions of induction, promotion, separation, and reunion. These rituals are acts of celebration that embrace group solidarity and loyalty, expressing and confirming the members in commitment to shared ideals and objectives. Such acts are important means of sustaining morale and of increasing the motivation of the participants. There are also rituals performed in schools that reflect wider community loyalties, as, for example, the Pledge of Allegiance, the salute to the flag, and the singing of patriotic anthems, which are symbols of devotion to the nation.

As indicated earlier, the general principle in American society regarding ritual practices in schools is that religious rites belong only in nonpublic schools, where it may be presumed that those who participate in them belong to, or on their own initiative associate with, a particular community of faith; and that they are not appropriate in public schools, which in the secular state are obliged to assume a position of strict neutrality with regard to religious celebration and inculcation. Furthermore, it is clear that while nonreligious symbolic acts, such as specifically academic ceremonies and patriotic acts, are appropriate in both public and nonpublic schools, it is essential in public schools to excuse from any such acts students who for reasons of conscience cannot participate in them, as in the case of Jehovah's Witnesses who object to the flag salute on the ground that it constitutes idolatry.

In practice, it is not always easy to distinguish religious from secular acts. Thus, it might seem that reading from the Bible as one of the great books of Western civilization could be regarded as secular, and indeed this may be the case, but only provided it is done as academic study, with appropriate opportunity for analysis and discussion, and not as an act of veneration or celebration. More problematic are the cases of sacred symbols that have become part of the general cultural inheritance, such as those associated with the celebration of Christmas and Easter. For example, is it permissible in a public school to sing Christmas carols or to set up a creche? The answer is clearly no, because these are expressions of faith within the Christian community, and do not correspond to the faith of such groups as the Jews and Humanists. To use the symbols of one religious group in a public school is to place students who belong to other groups in the position either of being excluded, explicitly or tacitly, or of having to participate or acquiesce in acts contrary to their own traditions and commitments. It does not matter that some of these symbols have become widely diffused throughout the culture and taken for granted as part of the common patrimony. If any institution in society ought to foster a true understanding of the meaning of symbols, it is the school. One may understand and perhaps forgive business establishments that turn religious festivals into opportunities for commercial advantage, but one cannot justify a school's treatment of these occasions as folk celebrations devoid of their authentic symbolic meanings. It is precisely the function of the school to emphasize the true meanings and to set itself against the tide of vulgarization.

On the other hand, the fact that public schools ought not to engage in religious practices as such does not entail excising all references to such practices or excluding them as demonstrations of the ways certain groups express their faith. On these grounds, it would be quite appropriate for a choral group to sing Christmas carols to illustrate the religious heritage of Christians or for students who wished to do so to construct a creche to portray visually one aspect of the Christian epic. It would be equally fitting, and usually more productive educationally, to render the music and create visual expressions of the faith of other than the majority religious groups, such as Jews, Muslims, and Buddhists. The central point is that there is no need to eliminate religious symbols and acts from public schools insofar as they are deliberately introduced as illustrative materials for study within the secular program and not as presumed expressions of the faith of the students as a worshipping community.

The Teacher and His Religion

The reader will recall that experientially conceived religion is concerned with a person's comprehensive and ultimate orientation toward life. It follows that in the last analysis everyone has some kind of religion —some standpoint of faith in terms of which he directs his life—and that this basic outlook and commitment shapes and colors whatever he does. This being the case, it is clear that a teacher cannot possibly teach in total independence of his faith. He cannot leave his ultimate commitments at home when he goes to school. Rather, his behavior as a teacher is bound to express what he believes and cares for at the deepest levels of his existence.

There is a sense, therefore, in which every teacher inescapably teaches religion. In his actions he communicates the faith that animates him as a living, choosing person. This is as true of the teacher in public schools as of those in nonpublic schools, and it applies as much to the traditional theist and practicing member of an organized religion as to the teacher who is a professed atheist or agnostic and without any formal religious affiliation. Every teacher bears tacit witness to what he values most highly in the choices he makes and in the way he handles such basic life problems as anxiety, guilt, doubt, and estrangement. His faith shines through in his relations with students, with colleagues, and with the materials of instruction. No one can miss the lesson of a teacher's unswerving devotion to truth regardless of consequences, of his untiring patience and concern for the well-being of even an unpromising student, or of his rapt absorption in the contemplation of a work of surpassing beauty. Nor can one miss the lesson of other types of life commitment—of a teacher whose first concern is his own comfort and security or of a teacher who supinely and without question submits to the authority of his supervisors. These revelations of the teacher's own life are, in fact, what he most directly and impressively teaches. In comparison with these lessons, those of the "objective" curriculum are of minor importance. Deeper than the easily forgotten and superficially learned materials of instruction lies the image of the teacher whose life, for good or for ill, impresses itself upon the learner through the personal encounter of teacher and student.

Granting this ineluctable witness of the teacher to his faith through his personal and professional life, it is still important to ask how far this tacit witness may properly be accompanied by explicit declarations of faith by the teacher in the school. Should a teacher make known to his students his personal religious commitments, convictions, and affiliations? It seems obvious that bearing such explicit witness may well be construed as a form of religious indoctrination. Since the teacher occupies a special position of influence and authority, his declarations of faith may be presumed to have unusual weight. In nonpublic schools there can be no objection on constitutional grounds to such witnessing. In public schools, on the other hand, this inculcation is not permissible, and the teacher is under obligation to avoid it. Even in nonpublic schools it can be argued on educational and even on religious grounds that the teacher would do well to exercise a degree of reticence about his personal religious commitments, in order that his students may be encouraged to seek their own path of faith rather than to adopt that of the teacher as an authority figure.

On the other hand, it can be argued that the teacher has a right to be himself, even in a public school classroom, and that there is no law against letting his personal beliefs be known on any subject, including religion, provided he does not represent them as matters to be believed by the students. It can be urged that a teacher who feels himself muzzled in regard to questions of deep import will lack the authenticity and vitality that make for effective teaching, and that it is quite possible for a teacher to find appropriate ways of expressing his personal convictions freely and openly without diminishing, but instead even heightening, the student's sense of his own freedom of belief and of the importance of finding and articulating his own faith. How easily this two-sided openness and freedom may be achieved depends both on the age of the students and on the general intellectual and emotional climate prevailing in the community, in the school, and in the particular classroom. The frank expression of convictions by the teacher is less hazardous with older students, whose own beliefs are more developed and who are likely to be more critical of indoctrination than are younger ones. Also, open expressions of faith are less likely to have a propagandist effect in a general climate that encourages diversity and individuality and are more questionable in situations that press for conformity and that encourage submission to authority.

The Objective Study of Religion

From the standpoint of the Constitution, as pointed out above, it is quite permissible to include religion in the public school program, provided it is treated objectively as part of the secular curriculum. Nonpublic schools may conduct religious education in the sense of propagation of a particular faith, but public schools may not. In this regard, it is worthy of remark that even in religious schools it may be educationally and religiously more effective to present religion in the objective manner rather than as indoctrination. For the case can be made that indoctrination may have the contrary effect of inoculation, so that students who are expected to accept official doctrine will, in the exercise of their inner freedom, decide to reject the proffered teaching. If, on the other hand, a faith is presented objectively, along with other options, as a way of belief and practice to be freely chosen, it may have a better chance of being intelligently and wholeheartedly accepted. From this standpoint, then, the objective study of religion is the indicated approach not only in public schools but in nonpublic schools as well. Indeed, if one takes the position that education is the best form of persuasion, and that good education has universal rather than partisan norms, it should follow that the best way to conserve and extend the truth of a faith is to teach it responsibly according to the principles that prevail in sound education, both public and nonpublic.

What, then, are those principles? What does it mean to teach religion objectively, as part of a secular curriculum, that is, as an element in a course of studies not designed to promote the special interests of organized religious groups? The word "objective" is often interpreted as signifying freedom from emotional reactions. One is said to be objective if he is cool and detached and without any personal stake in the matter, if he is concerned only with the hard facts and not with commitments or preferences. It is difficult to see how this conception of objectivity can be defended in any field of study, let alone in religion. No person is ever free of interests and commitments. Objectivity itself is an ideal of a particular kind to which inquirers are committed. There are no facts wholly free of values. A fact is, indeed, a proposition to which truth-value is ascribed.

We can usefully approach the meaning of objectivity by contrasting it with subjectivity. A person is said to be objective if he succeeds in transcending his subjective reactions, that is, if he is able to enter into the being of other persons and situations that lie beyond the limits of his own private life. Clearly, then, objectivity does not mean noninvolvement and lack of commitment. It means, rather, involvement in the interests of others and commitment to the community of persons who endeavor to understand the nature of things as they are and not for purposes of group propaganda and advantage. Interpreted in this way, objectivity can be regarded as a form of controlled intersubjectivity, that is, a process of becoming aware of the subjectivities of others, controlled so as to create common understanding on the part of all inquirers.

Objectivity of this kind is the hallmark of scholarly inquiry and the central obligation of the academic community. Furthermore, the norms of scholarship and of academic excellence are not sectarian. They are identical for all inquirers and teachers regardless of the arrangements of support, control, or sponsorship within which they work. It follows that the objective study of any subject, including religion, ought not to differ in public schools and nonpublic schools. Nor should a teacher's own religious commitment determine how he will teach religion. The academic teaching of religion by a responsible Christian scholar should not differ from that of a responsible Jew, or Buddhist, or atheist, since all are committed as scholars to the same objective canons of inquiry.

How is this objectivity achieved? The usual term for a responsible community of inquiry is a "discipline." Scholarship is disciplined when it proceeds according to canons that permit public checking of an inquiry by any other person who wishes to do so, according to criteria agreed on by the relevant community of scholars. In the case of religion, inquiry can be based on concepts and methods distinctive of the religious phenomenon itself or on those that are derived from other fields of experience. Each of these approaches is capable of yielding objective understanding of religious realities.

According to the first approach, a discipline of "religious studies" is organized, using concepts that are appropriate to religion as distinct from other fields of study. Examples of such concepts are "the holy" or "the sacred," "the divine," "God," "the soul," "spirit," "transcendence," "ultimacy," "creation," "revelation," "faith," "sin," "the demonic," "eternal life," and "miracle." Within the context of any given community of faith, the exposition and development of such ideas is generally referred to as "theology." Thus, the disciplined study of the faith of the Christian community constitutes Christian theology, of the Hindu community, Hindu theology, and so on.

Religious studies, including the theologies of the various faiths and the comparative analysis of them, provide the means for illuminating and clarifying the significance of the experiences, beliefs, practices, and institutions of the religions of mankind, by entering as fully as possible into the faiths as they are inwardly held by the devotees themselves. To carry on these studies, there exists a well established community of scholars in religion and theology and a highly developed body of scholarly literature. These studies are carried on not only in theological seminaries and institutes, but also increasingly in colleges and university departments of religion, in both public and private institutions. Anyone who would teach religion responsibly, at any level of the educational system, needs to depend on the work done by scholars in the discipline of religion, exactly as the teachers of physics or of music must depend on the contributions of recognized scholars in those disciplines. The teacher of religion is no more exempt from the requirements of academic competence than is the teacher of any other school subject, and in the field of religion, the same kinds of opportunities exist for the use of objective methods of study as in any other curriculum area.

The other approach to the disciplined study of religion is through the application of concepts and methods of relevant disciplines other than those of theology and religious studies. Of these, the most significant are history, literature, music, art, anthropology, sociology, psychology, and philosophy. Each of these "secular" disciplines yields certain distinctive insights into religion. Thus, history locates religious events in time and interprets them in relation to other events. Sociology studies the nature of religious institutions and shows how the character of religious experience is conditioned by social structures and processes, and vice versa. Philosophy analyzes the meaning and truth of theological statements and supplies categories for the more adequate interpretation of religious phenomena.

The academic study of religion by means of these disciplines may occur either in special courses or units on religion—as in a series of lessons on "Religious Art of the West"—or incidentally in the normal course of study—as in the inclusion of religious poetry in a general course on poetry. In either case the same canons of scholarly responsibility apply to the religious subject matter as to ostensibly secular materials.

There are two pitfalls to be avoided in the use of the secular disciplines for the study of religion. The first is the temptation so to concentrate on the discipline that the proper goal in using it—to understand religion as a living human reality—is lost sight of. For example, a teacher in his enthusiasm to show the use of anthropological concepts to interpret religious rituals may forget that these tools are not themselves the primary objects of study, but are windows through which to see more clearly the realities to which the inquiry is directed.

The other tendency to be resisted is that of reducing religious realities to the aspects surveyed by means of the discipline. In studying religion by the tools of sociology, for example, it is easy to conclude, as did Durkheim and many others, that religion is *nothing but* the spirit of the group, rather than recognizing that the undeniable social effects of religion may well be merely limited aspects and concomitants of a much wider reality. Each discipline succeeds in exhibiting certain partial aspects of the religious phenomenon, and needs to be supplemented by other disciplines, including the overarching one of theological studies, in order to gain a comprehensive understanding.

As in all studies, the objective study of religion through the disciplines needs to be organized with due regard to the learner's level of maturity. For young children, music and art usually provide the most promising introduction to the understanding of religion in its authentic inwardness, since these studies lead the student into the realm of devotion where faith dwells, and since they comprise concrete presentations more easily grasped by children than verbal abstractions. Next in order would normally come literature and history, and only later the social sciences and psychology. Philosophy and theology are appropriate only for the most mature students, dealing as they do with the most abstract aspects of religion and with questions of truth that cannot be effectively considered in the absence of solid grounding in the intersubjective appreciation of the claims of the living faiths of mankind achieved through the other disciplines—chiefly the humanistic ones of history, literature, and the arts.

The objective study of religion presupposes, of course, consideration of the varieties of faith and of its expressions. Whatever disciplines are employed to gain intersubjective understanding, it is of the essence of the objective approach to treat the various faith options, including not only the principal historic religions but also secular faith orientations such as naturalistic humanism, atheistic existentialism, and Marxism. It is seldom if ever practicable to consider all the major options, but it is always essential, in religious studies, to acknowledge the alternative possibilities and to regularly illuminate the faiths being studied by illustrative reference to contrasting orientations.

Religious Perspectives in Secular Studies

In addition to conducting a study of the explicit religions of mankind as objective realities of culture, it is important to recognize the implicit religious dimensions in what are regarded as secular studies, such as language, science, social studies, and the arts. Recalling the basic experiential meaning of religion discussed early in this chapter, it can be seen that any secular study pursued with seriousness and with regard to its most comprehensive significance becomes an occasion for the expression of one's ultimate commitments. Since certain faith presuppositions are implicit in the dedicated pursuit of ostensibly secular inquiries, the teacher in any school, public or nonpublic, is inevitably presented with questions of ultimate concern in the treatment of his curriculum materials. In this sense no clear separation can be made between secular studies and sacred studies, for the secular ones can always be seen in the perspective of the sacred.

For example, science presupposes dedication to the ideals of truth and of loyalty to the canons of investigation in a universal community of inquiry, both of which attitudes are at least analogues of the religious spirit. Again, the arts present occasions for creation, for the incarnation of forms, and for the expression of unique personal authenticity, all of which may be regarded as manifestations of human spirituality essentially identical with those of religion in its explicit forms. While a teacher may on occasion wish to employ some of the traditional theological terms to interpret the ultimate meanings of the secular studies, this is not necessary to the realization of the implicit religious values in teaching. What is important is that the student be helped to sense the momentousness and the wonder in the pursuit of learning.[19]

Religion in the Preparation of Teachers

In the last analysis, the key to the competent handling of religion in education is the teacher. In the past, and to a large extent at the present time, most teachers have not been prepared to deal with religious questions in an academically competent manner. This is quite understandable, in view of the prevalence of the essentially sectarian, indoctrinating concept of religious education. Under these circumstances, most teachers have been reluctant to deal with religious matters, at least within the public school, and where they have ventured into the subject they have frequently been challenged by parents and ecclesiastical functionaries who object to religion being taught their children by persons of other faiths

---

[19] In *A Common Faith,* Yale, New Haven, Conn., 1934, John Dewey argues, from a naturalistic perspective, the case for the religious dimensions in what are usually regarded as nonreligious activities. See also, from a different perspective, Philip H. Phenix, *Education and the Worship of God,* Westminster, Philadelphia, Pa., 1966, where religious aspects of five curricular areas are discussed.

or of no religious affiliation. The consequence has been a tendency to divest the public school curriculum as much as possible of references to religion, and to treat such religious matters as cannot be avoided in a gingerly fashion, referring them as quickly as possible to parents and clergy.

This situation is manifestly unhealthy from an educational standpoint, since it entails a distorted view of personal and cultural realities and an avoidance of issues that, though not easy to handle and often fraught with tension and controversy, present rich opportunities for enlarging and deepening the student's experience. Fortunately, in recent years a revolution has occurred in the teaching of religion in colleges and universities, so that now across the nation a substantial proportion of the leading institutions, both public and private, offer religion courses taught as an objectively defined discipline by academically competent professors specifically trained in religious studies.

The clue to the responsible handling of religion in the schools lies in the preparation of teachers who either through general education or through specialized courses have become knowledgeable about religion as a fundamental human phenomenon. Such teachers will be competent to deal with religion as fairly and sympathetically as they would with any other important human concern, not in order to inculcate their own commitments in the students, but in order to illumine mankind's paths of faith so that their students may better know the world, in all its rich variety, and be more capable of carving out their own distinctive destinies.

References

❖❖❖

American Association of School Administrators, *Religion in the Public Schools,* Harper, New York, N.Y., 1964. A clear statement by an important commission of public school administrators of a constructive policy toward religion in American public schools, in the light of legal principles and of America's religious pluralism.

Butler, J. Donald, *Religious Education: The Foundations and Practice of Nurture,* Harper, New York, N.Y., 1962. A comprehensive text on religious education from the standpoint of Protestant Christianity, but generally useful also to religious educators of other faiths.

Clayton, A. Stafford, *Religion and Schooling: A Comparative Study,* Blaisdell, Waltham, Mass, 1969. A refreshing study of religion and the schools in England, the Netherlands, and Sweden, with analysis of the significance of these systems for American public school policy.

Kliebard, Herbert M. Ed., *Religion and Education in America: A Documentary History,* International, Scranton, Pa., 1969. An excellent collection of basic documents on the issues of church and state in American education from colonial times to the present, with useful introductory commentaries.

Loder, James E., *Religion and the Public Schools,* Association Press, New York, 1965. A searching analysis of political, legal, educational, and religious aspects of religion in public education, based on discussions of the New Jersey Committee for the Study of Religion in the Public Schools.

Panoch, James V., and David L. Barr, *Religion Goes to School: A Practical Handbook for Teachers,* Harper, New York, N.Y., 1968. A practical manual suggesting methods and materials for effectively dealing with religion in public school classrooms. Includes an extensive annotated bibliography.

Sizer, Theodore R. Ed., *Religion and Public Education,* Houghton Mifflin, Boston, Mass., 1967. Essays by leading authorities on the central issues concerning religion in American education.

175

8

The Law and the Courts

Michael L. Simmons, Jr.

❖❖

School law—the part of public law that pertains to schools—cuts across the various divisions of law. It finds its source in constitutional requirements, in legislative enactments, in judicial decisions on both federal and state levels, and in the actions of the legally constituted local educational authorities. It finds its application in practically every educational decision that is made, be it pedagogic, curricular, financial, or administrative.

In this chapter, politics and religion, two basic constituents of educational theory and practice, will of necessity be revisited, for a large part of the chapter's objective is to show how they relate *legally* to education. Much of the focus here is on the significance of the Bill of Rights, the interaction of judicial processes and public policy, and the meaning of a separate church and state as they affect education. This chapter complements the two previous chapters, but the context—that of public law—is new, and thus the reader is able to advance his total understanding of the educational endeavor.

At the outset it should be noted that the short noun *law* lends itself to no simple definition. Law has been considered to be basically the codification of custom, or a decree born of reason and directed to the common good, or one means by which a ruling class attempts to realize its interests, or as an accurate prediction of what the courts will say and do. For our purposes we shall say that law comprises all the rules and regulations that are intended to maintain and perpetuate the social order and that have the coercive power of government behind them. The "social order," it must be remembered, comprises social classes, groups, and individuals that have a history of conflicting social and economic interests, philosophical orientations, and varying degrees of power to achieve their will. Thus it is to be expected that court decisions in important areas of life will frequently evoke sharp disagreement from different sectors of the populace.

Legal theory and the living law cannot be understood if their relation to political theory is ignored. The Bill of Rights is both a political and a legal limitation of government power in favor of personal freedom and liberty. That the rights that are to be cherished have to be guaranteed underlines their precarious status in our community. These rights have been attained in a sociohistorical process that is by no stretch of the imagination purely rational or logical. The overall "logic" of law, like that of education, is the "logic" of action that comprises the rational and the irrational, and in which the active use of reason, interest, and power are combined.

To fully understand the working of law in education, as in the famous *Brown* desegregation decisions, one must grasp both the legal reasoning involved and the significance of the extralegal factors that contributed to the decisions. Not to understand the relation of these factors is to risk, on one hand, taking a self-defeating position of total legal relativism, or, on the other hand, to believe that law is established by purely logical entities that know neither flesh nor blood nor the company of men.

Legal Foundations of American Public Education

Under the Tenth Amendment to the Constitution, which reserves to the individual states and the people those powers neither delegated to the Federal Government nor prohibited by it to the states, education has come to be primarily a function of the individual states. Within the individual states it is the constitution, expressing the will of the people, that usually gives the legislature responsibility and authority to provide education for the populace. Generally acknowledged to have supreme authority in educational matters, the legislatures also have great freedom of action. They have only to observe limitations set by the federal and state constitutions. State legislatures have the power to establish school districts and give them responsibility for providing schools and education for their residents. They can delegate adminstrative power to collect taxes and the right of eminent domain to school districts, which are considered to be political subdivisions of the state. A state legislature, however, cannot delegate its legislative power to another body.

Education also has long been considered a national concern by the Federal Government. Through federal action, education has been encouraged and financially supported from the first Northwest Ordinance in 1785 to the present day. Article 1, Section 8 of the Constitution has granted Congress the power to lay and collect taxes to provide for the general welfare of the United States. It is under this "general welfare" clause that the Federal Government has assumed the power to initiate educational activity in its own right and also to participate jointly with states, agencies, and individuals in educational activity.

Of special importance to education are the First, Fifth, and Fourteenth Amendments, which establish freedom of religion and speech, assure individuals that they need not bear witness against themselves, guarantee individuals that they cannot be deprived of life, liberty, and property without due process of law, and prohibit states from making and enforcing laws that abridge the rights of citizens. We must also note the clause in Article I, Section 10 of the Constitution, which asserts that no state can pass any law impairing the obligation of contracts. In other words, a state cannot alter the terms of a contract without the consent of the other parties to the contract.

Constitutionally guaranteed rights are a mixed blessing if they cannot be enforced and used. Under our legal system a person who believes he has been denied his legal rights can turn to the courts for assistance. The judiciary, and ultimately the U.S. Supreme Court, the court of last resort, stands as a major guarantor of civil liberties in the United States. The courts have the right, established in statute and in practice, to find legislation unconstitutional or to find that a given process of government at any level violates constitutionally guaranteed rights. However, the courts remain silent until asked to speak by an aggrieved party, a plaintiff.

It is sometimes argued that the courts' role is "not to create law" but, in Chief Justice Marshall's words, "to say what the law is." However, any institution with the power to prohibit traditional social practice and to require that specific action be undertaken, as the Supreme Court has in its desegregation decisions, is in fact creating law. Although judicial decisions can create social problems, it would be more accurate to say that vital court decisions generally throw social problems of great magnitude into ever sharper relief.

The Student and the Law

Relation of Church and State in Public Education

Church and state relations in public education provide us with a particularly complex and important set of issues because it is at this point that constitutional interpretation, the ultimate nature of religious belief, and the importance of the child to his parents converge. Further, the facts of ethnic membership, community identity, and the political use of institutional religious power are also joined here. Most Americans are religious and claim church affiliation. The morality our public schools is expected to inculcate is generally considered by the lay public to be both historically rooted in, and logically justified by, religious sources. Our churches have tax exemptions, and the pledge of allegiance now asserts that we are one nation "under God." But nowhere in the language of the Constitution or Bill of Rights do we find a claim that it is religious belief or church support that justifies our form of government. Though federal and state governments obviously view religion favorably, we have no established church or churches in the United States. The First Amendment states that "Congress shall make no law respecting an establishment of religion, or prohibiting the free exercise thereof." Our government is, in fact, secular, that is, civil and nonecclesiastical.

An important body of law has developed through court response to allegations that existing laws or statutes, or school practices, deprive the plaintiff of rights guaranteed under the First Amendment and sometimes those guaranteed by the due-process clause of the Fourteenth Amendment. Most of the education cases dealing with church-state relations fall into two general categories. One is concerned with the question of public support of parochial schools. The other is concerned with the introduction of religious instruction into school curricula. But before we consider some of these cases we must ask the meaning of the First Amendment for religion and education.

Much disagreement centers on the interpretation of the meaning of the First Amendment for church-state relations in general and, specifically, in education. Justice Black, speaking for the Supreme Court in a crucial education case said:

> The "establishment of religion" clause of the First Amendment means at least this: Neither a state nor the federal government can set up a church. Neither can pass laws which aid one religion, aid all religions, or prefer one religion over another. Neither can force nor influence a person to go to or to remain away from church against his will or force him to profess a belief or disbelief in any religion. . . . No tax in any

amount, large or small, can be levied to support any religious activities or institutions, whatever they may be called, or whatever form they may adopt to teach or practice religion. . . . In the words of Jefferson, the clause against establishment of religion by law was intended to erect "a wall of separation between Church and State" . . . .[1]

Not all people who accept Justice Black's interpretation necessarily agree on specific application of the principles enunciated. Several major positions respecting the meaning of the "wall of separation" will now be presented.

A position that we shall identify as "strict separationist" contends that the state is not competent to judge the value of religion or nonreligion. Religious freedom in thought and practice is noted to have flourished in the United States under "separation," and it is generally argued that public support of church-connected schools would be socially divisive. The rights of parents to enter their children in church-connected schools is supported, and it is recognized that this may impose a financial burden on parents choosing to exercise this right. The First Amendment is judged to prohibit both *direct* and *indirect* financial support for any or all religious sects or denominations. This position rejects the logic of the "child-benefit theory,"[2] which contends that indirect support to church-connected schools, such as the state purchase of textbooks for parochial school pupils, is not an aid to the school but to the children themselves.

Opposing the strict separationist position are a number of arguments. Some claim that the parental right to determine the nature of a child's education is a natural right. To make this right a reality, not just a formal freedom, parents should have the opportunity to indicate the school or school system to which their tax monies should go. Government can and should give equal support on a nonpreferential basis to all qualified schools, church-connected and otherwise. Religious schools are said to perform a *public* service in that they educate a sizable section of the public's children. Parents who enroll their children in church-connected schools, in fact, suffer what can be called "double taxation."

A third position argues that indirect support for certain aspects of church-school education is both legal and desirable. This position claims to be in keeping with the American tradition, which includes church

[1] *Everson v. Board of Education of the Township of Ewing et al.*, 330 U.S. 1, 67 S. Ct. 504 (1947).

[2] *See Cochran et al. v. Louisiana State Board of Education et al.*, 281 U.S. 370 (1930) for the birth of the "child-benefit theory." *Cochran* is the textbook case. *Everson* justified public payment of transportation costs for children attending parochial schools.

tax exemptions, the public support of chaplains in the armed services and prisons, and the use of prayer in Congress. Separation was never intended to be absolute. This position supports the logic of the "child-benefit theory" and has been called a "wavy line" interpretation. It has been summed up in this fashion:

> Between the poles of "non-establishment" and "free exercise" lies a vast realm of functional interaction which cannot—and should not—be proscribed by legal and judicial acts. Instead of a "wall" we ought to have a "wavy line" between church and state. They are in dynamic relation to each other and the boundaries of their respective spheres cannot be determined for once and for all.[3]

The above issues are now being argued before state and federal courts. At issue in the most important cases is the constitutionality of Titles I and II of the Elementary and Secondary Education Act of 1965 (Public Law 89-10 [1965]). This act authorizes the use of over one billion dollars of federal funds to improve the education of school children (for the most part children in low-income areas, in both public and private, including church-connected, schools. Among the services and materials to be provided are textbooks, additional library resources, instructional materials, language, reading, and science laboratories, school plan improvements, and preschool training programs. Both Titles place administrative supervision and control of the programs in public agencies. They also state that property constructed and materials purchased are to be loaned, not given, to participating schools.

In *Flast v. Cohen* plaintiffs have contended that both Titles contravene the "establishment" and "free exercise" clauses. The Supreme Court has agreed that there are sufficient grounds in the complaint to involve the jurisdiction of a federal court, but it has not yet ruled on the substantive issues raised.[4]

Classroom Prayer and Bible Readings. In many public schools the

---

[3] Ray Gibbons, "Protestantism and Public Actions," *Social Action* (February 15, 1949), 4-27, cited in Philip Jacobson, *Religion in Public Education: A Guide for Discussion*, The American Jewish Committee, Institute of Human Relations, New York, 1969, p. 9.

[4] *Flast v. Cohen*, 88 S. Ct. 1942 (June 10, 1968). A most thorough analysis of this Act is found in George R. La Noue, "Church-State Problems in New Jersey: The Implementation of Title I (ESEA) in Sixty Cities," *Rutgers Law Review*, **XXII** (Winter 1968), 219-280. Among Professor La Noue's conclusions is the statement: "If tested by *Everson* standards, at least half of the sixty cities are operating unconstitutional projects." p. 271. The article has been reprinted in pamphlet form by the American Civil Liberties Union.

school day has traditionally started with a prayer. In 1951 the New York Board of Regents composed a prayer that reads as follows:

> Almighty God, we acknowledge our dependence upon Thee, and we beg Thy blessings upon us, our parents, our teachers, and our country.

This prayer was written, according to the Board, as part of an attempt to meet an atheistic attack on our way of life, a rise in juvenile delinquency, a rise in crime, and other ills besetting American society. The Supreme Court found it to be unconstitutional in 1962.[5]

Reading from the Bible without comment or recitation of the Lord's Prayer has also been found unconstitutional. Here the Court rejected the contention of school authorities that the readings were not religious exercises, but merely attempts to promote moral values. In both of these decisions the fact that pupils could be excused from the activity was found to be immaterial.[6]

Released Time. For over half a century children desiring to receive religious instruction during the school day have been excused from part of the school program to receive such training. Students not participating in such "released-time" programs are given other work to do during these periods. A released-time program with privately paid teachers, held during the school day in the public building, with supervision of the records done by public personnel, was found by the Supreme Court to be a "utilization of the tax-established and tax-supported public school system to aid religious groups to spread their faith." It was ruled unconstitutional.[7] A program that removed instruction from the public school building and put general supervision in the hands of religious authorities or their agents was not construed by the Court to be an establishment of religion.[8]

Religious Holidays. Lower court rulings have found that the singing of religious songs and hymns during Easter and Christmas did not violate pupils' rights because they were not compelled to attend such exercises. The presence of such religious symbols as the cross, the star of Bethlehem, or the star of David, were not considered a violation of pupil's rights. However, courts have enjoined pageants and programs intended to cele-

---

5 *Engle v. Vitale*, 370 U.S. 421, 82 S. Ct. 1261 (New York 1962).

6 *School District of Abington Township, Pennsylvania v. Schempp; Murray v. Curlett* (Maryland), 374 U.S. 203 (1963).

7 *People of State of Illinois ex rel. McCollum v. Board of Education of School District No. 71, Champaign County, Ill., et al.,* 333 U.S. 203, 608 S. Ct. 461 (1948).

8 *Zorach v. Clauson*, 343 U.S. 306 (1952).

brate religious holidays. Another issue on which controversy and some confusion continues is whether a school board has the right to prevent public school teachers from wearing religious garb in the classroom. The constitutionality of regulations prohibiting such dress in the classroom has been upheld by various courts. However, where there are no regulations to the contrary, school boards may permit teachers to appear thus attired in public school classrooms.[9]

Religious Conviction Versus the Flag Salute and the National Anthem

In *West Virginia State Board of Education v. Barnette*,[10] the Court ruled in favor of Barnette, against whom legal action had been taken because his children had remained away from school rather than salute the flag. The freedom to differ, in order to have real significance, should not be restricted to matters of little import, stated Justice Jackson for the Court, but must "touch the heart of the existing order." Barnette's spiritual and intellectual liberties guaranteed by the First Amendment had been denied him by the action of the school board. Justice Jackson's interpretation of the meaning of the First Amendment included the now famous statement that

> If there is any fixed star in our constitutional constellation, it is that no official, high or petty, can prescribe what shall be orthodox in politics, nationalism, religion, or other matters of opinion or force citizens to confess by work or act their faith therein. If there are any circumstances which permit an exception, they do not now occur to us.

West Virginia v. Barnette was said to rule in a situation where public school students who were members of Jehovah's Witnesses refused on religious grounds to stand during the singing of the national anthem. The students were suspended from school for insubordination. Although the court claimed that singing the anthem was a patriotic, not a religious ceremony, it also stated that the students had the constitutional right to object to standing on religious grounds. Their expulsion was thus inter-

---

[9] For a thoughtful discussion of the above issues, the reader is referred to *Religion in the Public Schools, A Report by the Commission on Religion in the Public Schools,* American Association of School Administrators, Washington, D.C., 1964.

[10] *West Virginia State Board of Education v. Barnette,* 319 U.S. 624, 63 S. Ct. 1178 (1943).

preted to be a denial of their rights and the school board was enjoined from excluding them from school.[11]

The way in which students may express their beliefs has been extended by a federal court judge who granted a temporary injunction to three high school students who objected to a school regulation that students must either stand during the Pledge of Allegiance or leave the room while it was being recited. The students claimed that the words "with liberty and justice for all" did not apply to the nation today and to stand during the pledge would constitute participation in a "lie." Leaving the room, they claimed, would be a punishment for their exercise of free speech. Judge Orrin G. Rudd said the students had the right to express their beliefs in "their own way" as long as they did not disrupt the school or interfere with the rights of others.[12]

Power of Public School Authorities

The fundamental question, can a state compel a child to attend school, has never been answered directly by the Supreme Court. Lower courts have on numerous occasions upheld state legislation demanding school attendance of children of specified ages. A Compulsory Attendance Act in Oregon that in effect compelled all children to attend public school until completion of the eighth grade was found unconstitutional by the Supreme Court. This decision, stating that parents possessed the right and liberty to direct the upbringing and education of their children, thus guaranteed the rights of children to attend private schools. This historic decision also made clear that there was no question about the state's right to regulate, inspect, and supervise all schools, public or private.[13]

On numerous occasions parents have kept their children home to be educated. In deciding whether this was in keeping with current law, courts have had to address themselves to a basic question: what is a school? There is no single legal definition upon which all courts have agreed. In deciding these cases, the courts have asked whether parents have been properly trained and equipped to teach, whether other children were present, whether there was a regular schedule of studies, and whether proper educational materials were present. There is no single line

---

[11] *Sheldin v. Fannin,* 221 F. Supp. 766 United States District Court, D. Arizona, Prescott Division.

[12] "Flag-Pledge Refusal Is Upheld," *Buffalo Evening News,* December 11, 1969, p. 14.

[13] *Pierce v. Society of the Sisters of the Holy Names of Jesus and Mary.* 268 U.S. 501, 45 S. Ct. 571 (1925).

of thought that can be pointed to in these cases. It does seem to be the case, however, that courts can compel children to receive some form of education. In those states where this has been equated with attendance at a formal school, there are always mitigating circumstances that are recognized as justifying nonattendance. Illness, of course, is one. Demonstrated inability of the child to benefit from instruction, due to physical or mental incapacity, is another unless the state makes provision for special instruction.

Parents have frequently resisted the demand that a child be vaccinated against smallpox as a condition of enrollment when school attendance is compulsory. The claim that establishment of such a criterion for public school enrollment is a denial of individual liberty as guaranteed under the Fourteenth Amendment has been uniformly rejected by the courts. The courts have viewed the demand for vaccination as in keeping with the police power of the state to protect the health of the community. Courts, using the same rationale, have also upheld school boards' demands that children have a physical examination by a private or school physician as a condition of entrance, as they have also affirmed the requirement that students seeking to enter a state university have a chest X ray.

Public school authorities enjoy a wide range of power with respect to the students in their care. Schools can reject children who do not meet requirements established by the state with respect to health, cleanliness, residence, and the ability to benefit from instruction. Children with physical or emotional defects can be required to attend special public schools or classes established for them unless they are enrolled in special private educational activities. The school has the authority to make the proper grade placement for the student and to demote or refuse to advance the student, although such action may run counter to parental desire. Courts have defended the school's right to punish children for behavior off the school ground and after school hours when such conduct is shown to have a detrimental effect on the morale and performance of other children.

Discrimination in Public Education

In education, as in other walks of life, it has been the black American who has felt the severest restrictions and denials of his liberty. From 1661, when a Virginia statute recognized the legality of slavery, through the 19th century, a mass of legislation was enacted to establish and maintain the distinct status of black Americans as second-class citizens. In some Southern states, for example, it was a crime to teach a slave or a free Negro to read or write.

Not all legislation that focused on the Negro was in the form of "Black Codes" and "Jim Crow Laws." In 1865, Congress created a Bureau of Refugees, Freedmen, and Abandoned Lands that, among its many activities, organized schools for Negroes. Slavery was abolished by the Thirteenth Amendment, and the Fourteenth Amendment makes citizens of all persons born in the United States; it further proclaims that "No State shall enforce any law which shall abridge the privileges or immunities of citizens of the United States. . . ." However, the battle for equal rights in education, as in other aspects of social life, has taken place in a legal context that originally denied these rights.

The concept "separate but equal" long figured importantly in relations between the races. The Supreme Court gave it sanction in 1896, declaring that a Louisiana statute authorizing Jim Crow railroad cars was not a denial of constitutional guarantees.[14] In effect, the Court reconciled segregation with equality. For a long period of time the Court seemed to place the concept beyond the point of possible change because it refused to consider the possibility that racial segregation in education was a denial of individual liberty. It was not until the late 1930s that the Court began to recognize that segregated schools denied black students equality in those personal, social, and professional realms—sometimes identified as "intangible" by the Court—associated with education.[15]

In the historic *Brown v. Board of Education*[16] decision, the Supreme Court finally destroyed the legality of the separate-but-equal doctrine. The Court upheld the contention of the black plaintiffs that the segregated schools they were forced to attend were not equal and could not be equal and that such schools deprived them of equal protection of the laws as guaranteed by the Fourteenth Amendment. Calling education "perhaps the most important function of state and local governments," the Court added that where the state provides public education, it is a "right which must be made available to all on equal terms." Segregation of children solely on the basis of race, no matter what the equality of physical and tangible factors, was said to deny minority-group children equal educational opportunities. Citing a lower court decision that observed that the policy of separating the races is "usually interpreted as denoting the inferiority of the Negro group," the Court concluded that "in the field of public education the doctrine of 'separate but equal' has no place. Separate educational facilities are inherently unequal."

14 *Plessy v. Ferguson,* 163 U.S. 537, 16 S. Ct. 1138 (1896).

15 *Missouri ex rel. Gaines v. Canada,* 305 U.S. 337, 59 S.Ct. (1938); *Sweatt v. Painter,* 399 U.S. 629, 70 S. Ct. 848 (1950); *McLaurin v. Oklahoma State Regents,* 399 U.S. 637, 70 S. Ct. 851 (1950).

16 *Brown v. Board of Education of Topeka,* 347 U.S. 483, 74 S. Ct. 686 (1954).

This decision made unconstitutional the laws demanding separation of the races in seventeen states and the District of Columbia. However, the decision said nothing about desegregation or integration. In 1955, after hearing further evidence from the concerned parties, the Court ruled that the children involved had to be admitted "to public schools on a racially nondiscriminatory basis with all deliberate speed." The Court further said that school authorities had the prime responsibility for assessing and solving the problems, and that the lower federal courts should see that the decisions were complied with.[17]

Desegregation means that legally required dual school systems have to be replaced by unitary systems—single systems for black and white students and teachers. The major response to the *Brown* decisions was the enactment of "pupil-assignment laws." These laws gave school authorities the power to assign individual students to school on the basis of a host of administrative and educational factors. In the deep South they produced little desegregation and less integration. In practice, the burden was put on black students and parents to demonstrate that school authorities were denying them their rights.

"Freedom of choice" plans were later developed and were at first supported by the Office of Education. These plans enabled students and their parents to select schools of their choice within their districts. Thus, theoretically, black students could attend schools with whites. These plans failed to produce any sizable progress toward desegregation or integration. The rationale for both of these responses was based on the view that the Constitution forbids discrimination but does not require integration. Such segregation that occurs as a result of voluntary action is not unconstitutional. When applied to the North, this line of reasoning would deny the claim that *de facto* segregation denies equal protection of the law and equal educational opportunity.

Under the second *Brown* decision, lower courts were to insure that local school authorities, those persons least able to withstand political and social pressure against desegregation, obeyed the new law. Further, local courts offered no firm guidelines by which accomplishment could be measured. For years these courts were satisfied with the production of "theoretically sound minimal" plans for desegregation.[18]

As we have said, desegregation in the Southern States has been dismally slow. Five years after the first *Brown* decision, only 144 of the 2095 dual school systems in the eleven former Confederate states were desegregated

[17] *Brown v. Board of Education,* 349 U.S. 294 (1955).
[18] Theodore A. Smedley, "Enforcement Fell Heavily on the Courts," *Southern Education Report,* **IV**, 10 (June 1969), 32.

and fewer than 3500 of the 2.5 million black schoolchildren were in schools with whites. Ten years after *Brown,* about twenty percent of the school districts abolished their dual systems, but less than 30,000 black children were in schools with whites.[19]

The greatest impetus to desegregation in the South has come from Title VI of the Civil Rights Act of 1964, which bars discrimination in federally assisted programs, permits the government to withhold funds, and also provides for the Department of Justice to initiate court suits to enforce provisions of the Act. As of June, 1969, some 20.3 percent of the South's black children are said by the federal government to be attending schools in which at least fifty per cent of the enrollment is white. Of the 4529 school districts in the seventeen Southern and border states, 3004 were operating unitary school systems by June 1969. Of the remaining districts, 1105 were desegregating under court order or according to voluntary plans approved by H.E.W., and 505 were "in compliance or in questionable compliance with the law."[20]

In the last three years the courts have demanded a "showing of substantial desegregation of all aspects" of the public school systems. The shift of focus from means to ends was stated succinctly in the important *Green* decision, which stated that the "transition to a unitary, nonracial system of public education was and is the ultimate end to be brought about. . . . School boards . . . [are] . . . clearly charged to take whatever steps might be necessary to convert to a unitary system in which racial discrimination would be eliminated root and branch."[21] Freedom-of-choice plans were not found to be unconstitutional per se but could not be considered ends in themselves.

The earlier held view that the second *Brown* decision did not require integration has been increasingly rejected by the courts. The change in interpretation has been expressed in this way:

> The central constitutional fact is the inadequacy of segregated education. That it is not coerced by direct action of an aim of the state cannot, alone, be decisive of the issue of deprivation of constitutional right. . . . The educational system that is thus compulsory and publicly afforded must deal with the inadequacy arising from adventitious segregation; it

[19] Benjamin Muse, "The South's Troubled Years," *Southern Education Report,* **IV,** 10 (June 1969), 16-17.

[20] James K. Batten, "The Nixonians and School Desegregation," *Southern Education Report,* **IV,** 10 (June 1969), 27-28.

[21] *Green v. School Board of New Kent County, Va.,* 88 S. Ct. 1689 (1968), cited in Smedley, op. cit., p. 33.

cannot accept an indurate segregation on the ground that it is not coerced or planned but accepted.[22]

Clearly, this new line of reasoning will have serious ramifications for education in the North, where segregation in the schools follows residential living patterns and has been largely *de facto*. In our largest cities there are hundreds of elementary and secondary schools with student bodies that are ninety percent black. In recent years the segregation in these schools has increased as the more affluent whites have fled to the suburbs.

The issue was joined on February 11, 1970, when Superior Court Judge Alfred E. Gitelson ordered the Los Angeles, California, school district to present a plan by June 1, 1970, for the integration of its schools. The plan is to take effect in September 1970 and no later than September 1971. In his opinion, Judge Gitelson dismissed the importance of the distinction between legally and *de facto* supported segregation. Los Angeles Superintendent of Schools Robert F. Kelly claimed that the order would require busing more than one third of the children in the district and that the added costs "would mean the virtual destruction of the school district." He announced that he would recommend an appeal of the ruling at the earliest possible time.[23]

School authorities have used several methods to achieve racial balance in the schools. Districts have been rezoned, schools have been "paired," and children have been transferred to less crowded schools. It is sometimes argued that in cases not requiring action to alleviate legally enforced segregation it is unconstitutional to consider race or color in making plans for such undertakings. Official action, it is sometimes said, must be color blind. This argument, however, misses the essence of the problem. "Courts will not say in one breath that public school systems may not practice segregation and in the next that they may do nothing to eliminate it."[24] It is clear that a problem cannot be solved by ignoring one of its basic dimensions.

Although the Supreme Court, in *Brown* and subsequent decisions, has spoken unequivocally for Constitutional support for equal educational opportunity for black students, it is apparent that the nation as a whole

---

[22] *Branche v. Board of Education of Town of Hempstead*, 204 F. Supp. 150, 153 (E.D.N.Y. 1962) as cited in Robert L. Carter, "Equal Educational Opportunity for Negroes—Abstraction or Reality," *The University of Illinois Law Forum*, **1968** (Summer 1968), 169-170.

[23] *New York Times*, February 12, 1970, p. 1.

[24] *Wanner v. County School Board*, 357 F. 2d 452, 455 (4th Cir. 1960), as cited in Carter, op cit., p. 186.

has not been willing, and perhaps is not able, to take the steps necessary to make this ideal a reality. The stance of the present executive branch of the federal government has been difficult to identify. In late 1969, when H.E.W. announced that it would rely on its seldom-used power to withhold funds from a number of deep-South school districts that were ignoring previously agreed-on desegregation plans, the Attorney General's office asked the courts to give the districts more time to draft additional plans. With respect to some of the districts involved, the conflict was resolved by the Supreme Court, which demanded that desegregation plans be implemented immediately.

Without the support of the courts, few of the gains that have been realized would have been achieved. The social psychologist Kenneth B. Clark has argued that if the courts had been firmer from the outset, demanding concrete evidence of desegregation within stipulated time periods, the resistance to desegregation, both violent and nonviolent, could have been lessened.[25] There is evidence that many Southern school authorities who have been willing to act in keeping with the Constitutional commitment to equality have retreated when it became clear that the Justice Department was not willing to back them up.[26] Until it is recognized by the populace in general and by educators, as well as by the courts, that the overall quality of American public education cannot be improved without attacking the substance of racial discrimination, it is clear that court decisions alone cannot solve the problems and issues they speak to.

The Rights of Students

Teachers and schools have long been recognized as standing *in loco parentis*—in the place of the parent—to students. Theoretically this relationship should hold only with respect to matters specifically germane to educational practices. Increasingly students have gone to court contending that school requirements and standards go beyond their proper limits, thus constituting a denial of personal and constitutional rights.

In the *Tinker* case the Supreme Court for the first time asserted that the free-speech clause of the First Amendment applied to schoolchildren. The Tinker children wore black armbands to class as a "form of witness"

[25] Kenneth B. Clark, "Fifteen Years of Deliberate Speed," *Saturday Review,* **LII,** 51 (December 20, 1969), 59-61, 70.

[26] Gary Orfield, "The Politics of Resegregation," *Saturday Review,* **LII,** 38 (September 20, 1969), 58-60, 77-79.

against the Vietnam war and also to influence the views of their class-mates. They were suspended until they removed the armbands. The Court found that the armbands were symbolic speech that in no way disrupted school activities and that school authorities had denied the children their constitutional right to express their opinion.[27]

For years the courts have supported school authorities who have imposed restrictions on styles of dress and grooming on the grounds that they can disrupt school activities. However, in late 1969, five different federal courts found in favor of students who claimed that wearing long hair was symbolic speech and thus deserved protection. The courts noted that long hair did not in fact create disturbances in the school, and thus the doctrine of *in loco parentis* had no applicability.

The authority of a teacher to search a student or his locker is not clearly defined by court decisions. The Fourteenth Amendment only prohibits unreasonable search, and courts have supported the right to search a student for dangerous instruments.[28] Schools have the right to suspend or expel students on numerous grounds including academic incompetence. Students must be notified of such action and granted hearings only where statutes demand such procedures. Students do not have the legal right to be represented by counsel, and such hearings may be informal.

In the past, courts have supported colleges and universities that expelled students for not attending chapel or for off-campus political activity on the ground that a student who voluntarily entered a university "necessarily surrenders very many of his individual rights."[29] Clearly, with the barest exception, such reasoning no longer holds on campus or in the courts. The campus today is a highly political place. Student political activities have taken many forms, as have the responses to them of campus officials and local law-enforcement agencies. As students have been disciplined by university authorities for violations of campus rules and regulations, they have gone to court raising a number of important

[27] *Tinker v. Des Moines Independent Community School District,* 89 S. Ct. 733 (1969).

[28] See LeRoy J. Peterson, Richard A. Rossmiller and Marlin M. Volz, *The Law and Public School Operation,* Harper and Row, New York, 1969, pp. 412-414 for a summary analysis of this issue.

[29] *North v. Board of Trustees of Illinois,* 137 Ill., 296, 27 N.E. 54, 56 (1891) as cited by William W. Van Alstyne, "Student Academic Freedom and the Rule-Making Powers of Public Universities: Some Constitutional Considerations," *Law in Transition Quarterly,* 2, 1 (Winter 1965), 3. An excellent overview of the issue is presented in this article. See also "Draft Statement on the Academic Freedom of Students," *A.A.U.P. Bulletin,* 51 (December 1965), 447-449; and the A.C.L.U. pamphlet, *Academic Freedom and Civil Liberties of Students in Colleges and Universities,* New York, 1970.

issues. We have space here to indicate only briefly some of the major findings respecting the rights of college and university students. Attendance at a state university has been termed a right as opposed to a privilege. A student cannot be expected to waive his constitutional rights as a condition of attending a state university. The right to demonstrate on university property is not absolute. Private universities that receive significant governmental financial support and that serve a public function are bound by the criteria of due process.

The relation of substantive student rights and procedural due process has been increasingly dealt with by the courts. Perhaps the most inclusive statement of due process for college students appeared in the *Esteban* case, in which the court said students were entitled to due process before they could be expelled from school. The essential elements of due process were summarized in this fashion:

> (1) written charges; (2) 10 days' notice of hearing and charges; (3) hearing before the President (the final authority); (4) student's rights to advance inspection of the college's affidavits or exhibits; (5) student's right to counsel; (6) student's right to call witnesses, or introduce affidavits or exhibits; (7) right to confrontation and cross-examination of witnesses; (8) determination solely on evidence in the record; (9) written findings and disposition; (10) either side may make a record at its expense.[30]

The Teacher and the Law

The public school teacher has certain rights and responsibilities that are well established by law. It is to these that we first turn our attention. Then we shall deal with teacher loyalty oaths.

Rights and Responsibilities

Contracts. School teachers are generally considered employees, and not officers, of the district hiring them. They work under contracts whose form and content are usually determined by state legislation. In all states there are statutes establishing the requirements that must be met to earn a teaching certificate. Once the requirements have been met, the cer-

---

[30] *Esteban v. Central Missouri State College*, 277 F. Supp. 649 (W.D. Mo. 1967). The summary appears in the A.C.L.U. pamphlet, *Recent Court Decisions on Student Rights*, New York (November 1969), p. 2.

tificate cannot be withheld arbitrarily. Teachers who do not possess certificates may not be issued legal contracts by school boards. Contracts usually designate the salary, duration of employment, date of effectiveness, and legal capacity of the person hired. General tenure-continuing contracts, in essence, assure the teacher of his job under good conduct. Usually they are acquired after the successful completion of a probationary period that can last from one to five years.

Tenure. Although tenure provisions vary from state to state, they usually entitle the teacher to a notice, a statement of charges, and a hearing before he is dismissed. Reasons for dismissal, when specified, include incompetency, neglect of duty, unprofessional conduct, immorality, insubordination, and physical disability. Some tenure regulations merely state as reasons for dismissal, "for cause" or "for good and just cause." A tenure law providing for the dismissal of women teachers because of marriage is now a rarity.

Political and Union Activity. The right of teachers to participate in political campaigns, including active support of candidates for the board of education, has generally been established by court decision. The teacher's classroom, of course, cannot be used for active campaigning. School boards have required that teachers running for public office take a leave of absence during their campaign on the grounds that such strenuous political activity interferes with their professional preparation and work. In better than three fourths of the states, teachers are permitted to serve as legislators. In more than half of the states with no law on the subject, teachers serve in state legislatures.

Teachers, under the First and Fourteenth Amendments, have the right to organize; in all but a few states they may join trade unions. There is presently a strong national trend toward acceptance of the right of public employees, including teachers, to bargain collectively, although the bargaining system is more restricted than that found in private enterprise. Teachers may still not legally strike, but in fact, in recent years there has been a strong trend of teacher "activism," including walkouts, holidays, calling in sick, and the actual calling of strikes. From 1955 to 1965, thirty-five national teacher work stoppages were counted. In 1967 there were 100, with the number increasing each year thereafter.

In Loco Parentis. Both the importance and the scope of the teacher's role are underlined by the statement that he stands *in loco parentis* to his students. Let us consider two aspects of this role, the right of the teacher to inflict corporal punishment on the student and the teacher's responsibility for the pupil's physical well-being. In most states and school districts, corporal punishment is permissible with qualification. The qualifications usually state that the punishment not be excessive and that it be administered in good faith by a teacher using discretion and good judgment. Punishment must be suitable to the sex and age of the pupil. The pupil must understand why he is being punished, and punishment must be in accordance with statutory enactments. Teachers and school principals frequently have been sued for administering corporal punishment. Usually courts have acted on the assumption that a teacher is not liable for an error in judgment in the matter of punishment. It is supposed that the teacher has acted in good faith, that his actions were correct, and that excessive punishment is not a crime unless it produces a lasting injury or can be shown to have been administered without just cause and with express or implied malice.

Of great importance is the teacher's responsibility for his student's physical well-being. If a pupil is injured because of a teacher's negligence, the teacher is legally responsible. In most states he must pay for the damages himself. Most teachers are insured against such an eventuality.

But the student has certain responsibilities, too. He is supposed to exercise the degree of care in a given situation that can be expected of the average child of the same age, intelligence, and experience. If a teacher who is accused of negligence can demonstrate contributory negligence on the part of the student, he will not be found liable for payment of damages in a majority of cases.

Loyalty Oaths. Loyalty oaths for teachers, although not new in the United States, became a subject of controversy in the uneasy years following the Second World War. In the 1960s more than half of the states had some form of teacher oath as a requisite for working in the public schools. "Positive oaths" usually require sworn promises to uphold the federal and state constitutions and a further statement that the teacher does not believe in, or advocate, the overthrow of government by force and violence. Many "negative loyalty oaths" focused on disclaimer affidavits that require a statement that the teacher does not belong to a subversive organization and will not join one in the future. Of the three major professional organizations for teachers, it has been the American Association of University Professors that has consistently maintained the position that a teacher's or professor's professional competency, and not his political beliefs or affiliations, should be the major condition of his employment.

In recent years the Supreme Court has struck down a number of "negative oaths" on the grounds that they were unconstitutionally vague. In the *Keyishian* decision the Court also annulled a statute that made Communist Party membership alone evidence for disqualification for teaching in the public schools.[31] The Supreme Court, however, has not reversed lower courts that have upheld "positive oaths" for teachers in a tax-exempt private institution in New York and also at the State University of Colorado.[32]

[31] *Keyishian v. The Board of Regents of the University of the State of New York*, 385 U.S. 589 (1967); *Elfbrandt v. Russell*, 86 S. Ct. 1238 (1966).

[32] *Knight v. Regents of the University of the State of New York*, 269 F. Supp. 339 (S.D.N.Y. 1967); 390 U.S. 36 (1968) and *Hosack v. Smiley*, 276 F. Supp. 876 (D. Colo. 1967); 36 USLW 3411 (1968). For a detailed analysis of the manner in which H.E.W. was led to exchange its secretive security procedures for procedures more akin to those involving "negative" affidavits, see Bryce Nelson, "HEW: Blacklists Scrapped in New Security Procedures," *Science*, **167** (January 9, 1970), 154-156.

References

❖❖❖

Blaustein, Albert P., and Clarence Clyde Ferguson, Jr., *Desegregation and the Law*, second edition revised, Vintage Books, Random House, 1962, 359 pp. Presents good historical material with focus on the *Brown* decisions.

Carter, Robert L., "Equal Education Opportunity for Negroes—Abstraction or Reality," *The University of Illinois Law Forum*, Vol. 1968 (Summer 1968), 160-188. A highly critical evaluation of the present status of desegregation and integration by the former general counsel of the NAACP.

"Developments in the Law—Academic Freedom," *Harvard Law Review*, Vol. 81, 5 (March 1968), 1045-1159. An excellent summary analysis with a substantial section on the rights of students.

Emerson, Thomas I., David Haber, and Norman Dorsen, *Political and Civil Rights in the United States*, third edition, Little, Brown and Co., 1967, two volumes. This basic text has copious selections from the major court decisions. Excellent bibliography.

Oaks, Dallin H., Ed., *The Wall between Church and State*, Phoenix Books, The University of Chicago Press, 1963, 179 pp. Highly sophisticated analyses of the issues, presenting major points of view.

Peterson, Leroy J., Richard A. Rossmiller, and Marlin M. Volz, *The Law and Public School Operation*, Harper and Row, 1969, 590 pp. A good general introduction covering every conceivable issue in school law.

Weinberg, Meyer, Ed., *Integrated Education*, Glencoe Press, 1968. A highly diversified collection of articles selected from the journal of the same name.

PART THREE

PHILOSOPHIC
FOUNDATIONS

9

The Relevance of Philosophy

George F. Kneller

◆◇◆

From time to time every teacher and student asks himself questions that are implicitly philosophical. The teacher wonders, "Why am I teaching? Why am I teaching history? What is teaching at its best?" And the student asks, "Why am I studying algebra? What am I going to school for anyway?" Taken far enough, these questions become philosophical. They become questions about the nature of man and the world, about knowledge, value, and the good life.

Modes of Philosophy

Unfortunately, nothing illuminating can be said about philosophy with a single definition. Let us therefore think of philosophy as an activity in three modes or styles: the speculative, the prescriptive, and the analytic.

Speculative Philosophy. Speculative philosophy is a way of thinking systematically about everything that exists. Why do philosophers want to do this? Why are they not content, like scientists, to study particular aspects of reality? The answer is that the human mind wishes to see things as a whole. It wishes to understand how all the different things that have been discovered together form some sort of meaningful totality. We are all aware of this tendency in ourselves. When we read a book, look at a painting, or study an assignment, we are concerned not only with particular details but also with the order or pattern that gives these details their significance. Speculative philosophy, then, is a search for order and wholeness, applied not to particular items or experiences but to all knowledge and all experience. In brief, speculative philosophy is the attempt to find a coherence in the whole realm of thought and experience.

Prescriptive Philosophy. Prescriptive philosophy seeks to establish standards for assessing values, judging conduct, and appraising art. It examines what we mean by good and bad, right and wrong, beautiful and ugly. It asks whether these qualities inhere in things themselves or whether they are projections of our own minds. To the experimental psychologist the varieties of human conduct are morally neither good nor bad; they are simply forms of behavior to be studied empirically. But to the educator and the prescriptive philosopher some forms of behavior are worthwhile and others are not. The prescriptive philosopher seeks to discover and to recommend principles for deciding what actions and qualities are most worthwhile and why they should be so.

Analytic Philosophy. Analytic philosophy focuses on words and meaning. The analytic philosopher examines such notions as "cause," "mind," "academic freedom," and "equality of opportunity" in order to assess the different meanings they carry in different contexts. He shows how inconsistencies may arise when meanings appropriate in certain contexts are imported into others. The analytic philosopher tends to be skeptical, cautious, and disinclined to build systems of thought.

Today the analytic approach dominates American and British philosophy. On the Continent the speculative tradition prevails. But whichever approach is uppermost at any time, most philosophers agree that all approaches contribute to the health of philosophy. Speculation unaccompanied by analysis soars too easily into a heaven of its own, irrelevant to the world as we know it; analysis without speculation descends to minutiae and becomes sterile. In any case few philosophers are solely speculative, solely prescriptive, or solely analytic. Speculation, prescription, and analysis are all present to some degree in the work of all mature philosophers.

Philosophy and Science

A great deal of information has been gathered by various sciences on subjects treated by philosophy, particularly human nature. But when we look at this information, we find that psychology gives us one picture of man, sociology another, biology another, and so on. What we have after all the sciences have been searched is not a composite picture of man but a series of different pictures. These pictures fail to satisfy because they explain different aspects of man rather than man as a whole. Can we unify our partial pictures of man into one that is single and complete? Yes, but not by using scientific methods alone. It is through philosophy that we unify the separate findings of science and interrelate the fundamental concepts these findings presuppose.

The philosopher considers questions that arise before and after the scientist has done his work. Traditional science presupposes, for example, that every event is caused by other events and in turn causes still other events. Hence, for science no event is uncaused. But how can we be sure of this? Do cause and effect exist in the world itself or are they read into the world by men? These questions cannot be answered scientifically because causality is not a finding but an assumption of science. Unless the scientist assumes that reality is causal in nature, he cannot begin to investigate it. Again, science deals with things as they appear to our senses and to our instruments. But are things in themselves really the same as they appear to us? The scientist cannot say, because things in themselves, as opposed to their appearances, are by definition beyond empirical verification.

Philosophy, then, is both natural and necessary to man. We are forever seeking some comprehensive framework within which our separate findings may be given a total significance. Not only is philosophy a branch of knowledge along with art, science, and history, but also it actually embraces these disciplines in their theoretical reaches and seeks to establish connections between them. Once again, *philosophy attempts to establish a coherence throughout the whole domain of experience.*

Philosophy of Education

Beside having its own concerns, philosophy considers the fundamental assumptions of other branches of knowledge. When philosophy turns its attention to science, we have philosophy of science; when it examines the basic concepts of the law, we have philosophy of law; and when it deals with education, we have philosophy of education or educational philosophy.

Just as formal philosophy attempts to understand reality as a whole by explaining it in the most general and systematic way, so educational philosophy seeks to comprehend education in its entirety, interpreting it by means of general concepts that will guide our choice of educational ends and policies. In the same way that general philosophy coordinates the findings of the different sciences, educational philosophy interprets these findings as they bear on education. Scientific theories do not carry direct educational implications; they cannot be applied to educational practice without first being examined philosophically.

Educational philosophy depends on general or formal philosophy to the extent that the problems of education are of a general philosophical character. We cannot criticize existing educational policies or suggest new ones without considering such general philosophic problems as (a) the nature of the good life, to which education should lead; (b) the nature of man himself, because it is man we are educating; (c) the nature of society, because education is a social process; and (d) the nature of ultimate reality, which all knowledge seeks to penetrate. Educational philosophy, then, involves among other things the application of formal philosophy to the field of education.[1]

Like general philosophy, educational philosophy is speculative, prescriptive, and analytic. It is speculative when it seeks to establish theories of the nature of man, society, and the world by which to order and interpret the conflicting data of educational research and the behavioral sciences. It is prescriptive when it specifies the ends that education ought to follow and the general means it should use to attain them. It is analytic when it clarifies speculative and prescriptive statements. The analyst, as we shall see, examines the rationality of our educational ideas, their consistency with other ideas, and the ways in which they are distorted by loose thinking. He tests the logic of our concepts and their adequacy to the facts they seek to explain. Above all, he attempts to clarify the many different meanings that have been attached to such heavily worked educational terms as "freedom," "adjustment," "growth," "experience," "needs," and "knowledge."

We are now ready to consider the various branches of philosophy, particularly metaphysics, as they relate to education.

The Nature of Reality

Metaphysics is mainly the province of speculative philosophy. Its central concern is the nature of ultimate reality. Metaphysics seeks to answer

---

[1] Educational philosophy derives also from the experiences of education. See Chapter 11 on "Contemporary Theories."

such questions as these: Does the universe have a rational design or is it ultimately meaningless? Is what we call mind a reality of its own or merely a form of matter in motion? Is the behavior of all organisms causally determined, or do some organisms, such as men, possess a measure of freedom?

With the rise of science many people believed metaphysics to be outmoded. Scientific findings seemed trustworthy because they could be measured, whereas metaphysical notions seemed to be unverifiable and to have no practical application. Today, however, we recognize that metaphysics and science are two different activities, each valuable in its own right. Both seek to make general statements, but metaphysics deals with concepts whose instances cannot be measured, such as "reality," "change," "self," and "spirit." This does not mean that metaphysicians disregard science. On the contrary, science itself often gives rise to problems about the nature of reality that metaphysicians seek to resolve.

Science also rests on metaphysical assumptions. Many people do not realize this fact. In his *Adventure of Ideas* Alfred North Whitehead writes: "No science can be more secure than the unconscious metaphysics which tacitly it presupposes." The nuclear physicist Max Planck agrees:

> The scientific world picture gained by experience . . . remains always a mere approximation, a more or less well divided model. As there is a material object behind every sensation, so there is a metaphysical reality behind everything that human experience shows to be real. . . .[2]

Many of our greatest scientists, notably Albert Einstein, have felt compelled to formulate metaphysical conceptions *in consequence of* their scientific discoveries.

Certain philosophers, it is true, regard metaphysics as superfluous. They confine their attention to logic and the theory of knowledge. This position is defensible, but it is not widely held. Most philosophers maintain that theories of logic and knowledge inevitably are derived from metaphysical assumptions. There is, says Bertrand Russell, a "concealed metaphysic, usually unconscious in every writer on philosophy. Even if

[2] Max Planck, "The Meaning and Limits of Exact Science," *Science* (1949), 319-327. Cf. Everett W. Hall, "Metaphysics," in Dagobert D. Runes, Ed., *Living Schools of Philosophy*, Littlefield, Adams, Ames, Iowa, 1956, p. 130: "Metaphysics affects action not by giving control over nature, not by offering physical devices which can be used for various purposes, but by shaping views as to what nature is and how it can and ought to be controlled, by indicating appropriate ends. It does so through a theory of ethics, based in a theory of values which, in turn, is based in a set of views concerning the nature of existence and of knowledge."

his subject is metaphysics, he is almost certain to have an uncritically believed system which underlies his explicit arguments."[3]

In recent years metaphysics has regained much of its former standing. Science no doubt has brought great material progress, but even if all man's material wants were satisfied, he would not be completely at home in the world. By nature man is a metaphysical being, possessed by a desire to draw from the diverse realms of public knowledge and private experience some understanding of the *ultimate* nature of things.

Metaphysics and Education

In educational theory and practice metaphysics generates discussions of questions that lack scientific answers. For example, the metaphysical question whether human life has any purpose and, if so, what, is implicit in any study of biological evolution. If a student concludes from his study of evolution that the universe has no purpose, he may conclude that his life has meaning only as he personally puts meaning into it. In this case he must ask himself what goals in life he should pursue. Taking a metaphysical position will help him answer such questions.

Again, take the problem of the nature of mind. Teachers often say, "If Johnnie would keep his mind on his work, he would have no trouble at all in school." But what does the teacher mean here by "mind"? Is the mind different from the body? How are the two related? Is the mind the actual source of thoughts? Perhaps what we call "mind" is not an entity at all. Physiological and psychological studies of the brain have given us factual information and cyberneticians have compared the mind (or brain) to a computer. But such comparisons are crude; they do not satisfy our concern about the ultimate nature of the mind. Here again, knowing metaphysics and being able to think metaphysically helps the teacher when he is considering questions of ultimate meaning.

All teachers entertain notions about the nature of reality. They have views, however vague, about the nature of the universe, the destiny of man, the natural and the supernatural, permanence and change, and the ultimate purpose of things—matters that have concerned metaphysicians throughout the ages. Nothing, in fact, contributes more to continuous, patient, and careful reflection than the treatment of an educational problem in its metaphysical dimensions.

The number of metaphysical ideas is legion. For our purposes, how-

---

[3] Bertrand Russell, "Dewey's New Logic," in Paul Schilpp, Ed., *The Philosophy of John Dewey*, Northwestern University Press, Evanston, Ill., 1939, p. 138.

ever, they can be grouped according to certain "schools" of philosophic thought. The main schools, each with many subdivisions, are "idealism," "realism," and "pragmatism." If we consider what these schools have to say about the nature of reality and its relation to education, we shall be able to think more clearly about the question ourselves.

Before beginning our presentation, one word of caution: we are grouping philosophies into schools of thought for purposes of convenience, for ease of understanding. Philosophers also have to be studied separately and in their own right. Locke and Kant, for example, created systems that solved traditional philosophic problems afresh. Rousseau and Nietzsche were even more individualistic. And although both Kierkegaard and Sartre are existentialists, they differ in their views as much as they agree. After the student has studied philosophers in schools, he should go on to study them as individual thinkers.

Idealist Metaphysics and Education

The philosophic idealist claims that ultimate reality is spiritual in nature rather than physical, mental rather than material. When the ancient Eleatic philosopher Parmenides said, "What cannot be thought cannot be real," and when Schopenhauer proclaimed, "The world is my idea," they expressed the metaphysical outlook of idealism. The idealist does not deny the existence of the physical world around us—the world of houses, hills, stars, and cities with which our senses acquaint us. But he maintains that, real as these things are, they are not *ultimately* real. They are manifestations of a more fundamental incorporeal reality.

This reality may be either personal or impersonal. For the Christian idealist, ultimate reality is the God of three persons. It is not, as it is for Hegel, an impersonal Spirit. The Christian idealist agrees with other idealists in their conviction that man is a spiritual being who exercises free will and is personally responsible for his actions. Plato regards man's spirit as a "soul" emanating from an empyrean of perfect and external "ideas." Berkeley takes the orthodox Christian view that the soul is immortal, having been created by God to enjoy eternal life after probation on earth. According to Kant, man is both free and determined—free insofar as he is a spirit, determined to the extent that he is also a physical being subject to natural law. The Hegelian idealist regards man as a vital part of the Absolute—a spark, as it were, of an Eternal Spirit into which he is reabsorbed at death. Thus idealists agree that man is a spiritual being, but they disagree as to exactly how he is related to the ultimate spiritual reality from which he springs.

Idealists believe that the child is part of an ultimately spiritual universe and that he has a spiritual destiny to fulfill in accordance with his own potentialities. For this reason education must instill a closer intimacy between the child and the spiritual elements of nature; it must emphasize the innate harmony between man and the universe. When the child studies the natural world, he should not regard it as an enormous machine functioning soullessly and aimlessly. He should see the universe as possessing meaning and purpose.

The idealist teacher presides like Socrates over the birth of ideas, treated not as principles external to the student but as possibilities within him that need to be developed. The idealist teacher is also supposed to embody as fully as possible the finest characteristics of mankind and therefore to be worthy of emulation. With Socrates, Plato, and Kant he believes that knowledge is best "wrung out" of the student rather than "poured into" him. However, it is primarily *approved* subject matter that the teacher may "wring out," not usually the kind a student chooses for himself.

In view of prevailing skepticism about patriotism and love of country, we should note that many idealists uphold a philosophy of loyalty. Because in the long run the state is said to be a personality greater than any individual—a whole more important than any of its parts, the student should be taught to respect his country and the community into which he is born. He should study *sympathetically* the cultural foundations and ideals of his country and his community. His own freedom will grow only in proportion as he develops a sense of personal service to both community and nation.[4]

What, then, does education mean to the idealist? I know of no better definition than that of Herman H. Horne (1874-1946): "Education is the eternal process of superior adjustment of the physically and mentally developed, free, conscious, human being to God, as manifested in the intellectual, emotional, and volitional environment of man."[5]

Realist Metaphysics and Education

The basic principle of philosophic realism is that matter is the ultimate reality. Hills, trees, cities, and stars are not simply ideas in the minds

[4] Josiah Royce, *The Philosophy of Loyalty*, Macmillan, New York, 1908. Students interested in this particular phase of idealism would do well to study Royce's philosophy of loyalty. Royce insists that our allegiances should be not only local and national but also international.

[5] Herman H. Horne, *The Philosophy of Education*, Macmillan, New York, p. 285. Beginning p. 257 Horne analyzes the meaning of nearly every word in his definition. Especially valuable is his analysis of "freedom."

of observing individuals, or even in the mind of an Eternal Observer. They exist in and of themselves, independently of the mind. Although realists agree about the reality of matter, however, they disagree in some other respects and so may be divided into various subschools. Today the major groupings are "rational realism" on the one hand and "natural" or "scientific realism" on the other.

Rational Realism. This tradition may be divided into "classical realism" and "religious realism." The main form of religious realism is "scholasticism," the official philosophy of the Roman Catholic Church. Both schools bear the imprint of the Athenian philosopher Aristotle. But whereas rational realists look directly to Aristotle, the scholastics do so only indirectly, basing their philosophy on that of St. Thomas Aquinas. By harnessing the doctrines of Aristotle to the theology of the Church, Aquinas created a new Christian philosophy, later called "Thomism," in opposition to the modified Platonism espoused by most theologians of his time.

Classical and religious realists agree that the material world is real and exists outside the minds of those who observe it. Thomists, however, maintain that both matter and spirit have been created by God, Who constructed an orderly and rational universe out of His supreme wisdom and goodness. The fact that God created the universe is proof enough of its reality, for, say Thomists, anything divinely created must be real. Although not exactly more real than matter, spirit nevertheless is more important; it is a "higher" mode of being, because God himself is Spirit and He is perfect in every way. How do Thomists know all this? By revelation—from Biblical history, prophecy, and the teachings of Jesus Christ, which they affirm to be God's word for all mankind. But their knowledge, they state, is also attained by means other than faith; they get it from reason and experience, which are used not to contradict their faith but to support it. Thomists also declare that man is a fusion of the material and the spiritual, with body and soul forming one nature. We are free, they say, and responsible for our actions; but we are also immortal, having been placed on earth to love and honor our Creator and so earn immortal happiness.

Natural and Scientific Realism. This branch of philosophic realism accompanied the rise of science in Europe during the fifteenth and sixteenth centuries. Its leading spokesmen have been Francis Bacon, John Locke, David Hume, and John Stuart Mill. In this century they include Ralph Barton Perry, Alfred North Whitehead, and Bertrand Russell.

Skeptical and experimental in temper, natural realism maintains that philosophy should seek to imitate the rigor and objectivity of science. Since the world around us is real, it is the task of science rather than philosophy to investigate its properties; philosophy's function is to co-ordinate the concepts and findings of the different sciences. The most significant feature of the universe is that it is permanent and enduring. Change is real, but it takes place in accordance with permanent laws of nature, which give the universe a continuing structure. The world's permanence is the background against which changes occur and may be assessed. Natural realists either deny the existence of a spiritual realm or else maintain that its existence cannot be proved, so that it is of no importance philosophically.

Natural realists declare that man is a biological organism with a highly developed nervous system and an inherently social disposition. There is no need to suppose that his cultural achievements are due to a separate entity known as mind or soul. What we call "thought" is really a highly complex function of the organism that relates it to its environment —similar in kind, though not in degree, to such other functions as respiration, assimilation, and metabolism. Most scientific realists deny the existence of free will; they argue that the individual is determined by the impact of the physical and social environment on his genetic structure. What seems to be freedom of choice is really causal determinism.

Since in the realist view the world exists independently of man and is governed by laws over which we have little control, the school should transmit a central core of subject matter that will acquaint the pupil with the world around him. The Catholic realist adds that since the order and harmony of the universe are the result of Divine creation, we should study nature as God's handiwork. In his view the prime purpose of education is to prepare the individual person for life in the hereafter. For the classical realist the purpose of education is to enable the pupil to become an *intellectually* well-balanced person, as against one who is simply "well adjusted" to his physical and social environment. Individual spontaneity and creativity are prized, as they are in other philosophies, but the products of these elusive attributes are subject to greater scrutiny.

Pragmatist Metaphysics and Education

Although philosophic pragmatism is often regarded as an indigenous American philosophy, it is actually an outgrowth of the British empiricist tradition, which maintains that we can know only what our senses experience. In its theory of perpetual change, pragmatism looks back to Heraclitus, who lived before Socrates. The leading American pragmatists are Charles Sanders Peirce, William James, and John Dewey, all of whom differ in their methods and conclusions. Peirce's pragmatism is influenced by physics and mathematics, Dewey's by social science and biology. James's philosophy is personal, psychological, even religious. To a greater extent than realism or idealism, pragmatism has been influenced by conditions of the twentieth century. During the 1920s, for instance, it advocated individualism, while during the Depression it called for a greater social consciousness.

Pragmatism has been known by a variety of names, from "pragmaticism" (coined by Peirce) to "instrumentalism," "functionalism," and "experimentalism." In his later years, Dewey preferred "experimentalism" to "instrumentalism," partly because the latter sounded too materialistic. The principal themes of pragmatism are (1) the reality of change, (2) the essentially social and biological nature of man, (3) the relativity of values, and (4) the use of critical intelligence.

Pragmatists maintain that the world is neither dependent on nor independent of man's idea of it. Reality amounts to the "interaction" of the human being with his environment; it is the sum total of what we "experience." Man and his environment are "coordinate;" they are equally responsible for what is real.

The world has meaning only to the extent that man reads meaning into it. If the universe itself possesses some deeper purpose, it is hidden from man; and what man cannot experience cannot be real for him. Humanist in temper, pragmatism subscribes to the maxim that "man is the measure of all things." William James emphasizes the right of the educated individual to create his own reality, whereas Peirce and Dewey declare that the facts of reality are best established by experts, especially scientists.

The pragmatist believes that change is the essence of reality and that we must always be prepared to alter the way we do things. The ends and means of education must be flexible and open to continual revision. They must be pursued rationally and scientifically. Means are indigenous to their ends, and ends may derive from their means. Thus education itself is both an end and a means—an end in that it aims to improve man, and a means in that it is a way of doing so. Within education, discipline generally should not be opposed to the student's felt interests but should grow out of them.

The pragmatist maintains that since reality is created by a person's interaction with his environment, the child must study the world as it affects him. Just as the child cannot be considered apart from the environment in which he lives, so the school cannot be separated from life itself. Education *is* life and not a preparation for it. Formal subject matter should be linked wherever possible to the immediate problems that the child faces and that society is concerned to solve.

Unlike the realist and the idealist the pragmatist believes that human nature is fundamentally plastic and changeable. The pragmatist regards the child as an active organism, continually engaged in reconstructing and interpreting his own experiences. Because the child grows only by associating with others, he must learn to live in a community of individuals, to cooperate with them, and to adapt himself intelligently to social needs and aspirations.

The world view of pragmatism has certainly proved more congenial to American students than the philosophies of realism or idealism. Also pragmatist philosophy has animated most programs in teacher education. It is not hard to see why this should be so. American culture is pluralist and heterogenous. America has no national religion, no ancient monarchy, and little veneration of the past. A dynamic and skeptical society appreciates a philosophy of change rather than of permanence; a calling into question of all things; and a theory that man by nature is enterprising and exploratory. When William James said that pragmatism implied an open-ended universe—a universe "with the lid off"—his American audience was delighted, for this was the world that many of them believed they lived in. Just as the American frontier could be pushed west to the limitless Pacific, so the world seemed full of infinite possibilities. Ingenious, optimistic, experimental, this was the pragmatist temper, and it was the temper of the American people.

Conclusion

From this brief overview we can see that although philosophy as a whole does not provide us with final answers to the questions it asks, it does offer a range of different possible answers that enlarge our thoughts and assist us in making personal choices. As I shall show in the next chapter, learning means more than accumulating facts that have been scientifically established; it also means speculating and advancing beyond the limits of such findings.

What, then, is the kind of knowledge that philosophy aims to achieve? It is the kind that, as Bertrand Russell so well says, results from a "critical examination of the grounds of our convictions, prejudices, and beliefs." Questions that can be answered definitely belong mostly to science; other questions, speculative, prescriptive, and analytic, belong to philosophy. A study of the philosophy of education alerts us to the importance of these questions for the theory and practice of education. It enables us to examine philosophic questions for the light they throw on educational problems.

References

❖❖❖

The entire issue of the *Harvard Educational Review*, XXVI, 2 (Spring 1956), is devoted to the relationship between philosophy and education. It contains essays by philosophers of different schools. Two recent comprehensive anthologies are Thomas O. Buford, Ed., *Toward a Philosophy of Education* (Holt, Rinehart and Winston, 1969, 518 pp.), and Christopher J. Lucas, Ed., *What is Philosophy of Education?* (Macmillan, 1969, 313 pp.). Buford's text has a glossary and extensive biographical notes; Lucas' has an excellent introduction.

The best textbook treating metaphysical aspects of education is Samuel Shermis, *Philosophic Foundations of Education* (American Book Co., 1967, 292 pp.), chs. 1-4.

On the schools of philosophy I recommend the following monographs: J. Donald Butler, *Idealism in Education* (1966, 145 pp.); Ernest E. Bayles, *Pragmatism in Education* (1966, 145 pp.); and William Oliver Martin, *Realism in Education* (1969, 198 pp.), all published by Harper and Row. The classic text covering the entire field is John S. Brubacher, *Modern Philosophies of Education*, first published, 1939, now in its 4th edition (McGraw-Hill, 1969, 393 pp.).

Students majoring in educational philosophy will find a useful, well organized handbook in *Philosophy of Education: An Organization of Topics and Selected Sources* by Harry S. Broudy, Michael J. Parson, Ivan A. Snook, and Ronald D. Szoke (University of Illinois Press, Urbana, 1967, 287 pp.).

Students who desire to learn more about philosophy itself, and to have fun doing so, will enjoy C. E. M. Joad's *Philosophy* (Fawcett World Library, New York, 1962). Students with an interest in metaphysics will find much to challenge them in W. E. Kennick and M. Lazerowitz, *Metaphysics: Readings and Appraisals* (Prentice-Hall, 1966, 387 pp.).

211

10

Knowledge and Value

George F. Kneller

❖❖❖

In the previous chapter I argued that the theory and practice of education presuppose ideas about human nature and the nature of reality that are ultimately of a philosophical character. I pointed out that if the teacher is to do his life's work wisely and well, he must confront and debate and perhaps change the metaphysical assumptions by which his conduct is partly guided. To help the teacher do this, I considered some important metaphysical theses that have in fact influenced education. But education presupposes more than metaphysics; it also presupposes ideas about the nature of knowledge and the nature of what is valuable. To understand these ideas in their clearest and most general terms, we turn to philosophy.

Knowledge is the principle stock in trade of educators. A teacher is preoccupied chiefly with the intellectual development of his students. Even when he is concerned with their physical health and emotional well-being, he must base his judgments on reliable knowledge. It is therefore important for the teacher to think out for himself philosophically what knowledge ultimately amounts to.

The branch of philosophy that deals with knowledge is called "epistemology." The philosopher as epistemologist reflects on the nature of knowledge as such. What is there, he asks, that is common to all the different activities that are involved in knowing? What is the difference between knowing and, say, believing? What can we know beyond the information provided by the senses? What is the relation of the act of knowing to the thing that is known? How can we show that knowledge is "true"?

Unlike the scientist, the epistemologist is interested in concepts rather than facts. The task of the psychologist, for example, is to find out how people actually think and feel. The task of the epistemologist, on the other hand, is to consider what is meant by such psychological concepts as "feeling," "perception," "learning," and "reinforcement," and to judge whether the psychologist is applying them correctly. If the psychologist is not doing so, he is misdescribing the facts.

From the point of view of the teacher, one of the most important distinctions made in epistemology is that between the different types of knowledge. As an introduction to epistemology for education, we will consider what these types of knowledge are. We will then look more generally at the epistemologies proposed by the leading schools of philosophy.

Types of Knowledge

Revealed Knowledge. Simply put, revealed knowledge may be described as knowledge that God has disclosed to man. In His omniscience God inspired certain men to write down truths that He revealed to them, so that these truths might be known thereafter by all mankind. For Christians and Jews the word of God is contained in the Bible, for Mohammedans in the Koran, for Hindus in the Bhagavad-Gita and the Upanishads. Because it is the word of God, it is true forever. If it were not, God would be either ignorant or deceitful, which is to say that He would not be God. But although the truths recorded are supernatural, the language in which they are written is not. Hence religious scholars spend much time arguing over the precise meaning of words and expressions in the sacred texts. These arguments are not exercises in hairsplitting. For the religious believer the most important truths in the world lie in the words over which theologians argue. The essence of textual interpretation is to bring to light the eternal truths that are locked in these words.

Intuitive Knowledge. Revealed knowledge is God-given and external to man. Intuitive knowledge is knowledge that a person finds within himself in a moment of insight. Insight or intuition is the sudden eruption into consciousness of an idea or conclusion produced by a long process of unconscious work. All of a sudden we see the solution to a problem with which our unconscious has been at grips for days, months, or even years. It is this prior labor of the unconscious that gives the moment of insight its exhilaration and its seeming certainty. We feel sure of our insights just because, without being aware of it, we have worked so hard for them. We are exhilarated by them because the psychic energy, so long invested in the search for a solution, is released suddenly in the sheer pleasure of discovery. We are exhilarated, too, because this very discharge of energy gives us a sense of the fullness of our mental powers.

We must distinguish, however, between the act of intuition and intuitive knowledge proper. Some formative insight or illumination seems necessary to all great intellectual achievements. Philosophic theses, scientific theories, and works of art all seem to be generated out of some primary intuition, which is then elaborated and refined. But whatever its origins, a completed scientific theory is not a form of intuitive knowledge. It is logically consistent and is testable by observation or experimentation or both. When a scientific theory is proposed as a claim to knowledge, it is submitted not as a personal insight of its creator but as a publicly verifiable hypothesis.

What, then, is intuitive knowledge? It is knowledge that is proposed, and accepted, on the strength of the imaginative vision or private experience of the person proposing it. The truths embodied in works of art are a form of intuitive knowledge. All great writers—Homer, Shakespeare, Proust—tell us truths about the heart of man. We would not dream of testing these truths by observations or calculations or experiments, because these truths are not hypotheses. They are offered as insights, and we ourselves recognize them as true intuitively. Mystical writings, autobiographies, and essays of all kinds are reflections of intuitive knowledge.

We ourselves also possess a good deal of intuitive knowledge of our own, especially about people. It is knowledge that we have picked up from our experience of others and our experience of ourselves. We have reflected on it, certainly, but we have not submitted it to any systematic rational scrutiny or observational testing. We have not done so because we do not need to. It is a knowledge or awareness that we deepen, broaden, and correct in the course of our experience.

Rational Knowledge. This is knowledge that we obtain by the exercise of reason alone unaccompanied by observation of actual states of affairs. The principles of formal logic and pure mathematics are paradigms of rational knowledge. Their truth is demonstrable by abstract reasoning alone. Take the logical principle that two contradictory statements cannot both be true at once, that the statements "Fido is a dog" and "Fido is not a dog" cannot both be predicated of the same object at the same time. Or take the principle that if *A* is greater than *B* and *B* is greater than *C*, then *A* is greater than *C*; for example, if a Boeing 747 is bigger than a Flying Fortress, and a Flying Fortress is bigger than a Piper Cub, then a 747 is bigger than a Piper Cub. Both these principles can be illustrated by actual instances, but both are true independently of such instances. The principles of rational knowledge may be applied *to* sense experience, but they are not deduced *from* it. Unlike the truths of intuitive knowledge, they are valid regardless of our feelings about them and they are valid universally.

Rational knowledge is not without its limitations. It is fundamentally abstract and formal. It deals with logical relations and impersonal meanings and disregards emotional needs and actual states of affairs. Because we live emotionally among states of affairs, rational knowledge alone is hardly sufficient. We also need intuitive and empirical knowledge, and often we need them more. It is also open to debate how much rational knowledge actually is valid universally and how much merely seems so. All of us are to some extent culture-bound, and it may be that even the principles of formal logic are valid only for persons who use European languages and think in the mental categories that these languages embody. It has also been questioned whether rational knowledge ultimately rests on rational demonstration. According to one school of thought, for example, the principles of pure mathematics are grounded in a basic *intuition* of successiveness.

Empirical Knowledge. Especially important nowadays is empirical knowledge or knowledge that is confirmed by the evidence of the senses. By seeing, hearing, smelling, feeling, and tasting, we form our conception of the world around us. Knowledge, therefore, is composed of ideas formed in accordance with observed—or sensed—facts. Whereas the rationalist tells us to "think things through," the empiricist advises us to "look and see."

The paradigm of empirical knowledge is modern science. Scientific hypotheses are tested by observation or by experiments to find which hypothesis accounts most satisfactorily for a certain set of phenomena. Nevertheless, a hypothesis is never proved or disproved absolutely. It is only shown to be more or less "probable." Empirical probability may come close at times to certainty but can never actually attain it. The reason for this is that we can never be certain that the future will resemble the past, and hence we can never be absolutely sure that phenomena that have behaved in certain ways hitherto will behave in exactly those ways hereafter.

It should also be pointed out that our senses may at times deceive us, as when a stick that is really straight looks bent in water. As Socrates asked just before he drank the hemlock, "Have our senses truth in them? Are they not . . . inaccurate witnesses?" Moreover, our senses are conditioned by our preconceptions. We tend to perceive what it is within our power to conceive. Thus we perceive space as a permanent background within which unique events occur sequentially in time. This apprehension of space and time is almost certainly a phenomenon of our culture at a certain stage of its development.

Authoritative Knowledge. We accept a good deal of knowledge as true not because we have checked it out ourselves but because it is vouched for by authorities in the field. I accept without question that Canberra is the capital of Australia, that light travels at 186,281 miles per second, and that the Battle of Waterloo took place in 1815. I feel no need to verify these facts, any more than I feel the need to work out for myself the table of logarithms. I take them for granted because I find them in encyclopedias and other works written by experts. I take the experts in turn at their word because I wish to preserve my psychic energy for personal projects that utilize or go beyond established facts. The world is too large a place for me to verify personally all that occurs in it.

What knowledge I take for granted depends on my needs and interests. If I want to know, as items of information, what Cubism is or what Newton's laws of motion are, I look up Cubism and Newton in an encyclopedia. But if information is all I am looking for, information is all I get. If I wish to *understand* Cubism or Newtonian mechanics, I must work out the principles of these things for myself. Needless to say, I do not reinvent Cubism or mechanics, but I think through the principles on which they are based until I see the "point" of them. I understand Cubism when I see the artistic objectives that the Cubists set themselves and the means they used to attain them. I understand Newton's laws of motion when I see the reasoning on which they are based, the conclusions to which they lead, and the evidence massed in their favor.

What I take for granted, however, is already knowledge. Newton's laws of motion have been confirmed scientifically; they are empirical knowledge. Thus the term "authoritative knowledge" is more psychological than epistemological in import. It denotes not the nature of those things that I know but the manner of my knowing them. It refers not to those cultural products we call knowledge as such but to the way in which I appropriate these products. "Authoritative knowledge" is established knowledge that I accept on someone's authority.

So far we have considered some of the different categories of what passes for knowledge. Let us now take a broader view and inquire what the leading schools of philosophy have said about knowledge in general and its relation to education.

Idealist Epistemology and Education

Within the idealist tradition different philosophers have produced different theories of knowledge. Plato, in agreement with Socrates, maintained that knowledge acquired through the senses must always remain uncertain and incomplete, since the material world is only a distorted copy of a more perfect sphere of being. True knowledge is the product of reason alone, for reason is the faculty that discerns the pure spiritual forms of things beyond their material embodiments.

Hegel elaborated the platonic concept that knowledge is valid only insofar as it forms a system. Since ultimate reality is rational and systematic, our knowledge of reality is true to the extent that it, too, is systematic. The more comprehensive the system of our knowledge and the more consistent the ideas it embraces, the more truth it may be said to possess. This principle usually is referred to as the "coherence theory" of truth. It is based on the view that a particular item of knowledge becomes significant to the extent that it is seen in its total context. Hence all ideas and theories must be validated according to their "coherence" within a continuously developing system of knowledge.

Following Kant, most modern idealists maintain that the essence of knowing is the imposition of meaning and order on information gathered by the senses. The purpose of teaching is not so much to present the student with a mass of information as to help him to impose order and meaning on it. Some idealists, known as "personalists," also maintain that the student should relate this information to his own previous experiences so that what he learns is significant to him personally.

Realist Epistemology and Education

The realist rejects the Kantian view that the mind imposes its own categories, such as "substantiality" and "causality," on the data of the senses. On the contrary, says the realist, the world we perceive is not a world that we have recreated mentally but the world as it is. Substantiality, causality, and the order of nature are not a projection of the mind but are features of things themselves. Admittedly, natural science yields a different picture of the world than everyday experience. The sturdy table on which I write these words is, for the physicist, a collection of invisible particles. But from this it follows only that with different instruments different aspects of the world are observed, not that these aspects are appearances synthesized by the observer himself.

For the realist, then, an idea or proposition is true when it "corresponds" with those features of the world that it purports to describe. A hypothesis about the world is not true simply because it "coheres" with knowledge. If new knowledge coheres with old, it is because the old is true, that is, it is because the old knowledge *corresponds* to what is the case. Coherence then does not create truth. It is rather that, when two or more theories about related features of the world correspond to the features they describe, they will naturally support one another.

True knowledge, then, is knowledge that corresponds to the world as it is. In the course of time the human race has put together a stock of knowledge whose truth has repeatedly been confirmed. To impart a selection of this knowledge to the growing person is the school's most important task. The initiative in education, therefore, lies with the teacher as transmitter of the cultural heritage. It is the teacher, not the student, who must decide what subject matter should be studied in class. If this subject matter can be made to satisfy the student's personal needs and interests, so much the better. But satisfying the student personally is far less important than imparting the right subject matter. To instruct the student in the knowledge that matters most is the true end of education; satisfying the student is only a means to this end, a useful teaching strategy.

Pragmatist Epistemology and Education

Pragmatists believe the mind to be active and exploratory rather than passive and receptive. The mind does not confront a world that is separate and apart from it. Rather, the known world is formed in part by the mind that knows it. Truth does not lie solely in the correspondence of human ideas to an external reality, because reality for man depends in part on the ideas by which he explains it. Knowledge is produced by a "transaction" between man and his environment, and truth is a property of knowledge. What then does truth amount to?

Pragmatists have been charged with claiming that an idea is true if it "works." The charge applies, if at all, only to William James, who maintained that an idea is true if it has favorable consequences for the person who holds it. Other pragmatists, such as Peirce and Dewey, insist that an idea is true only if it has satisfactory consequences *when objectively and if possible scientifically tested.* For the typical pragmatist, then, the truth of an idea depends on the consequences that are observed objectively when the idea is put into operation.

Pragmatists also maintain that the "method of intelligence" is the ideal way to acquire knowledge. We grasp things best, they say, by locating and solving problems. Faced with a problem, the intelligence proposes hypotheses to deal with it. The hypothesis that solves the problem most successfully is the hypothesis that explains the facts of the problem. It is what Dewey calls a "warranted assertion," a claim to knowledge that has been confirmed objectively and operationally and may serve as a basis for generating further hypotheses for further problems.

According to the pragmatist, the teacher should construct learning situations around patricular problems whose solution will lead his pupils to a better understanding of their social and physical environment. Instead of following the traditional structure of subject matter, both teacher and class should draw on whatever knowledge proves useful in solving the particular problem with which they are engaged, such as "transportation through the ages," "contemporary sexual mores," or "life in an Indian village." The same procedure should be followed in learning the skills of reading, writing, and arithmetic. All subjects, says the pragmatist, become more meaningful to the student and so more easily mastered when the student can use them as means for satisfying needs and interests of his own.

According to the pragmatist, a young person is a natural learner because he is naturally curious. He will learn most from whatever he feels stimulated to explore and think about. The teacher should foster this spirit of inquiry. Instead of instructing the student in subject matter prescribed for him by others, the teacher should encourage the student (a) to learn what he feels curious about and (b) to feel a curiosity about subjects that matter such as science, literature, and history. Precept (b) is important, because the teacher would be irresponsible if he encouraged the student to pursue his every whim and fancy. The point for the pragmatist is that the child should learn from curiosity, while the teacher should stimulate curiosity about subjects that will fully reward it.

Values and Education

Values abound everywhere in education; they are involved in every aspect of school practice; they are basic to all matters of choice and decision-making. Using values, teachers evaluate students and students evaluate teachers. Society evaluates courses of study, school programs, and teaching competence; and society itself is evaluated by educators. When we pass judgment on educational practices, when we estimate the worth of an education policy, what kind of values do we employ?

The general study of values is known as "axiology." It concerns itself with three main questions: (1) whether values are subjective or objective, that is, personal or impersonal; (2) whether values are changing or constant; and (3) whether there are hierarchies of value. Let us examine these issues briefly.

1. To say that there are objective values is to claim that there are values that exist in their own right regardless of human preferences. Such values as goodness, truth, and beauty are cosmic realities; they are part of the nature of things. Certain things are objectively true. Certain actions and certain qualities are inherently good. Certain things are beautiful in themselves. Education has an objective value; it is worthwhile in itself.

To maintain that values are subjective is to claim that they reflect personal preferences. To be valuable is to be valued by someone. Whatever is valuable is so not in itself but because we happen to value it. To say that education is valuable, for example, is to say that one values education oneself or that some people value education. It is not to claim that education is worthwhile regardless of whether anyone thinks so.

2. Some people argue that there are values that are absolute and eternal. These values are as valid today as they were in the past, and they are valid for everyone regardless of race or class. Charity, it is sometimes argued, is a good for all men everywhere at all times. Other people maintain that all values are relative to men's desires. As our desires change, so do the values that express them. Desires, and so values, change in response to new historical conditions, new religions, new findings in science, new developments in technology, advances in education, and so forth. These values may be arrived at empirically and tested publicly; they may be the creation of the rational mind; or they may be the result of strong belief. We may ask, for example, whether grading is valuable. We cannot say absolutely yes or no. It may or may not be, depending on the persons involved, the purposes it serves, the way it is handled, and the results it produces. How would we know? Chiefly by applying standards or criteria that educated men accept. Paradoxically, however, such standards are closely linked to absolute values, or at least to values that are more or less permanent. For how can we know the extent to which our values change if we do not have something permanent against which to assess the change?

As a rule, young people prefer to keep their values personal and relative. In the way they prize things they want to remain flexible and openminded. Indeed, the very thought of having anything absolute disturbs them profoundly . . . except, perhaps, when it comes to absolutes they may desire, such as freedom, love, peace, justice, and human understanding.

3. Just what attitude the thoughtful person takes to values depends on his general philosophy. As I shall show, the philosophic idealist maintains that there is a fixed hierarchy of values in which spiritual values are higher than material ones. The idealist ranks religious values high because, he says, they help us realize our ultimate goal, unity with the spiritual order. The philosophic realist also believes in a hierarchy of values, but he ranks rational and empirical values high because they help us adjust to objective reality, the laws of nature, and the rules of logic. The philosophic pragmatist denies that there is a fixed hierarchy of values. For him one activity is likely to be as good as another if it satisfies an urgent need and possesses instrumental value. He is sensitive to the values that society prizes, but he believes that it is more important to test values empirically than to contemplate them rationally. He believes so because he thinks that all particular values are merely instruments for the attainment of better values.

It is desirable to study values scientifically as well as philosophically. If, for example, we can show that Americans prize the same values as do other people elsewhere, we shall have come a long way toward establishing foundations on which international understanding can be built. Elaborate classifications have been made of what men *in fact* value highly as contrasted with what they *say* they value. The results are startling and should be studied by every educator. The findings of the social scientist provide both educator and philosopher with facts for deep reflection.[1]

1 For example, in 1969 Louis Harris & Associates surveyed a cross section of four thousand Americans on a wide range of attitudes and values. The poll revealed a continued preference for basic values, although the Puritan ethic of hard work and personal success did not rank as highly as might have been expected, coming below a desire for greater tranquility and more leisure time. Given a choice between making more money and getting more time off, only forty-five percent opted for the money. In short, we do not appear to be as compulsively dissatisfied and materialistic as we are often accused of being. Sixty percent of teen-agers and seventy-five percent of adults opposed pre-marital sex. Seventy-five percent of people considered the use of marijuana to be a "very serious" problem. There were, however, big differences between adults and young people and between whites and blacks, which suggests that many of the nation's values will change "dramatically" in the next decade, when present teen-agers become adults, when the number of blacks increases (from eleven

Ethics and Education

Education is widely regarded as a moral enterprise. Teachers are always drawing attention to what ought to be said and done and how students ought to behave. They are concerned with imparting moral values and improving individual and social behavior.

What kind of moral behavior should a teacher advocate in his classes? Should he seek to promote the behavior that he values or the behavior valued by his community? Should he encourage the growth of certain character traits that he believes are desirable or should he let the child's character form itself in response to the expectation of the classroom peer group? One's answers to these questions will depend on one's ethical attitudes. Any teacher who takes his vocation seriously must seek to answer the questions and justify his attitudes. He will be assisted in doing so by a formal study of ethics.

Ethics is the study of values in the realm of human conduct. It deals with such questions as: What is the good life for all men? How ought we to behave? It is concerned with providing "right" values as the basis for "right" actions. At one time ethical systems were linked to religions. Today, however, the ethical systems of the Western world, although largely derived from religious teachings, are usually justified on other grounds. As we have seen in the chapter on religion, the United States has separated church and state and as a result religious teaching has been banned in American public schools. But this ban in turn has stimulated a desire to substitute some kind of moral training.

Two types of ethical theory are important here: "intuitionism" and "naturalism." Intuitionists assert that moral values are apprehended by the individual directly. We grasp the rightness or wrongness of something by means of an inborn moral sense. The moral values we apprehend in this way are right in themselves. Their rightness cannot be proved logically or tested empically; it can only be intuited.

Naturalists maintain that moral values should be determined by careful studies of the ascertainable consequences to which they give rise. For example, if one believes that premarital sexual relations are morally wrong, one should do so not because of ethical judgments already made on the subject but as a consequence of personal observation or scientific studies of the effects of such relations. A person who accepts the naturalistic interpretation of ethics chooses or justifies moral values according

percent of the population to an estimated seventeen percent), and when the college-educated will form forty-five percent of the population instead of the present thirty percent.

to what scientific investigations reveal about right and wrong behavior and what *examined* life experiences suggest is the best way for human beings to conduct themselves. In brief, the naturalist maintains that moral values should be founded on an objective examination of the practical consequences of any act of human conduct.

Can moral values be taught in the same sense that factual knowledge is taught? Socrates sought to answer this question. Assuming that moral virtues were latent in each individual, he maintained that the teacher could bring these values into the student's consciousness. Virtue, we may say, can be taught, if by teaching virtue we mean helping students become aware of it. But will the student act on what he has learned? We all recognize that a student can hardly be said to have really learned something unless he is able to act on it.[2] Here then is the rub. If by teaching and learning we mean simply imparting and acquiring knowledge of what morals are, then values are teachable. Teachers can also test students to find out how much they know about moral values and can assist them in choosing between alternative courses of action. But no teacher can guarantee, even after performing his task assiduously, doing all he can to get a student to know what ethical values are, and helping him to choose certain values for his own life, that a student will not cheat on a test. The most a teacher can expect is that the student (a) *knows* what is right and what is wrong, (b) knows *why* it is so, and (c) has some idea of what he *ought* to do about what he knows. If, in addition, the student actually engages in right conduct, the teacher will have been more than amply rewarded for his efforts.[3]

Aesthetics and Education

Aesthetics is the study of values in the realm of beauty. Aesthetic values usually are difficult to assess because they are likely to be personal and subjective. A particular work of art evokes varying responses from different people. *De gustibus non disputandum est.* Who is to say which response is the more appropriate?

Who, indeed, unless we believe that there are objective aesthetic

[2] Socrates also thought that, assuming that the teacher himself were virtuous, then the more virtue were taught to the student, the more virtue the student would practice. I would reply: The more the virtuous teacher presides over the *practice* of virtue, the more virtue the student will practice.

[3] I discuss these ideas in my treatment of the concept of teaching in the chapter on analysis.

values, in which case we may choose to rely on the decision of experts as to what is good art. We may judge beauty by using criteria said to be authoritative, and may claim that any work of art that scores low on these criteria will have a hard time finding its place in history. Objective criteria are useful to the novice, and they serve as enduring standards of criticism. Textbooks in literature, art, and music rely on these standards when informing students on matters involving assessment and appreciation. The fact, however, that authoritative critics may differ widely when assessing a work of art brings us back to our previous question: Who is to say which response is truly appropriate? Unfortunately we cannot look to science for answers to this question. Scientific knowledge is largely irrelevant to the judgment of a work of art.

Through the centuries an important question discussed in aesthetics has been this: Should art be representative, or should it be the product of the creator's imagination? According to the first view, art should faithfully reflect life and human experience. We should clearly recognize the autumnal scene or fading sunset depicted in a landscape painting. We should be delighted by a still life of a bowl of flowers, each flower etched so well, its petals so lifelike, that we feel impelled to reach out and touch them! According to the second view, the artist expresses himself spontaneously about any aspect of life that interests him. "A picture," said Degas, "must never be a copy . . . . The air we see in the paintings of the old masters is never the air we breathe." The artist is on his own. He creates out of his personal drives and experiences. He expresses his feelings about the beauty or ugliness of the world and, perhaps, shows what he thinks the world should be. In this view, the creator enjoys limitless freedom to use his medium in a way that fulfills the creative urge within him.

In both views, questions arise as to the proper subject matter and scope of art. Some people maintain that if art is an expression of life, it should deal with *all* of life: the ugly, the aberrant, the grotesque, and the unique. Others believe that art should perform a social function. The artist should speak to all the men of his time, not to a tiny clique now or hereafter. Still others are skeptical of the so-called social responsibility of the artist. Society changes. An artist born in one generation may be creating for the next. Shall he be condemned for failing to please his contemporaries? An artist who has pleased his critics is probably at the end of his inventive powers, for critics tend to judge in accordance with accepted standards. Indeed, the artist rejected by the critics may well be the true innovator.

Teaching, too, is an art; it has its own aesthetic dimensions. The good teacher, we say, is an artist at his work. Just what this means will be revealed in Chapter 14, "The Aesthetic Component." In the meantime, I must fulfill my promise to discuss theories of value and ethics by outlining the various points of view taken by the three philosophic schools.

Idealist Values and Education

For the idealist, values and ethics are absolute. The good, the true, and the beautiful do not change fundamentally from generation to generation, or from society to society. In their essence they remain constant. They are not man-made but are part of the very nature of the universe.

The student, says the idealist, should be taught enduring values and how to live by them, for they put him in harmony with the greater spiritual whole to which he belongs. He should realize that evil offends not merely himself, or society, or even mankind as a whole, but the very soul of the universe. His values become significant only to the extent that they relate to the ultimately spiritual order of the universe, an order that the teacher can illuminate for the student.

Evil, says the idealist, is incomplete good rather than a positive thing in itself. It results from the disorganization and lack of system still present in the universe. As the Spirit present in the universe expresses itself more and more fully, the world will become more rational and less imperfect, and evil will gradually disappear. In any school system there are, for the idealist teacher, no really bad children, but only those who have strayed away from, or do not fully comprehend, the fundamental moral order of the universe.[4]

Plato maintained that the good life is possible only within a good society. In *The Republic*, he describes an ideal society ruled by a highly virtuous elite of philosopher-kings. Hegel declared that the individual derives his understanding and practice of virtue from the virtuous state of which he is a part. Kant's ideal community consisted of men who treated one another as ends rather than means. His famous "categorical imperative" states that we should always act as though our individual actions were to become a universal law of nature, binding on all men in similar circumstances.

---

[4] The same is true of ugliness, which, says the idealist, is beauty incomplete or disorganized. Cf. J. Donald Butler, *Four Philosophies and Their Practice in Education and Religion*, Harper, New York, 1957, pp. 534 ff. As a religious idealist, Butler asks, "Since the One who alone . . . has ultimate being, is good, how can evil have ultimate being?"

Assuming that no one would wish to see his own wrongdoing universalized, we should expect anyone following Kant's maxim always to refrain from doing evil. When a pupil misbehaves, the teacher would ask him what would happen if *everyone* behaved in this way. Is he setting a good example for his classmates to follow? (The teacher might also ask himself whether *he* is a good example for his students to follow!) Infractions of discipline are conceived as expressions of selfishness, to be punished in accordance with the moral principles that have been incorporated in the common culture over time. In the idealist view these principles are generally rooted in religion or at least in a view that life is eternal. In this respect here is a beautiful passage by Herman H. Horne, reflecting as well as any passage I know the prevailing mood of idealism:

> No man is ever all he can be . . . . His purposes are not ended with his life, nor does he live in a spent world . . . . Age does not wither, nor custom stale, the philosopher's love of truth, the artist's love of beauty, or the saint's love of virtue . . . . There is always more to know, and to love, and to do . . . . Man does not limit his will to know, to enjoy, to achieve, to his life's unknown term of years. His plans bridge the chasm of death; they call for unending time . . . .[5]

Realist Values and Education

Realists agree with idealists that fundamental values are basically permanent, but they differ among themselves in their reasons for thinking so. Classical realists agree with Aristotle that there is a universal moral law, available to reason, that is binding on all of us as rational beings. Christian religious realists agree that we can understand much of this moral law by using reason, but they insist that the law has been established by God, Who has endowed us with the rational faculty to apprehend it. We may be able to understand the moral law without divine aid, but because our nature has been corrupted by Original Sin, we cannot practice it without the help of God. Scientific realists deny that values have any supernatural sanction. Good is that which accommodates us to our environment, evil that which estranges us. Because both human nature and physical nature are constant, the values that accommodate the one to the other are constant also. It is true that social institutions and practices vary considerably in various parts of the world, but basic values remain the same. Whereas idealists hold man to be perfectible, scientific realists accept him as he is, imperfect.

---

[5] Herman H. Horne, *The Philosophy of Education*, Macmillan, New York, 1927, p. 278.

Realists agree that teachers should impart certain well-defined values. The basic moral and aesthetic standards that we teach the child should not be affected by temporary issues. The child should understand clearly the nature of right and wrong, respecting what is objectively good and beautiful regardless of changes in moral and aesthetic fashion.

Classical realists insist that despite concentration on subject matter, schools should produce individuals who are well-rounded, in the Aristotelian sense of being moderate and temperate in all things. The child should be taught to live by absolute and universal moral standards, because what is right is right for man in general and not simply for the members of a particular race or society. It is important for children to acquire good habits, for virtue does not come automatically to man but has to be learned.

Christian religious realists declare that naturalistic ethics are inadequate, for man has been created to transcend the natural and attain the supernatural. The true purpose of moral education is the salvation of souls. The child should be taught to keep his soul in a state of grace, that is, filled with Divine Grace and free from mortal sin. He should seek good and avoid evil, not only because reason prescribes this but also because it is God's will that he should.

The Christian religious realist trains man's will as well as his intellect. Although God offers salvation, the individual must decide whether to accept or reject it. The will should therefore be "habituated" to making the right choices. Because human nature has been corrupted by Original Sin, education has an essentially corrective role to play. Firm discipline is needed to eliminate bad habits and cultivate good ones. But reason is not sovereign. Indeed, a complete understanding of the nature of things lies beyond the power of reason, and we must depend on faith to carry us through. Reason should support faith, for God has given it to us so that we may come to know Him better.

The scientific realist teaches that right and wrong come from our understanding of nature and not from religious principles. Morality should be based on what scientific investigation has shown to be beneficial to man as the highest species of animal. Disease is evil and health is good. We must promote the good by taking measures to improve our genetic constitution and overcome evil by improving the environment in which we live.[6]

---

6 Many scientific realists are also religiously minded. If so, they treat religion and science as two different aspects of truth. Not necessarily in conflict with one another, religion and science lead to a greater understanding of the ultimate mystery

I close this sketch of realist values by asking, with realist Harry S. Broudy, "How can life be both subjectively and objectively good?" The answer, he says, is "self-cultivation"—cultivation of the individual's capacity to achieve enduring values in both intellectual and moral realms of experience:

> For education, this has always meant the appropriation by the individual of the best and noblest of the cultural resources of his time. It has meant becoming a connoisseur in every area of human life, so that the individual not only lives but lives well . . . . [But] there is a sense in which problems and answers are neither old nor new; it is the sense in which they are timeless structures revealed in a timeless insight into the form of universal truths.[7]

Pragmatist Values and Education

For the pragmatist, values are relative. Ethical and moral canons are not permanent but must alter as cultures and societies change. This is not to claim that moral values should fluctuate from month to month. It is to say that no particular precept should be regarded as universally binding irrespective of the circumstances in which it is exercised. "Thou shalt not kill" is not an absolute principle; on occasion it may be right to kill, in order to defend oneself, for example, or to save the life of another. The child should learn how to make difficult moral decisions not by recourse to rigidly prescribed principles but by deciding which course of action is likely to produce the best results for human beings.

Pragmatists urge us to test the worth of our values in the same way that we test the truth of our ideas. We should consider the problems of human affairs impartially and scientifically and choose the values that seem most likely to resolve them. These values should not be imposed on us by a higher authority. They should be agreed on after open, informed discussion, based on objective evidence.

The more complex a society becomes, the greater the demands it makes on the individual. But the pragmatist rejects any concept of individualism that leads to social exploitation and also any social arrangement that submerges the individuality of the person. Dewey calls the blending of

of the universe: "The heavens declare the glory of God and the firmament showeth His handiwork."

[7] Harry S. Broudy, "New Problems and Old Solutions," The Kansas State College, Emporia, *Studies in Contemporary Educational Thought,* **XL,** 11 (November 1960), 20-24.

individual thought and group sanction a "critical engagement." The utopian community he envisions is built by people who have the courage to think independently and yet relate themselves to the group.

"My belief in the Absolute," wrote William James, "must run the gauntlet of my other beliefs." It "clashes with other truths of mine whose benefits I hate to give up on its account." Such is the moral attitude of the pragmatist, whose doctrine, says James, "unstiffens our theories," and, if anything, "widens the search for God." What, then, is the moral ground of the pragmatist? Let William James describe his doctrine in his own inimitable way:

> She [pragmatism] has in fact no prejudices whatever, no obstructive dogmas, no rigid canons of what shall count as proof. She is completely genial. She will entertain any hypothesis, she will consider any evidence . . . . Her only test of probable truth is what works best . . . what fits every part of life best, and what combines with the collectivity of experience's demands, nothing being omitted . . . . You see how democratic she is. Her manners are as various and flexible, her resources as rich and endless, and her conclusions as friendly as those of mother nature.[8]

These last two chapters have given us some idea of philosophy's contribution to education. This contribution will be spelled out in greater detail in the next chapter on theories of education, where the views of educators themselves are examined. Although these theories are related to the philosophic themes we have discussed, they deal with issues specific to the actual practice of education.

---

[8] William James, *Pragmatism,* Longmans, Green, New York, 1907, pp. 80-81.

References

❖❖

On general epistemology I recommend three works: Roderick Chisholm, *Theory of Knowledge* (Prentice-Hall, 1966, 117 pp.); Michael Polanyi, *Personal Knowledge* (University of Chicago Press, 1958, 428 pp.); and John V. Canfield and Franklin H. Donnell, Ed., *Readings in the Theory of Knowledge* (Appleton-Century-Crofts, 1964, 520 pp.).

There are few comprehensive treatments of the significance for education of philosophic theories of knowledge. The most helpful discussion of the subject is probably Philip G. Smith, *Philosophy of Education: An Introduction* (Harper and Row, 1965, 276 pp.), ch. 4. (Ch. 7 on values is also good.) A useful book of readings is Donald Vandenburg, Ed., *Theory of Knowledge and Problems of Education* (University of Illinois Press, 1969, 302 pp.). On criteria for "true" knowledge from the analytic point of view, see Israel Scheffler, *Conditions of Knowledge: An Introduction to Epistemology and Education* (Scott, Foresman, 1965, 117 pp.).

On values and ethics, see William K. Frankena, *Ethics* (Prentice-Hall, 1963, 109 pp.) and A. Oldenquist, Ed., *Readings in Moral Philosophy* (Houghton, Mifflin, 1965, 364 pp.). My favorite is Jacob Bronowski's well written *Science and Human Values* (Harper, 1965, 119 pp.).

On values in relation to education, see R. S. Peters, *Ethics and Education* (Scott, Foresman, 1967, 235 pp.); John Wilson et al., *Introduction to Moral Education* (Penguin, 1967, 463 pp.); John Martin Rich, *Education and Human Values* (Addison-Wesley, 1968, 163 pp.); and three anthologies: Theodore Brameld and Stanley Elam, Eds., *Values in American Education: An Interdisciplinary Approach* (Phi Delta Kappa, Bloomington, Indiana, 1964, 180 pp.); Michael Belok et al., Eds., *Approaches to Values in Education* (Wm. C. Brown, Dubuque, Iowa, 1966, 322 pp.); and Philip G. Smith, Ed., *Value Theory and Education* (University of Illinois Press, 1970). In Donald Arnstine's *Philosophy of Education: Learning and Schooling* (Harper and Row, 1967, 388 pp.) chs. 6, 7, and 8 are especially good on aesthetics and curiosity.

11

Contemporary Educational Theories

George F. Kneller

❖❖❖

The word "theory" has two central meanings. It can refer to a hypothesis or set of hypotheses that have been verified by observation or experiment, as in the case of the theory of gravitation. It can also be a general synonym for systematic thinking or a set of coherent thoughts. As regards theory in the first sense, education awaits development, and we shall discuss what there is of it in Part Four. As regards theory in the second sense, education has harvested a veritable cornucopia.

In this chapter I shall explore four educational theories that lead or have led to programs of reform. Although these theories tend to flow from formal philosophies, they take on a special character because they are conditioned largely by experiences unique to education. Two other modes of thinking about education—existentialism and analysis—I will leave for separate treatment.

In this country the first educational theory to excite widespread attention was that of "Progressivism." The progressive movement, to be analyzed presently, burst upon the educational scene with revolutionary force. It called for the replacement of time-honored practices by a new kind of education based on social change and the findings of the behavioral sciences. The very force of the progressive movement and the publicity that it received paved the way for a counterrevolution. A revived conservatism decried the excesses for the progressivists, at the same time accepting some of their more moderate doctrines. This movement was known as "Perennialism." I will discuss it now because its fundamental themes antedated those of progressivism.

Perennialism

Against the progressive emphasis on change and novelty, perennialists call for allegiance to absolute principles. Despite momentous social upheavals, permanence, they say, is more real than change. It is also more desirable as an ideal. In a world of increasing precariousness and uncertainty nothing can be more beneficial than steadfastness of educational purpose and stability in educational behavior.[1] The basic principles of perennialism may be outlined in six categories.

1. *Despite differing environments, human nature remains the same everywhere; hence, education should be the same for everyone.* "The function of a citizen or a subject," writes Robert M. Hutchins,

> . . . may vary from society to society . . . . But the function of a man, as a man, is the same in every age and in every society, since it results from his nature as a man. The aim of an educational system is the same in every age and in every society where such a system can exist: it is to improve man as man.[2]

Or, in Mortimer Adler's words,

> If man is a rational animal, constant in nature throughout history, then there must be certain constant features in every sound educational program, regardless of culture or epoch.[3]

Knowledge, too, is everywhere the same. If it were not, learned men

[1] Perennialism's philosophic foundations are embedded in classical realism; the philosophers most quoted are Aristotle and Aquinas. Among its leading spokesmen are Robert Maynard Hutchins, Mortimer J. Adler, and Sir Richard Livingstone, an English classicist who has won an appreciable following in the United States. Although perennialist ideas are in practice nearly everywhere, they have been applied most consistently at St. John's College, Annapolis, Maryland.

[2] Robert Maynard Hutchins, *The Conflict in Education*, Harper, New York, 1953, p. 68.

[3] Mortimer J. Adler, "The Crisis in Contemporary Education," *The Social Frontier*, V, 141-144 (February 1939).

could never agree on anything. Opinion, of course, is different; here men may disagree. (But when they do agree, opinion becomes knowledge.) Admittedly, the acquisition of knowledge is not easy and some children are apt to resist it. Admittedly, too, some children take longer to learn than others. But this only means that we must spend more time with them. Are we not, asks the perennialist, fostering a false notion of equality when we promote children on the basis of age rather than intellectual attainment? Is it not likely that they will gain greater self-respect from knowing that they have *earned* promotion by passing the same tests as those given to other children of their age?

2. *Since rationality is man's highest attribute, he must use it to direct his instinctual nature in accordance with deliberately chosen ends.* Men are free, but they must learn to cultivate reason and control their appetites. When a child fails to learn, teachers should not be quick to place the blame on an unhappy environment or an unfortunate psychological train of events. Rather, the teacher's job is to overcome these handicaps through an essentially intellectual approach to learning that will be the same for all his pupils. Nor should teachers become permissive on the grounds that only thus may a child relieve his tensions and express his true self. No child should be permitted to determine his own educational experience, for what he wants may not be what he should have.

3. *It is education's task to impart knowledge of eternal truth.* In Hutchins' celebrated deduction,

> Education implies teaching. Teaching implies knowledge. Knowledge is truth. The truth is everywhere the same. Hence, education should be everywhere the same.[4]

Education should seek to adjust the individual not to the world as such but to what is true. Adjustment to truth is the end of learning.

4. *Education is not an imitation of life but a preparation for it.* The school can never be a "real-life situation." Nor should it be; it remains for the child an artificial arrangement in which he becomes acquainted with the finest achievements of his cultural heritage. His task is to realize the values of this heritage and, where possible, add to its achievements through his own endeavors.

5. *The student should be taught certain basic subjects that will acquaint him with the world's permanencies.* He should not be hustled into studies that seem important at the time. Nor should he be allowed

---

[4] Robert Maynard Hutchins, *The Higher Learning in America*, Yale University Press, New Haven, Conn., 1936, p. 66.

to learn what appeals to him at a particular age. He should study English, languages, history, mathematics, natural science, philosophy, and fine arts. "The basic education of a rational animal," writes Adler,

> . . . is the discipline of his rational powers and the cultivation of his intellect. This discipline is achieved through the liberal arts, the arts of reading and listening, of writing and speaking, and, perforce, of thinking, since man is a social animal as well as a rational one and his intellectual life is lived in a community which can exist only through the communication of men. The three R's, which always signified the formal disciplines, are the essence of liberal or general education.[5]

Vocational, industrial, and similar types of education may be included, provided their instruction is intellectually sound. However, the school does not exist to train for occupational tasks; these are best left to practitioners in the field. Nor should the school stump for social reform. Democracy will progress because people are properly educated and not because they have been taught to agitate for social change.

6. *Students should study the great works of literature, philosophy, history, and science in which men through the ages have revealed their greatest aspirations and achievements.* The message of the past is never dated. By examining it, the student learns truths that are more important than any he could find by pursuing his own interests or dipping into the contemporary scene. Mortimer Adler summarizes this view admirably:

> If there is philosophical wisdom as well as scientific knowledge, if the former consists of insights and ideas that change little from time to time, and if even the latter has many abiding concepts and a relatively constant method, if the great works of literature as well as of philosophy touch upon the permanent moral problems of mankind and express the universal convictions of men involved in moral conflict—if these things are so, then the great books of ancient and medieval, as well as modern, times are a repository of knowledge and wisdom, a tradition of culture which must initiate each new generation. The reading of these books is not for antiquarian purposes; the interest is not archaeological or philological . . . . Rather the books are to be read because they are as contemporary today as when they were written, and that because the *problems they deal with and the ideas they present are not subject to the law of perpetual and interminable progress.*[6]

In short, say the perennialists, the minds of most young Americans

---

[5] Adler, op. cit., p. 62.

[6] Ibid., p. 63. Thus Adler expounds what has been called the "Great Books" Theory.

have never really been exercised in intellectual matters, largely because teachers themselves are indifferent and give up too quickly. It is much easier to teach students at their own pace and in accordance with what they want to learn. Yet, in allowing the child's superficial inclinations to determine what he learns, we may actually hinder him from developing his real talents. Self-realization demands self-discipline, and self-discipline is attained only through external discipline. Those higher interests—literary, artistic, political, and religious—one or more of which are latent in everyone, do not emerge without hard work and application. It is all too easy to underestimate the child's abilities in these directions. Why not make every man a king in some intellectual realm? This, surely, is a worthier goal than settling for intellectual mediocrity and falsely equating such mediocrity with individual freedom.

Critique of Perennialism

Perennialists may be accused of fostering an "aristocracy of intellect" and unreasonably restricting their teaching to the classical tradition of the Great Books. They fail to appreciate that, although many children lack the particular intellectual gifts perennialism emphasizes, they nevertheless become good citizens and productive workers. To subject them to the same sort of rigorous academic training as that given to students of university caliber is to ignore this difference and perhaps to injure their personal growth. Indeed, such a practice actually may retard the development of attributes that are equally as valuable as any academic qualities they may have acquired in school. The intellect is only one side of a man's personality. And although rational behavior is indispensable to human progress, the affective and uniquely personal side can ill afford to be subordinated.[7]

Progressivism

By the turn of the century a number of educators already had rebelled against the excessive formalism of traditional education, with its emphasis on strict discipline, passive learning, and pointless detail. As far back as

---

[7] Many other criticisms may be leveled at perennialism, but they are inherent in the tenets of rival doctrines, as outlined in this chapter. On the matter of the sameness of human nature everywhere, however, I cannot refrain from citing a retort attributed to the anthropologist Clyde Kluckhohn: "Every man is in certain respects (a) like all other men, (b) like some other men, (c) like no other man."

the 1870s Francis W. Parker was advocating school reforms later to be revised and formalized by John Dewey. However, Dewey's first major work, *Schools of Tomorrow,* was not published until 1915, and another four years went by before the Progressive Education Association was founded. Thus, progressivism had been on the move for 30 years before its impact actually was felt. In its early stages it was largely individualist in temper, reflecting the bohemianism of the age; it was at this point that it attracted the support of William Heard Kilpatrick of Columbia University.

With the onset of the Depression, however, progressivism swung its weight behind a movement for social change, thus sacrificing its earlier emphasis on individual development and embracing such ideals as "cooperation," "sharing," and "adjustment." During this period it was joined by John L. Childs, George Counts, and Boyd H. Bode. The Progressive Education Association has long been disbanded, and the movement suffered a major reversal after the USSR displayed its sputnik,[8] but progressivism continues to exercise considerable influence through the individual work of such contemporaries as George Axtelle, William O. Stanley, Ernest Bayles, Lawrence G. Thomas, and Frederick C. Neff.

Taking the pragmatist view that change, not permanence, is the essence of reality, progressivism in its pure form declares that education is always in the process of development. Educators must be ready to modify methods and policies in the light of new knowledge and changes in the environment. The special quality of education is not to be determined by applying perennial standards of goodness, truth, and beauty, but by construing education as a *continual reconstruction of experience.* As Dewey expresses it,

> We thus reach a technical definition of education: it is that reconstruction or reorganization of experience which adds to the meaning of experience, and which increases the ability to direct the course of subsequent experience.[9]

---

8 Progressivism always attracted a lion's share of criticism, but never more so than during the days of mingled amazement and humiliation that followed the launching of the first Soviet sputnik. Americans had been convinced that Russian education was undemocratic and authoritarian and, therefore, ineffective. But how could such success in science and technology be explained? Could it be that American schools were paying too much attention to the children they taught and too little to the subjects they taught them? There was a revulsion against the "child-centeredness" identified with progressivism. Americans, it was said, had pandered to their children too long; the nation was going soft; the rot must be stopped.

9 John Dewey, *Democracy and Education,* Macmillan, New York, 1916, p. 89.

However, during the course of its development progressivism began to make some assertions of its own, six of which I will now discuss.

1. *Education should be life itself, not a preparation for living.* Intelligent living involves the interpretation and reconstruction of experience. The child should enter into learning situations suited to his age and oriented toward experiences that he is likely to undergo in adult life.

2. *Learning should be directly related to the interests of the child.* Progressive educators introduce the concept of the "whole child" as an answer to what they consider partial interpretations of the child's nature.[10] Thus Kilpatrick advocates the "child-centered" school, in which the process of learning is determined mainly by the individual child. A young person, he says, is naturally disposed to learn whatever relates to his interests or appears to solve his problems; at the same time, he naturally tends to resist whatever he feels to be imposed on him from above. The child, then, should learn because he needs and wants to learn, not necessarily because someone else thinks that he should. He should be able to see the relevance of what he learns to his own life and not to an adult's conception of the sort of life that a child of his age should be leading.

This does not mean that the child should be allowed to follow every prompting of his own desires, if only for the fact that he is not mature enough to define significant purposes. And although he may have much to do in determining the learning process, he is not its final arbiter. He needs guidance and direction from teachers who are equipped to perceive meaning in his discrete activities. The child experiences a continuous reconstruction of his private interests as they move to embrace the logical content of subject matter.[11]

[10] William Heard Kilpatrick, "The Essentials of the Activity Movement," *Progressive Education,* **II** (October 1934) 357-358: "The conception of 'the whole child' carries two implications which at bottom agree: one, that we wish at no time to disregard the varied aspects of child life; the other, that the child as an organism properly responds as one unified whole."

[11] The view that the individual child should be the center of the school's activity is much older than the writings of either Dewey or the progressivists. It was advocated, for varying philosophical reasons, by Rousseau, Froebel, Pestalozzi, Francis Parker, and G. Stanley Hall. However, it underwent a radical shift in meaning within the context of the moral relativism advanced by the progressive movement. When Froebel, for instance, argued for the free unfolding of the child's nature, he did so with an absolute goal in mind—that of allowing the child to unite himself spontaneously with God under the inspired guidance of his teacher. Progressivism acknowledges no absolute goal, unless it is social progress attained through individual freedom.

Even so, the progressivist teacher influences the growth of his pupils not by drumming bits of information into their heads but by controlling the environment in which growth takes place. Growth is defined as the "increase of intelligence in the management of life" and "intelligent adaptation to an environment." Dewey advised the teacher: "Now see to it that day by day the conditions are such that their own activities move inevitably in this direction, toward such culmination of themselves."[12]

3. *Learning through problem solving should take precedence over the inculcating of subject matter.* Progressivists reject the view that learning consists essentially of the reception of knowledge and that knowledge itself is an abstract substance that the teacher loads into the minds of his pupils. Knowledge, they declare, is a "tool for managing experience," for handling the continuously novel situations with which the mutability of life confronts us. If knowledge is to be significant, we must be able to do something with it; hence, it must be wedded to experience. Dewey says that we have learned all this from experimental science:

> The most direct blow at the traditional separation of doing and knowing and at the traditional prestige of purely "intellectual" studies, however, has been given by the progress of experimental science. If this progress has demonstrated anything, it is that there is no such thing as genuine knowledge and fruitful understanding except as the offspring of doing . . . . Men have *to do* something to the things when they wish to find out something; they have to alter conditions. This is the lesson of the laboratory method, and the lesson which all education has to learn.[13]

Thus, the search for abstract knowledge must be translated into an active educational experience. If the student is to gain any real appreciation of social and political ideas, the classroom itself must become a living experiment in social democracy. Indeed, experience and experiment are the key words of the progressivist method of learning. Dewey does not reject the content of traditional subject matter; on the contrary, he insists that much of it be retained. But, he says, subject matter constantly changes in terms of what men do with their environment. Consequently, education cannot be limited to a recollection of information obtained solely from a teacher or a textbook. It is not the absorption of previous knowledge that counts but its constant reconstruction in the light of new discoveries. Thus, problem solving must be seen not as the search for merely functional knowledge, but as a "perpetual grappling"

12 John Dewey, *The Child and the Curriculum*, University of Chicago, Chicago, Ill., 1943, p. 31.
13 Dewey, *Democracy and Education*, op. cit., pp. 321-322.

with subject matter. Grappling is to be understood not only as physical motion, that is, handling test tubes, or counting money, or raising one's hand to vote, but also as critical thinking, reconstruction of previously held ideas, and discovery .

Instead of teaching formal subject matter, we should substitute specific problem areas such as transportation, communication, and trade. But not even these can be fixed too far in advance. "Thus a curriculum," declares Lawrence G. Thomas,

> . . . cannot be more than outlined broadly in advance by the teacher and will consist largely of an array of resources which the teacher anticipates may be called upon as the current activities of the class lead on to new interests and new problems. The actual details of the curriculum must be constructed cooperatively in the classroom from week to week.[14]

Kilpatrick suggests that, instead of trying to grasp abstract principles on a theoretical level, the child should study particular topics or situations, such as Galileo's method of experimentation or the way in which the Hopi Indians gather and prepare food. The purpose is to enable the student to cope with his own problems by observing how others have done so elsewhere and at other times. The student engages in projects that (a) spring from his natural curiosity to learn and (b) acquire significance as they are worked out in cooperation with other members of the class and under the guidance of the teacher. Thus, all projects should be both personally and socially significant.

4. *The teacher's role is not to direct but to advise.* Because their own needs and desires determine what they learn, children should be allowed to plan their own development and the teacher should guide the learning involved. He should employ his greater knowledge and experience to help them whenever they reach an impasse. Without directing the course of events, he works with the children for the attainment of mutually agreeable ends. "In the Progressive view," declares Lawrence G. Thomas,

> . . . the teacher merely has superior and richer experience to bring to bear on the analysis of the present situation . . . . The teacher is vitally important as stage setter, guide, and coordinator, but he is not the sole source of authority.[15]

[14] Lawrence G. Thomas, "The Meaning of 'Progress' to Progressive Education," *Educational Administration and Supervision,* **XXXII**, 7 (October, 1946), 399.

[15] Op. cit., 398.

5. *The school should encourage cooperation rather than competition.* Men are social by nature and derive their greatest satisfaction from their relations with one another. Progressivists maintain that love and partnership are more appropriate to education than competition and personal gain. Thus education as the "reconstruction of experience" leads to the "reconstruction of human nature" in a social setting. The progressivist does not deny that competition has a certain value. He agrees that students should compete with one another, provided that such competition fosters personal growth. Nevertheless, he insists that cooperation is better suited than competition to the biological and social facts of human nature. Rugged individualism is permissible only when it serves the general good.[16]

6. *Only democracy permits—indeed encourages—the free interplay of ideas and personalities that is a necessary condition of true growth.* Principles 5 and 6 are interrelated, because in the progressivist view democracy and cooperation are said to imply each other. Ideally democracy is "shared experience." As Dewey puts it, "A democracy is more than a form of government; it is primarily a mode of associated living, of conjoint communicated experience." Democracy, growth, and education are thus interrelated. In order to teach democracy, the school itself must be democratic. It should promote student government, the free discussion of ideas, joint pupil-staff planning, and the full participation of all in the educative experience. However, schools should not indoctrinate students in the tenets of a new social order. To instruct them in a specific program of social and political action would be to adopt an authoritarianism that progressivism specifically rejects.

Critique of Progressivism

I have already stated that some of Dewey's followers carried his teachings to lengths he himself never intended. This is particularly true of his "doctrine of interest." One result was the much criticized "child-activity movement" that flourished during the 1930s and early 1940s. Self-activity may well lead to individual improvement, social betterment, and

[16] Progressivism rejects the social Darwinist view, developed by Herbert Spencer, that society should imitate nature and encourage competition. Life in the jungle does indeed appear "red in tooth and claw," but only when animals are hungry, angered, or mating. Even if nature did possess the characteristics imputed to it by social Darwinism, the argument that since ruthlessness is present in nature, it is therefore desirable in society, would still be untenable. Because they are unable to control their condition, animals cannot improve it; man, who is, can.

the good life. But how are "improvement," "betterment," and "the good life" to be defined? If the child is to be permitted freedom for self-activity, there should be a fixed goal for him to attain. The conception of child activity admirably illustrates the progressivist theory that growth should lead to more growth. Yet the entire process seems circular in nature. Growth as such cannot be self-justifying, for we need to know to what end it is directed. We require the assurance that, when we strive to achieve a certain goal, it will be desirable in itself when we actually attain it and not liable to replacement by another goal.

The progressivist has good psychological grounds for his claim that the child is not a little adult and that he must not be treated simply as a scholar. Rousseau was one of the first to call this fact to our attention. He also stated that it was useless to expect a child to indulge in abstract intellectual pursuits until he had reached the age of reason. Instead, a child should learn the things he is capable of understanding through personal discovery. However, his life displays many features, not the least of which is a process of intellectual growth and change. Is it not risky, therefore, to allow the child's interests so great an influence over what he learns? Viewed in retrospect, today's interests may seem as dull as yesterday's newspaper. How far should we give way to the child's desire to be a cowboy? How far should we encourage his desire to shoot Indians? Progressivists themselves are aware of the dangers of too great an emphasis on "presentism" in educational practice. Boyd Bode points out that the school should lead the child not merely to live but also to "transcend" his immediate existence and outgrow any habit that might keep him immature. It is part of the intelligent life, and therefore of education itself, to heed the demands of the future as well as those of the present.

It is also difficult to see how the school could be a replica of life, even if it tried. Inevitably the school is an artificial learning situation, beset with restrictions and prohibitions different from those encountered in life as a whole. Not only is it simply one life situation, it is also only one educational agency. It assumes tasks that other social agencies cannot handle. Indeed, the logic of the progressivist leads him to an odd dilemma. On the one hand, he advocates a real-life situation; on the other, he calls for types of tolerance, freedom, and control rarely permitted by the stern exigencies of life.

Progressivists claim that learning through problem solving leads to more genuine intellectual attainment than do other methods of learning. But this claim cannot be verified. Protagonists point to such experiments as the Eight-Year Study of 1933 to show that students who have been prepared for college by progressive methods do as well as, or better than, those prepared in the traditional way.[17] But the study is not definitive. Critics insist that the number of uncontrolled variables in the experiment nullifies its validity. Even so, Dewey did not intend that learning should remain indefinitely at the level of problem solving. On the contrary, problem solving is a means by which the child is led from practical issues to theoretical principles, from the concrete and sensory to the abstract and intellectual.[18]

The progressivist cites in his defense the fact that education culminates at the graduate level, where the professor acts more as a resource person than as a dictator of studies. Although graduate education permits the student considerable personal freedom, it is debatable whether elementary and secondary education should adopt the same procedure. We allow graduate students this freedom because they are intellectually mature and presumably can recognize where their true interests lie. The progressivist could reply that his methods of learning accustom the child to independent research and self-reliance from the very beginning of his school career; they enable him to reach this intellectual maturity earlier than he is permitted to at present. The core of the dispute reduces itself to the question of how far the self-discipline necessary to intellectual maturity can be self-taught and how far it should be developed through external discipline. However, since the ability to discriminate between essential and nonessential knowledge is largely an adult achievement, it would seem that the teacher himself should impart the bulk of what the child learns.

On the matter of cooperation as opposed to competition I will mention only one point. The individual wishing to contribute to the general good may on occasion be unable to cooperate, precisely because his ideals and life style are unacceptable to the group. The tyranny of the group has dangers of its own; it is not necessarily more clear-headed than the

---

17 W. Aiken, *The Story of the Eight-Year Study*, Harper, New York, 1942. Aiken concluded that what was important was not the type or number of subjects studied but the quality of the work done.

18 Cf. Foster McMurray, "The Present Status of Pragmatism in Education," *School and Society*, LXXXVII (2145) (January 17, 1959), 14-15: "Clearly the intent of Dewey's theory was to stimulate more and better learning of arts, sciences, and technologies. There was in this program no concern for immediate practical or directly utilitarian bits of information and technique, nor any process of choosing and organizing information around characteristic activities of daily life. On the contrary, in Dewey's version of pragmatism, characteristic activities of daily life were psychologically useful starting points for moving the learner to a consideration of meanings increasingly remote, abstract, and related to one another in impersonal systems rather than to practical daily use."

individual. The mass mind at times may wear moral and intellectual blinders that a single mind does not. We must therefore make sure that our cooperation is free and unforced—in short, that it does not become conformism.

Finally, Dewey's definition of democracy may be more comprehensive than most; nevertheless, although his theory of democracy leads him to certain conclusions about behavior in the school, other doctrines are equally as democratic. Until recently French education has been authoritarian (judged by progressivist standards), but France is surely a democracy, and her educational system corresponds to the wishes of the majority of her people. Perennialism, which has been criticized as reactionary and antidemocratic, is committed just as firmly to democracy as is progressivism. Indeed, it would be difficult to find a more vigorous defender of the democratic way of life than Robert M. Hutchins. The point is that different thinkers advance different interpretations of the democratic way of life; all of them are permissible, but none is definitive. American democracy has room for all sorts of responsible educational ideas.

Even so, progressivism has introduced many worthwhile reforms into American education, reforms that other outlooks must consider if they wish to retain their influence. By drawing attention to the currents of change and renewal that run constantly through the universe and through education itself, and by continually challenging the existing order, progressivism expresses an educational attitude of abiding significance.

Essentialism

Essentialism is not linked formally to any philosophic tradition, but is compatible with a variety of philosophic outlooks. Unlike perennialism, some of whose views it rejects, it is not opposed to progressivism as a whole but only to specific aspects. In maintaining that there are certain essentials that all men should know if they are to be considered educated, it does not repudiate Dewey's epistemology so much as the pronouncements of his less cautious followers. The essentialists devote their main efforts to (a) reexamining curricular matters, (b) distinguishing the essential and the nonessential in school programs, and (c) reestablishing the authority of the teacher in the classroom.

Founded in the early 1930s, the essentialist movement included such educators as William C. Bagley, Thomas Briggs, Frederick Breed, and Isaac L. Kandel. It also won the support of Herman H. Horne. In 1938, these men formed the Essentialist Committee for the Advancement of

American Education. The tradition continues in the writings of William Brickman, editor of *School and Society*. The Council for Basic Education, whose most active members are Arthur Bestor and Mortimer Smith, may also be considered essentialist in spirit, although members are skeptical of the value of formal educational studies by specialists in education. In fact, they say, the "educational establishment," consisting chiefly of schools and professors of education, is largely responsible for what they believe to be the sorry state of American education today.[19]

Like perennialism, essentialism stands for the reinstatement of subject matter at the center of the educational process. However, it does not share the perennialist's view that the true subject matter of education is the "eternal verities" preserved in the "great books" of Western civilization. These books should be used, but not for themselves. They should be made to relate to present realities.

Some essentialists turn to educational psychology for knowledge about the process of learning and the nature of the learner. Others are less confident. Although not denying the relevance to education of the findings of the behavioral sciences, they nevertheless view them more critically. In a field such as psychology, where little is claimed that is not instantly disputed, the educator, they say, would be wise to tread cautiously. Field theory conflicts with behaviorism and functionalism with psychoanalysis, so that it is impossible to tell which provides the more reliable knowledge. Until the findings of educational psychology become more genuinely scientific, some essentialists will regard them with considerable skepticism.

Essentialists have no united front. Since they hold different philosophies, it is not surprising that they disagree on the ultimate nature and value of education. Agreement is reached, however, on four fundamental principles.

---

[19] Critics of education as a formal study usually advocate that "what little there is of it" should be incorporated into other disciplines. The philosophy of education, then, would be taught by professors of philosophy in the department of philosophy; the history of education would be handled in a department of history; and so on. But why stop with education? The philosophy of science, of history, of politics, etc., by this reasoning, would all be taught in a philosophy department. Indeed, since all subjects are usually taught in English, why not deal with them all in an English department? Conversely, since all disciplines are educational, why not teach them all in a department of education? Bestor, a historian, would substantially reduce the number of professional courses taken by student teachers and curtail the influence of educationists on the practice of education. Brickman, an educationist, calls for more data and fewer polemics from writers such as Bestor who, in his view, are not qualified to make responsible judgments about a field as complex as education.

1. *Learning, of its very nature, involves hard work and often unwilling application.* The essentialist insists on the importance of discipline. Instead of stressing the child's immediate interests, he urges dedication to more distant goals. Against the progressive emphasis on personal interest, he posits the concept of effort. He agrees that interest in a subject does much to create the effort needed to master it, but points out that higher and more enduring interests are not normally felt at the outset; they arise through hard work from beginnings that do not in themselves attract the learner. Thus, the command of a foreign language, once attained, opens new worlds for the mind; yet the beginner often must overcome initial apathy and probable distaste. As the Frenchman says, "The appetite comes while eating."

Among living things man alone can resist his immediate impulses. If we do not encourage this capacity in the child, we make it harder for him to attain the self-discipline necessary to achieve any worthwhile end. The vast majority of students attain personal control only through voluntary submission to discipline intelligently imposed by the teacher.

2. *The initiative in education should lie with the teacher rather than with the pupil.* The teacher's role is to mediate between the adult world and the world of the child. The teacher has been specially prepared for this task and is, therefore, much better qualified to guide the growth of his pupils than they are themselves. Isaac L. Kandel maintains that:

> The essentialist is no less interested than the progressive in the principle that learning cannot be successful unless it is based on the capacities, interests, and purpose of the learner, but he believes those interests and purposes must be made over by the skill of the teacher, who is master of that "logical organization" called subjects and who understands the process of educational development.[20]

Thus, the essentialist teacher wields greater authority than does his progressivist colleague.[21]

3. *The heart of the educational process is the assimilation of pre-*

---

[20] Quoted by William W. Brickman, "Essentialism—Ten Years After," *School and Society,* **XLVII** (May 15, 1948), 365.

[21] William W. Brickman, "The Essentialist Spirit in Education," *School and Society,* **LXXXVI** (October 11, 1958), 364: "Essentialism places the teacher at the center of the educational universe. This teacher must have a liberal education, a scholarly knowledge of the field of learning, a deep understanding of the psychology of children and of the learning process, an ability to impart facts and ideals to the younger generation, an application of the historical-philosophical foundations of education, and a serious devotion to his work."

scribed subject matter. This view accords with the philosophic realist's position that it is largely man's material and social environment that dictates how he shall live. The essentialist agrees that education should enable the individual to realize his potentialities, but such realization must take place in a world independent of the individual—a world whose laws he must obey. The purpose of the child's attending school is to get to know this world as it really is and not to interpret it in the light of his own peculiar desires. Nor can he assimilate such knowledge haphazardly in whatever order he likes. It must be presented to him in accordance with the logical organization of subject matter (see pp. 267-8).[22]

Essentialists emphasize the importance of "race experience"—the "social heritage"—over the experience of the individual. This heritage summarizes the experiences of millions in attempting to come to terms with their environment. The wisdom of the many, tested by history, is far more reliable than the untested experience of the child.

4. *The school should retain traditional methods of mental discipline.* There are, it is true, certain advantages to the progressive method of problem solving, but it is not a procedure to be applied throughout the entire learning process. Of its very nature, much knowledge is abstract and cannot be broken up into discrete problems.

Although "learning by doing" may be appropriate in certain circumstances and for certain children, it should not be generalized. Must the child actually build a wigwam in order to learn how the Indian becomes domesticated? There is no doubt that doing so will help him to understand the Indian's way of life, but such an experience should support the learning process rather than constitute its essence. The child should be taught essential concepts, even if such concepts have to be adapted to his own psychological and intellectual level.

How does essentialism differ from perennialism? First, it advocates a less totally "intellectual" education, for it is concerned not so much with certain supposedly eternal truths as with the adjustment of the individual to his physical and social environment. Second, it is more willing to absorb the positive contributions that progressivism has made to educational methods. Finally, where perennialism reveres the great creative achievements of the past as timeless expressions of man's universal in-

---

[22] Isaac L. Kandel, *Conflicting Theories of Education,* Macmillan, New York, 1938, p. 99: "Since the environment carries in itself the stamp of the past and the seeds of the future, the curriculum must inevitably include that knowledge and information which will acquaint the pupil with the social heritage, introduce him to the world about him, and prepare him for the future."

sights, essentialism uses them as sources of knowledge for dealing with problems of the present.[23]

Reconstructionism

As far back as 1920 John Dewey suggested the term "reconstructionism" in the title of his book, *Reconstruction in Philosophy*. In the early 1930s, a group known as the "Frontier Thinkers" called on the school to lead the way toward the creation of a "new" and "more equitable" society. Their leading spokesmen were George Counts and Harold Rugg. Counts had written *The American Road to Culture* (1930) and *Dare the Schools Build a New Social Order?* (1932), and Rugg had published *Culture and Education in America* (1931). At this time progressivists such as W. H. Kilpatrick and John Childs were also urging education to become more aware of its social responsibilities. But they disagreed with the contention of Counts and Rugg that the school should commit itself to specific social reforms; they preferred instead to stress the general end of social growth through education.

Two decades later, as the progressive movement lost its momentum, further attempts were made to extend Deweyan philosophy into socially committed educational theories. In his major work, *The Ideal and the Community* (1958), Isaac B. Berkson sought a *rapprochement* of progressivism and essentialism, suggesting that although the school itself should not take the lead in social reform, it could cooperate with movements already underway that advocated a more thorough realization of liberal cultural values. However, it was Theodore Brameld who laid the foundations of "social reconstructionism" with the publication of *Patterns of Educational Philosophy* (1950), followed by *Toward a Reconstructed Philosophy of Education* (1956) and *Education as Power* (1965).[24] My résumé

---

23 Most attacks made on public education in the United States are likely to be essentialist in nature. The criticism of commentators such as Paul Woodring and James B. Conant is more conciliatory and could be placed halfway between the progressive and the essentialist points of view. Admiral Hyman G. Rickover, although not a professional educator, has affinities with both essentialism and perennialism. Like many essentialists, he esteems the contributions made to educational practice by the physical sciences more highly than he does those made by the behavioral sciences. He advocates more emphasis on knowledge for its own sake. Speaking as a professor of English, Jacques Barzun leans toward perennialism rather than essentialism, largely because he places the humanities at the center of the curriculum and believes in studying them for their own sake.

24 In his *Patterns of Educational Philosophy*, World Book, Yonkers, N.Y., 1950,

of reconstructionism will be limited to five of the main theses that Brameld puts forward.

1. *Education must commit itself here and now to the creation of a new social order that will fulfill the basic values of our culture and at the same time harmonize with the underlying social and economic forces of the modern world.* Claiming to be the philosophy of an "age in crisis," reconstructionism sounds a note of urgency not heard in other educational theories. Civilization, it declares, now faces the possibility of self-annihilation. Education must lead to a profound change in the minds of men, so that the enormous technological power at our disposal may be used to create rather than to destroy. Society must be transformed, not simply through political action, but more fundamentally through the education of its members to a new vision of their life in common. This commitment to the new order is not tenuous but urgent and direct. Reconstructionism, writes Brameld,

> . . . commits itself, first of all, to the building of a new culture. It is infused with a profound conviction that we are in the midst of a revolutionary period out of which would emerge nothing less than control of the industrial system, of public services, and of cultural and natural resources by and for the common people who, throughout the ages, have struggled for a life of security, decency, and peace for them and their children.[25]

2. *The new society must be a genuine democracy, whose major institutions and resources are controlled by the people themselves.* Anything that sufficiently affects the public interest, whether pensions, health, or industry, should become the responsibility of elected popular representatives. Thus Brameld declares:

> Control by the largest possible majority of the principal institutions and resources of any culture is the supreme test of democracy . . . the working people should control all principal institutions and resources if the world is to become genuinely democratic.[26]

p. 204, Brameld criticizes progressivism as "dilatory" and "inefficient." It is, he says, "the educational effort of an adolescent culture, suffering from the pleasant agonies of growing up, from the cultural period of trying and erring when the protections of infancy have been left behind but the planned autonomies of maturity await future delineation and fulfillment."

[25] Theodore Brameld, "Philosophies of Education in an Age of Crisis," *School and Society*, LXV (June 21, 1947), 452.

[26] Theodore Brameld, *Toward a Reconstructed Philosophy of Education*, Dryden, New York, 1956, pp. 328-329.

Since the ideal society is a democracy, it must also be realized democratically. The structure, goals, and policies of the new order must be approved at the bar of public opinion and enacted with the fullest possible measure of popular support. A revolution that takes place in the minds of a people is more profound and lasting than any change brought about by politicians alone. And the logical end of national democracy is international democracy, a form of world government in which all states will participate.[27]

3. *The child, the school, and education itself are conditioned inexorably by social and cultural forces.* Progressivism, says Brameld, overstates the case for individual freedom and understates the extent to which we are all socially conditioned. In its concern to find ways in which the individual may realize himself in society, it overlooks the degree to which society makes him what he is. Since civilized life by and large is group life, groups should play an important part in the school. "We should recognize groups for what they are," writes Brameld, "We should neither cynically condemn them nor passively accept their behavior as inevitable, but through sound diagnosis aim to build a social and educational program that will help resolve their longings, reduce their immoralities, and release their humane potentialities."[28] Thus education becomes "social self-realization"; through it the individual not only develops the social side of his nature but also learns how to participate in social planning.

4. *The teacher must convince his pupils of the validity and urgency of the reconstructionist solution, but he must do so with scrupulous regard for democratic procedures.* Under what Brameld calls the principle of "defensible partiality," the teacher allows open examination of the evi-

---

[27] Theodore Brameld, *Education as Power*, Holt, Rinehart and Winston, New York, 1965, p. 6: "The majority of peoples should, through their freely chosen representatives, control all fundamental economic, political, and social policies, and they should do so on a planetary scale. This is the supreme goal of education for the current decades. As long as our schools avoid recognition of this purpose; as long as teachers and professors skirt the subject because it is controversial; as long as educational theorists say, 'Oh, no, we must be concerned with training mental faculties,' or 'We must support the power struggle to glorious victory for our side,' then they are, in my judgment, denying a central purpose of education. To find a way to enlist and unite the majority of peoples of all races, religions, and nationalities into a great democratic world body with power and authority to enforce its policies— what greater mandate to us in the profession of education can be imagined than this?"

[28] Theodore Brameld, *Patterns of Educational Philosophy*, World Book, Yonkers, N.Y., 1950, p. 425.

dence both for and against his views; he presents alternative solutions fairly; and he permits his pupils to defend their own ideas. Moreover, since all of us have convictions and partialities, we should not only express and defend them publicly but also "work for their acceptance by the largest possible majority."

5. *The means and ends of education must be completely refashioned to meet the demands of the present cultural crisis and to accord with the findings of the behavioral sciences.* The importance of the behavioral sciences is that they enable us to discover those values in which men most strongly believe, whether or not these values are universal. Thus, Brameld declares,

> . . . the behavioral sciences are beginning to prove, really for the first time in history, that it is possible to formulate human goals not for sentimental, romantic, mystical, or similarly arbitrary reasons, but on the basis of what we are learning about cross-cultural and even universal values. Though studies in this difficult field have moved only a little way, they have moved far enough so that it is already becoming plausible both to describe these values objectively and to demonstrate that most human beings prefer them to alternative values.[29]

We must look afresh at the way in which our curricula are drawn up, the subjects they contain, the methods that are used, the structure of administration, and the ways in which teachers are trained. These must then be reconstructed in accordance with a unified theory of human nature, rationally and scientifically derived. It follows that we must construct a curriculum whose subjects and subdivisions are related integrally rather than treated as a sequence of knowledge components:

> A theory of unified man, both derived from and contributing to our experimental knowledge of human behavior in its multiple perspectives, not only should integrate all other fields of knowledge; it should provide them with a fresh and potent significance.[30]

Critique of Reconstructionism

Reconstructionism is stirringly expressed. Its appeal is all the more compelling because it claims to be based on reliable findings in the behavioral sciences. Such a claim, if true, would be difficult to counter. Unfortunately it is vitiated by the fact that these findings permit a variety

[29] Theodore Brameld, "Imperatives for a Reconstructed Philosophy of Education," *School and Society,* **LXXXVII** (January 17, 1959), 20.
[30] Ibid.

of interpretations, of which Brameld's is only one. As has already been pointed out and as Brameld himself admits, the established empirical conclusions of the behavioral sciences are scant indeed, and they carry no certain implications for education. There are, in addition, as many disagreements among behavioral scientists as there are among educators—and those, surely, are enough. What one sociologist or economist holds to be true is easily refuted by another; and psychologists do not agree about the kinds of behavior that are basic to a planned society. Science has yet to answer such questions as: What are the best values for men to accept? What social institutions best aid their realization? The boast of reconstructionism—that it is based on reliable scientific knowledge of human behavior—cannot be sustained.

Whether reconstructionism is as squarely in the mainstream of the American cultural tradition as its supporters claim is likewise open to doubt. Actually, liberal individualism is just as much a part of our tradition as is the commitment to democratically determined social ideals. It is difficult, indeed, to envisage a democracy as pluralist as the United States coming to any agreement on the far-reaching changes suggested by reconstructionists. It is one thing to vote yes or no for a political candidate or a bond issue but quite another to do so on the issues of education, affected, as they are, by a host of moral, religious, esthetic, and social—not to mention personal—considerations. How could the many competing interests in American society find a national educational system that pleased them all?

Perhaps the kind of permissive indoctrination that Brameld advocates is really a contradiction in terms. Reconstructionism as a doctrine demands commitment; a reconstructionist teacher cannot teach the doctrine without being committed to it himself and without hoping to commit his students also. However hard he may try to attain detachment in the classroom, he cannot, in the nature of things, be both scientifically detached and ideologically involved. Inasmuch as our society is deeply divided over social values, nothing less than capitulation to a totalitarian movement is ever likely to unite it. Our entire political structure would have to change, and individual enterprise would be severely enfeebled. In my view, reconstructionism seems to lead to a collectivist society, in which men would believe anything to be true provided it was attained by scientific methods and achieved through informed social consensus when persuasively presented.

References

◆◆

For recent publications on contemporary educational theories, see Frederick C. Neff, *Philosophy and American Education* (The Center for Applied Research in Education, New York, 1966, 168 pp.); and G. Max Wingo, *The Philosophy of American Education* (D. C. Heath, 1965, 438 pp.). These two volumes use the "schools of philosophy" approach. John P. Wynne's *Theories of Education* (Harper and Row, 1963, 521 pp.) is an imposing study of educational theory in all its historical, philosophic, social, and scientific dimensions. (Wynne says it took him thirty years to write the book, and I can believe it.) Of the many anthologies available, I will mention three: Joe Park, Ed., *Selected Readings in the Philosophy of Education* (Macmillan, 1968, 433 pp.); John Martin Rich, Ed., *Readings in the Philosophy of Education* (Wadsworth, 1966, 393 pp.); and Van Cleve Morris, Ed., *Modern Movements in Educational Philosophy* (Houghton Mifflin, 1969, 381 pp.). Like Wingo and Neff, Park structures his text according to schools of philosophy, whereas Rich and Morris use a topical or problems approach. Although Rich includes valuable discussion questions, his book suffers from the absence of biographies and an index.

12

The Challenge of Existentialism

George F. Kneller

❖❖

Most traditional philosophies have been of two kinds, metaphysical and skeptical. Metaphysical philosophies seek to explain certain fundamental features of experience by arguing that they derive from some further reality that this experience does not affect. Skeptical philosophies maintain that, since all human experience is deceptive, nothing can be known for certain and all metaphysical conceptions are provisional. Existentialism rejects both these courses. It argues against skepticism by claiming that men can discover the fundamental truths of their own existence. Against traditional metaphysics it argues that the real is what we experience. Reality, it claims, is *lived* reality. To describe the real we must describe not what is beyond but what is *in* the human condition.

Existentialism also differs *stylistically* from traditional philosophy. Because it is concerned with lived reality and with states of feeling in which this reality is fully apprehended, existentialist philosophy is generally more personal in style than traditional philosophy, being closer, in fact, to literature. I do not mean by this that existentialist philosophy is either less technical or more elegant than traditional philosophy. Martin Heidegger and Jean-Paul Sartre are highly technical philosophers, and Heidegger certainly is no model of clarity. Nevertheless, each writes in a personal and literary way, for each seeks to convey states of feeling as well as arguments, and each has forged a highly charged prose that is unmistakably his own.

I must also mention that existentialist philosophers have written little on education as such. Martin Buber is an exception. Gabriel Marcel frequently refers to education in passing. Jean-Paul Sartre has defined the educational significance of literature. Karl Jaspers has published a book on *The Idea of the University*. And Friedrich Nietzsche wrote a polemical essay on educational institutions that is radical and caustic enough to be relevant to our own day. This neglect of education is surprising when one considers how many traditional philosophers, such as Plato, Locke, Kant, and Dewey, have addressed themselves to educational problems. It becomes all the more surprising when one reflects that as a philosophy of personal life, existentialism is bound to yield insights into education, a process in which persons can either be made or make themselves. Perhaps the explanation is that a new school of thought is almost bound to concentrate on the theoretical problems it has raised and to leave till later or to others the application of its principles in realms where thought and practice converge, such as politics, law, and education. Be that as it may, the opportunity is all the greater for educators themselves to explore and synthesize the educational insights with which existentialism abounds. To do this, we must approach the doctrine on its own terms and attend to those themes with which it is most concerned.

The World View

Existentialism springs from the iconoclastic works of the Danish philosopher, Søren Kierkegaard (1813-1855) and the German thinker Friedrich W. Nietzsche (1844-1900). Both men turned against ecclesiastical Christianity and the speculative philosophy of Hegel. Kierkegaard strove to revitalize Christianity from within; whereas, Nietzsche denounced the otherworldliness of Christianity and advocated the yea-saying morality of the superman. The leading existentialists of our time are Martin Heidegger, Jean-Paul Sartre, Karl Jaspers, and Maurice Merleau-Ponty. Other existentialists are Gabriel Marcel and Paul Tillich, both Christian, and Martin Buber, Jewish.

Existentialists reject the traditional view that philosophy should be calm and detached above all. Philosophy, they say, should be reason *informed by passion,* because it is in passion, in states of heightened feeling, that ultimate realities are disclosed. Passionate reason is not unreason but the reason of the whole man. It is reason at grips with those fundamental realities of freedom, death, and other people with which human beings must contend. It is the opposite of dispassionate calculation, which manipulates abstractions and ignores the human predicament.[1]

For existentialism the physical universe, the world apart from man, has neither meaning nor purpose. It is a contingency, something that happens to be there. This is not to say that it is capricious. The regularities discovered by science are genuine enough. But they have no direct human significance. Understood properly, they correspond to no human ideals or desires save the desire for security, which is the desire to escape from the true freedom and the true terror of the human condition. In the universe man happens by chance. There is no world order, no natural scheme of things, into which he is born. A man therefore owes nothing to nature but his existence. His existence, then, precedes his essence, in the sense that he must exist if he is to be anything at all. But existence does not make him. Existing, he makes himself. As Sartre has said:

> What is meant here by saying that existence precedes essence? It means that, first of all, man exists, turns up, appears on the scene and, only afterwards defines himself. If man, as the existentialist sees him, is indefinable, it is because at first he is nothing. Only afterwards will he be something and he himself will have made what he will be. . . . Not only is man what he conceives himself to be, but he is also what he wills himself to be after this thrust toward existence. Man is nothing other than what he makes himself.[2]

What a man becomes is his own responsibility. Either he makes himself or, in a sense, he allows himself to be made by others. He chooses what he will be (his "essence") or, again in a sense, allows it to be chosen for him. But in either case he chooses, for acquiescence is not choice renounced but weak choice. Acquiescence is the unavailing flight from freedom. A man who is made by others is still the author of himself, for he chooses to be what they make him. He is, one might say, manufactured by choice.

If we accept this world view, what follows? As free men and free

---

[1] For Heidegger, philosophy begins and ends not in reason or logic but *wonder*: "Wonder pervades and maintains it. . . . Logic is only one explanation of the way we think. . . . 'Exact' thinking is never the strictest thinking . . . it is limited to the mere calculation of what-is and ministers to this alone" (*What is Philosophy?*, Twayne, New York, 1958, pp. 83-85).

[2] Jean-Paul Sartre, *Existentialism*, Philosophical Library, New York, 1947, p. 18.

teachers we must seek to expose and combat all those forces in culture and society that tend to dehumanize men by denying their freedom. We must repudiate the subordination of the person to economic "laws," the tyranny of the majority over the dissenting minority, and the stifling of individuality by social conformism.[3] We must urge our students to recognize and fulfill the freedom that is theirs as persons. What we urge we must also practice by respecting their freedom as we value our own.

Choosing

In itself freedom is neither a goal nor an ideal. It is the *potential for action*.[4] I am what I *do*. My character is the sum of my own actions and it is therefore self-created. My character can change because I can always act differently. My destiny is my own. Freedom, therefore, is "dreadful," for I am responsible for what I become.[5] The drunkard, the neurotic, the drug addict, the man in a rut, the man at the end of his tether, you and I, all of us have made ourselves and can make ourselves again.

I am free, therefore I become. When I choose, I throw myself into the future, I make myself other than I am. I "ex-ist." I summon into being that which was mere possibility. I am *homo viator*, the self forever in transit.

The moment for choice is important. As Kierkegaard says, "There is danger afoot" (*Either/Or*). I may lose my nerve and choose wrongly, or

[3] Cf. Kierkegaard ("Concluding Unscientific Postscript" and "The Individual"): "A Crowd . . . in its very concept is the untruth . . . it renders the individual completely impenitent and irresponsible, or at least weakens his sense of responsibility by reducing it to a fraction. . . . Thereof was Christ crucified because, although He addressed himself to all, He would have no dealings with the crowd. . . . He would not found a party, did not permit balloting, but would be that He is, the Truth, which relates itself to the individual."

[4] No one expresses this view more passionately and pointedly than Martin Buber (*Between Man and Man*, Macmillan, New York, 1965, pp. 91-92): "Freedom—I love its flashing face. . . . I am devoted to it. I am always ready to join in the fight for it. . . . I give my left hand to the rebel and my right to the heretic: Forward! But I do not trust them. They know how to die, but that is not enough. . . . They must not make freedom into a theorem or a program. To become free of a bond is destiny; one carries that like a cross, not like a cockade. . . . Life lived in freedom is *personal* responsibility."

[5] In Sartre's *The Flies*, Orestes says to Zeus: "I *am* my freedom. No sooner had you created me than I ceased to be yours . . . And there was nothing left in heaven, nor anyone to give me orders . . . But I must blaze my trail. For I, Zeus, am a man, and every man must find out his own way."

I may fail to see the opportunity and so let circumstances take their way. Choose I must and choose in time. Kierkegaard tells the story of a ship's captain who has to decide just when his ship must come about. The vessel makes headway all the time. He has a few moments to make up his mind: "If he forgets to take account of the headway, there comes at last an instant when there no longer is any question of either/or, not because he has chosen but because he has neglected to choose, which is equivalent to saying, because others have chosen for him, because he has lost himself."

Most choices we make are admittedly trivial and inconsequential— choice of a necktie, choice of a restaurant, choice of a movie. A serious choice is a choice between actions involving fundamental values. It calls for deep concentration, a looking into oneself. However, I must not be content merely to apply an abstract moral principle. This is a weak choice, reliance on a rule rather than on myself. I should choose the course of action that seems uniquely right in this particular situation. I should seek not *the* way but *my* way.[6]

The hardest choices to make are often those between alternative goods. Two courses of action seem to have an equally good claim on us—which course do we take? Sartre tells the story of a young man who must decide whether to stay home and support his destitute mother or join the Free French. Kant's categorical imperative will not help him, nor will the Golden Rule. What must he do? He must act according to his strongest feeling. The young man reflects: "I ought to choose whatever pushes me in one direction. If I feel that I love my mother enough to sacrifice everything else for her—my desire for vengeance, for action, for adventure— then I'll stay with her." And so he did.

If I am an existentialist teacher, I urge the student to take responsibility for, and to deal with, the results of his actions. To act is to produce consequences. He must accept that these consequences are the issue of his choice, but at the same time he must not submit to them as unalterable, for this is to assume that freedom is exhausted in a single act. Freedom is never exhausted, and each consequence poses the need for further choice. I would teach him that his life is his own to lead and that no one else can

---

6 I should point out that the existentialist does not reject moral principles as such, only abstract ones. Buber, writing on education for character, puts this well: "No responsible person remains a stranger to norms. But the command inherent in a genuine norm never becomes a maxim and the fulfillment of it never a habit. Any command that a great character takes to himself in the course of his development does not act in him as part of his consciousness or as material for building up his exercises but remains latent in a basic layer of his substance until it reveals itself to him in a concrete way." (*Between Man and Man,* op. cit., 1965, p. 114.)

lead it for him. It is pointless to blame his failures on environment, family, temperament, or the influence of others. These conditions are for choice to challenge. Whatever may have happened to the student in the past, the future is his to make.

Does this attitude lead to a ruthless disregard of others, to *my* fulfillment at the expense of yours? Not at all. True freedom implies not egoism but *communion*. The egoist is driven by a narrow self-interest. With him choice is not self-fulfillment but self-limitation. Freedom, open and dynamic, longs for other centers of freedom, other persons. It does not calculate but gives. The fulfillment of freedom is communion with others.

But we should not confuse this communion with mere familiarity. Communion is a certain intimacy with another person called by Buber "inclusion" and by Marcel "presence." You and I are in communion when we meet as independent selves to share a single experience. Each of us preserves his uniqueness.[7] I do not absorb you, nor do you me. Our communion is not an obliteration of selfhood in passion, but a dialogue in which I hear what passes in your mind and heart and you what passes in mine.[8] Listen to Buber: "The inner growth of the self is not accomplished, as people like to suppose today, in man's relation to himself, but . . . in the making present of another self and in the knowledge that one is made present by his own self to the other."[9]

Familiarity is not to be despised. It is natural and socially desirable. Nevertheless, it is incomplete, not a fulfillment of the self but a potential "waiting to be used." If as a teacher I assume the style and gestures for which convention calls, I may touch only the surfaces of my students' lives. I must go beyond familiarity and open myself to them. I must come

---

[7] Nicolas Berdyaev, *Slavery and Freedom*, Scribners, New York, 1944, p. 42: "Egoistic self-containment and concentration upon the self, and the inability to issue forth from the self is original sin, which prevents the realization of the full life of the personality and hinders its strength from becoming effective. . . . Personality presupposes a going out from the self to another and to others. It lacks air and is suffocated when left shut up in itself."

[8] Cf. Maurice Merleau-Ponty, *Phenomenology of Perception*, Routledge & Kegan Paul, London, 1962, p. 334: "In the experience of dialogue there is constituted between the other person and myself a common ground; my thought and his are interwoven into a single fabric, my worlds and those of my interlocutor are called forth by the state of the discussion, and they are inserted into a shared operation of which neither of us is the creator . . . we are collaborators for each other in consummate reciprocity. Our perspectives merge into each other, and we co-exist through a common world."

[9] Martin Buber, "Distance and Relation," *The Hibbert Journal*, **XLIX** (January 1951), 112 f.

to them unreservedly, creating the trust from which spring communion and true self-fulfillment.

According to the existentialist a moral act may be performed for itself or for an end. But a man must create his own ends. If he adopts the ends of a group or of society, he must make these ends his own by deciding in any situation that *this* is the end to aim at. The end is seized in the situation. It is not a standard to which acts conform but a goal at which an act is aimed. When moral principles are treated as external standards requiring certain sorts of behavior, they are turned into instruments of enslavement. Action becomes mere conduct and the individual submits to what is external to him.

As a teacher, then, I must not simply impose discipline. Rather, I must ask each student to accept the discipline that he sees as worthwhile in itself or as worthwhile for some end, such as his own intellectual development or the harmony of the class. It will be said by some that this is a counsel of perfection. Of course it is. It is an ideal to be striven for. Often I will fail to attain it, and so will my students. I may become a martinet; they may become anarchists. But we must try again. Neither repression nor anarchy is the answer. We must aim for the freedom and fulfillment of all, teacher and students together.

Knowing

As existentialists we must rethink our conception of knowledge. Properly conceived, knowledge enhances freedom, for it delivers man from ignorance and enables him to see himself as he is. Subject matter, codified knowledge, should be treated neither as an end in itself nor as a means of preparing the student for an occupation or career. It should be used, rather, as a means toward self-development and self-fulfillment. Instead of subjecting the student to the matter, let the matter be subject to the student. Let the student "appropriate" to himself any knowledge he studies, that is, let him make it his own. In the process of learning, the person must be sovereign over the textbook.

School subjects, then, should become tools for the realization of the person, not impersonal disciplines to which all must submit alike. Let the growing person think out truths for himself, not Truth in the abstract but *his* truths. I do not mean by this that we should encourage him to believe whatever he likes. Rather, we should say to him, "These things have been found true by many people; now see for yourself whether they are true or not. If you do not find them true, say so, and let us discuss them together."

For example, it is not enough for Newton's laws of motion to be true for scientists. The student must find them true for himself. He must be able to incorporate them within his view of the world.

This is what the pure specialist does not do. Specialization diminishes a man. The specialist is the creature of his knowledge, not the master of it. As Nietzsche pointed out, "A specialist in science begins to resemble nothing but a factory workman who spends his whole life in turning one particular screw or handle on a certain instrument or machine."[10] The school must see to it that the pupil who specializes continues to advance in knowledge of the human condition. Specialized studies must go hand in hand with humane ones, and specialization must be humanized as much as possible. The man must be master of his specialty. On this Karl Jaspers has spoken clearly (*Man in the Modern Age*): "For his activities in every situation and in all occupations man needs a specific expert knowledge concerning things and concerning himself. But expert knowledge alone is never adequate for it only becomes significant in virtue of him who possesses it."

Education should also provide an insight into those experiences in which man is most aware of the human condition, experiences such as suffering, conflict, guilt, and death. These are always with us. Death may strike you or me at any time. Death places life in question; it confronts us with the contingency of our existence. Guilt is always with us. Where have we gone wrong? Are we now right? What is our responsibility to the black man? To the Japanese maimed at Hiroshima? To the millions shattered in Vietnam? To the people we have used, the pupils we have failed? We cannot escape suffering, conflict, guilt, and death. We must seek to understand them and meet them with wisdom.

Teaching and Learning

For one existentialist's conception of teaching and learning we turn to Martin Buber's theory of the "dialogue." A dialogue is a conversation be-

---

[10] Friedrich Wilhelm Nietzsche, *On the Future of Our Educational Institutions*, Macmillan, New York, 1924, p. 39. Note that the existentialist does not condemn science as such, only the failure to educate scientists to be whole men as opposed to technicians. In *The Myth of Sisyphus* Camus puts the matter this way: "All the knowledge of this earth will give me nothing to assure me that this world is mine. You enumerate its laws and in my thirst for knowledge I admit that they are true. You take apart its mechanism and my hope increases. . . . But I realize that if through science I can seize phenomena and enumerate them, I cannot, for all that, comprehend the world."

tween persons in which each person remains a subject for the other, a conversation, in Buber's terms, between an "I" and a "Thou."[11] The opposite of a dialogue is an act of verbal manipulation or dictation in which one person imposes himself on another, turning the latter into an object of his will expressed in speech. By Buber's standards most teaching is manipulation or dictation. The child is compelled to submit either to the will of the teacher directly or to a body of inflexible knowledge of which the teacher is custodian. Sometimes, of course, the tables may be turned and the teacher himself may become an object of the scorn or anger of his class.

Most of us are opposed to personal tyranny in the classroom, but Buber also opposed what he believed to be the tyranny of impersonal knowledge. Teaching, he said, could not be a true dialogue if the teacher were construed as an instructor, one who simply mediates between the pupil and the subject matter. When teaching is understood as instructing, the teacher is devalued into a means for the transfer of knowledge and the pupil is devalued into the product of this transfer. Knowledge is sovereign and persons become means and products. How, then, is knowledge to be transmitted? It is not to be transmitted at all but "offered." The teacher, said Buber, must familiarize himself fully with the subject he teaches, and take it into himself as the rich fruit of human activity. When the teacher has made the subject he teaches a part of his inner experience, he can present it to the pupil as something issuing from himself. Then teacher and pupil can meet as persons because the knowledge the teacher offers is no longer something external to him but an aspect of his own condition.

When discussing a subject with his class, when teaching an aspect of literature or history, for example, the teacher seeks to introduce as many points of view as he can. He seeks to present the subject as a product of the thought of many men and as a focus of continuing thought. This indeed is the status of all knowledge that matters, for if knowledge is to

---

11 Although Buber's philosophy is highly personalistic, it is nevertheless a philosophy of human relations. In his view, true community could not come to pass until each individual accepted full responsibility for his neighbor. "Spirit is not in the *I* but between *I* and *Thou*. It is not like the blood that circulates in you but like the air in which you breathe." Social reality, then, is *mutuality*: "Through the Thou a man becomes I." But the I-Thou dialogue is not a mere verbal engagement. It is experiential, concrete, lodged in the "depth of living." See Martin Buber, *I and Thou*, Scribner's, New York, 1958, p. 64 especially. In *Between Man and Man*, op. cit., Buber writes (p. 88): "What teaches us the saying of *Thou* is not the instinct of origination but the instinct of communion."

endure, it must be reinterpreted and yield fresh significance in use. But it is not the teacher's intention to let the pupil choose whatever view of the subject he wishes. This would be irresponsible because the pupil is not an expert in the field. At the same time the teacher does not impose an interpretation or slip one past the pupil's guard, for this would devalue the student into an object of a teaching stratagem. Instead, after full discussion the teacher offers the pupil what he believes to be the best view of the subject and asks him whether he will accept it.

The teacher presents the class with a variety of views to bring about a genuine discussion of the subject matter. The teacher has read widely and can set the subject before the class adequately. But he submits it for discussion. After discussion he offers the class the view that he himself has formed of the subject after long reflection. He asks each student to test this view against his own experience, including the knowledge he has gathered in this class and in previous ones.

Suppose the student rejects the teacher's interpretation of the subject? Well, then, he rejects it. It is his right to do so. Existentialism insists not that the teacher be "successful" but that he be *honest*. Nevertheless, honesty leads to success, for if the teacher is honest with the pupil, he trusts him, and trust breeds its return. In an atmosphere of mutual trust the student knows that the teacher's interpretation of a subject is a wise one, and the teacher knows that the student will weigh this interpretation with the respect it deserves. Thus the dialogue that is education rests on trust between persons, a trust that the teacher must earn by integrity and create with skill.

What about subject matter? In the existentialist view no subject is more important (in itself) than any other. The subject that matters is the one in which the individual finds self-fulfillment and an awareness of the world. For some this subject is natural science; for many, it is history, literature, philosophy, or art. In these latter subjects the student becomes acquainted with the insights of great writers and thinkers into the nature of man in the world, into freedom, guilt, suffering, conflict, triumph, and death—themes that should engage the student intellectually and emotionally. The existentialist sees history, for example, in terms of man's struggle to realize his freedom. The student must commit himself to whatever period he is studying and immerse himself in its problems and personalities. The history he studies must fire his thoughts and feelings and become part of them.

When discussing the nature of human life, teachers should show that life is compounded of growth and decay, joy and tragedy. "Education for happiness" is a delusion. There is no happiness without pain, no ecstasy without suffering. Are the greatest achievements the work of happy men? Or of unsatisfied men striving for fulfillment? Education for security? For personal contentment? How illusory!

How does the existentialist teacher approach the subject of death? He suggests to his students that a knowledge of death increases one's awareness of life. If a student thinks hard about death, he becomes more conscious of the meaning of life. He ceases to drift; he is ready to sift the essential in his life from the trivial. That is why Blaise Pascal declared, "Live today as if you were to die tomorrow." The fact of death tells the student that he must make his life now.[12]

The teacher encourages the pupil to think for himself by engaging him in a dialogue. He questions the student about his ideas, proposes other ideas, and so leads him to choose between alternatives. The student sees then that truths do not happen to men, they are chosen by them. More than this, he becomes an actor in the drama of learning, not a spectator. He must work as hard as his teacher.

Unfortunately too many students think that learning is just a matter of "soaking it up." They are wrong. Knowledge is acquired by active effort, by never closing the mind or heart, and by always seeking profounder truths than those one possesses. Some students keep this search to themselves. They do not open themselves to their teachers. However well they do in their work, they miss the opportunity for communion in the classroom. I always regret this. I believe that students and teachers should constantly interrogate one another.

The more I consider the troubled state of public education today, the more I am convinced that existentialists show the way to reform. Our children are herded into educational factories, where they are processed and fashioned alike regardless of their personal uniqueness. Our teachers are forced, or think they are forced, into teaching along lines laid down

---

[12] In handling the topic of death the teacher could engage his students in debates or discussions on statements made by many thinkers throughout history. For example, the attitude of Judaism is expressed in Ecclesiastes: "There is a time to live and a time to die." When, indeed, *is* this time? Vespasian once declared, "An emperor should die standing up." What implication does this remark have for the practice of euthanasia? Marcus Aurelius was a bit ruthless: "Thou hast embarked, thou hast made the voyage, thou art come to shore; now get out." Would suicide be an appropriate way to "get out"? The celebrated modern French author François Mauriac said recently that he was "fascinated" with the prospect of dying. He was in fact (at 80-odd years of age and sick in bed) eagerly awaiting his encounter with death. To what extent can we sympathize with such a view?

for them. This system alienates both pupil and teacher.[13] It is time to change it for a better one.

Like Marcel, I believe that, in its present form, the school should be abolished. I would preserve a few of the facilities of the school—the library, the assembly hall, the gymnasium, the playing field—but as facilities only. Young people could use these for studying and for group activities, such as games, play-acting, and musical performances. Instead of going to school for an education, the young person would go to a teacher. Student and teacher would meet in the teacher's home, or in the student's, or, if appropriate, on location. Sometimes the student would come alone, and sometimes with friends. I believe that under this arrangement the student would accomplish much more and in much shorter time than he does now. For the teacher would meet the student where he individually *is*.

I realize that this is a highly radical proposal and will be called impractical. But today's public schools are little more than a hundred years old and when first conceived, were also called radical and impractical. I cannot help recalling the kind of school that J. D. Salinger's Teddy wanted. He would first "assemble" the students and "show them how to meditate." He would "try to show them how to find out who they *are*, not just what their names are and things like that. . . ." He would even try to "get them to empty out their heads" of all the stuff their parents and others had told them. If, as Camus said, "There is a whole civilization to be remade," Teddy's school would be an ideal way to start remaking it. As I have said in Chapter 3 on culture, teachers alone cannot rebuild a civilization. But they can do much to educate individual pupils who may one day set about doing so.

---

[13] Clark Moustakas eloquently expresses my point of view ("Alienation, Education, and Existential Life," Merrill Palmer Institute, Detroit, n.d., p. 16): "As it now stands the school is a powerful reinforcer of alienation in modern society. The teacher is alienated in himself; he does not exist as a real person in the classroom; he plays a part, a role; he fulfills duties and follows instructions. The teacher is alienated from his subject matter; it is external to his real world of feelings—anger, joy, sadness, loneliness, imagination, excitement, compassion—it is outside himself. The teacher is also alienated from the child; the child is perceived in categories and evaluative terms, as slow or fast, as an outstanding achiever or an underachiever, as average or retarded, and in many, many other traits and classifications, all of which have relevance in the object relationship but not in encounter and in self-actualization. In such a setting, where the teacher is alienated from himself, from the subject matter and from his pupils, gradually but definitely, the teacher becomes an object among objects, a thing among things."

References

❖❖

There are many articles on the meaning of existentialism for education but only two full-length books: my own *Existentialism and Education* (Wiley, 1965, 170 pp.), originally published in 1958; and Van Cleve Morris, *Existentialism in Education* (Harper and Row, 1966, 163 pp.). The only anthology I know, and one that has helped me in writing this essay, is Maxine Greene, Ed., *Existential Encounters for Teachers* (Random House, 1967, 174 pp.). The selections are from original writings by authors with existentialist views, and Greene's commentary is perceptive. There are many general studies of existentialism as such. My students particularly like William Barrett's *What Is Existentialism?* (Grove, 1965). *Existentialism from Dostoievsky to Sartre*, edited by Walter A. Kaufmann (Meridian Books, World Publishing Co., Cleveland and New York, 1956) is an excellent anthology. For ambitious students with a good background in formal philosophy I recommend George A Schrader, Ed., *Existential Philosophers: Kierkegaard to Merleau-Ponty* (McGraw-Hill, 1967, 437 pp.).

265

13

Logic and Analysis

George F. Kneller

❖❖❖

Logic and Psychology

I have often wondered why teachers in training are usually taught so much psychology and so little logic. One explanation is that psychology, the study of individual behavior, tells teachers important things about how their students are likely to behave. Another explanation is that, whereas psychologists always have been interested in education, logicians, at any rate since the Middle Ages, have generally ignored it. There is also a third explanation. Psychology studies the *process* of thinking as it actually occurs. Formal logic, on the other hand, considers the *forms* taken by the ideas or arguments that thought produces. As a result, formal logic has seemed less applicable to the problems of teachers at work. Nevertheless, any notion that logic has little or nothing to say to the teacher in the classroom is profoundly mistaken. This chapter will, I hope, show that the study of logic and of the logical use of language has much to contribute to both the theory and the practice of education.

Whereas psychology studies the actual process of thinking, formal logic supplies rational forms for ordering the results of thought. Formal logic considers what sorts of arguments are valid. How any person actually thinks in order to produce these arguments is irrelevant to the logical validity of the arguments themselves. Admittedly, if a person is to produce logical arguments, he must be motivated to do so. But whether or not he produces them by intuition or slow calculation does not matter from a formal logical point of view. What matters is that he should wish to reach conclusions that are valid and should know when he does so. To implant the wish and to cultivate the knowledge are tasks of teaching.

At first a teacher may reward a student for thinking logically, that is, for drawing valid conclusions, and the student may for a while think logically in order to receive the reward. Gradually, however, if he is properly taught, the student may find such thought satisfying not only because it is rewarded but also because it is intellectually fruitful. He will find that one valid conclusion begets another, whereas inconsistency leads nowhere. Thus the *habit* of thinking logically can be cultivated by psychological means, that is by specific tactics of teaching based on an understanding of human behavior.

Indeed, a knowledge of and a training in logic can in themselves affect a person's behavior. Other things being equal, a person who has studied logic will tend to be more rational and more intellectually aware than one who has not. He will be more likely to question his own prejudices and rationalizations. He will be less influenced by the specious pleading of others and more competent to spot fallacies and inconsistencies in their arguments.

In education the question is often asked: Is it better to introduce content on the basis of an order present in the subject matter itself or according to the stage of development reached by the learner? Should the study of physics, for example, always follow that of algebra (logical order), or should these subjects be taught any time the learner is ready for them (psychological order)?

The logical presentation of subject matter is based on the theory that logical order already is built into it. Such order is a part of nature, we hear, or is assumed to be. Algebra, for example, has many components and we must know certain ones before we can understand others. We can also grasp certain operations in physics only after we know algebra.

Those who hold this theory are confident that if a student masters knowledge in this fashion, he will automatically think logically. The more extreme among them reject virtually all psychological considerations that interfere with this approach. They maintain that one of the chief purposes of learning subject matter is to give order to a mind that comes to it in a state of disorder. It is folly, they say, to allow an unordered, untrained mind to dictate what the order of subject matter should be or how it should be learned.

Psychological order, on the other hand, relates subject matter to the aims, interests, and experiences of the student. The learning process, astutely manipulated by the teacher, is initiated by the learner; his interest is aroused; his reflective powers are challenged; and his curiosity is gratified. The student and the subject matter "interact."

That logical and psychological order should not conflict but should go hand in hand is a proposition supported by most observers.[1] John Dewey identified the "psychological and logical" with "process and product" respectively. The psychological process, he said, becomes the means of understanding subject matter in its logical form. For the learner, the latter is an ideal to be achieved and not a starting point from which to proceed.[2] The learning process is "the progressive development of what is already experienced into a fuller and richer and more organized form, a form that gradually approximates the subject matter presented to the skilled, mature person."[3]

The Logic of Inquiry

"Logic," said the iconoclastic English pragmatist F. S. C. Schiller, "is so much technical trivia . . . fit only to confuse students in examinations and inappropriate for a world of chance and change. We have no proof," he continued, "that the universe is logically organized. It may or may not be. In order to find out, we must experiment with the world, 'try it out', as it were."

Schiller was, of course, condemning only *formal* logic. But his remarks pave the way for us to seek answers through what has been called the "logic of inquiry," formulated by John Dewey. The subject of the logic of inquiry is the *process of inferring*. Where formal logic deals with the forms of arguments, the logic of inquiry seeks to establish the principles

---

[1] John Dewey, *How We Think*, Heath, Boston, Mass., 1933, p. 84: "[They] are connected as the earlier and the terminal stages of the same process of learning."

[2] John Dewey, *Democracy and Education*, Macmillan, New York, 1916, p. 257.

[3] John Dewey, *Experience and Education*, Macmillan, New York, 1951, p. 87. Dewey's "activity principle" springs from the concepts just outlined, according to which students should learn actively. They must become consciously involved when a lecture is being presented and not just sit and take notes. They must "activate" their intelligence; in other words, they must prepare themselves psychologically to deal with subject matter in all its essentially logical nature.

that men *ought* to observe in order to reach valid conclusions. Thus the logic of inquiry is prescriptive in that it recommends principles for men to follow. But it is also descriptive, since these, in Dewey's view, are the principles that men do in fact follow when they inquire successfully.

To inquire, said Dewey, is to resolve a problematic situation. This takes six steps, which will now be described in a school setting.[4]

1. In the Deweyan view all thinking is a response to some difficulty that cannot be surmounted by instinct or routine. The student encounters such difficulties all the time, for he is always learning something new. Suppose, then, that I am a student in high school studying the events leading to World War II. I learn about the Versailles Treaty, the Depression, the inaction of the League of Nations, the Munich Agreement, and so forth. Still, I am dissatisfied. I have many supposed facts before me—the fact, for instance, that the Versailles Treaty imposed crippling reparations on Germany, and the fact that France and Britain acquiesced in the German occupation of Czechoslovakia. But these facts are not yet organized in a way that makes sense to me. They are "inert." They do not explain anything.

2. After a while I cease to be merely dissatisfied. I realize that the matter I am learning needs somehow to be given significance. Now, if I have been taught to think logically, I do not dismiss my dissatisfaction, but put it in the form of a problem or a question to be resolved: Why did World War II happen?

3. Having formulated the problem, I must find information to solve it. True, I already have learned much in class. But the very act of defining the problem suggests other areas to be explored; in this case, the events leading to the outbreak of war and the conditions that made those events possible, such as rearmament, mass unemployment, and the rise of totalitarian ideologies. The information I gather suggests possible solutions to the problem. For example, in considering the ideology of National Socialism, I encounter the concept of *Lebensraum* ("living space") and the principle that Germany must defend Western Europe against Asiatic invaders. These ideas may suggest that Germany went to war in order to

---

[4] Dewey defined inquiry as "the controlled or directed transformation of an indeterminate situation into one that is so determinate in its constituent distinctions and relations as to convert the elements of the original situation into a unified whole." All logical forms, he said, "arise within the operations of inquiry and are concerned with control over inquiry so that it may yield warranted assertions." John Dewey, *Logic: The Theory of Inquiry*, Holt, New York, 1938, pp. 3-4, 104.

forestall a threatened assault on Europe by the Soviet Union. Still, this is only one of a number of possibilities that I consider.

4. My next step is to evaluate these possibilities to see how consistent each is with the facts at my disposal and with the other hypotheses that have occurred to me. Clearly, I will find a number of causes of World War II, some of which will be more important than others. Hence I will consider each hypothesis in relation not only to the facts it covers but also to the other explanations with which it will cohere. In the process a number of hypotheses will be rejected—the hypothesis, for example, that Germany declared war in 1939 because a severe depression earlier had led to the formation of an authoritarian and warlike regime. This hypothesis breaks down because it fails to account for the fact that Britain, France, and the United States all suffered from a depression and yet became pacifist or isolationist rather than belligerent. A more likely hypothesis might be that Hitler only intended to attack Russia and that he found himself at war with the Western powers as a result of diplomatic misunderstandings. Another hypothesis might be that the failure of the Western powers to act at the time of Hitler's movements into Austria and Czechoslovakia encouraged the National Socialists to embark on a plan of world conquest.

5. I then test the more promising hypotheses experimentally by deducing their probable consequences and verifying whether these consequences hold good. Suppose I consider the hypothesis that World War II was caused by Hitler's desire to make Europe an Aryan fortress. First, I deduce the likely outcomes of this hypothesis: that Hitler would cooperate for a time with other Aryan peoples in Europe, that he would make all non-Aryan populations servants of the master race, and so forth. Then I check whether these consequences in fact took place. I investigate whether Hitler offered to cooperate with other Aryan nations, whether he in fact turned Slavic countries into vassal states, and so on.

6. Finally, I coordinate the hypotheses that I have verified objectively. They now constitute "warranted assertions," meaning that they are justified on the basis of the information I have examined and the range of hypotheses I have proposed to explain it. All such assertions, however, are tentative, since further information, broader or more penetrating hypotheses, or simply finer thinking, might invalidate them wholly or in part. Thus the knowledge I have acquired is provisional. But it is a basis for further inquiry, because it offers a means for exploring the same ground more thoroughly and because it provides a vantage point for much broader generalizations, as, for example, about the causes of *all* wars.[5]

---

[5] Recently the factor of *relevance* has taken on greater significance for the logic

What are the special characteristics of this kind of thinking? First, it is *scientific*. It leads me to define a problem, gather information, propose hypotheses, predict their consequences, verify the latter experimentally, and coordinate the findings. Second, it is *critical*. It makes me consider alternative possibilities, examine as many facts as I can, delay judgment until the facts have been verified, and verify ideas with reference to facts rather than personal preferences. It makes me unwilling to take things for granted and leads me to consider all knowledge as tentative and open to revision. Finally, it is *reflective*. It stops me from jumping to conclusions. Instead of doing the first thing that enters my head, I pause to consider whether there are better alternatives.

Many problems within individual disciplines lend themselves to this kind of thinking—the sociological problem, for instance, of population mobility and its probable effect on the education of youth. Clearly, a question as complicated as this should not be attempted without several years' study of sociology together with some knowledge of other social sciences. But there are simpler sociological problems to which the method can be applied at an earlier age. In other words, once the pupil has been introduced to some area of study, he can use the problem-solving method not only to handle what he knows but also to explore further.

The problem-solving method may be applied to issues in contemporary life, such as civil rights, taxation, and Federal aid to schools. These are "molar" problems, so called because they cut across a range of disciplines. Problems of taxation, for example, call for a knowledge of law, finance, economics, and accounting. Problems of Federal aid to education require a knowledge of history, political science, sociology, and economics. One of the main tasks in dealing with such problems is to judge what knowledge and what disciplines are relevant to them, an art that can be

of inquiry. See Joseph J. Schwab, "The Structure of the Natural Sciences," in G. W. Ford and Lawrence Pugno, Eds., *The Structure of Knowledge and the Curriculum*, Rand McNally, Chicago, 1964, pp. 38-39, where Schwab summarizes his criticisms and gives implications for a "revised version of the schoolbook study of the short-term syntax of the sciences." Existing versions, he says (p. 37), omit a step preceding step one, which "refers to the discrimination of relevant data but fails to tell us in what way relevance and irrelevance are determined." Relevance, in other words, must have a reference. Schwab then outlines his own version: "(1) The formulation of a problem (from juxtaposing a principle of inquiry—a substantive structure—and index phenomena); (2) the search for data that will suggest possible solutions to this problem; (3) reformulation of the problem to include these possible solutions; (4) a determination of the data necessary to solve the problem; (5) a plan of experiment that will elicit the data required; (6) execution of the experiment and accumulation of the desired data; (7) interpretation of the data by means of the guiding substantive structures together with previous knowledge possessed by the investigator."

learned only by actually handling problems that involve a number of disciplines.

Educators might help here by offering a problems course in such topics as juvenile delinquency, disarmament, and central-city decay. The primary purpose of such a course would be to nurture an intelligent and flexible cast of mind rather than to provide knowledge or ready-made solutions.[6] In particular, it would help cultivate the ability to think logically, interpret a problem through different intellectual frames (sociological, ethical, and so forth), and decide matters in concert with others. To be effective, the course would probe only a few problems in depth. The pupils would engage in such operations as defining the problem to be solved, tracing its implications, gathering relevant facts and theories, examining the causes of disagreement, proposing alternative solutions, and evaluating them.[7]

Logic in Teaching

Logic may also be applied to the *act of teaching,* where teaching is understood to be a special way of making things known to others. Here teaching may be considered a system of actions varied in form and content but directed toward learning. It is in the performance of these actions and in the interactions of the teacher with his students that learning takes place. These actions and interactions are of course personal. But they are

---

[6] Cf. Harry S. Broudy, B. Othanel Smith, and Joe R. Burnett, *Democracy and Excellence in American Secondary Education: A Study in Curriculum Theory,* Rand McNally, Chicago, 1964, pp. 241-243. A problems course may also be instituted to coordinate the different disciplines and accompany the general education program throughout the junior and senior high school. See Arno A. Bellack, "Knowledge Structure and the Curriculum," in Stanley Elam, Ed., *Education and the Structure of Knowledge,* Fifth Annual Phi Delta Kappa Symposium on Educational Research, Rand McNally, Chicago, 1964, pp. 275-276.

[7] The utility of the logic of inquiry is still disputed. Critics maintain that in practice it is less effective than the techniques of problem solving formulated within the disciplines themselves. It also tends, they say, to constrict the inquiring mind. My own reply would be that it is *adaptable* (if not immediately applicable) to any subject matter at almost any level. And *any* formulation of a way of thinking by its very nature can be accused of constricting the mind. But the argument is too lengthy to pursue here. For a philosophic analysis of Dewey's theory of inquiry and resultant debates see Robert R. Wellman, "Dewey's Theory of Inquiry: The Impossibility of Its Statement," *Educational Theory,* **XIV,** 2 (April 1964), 103 ff., answered by Philip Eddy, "On the Statability of Dewey's Theory of Inquiry," *Educational Theory,* **XV,** 4 (October 1965), 321 ff., and rebutted by Wellman, op. cit., 327 ff.

also logical, in that they have a certain structure, a certain order, such that no matter where in the world teaching takes place, it does so in accordance with operations that reflect the very nature of a teaching-learning situation.

What are these logical operations? How may they be analyzed?[8] The act of teaching may be said to involve three variables: (1) the teacher's behavior, which is the independent variable, (2) the pupil's behavior, which is the dependent variable, and (3) various postulated entities, such as memories, beliefs, needs, and inferences, which are intervening variables.[9]

In the course of teaching, these variables—the teacher's acts, the pupil's acts, and the postulated entities—are related in many ways. The teacher's acts are followed by various postulated states in the pupil which cause him to behave in certain ways. The teacher cannot observe these states directly; he cannot personally witness interests, needs, motives, and the like; but he can, and often does, *infer* them from the pupil's overt behavior. For example, he may infer from the pupil's reactions that he is interested in what he is doing or that he would prefer to do something else. The pupil's actions in turn lead to various postulated states in the teacher, which then give rise to actions. The cycle begins again, as the teacher's behavior produces postulated states in the pupil, and so on. The process of teaching continues in this fashion until the teacher concludes either that the pupil has learned what he intended him to learn or that there is nothing to be gained from teaching him any more at the moment.

Independent variables in the teacher's behavior consist of "verbal," "performative," and "expressive" acts. *Verbal acts* are of three kinds: (1) logical operations, such as defining, classifying, explaining, and the like; (2) directive operations instructing the pupil in what he is to do, such as write on a blackboard, read a poem, or recite a multiplication table; and (3) admonitory operations, such as praising, blaming, reassuring, and so on. *Performative acts* are of the motor variety but may be accompanied by words. The teacher shows the pupil how to do something,

---

[8] For a complete account, see the works of B. Othanel Smith (and others) cited in the References at the end of this chapter. For an earlier brief statement, see B. Othanel Smith, "A Concept of Teaching," in B. Othanel Smith and Robert H. Ennis, Eds., *Language and Concepts in Education*, Rand McNally, Chicago, 1961, pp. 86-101.

[9] It should be pointed out that the expression 'intervening variable" has been used in so many difffferent ways that psychologists as a whole now tend to avoid it. (It has always struck me as rather like "phlogiston" or Hull's "black box"—a place to put vague concepts that refer, as John Locke said of "substance," to "I know not what.")

such as regulate a Bunsen burner. *Expressive acts* reveal the psychological state of the teacher, exemplified in facial expression, tone of voice, body movements, and so forth.

The dependent variables can be similarly classified. The learner performs many verbal actions. Some of them are logical operations, and their purpose is to indicate that the pupil understands what he is being taught. He rarely performs verbal actions that are directive or admonitory, since telling-how-to and praising or blaming are typically the teacher's responsibility. When the pupil behaves performatively (taking part in athletics, for example, or setting up laboratory equipment), he normally does so to practice the actions themselves rather than to instruct anyone. The pupil also behaves expressively. He smiles or frowns, slumps or sits erect, speaks firmly or uncertainly, and so on. Such behavior, though rarely addressed to anyone, indicates to the teacher how the pupil is feeling.

Admittedly, "logic" used in this sense is not the rigorous enterprise normally understood when we use the word, but it does involve such elements as structure, propriety, and rationality when dealing with events like teaching. Thus, when we construe teaching as a system of actions intended to induce learning, and analyze the model of the teaching process based on it, we emerge with an objective approach to the study of teaching. Where previously research into the effectiveness of teaching methods has proceeded from definitions of teaching that reflect a preference for one method or another, the findings being inconclusive, we now see the actions of the teacher as they really are, relatively undistorted by our preconceptions. Thus we are, or should be, able to assess more accurately the strengths and weaknesses of different teaching methods.[10]

Analysis and Language

In the chapter on the Relevance of Philosophy I outlined three modes of philosophy, of which *analysis* was one. The hallmarks of philosophic analysis are a concern with logic and a concern with language. Analysis turns away from speculation and prescription. It refuses to offer theories

[10] The application of logic to the act of teaching is far from being as definitive as we would like, for teaching, being a human endeavor, resists our most earnest attempts to establish a structure for it. Also, the success of construing teaching as an act involving logical operations depends chiefly on the expertise of the teacher and the kind of subject matter he imparts. (Here I do not refer to method or purpose, but simply to a practical knowledge of what actually happens or comes close to happening when any teacher teaches.)

of the universe or rules for the good life. Its goal is to clarify thoughts. This goal has been aptly described by Ludwig Wittgenstein:

> The object of philosophy is the logical clarification of thoughts.
> Philosophy is not a theory but an activity.
> A philosophical work consists essentially of quotations.
> The result of philosophy is not a number of "philosophical propositions," but to make propositions clear.
> Philosophy should make clear and delimit sharply the thoughts which otherwise are, as it were, opaque and blurred.[11]

A concern with clear, logical thinking implies an equal concern with the language in which thoughts are expressed. It is pointless to look *through* language at thoughts or propositions if that language is opaque and blurred. One must also look *at* language.

In the combination of logical and linguistic analysis—analysis of the logic of arguments through analysis of the language in which they are expressed—philosophers of this persuasion believe that they have found a means of resolving most of the traditional problems of philosophy. Such problems, they say, are confusions in thought arising at least in part from confusion in language. Misleading constructions, obscure idioms, and ambiguous phrases generate philosophers' perplexities. These problems must be dissolved by investigating the logical implications of the sentences in which they occur. Among the leading exponents of this view are G. E. Moore, Ludwig Wittgenstein, Gilbert Ryle, Peter F. Strawson, and John L. Austin.

The analyst maintains that philosophic problems arise in the course of our attempts to order and explain known facts. These problems cannot be solved by an appeal to the facts themselves, because the point at issue is how the facts are to be described. The problems are created by the complexities of language. Since a given word or expression normally has a range of uses, it is easy to confuse these uses and to employ one where another is appropriate. For example, the word "growth" is used in a number of contexts from biology to education. If we transfer the biological sense of growth to the context of education, we unwittingly tangle two sets of logical implications, those of growth in biology and those of growth in education. To compare the growth of a child with that of a plant is misleading, because the word "growth" implies different things in these different contexts.

The role of analysis, then, is essentially therapeutic: to clear the mind

---

[11] Ludwig Wittgenstein, *Tractatus Logico-Philosophicus,* Humanities Press, New York, 1955, p. 77 (4.112).

by revealing the sources of conceptual perplexity. Analysis does not "solve" problems, it "dissolves" them. Analysis examines the customary uses of the expressions and types of expression that are involved in the problems of philosophy, and it seeks to indicate where philosophers have overextended or misapplied such expressions to produce paradox or perplexity. The standard of correct use is normally actual speech, or the ways in which words are customarily used in various contexts. Actual speech is the most reliable guide to meaning, for it must meet what for the analyst is the most stringent of all tests of effective communication, that of constant use.[12]

Analysis has answered readily to the study of education. As a discipline or branch of knowledge, education is highly practical, in the sense that the process it studies (that of being educated) is a normal experience in the life of every person. What is true of the study of education as a whole is true of its philosophy. The problems and the language of educational philosophy are for the most part those of general life. At the same time some fundamental concepts that occur in educational discourse also appear in a number of realms of inquiry, such as psychology, sociology, and economics. They include "knowing," "learning," "socializing," "valuing," and "ascertaining." When analyzing these concepts, the educator must examine their meanings in many different contexts. Then he will be able to spot the ambiguities that are caused when meanings appropriate to certain contexts are imported into others. Education also possesses concepts of its own, such as "subject matter," "mastery," "readiness," and "character training." These are not only topics of theoretical debate but also fiercely defended justifications of many practical school policies, a fact that adds to the difficulty of analyzing them.

Thus the study of education draws heavily on ideas in general currency as well as on the ideas of a range of related disciplines. As a result, not a few educational concepts carry a number of logical implications corresponding to the different spheres in which these concepts are used; and in consequence, they are highly ambiguous. One of these concepts is that of "adjustment," which is used, among other places, in psychology

---

[12] P. F. Strawson, "Construction and Analysis," in *The Revolution in Philosophy*, Gilbert Ryle, introd., Macmillan, London, 1956, p. 103. Cf. also J. L. Austin, "A Plea for Excuses," *Proceedings of the Aristotelian Society*, **LVIII** 8 (1956-57): ". . . our common stock of words embodies all the distinctions men have found worth drawing, and the connections they have found worth making . . . these surely are likely to be more numerous, more sound, since they have stood up to the long test of the survival of the fittest, and more subtle, at least in all ordinary and reasonably practical matters, than any that you or I are likely to think up in our armchairs. . . ."

and in education.[13] Another is that of "need." When a school says that it exists "to meet the needs of students," what is it really saying? That it has assessed *all* the needs of its students and can meet them? Or just *some* of the needs? If so, which ones? Perhaps "needs" could be dissolved into a statement about the aims of education as seen and practiced by School X. Or perhaps the word means nothing at all. Or take "adjustment." To which part of the school is Johnny supposed to adjust—the routine, the teacher, the curriculum, the athletic program, or what? Does he become less free by adjusting or more free? Does anybody—in fact, *can* anybody—adjust to an *entire* school? Even if a student could adjust to the school, is it not better for the school to adjust to the student?

The word "relevant," too, has become a fashionable term for judging the success or failure of schooling. But the term lends itself to almost as many meanings as there are people who use it. "Relevance" can be used to convey an emphasis on vocational studies, on a problems approach to learning, on learning for its own sake, on a theoretical analysis of the human condition, or on whatever the speaker regards as the end of a good education. Perhaps most often it is used to indicate that the school has an obligation to serve a particular community, or a special subculture, or a certain class of people. An education that is relevant, we hear, is one that goes out into the streets, into factories, homes, organizations, and settlements. It takes place in communes and collectives. It is geared to individual and racial hopes, aspirations, and special interests. It even serves or should serve to overthrow a "sick" society and to revolutionize the value system of our culture. Thus the slogan, "Education should be relevant to the needs of the community," can mean anything and everything. For what is meant by "education"? What precisely are the "needs" that education is physically and spiritually capable of meeting? And what is a "community"? Is it a place, a feeling, a condition, a unified set of purposes, an autonomous, self-subsistent society, or what?

Nevertheless, analysis is no substitute for factual knowledge. If we dispute how far education should "meet the needs" of the pupil, we must know what these needs are at different ages and whether they vary by region, by social class, by economic status, and so on. This knowledge can come only from factual inquiry. Nor can analysis provide us with the moral beliefs that are necessary for decisions about educational prac-

---

13 For an analysis of this concept, see C. J. B. Macmillan, "The Concept of Adjustment," in George F. Kneller, Ed., *Introduction to the Philosophy of Education*, Wiley, New York, 1964, pp. 82 ff. See also B. Paul Komisar, " 'Need' and the 'Needs-Curriculum'," in B. Othanel Smith and Robert H. Ennis, Eds., *Language and Concepts in Education*, Rand McNally, Chicago, Ill., 1961, pp. 24-42.

tice. For instance, the problem of adjustment is to a large extent a moral one. Analysis cannot provide us with the moral principles that we need to decide it. But it can make us aware of the assumptions and implications that these principles involve. It can clarify the concepts, slogans, exhortations, and the like that are put forward in arguments on "neutrality," "commitment," and so forth.

So far I have described what analysis is. Now I will do some analysis myself. I have chosen two concepts to analyze: "teaching" and "equality." My treatment must be short and simple to fit into this chapter. But perhaps I can say enough to challenge the reader to study these concepts further.

Concept of Teaching

Classic definitions state that teaching is "imparting knowledge," "training in a skill," "giving instruction." But they tell us very little about what imparting knowledge amounts to, what goes into the task of training in a skill, or what happens when one gives instruction. In fact, if we look up "impart," we find that one of its meanings is "teach." Under "instruct" the first synonym is also "teach." We are a little better off with the word "train," which dictionaries associate with "strong teaching." To train is to "subject to instruction" with the idea of producing "efficient performance." Still, we can have weak training, the kind that does not result in efficient performance. The dictionary, then, does not help us to distinguish among all the synonyms of teaching. In fact, it leads us round and round and back where we started. Let us therefore move out of the pages of the dictionary and into the more enlightening realm of analysis.

First of all, what does a teacher do when he teaches? Does he just talk, or tell, or relate, or what? Actually, he does all these things, but *with a purpose.* And that purpose is to get students to learn. Teaching, then, is an "intentional activity," one that aims to bring about learning. The teacher describes, explains, questions, and evaluates; he urges, threatens, and cajoles; in short, he does many things to get students to learn the sorts of things he thinks they should learn and in a manner of which he approves. Parents and others do this too, but with a difference. Teachers are more "professional," meaning that they know a great deal about (a) what they teach, (b) how to teach it, and (c) whom they are teaching. A teacher's primary task is to get students to know or to do things in a formal way. This means that he structures knowledge or skills in such a way as to cause the student not only to learn them but also to remember them and do something with them. The teacher also evaluates the student; hence, the student is challenged to learn and to remember because he knows that in one way or another he will be examined. In short, unlike other people, the teacher engages in what has been called "didactic," as distinct from "ordinary," discourse. That is, he avoids casual, unstudied conversation in favor of deliberate, weighed communication. He designs his teaching in such a way that the student will think hard about and remember what he is learning.

Now of course, all discourse is intended to influence people in some way. A question is meant to elicit a reply, a threat to deter, a condolence to comfort, and a promise to reassure. The purpose of didactic discourse is not merely to enable the student to repeat what he has been taught but also to say and do a number of things with it. When a teacher explains the use of the relative pronoun, his prime aim is not that the pupil should repeat this explanation (although no doubt he intends this too) but that the pupil should use the relative pronoun correctly. When he sets forth the causes of the French Revolution, he intends that the pupil should be able not only to repeat this knowledge in an examination but also, and more importantly, to use it in assessing other prerevolutionary situations past and present, in short to apply the knowledge he has received.[14]

Not all teaching is didactic discourse. We can teach by demonstration, by drill, by example, and by any method that results in the kind of learning we want to achieve. In essence, however, the language of teaching is didactic discourse. There are several advantages in accepting this view. For one thing, the content of didactic discourse is largely independent of the deliverer, the recipient, and the occasion of the delivery. Other things being equal, the information involved can be delivered by any appropriately qualified person to any properaly prepared learner on any suitable occasion. Thus if a student misses a lesson, he can make it up later. For another, the content can be preserved, compared, criticized, and added to, so that what is taught to one generation can be imparted to another generation years later, whereas mere talking, telling, and narrating are more greatly conditioned by who talks and when and where.[15]

14 Didactic discourse can also be internal. A person can teach himself to say and do things that differ from the style in which the teaching was given. For example, having taught himself elementary logic, he can then detect flaws in other people's reasoning. In fact, people often learn more through self-instruction than from a human teacher.

15 Didactic discourse also helps us to distinguish between kinds of human communication. It involves intellectual operations that, in the opinion of most educators, are "higher" than other kinds of behavior and indeed should govern them. In most

But, you will ask, where does learning come in? Teaching, I have said, is an effort to bring about learning. The converse, however, is not true. Efforts to achieve learning do not necessarily require a human teacher. Furthermore, although the achievement of learning is the hallmark of successful teaching, it is not sufficient in itself to determine *good* teaching. All depends on the appropriateness of the learning achieved. I might be able to teach Johnny the multiplication table, and then when he shows me that he has learned (and remembers) it, I can say I have taught him successfully. But I may not have taught him as well as I could all the things he should know about the concept of multiplication. I may not have allowed him to make discoveries on his own. I may have looked for quick results when I should have spent more time building sounder knowledge. So teaching now appears to involve "goodness" as well as "success."

What are some of the conditions of good teaching? The first is *continuity*. We do not teach a single lesson and let it go at that. We teach lessons both cumulatively and in order of difficulty. We take into consideration the age, aptitude, and ability of the educand, and we organize our activities over a relatively long span of time. This is quite different from the way nonteachers behave. Parents inform their children about many things, such a religion, morals, and sex. But under the conditions we have given for the application of the concept "teaching," parents do not usually teach. Indeed, this is one reason why, in the opinion of many, information on morals and sex should be taught in school. Here in theory, if not necessarily in practice, morality and sex may be learned as a consequence of good teaching. The second condition of good teaching is the *intentional practicalization* of what is taught (and learned). Telling, informing, and relating do not *require* learning—not even good telling, informing, and relating. But good teaching does, and teaching is good only when the pupil uses and lives out what he has learned freely and responsibly.

Good teaching involves yet a third condition, *concept formation*. The good teacher ensures that learners acquire patterns of thought and action that will not only endure but will also render specific commands superfluous. There is a vast difference between people who (a) have been told

civilized nations intellectual work is "highly" favored. It is the work of those who, like the readers of this essay, have received a "higher" education and can give it to others. If intellectual power as generated through didactic discourse ceases to be favored by a culture, that culture will atrophy. Cf. Gilbert Ryle, "The Intellect," in Israel Scheffler, Ed., *Philosophy and Education*, Allyn and Bacon, Boston, 1958, pp. 133-140.

to be honest, (b) have learned to be honest, and (c) have learned that they *ought* to be honest. I can tell Johnny to be honest (a command); but if I teach him well, he will learn (a) what honesty is, (b) why it is a good thing, and (c) why he *ought* to be honest. I would also expect him actually to *be* honest, because he has come to *believe* (as well as know) that he *should* be honest. The challenge then for the teacher is not only to inform students about honesty (or anything else, for the matter) but also to try to get them to be honest from their own convictions critically arrived at.

Now of course, it is possible to teach well only to have the student quite responsibly reject (a) the teacher, (b) the knowledge, and (c) the way the knowledge is presented. This is a risk all teachers must take. Indeed, having taken the risk, having encouraged critical reflection, impartial scrutiny, and the taking of positions, we find ourselves confronted today with rebellious students everywhere. But unless the rebels can be shown to be irresponsible and unreasonable, we must happily conclude that some teachers have done their job well—very well indeed. "Progress," we hear, "is the result of discontented minds."

In a nutshell, when we say that certain conditions are necessary for good teaching, we mean that students are taught the habits and norms of critical thought and behavior. We do not simply teach students *how* to be good citizens, as if citizenship were a set of skills, but also *to be* good citizens (or give good cause for being otherwise). We teach them not merely what voting is but also how to vote and what voting is worth as a norm in political life.

Does good teaching include indoctrination? Yes, for a good teacher cannot help indoctrinating. He will tell his class what he thinks is good and bad in our culture, but he will also praise the good and condemn the bad. Since education, as I have said, is essentially a normative affair, a teacher will always reveal his values. He will teach what he thinks students ought to learn (as well as what he is directed to teach).

Indoctrination, then, is not in itself contrary to good teaching. Rather, *it is the content of what is indoctrinated that matters, together with the method used.* Some people think that indoctrination in democracy is a contradiction in terms (since democracy implies freedom of teaching and learning). It is not. "The qualifications for self-government," said Thomas Jefferson, "are not innate. They are the result of habit and long training." Democracy rests on certain established principles, and we have every reason to teach for the acceptance of these principles, in short to inculcate a belief in them. This does not mean that we cannot criticize them. It means that the teacher has every right to use his influence on his students when he is teaching them about our political system. He is privileged and, some think, duty-bound to communicate the ideals of the culture, among which is included the right to criticize the culture. To the demurrer that teachers should remain "neutral," I can only reply that this too is taking a position, although not a very effective one. The neutral teacher quickly loses his appeal, for education is not a neutral but a value-laden enterprise.[16]

It should now be clear that teaching is also a method of inducing acceptable belief. But we must show how teaching differs from other methods of inducing belief, such as debating, threatening, forcing, propagandizing, bribing, and so forth. Teaching differs from these primarily because it involves rationality, judgment, critical dialogue, and defensibility. Teaching induces belief through the exercise of free, rational judgment by the student. The teacher too gives reasons for the beliefs he wants to transmit, thus submitting his own judgments to the critical assessment of his students. The teacher then actually risks his own beliefs, for student criticism can be devastating.

But overly rational teaching has its own limitations. It is hardly applicable to children in the early grades. If, as I have said, teaching is any activity that brings about learning, teaching must be held to include other methods than the purely rational. In the first grade the teacher brings about the kind of learning a pupil needs at that age—socialization, perhaps, or acculturation, or good habit formation. When a first-grade child asks why he has been requested to do such and such, he does not expect to receive a highly rational reply. All he wants is an answer that he can understand, one that satifies his curiosity or his need for attention. The world of the child in the early grades is lively, animated, and imaginative, hardly a world dominated by reason.

Thus teaching is not simply the activity of deliberately inculcating habits, norms, information, and skills, even if we take into account the condition that what has been taught must be remembered. Some inculcation there must be, even some indoctrination, as against the evils of rape, venereal disease, and child abandonment, and for the goods of promise fulfillment, integrity, and physical health. Teaching is good when the

---

[16] I do not refer here to the so-called "neutrality" of science or the "objectivity" of factual knowledge. Certainly there can be no argument about many scientific and empirical facts, laws, and theories. I refer to the act of teaching and to the attitudes of teachers with respect to what they are teaching. I can teach Communism or Presbyterianism or the phlogiston theory objectively and didactically. But I would hardly be expected (and perhaps not allowed) to indoctrinate my class into a belief in them.

method of teaching is adapted to the kind of learning desired. Good teaching involves submitting subject matter to the independent judgment of students wherever it is suitable to do so. It also involves sorting out the various elements in this subject matter. In science, for example, we may teach (a) the straightforward facts of science, (b) the meaning of science (personal, social, epistemological, etc.), (c) the value of science, (d) how to think scientifically, and (e) how to solve problems in science. The good science teacher attends to all these elements. He knows which is which, how they are to be separated, and how they are to be unified.

The teacher also assumes a moral responsibility for the welfare of those in his charge. He is in a position of trust and is therefore likely to be judged severely if he abuses his position. A teacher is one who has a special knowledge of his subject and his pupils. When he is licensed or given a certificate, he does not simply go out and teach; he is morally obligated to teach well. He has accepted quite explicitly the responsibility to see that learning does indeed take place. Of course, no teacher can *guarantee* that learning will take place. He can encourage, even cajole, a pupil into learning, but he cannot in the long run *make* him learn. Only the pupil can do that for himself.

This means that control by the teacher, teacher authority, must be recognized as a necessary prerogative of teaching. A teacher is an authority not only with respect to his subject matter but also with respect to the classes he teaches. Some teachers, especially beginners, are fearful of losing the affection of their pupils, so they hesitate to use this authority. But a teacher's authority comes to him whether he wants it or not by virtue of his professional role. Parents and pupils *expect* him to be an authority, and pupils know they are in school to learn from him.

The teacher then, like the British householder, is king of his castle, with all the rights, privileges, and responsibilities that go with it. One of his rights is to be obeyed by those over whom he has authority. To secure obedience he may even use force or delegate its use. This is quite proper, for unless authority can have recourse to force, it may be flouted at will. Of course the teacher must exercise his authority wisely and responsibly. He must also remember that his authority is less than that of a parent. The teacher-pupil relationship may be affectionate, but it does not involve parental love and devotion. It is essentially temporary and limited: temporary in that a teacher does not normally teach a particular child more than a year or two, limited in that the learning that the teacher directs is, or should be, primarily intellectual. It is a relationship determined ultimately by the principles of a very old profession.

Concept of Equality

Now let us take the concept of equality. In this country belief in equality is so strong that the traditional policy of "separate but equal" schools for nonwhites is no longer officially accepted. In the name of equal educational opportunity the doors of most institutions of higher education are open to all secondary-school graduates. Everyone, it is said, has a right to attend school or college up to a point of obviously diminishing returns.[17]

Nevertheless, there is little agreement on what we mean by "equality" or "equal treatment." My dictionary states that "equal" means alike or same in quantity, degree, value, ability, etc. It gives other definitions too, such as "not having sufficient power or ability," as in the expression, "He was not equal to the task." For the moment, however, let us confine our attention to the first meaning, that of "likeness" or "sameness."

In the sense of sameness in degree or quantity, the term "equality" gives us no trouble. When we say, "John's IQ is equal to Mary's," we know that if John's IQ is 110 Mary's is 110 too. But what do we mean when we say, "The teacher gave equal treatment to John and Mary"? Do we imply that the teacher spent the same amount of time with each? That if he kept John after school he kept Mary too? That despite their different personalities he handled both pupils exactly alike? Obviously there is something puzzling about using "equal" in the sense of "same."

Perhaps there are times when we should give pupils *unequal* treatment. Surely Mary should not be kept after school just because John is. Yet if I said, "The teacher gave John and Mary unequal treatment," I would seem to be accusing the teacher of discrimination. "Equal," we see, is a word that usually connotes something fine and desirable. Human beings, it is said, are "born free and equal." People who think that men are not born this way are regarded as uncivilized. We may, it is true, remember the parable of the talents, which makes the point that some people, as a result of birth or environment, are more talented than others. But at least, we say, all people should be *treated* as equals. They should all have an equal *opportunity*, an equal chance, to make the best of whatever talents they possess.

---

17 Over the last decade the concept of equality has been much discussed by educational philosophers. Even though one essay is entitled "Too Much Equality" (B. Paul Komisar and Jerrold R. Coombs, *Studies in Philosophy and Education*, Fall 1965, 263 ff.), it is certain that other authors will assert that we do not have enough. Perhaps the most engaging contribution is Paul Nash's "Two Cheers for Equality," in *Teachers College Record* (December 1965), pp. 217 ff.

But this only compounds the difficulty, for opportunity is not something that can be quantified into a measure for you and the same measure for me. And what is an opportunity for me may not be an opportunity for you. How then can any opportunity or chance be equal? Indeed, we may first have to provide equality, whatever that is, before we can provide opportunity. Obviously, even when all children have "equal opportunity" to attend school, those children who are significantly disadvantaged will have less chance of succeeding in school than those who are not. Suppose we then do what we can to bring the disadvantaged to the same starting line as the advantaged. Do we not now fall into the trap of treating unequally those who already are at the starting line? A teacher has only so much time and energy. If in a class of 30 he concentrates on the disadvantaged, others in the class will be neglected. We live, let us remember, in a highly competitive society. Cooperation is a fine ideal, but if we want to get ahead (and who does not?), we must also compete. Even the finest minds need guidance and challenge, and students possessing such minds are in school for that purpose. Are we not, then, just as well off omitting "equal" before opportunity? The adjective seems both redundant and confusing. The best we can surely do is to provide an opportunity—equal or not—for everyone to get the kind of education to which he is *justifiably* entitled, about which more will be said in a moment.

To recapitulate, it seems that when we employ the term "equality" to mean "sameness," we not only use it narrowly but we also actually negate its dictionary meaning. We say that treating people equally means treating them the same, yet we find that in order to be fair to the disadvantaged we must treat them differently, that is, not the same, unequally. If Mary comes from a disadvantaged home and John comes from a comfortable middle-class home, the teacher is not as a rule expected to treat them equally but rather unequally in order to bring about a greater equality (social, economic, vocational, etc.) between them. This is the whole point of compensatory education.

Let us try a second approach, one that the alert reader may already have considered. If we say that the teacher treated Mary and John equally, perhaps what we really mean is that he treated them *justly*, or *fairly*, or *fittingly*. The teacher kept John after school, but it was not fair (or fitting) for him to treat Mary in the same way because Mary had not misbehaved like John. No trouble here. Now suppose I say, "The teacher gave equal treatment to both sides of an issue." This seems praiseworthy enough, for in a truly democratic society teachers are expected to do just this. But what does this equal treatment entail? That the teacher devotes twenty minutes to each side? That the teacher presents six arguments for and half a dozen against? That the teacher spends five minutes in turn describing, explaining, advocating, refuting one side and then five minutes doing the same with the other? Hardly. For one thing, the teacher may not need to explain one side because the students already have studied that side themselves. They may indeed have studied it so well that the teacher can devote all his time to the other side. At first reading this may sound pointless, but it is only a *reductio ad absurdum* of the way some people use the term "equality."

Since we cannot afford to be pointless, let us try a third approach. Why not let the student himself decide what equal treatment is? Why not ask the student what he understands by equal treatment and whether he is getting it? In this case, however, we assume that the student can *justify* his claim. It is no use just letting him sound off. Here, then, the student needs knowledge about justifying moral claims in general and his claim of equality in particular. There are some justifying principles that he may take from ethics. He might, for example, refer to Kant's categorical imperative, that we should act "only on that maxim which we can at the same time will to be a universal law." This imperative represents Kant's classic principle of impartiality and respect for persons, that no one shall demand favored treatment unless he can advance good reasons for it. In other words, we are obligated to treat people "equally" (that is, the same) until we have good cause to treat them differently. Obviously, if a student were disadvantaged in some understandable way, we would be justified in giving him different treatment. He is not an equal and therefore should not be treated equally.

So we return to such notions as justice, fairness, and fittingness. After all, when people demand equality, what they really want is justice, fair play, and treatment appropriate to their needs. But what makes our reasons good? We know that shrewd people can produce seemingly good reasons for what appear to be quite blatant acts of inequality. To this I reply that our reasons must be (a) relevant, (b) socially viable, and (c) defensible. *Relevance* best can be established by appealing to sound ethical principles. I could justify a statement that it is wrong to treat people as slaves by citing my ethical beliefs about the dignity of man. In my view slavery is an offense against human dignity. By *social viability* I refer to the possibility of obtaining some particular form of justice within a given society. Obviously, I cannot treat students equally in any sense of the word if law or custom prevents me. My reasons are *defensible* if I have reached them logically and if they are grounded in an ethical theory that I can rationally demonstrate to be beneficial to mankind. Now of course there may be some argument over whether my reasons are better than yours or whether I have proved my case. If so, we may have to have recourse to courts of law. The Supreme Court is a last resort when disputes have to be settled, and although the justices themselves in turn become disputants, majority opinion even here in the end prevails.

How comforting to be able to rely on the Supreme Court for answers! The settlement, however, is chiefly a legal one, and in reaching it the justices too have had to educate themselves. They have had to appeal to ethical principles, to philosophies of law and human conduct. Even so, very few cases involving equality actually reach the Supreme Court. Most of them have to be settled in the arena of education where the challenge is issued. Schooling is an urgent matter. Teachers cannot wait; emergencies arise every hour; decisions must be made on the spot. The teacher must have reflected on questions of equality and must be ready to draw on his fund of ethical knowledge.

Conclusion

There is no doubt that analysis has improved educational philosophy, making it more rigorous and also more sensitive to the manifold implications of educational terms. On the other hand, analysis alone is incomplete as a philosophy. It has illuminated individual educational concepts and concept pairs (for example, teaching and learning), but no analytic philosopher has yet sought to coordinate or systematize major educational concepts. In time analysts may undertake such systematizing; to date they have shown no taste for it.

Education is the conscious molding of man by men. It rests on conceptions of man and society that can be judged only by an educational philosophy that embraces the full range of philosophy's subject matter. Analysis has not invalidated this concern but rather has turned away from it. Thus the influence of analysis on present-day educational philosophy should not lead us to conclude that the other functions of educational philosophy, the speculative and the prescriptive, have been superseded. They have not. They are needed now as much as they have ever been.

References

‡‡

There are two major systematic studies of logic in education: my own *Logic and Language of Education* (Wiley, 1966, 242 pp.), and Robert H. Ennis' *Logic in Teaching* (Prentice-Hall, 1969, 520 pp.). B. Othanel Smith and his associates have published several studies on aspects of logic in teaching, such as *A Study of the Strategies of Teaching* (Bureau of Educational Research, University of Illinois, 1967) and *A Study of the Logic of Teaching* (Bureau of Educational Research, University of Illinois, n.d.).

On philosophic analysis in general I recommend John Hospers, *An Introduction to Philosophical Analysis* (Prentice-Hall, 1965). On logic and analysis with reference to education, see D. J. O'Connor, *An Introduction to the Philosophy of Education* (Routledge and Kegan Paul, London, 1957), and L. M. Brown, *General Philosophy in Education* (McGraw-Hill, 1966, 244 pp.), which is well equipped with exercises and discussion questions. In the field of language analysis Israel Scheffler's *The Language of Education* (Charles C Thomas, Springfield, Illinois, 1960, 113 pp.) opened the way for other works, such as Jonas P. Soltis, *An Introduction to the Analysis of Educational Concepts* (Addison-Wesley, 1968, 100 pp.), James Gribble, *Introduction to Philosophy of Education* (Allyn and Bacon, 1969, 198 pp.), and Glenn Langford, *Philosophy and Education* (Macmillan, London, 1969, 160 pp.). Like Soltis, Gribble and Langford focus entirely on the analysis of language and concepts in education. They do not consider other modes of philosophy. Beginning students may find Soltis the most readable. Gribble, influenced by R. S. Peters, is incisive. Langford brings analysis closer to the classroom.

288

14

The Aesthetic Component

Maxine Greene

❖❖

At a moment of "happenings," "politics as theater," and preoccupation with personal "life style," relationships between the aesthetic and the actual become increasingly obscure. Life afflicts many young people as if it were a spectacle, a whirl of discontinuous events, tolerable only to those who can remain inwardly detached and self-consciously "cool." Political activities are planned as if they were dramatic productions, intended to *present* frustration and outrage, to arouse and to shock rather than to persuade. Gestures, rituals, and styles of clothing substitute for a reasoned moral outlook; "beautiful" takes the place of "good" or "humane"; appearance becomes more meaningful than action or speech. At once, with the rise of participatory theater, "chance" or aleatory music, "history as novel,"[1] the "nonfiction novel,"[2] art itself becomes increasingly "anxious."[3] This means that people are becoming more and more aware

[1] See Norman Mailer, *The Armies of the Night: History as a Novel, The Novel as History,* The New American Library, New York, 1968.

[2] See Truman Capote, *In Cold Blood: A True Account of a Multiple Murder and Its Consequences,* Random House, New York, 1965.

[3] Harold Rosenberg, *The Anxious Object: Art Today and its Audience,* Horizon Press, New York, 1964.

289

of the indefiniteness of art's function in the world today, more and more uncertain of the differences between art and non-art, media, put-ons,— between, in the last analysis, art and life.

Our concern in this chapter is with the distinctions that can and ought to be made. It is with the several arts and the "pluralism of visions,"[4] the experiences they make possible for diverse human beings. It is also with the ways in which reflection on encounters with works of art may intensify aesthetic fulfillment and, at once, shed light on aspects of the teaching-learning process that would not become visible were it not for pondering the place of art in life. When we speak of "the aesthetic component," then, we are not simply referring to those parts of the curriculum that focus on literature, the visual arts, or music. We propose to consider a range of particular questions to which the mode of inquiry called "aesthetics" responds.

Aesthetics, George Kneller has written, "is the study of values in the realm of beauty and art. It deals with the theoretical aspects of art in its widest meaning, but it is not to be confused with the actual work of art or specialized criticisms of it." Using this statement as our starting point, we propose to move outward to wide-ranging questions involving the relationships between the worlds created by works of art and what we understand to be "reality," with expressiveness, form, and the imaginative transmutation of experience into sonatas, paintings, and poems. We shall touch, too, upon questions related to the structures and dimensions of created works, their internal relations, their levels of potential meaning, and the boundaries that separate them from the common sense world. We shall touch on related questions as well: those having to do with the kinds of perception, the kinds of "seeing" required for realizing works of art; those concerned with the events and confrontations that occur (when such works are fully realized) in the reader's, listener's, or beholder's "inner time."[5]

There is a profound educational relevance in questions of this kind for teachers preoccupied with enabling their students to learn how to learn. This is because they all ultimately involve sense-making, personal choosing, and the creating of order or form. They draw attention to a "vital center" of educational thinking in the late 20th century. (The "vital center" is Herman Melville's phrase, used on the last page of *Moby*

---

4 Dorothy Walsh, "The Cognitive Content of Art," in Francis J. Coleman, Ed., *Contemporary Studies in Aesthetics*, McGraw-Hill Book Company, New York, 1968, pp. 292-293.

5 Alfred Schutz, "Making Music Together," in *Collected Papers*, Vol. II, Martinus Nijhoff, The Hague, 1964, p. 170.

Dick, where Ishmael explains how he survived the wreck of the whaling ship: "So, floating on the margin of the ensuing scene, and in full sight of it, when the half-spent suction of the sunk ship reached me, I was then, but slowly, drawn towards the closing vortex. . . . Round and round, then, and ever contracting towards the button-like black bubble at the axis of that slowly wheeling circle, like another Ixion did I revolve. Till, gaining that vital centre, the black bubble upward burst; and now, liberated by reason of its cunning spring . . . the coffin life-buoy shot lengthwise from the sea, fell over, and floated by my side."[6]) As in the case of other contributors to this volume, we conceive the current concern with active, principled, "norm-regarding"[7] learning and the growing use of the "rule model"[8] by teachers eager to break with manipulative approaches to be, as it were, life buoys for American education. "The vital center," as we see it, is the point at which learning is treated as a conscious achievement, involving an engagement of the learner's own judgment and culminating in his own authentic sense-making, his achieved ability to order experience by means of principles he has consciously appropriated and put to work. It is the point at which the learner is seen to be constructing defensible semblances of the world as he knows it, using the conventions and norms made available by a teacher who respects him *and* his judgments. It is the point, in sum, at which both teacher and learner are conceived to be free agents: free to create themselves by means of thoughtful, goal-oriented action, and free to choose themselves in time.

Too frequently, when "art" is linked to "education," visions of spontaneity and expressiveness overwhelm all others. Before long, the "aesthetic" is made polar to the "cognitive." Experiences with the arts are discussed as humane alternatives to intellectual rigor, technological thinking, programming, and even rationality. Something very much like "grooving" or "digging" is defined as aesthetic appreciation. Children are encouraged to let sounds wash over them; multimedia images are allowed to flicker and to stimulate presumably dormant senses; open-eyed, moving with the "beat," they are thought to be responding—that is, "learning." "Sense" and "feeling" and immediacies become the desiderata. Intuiting, children are said to be "knowing." Ecstasy becomes a primary educational objective—or wonder, or joy. "To play, to dally, to caper—these are the

---

6 Herman Melville, *Moby Dick*, Random House, New York, 1930, p. 823.

7 Thomas F. Green, "Teaching, Acting, and Behaving," in Israel Scheffler, Ed., *Philosophy and Education*, Second Edition, Allyn and Bacon, Inc., Boston, 1966, p. 130.

8 Israel Scheffler, "Philosophical Models of Teaching," in Scheffler, op. cit., p. 109.

true modes of creation,"[9] writes one of the proponents of "ecstasy in learning." A tendency to dichotomize grows. Cognition is opposed to feeling, control to ecstasy, reflectiveness to intuitiveness, idea to image, and mechanization to art.

Unquestionably, indifference and impersonality must be combatted in the schools. Statistical thinking must be complemented by existential awareness; what Ralph Ellison calls "invisibility"[10] must be challenged; we must be forever vigilant, as Albert Camus's character Tarrou puts it, against the "plague."[11] Young people must be enabled to feel authentically, to see through their own eyes, to be spontaneous, and to express themselves. The cause of authenticity is, however, injured by the habit of dichotomizing. Aesthetic experiences (like learning experiences) become less likely if we permit "ruptures of continuity . . . [which] have their intellectual formulation in various dualisms or antitheses. . . . ,"[12] if we think in terms of an either/or. To think this way is to obscure or falsify what is involved. It may well deprive people of occasions for aesthetic experience and artistic pleasure. This is because a work of art cannot be realized by an "innocent eye"[13] or by merely passive contemplation or by reflex responses to external stimuli. If *Moby Dick* (or *The Great Gatsby* or *Catch-22*) is to be more than printed words on a page, if the Mozart "Clarinet Quintet" is to be more than a sequence of sounds, if Picasso's *Guernica* is to be more than brushstrokes on canvas, each one must be "noticed"[14] in a special way. It must be attended to for its own sake, perceived "in the mode of prehension."[15] Prehension is not the same as ordinary looking or hearing: when one prehends something, one becomes sharply aware of the medium, of "intensities or values of colors and sounds." One is concerned with "qualities"[16] that may become valuable in and of themselves or that may be brought into relationship with one another, harmonized, and given form. All this signifies that an aes-

---

[9] George B. Leonard, *Education and Ecstasy*, Delacorte Press, New York, 1968, p. 98.

[10] Ralph Ellison, *Invisible Man*, Signet Press, New York, 1952.

[11] Albert Camus, *The Plague*, Alfred A. Knopf, New York, 1948.

[12] John Dewey, *Democracy and Education*, The Macmillan Company, New York, 1916, p. 377.

[13] Ernst Gombrich, *Art and Illusion*, Pantheon Books, New York, 1965, pp. 174-175.

[14] Frank Sibley, "Aesthetics and the Looks of Things," in F. J. Coleman, Ed., op. cit., pp. 334-335.

[15] Virgil C. Aldrich, *Philosophy of Art*, Prentice-Hall Inc., Englewood Cliffs, N.J., 1963, pp. 6-9.

[16] John Dewey, *Art as Experience*, Minton, Balch and Company, New York, 1934, p. 120.

thetic experience is only possible for the person who is ready and perceptive, and who knows how to look and what to look for in a given work of art.

Moby Dick, for example, may exist in the world as a physical object known as a book, in any of the multiple editions in which it has appeared; but it does not exist as an aesthetic object until it is brought into being, realized, or concretized by someone willing and able to lend it his life. If no one were ever to read it attentively, with an ability to move into an illusioned world by means of the language, the metaphors, and the images out of which that world is made, *Moby Dick* as work of art would remain a dead thing, "unravished" and unconsummated, like Keats' Grecian urn.

Not only is it neccessary to know enough about the "language of fiction"[17] to penetrate below the surfaces of what is, on the face of it, a whaling story; it is also essential to be able to enter the work imaginatively, to avoid confusing the novel with a document. Imagination, as Sartre makes particularly clear,[18] is a mode of awareness radically different from memory and anticipation. Using his imagination, a person wrenches himself from day-to-day reality. "In order to imagine," Sartre says, "consciousness must be free from all specific reality and this freedom must be able to define itself by a 'being-in-the-world' which is at once the constitution and negation of the world; the concrete situation of the consciousness in the world must at each moment serve as the singular motivation for the constitution of the unreal."[19] The reader, breaking with the expectation that *Moby Dick* will offer him verifiable information about the whaling industry, breaking at once with ordinary reality (as a student in a library, a young man reading on the way to work), moves imaginatively into an alternate world. It is a world where he first encounters thoughts of suicide ("a damp, drizzly November in my soul"[20]), a decision to go to sea, a journey to New Bedford, Nantucket, and, at length, on board the Pequod. There is the launching; there is the appearance of "moody stricken Ahab," the scarred Captain "with a crucifixion in his face."[21] Then there is the long journey and being lost in the "un-

[17] David Lodge, *Language of Fiction,* Columbia University Press, New York, 1966, pp. 6-8.
[18] Jean-Paul Sartre, *The Psychology of Imagination,* The Citadel Press, New York, 1963.
[19] Op. cit., pp. 269-270.
[20] Melville, *Moby Dick,* op. cit., p. 1.
[21] Op. cit., p. 178.

shored, harborless immensities" not only of the "deep" but also of existence itself.

None of this would emerge for the reader if he could not negate his mundane existence in the course of his reading, if he could not break with his customary routines, his habitual modes of looking on the world. It is important to note, however, that the reader's realization of *Moby Dick* as an aesthetic object involves his shaping, out of the stuff of his own consciousness, a fictive world. He, as an individual, must reenact under Herman Melville's guidance the journey of the Pequod; he must lend to the ship's crew on that journey some of his distinctive life. He can do this only as he moves, in the imaginary mode, into his own consciousness; what he will discover (if he is perceptive and lucky) is his own white whale. When Sartre talks of the motivation for such an engagement arising out of "the concrete situation of the consciousness in the world," he means that only the person who is fully engaged with his own life-world is prepared to "posit an unreality" and journey into himself. Full engagement in this fashion is not the same as everyday living. It is an inward awareness of oneself in one's existential freedom; it is a readiness to take the risk of possibility. And, if the "unreal" world one enters by means of the work of art offers anything, it offers possibility. Dorothy Walsh writes:

> The possible, as it relates to an existential context, is the potential: the potential as capacity or tendency. This actually possible is sometimes called real possibility. The possible, as it relates to a conceptual context, may be called ideal possibility. I suggest that such ideal possibility may be classified as follows: (1) the formally possible, as, for example, in pure mathematics; (2) the hypothetical, as, for example, in scientific theory— this is the statement of what is probably actual; (3) the alternative, presented as I believe in art—this is an internally coherent or compossible scheme presented as alternative to the actual.[22]

Aware, ready, understanding what it is to penetrate the language of literature (or music or painting), the individual may be enabled to perceive *personal* possibility as he could never have perceived it in the "real" world. He may be enabled to see dimensions of his experience he could never otherwise have seen. Joseph Conrad once wrote:

> My task which I am trying to achieve is, by the power of the written word to make you hear, to make you feel—it is, before all, to make you see. That—and no more, and it is everything. If I succeed, you shall find there according to your deserts: encouragement, consolation, fear,

22 Dorothy Walsh, op. cit., p. 289.

charm—all you demand—and, perhaps, also that glimpse of truth for which you have forgotten to ask.[23]

The important point is that this kind of "seeing" is only possible for those who have learned to act consciously according to the "norms" or reading literature.

Many of these norms—or rules or principles—are communicated by critics or critic-teachers concerned with providing, as Arnold Isenberg puts it, "directions for perceiving"[24] by means of certain ideas that they impart. But the individual—reader, listener, or beholder—needs other concepts, other tools as well. He needs to be permitted to reflect, on whatever conceptual level is appropriate, on his own experiences with different works of art. How, for example, do his experiences with various works compare with one another? What criteria does he consult in choosing among what he considers to be desirable experiences? Why are certain ones so intensely meaningful and moving, while so many leave him cold? What are the grounds for recommending one experience to another person and discouraging pursuit of another? How is he to think about what arouses an aesthetic experience? How is he to recognize one? How is he to use the term "art"?

Questions of this sort are aesthetic questions, relating to the choosing and the development of taste. When they are asked with specific encounters in mind, they are likely to stimulate self-consciousness with respect to many aspects of the artistic-aesthetic and the role art plays in life. This type of self-consciousness is alien to those who associate aesthetic awareness mainly with feeling or the overflow of emotion. It is alien to those who think in terms of intuitions or a quietist passivity. But it is not and ought not to be alien to those interested in "rule models," or to those concerned with freeing young people to learn how to learn.

The concepts required for the "doing" of aesthetics are to be found through consideration of the various theories of art developed over time. We lay stress on "various," because, as Morris Weitz[25] and Morris H. Abrams[26] make eminently clear, no single theory can account for all the phenomena spoken of as works of art. No single trait or "essence," in other words, can be found that is common to Dante's *The Divine Comedy*,

[23] Joseph Conrad, "Preface to *The Nigger of the 'Narcissus'*," in James E. Miller, Jr., Ed., *Myth and Method*, University of Nebraska Press, 1960, pp. 30-31.

[24] Arnold Isenberg, "Critical Communication," in Copeland, op. cit., p. 150.

[25] Morris Weitz, "The Role of Theory in Aesthetics," in Coleman, op. cit., pp. 84-93.

[26] M.H. Abrams, *The Mirror and the Lamp*, The Norton Library, W.W. Norton & Company, 1958, pp. 3-8.

Handel's Oratorios, Michelangelo's David, Thomas Pyncheon's *V*, Arthur Miller's *Death of a Salesman,* and Antionioni's film, *Blow-Up.* As Weitz points out: "The very expansive, adventurous character of art, its ever-present changes and novel creations, make it logically impossible to ensure any set of defining properties."[27]

This does not, however, mean that the theories are not helpful as recommendations to attend to specific components of the artistic-aesthetic, the kinds of recommendations that nurture reflection and deliberative choice. The aim of a good aesthetic theory, writes Abrams, is "to establish principles enabling us to justify, order, and clarify our interpretation and appraisal of the aesthetic facts themselves."[28] This is quite different from making empirically verifiable statements about art; it is different from a search for "necessary and sufficient properties." Weitz says:

> If we take the aesthetic theories literally . . . they all fail; but if we reconstruct them, in terms of their function and point, as serious and argued-for recommendations to concentrate on certain criteria of excellence in art, we shall see that aesthetic theory is far from worthless. Indeed, it becomes as central as anything in aesthetics, in our understanding of art, for it teaches us what to look for and how to look at art.[29]

It seems to us to be entirely appropriate for a teacher or a student of one of the arts to ponder what is frequently the conventional wisdom where art is concerned. Most conventional is the view that a work of art imitates or represents great recurrent patterns of cosmic life, that which is fundamentally "real." Those who hold this view tend, like Aristotle, to distinguish works of art from other representations by what they imitate. "Tragedy," he wrote, "is essentially an imitation not of persons but of action and life, of happiness and misery. All human happiness or misery takes the form of action; the end for which we live is a certain kind of activity, not a quality."[30] The action imitated, Aristotle went on, had to be "serious, complete, of a certain magnitude." The tragic writer's function was not to describe what actually happened, as was the historian's. A play like *Oedipus Rex* described what *might* happen, "what is possible as being probable or necessary." Poetry (art) was more significant than

27 Weitz, op. cit., p. 90.

28 Abrams, op. cit., p. 4.

29 Weitz, op. cit., p. 94.

30 Aristotle, *Poetics,* in Albert Hofstadter and Richard Kuhns, Eds., *Philosophies of Art and Beauty,* The Modern Library, New York, 1964, p. 103.

history, "since its statements are of the nature rather of universals, whereas those of history are singulars."[31]

Although most people realize that Aristotle's theory of *mimesis* was a function of a conceived universe governed by a *logos,* orderly, purposeful, and just—a universe utterly different from the one we posit today— they somehow want to believe that great works of art are windows through which they can look out upon the ultimate. The shapes of eternal Good should (they believe) be visible through such windows; so should Beauty; so should Truth. Often, when the humanizing function of the arts is discussed, someone will bring up the ancient notion of "humanitas," referring to that believed to be the essence of humanity, or the perfection of "Man" in the abstract. According to classical tradition, the human essence was to be found in man's "rational soul"; and even today there are persons who want to believe that the arts humanize by moving men somehow upward, closer to purity, to Form, to the Ideal. George Steiner has something relevant to say in this regard:

> The simple yet appalling fact is that we have very little solid evidence that literary studies do very much to enrich or stabilize moral perception, that they *humanize.* We have little proof that a tradition of literary studies in fact makes a man more humane. What is worse—a certain body of evidence points the other way. When barbarism came to 20th century Europe, the arts faculties in more than one university offered very little moral resistance, and this is not a trivial or local accident. In a disturbing number of cases the literary imagination gave servile or ecstatic welcome to political bestiality. That bestiality was at times enforced and refined by individuals educated in the culture of traditional humanism. Knowledge of Goethe, a delight in the poetry of Rilke, seemed no bar to personal and institutionalized sadism. Literary values and the utmost of hideous inhumanity could coexist in the same community, and in the same sensibility; and let us not take the easy way out and say "the man who did these things in a concentration camp just said he was reading Rilke. He was not reading him well." That is an evasion. He may have been reading him very well indeed.[32]

Steiner's comment does not prove, of course, that the arts have no positive effect on human beings; nor does it suggest a cause-and-effect relation between literary values and "hideous inhumanity." It does, however, pose a considerable challenge, not only to conventional wisdom but also

---

[31] Op. cit., p. 106.
[32] George Steiner, *Language and Silence,* Atheneum, New York, 1967, p. 61.

to customary "justifications" for teaching the arts in schools. Also, it sharpens the questions that must be asked by the reader (or the listener, or the beholder) intent on clarifying the value of the "aesthetic component" in his thinking, his feeling, and his life.

Although it is extremely difficult to validate the claim that art can be defined by what it imitates (for all the conventional wisdom respecting art), the ancient theory *does* draw attention to the relation between works of art and "reality," however conceived. Even those who challenge imitative theories for focusing concern on what lies beyond rather than on the "work itself" recognize that significant questions can be asked about the connection between any given work and its "world." If, say, *A Farewell to Arms* "holds a mirror up to nature" (as Hamlet put it), reflecting the "form and pressure" of the retreat at Caporetto, how does the rendering of that retreat resemble a historian's rendering? How does Hemingway's "truth" relate to the "truth" of the military historian? To what extent does a Monet painting capture the actuality of a misty Paris street? Does a Bach fugue represent mathematical laws that exist objectively in time? What light, if any, does an artist's forming of his own perceptions cast on life in a school, for example, or on the sea, or in a mental institution?

There are those who say that works of art make possible an awareness of the particularities of the world: the details of a Russian household in *War and Peace;* the immediacies of "coffee and oranges in a sunny chair" in Wallace Stevens' "Sunday Morning"; the thrusting planes of a tablecloth in a Cezanne still life; the sounds of summer in the Beethoven Sixth. There are others who point to the ways in which novels, yes, and certain paintings enable one to perceive life in its fullness and interconnectedness, as works of history can never do. Still others discover analogues in works of art, semblances of empirical reality; and many, particularly today, find alternative universes in created things, what W. H. Auden calls "secondary worlds."[33]

Since the 18th century, of course, when faith in an orderly, knowable universe began to erode, attention has shifted to the men who create works of art or to the works of art themselves. Nurtured in diverse romanticisms, expressivist theories began competing with the classical views when William Wordsworth and others began stressing the ways in which poems and paintings express "emotions recollected in tranquillity."[34] Once one begins

33 See W. H. Auden, *Secondary Worlds,* Random House, New York, 1969.

34 William Wordsworth, "Preface to the Lyrical Ballads," in Carlos Baker, Ed., *William Wordsworth's The Prelude with a Selection from the Shorter Poems,* Holt, Rinehart and Winston, New York, 1962, p. 25.

to pay heed to the artistic process itself and to consider the feelings or perceptions or inward vision being imaginatively transmuted and formed, one cannot but revise one's conception of art as a mirroring or a reflection. The reader of *A Farewell to Arms* is compelled to turn his attention away from the Italian scene in World War I to the emotive components of his own experience with the "traps" presented in the book, to the sensuous qualities it organizes, to the sense of dark fatality communicated by the images of retreating soldiers, rainy streets, a black cape in the mountains, a hospital waiting room. No longer is he likely to seek outside the book for the action "of a certain magnitude" being imitated; no longer is he likely to look beyond for an overarching "meaning."

According to expressivist theories, art is a mode of communication; but that which is communicated is not to be confused with conceptual knowledge. By means of image, metaphor, or symbol, "import" is communicated, not "meaning" in any discursive sense. The art work, says Susanne Langer, is itself a symbol, expressing a conception of inward reality, presenting feeling to the understanding.[35] Others speak of art as a specialized language. For them, each work is a sign or an image of what is being designated; value is embodied in a medium that permits it to be directly inspected.[36] All who put their emphasis on expressiveness speak often of creative or poetic vision, of sincerity, of unions between the inner and outer worlds. But they also insist on the role of imagination, on representative or formal elements as the *means* of expression. They make sharp distinctions between "mere" self- expression and the embodiment of what is being expressed in objective forms.

Theories of this sort throw considerable light and nurture the sorts of questions that move the individual to attend both to what is communicated by a work and what he experiences in his own "inner time." But, like the mimetic theories, they cannot explain or account for every phenomenon experienced as art. It is impossible to verify the claim that, in order to *be* a work of art, a novel or a painting or a musical piece must be expressive of something in an artist's innerness, must present (sincerely) a subjective valuation or feeling given form. Just as mimetic theories cannot explain or account for confessional or lyrical pieces (or William Burroughs' *Naked Lunch,* or Manet's "Luncheon on the Grass," or Beckett's *Waiting for Godot*), so are expressive theories unable to account

---

[35] Susanne K. Langer, *Problems of Art,* Charles Scribner's Sons, New York, 1957, Chapter 2.

[36] See, for instance, Charles W. Morris, "Science, Art, and Technology," in Melvin Rader, Ed., *A Modern Book of Esthetics,* 3rd Edition, Holt, Rinehart and Winston, New York, 1965, pp. 241-245.

for self-sufficient literary works like James Joyce's *A Portrait of the Artist as a Young Man*, T. S. Eliot's *Four Quartet's*, and Nabokov's *Pale Fire*. Nor can they account for abstract, "minimal," or "pop" art, nor for serial music, nor for John Cage's aleatory works. Again, the point to be stressed is that, although each theory makes an assertion about some quality conceived to be "necessary and sufficient," it remains impossible to discover a single "essence" present in every work that has ever been categorized as art.

Nevertheless, expressive theories, when taken to be "recommendations," do support the individual's effort to discover criteria of evaluation —and to discover more about the meaning of "art." Because, too, of their focus on the objectification of subjectivity or feeling, they hold a variety of implications for conceptions of classroom performance and teacher activity. Too frequently, as we have said, educators turn to one or another form of expressiveness to counter the culture's emphasis on technique, "manipulation," and "processing." Too frequently, they view art (because it is expressive) as primarily emotive in nature. Without realizing it, many times, they take a position much like that of the British critic-philosopher I. A. Richards, when he was distinguishing literary communication from the sciences by saying that literature was, by definition, "emotive," while the sciences were "descriptive" in nature.[37] He meant that literary works provided no factual information, because they were not composed of propositional statements. Addressing themselves to interests and attitudes rather than to the intelligence, they were empirically "meaningless." Richards' mainly linguistic distinction was picked up, as is well known, by a number of British positivists[38] who talked for a decade or more about the "pseudo-statements" to be found in both art and ethics as they worked to clarify what "meaning" entailed. Their primary aim was to clarify the language used in philosophy and the language used for making knowledge-claims. They were empiricists, with a strong commitment to clarification, analysis, and what might be called the "cognitive" side of life. This makes it particularly strange to see educators (of romantic and other persuasions) applying something resembling the "emotive theory" in opposition to the cognitive.

The teacher who proposes to conceive his own teaching as art because he sees the teaching act as an act of self-expression, and hopes that his own

---

[37] I. A. Richards, *Principles of Literary Criticism,* Harcourt, Brace and Company, New York, 1926, pp. 107-113.

[38] See, for example, Alfred Jules Ayer, *Language, Truth and Logic,* Victor Gollancz Ltd., London, 1950.

spontaneity and emotionality will arouse his students to feeling and awareness, would be well advised to consider expressivist theories of art. They
make it perfectly clear that an artist cannot create a work of art "spontaneously," although the imagery and the language he chooses may well
communicate a sense of spontaneity. Coleridge's "Ode to Dejection" is
something quite different from an expression of melancholy by the living
Coleridge. Yeats's "Second Coming" is entirely different from an outcry
by the living Yeats regarding the disorder of his time and the loss of the
"ceremony of innocence." Picasso's "Guernica" is not the same thing as
an expression of Picasso's despair and anger at the moment of the bomb-
ing. ("And that masterpiece," wrote Sartre, " 'The Massacre of Guernica,'
does any one think that it won over a single heart to the Spanish cause?
And yet something is said that can never quite be heard and that would
take an infinity of words to express."[39])

The student, like the teacher, can learn from consideration of expressivist theories of art that artistic communication can never take place
without the forming of a presentation, the kind of forming that takes
place after a period of gestation, brooding, play with the medium, shaping, and reshaping. An encounter with a Dylan Thomas poem or an
Andrew Wyeth painting is not to be equated with a direct encounter with
the poet or the painter. There may be, as Alfred Schutz says,[40] a mode of
"tuning-in" with the stream of consciousness of the artist, a moment when
it *seems* as though the reader, listener, or beholder exists in a shared
present with the creator, in an instant of "vivid time." But this can only
occur if and when the reader, listener, or beholder reenacts the work of
art, and attends to it step by step, aspect by aspect. Although direct
"I-Thou" encounters may occur in a classroom, the teacher ought not to
confuse what he is doing with an artist's expressive act.

Nor ought he, in considering works of art, become so preoccupied
with the creative process that gave birth to them that he overlooks the
works themselves. There is a group of theories, described as formalist or
objectivist, that were framed in reaction against precisely such neglect.
They attempt to counter, in fact, the stubborn tendency to talk "about"
art rather than to confront it. They are often critiques of the habit of
using a work of art as a mere occasion for the examination of a social
condition, a historic event, or some other aspect of the universe. As often,
they challenge efforts to explain works of art by pointing to the biogra-

[39] Jean-Paul Sartre, *Literature and Existentialism,* The Citadel Press, New York,
1965, p. 11.
[40] Alfred Schutz, "Making Music Together," op. cit.

phies or the presumed "intentions"[41] of their makers, or to cultural forces pressing to assert themselves through various forms and styles. The origins of such theories are probably to be found in Aristotle's concern with the form, language, and "plot" of the tragedy; but they began to take on wide significance in the 19th century, when artists like Charles Baudelaire and Gustave Flaubert began rebelling against unbridled expressiveness and, at once, genteel sentimentality. "I have no desire either to demonstrate, to astonish, to amuse, or to persuade," wrote Baudelaire.[42] Writing about *Madame Bovary* ("a totally fictitious story"), Flaubert said that it contained none of his feelings and no details from his own life. "The illusion of truth (if there is one) comes, on the contrary, from the book's impersonality. It is one of my principles that a writer should not be his own theme. An artist must be in the work like God in creation, invisible and all-powerful; he should be everywhere felt, but nowhere seen."[43]

In a well-known passage from Joyce's *A Portrait of the Artist as a Young Man,* something similar is said: " 'The narrative is no longer purely personal,' " Stephen Daedalus is saying, in a discussion of epical and dramatic literary forms. Then:

> "The personality of the artist, at first a cry or a cadence or a mood and then a fluid and lambent narrative, finally refines itself out of existence, impersonalises itself, so to speak. The esthetic image in the dramatic form is life purified in and reprojected from the human imagination. The mystery of esthetic like that of material creation is accomplished. The artist, like the God of creation, remains within or behind or beyond or above his handiwork, invisible, refined out of existence, indifferent, paring his fingernails." "—Trying to refine them also out of existence," said Lynch.[44]

And, to clarify the approach even further, there is T. S. Eliot on the objective correlative: "The only way of expressing emotion in the form of art is by finding an 'objective correlative'; in other words, a set of objects, a situation, a chain of events which shall be the formula of that *particular*

---

41 See John Wain, F. W. Bateson, and W. W. Robson, " 'Intention' and Blake's Jerusalem," in Marvin Levich, Ed., *Aesthetics and the Philosophy of Criticism,* Random House, New York, 1963, pp. 375-383.

42 Charles Baudelaire, "Three Drafts of a Preface," in *The Flowers of Evil,* New Directions Books, New York, 1958, p. xvi.

43 Gustave Flaubert, Letter to Mlle. de Chantepie (1857), in Francis Steegmuller, transl., *Selected Letters,* Hamish Hamilton Ltd., London, 1954, p. 195.

44 James Joyce, *A Portrait of the Artist as a Young Man,* The Viking Press, New York, 1947, p. 482.

emotion; such that when the external facts, which must terminate in sensory experience, are given, the emotion is immediately evoked."[45]

These views all center on the "impersonality" of art forms and attempt, frequently, to define works of art in terms of what Clive Bell called "significant form."[46] Attention is directed to the forms, the internal relations within each work of art, rather than to its representative aspect or to the emotions "behind the forms." The artist's intention is considered to be objectively present in the work, experienced as its "focal effect."[47] The aesthetic response is described as the unique response evoked by a contemplation of lines, colors, shapes, volumes, images, symbols, cadences, and rhythms in the intricate interior relationships identified as form. Those who look on literature, for example, from a formalist vantage point, stress the work of art's existence within a "frame of fictionality" that takes it out of the world of empirical reality.[48] Painting, similarly, becomes a formal or sensuous adventure in line, shape, and intensity of color. The formal and sensuous values of a Raphael Madonna or a De Kooning woman or an Auden poem or a Hawthorne short story, it is said, satisfy an interest aroused by something in the work itself, an interest that is uniquely aesthetic. Associations to events, persons, conditions, or objects external to the work are conceived to be distracting and irrelevant. What Immanuel Kant called the "disinterestedness"[49] of pure aesthetic experience is here given a peculiar centrality, as is the notion of "psychical distance," a mode of seeing outside the context of personal needs and concerns.[50]

The individual, teacher or student, who derives tools of inquiry from formalist theories as he reflects upon his own experiences with works of art is compelled to attend to the works themselves in their integrity. He is reminded that, if they are truly to be "known," realized, and concretized in his experience, they cannot be subordinated to anything beyond themselves. Once again, the notion that one particular essence

[45] T. S. Eliot, "Hamlet," in *Selected Essays*, Harcourt, Brace & World, Inc., New York, 1960, p. 124.

[46] Clive Bell, *Art*, Chatto & Windus, London, 1914, Chapter 1.

[47] Richard Kuhns, "Criticism and the Problem of Intention," in Ralph A. Smith, Ed., *Aesthetics and Criticism in Art Education*, Rand McNally & Company, Chicago, 1966, p. 387.

[48] Rene Wellek and Austin Warren, *Theory of Literature*, Harcourt, Brace & World, Inc., New York, 1956, pp. 26-27.

[49] Immanuel Kant, selections from *Critique of Aesthetical Judgment*, in Hofstadter and Kuhns, op. cit., pp. 281-282.

[50] Edward Bullough, " 'Psychical Distance' as a Factor in Art and an Aesthetic Principle," in *British Journal of Psychology*, V, 1912, pp. 87-98.

(in this case "significant form") can be isolated and that all art can be defined in terms of that essence must—on Morris Weitz's grounds and others—be rejected. This does not take away from the power of formalist concepts to make a great many things clear.

Often concerned with the "structure" of a given work, and with the levels of significance or meaning potential in each one, the objectivist may speak of a "system of norms." By "norms" he may mean "implicit norms which have to be extracted from every individual experience of a work of art and together make up the genuine work of art as a whole."[51] He means by this that no single poem (or painting or musical work) is fully realized in any individual's experience. Over the centuries, for example, numbers of human beings have encountered the play *Hamlet* and discovered within it an infinite variety of different things. It is impossible to speak of a "common denominator" of these multiple experiences; it is difficult to identify positively some "Ideal Reader" to establish a standard of interpretation for all others to attempt to meet. But it *is* possible to speak of *Hamlet* as a potential cause of aesthetic experience in each individual case, and to imagine a world of cumulative meanings developing over time. Henry D. Aiken, discussing cultural differences "which determine the subjective contexts of individuals" at different moments in history, talks in terms of a degree of objectivity where "the public work of art" is concerned. He writes:

> Our experience of art, both personal and collective, is, to borrow a felicitous term from Professor Pepper, a "funded" experience. Unlike automatic responses to physical stimuli, the later perceptions of a work of art are themselves functions, not merely of a general cultural and aesthetic context, but also of previous transactions with the work of art itself. In short, part of the subjective context of each individual encounter with the work will be the earlier encounters, each of which leaves a fresh deposit of meaning and expression or, in the case of "perishable works," a lowering of vividness and vitality. So, also, although the mechanisms of transmission and accumulation are obviously different, there is such a thing as funding in the responses of successive generations of critics.[52]

What appears to be particularly relevant here is the stress on norms as well as on funding. Like other subject matters, the arts are seen to be structured or layered. The components of, for example, literary art are

---

[51] Wellek and Warren, op. cit., pp. 150-151.
[52] Henry D. Aiken, "A Pluralistic Analysis of Aesthetic Value," in Copeland, Ed., op. cit., pp. 127-128.

not, however, to be conceived of as concepts logically related to one another in terms of decreasing generality or any other such principle. There are, rather, levels of meaning, as poets as far apart in time as Dante and T. S. Eliot have said. The surface level of a poem is the so-called "sound stratum," which makes it possible for units of meaning to be penetrated (patterned in sentences and stanzas). Below these—and arising out of engagement with them—is the fictive "world" created and presented from a particular vantage point, explicit or implied within the poem.[53] Consider the first lines of Matthew Arnold's "Dover Beach":[54]

> The sea is calm tonight.
> The tide is full, the moon lies fair
> Upon the straits;—on the French coast the light
> Gleams and is gone; the cliffs of England stand
> Glimmering and vast, out in the tranquil bay.

Most people, well informed or not, will be able to respond on a sensual level to the slow rhythms, the legato of those lines. With a sense of the expansive sweep and of tranquillity, some will be able to interpret not only the single words, but also the entire syntactic structure of meanings: the calm sea moving slowly into a "tranquil bay"; the steady moon and the ephemeral gleam across the straits; the hugeness of the chalk cliffs. Engaging with that structure, those interrelationships of meaning, a few will be able to move imaginatively into themselves and shape—not a postcard representation of the Dover Cliffs—but the contained expanse of that sea as perceived by a man whose serenity is precarious and whose melancholy is about to overcome him. And a few more, once they read the entire poem, will be capable of perceiving ever-widening significance: the symbols (sea, land, pebbles, naked shingles, darkling plain, and clashing armies) will lead continually further out, until at length they confront such readers with a dimension of the human condition itself.

At each level, some kind of enjoyment is possible; but it is a function of a particular subjective context, of experience in the reading of poems, of perceptiveness in attending to them. The more perceptions that have been funded, the deeper the reader will move into the work of art and the closer he will come to achieving it as an aesthetic object. No single person, however, can ever exhaust it or see all there is to see. There are forever

---

[53] See discussion of Roman Ingarden's approach in Wellek and Warren, op. cit., pp. 151-152.

[54] Oscar Williams, Ed., *Immortal Poems of the English Language,* The Pocket Library, New York, 1959, p. 428.

new possibilities, increasingly available to the one familiar with the cumulative meanings of the poem, which are the "responses of successive generations of critics," existing in some sense simultaneously in the literature dealing with literary art.

A normative approach of this kind, combined with regard for works of art in their autonomy, may well hold implications for conceptions of curriculum. Is not a discipline, as presented to a group of students, somewhat like a system of norms? Is it not the case that a "mastery" of the concepts composing history or geography or chemistry is contingent on funding, and on the ability of the individual to engage himself more and more consciously with the "doing" of the discipline until "he has mastered the moves made by his predecessors which are enshrined in living traditions"? R. S. Peters writes, in this regard: "The pupil has gradually to get the grammar of the activity into his guts so that he can eventually win through to the stage of autonomy."[55] Not only does this apply as much to the "grammar" of reading, listening, and beholding as it does to the study of history; it suggests a way in which the process of achieving an aesthetic object can become exemplary in education.

Something, however, must be added. One difficulty with the formalist approach where the arts are concerned is that it tends to neglect the "implicit but constant requisition of a serious literary work upon our predispositions and beliefs. . . ."[56] Somewhat the same thing may be said with respect to serious painting, sculpture, music, and dance. This requisition is not to be conceived as an end in itself, "but a necessary means to engage our interests and feelings, in order to move them towards a resolution."[57] No matter what the degree of "impersonality" claimed for his work by an artist, he is making his presentation for other human beings; and he is doing so as a human being. Moreover, the only way of actualizing the work of art, as we have seen, is by engaging with it emotively, sensually, *and* cognitively, with one's whole self. There must be some recognizable human center of reference on which the imagination or the consciousness can rest, if the individual is to be fully engaged. To say this is not to deprive formalist theories of their value, nor even to deny the possibility of a specifically aesthetic experience aroused by sensuous and formal elements in the "work itself." It is simply to suggest that the

55 R. S. Peters, "Education as Initiation," in Reginald D. Archambault, Ed., *Philosophical Analysis and Education*, Routledge & Kegan Paul, London, 1965, p. 109.

56 M. H. Abrams, "Belief and the Suspension of Belief," in Abrams, Ed., *Literature and Belief*, Columbia University Press, New York, p. 30.

57 Ibid.

aesthetic experience has, at once, an integral character: "its domain," as Aiken has written, "is sufficiently commodious to include not merely the sensuous surfaces and emotive meanings of signs, but also the full range of what, all too obscurely, we lump together under the rubric of cognitive meaning."[58] The fundamental relevance of art, it would appear, is a function of this commodiousness, at least for those who know how to attend.

We return, therefore, to our starting point: to the significance of aesthetic experiences (when reflected upon) in a human life. Throughout, we have taken issue with the romantic approach: that the aesthetic experience is predominantly one of unleashed "feeling"; that the primary function of art is to enable us to recapture our lost paradise, to "gaze like children."[59] It is indeed the case that perceptive encounters with works of art may make possible an awareness of a person's authentic self, what some call his "true" or his "original" personality. But this occurs only when innocence and foolishness are abandoned, when the highly conscious individual develops the capacity to "bracket out"[60] the mundane and the ordinary. It occurs only when he breaks, as John Dewey suggested, with the stereotyped and with routine, merely conventional ways of seeing.[61] Spontaneity, paradoxically, can be rediscovered only at those moments when the aesthetic posture is rendered self-conscious. The reader, listener, or beholder must not simply be aware of the boundaries that separate works of art from the everyday world. He must be equally aware of the great unsettled questions with regard to the very concept "art," of the peculiar ways in which art reveals without reflecting, engages interest on the part of the "disinterested," and makes confrontations possible while "distancing" important dimensions of life.

The uses of the "aesthetic component," then, may be manifold. Most fundamentally, it confronts the human being with his own consciousness of his life situation, and it provides occasions for his imposing order upon the chaotic materials of his experience. There are, in the course of his education, many other opportunities for ordering and sense-making; but the aesthetic occasion is the only one that moves him into himself. Only when engaging in works of art as unreal objects, does he become

[58] Henry D. Aiken, "The Aesthetic and the Cognitive," in Morris Philipson, Ed., *Aesthetics Today,* Meridian Press, New York, 1961, p. 273.

[59] See Tony Tanner, *The Reign of Wonder,* Cambridge University Press, New York, 1965, Chapter 2.

[60] See Maurice Natanson, *Literature, Philosophy and the Social Sciences,* Martinus Nijhoff, The Hague, 1962, Chapter 7.

[61] John Dewey, *Art as Experience,* op. cit., Chapter I.

existentially open to himself, in the way of understanding the *objects* of his consciousness and feeling. Only then is he likely to express what he has come to understand. The order he is enabled to create and, perhaps, to articulate is the "commodious" one that Aiken has described. Contained in such an order are feelings that have become more than mere sentiency, more than vague outrage, happiness, and despair. Contained as well are moral dispositions and commitments, related in complex ways to feeling, to action, and to authentic perceptions of the "world." An order of this kind is organic and vivid. The person who can pattern the materials of his selfhood in such a manner is one who cannot easily be manipulated from without. At once, he is one capable of avoiding statistical and abstract seeing when they are irrelevant, as they so often are in the social domain. Just as significantly, he is likely to be self-conscious about the ordering process itself, of the many modes there are of sense-making, and of the diverse "fictions" by means of which men live.[62] Frank Kermode speaks eloquently about the need to be knowledgeable about the "fictive," so as to be clearer about our interpretations of our reality and to "purge the trivial and stereotyped from the arts of our own time." He writes of the danger of confusing conventional ways of making sense with myths (which are fossilized fictions) and of the need to understand the value of particular fictions in our lives. "The critical issue," he says, "given the perpetual assumption of crisis, is no less than the justification of ideas of order. They have to be justified in terms of what survives, and also in terms of what we can accept as valid in a world different from that out of which they come, resembling the earlier world only in that there is biological and cultural continuity of some kind. Our order, our form, is necessary; our skepticism as to fictions requires that it shall not be spurious."[63]

Justifications of ideas of order require choices; choices, as we have seen, require a spectrum of insights and awarenesses. Among these are the ones that may be developed in the process of pondering responses to works of art and attempting to justify the recommendations we make. Recommendations ought to rest not simply on enjoyment or immediate satisfaction. They ought to arise out of considered preferences; and our point has been that considerations of aesthetic preferences heighten aesthetic fulfillments as they intensify self-consciousness about our encounters with art. Because, according to most scholars of the arts today, art cannot be

62 See Frank Kermode, *The Sense of an Ending: Studies in the Theory of Fiction*, Oxford University Press, New York, 1967.

63 Frank Kermode, op. cit., p. 124.

conclusively defined, and because the most urgent questions about it cannot be finally answered, the process of inquiry and evaluation must continue.

Doing aesthetics, the teacher or the student engages, therefore, in a continuing quest for paradigm cases in his effort to identify the criteria by which he can recognize new works of art. Searching in this way, tracing "strands of similarity,"[64] he is likely to keep discovering new dimensions of both the paradigms and the works that defy convention and seem to break with traditional categories. He might, as people often do, take *Hamlet* as a paradigm case of a dramatic work in an attempt to determine whether Harold Pinter's *The Caretaker* is to be considered either drama or art. It is simple enough to determine obvious similarities: both are designed to be performed on a stage; both are largely enacted by means of dialogue; both are divided into acts and scenes. But *The Caretaker* breaks with the tradition demanding "crisis" and "climax" in a play. It possesses no definite beginning, middle, or end. Its characters are not individualized in psychological terms; their histories, if existent, are wholly unclear. They are presented; they perform a type of oral ballet; they communicate without understanding one another; their language lacks ordinary logic; their predicament makes no "sense." Nevertheless, *The Caretaker* would not come into being as a play if there were no dramatic tradition; it would not defy expectation if no expectations were brought to it by those who read or watch. Yet its place in art history or in the dramatic tradition cannot be finally determined, at least not yet. All one can do is apply the principles provided by the various theories of art, and look through the lenses they provide at the play's relation to "reality," at its emotional depth and sensuousness, at the intricacy of its interior relations, and at its impact upon the imagination. Looking in that fashion, the student will surely "see" more in the play—and, more than likely, in plays in general. He will also become more aware than he has been of what it means to evaluate, to categorize, and to choose.

Everything finally, it appears, rests on choice. The "aesthetic component" will not be significant in an individual's life and education if "good taste" is simply imposed on him, if ideals or exemplars are presented as preexistent, "given." It will only be meaningful and make a difference if he is equipped for perceptiveness, aroused to sensitivity, and freed to reach out—by means of art—for his own authentic being. This cannot be done simply by developing technical mastery nor by exposing him to exemplars and "great art." Nor can it be done simply by "point-

---

[64] Morris Weitz, "The Role of Theory in Aesthetics," op. cit., p. 89.

ing" (as critics point and as teachers must do) to formal and expressive elements in particular works. It can surely not be done by identifying teaching with the making of art or the teacher with the artist. The student must be engaged with the teacher in sense-making with respect to art, in conscious exploration of the possibilities of many media,[65] in pondering concrete experiences, and in making reasonable choices as he moves. For the rest—there are the moments of private possession, the shaping of orders, the recovery of the self. There is the dimension of the possible; there are what Wallace Stevens called "significant landscapes" to perceive. He wrote:

> Rationalists, wearing square hats,
> Think, in square rooms,
> Looking at the floor,
> Looking at the ceiling.
> They confine themselves
> To right-angled triangles.
> If they tried rhomboids,
> Cones, waving lines, ellipses—
> As, for example, the ellipse of the half-moon—
> Rationalists should wear sombreros.[66]

The idea is not to oppose the aesthetic to the cognitive, the emotive to the rational. The idea is to break with constraints and mechanism, to pursue a wider vision. A rationalist who wears a sombrero does not stop being a rationalist; he does not opt for irrationality. He opts, quite simply, for more alternatives, for more choices. He reaches out for a wider world.

---

[65] See Max Black, "Education as Art and Discipline," in Scheffler, Ed., *Philosophy and Education,* op. cit., p. 41.

[66] Wallace Stevens, "Six Significant Landscapes," in *The Collected Poems,* Alfred A. Knopf, New York, 1964, p. 75.

References

❖❖

Coleman, Francis J., Ed., *Contemporary Studies in Aesthetics*. McGraw-Hill Book Company, New York, 1968. Mainly analytic essays on such matters as criticism, literature, the aesthetic experience, and the nature of theory.

Jacobus, Lee A., Ed., *Aesthetics and the Arts*. McGraw-Hill Book Company, New York, 1968. An introduction to philosophic thinking about art, divided into sections on the dance, literature, music, the visual arts, architecture, and film.

Levich, Marvin, Ed., *Aesthetics and the Philosophy of Criticism*. Random House, New York, 1963. An approach to aesthetics by way of criticism, organized in terms of discussions of form, content, style, critical judgment, and definition.

Smith, Ralph A., Ed., *Aesthetics and Criticism in Art Education*. Rand McNally & Company, Chicago, 1966. Varied articles on definition, explanation, and criticism, with introductory essays indicating relevance for art education.

Weitz, Morris, Ed., *Problems in Aesthetics*. The Macmillan Company, New York, 1959. Introductory readings covering basic concepts and including statements by several artists as well as by critics and philosophers.

Epilogue

◆◇

The past few chapters have set out the principles of a range of educational philosophies. Some readers may find one or other of these philosophies especially persuasive. Other readers may be attracted variously by several or even by all of them. Such readers will tend to bring together ideas from a number of different philosophies in the hope of forming a single reflective attitude toward education. This is the way of the eclectic and it is a reasonable first step in working out a true philosophy of education.

If we are to have such a philosophy, however, we must make sure that each of its ideas is consistent with the rest. To superimpose Hutchins' educational values on Dewey's theory of knowledge is to combine incompatibles, because Hutchins and Dewey proceed from very different premises about the true nature of education. On the other hand, since all philosophies tend to start eclectically, each reader will have to begin his work of creation by selecting from the philosophies he has studied and from his own life experience those ideas which, put together, best answer to his own thoughts and feelings about education.

However, no one is forced to build a philosophy of education according to the method used in this text, which is at heart traditional. Many philosophers of education, especially those influenced by pragmatism or analysis, maintain that educational philosophy should take its departure from problems, themes, and concepts that are germane to education. One can decide which method is better only after making a careful study of both.

Whichever method we use to build our philosophy of education, what else must we do? First, we must examine our own lives to find out what purpose, if any, we have in living, what it is that we value most highly, and what knowledge we consider to be most worthwhile. We must ask ourselves what real concern we have for the well-being of humanity. When we say that we "like people," what do we really mean? What does it mean to "love children"? Unless we answer such questions critically, we may fail in our effort to improve the quality of teaching.

Whatever the outcome, this self-analysis must do us good. In any walk of life we need a philosophy of our own in order to know where we are going. If a teacher or an educational leader has no philosophy of education, he is headed nowhere in particular, and his pupils will have to follow him aimlessly or put their big questions to someone else.

Philosophy is important because it frees the mind and also guides it. Philosophy liberates us from the hold of unexamined attitudes and at the same time leads us to think rationally. Bold in conception, rigorous in proof, philosophy is thought at its purest and most daring. By taking problems of education to a philosophical plane, the teacher sees these problems in ampler perspective. By thinking philosophically he applies his mind vigorously and clearly to issues of importance. As a result of philosophy he becomes a more thoughtful person and, in all probability, a more stimulating teacher.

PART FOUR

SCIENTIFIC FOUNDATIONS

15

The World of Science

George F. Kneller

❖❖

One word characterizes more than any other what is unique about the contemporary world, and that word is "science." Not only have more scientific discoveries been made in the past century than in any previous time, but the findings of science have been used markedly to transform the conditions in which men live and work, and they have become indispensable to the practice of nearly every public activity. The modern world was made by science, it makes science, and it relies on science. If we are to understand the world and be at home in it, we must have some insight into the nature of the science that pervades it.

Something as pervasive as science defies precise definition. Let us therefore say very generally that it is man's interrogation of the world and the knowledge this interrogation produces. The scientist interrogates the world by proposing and testing hypotheses about connections among the phenomena of which the world is observed to consist.

Owing to the range of its findings and the variety of its techniques, science has been divided into a number of branches, notably the physical sciences of chemistry, physics, and geology, and the biological sciences of botany, zoology, and physiology. Nature itself, however, is a whole, and therefore these divisions, which are drawn for convenience, are spanned

317

by intersciences, such as biochemistry and biophysics, and interdisciplines, such as the history and philosophy of science. In addition to the so-called natural sciences, there are the sciences of human behavior, including psychology, sociology, anthropology, economics, and linguistics. All these divisions of subject matter enable us to see the sciences spread out in a panorama according to the phenomena they study.

When the scientist seeks knowledge without regard for ways in which it may be applied, he is engaged in "pure" or "basic" science. But when he studies the behavior of a phenomenon, such as the electron, in order to acquire knowledge that may *eventually* be put to some practical use (for example, in the construction of electronic circuits for computers), he is engaged in "fundamental applied science" or "mission-oriented research." Finally, when he studies a phenomenon with the intention of producing knowledge *immediately* applicable to the solution of a technical problem, he is engaged in "applied science." The recent isolation of the gene is a fine example of fundamental applied science. Not a significant advance in basic or pure science, it is rather a technical feat arising from a desire further to understand the genetic mechanisms of viruses and their hosts so that one day these mechanisms may be controlled.[1]

What are the insights of pure science? They are the laws and theories that display the fundamental workings of the universe. Not facts and events as such, but the order that facts exemplify, is the goal of scientific inquiry. A fact or an event is important as an instance of a "regularity." It is not the unique that matters but rather whatever is general and repeatable and therefore subject to law.

There are at least two reasons for this. One is that the scientist is interested in accurate prediction, and only the recurrent can be predicted. The other is that the events studied by natural scientists are rarely of interest in themselves. Gas molecules, polymers, and pea plants exist as particulars rather than as individuals. They are entities without self-consciousness and therefore cannot be unique. The behavior of gas molecules in a flask or the transmission of the hereditary characteristics of pea plants is important only insofar as it indicates a universal regularity.[2]

---

[1] Actually the knowledge and tools for employing genetic engineering to modify the heritable characteristics of man are not available at present and probably will not be for many years to come. Thus the social consequences of the isolation of the gene will be a problem of the 21st century (although the earlier we consider them the better!). See *Science*, **167** (March 27, 1970), 168.

[2] Granted, the scientist will sometimes study a nonrecurring event, like a supernova, or a rare particular such as a coelacanth. But the fundamental import

What is a "regularity"? Broadly speaking, it is a connection either between certain things (or events) and certain properties, or between those things and certain other things possessing properties. For example, scientists have established that every benzene molecule is composed of six atoms of carbon and six of hydrogen. This is a regularity of the first kind. Scientists also have established that a certain amount of mechanical energy, or the energy of a body moving against resistance, produces a certain amount of heat energy and vice versa. (If I rub my hands together on a cold day they become warm, because the mechanical energy given off in rubbing creates heat.) This is a regularity of the second kind, for the connection noted holds between events, in this case between two events occurring more or less simultaneously, the doing of work and the production of heat.

These two regularities, the chemical composition of the benzene molecule and the interconvertibility of mechanical work and heat, are aspects of the order of nature. To say that nature is orderly is to say in part that it is characterized by regularities such as these. Nevertheless, they are limited in scope, for each regularity holds only for a fairly restricted domain of phenomena. The structure of the universe is displayed in depth only when a limited regularity is shown to exemplify a far more general uniformity, such as that expressed by the law of the conservation of energy (that whenever a certain amount of one form of energy disappears, it is replaced by an equal amount of energy in other forms). The conversion of mechanical energy into heat energy is a special case of this law, which applies to all forms of energy whatever, including nuclear, chemical, electric, and radiant energy.[3]

of the event is that it suggests, confirms, or calls into question an empirical or theoretical hypothesis about the conditions under which stars collapse or a more general hypothesis about the origin of the universe. The coelacanth, again, is interesting to a biologist because it is rare, that is, because it is an unusual specimen of a species that has been or can be classified. It is also true that a biologist is often as interested in the differences between members of a species as he is in their common characteristics. But even then, when he is observing and experimenting on a particular organism, the process or state he is investigating, such as reproduction or cell division, is a repeatable one, which may be observed in other organisms.

[3] A uniformity still more fundamental is expressed in the equation, $E = mc^2$, which is part of Einstein's Special Theory of Relativity. This equation expresses the equivalence of mass and energy. It states that energy equals mass multiplied by the square of the velocity of light. This means that a moving body gains mass, or amount of matter, in proportion to its acceleration. It means also, as has been demonstrated in the explosion of nuclear bombs, that energy is released proportionate to the loss of mass. To have established that mass and energy are everywhere equivalent is to have attained a profound insight into the nature of the physical universe.

The search for order in nature leads to abstraction. In order to discover and express a fundamental regularity holding for a range of phenomena, the scientist must concentrate on a few properties of these phenomena to the exclusion of a great many others. Thus the law of the conservation of energy makes no mention whatever of the processes in which energy is manifest. From every action and reaction of every material body and every particle anywhere in the universe the law abstracts the single property of energy. Taken, then, as a description of the phenomena to which it applies, the law is incomplete. Where in this law are the running horses, the striking flints, and the turning mill wheels? Where, indeed, is any phenomenon whatever in which energy is manifest? None of them is present, because in order to describe the regularity of which the phenomena are instances, a law must ignore the instances themselves. If it did not, the statement would cease to be a law and would become a list. And a list is precisely what a law obviates, for a law states what is characteristic of listable items and therefore saves us the labor of listing them.

Insofar, then, as science is an abstraction, it does not reveal our full experience of the world but only an order that *appears* to exist in the world. Insofar as this abstraction is made from the physical universe, it does not represent the essence of the real. For the real is not only the reality of the material world, it is also reality-for-man; it is the reality of the heart and spirit of man, as well as the reality of the atoms and stars that physical science has sought so magnificently to schematize. This other reality is experienced by all of us. It is the reality of love, sorrow, and heroism. It is described in philosophy and represented in art. It is the human meaning of things.[4]

A Method of Inquiry

The actual process of scientific investigation, the day-to-day activity of setting up instruments, taking readings, looking at specimens, making calculations, and so on, may seem to the outsider a rather unplanned affair. But behind this tinkering there is a method, the most successful of all methods for finding out how the universe works. The method may be summed up in the formula, "observation-hypothesis-deduction-check."[5]

[4] See my remarks on metaphysics and its relation to science on pp. 200-204.

[5] The seeming planlessness of most actual research is well described by the biologist, J. Z. Young, *Doubt and Certainty in Science,* Oxford University, 1951, pp. 1-2: ". . . in his laboratory he [the scientist] does not spend much of his time thinking about scientific laws at all. He is busy with other things, trying to get some

What does this formula mean? It means that in a typical piece of research the scientist observes something surprising, thinks of an explanation of it, asks what this explanation implies, and examines whether the implications are borne out in fact. Let us see what these activities involve.[6]

Observation. All scientific research begins with something that is observed. Either in the ordinary course of events or in the course of investigating some other scientist's conclusions, the scientist comes across a phenomena that puzzles or actually astonishes him, as Ernest Rutherford was astonished when he learned that some of the alpha particles fired by his assistant at a sheet of metal foil were ricocheting backwards. "It was," he said, "quite the most incredible event that has ever happened to me in my life. It was as incredible as if you had fired a 15-inch shell at a piece of tissue paper and it had come back and hit you!"[7] He remained perplexed for several days until it struck him that these particles were recoiling from a powerful electric charge at the core of the atoms in the foil while the other particles were passing through the atoms. This meant that, contrary to what everyone had thought, the electrical energy of the atom, instead of being distributed uniformly, was concentrated almost entirely at a single point. This proved to be one of the most momentous discoveries in modern nuclear physics.

Rutherford was hardly prepared for what he found, and it was only by an act of genius that he was able to lift his mind out of the frame of thought of his time. As a rule, however, the scientist who makes some chance discovery, and it is surprising how many scientific discoveries are made by chance,[8] perceives the significance of an oddity because certain contemporary ideas predispose him to do so.

piece of apparatus to work, finding a way of measuring something more exactly, or making dissections that will show the parts of an animal or plant more clearly. You may feel that he hardly knows himself what law he is trying to prove. He is continually observing, but his work is a feeling out into the dark, as it were. When pressed to say what he is doing he may present a picture of uncertainty or doubt, even of actual confusion."

6 Two excellent books on the scientific method are W. I. B. Beveridge, *The Art of Scientific Investigation*, Modern Library, New York, 1957, and P. B. Medawar, *Induction and Intuition in Scientific Thought*, American Philosophical Society, Philadelphia, 1969. For case histories of some actual scientific discoveries, see James B. Conant, *Science and Common Sense*, Yale University, New Haven, Conn., 1961.

7 Edward Neville da Costa Andrade, *Rutherford and the Nature of the Atom*, Doubleday Anchor, New York, 1964, p. 111.

8 Galileo, for example, discovered the principle of the pendulum while watching the oscillation of a candelabra in the cathedral at Pisa. In 1781, while surveying the northern heavens, the astronomer William Herschel observed an oversized and

Take the discovery of the X-ray. Wilhelm Konrad Röntgen, an obscure professor of physics at the University of Würzburg, was repeating another scientist's experiment on some recently discovered particles now known to be cathode rays. His intention was to discern their effects on fluorescent salts, which glow in response to certain light waves. As a check on one of his experiments he shielded the cathode tube entirely in blackened cardboard, shutting in the light. On November 8, 1895, he noticed to his amazement that a sample of salts twelve feet from the covered tube was glowing in the darkness. Where could the "light" be coming from? In order to find out he experimented feverishly for seven weeks. One of the things he did was to set a photographic plate facing the tube and put his hand in front of it. He was astonished to see the world's first X-ray picture.

At the end of these experiments he announced that he had discovered a hitherto unknown agent, the X-ray, which bore at least some resemblance to light. His discovery amazed people. The greatest physicist of the time, Lord Kelvin, even denounced it as a hoax. But Röntgen's insight was not unprecedented. As early as 1822, Michael Faraday had sought to find a relationship between magnetism, electricity, and light, and in 1864 James Clerk Maxwell had demonstrated that light was indeed a form of electromagnetic radiation. Faraday had actually spoken of "rays," and Röntgen at once named this new light-resembling phenomenon, the "X-ray." Being well acquainted with the idea that light was electromagnetic radiation, Röntgen swiftly perceived the significance of the glow that he noticed by chance.

Although Rutherford and Röntgen soon thought of solutions to their problems, other scientists have had to gather a great many facts before satisfactory explanations occurred to them. So it was with Darwin. Between 1831 and 1836 the young Darwin served as a naturalist aboard the *Beagle,* a British naval vessel surveying the coast of South America and the Pacific archipelagoes. During the voyage he filled the ship with fossils and specimens of all kinds. The evidence these presented led him to accept the then highly controversial theory that the earth had evolved geologically. While visiting the Galapagos Islands he noticed something

anomalous planet that was later named Neptune. Oliver Evans first thought of the steam engine when he noticed steam blow a cork out of a gun barrel filled with boiling water. Alexander Graham Bell was in his laboratory improving the telegraph when a chance occurrence, the sticking of a reed vibrated by an electric current, gave him the idea of the telephone. Alexander Fleming discovered penicillin after noticing that a little green mold had destroyed some bacteria he was breeding in a dish.

particularly strange. Although the islands shared a similar soil and climate, they were inhabited by many different kinds of plants and animals. Some islands even contained varieties unique to themselves. "I never dreamed," he wrote later, "that islands, about fifty or sixty miles apart . . . formed of precisely the same rocks, placed under a similar climate . . . would have been differently tenanted. . . ."

He remained puzzled by this until he returned to England. Then it occurred to him that, since the plants and animals he had seen on the islands resembled in essentials those he had observed on the mainland, the ancestors of the island species must have been carried from the continent by wind and tide. Moreover, since the plants and animals varied from island to island, they must have diverged as a result of the process of evolution in which each island, cut off from its neighbors, had developed variants of its own. But, if this were the case, not only had the earth itself evolved, but so had some of its species. If some, why not all? And if all had evolved, how had they done so?

Equipped with the very general hypothesis that species had evolved, Darwin now sought to form a precise hypothesis as to how this evolution had occurred. His search was for the evolutionary mechanism. He collected as many facts as he could about variation in animals and plants in the hope that the mechanism would reveal itself. Here, in his own words, is how he made the crucial discovery:

> In October, 1838, that is fifteen months after I had begun my systematic inquiry, I happened to read for amusement Malthus on population, and being well prepared to appreciate the struggle for existence which everywhere goes on from long continued observation of the habits of animals and plants, it at once struck me that under these circumstances favorable variations would tend to be preserved and unfavorable ones to be destroyed. The result of this would be the formation of new species. Here, then, I had at last got a theory by which to work.

Hypothesis. Darwin's words tell us two important things about the formation of a scientific hypothesis. The first is that phenomena do not dictate their own explanation. Granted, the scientist must be familiar with phenomena if he is to grasp the principle that accounts for them. Nevertheless, this principle is not absorbed from phenomena; it is read into them. Darwin collected more and more information in the hope that the secret of evolution would come to him, and so it did—by way of Malthus!

Amassing facts produces nothing but facts, bits of information without significance. Facts become significant only when they are interpreted, and interpretation presupposes an idea in the mind of the interpreter.[9] This idea may be only a shadow of the hypothesis to come, but it enables the scientist to look among phenomena for single significant threads from which he will later weave his imaginative design. A hypothesis, then, is a pure creation of the mind—a creation that is accepted if shown true to fact but that is formulated before this truth is known.

Second, forming a hypothesis is an act of pure intuition. There is no formula for producing scientific ideas; there are no logical steps to be taken at the end of which a hypothesis will be found waiting. The solution to a problem often dawns on the scientist when he is least expecting it. Here is August Kekulé's account of his discovery (in 1865) that the atoms in a benzene molecule constitute a ring, a discovery that was to underlie all subsequent study of the great range of so-called "aromatic" compounds derived from benzene:

> I was sitting writing at my text-book; but the work did not progress; my thoughts were elsewhere. I turned my chair to the fire and dozed. Again the atoms were gamboling before my eyes. This time the smaller group kept modestly in the background. My mental eye, rendered more acute by repeated visions of the mind, could now distinguish larger structures of manifold conformation: long rows, sometimes more closely fitted together; all twisting and turning in snake-like motion. But look! What was that? One of the snakes had seized hold of its own tail, and the form whirled mockingly before my eyes. As if by a flash of lighting I awoke; and this time also I spent the rest of the night in working out the consequences of the hypothesis.[10]

Nevertheless, a hypothesis only occurs to the mind that has striven for it. What happens, so far as we know, is that, given a problem to solve and given a knowledge of relevant facts, the unconscious mind goes to work during periods when the conscious mind is otherwise engaged, and eventually, if the scientist is lucky, it produces a solution. This solution, which appears to the scientist to be a gift, is really the product of a persisting mental activity of which he is unaware.[11]

[9] Paul K. Feyerabend, "Problems of Empiricism," in Robert Colodny, Ed., *Beyond the Edge of Certainty*, Prentice-Hall, Englewood Cliffs, N.J., 1965, p. 156.

[10] Quoted by Magnus Pyke, *The Boundaries of Science*, Penguin, Harmondsworth, Middlesex, 1963, p. 197.

[11] Henri Poincaré's words on mathematical creation apply equally well to creation in science: "Most striking at first is the appearance of sudden illumination, a manifest sign of long, unconscious prior work. The role of this unconscious work in mathematical invention appears to me incontestable." Quoted by Jacques Hadamard, *The Psychology of Invention in the Mathematical Field*, Dover, New York, 1954, p. 14.

Deduction and Check. The scientist has now made an informed guess, but has he guessed right? If he has, his hypothesis should apply not only to this particular situation but also to a range of others, for, as we have seen, claims to scientific knowledge are usually claims to a knowledge of regularities. The scientist therefore asks himself, "To what situations should my hypothesis apply, and does it actually do so?" To answer this question, he first deduces from the hypothesis what states of affairs can be expected to occur if the hypothesis is true. These deductions amount to predictions that, given the truth of the hypothesis, such and such phenomena should be observed under such and such conditions. He then looks for the conditions. Sometimes he seeks them in the ordinary course of nature, and sometimes he elicits them himself by means of an experiment. Having found the conditions or having brought them about, he observes whether the phenomena occur. If they do, he regards the hypothesis as to that extent confirmed. If they do not, he either revises the hypothesis and tests it again, or he invents a new hypothesis and tests that.

Let us take two actual hypotheses and see how they were tested. The first hypothesis was proposed to account for a seeming anomaly in an otherwise well-confirmed theory. In 1820 during a routine survey of the heavens, the French astronomer, Alexis Bouvard, noticed that the supposed outermost planet, Uranus, was not where it should be according to the laws of Newtonian mechanics. The deviation was slight, but it had scientists by the ears. Since Newton's theory had been so often corroborated, scientists were reluctant to abandon it in the face of one seeming counterinstance. Instead, two scientists working independently, John Couch Adams in England, and Urbain Leverrier in France, proposed the hypothesis that beyond Uranus there lay another planet whose gravitational pull was the cause of Uranus' observed position. Deducing the implication of this hypothesis was not easy. It was necessary to work out mathematically, from the size and position of Uranus and from Newton's laws, the precise spot at which a planet of certain dimensions should be observed. The calculation was completed by Leverrier and sent to the Berlin observatory. The big telescope there was trained on the spot where the planet should be, and, sure enough, on September 23, 1846, the new planet, Neptune, was observed less than one degree from the place pre-

Some good symposia on creativity in science are Calvin W. Taylor and Frank W. Barron, Ed., *Scientific Creativity: Its Recognition and Development*, Wiley, New York, 1963; and *The Way of the Scientist*, selected and annotated by the Editors of *International Science and Technology*, Simon and Schuster, New York, 1966. See also George F. Kneller, *The Art and Science of Creativity*, Holt, Rinehart and Winston, New York, 1965.

dicted. The discovery was a triumph of mathematical deduction and a remarkable vindication of Newtonian mechanics.

This example shows that the act of observation in science is both disciplined and technical. The scientist testing a hypothesis does not merely look about him; he looks to see whether a particular event is occurring or not. Often he observes by means of an instrument such as a microscope or telescope, and sometimes by means of an instrument thousands of miles away from him, such as an orbiting camera or a radar transmitter dropped on another planet. The observation may be made in the world outside or in a laboratory. The thing observed may be an independent physical occurrence or it may be some fact about a recording instrument that is interpreted as the effect of such an occurrence. For example, the shift of starlight to the right or red end of a spectrograph (the so-called Doppler effect) is taken as evidence that the star from which the light comes is receding fast into deep space, a sign in turn that the universe is expanding.

Let us now see how a hypothesis is tested experimentally. The reasoning behind the conduct of an experiment is as follows. When the scientist seeks to establish a connection between sets of events, he usually seeks to establish that one of these sets is the cause of the other. That is, he seeks to show that an event of one sort, A, is always accompanied by an event of another sort, B, and that an instance of B never occurs unless an instance of A also occurs. A, then, causes B when A is the condition that must be present if B is to happen and in the absence of which B never happens.

To show that one event is the cause of another is by no means easy. Any event, B, in nature usually occurs in combination with so many other events that it is hard to tell which of these other events is the cause of B and which of them accompany B by chance. One way of finding out is to create a situation in which we ourselves control the accompanying events (or conditions). We can then manipulate them one after another in order to ascertain which produces B and which does not. What we do is to produce a change in the condition we think is the cause of B, while at the same time we keep all other conditions from changing. If we then observe a change in the event, B, that follows, we may attribute it to the change we produced. This is our first experiment. We may then carry out a second experiment by varying some condition that we think has no significant influence on B, while holding unchanged the condition which we think produces B. If we then observe no significant change in B, we infer that B is significantly affected by a change in the original condition only and not by a change in any other.

When the scientist conducts an experimental test, he first deduces what his hypothesis implies for a given experimental situation and then manipulates the situation to see whether the implication is correct. Let us consider one of the most famous of all experimental tests, the experiment in vaccination carried out by Louis Pasteur at Pouilly-le-Fort, France, in 1881. Pasteur wished to prove that vaccinating an animal with attenuated anthrax bacteria would make the animal immune to the disease of anthrax itself. Given 60 sheep by the local agricultural society, he divided the animals into three groups: (1) a control group of ten sheep that were to receive no treatment whatever; (2) an experimental group of 25 that would be vaccinated and then inoculated with a highly virulent culture of the anthrax germ; and (3) another group of 25 that would not be vaccinated, but would receive the same dose of the germ. The experimental group would be vaccinated twice with anthrax bacteria of decreasing attenuation, at intervals of ten or 15 days, and would be injected with a virulent dose of the germ twelve to 15 days later. Pasteur predicted that the 25 vaccinated sheep would all survive and the 25 unvaccinated ones would die. The survivors would then be compared with the ten control sheep to show that vaccination had done them no harm.

The first vaccinations were carried out on May 5 before a large crowd, and were followed later by the second set of vaccinations and the administration of the germ itself. On June 2 Pasteur arrived to see the results. His predictions were fulfilled to the letter, as an eyewitness has described:

> When Pasteur arrived at two o'clock in the afternoon . . . accompanied by his young collaborators, a murmur of applause arose, which soon became loud acclamation, bursting from all lips. Delegates from the Agricultural Society of Melun, from medical societies, veterinary societies, from the Central Council of Hygiene of Siene et Marne, journalists, small farmers who had been divided in their minds by laudatory or injurious newspaper articles—all were there. The carcasses of twenty-two unvaccinated sheep were lying side by side; two others were breathing their last; the last survivors of the sacrificed lot showed all the characteristic symptoms [of anthrax]. All the vaccinated sheep were in perfect health . . . . The one remaining unvaccinated sheep died that same night.[12]

An experiment makes an effective test of a hypothesis about a causal connection, for the experimenter can insure that whatever effects he observes are caused by the conditions he manipulates. The ideal experiment

---

[12] Quoted by Magnus Pyke, *The Boundaries of Science*, Penguin, Harmondsworth, Middx., 1963, pp. 82-83.

is one that confirms a single hypothesis and disconfirms alternatives. It is known as a "crucial" experiment (from the Latin *crux*, a cross), because it is conducted at the crossing point of several hypotheses and shows which of them to take.

But experimentation is not a *sine qua non* of scientific testing. Often it is physically impossible for the scientist to manipulate and control the circumstances of the phenomenon he wishes to explain, or, if it is possible, to do so without distorting them. On other occasions experimentation is not only physically impossible, but also logically inappropriate. This is the case when the scientist is seeking to explain some particular event that has occurred in the past, such as the event or events indicated by the presence of certain fossils in a certain stratum of the earth. Since this event is nonrecurring, it cannot, as a matter of principle, be repeated in an experiment.

Indeed, some hypotheses cannot be tested decisively even by observation. Take Darwin's theory of evolution by natural selection. Although there is abundant evidence that species evolve, evolution, as such, is almost impossible to observe, for a variation only establishes itself over the course of many generations, and we cannot be around to watch the entire process. Nevertheless, although the theory has not been decisively tested, it is taken to be extremely well confirmed, for by its means many phenomena have been explained that would otherwise remain inexplicable. The theory works, not because it is decisively testable, but because it renders intelligible what could not be understood without it. The weight of the evidence, collected by Darwin and accumulated since, is overwhelmingly in its favor.

A single prediction verified serves as a first confirmation of a hypothesis but hardly establishes it as a scientific finding. A hypothesis normally graduates to a law or theory only after it has been tested and confirmed by a variety of scientists under a variety of conditions. A hypothesis, for example, that an agent such as nicotine or cyclamate is cancer-producing is usually tested in a number of laboratories against a range of animal species to determine whether the hypothesis applies to one species or several or all. If the hypothesis is well-confirmed by a variety of tests, it is regarded as a law, and the search then begins for a theory to explain the mechanism by which the agent produces its effects.

But whatever law or theory is established, it will always be a provisional truth, never a dogma. By a provisional truth, we mean a truth that is permanently open to refutation by factual evidence or rational discussion. We mean one that is so formulated as to indicate the sort of evidence that, if found, will confute it. For the aim of science is to seek truth by eliminating error, and a truth may be regarded as error-free only so long as anyone can find error in it but no one has. It is this permanent possibility of refutation that gives the findings of science their authority. We accept the truth of Newtonian mechanics because we know that Newton's laws have been, and are being, confirmed over and over again; and we accept the truth of the confirmations because we know that every test is repeatable and therefore repeatable with potentially different results.

A Social Institution

The Scientific Community. Publication makes a tested hypothesis a candidate for the title of knowledge, but it does not confer that title. A hypothesis becomes scientific knowledge only when a majority of scientists competent to judge it are satisfied that it is correct. It is through the scrutiny of his peers that the errors of the individual scientist are brought to light and eliminated; through the scrutiny of future scientists the errors of this scientific generation will be revealed and eliminated in turn.[13]

Thus the objectivity of science is a product of the method and not of the man. The individual scientist is as prone to error and bias as is the individual historian, philosopher, or literary critic. If he has labored over a hypothesis, he wants it to be right. If it is criticized, he hastens to defend it. What checks the frailty of the individual scientist is the more detached scrutiny of the scientific community. In science unsatisfactory hypotheses are eliminated because they are tested in agreed-on ways, not by their authors alone, but by many different scientists.[14]

But these scientists are not above bias, either. They tend to think ac-

[13] For studies of the scientific community, see Bernard Barber, *Science and the Social Order,* Free Press, New York, 1952; "Resistance by Scientists to Scientific Discovery," *Science,* **CXXXIV** (1961); Robert K. Merton, *Social Theory and Social Structure,* Free Press of Glencoe, New York, 1957, Part IV; Norman W. Storer, *The Social System of Science,* Holt, Rinehart and Winston, New York, 1966; Gordon Tulloch, *The Organization of Inquiry,* Duke University, Durham, N.C., 1966; and J. M. Ziman, *Public Knowledge: An Essay Concerning the Social Dimension of Science,* Cambridge University Press, New York, 1968.

[14] Hans Reichenbach, *The Rise of Scientific Philosophy,* University of California, Berkeley and Los Angeles, 1956, p. 118: "The social character of scientific work is the source of its strength; the limited power of the individual is supplemented by the resources of the group, the slips of the individual are corrected by his fellow workers, and the resultant of the contributions of the many intelligent individuals is a sort of superpersonal group intelligence, which is able to discover answers that a single individual could never find."

cording to the paradigm (model or example) of their field, so that if a hypothesis challenges that paradigm, it tends for that reason to be resisted. The history of science is full of brilliant breakthroughs that at first were received by the scientific community with indifference or contempt. Copernicus' heliocentric theory did not win general acceptance until a century after his death. William Gilbert's studies of magnetism and electricity were dismissed by Lord Bacon as "so many fables." Newton's theory was not taken seriously on the Continent until half a century after the publication of his *Mathematical Principles of Natural Philosophy*, now ranked as one of the greatest works in the history of science. Probably no work was more vilified than Darwin's *The Origin of Species*. An anonymous reviewer in the *Edinburgh Quarterly Review* debunked it as a "rotten fabric of guess and speculation . . . dishonorable to natural science." Darwin's former geology professor wrote to him from Cambridge, "I laughed . . . till my sides were almost sore . . . utterly false and mischievous . . . deep in the mire of folly."[15]

Happy, then, is the scientist who disarms his opponents as ingeniously as young Ernest Rutherford disarmed Lord Kelvin, the Grand Old Man among the physicists of his day. Kelvin had calculated, from the amount of heat flowing from the earth's interior, that the earth was 24 million years old. This was well short of the span proposed by Darwin, whose theory of evolution Kelvin rejected. But Kelvin had not known what Rutherford discovered in 1904, that the earth contains radioactive substances such as uranium and potassium, which release enough heat to extend the time of the cooling of the earth far beyond Kelvin's estimate. Rutherford discussed the implications of his discovery in a lecture that Kelvin attended. This, in his own words, is how he went about it:

> I came into the room, which was half dark, and presently spotted Lord
> Kelvin in the audience and realized that I was in for trouble at the

15 And so it goes. Mendel's discoveries in genetics were ignored by biologists. Pasteur's theory of fermentation was rejected by chemists and his germ theory was denounced by physicians. Alfred Wegener's theory that the continents of Africa and South America had once been joined was regarded as fiction until after the Second World War, although it had been proposed in 1912. On this record see Max Planck (*Scientific Autobiography and Other Papers*, F. Gaynor, transl. Philosophical Library, New York, 1949, pp. 33-34): "A new scientific truth does not triumph by convincing its opponents and making them see the light but rather because its opponents eventually die and a new generation grows up that is familiar with it." N. R. Hanson's *The Concept of the Positron*, Cambridge University Press, New York, 1963, includes an excellent account of how the evidence for the positron was ignored for seven years from 1926 to 1933.

last part of my speech dealing with the age of the earth, where my views conflicted with his. To my relief, Kelvin fell asleep, but as I came to the important point, I saw the old bird sit up, open an eye and cock a baleful glance at me! Then a sudden inspiration came, and I said Lord Kelvin had limited the age of the earth, provided no new source was discovered. That prophetic utterance refers to what we are now considering tonight, radium! Behold! the old boy beamed upon me![16]

Ultimately, however, the scientific method of public criticism and test is self-correcting. Although the scientific community may resist its geniuses, it does not resist them forever. Paradigms do change and younger men, less committed to past ideas, judge new hypotheses on their merits. Because the scientific community is committed to the scientific method, an unreasonable consensus, such as the agreement to ignore Mendel's hypothesis or to dismiss Wegener's is eventually overthrown. Even a theory as seemingly unassailable as Newton's is modified by an Einstein. In the long run, then, the method is proof against the prejudices of its practitioners, and as the errors of the individual scientist are detected by his peers, so the weaknesses of a school or a generation of scientists are eventually corrected by their successors. As with a river, so with science, what matters most is the current of thought rather than the content—not the paradigms, but the mode of regenerative thinking that produces them.

Science and Human Values

In writing this final section, I own that I have said nothing about education. I make no apology for this because my main purpose is to provide future teachers with a conception of science that all of them should possess. The nature, methods, and uses of science should be known by every teacher today, regardless of what subjects or grades he teaches. However, since education deals with problems of value, I must seek to answer two questions: What is the relation of science to human values? What is the scientist's responsibility to society?

The very practice of science presupposes an adherence to certain values, that is, to certain standards regarded as worthwhile. But these values are not ethical ones, for science in its pure form, or science for its own sake, is not an ethical enterprise. It does not seek to discover or to realize either personal goodness or social justice. Its values are there-

[16] Quoted by Robert Jastrow, *Red Giants and White Dwarfs: Man's Descent from the Stars*, New York, Signet, 1969, pp. 146-147.

fore intellectual ones. They are principles that scientists must observe if they are to discover the sort of truths they seek.[17] What are these principles? They are those to which the individual scientist commits himself in the formulation and testing of his own hypotheses. They include objectivity in deciding which observations are significant, care and accuracy in recording them, soundness in reasoning, and scrupulousness in generalization (for example, refusing to propose a universal hypothesis where the evidence warrants only a statistical one). Still others are principles to which the scientist commits himself when employing or testing the hypotheses of others, notably the principle that any such hypothesis is to be considered strictly on its merits and not on the intellectual eminence or social prestige of the person proposing it (for instance, $E = mc^2$ not because Einstein said so but because the proposition has been amply confirmed by experiments). Then there is the general principle that whatever is random and capricious has not been scientifically explained and should be accounted for if possible as an instance of some general regularity. There is also the principle that of a number of hypotheses equally consistent with the evidence available, the best is always the simplest one. Finally, there is the principle of rationality, that any claim to knowledge must always be open to criticism or refutation by anyone who can bring either logical objections or empirical evidence against it. None of these principles is derived from the facts, but all are brought by the mind to the consideration of facts. None has been established by the act of scientific inquiry itself.

These intellectual values inform the enterprise of science; they make science what it is. If we accept science, then, we must accept the values that make it science. But should we accept science? When we put this question, we move outside the scientific order to ask whether science as such has a moral value. This question cannot be raised scientifically, for science is concerned with the truth of particular hypotheses about the world, and the nub of the question is whether scientific truth itself is good. Scientific truth is good, I believe, not because it makes men happier (for there seems to be no way of telling whether it does), but because it makes them freer. Knowledge leads in principle to freedom, because the more we know of the world and of ourselves, the better we are able to foresee the consequences of our actions and so to choose those courses of action that are in our best interest. Even if such knowledge were to reveal how little there is that we could change, we should still be freer than we were when ignorant, for we should now be able to adapt

---

[17] Cf. Jacob Bronowski, *Science and Human Values,* Harper, New York, 1959.

rationally to the unalterable and so to take full advantage of the freedom we possessed. Knowledge, then, increases man's power to use natural forces and social institutions freely and purposefully. Insofar as science gives him this knowledge, science may be regarded as good.

But although scientific knowledge may be justified as instrumental to freedom, freedom is not the only good in the world; it must be tempered by justice and charity. Knowledge in general may be good, but it may be used for unjust or selfish ends and, even when used for good ones, it may have harmful results. In the real world, then, science must be judged by its consequences. Let us therefore consider the consequences of science, or what happens when science is applied.

The activities of applied science and technology, if we consider them for a moment separate from their products, are social processes having a profound influence on the character and evolution of the society we live in. In armaments, atomic energy, and aerospace, applied scientific research and technological development have acquired a momentum of their own, affecting political decisions, the conduct of war, and the thinking of millions of people. Modern technology also tends to bureaucratize society. The expense and complexity of modern technology, and the premium it places on efficiency, lead to the creation of large, highly integrated organizations of specially trained people, organizations that seek to control as many possible materials and processes on which their technologies depend. Applied science and technology also influence ways of thinking. Because science and technology enter into so many activities, people tend to think that all activities and problems are amenable to scientific and technological treatment, and they tend to regard quantifiable, utilitarian considerations as more important than spiritual or aesthetic ones. Finally, science and technology are both inherently changeable, since the one is forever seeking greater knowledge and the other greater efficiency. Consequently, the society that depends on them is subject to the changes they introduce. In agrarian societies a man grows up and grows old in a world that his father knew and that his children will know in turn. But in industrial societies today, a man in middle age is likely to have lost not only his childhood but the world in which he was a child.

Then we must consider the products of technology. Technology can be used to do good, to cure diseases, to raise the standard of living, and to provide comfortable transportation. It can also be used destructively; for example, to wage nuclear war. In addition, it can have side effects that were not foreseen. The car, for instance, which provides freedom of movement and comfortable travel, also causes traffic accidents and air pollution.

Our environment today is increasingly affected by technology. We are beginning to realize that man cannot go on exploiting nature indefinitely, for man himself depends on the balance of nature. If nature is treated recklessly, that balance is upset, to man's peril. Pesticides and industrial waste upset the chain of organisms that provide our supply of food; car exhausts and factory smoke pollute the air we breathe. Man, it is becoming clear, must cooperate with nature, not try to dominate it.[18]

Two important steps can be taken to see that scientific knowledge and technological products are used wisely. One step is to anticipate the consequences of developments in pure and applied science and technology. This will enable us to prepare ways of mitigating or cancelling the undesirable side effects of otherwise desirable projects. The second step is to decide which fields of pure science, applied science, and technology are most worth supporting, and to put public money into these rather than others.

Does the scientist have a professional responsibility to see that these steps are taken? He does indeed, since he originates the scientific and technological developments in question and knows most about them. How can he discharge this responsibility? He can inform the public of those forms of research that he believes are in the general interest and so deserve to be supported with public money. He can also warn of the undesirable consequences that are likely to ensue from technological products whether projected or in use. Finally, he can join with his colleagues and with the public in forming pressure groups to bring these concerns to the attention of the government so that something is done about them.

Summary

We have seen in this chapter that the prime purpose of science is to obtain reliable knowledge about the behavior of nature and the behavior of men. Through its special method of inquiry science replaces intuition, revelation, and crude common sense with generalizations and theories confirmed by repeated testing. No matter how elegant or daring a hypothesis may be, it must be confirmable by observation or remain a guess. As Thomas H. Huxley once said, the great "tragedies" of science are the slaying of beautiful theories by ugly facts. But the slaying is necessary

[18] On the care for the natural environment, see especially Barry Commoner, *Science and Survival*, Viking, New York, 1966.

and it is done to insure truth to fact. Unlike other kinds of knowledge, then, the findings of science are the result of close observation and careful experimentation. The degree to which findings are confirmed, and the confidence with which they are held, depend on the weight of the empirical evidence that supports them.

In science phenomena are explained by means of laws and theories, which are sometimes ordered in hierarchical systems. Indeed, science of its nature aims at generality and systems, because it seeks comprehensive and far-reaching theories within which less extensive generalizations may be subsumed.

The knowledge that scientists possess today has been built up year after year by the investigations of scientists in the past. Without it the scientist of today could not propose his hypotheses, for these have meaning only insofar as they cohere with, or deviate from, laws and theories that have been established already. This growing body of knowledge is produced by a community of scholars using a range of procedures exemplifying the scientific method. The essence of this method is "observe, hypothesize, confirm." Having confirmed his hypothesis, the scientist submits it to the verdict of scientists the world over and of scientists yet unborn.

Finally, although science is an intellectual and not a moral activity, in relation to society science is a social force with far-reaching consequences. The scientist therefore has a moral responsibility to press for the wise use of scientific knowledge. He has a responsibility, for example, to provide the layman with vital information on the consequences of his discoveries. He should come out of his laboratory long enough to show how his findings may affect the way we live. Unfortunately, the rank and file of our scientists are not forceful enough in this regard. As members of the human community, they must learn to discharge their special responsibilities with greater vigor and conviction. Since teachers of science are in an ideal position to do all this, we look to them for leadership.

References

❖✿

For a highly readable account of where science stands today, I recommend Ritchie Calder's *Man and the Cosmos: The Nature of Science Today* (Mentor, New York, 1968, 277 pp.).

A key work for understanding the history of science is Thomas S. Kuhn's *The Structure of Scientific Revolutions* (University of Chicago Press, 1970, 210 pp.).

John G. Kemeny's *A Philosopher Looks at Science* (Van Nostrand, 1959, 272 pp.) is a well-written introduction to the philosophy of science, including such topics as the structure of scientific knowledge and the nature of scientific laws and theories.

For a readable study of the scientific method, see P. B. Medawar, *Induction and Intuition in Scientific Thought* (American Philosophical Society, Philadelphia, 1969). James B. Conant provides some "case histories" of actual scientific discoveries in his *Science and Common Sense* (Yale University, New Haven, Conn., 1961). James D. Watson's *The Double Helix: A Personal Account of the Discovery of the Structure DNA* (Atheneum, New York, 1968) is an inside view of the greatest achievement of postwar science.

The best study of the scientific community is probably Norman W. Storer's *The Social System of Science* (Holt, Rinehart and Winston, New York, 1966).

16

Teaching and Technology

George F. Kneller

❖❖❖

Pure science, as we saw in the last chapter, is the study of nature for it own sake. Applied science is the study for practical ends of areas that pure science has opened up. Its purpose is to produce knowledge that can be employed to increase human well-being and satisfy human desires. Technology is the use of this knowledge to build artifacts and organize human activities. The technology of electronics, for example, is the use of knowledge about electrons—the applied science of electronics—to construct devices for the transmission of images (television), the recording and reproduction of sound (tape recorders and high fidelity systems), the storing and treatment of information (computers), and the control of industrial, commercial, and other processes (automation).

Education remained untouched by technology until the Renaissance. During the Middle Ages and before, education was conducted almost entirely by word of mouth. The teacher would read from a manuscript and the students would memorize what he said. There were no printed books, and teachers' manuscripts were scarce.

This was changed by the invention of the printing press in the middle of the fifteenth century. A century later the printed textbook had become the basic medium of instruction, and has remained so ever since. In recent decades, however, educators have begun to explore the possibilities of alternative means of instruction, such as radio, film, records, television, video and audio tape, teaching machines, and computers.

What has led to this exploration? In part, the march of technology. The very existence of new media of communication tempts some educators to experiment with them. But technological advance alone is not responsible for the interest shown in these inventions. What has really impelled schools to try them out is social progress and economic need, or the demand of more people for more education and the need of an increasingly sophisticated economy for a better educated labor force.[1] To close the gap between the demand for education and the supply of it, educators have decided to reap the harvest of the 20th-century revolution in communications.

Serious experimentation started in the 1930s when a few schools tried out a number of devices with a potential for mass instruction—records, films, and radio. During the war these media were used widely for military and industrial training. Impressed by the results, some educators sought, after demobilization, to use similar methods in the schools. Commercial television, made available to the public in 1948, was taken up by educators rather more enthusiastically than radio had been. In 1954 the Ford Foundation helped establish a now-famous television center serving the schools of Hagerstown, Maryland. Education television had "arrived."

Late in the 1950s there was a second burst of technological innovation. Its results were two devices for individual instruction: the language laboratory, a means of learning grammar and pronunciation by tape recorder, and the teaching machine, an instrument for presenting subject matter in easy-to-learn, step-by-step sequences.

The teaching machine has since been outdated by the computer. Because the computer is able to evaluate, store, and reactivate vast quantities of information, it is capable in principle of adapting complex learning programs to the needs of individual students in a way that the teaching machine never could. Computers were first employed for record-keeping in libraries and administrative offices. Then in 1966 in a Palo Alto (California) elementary school, Richard Atkinson and Patrick Suppes used an IBM 1500 computer to present programs in mathematics and reading

---

[1] Between 1950 and 1965, high school enrollment almost doubled, rising from 6.7 million to 13 million. During the same period, enrollment in colleges and universities increased by 60 percent. See Philip M. Hauser and Martin Taitel, "Population Trends—Prologue to Education Problems," in Edgar L. Morphet and Charles O. Ryan, Eds., *Prospective Changes in Society by 1980*, Denver, 1966, pp. 52-53.

to children in the first grade. This experiment and others like it suggested that here was a means of basic instruction with a greater potential than any medium since the textbook.

Both the teaching machine and the teaching computer are devices for programmed instruction. How effectively they teach depends on the quality of the program they present. Let us therefore consider what an instructional program is.

The Instructional Program

An instructional program is the representation for learning purposes of a complex subject matter as a sequence of its simple components. A program may be short or long; it may contain the matter for a single lesson or for an entire course. Each item of information in the sequence, or each component of the represented subject matter, is called a "frame." A program may contain anything from several hundred frames to several thousand. How much information is put in a given frame depends on the program writer's estimate of the mental step that the learner may now take as a result of having mastered the information in previous frames. Some programs provide a minimum of information per frame in order to elicit a series of limited correct inferences. Others present rather more information per frame in order to stimulate the learner to think more deeply and run the risk of error.[2]

An instructional program is constructed on the premise that a subject matter can be mastered provided that (a) it is broken into parts that are easy to learn, (b) these parts are arranged in a suitable order, and (c) the learner is informed regularly that he has learned correctly. Working on this premise, the program writer subdivides the subject matter into its constituent facts, concepts, and principles. He then arranges these constituents in the exact sequence in which it is believed the pupil will most readily comprehend them. The purpose of the program is to enable the learner to attain an intellectual grasp of the entire subject matter as a result of having mastered in sequence each of its constituent elements.

[2] A teaching machine is a typewriter-sized box with a window or screen (in which the matter of each frame is displayed) and a knob or button (which is manipulated to bring the next frame into view). Programs can also be presented by means of books: (a) "programmed textbooks," in which the student reads the top quarter or frame of all the pages in one chapter, then the next quarter, and so forth; (b) "scrambled books," in which the student is "branched" to a page or frame appropriate to the answer he has just given.

What stimulates the student to master a particular frame? What provokes his interest? What arouses the desire to learn? The stimulus is given by a question about the matter of the frame. To answer the question, the student must think about this matter in relation to the matter he has learned in previous frames. In most programs, then, each frame makes a point and then asks the student to answer one or more questions arising from it. As the program proceeds, the questions become more and more difficult relative to those of earlier frames, yet they always remain— in theory, at any rate—just within the learner's capacity to answer.

Each question or set of questions acts as a springboard propelling the student to the next frame. If the student has replied correctly, he is told so. If he has not, he is asked to try again, or told the right answer, or offered further information (another frame) that should lead him toward this answer. This instant appraisal of his reply, together with the advice he may receive if the reply is incorrect, gives the student an incentive to continue with the program. The student, it is said, likes to have his answers evaluated. If he has replied correctly, he appreciates recognition of this fact. If incorrectly, he welcomes a lead toward the answer he has missed. By providing him with a prompt feedback on all his answers the program motivates him to keep learning.

The general principles of programmed instruction have long been practiced. Teachers have been subdividing subject matter, reinforcing responses, and proceeding from easy to difficult matter ever since education began. What is new is the embodiment of these principles and others in carefully designed programs based on intensive research into the structure of subject matter and the psychology of learning, and open to continuous revision in the light of information about the performance of students using the programs. What is new, then, is the instructional program itself, a product of the application of scientific findings to the technique of teaching—a product, that is, of technology.

A *particular* instructional program can hardly be considered apart from the means that is used to deliver it. A program that is designed for communication by a computer cannot be presented by a textbook or even by a teaching machine. But the concept of a program as such, while *implying* the concept of a means of delivery, is logically independent of the notion of any particular means. If we prepare a particular program we must have a means of delivery in view, but that means is still subordinate to the program it delivers. All means whatever, however, are subordinate to the idea of a program as such. The heart of programmed instruction is the concept of an instructional program, for the concept of a program calls into being concepts of means, whereas means of delivery cannot be conceived at all unless there is first the concept of a program to be delivered. Let us therefore inquire what kinds of programs there are.

Linear Programs

Two main types of program have been designed so far: "linear" and "branching." The first linear programs were devised by the psychologist B. F. Skinner as a result of experiments he had conducted in animal learning. Skinner demonstrated that pigeons can be taught to perform surprising feats provided they are trained in very small steps taken one at a time and provided that each successful step is rewarded ("reinforced") with a grain of corn. If pigeons can be taught this way, said Skinner, so can children.[3] The technique is to break up a complex subject into very small pieces of information that can be learned step by step, and to reinforce success at each step not by presenting corn but by immediately telling the learner that his response is correct. By means of this technique the learner is led in a series of small and easy steps ("successively closer approximations") from an initial level of learned verbal behavior to the level of verbal behavior desired. In Skinnerian terms, the learner's verbal behavior is "shaped."

A linear program takes one route. All learners proceed through the same frames in the same order. The matter is so arranged that the learner makes only correct responses throughout the program and receives in consequence only positive reinforcement. To minimize the risk of error the steps in the program are made very small indeed. If a student does make a mistake in a particular frame, he may have to repeat the frame, or he may be told what the correct response is. In any case, he is not allowed to go to the next frame until he can respond correctly to the question(s) posed in the present one. Advocates of the linear program maintain that learning occurs mainly when behavior is "reinforced." By requiring minimal steps and ensuring that each of them is successful, the linear program allegedly *guarantees* that learning takes place.

Unfortunately the notion that learning must be rewarded at nearly every step on the way has yet to be proved, even for the learning performed by animals at the behest of experimenters. But if we forget Skinner's pigeons for a moment and think of real children, the disadvantages

[3] Skinner first expounded this view in "The Science of Learning and the Art of Teaching," *Harvard Educational Review*, **XXIV**, 2 (1954), 86-97. See also his *The Technology of Teaching*, Appleton-Century-Crofts, New York, 1968.

inherent in linear programs become more apparent. One is that linear programs soon tend to bore most children, especially intelligent ones. There is precious little reinforcement to be gotten from answering correctly if the chances of not doing so are minimal. Another disadvantage is that a number of small learning steps need not add up to a large one. It is often necessary for a student to grasp a whole structure first in an incomplete way if he is to think at all creatively about the constituent parts he learns. A linear program is more suited to rote learning than to the creative understanding of a structure of ideas. Again, to insure that the learner responds correctly, the linear program asks questions that normally require very little effort to answer. Yet what genuine learning is without effort and a little frustration? Skinner's promise that the linear program makes learning "active" amounts in practice to little more than the truism that one cannot operate a teaching machine without answering it. Whether that answer involves effort, and therefore an active coming to grips with the program, depends entirely on the kind of question that is asked.[4]

Branching Programs

Branching programs were invented by Sidney L. Pressey for use with his original teaching machine of 1926. In the 1950s they were developed further by Norman A. Crowder, who was training American airmen to trace breakdowns in electronic equipment.[5] With a branching program the learner is moved forward if he answers correctly but is diverted ("branched") to one or more remedial frames if he does not. These frames explain the matter afresh, ask him questions to elicit the right answer and reveal his previous mistakes, and then return him to the original frame. Thus, in contrast to a linear program which is designed to produce only correct responses, a branching program is set up to make intelligent use of errors by leading the learner to see for himself where he went wrong.

Branching and linear programs differ in still another way. A linear

[4] An excellent critique of the linear program is Herbert A. Thelen's "Programmed Materials Today: Critique and Proposal," *The Elementary School Journal*, **LXIII** (January 1963), 189-196.

[5] Norman A. Crowder, "Automatic Tutoring by Intrinsic Programming," in Arthur A. Lumsdaine and Robert Glaser, Eds., *Teaching Machines and Programmed Learning: A Source Book*, Department of Audio-Visual Instruction, National Education Association, Washington, D.C., 1960, pp. 286-298.

program requires the learner to "compose" or "construct" his own answers to the questions put to him. It does not furnish him with alternative answers to choose from but, as we have seen, seeks to insure that he answers correctly by questioning him about minimal amounts of information. Many branching programs, on the other hand, ask the learner to pick an answer from a number of answers that are proposed to him. This procedure allows the learner to choose an answer that is wrong. It is defended, however, on the grounds that a person learns a subject better by exploring his mistakes than by being prevented from making any mistakes at all.[6]

Branching programs are in agreement with Gestalt rather than with associationist psychology. The Gestaltist rejects the notion that learning consists of forming responses under the control of stimuli. Learning, he says, is a purposive activity, influenced by stimuli but not caused by them, in which a person acquires "insights" into relationships. To gain an insight into a subject, one must explore its implications and consider it from many points of view. By providing more information per frame than a linear program, a branching program enables the learner to think about a subject in some depth. By branching him through special frames that depend on his answers, the program helps him think about it to some extent in his own terms.

The case for the branching program rests on the argument that the learner can reach a genuine understanding of the principles governing some area of knowledge only if he thinks his way through to them by exploring the implications of right and wrong responses. Genuine understanding of a principle implies the ability to use it in novel situations. Unless the learner has the opportunity to use the principle wrongly and to discover his own errors, he is not consciously using the principle at all but is merely responding correctly to particular situations in which the principle happens to be exemplified. There is a vast difference between (a) performing numerous exercises in the technique of long division and (b) understanding the arithmetical notions from which this technique is derived. To grasp the reasons for the technique the student must be able to perceive for himself why certain uses of the technique succeed and

---

[6] It should be pointed out that branching does not depend on multiple-choice questions. Branching programs presented by teaching machines incorporate questions of this kind because the machines provide feedback only for a limited number of responses. Computers, on the other hand, can be programmed to handle a much wider range of answers, and therefore in many cases they allow students to respond freely.

others fail. Otherwise he has merely been drilled to go through the motions without seeing the point of them.[7]

The chief weakness of most branching programs, especially those designed for teaching machines, is that they are still too inflexible. In order to produce a program that the teaching machine can handle, the program writer specifies for each question a few alternative answers from which the learner must choose and for which branching frames have been prepared. Requiring the learner to choose between set alternatives is better than conditioning him to make only one response per question, but it is still a long way from permitting him to explore and test a principle for himself.

The Verdict on Teaching Machines

In the early 1960s the teaching machine, a rather ordinary gadget, aroused great expectations. Supporters of the machine credited it with extraordinary powers. The machine, it was said, would teach any subject matter at all that had logical structure. Students in turn would relish learning from the machine because their answers would be instantly appraised. Also, each student would learn at his own speed instead of having to keep pace with the class as a whole, while a student who was put off by the personality of his teacher would welcome learning from an impersonal box.

Alas for these claims, the machines could only be made to present the most rudimentary programs. Linear programs were the most tedious, but branching programs too fell far short of the variety and interest that a normal teacher would provide. In the end, the machines proved most useful for giving extra practice to backward students in drill aspects of subjects such as grammar and arithmetic.

Program-carrying textbooks, especially scrambled ones, have proved much more popular. It is easier to absorb information from the pages of a book than from the window of a machine. Consequently the steps in a book can be made more complex and the program more sophisticated. A book is also more flexible, because one can always turn back the pages to review what one has read, whereas a machine does not reroll. Most important, a book is a personal possession. One can stuff it in one's pocket,

---

[7] Cf. Sidney L. Pressey, "Unresolved Teaching-Machine Problems," in *Theory into Practice*, The Ohio State University Bureau of Educational Research, I (February, 1962), 30-37.

take it home, and write liberating remarks in it. No machine is that obliging.

Computer-Assisted Instruction

Potentially the most effective device for presenting an instructional program is the computer. With its speed, accuracy, and storage capacity, a computer is in an entirely different class from a teaching machine. It can be made to handle a learning program of any degree of complexity. The only limits to the branching it can accommodate are set by the ingenuity of the program writer. Again, a computer can respond to the particular characteristics of the individual learner. This is because it can store, retrieve, and act on whatever data the learner feeds into it. Since the data are converted into electric pulses, they can always be activated. Also, a computer may be made to serve hundreds of users simultaneously with different programs, whereas a teaching machine can be used by only one learner at a time and must be reloaded for every user with a fresh copy of the program.[8]

How Computer-Assisted Instruction Works. Computer-assisted instruction operates as follows. At the computer's command a frame of the program, consisting of information and a question, is submitted to the learner. The learner considers this material, then relays his answer to the computer. The computer evaluates the answer and returns a comment. A fresh frame is then presented, remedial or advanced depending on the learner's previous answer, and the process of instruction continues.

The content of the program is usually stored outside the computer in the form of slides, printed matter, or films. However, if the content of a particular frame is designed to vary with the learner's responses, it is stored or generated electronically within the computer. For example, a geometric figure shown on a television screen may be made to change its shape according to the way in which the learner, using a typewriter, handles the variables in the equation the figure represents. In this case

[8] Computer-assisted instruction should be distinguished from computer-*managed* instruction. The latter is the use of a computer, not as an instructional device communicating with a learner, but as a teacher's aid in selecting material for students and evaluating students' work. Cf. William W. Cooley and Robert Glaser, "The Computer and Individualized Instruction," *Science,* **CLXVI** (October 31, 1969), 574-582; and Harvey J. Brudner, "Computer-Managed Instruction," *Science,* **CLXII** (November 29, 1968), 970-975.

the information constituting the figure is maintained within the computer, since it has to be modified and not merely delivered by the computer.

The program may be presented to the learner aurally through a tape recorder or headphones, or visually through a slide projector, typewriter, or cathode-ray tube. A cathode tube can display a drawing or diagram and then, at the direction of the computer, incorporate within it the student's responses made at a typewriter or with a light pen. Information may also be presented to eye and ear at once by means of television, video-tape recorders, or talking typewriters.[9] Response equipment is also varied. The learner may type an answer, press a key on a multiple-choice key box, write or draw with a photoelectric light pen, or press with his finger a picture displayed on a touch-sensitive screen. Indeed, in some instructional systems the learner now replies to the computer through a microphone.

What Computer-Assisted Instruction May Achieve. At present computer-assisted instruction is in the experimental stage. Scores of pilot projects are being carried out by institutions throughout the nation. The best known of these projects are the work of the Institute for Mathematical Studies in the Social Sciences at Stanford University. One such project is a drill-and-practice program in elementary mathematics for grades 1 through 6. In the academic year 1967-68 this experimental program was introduced to 1000 students in California, 1100 in Kentucky, and 600 in Mississippi. There is also a tutorial program in reading. At the college level there are first- and second-year tutorial courses in elementary Russian.[10] The programs are carried out in actual institutions but under

9 The talking typewriter is used to teach reading and writing. The typewriter pronounces words and at the same time presents pictures of what the words represent. For example, it may pronounce the word "door" and then reel off pictures of doors. The child sitting at the typewriter runs his fingers over the keyboard and finds all the letters locked except "D." He presses this key and the letter appears on the paper in the roller. With the keyboard locking for the remaining letters in turn, the child spells out the whole word.

10 For comprehensive reports of the Stanford programs, see P. Suppes, M. Jerman, and D. Brian, *Computer-Assisted Instruction at Stanford: The 1965-66 Arithmetic Drill-and-Practice Program*, Academic Press, New York, 1968; and H. A. Wilson and R. C. Atkinson, *Computer-Based Instruction in Initial Reading: A Progress Report on the Stanford Project*, Technical Report No. 119 (August 25, 1967), Institute for Mathematical Studies in the Social Sciences, Stanford University. A shorter and more recent account of the mathematics and Russian programs is given by Patrick Suppes and Mona Morningstar, "Computer-Assisted Instruction," *Science*, **CLXVI** (October 17, 1969), 343-350. Drill and practice programs provide just that,

specially controlled conditions. They are conducted by specialists instead of by the normal school staff, and they constitute only a small part of the total instruction received by these students. Until computer-assisted instruction has been fully tested under normal school conditions, we will not be able to compare its effects accurately with those of conventional instruction.[11]

Nevertheless, it is possible to make some conjectures based on our present knowledge both of education and of computers. One thing we may conjecture is that computers will be able to take over the time-consuming tasks of monitoring, marking, and presenting information. If these tasks are given to computers, the teacher will be able to devote himself to more creative forms of teaching, such as illuminating knowledge and discussing its significance for the student and for the culture. He will also have more time to work with individual students and with small groups.

A computer can also provide instruction to large numbers of students simultaneously, each if need be at a different point in the curriculum. A computer with 200 terminals can serve up to 6000 students a day, while forthcoming computers with a thousand terminals will be able to handle five times that number.[12]

A computer can also adjust an instructional program to the needs of the individual learner. It does so by remembering and evaluating the responses of each user. Having appraised the learner's performance, the computer presents him with appropriate material. If the pupil is bright, he is challenged to move ahead quickly. If he is slow, he is advanced more gradually. By appraising the pupil's answers and relaying material accordingly, the computer enables him to proceed at his own pace and in line with his own abilities.[13]

whereas tutorial programs introduce new concepts. The difference between these two sorts of program will be discussed shortly.

[11] Cf. John E. Coulson, "Computer-Based Instruction," *International Review of Education*, **XIV**, 2 (1968), 146-147; and R. C. Atkinson and H. A. Wilson, "Computer-Assisted Instruction," *Science*, **CLXII** (October 4, 1968), 73 ff.

[12] Patrick Suppes, "Computer Technology and the Future of Education," *Phi Delta Kappan* (April, 1968), 421.

[13] Cf. Patrick Suppes, on the Stanford drill-and-practice mathematics program, in "Discussion," *Harvard Educational Review*, **XXXVIII**, 4 (Fall 1968), 732: "Individualization takes place in three distinct ways. First, under computer control, the teletype types out an exercise. The student responds with an answer that is immediately evaluated . . . . If the student is wrong he is given a second chance. If his answer is correct, he is immediately given a new problem. The second aspect of individualization is the organization of the problems in terms of difficulty. At each grade level

As I pointed out earlier, however, from a teaching point of view a computer is only a device for presenting a program. It is the program that does the instructing. If a computer, then, is to handle the instruction of a wide range of students in, say, elementary algebra or elementary French, the program it presents must contain a wide range of appropriately sequenced information. However, a powerful computer and elaborate branching do not guarantee that each student will be branched through a sequence of frames that meets his needs exactly. He may in fact be switched through several sequences without being any the wiser about the material. We have to ensure that the computer is able to recognize the needs actually implicit in the student's responses and that the remedial sequence it then offers really clears up his doubts. That is to say, we have to insure that the frames submitted to the student are actually satisfactory to him. To do this we must have wide, factual knowledge about what misunderstandings students form regarding particular items of subject matter, and about how these mistakes are really rectified. We can then devise frames capable of clearing up the difficulties that different students encounter at the points where they encounter them.

Levels of Computer-Assisted Instruction. What sorts of instruction can computer-delivered programs provide? It is claimed that programs can be devised for instruction on three levels. The first level is that of drill and practice. At this level of computer-assisted instruction the teacher introduces and explains new concepts and skills, and the computer gives the student programmed exercises in practicing them. For example, in a course in French one lesson may be devoted to a class discussion of the use and conjugation of the imperfect tense, and the next to computer-provided exercises in handling this tense. Here the computer has two advantages over the ordinary teacher. It can present exercises and evaluate the student's responses to them with no effort and in no time at all. The computer can also, it is said, give each student the exercises that he

the curriculum . . . is broken up into somewhat more than twenty concept blocks. Work in each concept block covers seven days. On the first day the student is given a pretest, and on the basis of his pretest score, he is placed on one of five levels for five days of training. During the training he moves up and down in the five levels depending upon his daily score. The third aspect of individualization is the selection of individualized review. While the student is working on a given concept block, he is also reviewing previous concepts on which his individual work was least satisfactory. For example, a fourth grader who is working on the twelfth concept block is concurrently reviewing the one concept block of the preceding eleven on which he scored lowest. For one student this review block might be multiple-digit multiplication; for another, problems of long division; and for another, solution of word problems."

is best equipped to handle, extending the capacities of the bright student with harder problems and encouraging the slower student with easier ones. In their beginning stages most school subjects, such as reading, grammar, spelling, mathematics, science, and foreign languages, require a good deal of practice in the use of basic concepts and skills. Providing such practice and grading the student's performance is likely to be the computer's first main job.[14]

On the second level of instruction the computer-delivered program introduces and explains the concepts and skills in which it then gives practice. At this level the computer is said to function like a "tutor," because it takes into account each student's difficulties and provides explanations and questions appropriate to his particular responses. Writing programs for computer "tutoring" clearly requires a great deal more knowledge and expertise than does writing programs for drill and practice. Subjects with a clear-cut logical structure, such as science, mathematics, and foreign languages, together with the factual sides of arts subjects like history, have been proposed as suitable matter for computer "tutoring."[15]

Within a few years computers will be capable of "tutoring" after a fashion. This will undoubtedly be a mechanical achievement. But the question remains, do we want this sort of tutoring? The answer surely is, not if we can help it. So far as we know, most adults and most children (once the novelty of the machine has worn off) would rather be taught by a person than by a machine. It would be surprising if they did not. The only good reason for using machines is to compensate for a shortage of teachers or the inadequacy of personal teaching.

Computers are suitable for drill and practice because here no real teaching is being done. The ideas or rules have been explained by the teacher, and the student has asked questions about what he does not

---

[14] Certain skills in the writing of expository prose may also be taught by computer. By applying a light pencil to a cathode ray tube, a pupil can rearrange the sentences in a purposely disordered paragraph. He can also learn to discriminate between more and less satisfactorily organized paragraphs. He can then apply what he has learned to his own compositions.

[15] The Palo Alto project in computer-assisted instruction includes a first- and second-year college course in elementary Russian, in which all elements except pronunciation (handled in the language laboratory) and the teaching of the Cyrillic cursive script are dealt with by the computer itself. These elements include comprehension of written and spoken Russian and mastery of grammar and syntax. See Patrick Suppes and Mona Morningstar, "Computer-Assisted Instruction," *Science*, **CLXVI** (October 17, 1969), 343-350; and Patrick Suppes, "Discussion," *Harvard Educational Review*, **XXXVIII**, 4 (Fall 1968), 734-5.

understand. Now he is ready to try out his knowledge on a set of exercises. But where tutoring is concerned, it is up to the advocates of computers to show that computers can do the job as well as teachers, if not better. A great deal of research needs to be carried out into the teaching potential of computer-assisted instruction. But it is a fair guess at present that computers are better suited to give practice than to provide true teaching.[16]

At the highest level of instruction, it is claimed, the student and the computer will actually discuss the subject matter of the program. First, however, computers must be built that not only recognize the words the student is speaking but also understand the meaning of the questions he is asking. Then programs must be written that anticipate all the questions he is likely to put. If we succeed in doing these things, we shall have demonstrated our technical skill, but it is hard to see what we will have gained for education. Conversing computers seem likely to prove about as useful as clockwork birds, which are triumphs of ingenuity with little practical application.

Computer-assisted instruction at present is also very expensive.[17] According to a recent study, computer-given drill and practice costs about $400 annually per student, and computer tutoring about $1000. If computer-assisted instruction were to be installed in all American public schools, the annual cost could range from $9 to $24 billion. This compares with a current annual expenditure of $30 billion, or $600 per pupil, on public school education as a whole. Admittedly, the price of computer-assisted instruction will fall. It is, after all, a law of modern technology that the cost of an innovation tends to vary inversely with the extent of its development and the scale of its manufacture. Nevertheless, computer-assisted instruction seems expensive enough now to remain an educational luxury for at least a decade.[18]

---

[16] On the concept of "teaching," see pp. 278ff.

[17] "Innovation in Education: New Directions for the American School," a report by the Committee for Economic Development, July, 1968, U.S. Office of Education, U.S. Department of Health, Education, and Welfare, Washington, D.C., 1968.

[18] Computers also are used in education for purposes other than instruction, such as for information storage and retrieval in libraries, and for data processing in administration and research. These uses, however, fall outside the scope of this chapter. The following works are recommended for further reading: Don D. Bushnell and Dwight W. Allen, Eds., *The Computer in American Education*, Wiley, New York, 1967, Part IV, "Information Processing for Education Systems"; John I. Goodlad, John F. O'Toole, and Louise L. Tyler, *Computers and Information Systems in Education*, Harcourt, Brace and World, New York, 1966; *International Review of Education*, **XIV**, 2 (April, 1968), special issue, edited by Richard Wolf, on "Uses and Values of the Computer in

Other Instructional Media

Television

Educational television was introduced early in the 1950s with the backing of the Ford Foundation. In schools it has been used mainly to compensate for the shortage of teachers. In rural areas especially, where a teacher must often struggle single-handedly with enough tasks for half a dozen people, television brings carefully prepared lessons not otherwise obtainable. In many schools, too, it can be used to teach special subjects, such as Russian or advanced mathematics, for which qualified teachers are not available.

Another use of television is to provide educational experiences that are outside the scope of the ordinary school. Television can broadcast performances of plays and ballets by the finest troupes. It can demonstrate complex and expensive scientific experiments that are beyond the range of the school laboratory, and it can show the uses of science in industry. It can bring together experts to discuss subjects of wide interest. For example, a historical turning point such as the Industrial Revolution or the collapse of the Roman Empire can be discussed by a historian, an economist, a literary critic, and a sociologist, each placing it in a different perspective.

Educational, or noncommercial, television can be broadcast on an open or a closed circuit. Open-circuit, noncommercial television is beamed to the general public. Anyone who wishes may tune in. Closed-circuit television is broadcast only to people in certain places, such as a particular building or the schools in a certain community.[19] Most noncommercial television stations are owned by communities, universities, or school systems.

There are now about 200 noncommercial open-circuit stations, compared with over 600 commercial stations. A national noncommercial network is slowly being established. At present National Educational Television (NET) distributes programs by telephone line to most noncommercial stations for two hours every evening except Friday and Saturday, and for six months of the year. Unfortunately, this amounts to no more than

Education"; and John W. Loughary, *Man-Machine Systems in Education*, Harper and Row, New York, 1966.

[19] The commercial networks also have broadcast some instructional programs. For example, the National Broadcasting Company, cooperating with the American Association of Colleges for Teacher Training, broadcast a series of college courses for credit. One of these courses, "Physics for the Atomic Age," proved especially popular.

ten hours of television a week. Unfortunately, too, noncommercial television is very short of money. During 1968 the Corporation for Public Broadcasting, which is allowed to spend tax money on broadcast programs if Congress approves, was allocated only $5 million, enough to finance one good weekly program a year. Eventually national noncommercial television may have to pay for itself by carrying advertisements in the European manner, which means gathering the advertisements into groups and denying the advertisers any influence over the programs surrounding their commercials.

One of the latest advances in open-circuit technology is the transmission of programs via communications satellites. A transmitting station sends programs to one or more satellites for relay to receiving stations on the ground that rebroadcast them to television sets at home and in school. Sets can also be made to receive programs directly from the satellite. Nationwide satellite systems offer the chance to educate and unify the diverse, isolated, and largely illiterate peoples living within the boundaries of some of the developing nations. In India an experimental satellite project will shortly be broadcasting advice on birth control and farming to 5000 villages. Similar projects may soon be set up in Brazil and Indonesia.

In the United States, however, open-circuit noncommercial television has supplied little in the way of formal classroom instruction. Instead it has concentrated on programs of a general cultural nature aimed at an adult audience—discussions of art, literature, and current events, long interviews, travelogues, concerts, plays, and so forth. This policy has limited its usefulness to the schools.[20]

Closed-circuit television, on the other hand, has been used by universities and school districts to provide programs in academic subjects to meet local needs. I have already mentioned the closed-circuit station serving the schools of Hagerstown, Maryland. Set up in 1954 with the aid of the Ford Foundation, this station offers courses in all academic subjects at every level. It can transmit six programs simultaneously. Another closed-circuit system is the Midwest Program on Airborne Television Instruction, or MPATI (Empatty). In this system a station on the ground transmits programs to a DC-6 flying several miles above Montpelier, Indiana. The aircraft, carrying two transmitters, relays a couple of

20 Cf. Malcolm S. Knowles, "Adult Education," in Peter H. Rossi and Bruce J. Biddle, Eds., *The New Media and Education: Their Impact on Society*, Doubleday Anchor, Garden City, N.Y., 1967, pp. 238-239.

programs at a time to nearly 17,000 classrooms in the rural schools of half a dozen midwestern states. The programs, which consist of taped lectures, allow the classroom teacher twenty or thirty minutes' discussion time. They are broadcast as semester or full-year courses covering all grades from elementary school to college.

Closed-circuit stations usually serve school districts. Individual schools, however, can also secure particular programs on videotape. The tapes can then be relayed from playback decks at some central point in the school to monitor TV sets in the classrooms. The taped programs are distributed, and in many cases made up, by an agency serving the schools of a city, county, or state.

Films

Motion pictures were taken up by educators between the two wars and became especially popular in the late 1940s. During the next decade they lost ground to television, but recently they have made a comeback owing to the development of new and cheaper kinds of film, notably 16 millimeter and 8 millimeter, together with appropriate cameras and projectors. Super-8 millimeter film is particularly useful because it is cheap, easily soundtracked, and in color. Sixteen-millimeter and especially 8-millimeter cameras and projectors are now within the financial range of quite a few schools and colleges wishing to make their own instructional films.

Both still pictures and moving ones have their special advantages. A motion picture is best used to display a process that must be grasped as a whole. A still, on the other hand, permits the analysis at length of a complex entity. An athlete or dancer who wishes to study form will be served better by a motion picture than by a series of equivalent stills. However, a class studying a machine, or an architectural style, or a complex equation, will naturally look to a still picture that they can analyze over and over again.

Schools can make their own films. They can also make their own videotapes. Instead of delivering a lecture several times a year to different classes, a teacher can deliver it once to a video recorder. Videotaping can also be used to analyze and correct the performances of pupils in physical education, public speaking, and the performing arts. A teacher can record the style of a hurdler or a discus thrower and show him the tape immediately afterward. A violin student can play a passage in front of the recorder, and then see and hear his performance on the television set.

Language Laboratories

The language laboratory is based on the principle that a language is best learned by being spoken, and that particular speech forms are best acquired by constant repetition. The laboratory consists of a booth equipped with a dual-track tape recorder, microphone, and earphones, in which a student listens to a tape recording of a foreign language, records his own performance, and plays this performance back to himself.

The laboratory usually provides drill and practice. The basic exercise is to substitute or transform the variable in a given linguistic structure. For example, the student of French may practice using the subjunctive mood after a verb of volition by substituting the appropriate forms of verbs like "courir" and "sortir" for the verb "partir" in a sentence such as "je veux qu'il parte" ("I want him to leave"). Or he may practice using the imperfect tense of verbs by employing this tense in different contexts—with negatives, to ask questions, with different persons, and so forth.

The student begins the drill by listening to the problem sentence on the tape. He then stops the tape, works out the answer in his mind, restarts the tape, listens to the correct answer recorded by the instructor, and repeats this answer as he records it in the space provided on the tape. When he has finished the exercise, he rewinds the tape and hears in sequence the problem, the instructor's answers, and his own answers. By comparing these answers he is able to correct his own pronunciation. On a dual-track tape recorder the master program cannot be erased. Only the practice track is erased automatically by the next student as he listens to the master program.

The language laboratory was developed during World War II in the language-training programs of the United States Army. When peace returned, the laboratory was adopted by colleges and schools, gradually at first, but then more enthusiastically as a result of the financial support given by the National Defense Education Act of 1958. In recent years the tape recorder has been supplemented by further instructional devices, while the laboratory study carrel has been used for teaching subjects other than languages, such as typing. Some laboratories are now linked to computers, enabling the student to summon both taped and pictorial materials from a central storage point.

Although language laboratories have proved effective enough at giving drill and practice, they have not been successful in introducing and explaining rules and concepts. They can be used to exercise the student in what he has learned already, but they do not, or do not yet, provide real tutoring or true teaching. This is due to the programs rather than to the mechanical mode of presentation. There is nothing intrinsically antipedagogical about educational machinery. If the student can learn from a textbook, he can learn from a well-programmed machine, particularly if the latter is used, like a textbook, to supplement the teacher and not to replace him. But the machine must indeed be well programmed, for once again, it is the program rather than the machine that does the teaching.

Unfortunately most programs used in language laboratories have been based on the unsatisfactory behaviorist hypothesis that languages are learned through the formation and reinforcement of connections between certain linguistic and nonlinguistic stimuli and certain linguistic responses. This hypothesis may conceivably apply to the more primitive kinds of rote learning, but it does not account for the creative, exploratory thinking involved in the primary understanding of rules and concepts.[21]

Conclusion

During the last two decades educators have turned to a variety of technical means to help provide an improved education for the increasing number of those who demand it. These means include films, television, language laboratories, video recorders, teaching machines, and computers. Of these devices, undoubtedly the most important is the computer, which is or will be capable of furnishing individualized drill and practice as well as individual tutoring in elementary subject matters. Let it be emphasized that these devices do not replace the teacher, but assist him. Their main function is to relieve him of the repetitive duties of instruction and to free him for more creative teaching.

The expanding market for technical goods and services in education has led to the emergence of an education industry, consisting mainly of electronics companies that have joined, or have taken over, publishing houses and other educational suppliers in order to invent, promote, and sell hard- and software. Although most educators welcome this infusion of funds and talent, some have opposed it as being motivated by a desire to profit from education rather than to improve it. The threat to educational standards is admittedly there. The best way to meet it, however, is not to boycott inventions that deserve to be tested but to put greater pressure on the industry to produce goods and services that educators can usefully adopt. In particular, companies must be persuaded to co-opt more

21 Cf. Jacob Ornstein, "Programmed Instruction in the Language Field," *The Modern Language Journal,* **LII** (November 1968), 401-410.

educators as consultants and designers. This should not be hard to do in what seems to be a buyer's market.[22]

[22] For a discussion of the education industry, see the *Harvard Educational Review* (Winter 1967), 107-124.

References

❖❖

There are two good symposia containing essays on all aspects of contemporary educational technology: H. Thomas James et al., *The Schools and the Challenge of Innovation*, A Supplementary Paper Issued by the Research and Policy Committee of the Committee for Economic Development (McGraw-Hill, New York, 1969, 341 pp.); and Peter H. Rossi and Bruce J. Biddle, Eds., *The New Media and Education: Their Impact on Society* (Doubleday Anchor, Garden City, N.Y., 1967, 460 pp.).

On concepts of the instructional program and teaching machines, I recommend Phil C. Lange, Ed., *Programmed Instruction*, The Sixty-Sixth Yearbook of the National Society for the Study of Education, Part II (University of Chicago Press, 1967); Robert Glaser et al., *Studies of the Use of Programmed Instruction in the Classroom* (Learning Research and Development Center, Pittsburgh, Pa., 1966); and Robert Glaser, Ed., *Teaching Machines and Programmed Learning II: Data and Directions* (National Education Association, Washington, D.C., 1965).

The outstanding work on computer-assisted instruction is Anthony G. Oettinger with Sema Marks, *Run, Computer, Run: The Mythology of Educational Innovation* (Harvard University Press, 1969). Oettinger maintains that in the long run, computer-assisted instruction will prove enormously beneficial but that its present performance is grossly overrated. Two symposia on computer-assisted instruction and other uses of computers in education are Don D. Bushnell and Dwight W. Allen, Eds., *The Computer in American Education* (Wiley, New York, 1967, 300 pp.); and Ralph W. Gerard, Ed., *Computers and Education* (McGraw-Hill, New York, 1967, 307 pp.).

On educational television, the best work is Wilbur Schramm et al., *The New Media: Memo to Educational Planners* (UNESCO and International Institute for Educational Planning, Paris, 1967). See also the three volumes of case studies in the use of educational television in different countries, called *The New Media in Action: Case Studies*

357

for Planners (UNESCO and International Institute for Educational Planning, Paris, 1967). For a recent summary of research on educational television, see Godwin C. Chu and Wilbur Schramm, *Learning from Television: What the Research Says* (National Association of Educational Broadcasters, Washington, D.C., 1968). The development of educational television in the United States is covered fully in Allen E. Koenig and Ruane B. Hill, Eds., *The Farther Vision: Educational Television Today* (University of Wisconsin Press, Madison, Wis., 1970, 387 pp.). For an incisive study of educational television in the United States and a plea for a system of public non-commercial television, see the Report of the Carnegie Commission on Instructional Television, *Public Television: A Program for Action* (Bantam Books, New York, 1967, 254 pp.).

On films in education the best study remains M. A. May and A. A. Lumsdaine, *Learning from Film* (Yale University Press, New Haven, Conn., 1958). See also D. W. MacLennan and J. C. Reid, *Abstracts of Research on Instructional Television and Film,* Institute for Communication Research (Stanford University, 1964, mimeo.).

On language laboratories I recommend Elton Hocking, *Language Laboratory and Language Teaching* (Monograph No. 2 Department of Audio-visual Instruction, National Education Association, Washington, D.C., 1964); and J. B. Carroll, "Research on Teaching Foreign Languages," in N. L. Gage, Ed., *Handbook of Research on Teaching* (Rand McNally, Chicago, 1963).

17

Perspectives from Sociology

Carl Weinberg

❖❖

EDITOR'S INTRODUCTION. The natural sciences—physics, chemistry, and biology—have made spectacular advances partly because in the beginning little was known about the phenomena they studied, such as gases, metals, and mammals. The behavioral sciences, on the other hand, have entered familiar ground. They have been preceded by every philosopher, moralist, historian, and poet who has sought to depict the passions and powers of men. They have been anticipated, too, by the wisdom of the race. There are countless common-sense generalizations about human nature that we absorb more or less consciously in the form of proverbs, tales, and general lore. We inherit this wisdom in the language we speak. The existence of different words for "envy" and "covetousness," let us say, or for "instinct" and "desire," testifies to a distinction that has been drawn between the mental states and dispositions to which these words refer.

We therefore already know in a general way a good deal about human nature. And so the behavioral scientist does not now and probably never will occupy the position in science of a Galileo, a Newton, or a Darwin. There is no discovery he is likely to make that will revolutionalize our conception of human nature in the way that the theory of universal gravitation revolutionalized mechanics or the theory of evolution trans-formed biology.[1]

The fundamental task of the behavioral sciences is to confirm, correct, and extend our existing knowledge of human nature by carefully constructing and testing hypotheses and by using those methods of exact observation that are the hallmarks of scientific inquiry. Many of our beliefs about human nature are well founded, but they need to be formulated more exactly and confirmed more rigorously. Others are bound to be mistaken and will need to be conclusively disproved. Moreover, there are aspects of the psyche, notably the unconscious, about which we have little common-sense knowledge. Here science has told us much and has much to tell us still.

Social processes are a good deal less familiar to us than the everyday behavior of individuals. They are also more subject to historical change. We therefore have much to learn from sociology about social institutions in general and about the social institutions of education in particular. This chapter shows how sociological concepts and methods contribute to our understanding of education, and the ensuing chapters, "Political Socialization" and "Economics," perform similar tasks on behalf of their own field of study.

The Meaning of "Context"

The pupil is a member of a classroom group; this is a "context." The classroom group exists within the context of the school, the school within the context of the community, the community within the context of the state, and the state within the context of the national society. Each of these contexts bears some relationship to the child. They help to explain many things about him, such as his aspiration, achievement, manners, likes and dislikes, language, values, and motivations.

The sociology of education is the study of these contexts. Sociologists who are interested in the way in which schools affect students, and social institutions affect schools, find the concept of context a useful way to focus on their problem. What, then, is a context?

A context is the sum total of all the forces that influence the adaptation of persons to their environment. A force is a condition that persons

---

1 For an elaboration of this general thesis see Michael Scriven, "Views of Human Nature," in T.W. Wann, Ed., *Behaviorism and Phenomenology: Contrasting Bases for Modern Psychology,* University of Chicago, 1964, pp. 163-183.

take into consideration in making decisions about how to behave. It does not have to be understood or even noticed by the individual to affect his behavior. For example, a group is a force. Most people, at some level of awareness, acknowledge the significance of the group in communicating to them how to behave when they are in the group. There are many things that we may be willing to do when we are alone but hesitate to do in a group. Undressing and cursing are two such behaviors. The force in question is simply the presence of others.

Every institution has its unique configuration of such forces. That is to say, when we are in a school we take the school into account in deciding how to behave. When we are in a church we use another configuration of forces; in the family we consult a third. The point here, and it may be a rather simple one, although not always obvious, is that the school exists as a social context, and its combination of forces or conditions influences people to act in regular ways that are different from the regular ways we behave in other social contexts. Educational sociology is a growing body of knowledge about these regular ways of behaving in schools, and about the relationships between these patterns of behavior and one or more forces in the school environment.

The Classroom Context

The child in school relates mainly to his assigned classroom. Even though forces greater than any contained in that classroom dictate what goes on in the class, the child sees the educational world through that classroom. One way of viewing the problem is to consider the classroom as the microcosm of all the forces in the school, community, and larger society. For it is here that the student receives his instruction about how to survive in the school environment, and eventually in the larger society.

The word "survive" was not chosen facetiously. It is quite accurate, for we are talking about survival skills. Without these skills the child becomes isolated from others and fails to achieve any of the goals that he is conditioned to admire and want. With these skills the child is able to become integrated into the only world he knows, his community and society. With these skills he can get a job; without them he cannot. With these skills he can receive from others the approval that he usually needs or is socialized to need; without them he is rejected, disapproved of, and left out of the mainstream of social life.

What are these skills? They are essentially of two kinds, "cognitive" and "moral." Cognitive skills are the "fundamentals": reading, writing, figuring, and speaking correctly. They are also skills associated with specific occupations such as medicine or automobile mechanics. Moral skills refer to citizenship qualities, such as industriousness, respect for authority, respect for property, good manners, and moral virtue.[2] The classroom is the context in which these skills are learned. This context is made up of physical, cultural, and social elements, each of which we will discuss in turn.

The Physical Element. The physical context of the classroom consists of the components that distinguish a classroom from, say, a cocktail lounge. Even though a bar may have chairs, the chairs are not arranged in the same way as they are in a classroom. In the classroom chairs are arranged in several ways. These different arrangements, which we might call the "ecology" of the classroom, suggest, or even influence, different patterns of classroom interaction. Take a classroom such as the one most of us know best, where chairs are arranged in long rows and the teacher's desk is centered in the front. What does that suggest about probable patterns of leadership and authority? How might a classroom where all chairs are arranged in a circle differ from the former with respect to the kinds of interaction this pattern might encourage?

In the same way that desk arrangement might influence behavior, other physical factors can play a significant role. Consider the dynamics associated with good and bad lighting, new and old facilities, and the presence or absence of educational materials, books, scientific equipment, and a view from the window.

The Cultural Element. Chapter 3 on the relevance of culture to education provides an orientation for this notion. In the classroom, culture is the accumulated values describing how persons should behave in the school class. Such values as how to treat teachers, how to conduct oneself in examinations ("thou shalt not cheat"), and how to react when frustrated, angered, or ecstatic ("thou shalt not show emotion") are representative.

Culture in the classroom is what might be referred to as the conventional wisdom of classroom interaction and the appropriateness of classroom goals. There is, in other words, a tradition in classroom life, a tradition of ways to do and things to want. The definition of the teacher as a moral leader, the desire to behave in ways that the teacher appears to represent, and the need to seek approval from the teacher are part of the classroom tradition. Students quickly learn these traditions. When the teacher says, "Children, do not speak out in class," the child hears two

---

[2] Talcott Parsons, "The School Classroom as a Social System, *Harvard Educational Review*, **29** (1959), 297-318.

things: that the teacher does not approve of speaking out in class, and that there is a way of behaving in school, a traditional way, which includes not speaking out in class.

The cultural habits of classroom life are maintained because they are consistent throughout a person's educational life. Students begin early to define the appropriate goal of classroom life as teacher approval, for example, or symbolic rewards, such as grades or prizes, and they conclude their educational career with the same definition. The reason new educational styles or goals are strongly resisted is that old values are deeply entrenched in the culture of classroom life.

As in all cultural systems, the classroom translates values into symbols. Success is translated into grades, awards, promotions, and entrance to college. Popularity is translated into leadership roles and friendship. Industriousness is signified by productivity, respect for authority, and institutionalized silence. Cleanliness and neatness are injected into the criteria for the evaluation of papers and the evaluation of persons. Show me a neat, well groomed first-grader who turns in neat, clean papers and I'll show you a student who will go to college.

The Social Element. The social forces within the classroom are those patterns of interaction that occur regularly as persons live and work through a school day. Some of these patterns are the "authority" pattern, the "work" or "task" pattern, and the "evaluation" pattern.

The *authority pattern* is the way teachers and students relate to each other. It has to do with such things as how directions for activity occur and how decisions are reached. There are several possibilities. Some observers use such criteria as student achievement, productivity, and morale.[3] Differences in style have been labeled "authoritarian" (when all direction comes from the teacher), "democratic," (when teacher and students together decide on tasks), and "laissez-faire," (when everybody appears to "do his own thing" with the teacher serving as a resource).

The *task pattern* has to do with various ways of conducting classroom affairs. How do students spend their time? Do they read books and write answers to questions at the end of the chapter? Do they listen to lectures, take notes, study those notes, and answer quizzes? Do they work independently or do they work on projects together, dividing the labor?[4]

---

[3] R. C. Anderson, "Learning in Discussions: A Resumé of Authoritarian-Democratic Studies," *Harvard Educational Review*, **29** (1959).

[4] Teachers have assumptions about how students learn. These assumptions appear to be linked to the kinds of activities that go on in their classrooms. However, this is not always the case. Many teachers conduct the affairs of the classroom as their own teachers did. The sociologist is interested in relating different task patterns to achieve-

The *evaluation pattern* deals with the various activities involved in evaluating and differentiating students along achievement lines. One consideration that does not appear to be directly linked to achievement is relevant here. This is the fact, mentioned earlier, that some persons are evaluated by moral rather than by cognitive criteria. Sociologists like to distinguish between "universalistic" and "ascriptive" criteria. "Universalism" applies a single standard to all persons independent of their particular qualities. "Ascription" evaluates persons differently, based on their special traits such as race, deportment, age, and sex.

Two evaluative modes are of contemporary interest. The current wave of student dissent speaks, among other things, to the way instructors evaluate students, which typically is competitive and unidimensional. Students would prefer cooperative, multidimensional ways of being evaluated. (Think about the way in which the evaluative mode becomes a context for decision-making. How does a competitive mode differ from a cooperative one in terms of the way students adapt to their everyday routines?) Competition produces a set of definitions about persons that are often loaded with antagonism, distrust, and prejudice. Cooperative learning tends to produce more favorable definitions.

Evaluation is used, of course, to differentiate students into categories that lead to different futures. Good students go to college; bad students get poor-paying jobs. At present society appears to need both types. Educators, however, often push for individualized instruction and individualized evaluation. Different patterns of evaluation, like different authority and task patterns, are likely to affect students in different ways. These are the kinds of problems educational sociologists like to consider.

The School as a Social System

The wider context for the classroom is the school. Within the school the child exists in two subsystems of the larger system, (1) the "formal" system of academic performance, including such activities as going to classes, doing homework, being graded, and being promoted, and (2) the "informal" system of peer relationships. If the student attends a secondary school or a college, he may be part of a third system that C. Wayne Gordon has called "semiformal." This is the system of clubs or organiza-

ment and morale outcomes. See C. W. Gordon, L. Adler, and J. McNeil, *Teacher Leadership in Classroom Social Systems*, A Report of the U.S. Office of Education, Washington, D.C., 1963.

tions, linked to the school in terms of sponsorship and support and linked to students in terms of interests.[5]

The Formal System. One aspect of the formal organization of the school is its hierarchical structure. This is the arrangement of positions in terms of power and authority. At the top is the superintendent; at the bottom is the student. In between are assistant superintendents, principals, vice principals, department chairmen, and teachers. One's position in this hierarchy determines many things—what he can or cannot do, who gives orders, and who obeys. For many students a teacher represents someone who has authority over him rather than someone who has knowledge to offer. Power relationships in education seem to lie at the base of much conflict between students and their schools. When many high school students from black and brown (Mexican-American) ghettos recently went on strike in several large cities it was not for an acknowledgment of ethnic contributions to world civilization, represented by something like an Afro-American studies center, but because the relationship between students and those who had power over them had become repressive. Where those who had power were white and those who did not were not, the conflict took on racial overtones. In many minority ghettoes black administrators, who may be less qualified and perhaps even more oppressive than white ones, are replacing their white counterparts. It is a matter of power politics as well as of better teaching and learning.

The Informal System. The system of peer-group affiliations plays an important role in the life of most secondary-school students. Adolescents have evolved their own society, the values of which compete with adults as well as the school for the loyalty of the student.[6] If one wishes to account for a school program, it can be done by examining the value structure of the adolescent group that attends a school; athletic students produce one that emphasizes sports. Students who historically have not experienced high rates of academic mobility seem to find themselves in schools that are organized to keep students out of higher education rather than get them into it. When the values of students are antiacademic, the school is hard pressed to push its own values forward. In a time when adolescents are alienated from adults, from the family, and from most institutions that are dominated by adults, the peer group offers

---

[5] See C. Wayne Gordon, *The Social System of the High School,* The Free Press, New York, 1957, for a description of the impact on high school students of participation in the several school systems.

[6] See James Coleman, *The Adolescent Society,* The Free Press, New York, 1961, for a description of the value structures of high school students and the way in which these values are translated into emphases within the school.

the adolescent personal security as well as information about how to survive within the institution. Students seem to organize themselves informally around a number of traits that they have in common. We have heard expressions such as the "athletic crowd," the "brainy crowd," the "hoods" or "delinquents," and the "popularity crowd." Often the traits that produce a homogeneous grouping are interest based, as in the case of a group of boys who like football. Often they are based on qualities of race or socioeconomic status. This latter type of grouping produces antagonisms, negative social typings, and frequent conflict.

The major point to be emphasized here is that a person's membership in a group of peers strongly influences his adaptation to the academic environment. If the peer group does not support values conducive to achievement, then achievement is rare. If the peer group stresses higher education as a social necessity, all members of the group set their sights on higher education, even when there is neither interest nor apparent advantage.

The Semiformal System. The system of extracurricular activities in high school and college is frequently the basis on which friendship groups form on one hand and ascribed achievement occurs on the other. It will be recalled from our earlier discussion that some criteria for attaining educational success are particularized. That is, persons are evaluated on the basis of who they are rather than what they do in a standardized competition.

Students who actively participate in extracurricular activities usually do well academically. There is no reason to believe that these students are brighter than those who do not participate. Rather, there seems to be a kind of involvement effect that transcends ability. All other things being equal, extracurricular participation provides students with a reputation that either aids them evaluatively or inspires them to do better work. Most college students who were members of the student government will recall how easy it was to get good grades, even when they spent most of their time out of class on "official" business. And many a school athlete moved on to higher education with grades earned by his popular reputation.

The Function of the School

Sociologists are interested in both structure and function. Structure is the way they conceptionalize the order of the school; function is the way they conceptualize the goals and processes. The function of the school in a period of rapid cultural change has been to attempt to integrate the dominant concerns outside the school into the school curriculum. In the last decade there has been a resounding cry for something called "relevance." This has come from public citizens as well as from teachers, writers, and students. The school, in its own slow-paced, conservative way, has tried to be responsive to this call. The term "conservative" here is not being used critically but descriptively. The school is tied to societywide structures in such a way as to render independent, innovative action almost impossible. At the same time, the school does change when desired programs seem consistent with many of the older established goals of education.

Most Americans believe in democracy. The school was organized to promote this social and political process. Unfortunately educators, like politicians, believe or have believed in the *principle* of democracy, not the practice of it. The relationship between schools and democratic institutions is practically nonexistent. Schools are run by administrative edict. This in part is what much of the current conflict in education is all about. The point is that schools are moving in the right direction, but slowly. There is student participation in the process of deciding on curriculum and in the organization and execution of rules for order. Other innovations in schools were brought about by publicized concerns of groups within the society. One of the cherished ideals of American society, and consequently one of the goals of education, is equality. Again, the structural hypocrisy of education has perpetuated the belief but done little about the practice. Education as an institution has been brought into direct confrontation with its hypocrisy and there are nationwide attempts to rectify the inconsistency. The government has acted with respect to integration, and school districts are responsive in greater or lesser degrees to the call to improve the quality of education for nonwhite minorities. These are simply examples of the way the function of education shifts slightly to accommodate social concerns.

Apart from the more dramatic examples of the school's concern with social problems, the major function of education remains one of funneling students through a filter. We put the gross product in one end and out the other comes a society of youth committed to everything Americans believe in, including such things as the intrinsic value of work, a respect for authority, a belief in our economic system, and a generalized willingness to defend our way of life against any political, social, or military threats to it. In the forthcoming section on education and disorganization we will take a look at how this filtering process is holding up in these critical times. Before we do this, however, there is one more context that we need to consider, the community.

The Context of the Community

Students view the world from the reference point of their communities. Many students who have grown up in suburban areas, and this includes a major portion of those who go on to college and study education, have never been in a ghetto. These students have a hard time grasping the notion that it is difficult to make it all the way to school without being in a fight, without being pressured to buy drugs, without being sexually propositioned, and without being requested to skip school and do something else.

Students bring to the classroom a view of the world and a concept of education that they receive from significant persons in their community environment. Young children from lower-income communities take to the classroom a sense of school as a hope but often the school becomes an enemy of that hope. Students from high-income communities come to view the school as a servant of their status aspirations, and the school seldom disappoints them.

The sociology of education views the community as a network of interacting forces that can be conceptualized as a set of traits: socioeconomic status, age distribution, racial composition, religious composition, and community function. This last trait, function, refers to the economic orientation of the community. Is the community oriented towards rural needs or urban needs? Is the community economy base one of recreation, as in Miami Beach, Las Vegas, or Atlantic City? Is the orientation towards shipping, as in Long Beach, California, or Norfolk, Virginia?

Most communities in an urban society are homogeneous. This produces a *de facto* socioeconomic and racial segregation. The consequences of this kind of segregation are the points of issue that have been stirring the educational community since 1954 when the Supreme Court decided against segregation. At this point it is well for the student to be able to conceive of the way community characteristics influence both the student and the school. Let us take an example from each of the trait categories.

Socioeconomic Status. Wealthy communities can afford to hire more counselors than can poor communities. The more counselors, the better is the advice about college. Lower-class persons are typically too busy or too disinterested in the business of the school to become a significant factor in administrator and teacher decisions. In suburban communities parents play the role of constructive watchdogs. This fact appears to guarantee that the school will provide students with everything they need to proceed normally towards a college career. At the same time it also appears to guarantee that teachers will take no chances with issues that might offend parents; ergo, there is practically no innovation.

Age. The kind of educational support offered by a community of senior citizens to its schools would vary considerably from the support forthcoming from a low-cost housing development where most parents have young children. The kind of educational opportunities available to children in communities where young adults leave for industrial areas often does not prepare students to meet college requirements.

Race. Mexican-American mothers are not able, socioculturally, to deal with the formal bureaucracy of the school. Although genuinely interested in their children's education, they find it distasteful and not their role to become involved in the affairs of the school. The forces of ghetto living, of a cultural system very different from the rules and expectations of white middle-class society, makes the child's adaptation to school expectations uncertain. The child is frequently punished for habits he has learned from others of his race.

Religion. This is a minor force in most urban educational settings. However, there is still an analytical issue in general and a real issue in some particular settings. Consider, for example, the education of children in Central Pennsylvania where the Mennonite sect is strong. Many of these people disapprove of any secular education for children beyond reading, writing, and figuring. Also consider the problems of gaining public school support in a city such as Boston, where there is a high Catholic population and parochial school education is prominent.

Function. The history of rural education has been the preparation of students for a life and a career in agriculture. Specific courses linked to this kind of life would be common in rural high schools and practically nonexistent in urban high schools. In urban areas there is a heavy concentration of vocational courses. In suburban communities we witness almost exclusively a college-preparatory education.

Not all communities have specific functions, but most have a personality. In "West Side Story" the notion of a personality for a community like the West Side of New York's Manhattan Island should be clear. Here we have a commercial style (small, independent shops), an ethnic style (black, brown, and white), an interpersonal style (fear, caution, and conflict), and an educational style loaded with stress, confusion, weak leadership, and weaker support.

Contrast this style with that of Long Island, not many miles away. The commercial style is large, modern shopping centers with large parking lots filled with station wagons. The ethnic style is pure white, mostly Anglo-Saxon, with several Jewish communities. The interpersonal style is polite, passive, superficial, and uninvolved. The educational style is academic, cooperative, and well supported. It is unidimensional in its goals, which are onward and upward, and relentless in its means, which are pressure and more pressure.

So much for the community context. The student should now have an academic framework within which to view the foci of sociological inquiry. He should also have a sense of the context that breeds widespread disorganization within the educational world.

Education and Disorganization

The most interesting and dramatic aspects of educational life are typically those dealing with social problems. Studies of race relations, student deviance, educational disruption, dropouts, drugs, and suicide are common in the socioeducational literature. In this next section we want to expose the dimensions of these problems as they emerge from ongoing social patterns in American schools.

Personal and Social Disorganization

In the context of school life, students often experience difficulty. If their problems can be explained by a configuration of qualities or traits that they do not share in common with others, we say that they are personally disorganized. A state of social disorganization exists when persons adapt to institutional life in a deviant way or when educational structures are incompatible with the needs or expectations of members of distinct social groups such as racial groups, socioeconomic groups, or age groups. If a person comes into conflict with the educational system or fails to adapt to the normal routines because he is black, poor, adolescent, or anything else that identifies him sociologically, we observe a pattern of social disorganization within the school.

Sociologists are only indirectly interested in problems of individual adjustment. If we hear about a student suicide and happen to know that this student grew up in a home where extensive pressure to succeed was always present, we might begin to formulate a hypothesis about the effects of pressure upon college students. Our interest, then, is in students, or in student suicides, not in the suicide of an individual.

Primarily, sociologists who study the school are interested in the way in which educational patterns affect persons who are present in the schools. These are primarily the students, although the adaptations of teachers and administrators are often the focus of sociological study.[7] The kinds of problems that involve the school as a context, and persons who occupy the roles in the educational drama, are typically those of race relations and alienation. We will return to these areas after a brief look at the structure and process of education. We need to understand the organism before we can begin to speculate about problems in its functioning.

Disorganization in the School

The school is organized to (1) differentiate students according to evaluative criteria such as ability, interest, and citizenship qualities; (2) instill in them certain commitments to do well in school and in the occupational world; and (3) allocate them to various places and positions in the adult society.[8] This has always proved to be an efficient system by which persons were processed from one institution, the family, through a second, the school, to a third, the economic order. When persons begin to disapprove of this kind of behavior or disapprove of the rewards of being managed in this way, disorganization erupts.

We observe disorganization when certain structures within the school no longer attain the goals they were created to serve. The critical component in this process is the structure of socialization. Socialization involves the development of a set of values or goals that students will aspire to achieve and a set of normative standards about how these goals shall be achieved. These we can call the means of goal seeking.[9] Teachers are also socialized to believe in these goals and in legitimate ways of attaining them. To ensure that persons do accept and internalize the goals and means of education, a set of rewards and punishments is established to ensure conformity and control deviance. Students receive A's or F's, smiles or frowns; teachers are promoted and fired; administrators move to higher posts or they do not.

---

[7] H. Becker, "The Career of the Chicago Public School Teacher," *American Journal of Sociology*, N. Gross, et al., *Explorations in Role Analysis: Studies of the School Superintendency Role*, J. Wiley and Sons, New York, 1958; and C. Weinberg, P. McHugh and H. Lamb, *Contexts of Teacher Alienation*, U.S. Office of Education Report, 1968, are examples.

[8] T. Parsons, "School Class as a Social System," op. cit.

[9] R. Merton, *Social Theory and Social Structure*, New York, The Free Press, 1959, 141-142.

Disorganization occurs when the process of socialization is inadequate to accommodate all social groups. It is at that point that rejection of many of the hitherto accepted values takes place. A student is taught to believe that hard work, good behavior, and respect for authority will be rewarded. But because his skin color may be different he has difficulty getting a job. Another student is taught that perseverance, hard work, and sacrifice will be rewarded with affluence. But he has grown up with affluence and his parents are unhappy, and perhaps he is unhappy. Affluence means little to him. Then why buy the beliefs that lead to affluence?

It is true that the American educational system continues to produce, without disruption, respectable, conforming citizens who take jobs and raise families. But it is also true that the schools are in greater trouble than ever before because of their failure to accommodate diverse groups of persons and because of their inability to develop the kind of flexibility required by changing cultural styles. It is becoming increasingly harder to socialize in the same way large groups of different kinds of people with differential opportunities. The problem occurs in the process of differentiating educational behavior in accordance with varying value-goals.

Differentiation

The history of changing educational patterns, discussed previously in Chapter 4, "Social Change," reveals a process of increasing specialization in every aspect of social life. What is true of the society at large is always reflected in prevailing educational patterns. As the division of labor became a prerequisite to industrial expansion, schools had to separate their own functions and allocate students to different tasks with different payoffs. At first, criteria for the differentiation of the student group was achievement, and then a combination of achievement and social style— something like manners. For many years the school pursued its task of allocating some students to the professions, others to general occupations, and still others to nowhere in particular. In the last decade educators, often with the data provided by sociological inquiry, began to consider the basis of differentiation and to ask certain questions about the appropriateness of the criteria on which students were differentiated. Some notions became quite obvious. First, a pattern of intergenerational consistency appeared. Sons of professionals became professionals and sons of unskilled workers became unskilled workers. This occupational pattern held up even when students were judged to be the same on achievement or intelligence criteria.[10] Second, persons who possessed a configuration of

---

[10] J. A. Kahl, "Educational and Occupational Aspirations of 'Common Man' Boys," *Harvard Educational Review*, 23 (Summer 1953).

"desirable" qualities (nice manners, willingness to work hard, ambition, appropriate language), were ascribed an educational superiority that smoothed the path to higher education. Those who were unable to simulate such qualities were seldom able to rise above their disadvantaged condition and attain the rewards of the educational system. Another popularized condition of the past decade was the fact, or issue, of "disadvantage." Some students, usually those with minority backgrounds, were found to be "ill-prepared" to gain the advantages of educational success. A current, and more realistic, perspective is that, rather than being ill-prepared (black children being as oriented to the Protestant ethic as white ones), they were ill-educated. Real and *de facto* segregation has provided the educational system with an easy mode of pursuing its sorting function. Rather than differentiating students within the same schools, it has become an easy job to sort them out according to the schools they attend. And since schools are known to vary considerably as to available human and material facilities,[11] it can be seen that the disadvantage lies not in intrinsic qualities but in the way Negroes and Latin Americans are defined and treated.

Differentiation and Status

The major problem with differentiation in education is that it rests on a foundation of invidious distinctions. It is not a matter of being sorted into a vocational career; it is more a matter of being sorted into a career that is defined by most members of the society as inferior. Hence the resentment of social segments of the society toward each other.

Status in American education is a duplicate of status in the larger society, and consequently supports a competitive and hence conflict-ridden structure. Disorganization in the schools can be directly linked to the patterns of competition that are intrinsic in almost everything students do. If there were no status distinctions there would be less competition; with less competition there would be less resentment or failure. In order for many youths to rationalize their failure in competition, they reject the criteria by which they are judged, thereby setting the stage for the emergence of delinquency modes. The process goes something like this.

A student enters school at the age of five, anxious to please and gain approval. He has trouble learning how to read. No one has been able to motivate him. He falls behind. By the fourth grade he is hopelessly behind. He begins to take intelligence tests. He discovers, perhaps by infer-

[11] James Coleman, *Equality of Educational Opportunity*, U.S. Office of Education Report, Washington, D.C., 1966.

ence from the way he is grouped, perhaps because his parents are given the information, that he is not very intelligent.[12] He begins to detect a difference between himself and others who receive good grades and rewards from teachers. He also begins to detect a commonality between himself and others who are in the same category that he is. More often than not, if the school is racially heterogeneous, he shares skin color in common. If the school is racially homogeneous he identifies with those who receive the same kinds of sanctions that he does, first disapproval for lack of achievement and then punishment for violations of the normative order of the school and classroom.

He begins to see that, in terms of the standards of achievement and behavior that he had been socialized to respect, he is losing in the competition for school rewards. His self-image is deflated and his self-worth is shaky. What can he do to preserve it? He begins to conceptualize the whole status game. Maybe he has been playing in the wrong game. If he cannot win in this one, why not get into one that promises him victory? He begins by denying that he wants to compete in the status game that the school has established. He then establishes a new system for himself, one that he can share with all others like himself. Now, how is status attained in the new system? Precisely by reversing the values and standards of the system that he must reject. What are those values? They are ambition, industriousness, cleanliness, passivity, honesty, morality, and so forth. His value system then becomes one that supports laziness, messiness, aggressiveness, dishonesty, and immorality—whatever that may mean to him and his peers. His status within his new group, sometimes referred to as a "delinquent subculture,"[13] is now based on the extent to which he behaves in terms of the new value system. It is obvious that such behavior leads him into direct conflict with school officials. But let us not think that only the failures suffer from the structure of status competition. Everyone does.

We have discussed the low-status child and his pattern of failure and delinquent activities. At least two other status groups are apparent, the middle-status student and the high-status student, the later obviously being the ostensible winner in the competition for educational rewards.

The Middle-Status Student. The middle-status student is the marginal student, the one who passes but cannot enter in. He is the student who

---

[12] D.A. Goslin and D.C. Glass, "The Social Effects of Standardized Testing in American Elementary and Secondary Schools," *Sociology of Education*, **40** (Spring 1967), 115-131.

[13] A. Cohen, *Delinquent Boys, The Subculture of the Gang*, New York, Free Press, 1965.

has achieved adequately enough to receive a high school diploma but does not meet the requirements of college entrance. At the same time he has majored in an academic curriculum that makes him untrained for vocational occupations. Recently a division of higher education called the junior college has emerged and assumed a prominent place in education. The junior college was created to accommodate the vast majority of middle-status students. Its major function is the "cooling out" of students who had higher aspirations than the educational system could handle.[14] Instead of becoming engineers they accept careers as technicians. The consequence of this kind of failure can be estimated by anyone who has set his mind to one goal and been forced to accept less.

The High-Status Student. The high-status student is one who has learned to survive and prevail in the competition by developing his intellectual skills and internalizing a dedication to get ahead through the established structures. He is the best socialized person in our system, and consequently the least free. He is the one most likely to attempt suicide over academic failure, lose sleep over grades, develop nervous habits, repress creativity, doubt his or her sexual capacity, set standards which he cannot meet, and delay the gratification that could come from daily living to a time that he will probably never see.

The high-status student is, in many ways, the worst victim of our educational policy. He has so internalized the values and commitments of competitive achievement and success that he is always running a race, even when there is no reason to keep running. It is no wonder that millions of young people, top students in the best universities, are declaring their own moratorium on education. But for the majority of students the years of delayed gratification and depersonalized student statuses are lengthening. Even medical students are becoming overwhelmed with the expectations laid upon them and are pushing their conservative staffs and faculty for a greater degree of personal freedom and participation in the affairs of the school. The college student no doubt is the victor in the educational game, but he is also the one most rebellious against the system that produced him.

Racial Differences and the School

Racial differences and the distribution of rewards according to these differences is a prominent theme in the socioeducational literature. A host

[14] B. Clark, "The 'Cooling-Out' Function in Higher Education," *The American Journal of Sociology*, **65** (May 1960), 569-76.

of studies reporting inequities in the reward system have been published in the last decade. The most prominent of these studies was conducted by James Coleman.[15] Some of the findings are instructive:

1. Most students attend schools that are racially segregated. Almost 80 percent of white students in grades 1 through 12 attend schools that are from 90 to 100 percent white. More than 65 percent of Negro pupils in first grade attend schools that are from 90 to 100 percent Negro. In the South most students still attend schools that are 100 percent white or Negro.

2. Segregation patterns are similar for teachers. Most Negro teachers teach in schools with predominently Negro pupils. For the nation as a whole the average Negro pupil attends a school where 65 percent of his teachers are Negro.

3. White students attend schools with a smaller pupil-teacher ratio than do minority-group students.

4. Minority-group students have less access to such facilities as laboratories and libraries than do their white counterparts.

5. Negro and Puerto Rican students are more frequently forced to attend schools that are not regionally accredited. They also have less access to a program of extracurricular activities (teams and clubs).

6. The Negro student, on the average, attends a school where teachers are less able, based on criteria of quality and quantity of training.

The pattern seldom changes, despite the fact that we have little or no evidence to support a thesis of the natural superiority of one race over another. Our conclusion must be that our institutions are structured to the advantage of one race over another, to reward members of one race more than members of another. This is what is usually meant by "institutional racism."

Racism in the Schools

"Racism" refers to social structure, not to the attitudes of persons. The evidence is clear that Americans who are not white generally do not do as well in school as do persons who are. This does not mean that teachers are prejudiced or that they discriminate against persons on the basis of race. Also, the mobility system is, theoretically, an open one. That is, if a Negro, Mexican-American, Indian, or Puerto-Rican student can get all

15 J. Coleman, op. cit.

A's in high school, score in the top five percent on a college entrance examination, and pay his way, the doors of almost any college are open to him. The problem is that, except for the very rare case, the nonwhite minority student does not usually get that far. Proportionate to his numbers, he is underrepresented on the college campus and in good jobs and overrepresented in the military and on the unemployment lines.

The question of racism can be resolved around the issue of equal opportunity. If one institution provides opportunities equally to whites and nonwhites, we designate that institution as nonracist. Racism is an emotionally charged word, and perhaps it is better to speak of equality of opportunity. At the same time, however, it is important to communicate across racial groups to recognize the meaning of ordinary language.

The institution of education as a whole does not appear to provide a similar pattern of mobility for whites and nonwhites alike. Some schools, usually in economically affluent communities, send forth a greater proportion of students to college than do schools in the ghetto. If a Negro pupil were enrolled in the white school, he would have as much chance to take advantage of the opportunities as does his white counterpart. For him the system would not be as closed as would be the case with his brothers in the ghetto. But schools in America, primarily in the urban North and the South, are segregated and the consequence of this has already been noted.

Compensatory Programs. Because political and educational leaders were unable to materially alter the structure of living patterns within the city, the notion of "compensatory" programs was introduced into ghetto schools. However, the evidence we have accumulated to date suggests that compensatory programs do not accomplish the goals sought by proponents of integrated schools.[16] These programs do not appreciably affect achievement, nor do they come to grips with the crucial problem of racial conflict. Segregation profoundly affects white children as well as black ones. Urban life is a heterogeneous and complex existence. The maintenance of sameness in one's experience inevitably leads to the definition of oneself and one's group as superior to others who are unlike one. This in turn distorts the patterns of interpersonal relations between persons who are different from each other and leads to ill-considered stereotypes.

Black Militancy. For the black child the integrated school situation means more than better facilities and better teachers. It means exposure to the world outside the black community; it means participation in a

---

[16] See *Racial Isolation in the Public Schools*, A Report of the U.S. Commission on Civil Rights, Washington, D.C., 1967, pp. 115-139.

multiracial society on an equal basis; it means a chance to view at first hand the very basis of democratic interaction. The argument of militant black leaders is essentially this. White society has created a number of institutions imbued with their own value systems and structured along lines that perpetuate white supremacy and reduce nonwhites to the level of second-class citizenship. Every attempt to introduce a single black face into the ranks of leadership of a multiracial society is viewed as "tokenism." The same definition is made of the increased number of nonwhites on college campuses. It is tokenism in that, for the most part it must be artificially managed (that is, by lowered admissions standards) rather than structurally produced in an ongoing way. In other words, blacks in college should be represented in proportion to their numbers in the population. If this is not occurring normally, a structural bias is operating in the system.

The role of sociologists who study problems of race as they relate to educational patterns has been to expose regularities in the distribution of rewards. The evidence stands out graphically against the American idea of equality. As Gunnar Myrdahl pointed out in his substantial study of the race problem in America, Americans never seem particularly concerned that their social scene is loaded with contradictions of what they purport to believe.[17]

Schools in the Cultural Revolution

As Chapter 4 suggested, change is occurring in a number of different ways. The direction most relevant to this section is away from the general culture or some segment of it. The adolescent subculture has had an extensive impact on secondary and higher education, and value changes in this section of the population have forced a confrontation with the schools. What are some of these values then and how have they affected or been affected by educational structures?

1. Belief in Power. Students have come to believe that they have an intrinsic right to influence decisions that affect their lives. Education is a critical component in determining life chances as well as in preparing persons to cope with the demands of the larger society. Student participation on important university committees has become a general practice in higher education. In racially segregated communities, high school students have engaged in walkouts and protests in order to influence the

---

[17] G. Myrdal, *An American Dilemma*, New York, Harper, 1947.

quality of the education they are receiving. Many schools where Negro pupils were in the majority have forced school boards to replace white administrators with black ones. White as well as black students in many urban high schools have pushed demands for greater participation in the establishment of codes for dress and deportment. The consequences of this thrust have been varied. Many schools have modified their codes; some schools have done away with them altogether, others resist fiercely. In the latter case, disorganization emerges as widespread alienation of a sort that tends to erupt later rather than sooner.

2. Belief in Relevance. The word "relevance" has been overused in recent days; nonetheless, this usage is in itself significant. It informs us that students are bothered by certain educational patterns that they construe to be not in their best interest. They find that their studies have little meaning, their activities are ritualistic and trivial, and their interpersonal relations are constrained. Educational structures are organized to pursue social goals at the system level. To conceive of an educational system that can simultaneously accommodate both system goals (socialization, skill training, occupational differentiation, and allotment to careers) and personal goals (the need for identity, affiliation, participation, and self-determination) is problematic. The maintenance of the present structure of schools and schooling requires personal goals to be treated as subsidiary to system goals. This is the unfortunate nature of monolithic institutions in industrial society.

3. Belief in Social Reconstruction. Unclear about the functional possibilities of institutions, students believe that education can somehow play an active part in solving some of the widespread social problems that confront our society. In many ways, possibly through a process of elimination of other institutions, the school is seen as the only organ of society that can make a difference. There are a number of reasons for this: everyone goes to school, the school has a powerful system of rewards and punishments with which to control behavior, it has access to a vast reservoir of resources, it supports the highest ideals of the society, and more than any other institution, it constitutes a minisociety.

Students see a world torn by strife and conflict, cities racked by riots, parents and children unable to communicate with each other, fellow students strung out on drugs, broken homes riddling family after family, and our nation involved in a war that has divided us as a people and calls upon them to choose between service, which may mean killing, or jail if they refuse.

To alleviate some of the most pressing complaints, the national government has poured millions of dollars into programs. But the question still remains: Can we solve new problems and take on new responsibilities with old programs and structures? Most social scientists see this as unlikely. Even so, increasing numbers of students as well as nonstudents believe that the school should more resolutely assume the burden of changing these programs and structures.

4. Belief in Freedom. Students want to be freer than they are at present. They want a world in which they can be free to pursue their own goals in their own way. But nobody, particularly in education, is going to give them their freedom if they do not demand it. In order to gain this freedom many adolescents remove themselves not only from the constraints of the school, but also from the constraints of institutions. The church and the family are forsaken in the same struggle. Because of its own inflexibility, the school has made it impossible for them to stay, and for some unknown reason students have been found the strength to do so. Precisely because the constraints against such a revolution are no longer effective, the cultural revolution is happening at a rapid rate. In the Columbia University rebellion students were threatened with arrest, court records, and dismissal if they persisted in their confrontation.[18] But to the utter surprise of bureaucrats and police alike, these threats went unheeded. When values change, particularly values toward school and career, where affluence is secondary to freedom, the sanctions once used so effectively become obsolete.

Conclusions

If we think back upon the school's role in social change, we perceive that education traditionally has played a passive role in advancing social or cultural change. This is true only in a direct sense; that it, schools do not encourage innovation, do not support it, and even punish persons who do.[19] But in this structural fact lies a latent condition that supports the cultural revolution. New ideas about living and working need an arena for exposure and a cause to develop commitment in others. By opposing change the schools provide both the arena and the issue around which persons aggregate. This has been referred to by radical students as "radicalizing" or "politicizing." It is, for example, within this context that the Columbia rebellion and the disruption of the Chicago Democratic

18 J. L. Avorn and R. Friedman, *Up Against the Ivy Wall,* Athenium, New York, 1969.

19 Schools may be enthusiastic about doing old things in new ways; unfortunately, this does not satisfy the notion of "innovation."

convention were considered victories for the political segment of the cultural revolution. In simpler terms, new structures or even proposals for new structures do not arise in a vacuum. Persons who are for the new must confront those who are for the old.

Now in what specific sense has the school stood in opposition to what we have called the cultural revolution? The following list should be sufficiently illustrative:

1. Students are encouraged to compete against each other.
2. Teachers rule; students obey.
3. School officials regulate; students conform.
4. School officials disapprove of dress or deportment; students are suspended, expelled, or forced to cut their hair.
5. Students express emotion; teachers disapprove.
6. Sex, institutionally, is avoided.
7. Students have no freedom in the curriculum, since college-admission prerequisites must be met.
8. Students are censured for political involvement in school.
9. Students are required to take courses that have little relevance to the critical problems of their lives.
10. Students are graded unidimensionally against a single standard, as if they had an equal chance at success.
11. Controversial issues are avoided formally and informally.
12. Interpersonal relations are formal and impersonal.

Students who have some interest in social change and who regard change as necessary, need to come to grips with the structures of schools that have to change. The sociology of education reveals the regularities of school life, and it is these regularities that communicate the culture of the school. The culture of the school is the conglomerate of values upon which social patterns are built. If we wish structures such as those outlined above to undergo a reconstruction in time with the cultural revolution, we need to speculate about ways to change the values of the larger society that support the school. If this can be achieved, revolution will not be necessary for social reconstruction. The structures will follow the values.

References

Coleman, James, *The Adolescent Society*, The Free Press of Glencoe, New York, 1961. This study reports the influence of adolescent value systems on the structure of high school education.

Clark, B., *Educating the Expert Society*, Chandler Publishing Co., San Francisco, 1962. A simple and straightforward text covering the main problem areas of the sociology of education.

Durkheim, Emile, *Sociology and Education*, The Free Press of Glencoe, New York, 1959. This essay on the function of education in society is one of the classic works on the subject. Durkheim provides the reader with a way of viewing education that is basic to understanding its relationship to other institutions and to the larger society.

Elkin, Frederick, *The Child and Society*, Random House, New York, 1961. A close examination of the socialization function of education.

Gordon, C. W., *The Social System of the High School*, The Free Press of Glencoe, New York, 1957. An analysis of the high school as a network of interacting systems. These systems are the formal, grades and achievements; the semiformal, extracurricular activities; and the informal, friendship patterns.

Weinberg, Carl, *Education and Social Problems*, The Free Press, New York, 1970. An analysis of the disorganizational aspects of American society and the relationship of these to educational policies.

18

Political Socialization

George F. Kneller

❖❖

By "political socialization" we mean the kind of learning that affects political attitudes and behavior. The term refers not only to formal learning (in civics, say, or current affairs) but also to the informal assimilation of political attitudes from the family, the peer groups, and others. It also refers to the development of certain social attitudes and personality characteristics.

As a field of study, political socialization may be considered a branch of social psychology. It is one of the fastest growing of the behavioral sciences. However, it is also very young and possesses neither laws nor theories (as outlined in Chapter 15). What it offers instead are a range of descriptive findings together with some hypotheses about particular influences and mechanisms in the political learning of young people. Neither the hypotheses nor the findings tell us definitely how political learning takes place, but they do suggest various ways in which it may take place. In this chapter we shall consider the part played by the school and the university in the political socialization of children and young people.

Elementary School Years

During the elementary school years, children form a number of political attitudes—towards the nation, the government, the law, political participation, and the party system. Let us see what these attitudes are and consider some ways in which they are acquired.[1]

Attitude to the Nation. By the time the child enters the elementary school he has already formed an attachment to the United States. This attachment is strengthened by various school practices such as the recitation of the Pledge of Allegiance, the display of the flag, and the decoration of classrooms with pictures of great Americans. The attachment is emotional rather than intellectual, for it is not based on any realistic comparison of this country with others. However, in the higher elementary grades the child comes at least to appreciate that America is not only his country but also a democracy whose citizens have the right to vote.

Attitude to the Government. The child tends to identify the government with certain people in authority, such as the President and the policeman. Most children regard these people as both powerful and benevolent. (In Appalachia, however, it has been found that elementary-school children actually regard the President as "malevolent.")[2] This attitude is, again, more emotional than intellectual. As the child grows older, however, he comes to realize that policemen do not make laws but only enforce them. He continues to regard the President as the most important figure in government, but he sees him as a man holding certain political powers by virtue of his office rather than as a man with certain personal qualities. He also appreciates that Congress and the Supreme Court play their separate parts in the government of the country.

This transition to a less personal and more institutional notion of gov-

---

1 Robert D. Hess and Judith V. Torney, *The Development of Political Attitudes in Children*, Aldine, Chicago, 1967. This study is based on a questionnaire given to a sample of 1000 elementary school children in eight American localities. Although this sample is large enough to virtually guarantee that the results obtained are unaffected by chance, the domain of the sample is restricted by the near or complete exclusion of black children, children from "ethnic" groups, and children from small towns. Thus, although the study may provide an accurate guide to the political attitudes of the children of middle-class WASPS, it needs to be complemented by equally broad studies of the political attitudes of children from other backgrounds. The data compiled by Hess and Torney are also analyzed in D. Easton and J. Dennis, *Children in the Political System*, McGraw-Hill, New York, 1969.

2 See D. Jaros, H. Hirsch, and F. Fleron, "The Malevolent Leader: Political Socialization in an American Sub-Culture," *American Political Science Review*, **LXII** (1968), 564-578.

ernment may be partly a result of education. Children learn in the class-room that America is governed through certain institutions, so they are less inclined to think of the government as simply the President. Nevertheless, education is only one influence at work. Two important findings need to be borne in mind: (1) although in the higher elementary grades most children come to take a more institutional view of government, their teachers at all grade levels claim to pay equal attention to the part played by institutions in government and the part played by persons;[3] (2) in Appalachia at any rate, throughout the elementary school years, most children identify the government with a malevolent President, so they evidently fail at this stage to develop an institutional conception at all.[4]

The child's view of government is also excessively idealistic. So far as the white middle-class child is concerned, the government can do no wrong. This is an attitude for which his teachers seem partly responsible. Nearly all elementary school teachers present a carefully edited and flattering picture of American politics past and present. American politicians are wise men seeking to do good rather than ambitious men seeking power. They strike no bargains and make no compromises with special interests. When dissension arises, one group is always in the wrong, and the wisdom of right-thinking people always prevails. This unrealistic picture naturally misleads the student. He should be shown that men are always fallible and sometimes venal, and that justice is rarely achieved without effort. He should also be shown that justice is achieved above all through wise political conduct, for politics is a process in which different interests are accommodated and through which men improve the conditions of their common life.

Attitude to the Law. The young white child regards the law as just, protective, and deserving of obedience. A lawbreaker, he thinks, will be caught and justly punished. In the higher grades of the elementary school the child becomes a little less certain that all laws are necessarily fair to all people and that all lawbreakers are always punished. He also stands less in awe of policemen. Nevertheless, he has no intention of breaking the law himself, no doubt because he regards the law as fundamentally protective rather than repressive. This disposition to obey the law seems to be formed in the family and is reinforced by the school at all grade levels. The child's tendency to think more critically of the law as he grows older is a part of his mental development. He then depends less on the opinions of his parents and teachers and so is more inclined to question them. His

---

[3] Hess and Torney, *op. cit.*, pp. 124-125.

[4] Jaros et al., *loc. cit.*

attitude to the law is apparently influenced also by the opinions of his peers and by the impressions he derives from television.

Attitude to Political Participation. The young child thinks of the good citizen as one who obeys the government. The older elementary school child regards the good citizen as one who votes. With this new view of citizenship comes the knowledge that individuals can affect both national and local government chiefly by voting but also by writing to congressmen and the press. The child is inclined to regard an interest in politics as a good thing, even if he does not have much interest in it himself.

Most elementary school teachers depict the good citizen as one who obeys the law, votes, and takes an interest in politics. Other forms of political participation, such as attending meetings, taking part in demonstrations, and joining interest groups, are ignored in the curriculum and receive little attention from teachers. Consequently, the white middle-class child comes to believe that people participate in politics as isolated individuals, a belief that is at odds with the actual influence of interest groups in American politics.[5] Since teachers themselves are aware of this influence, one presumes that, knowingly or unknowingly, they conceal it from their students just as they conceal other political realities.

The child who goes to school in a working-class area is likely to be even less well informed. He is taught that the essence of citizenship is obedience to benevolent authority. He hears little of his responsibility to participate in politics as a reasoning individual. Since political issues are rarely discussed in working-class homes, he is unlikely to form any other view of the duties of citizenship. Moreover, since he tends to drop out of high school early, he as often as not enters the adult world with no feeling that he has any part to play in the political life of his country. He is, in short, politically uneducated. If in later life he becomes unemployed or falls afoul of the law, this apathy may well turn into active resentment of all forms of authority seen as ranged arbitrarily against him.

Attitude to Political Parties. Young children believe that all people are either Republicans or Democrats. They also identify themselves with the party supported by their parents.[6] The older child is more independent. He believes that he would vote for the best man rather than for the candidate of a particular party. When asked which party he favors, he normally mentions the party supported by his parents. He claims, how-

---

5 See Robert A. Dahl, *Pluralist Democracy in the United States: Conflict and Consensus,* Rand McNally, Chicago, 1967, and T. Lowi, *The End of Liberalism: Ideology, Policy and the Crisis of Public Authority,* Norton, New York, 1969.

6 Hess and Torney, *op. cit.,* p. 99.

ever, that he is making up his own mind rather than following his parents' example.

When the child says that he would vote for the best man rather than the party candidate, he seems to be influenced by his education. Because party politics arouses strong feelings, it receives little attention in the elementary school. No doubt most teachers feel that if they discuss party politics they will sooner or later have to explain why they do not share the political views held by the parents of some of their students. They shy away from this because they do not wish to give the impression that American politics involves deep cleavages of opinion based on racial and class interests. Once again the elementary school fails to acquaint the child with the realities of American politics.

In sum, the white American child enters high school believing that his country fully deserves his loyalty, that the government is wise and the laws are just, that political life is harmonious, and that his duty as a citizen is to vote for the candidate he approves of. To call him conservative would be misleading, because this suggests that he holds certain political attitudes in opposition to others. In fact he doesn't oppose anything because he does not yet realize that conflict within agreed limits is the essence of democratic politics. It would be truer to say that he is a child of the Establishment without knowing it. He accepts the status quo because no one has suggested that he ask himself whether anything in the country needs to be changed.

Now I do not suggest that the role of the elementary school is to turn out young reformists and revolutionaries. Far from it. What I claim is that the elementary school should encourage children to think about political realities rather than accept pieties about the Constitution. Some children will think their way to conclusions that are conservative, others to conclusions that are liberal or radical. What matters is that they should think about politics critically but constructively, and that they should always be ready to think again. Unfortunately, our elementary schools have yet to handle the teaching of politics with this end in view. Let us hope that the current interest in the study of political socialization will lead shortly to a more enlightened attitude in this regard.

The High School Years

What attitudes, if any, emerge in the high school?[7]
Attitudes to the Nation, the Government, the Law. These attitudes

---

[7] Political socialization has been studied less in the high school than it has in the

seem to change very little. The student in high school is hardly more critical of authority than is the student in elementary school. He accepts equally both the rules and administration of his school and the laws and government of his country. In this he apparently accords with the wishes of his teachers.[8]

As before, working-class students attending schools in working-class areas are even less critical than middle-class students. However, working-class students in predominantly middle-class schools tend to take on the rather more independent attitudes of their middle-class peers. (The reverse does not hold. Middle-class students in working-class schools do not become any more subservient to authority.) Such at any rate was the conclusion drawn from a survey of high school students in Detroit.[9] It would be interesting to know whether a similar shift in attitude occurs under similar conditions in the elementary school, and still more interesting to know whether and in what direction attitudes are changed in schools that are racially or ethnically mixed.

Attitude to Political Participation. It would seem that few students are led by their high school experiences to believe that they can have an influence on government itself. In one survey adults in five countries (U.S., U.K., Germany, Italy, and Mexico) were asked what they thought their high schools had done for them in this respect.[10] Only those who had left school early believed that informal participation in school decision making had increased their confidence in their ability to affect the government. Do formal debates on political matters lead to the belief that one carries any political weight? Only, it would appear, if one is an active debater. What is the influence of teachers? In certain countries, such as the United States, teachers who make a point of discussing politics in class do seem to give their pupils some sense that they can contribute

elementary school. My main source of information is a survey of political attitudes among twelfth graders in the United States carried out in 1965 by the University of Michigan Survey Research Center under the direction of M. Kent Jennings. The results so far are reported.in M. Kent Jennings and R. Niemi, "Patterns of Political Learning," *Harvard Educational Review*, **XXXVIII** (1968), 443-467, and "The Transmission of Political Values from Parent to Child," *American Political Science Review*, **LXII** (1968), 169-184, and in K. Langton and M. Kent Jennings, "Political Socialization in the High School Civics Course," *American Political Science Review*, **LXII** (1968), 852-867.

[8] Cf. Edgar Z. Friedenberg, *Coming of Age in America: Growth and Acquiescence,* Viking, New York, 1963.

[9] Cf. K. Langton, *Political Socialization,* Oxford University Press, New York, 1969, especially p. 138.

[10] G. Almond and S. Verba, *The Civic Culture: Political Attitudes and Democracy in Five Nations,* Little, Brown, Boston, 1968.

to political life. But most of those sampled by the survey believed that they had learned more about their political influence while working than they had while attending high school.[11]

Moreover, a recent survey of American twelfth graders concludes that conventional civics courses do not increase the white student's belief that one can influence the government.[12] However, blacks who had taken such courses did feel rather more strongly that some influence could be exerted on the government. In sum, these various findings lead to the conclusion that one of the main incentives to political participation, the belief that a man can influence his government, remains untouched by present high school experiences, formal or informal, except perhaps among black students and those students who enjoy organized debates.

Are high school students interested in politics? All we know is that they show more interest than eighth-grade elementary school students and less interest than adults.[13] The precise causes of this growth in interest remain unknown, except that they do not seem to include high school civics courses. It has been found that white twelfth graders who have taken such courses show only marginally more interest in politics than white twelfth graders who have not. Among blacks interest increases if the student comes from the working class but actually drops off if he comes from a higher class.[14] It would seem that blacks with more social awareness are "turned off" by conventional civics, a finding that should surprise no one.

One's willingness to take part in politics may also depend on one's notion of responsible citizenship. Middle- and upper-class students are more likely to believe that the good citizen takes an active part in politics. Lower-class students tend to believe that he is obedient to the powers that be. According to one main source of information—a nationwide survey of twelfth graders carried out by the University of Michigan Survey Research Center—these attitudes are unaffected by high school civics courses, at

---

11 A recent study of Jamaican high school students found that a politically conscious school could help create a sense of political efficacy among students who by and large lacked this sense, but that the school was as a rule less effective in this respect than the family and that it had no influence at all on students whose confidence in their political efficacy was already high. See K. Langton, op. cit., pp. 140-160.

12 K. Langton and M. Kent Jennings, "Political Socialization in the High School Civics Course," op. cit.

13 M. Kent Jennings and R. Niemi, "Patterns of Political Learning," op. cit., 451-452.

14 K. Langton and M. Kent Jennings, "Political Socialization in the High School Civics Course," op. cit.

any rate among white students. Working-class blacks tend to regard obedience a little more highly after taking civics courses. With middle-class blacks the effect is the reverse.[15]

In short, although white students, especially those from the middle class, tend to grow more participation-minded while they are in high school, they do not for the most part seem to do so as a result of any experience in the school itself. Black students, on the other hand, do seem to be affected by their education. Exposure to civics courses leaves upper-status blacks less inclined to join in "the system" than they were before. These findings make it clear that the high school has signally failed to make political participation attractive to the young. If the generation now in its late teens and early twenties is more politically active than any of its predecessors, if its voice is indeed the conscience of the nation, this is not because of the American school but in spite of it.

Attitude to Political Parties. By the time he reaches the twelfth grade, the student can distinguish more clearly between the political parties than he could in the eighth grade. Nevertheless, the odds are still slightly against his being able to describe one party as liberal and the other as conservative. According to the Michigan University survey of twelfth graders, which we have mentioned already, less than half the students sampled could draw this distinction.[16]

Teenagers in high school are less likely than adults to identify with a political party. Most of them claim that they would vote for the best candidate, regardless of whether he were a Republican or a Democrat. By and large they remain political independents. They may be influenced in this by the precepts of their teachers. More than half the teachers sampled by the University of Michigan survey said that they taught their students to vote for the man rather than the party, notwithstanding that they themselves, the teachers, were no less partisan in their views than other

15 K. Langton and M. Kent Jennings, loc. cit. It should be pointed out, however, that an earlier survey of high school students in Boston found that those students in middle- and upper-class schools who had taken civics courses tended to be more favorably disposed to political participation than were those who had not. The survey also found that students in lower-middle and working-class schools remained unaffected in this respect. The survey concluded that civics courses create a belief in political participation only when they are taught in communities, usually of the middle and upper classes, that value participation and encourage the teaching of civics in their schools. See E. Litt, "Civic Education, Community Norms, and Political Indoctrination," *American Sociological Review*, **XXVIII** (1963), 69-75.

16 B. Massialis, *Education and the Political System*, Addison-Wesley, Reading, Mass., 1969, Ch. 6.

adults.[17] A more potent influence would seem to be the adolescent's tendency to reject or move away from the values, and so the political affiliations, of his parents.

In sum, our knowledge of political socialization in the high school remains rather sketchy. One of the few findings that stands out is that high school civics courses have virtually no effect on the political attitudes of white students who remain until the twelfth grade. Presumably these courses repeat what the student knows already or else duplicate what is presented more tellingly elsewhere.

The College Years

About the political effect of a college education we know still less. College-educated people certainly seem better informed politically, more liberal on civil rights and social services, less rigid in their party affiliations, more active politically, more likely to vote, less authoritarian and ethnocentric, less prone to make extreme statements when responding to questionnaires, more cautious in their interpretation of ambiguous items, and generally more likely to think critically.[18] What is less certain is the effect on these tendencies of the college experience itself. Perhaps they result from a college education, or perhaps from the socioeconomic background, personality traits, and intellectual skills of those who go to college. Again, if college experience does have a political effect, from what in the experience does the effect spring? From the attitudes of teachers? From those of friends? From the curriculum? From college life? From political activities on campus? At the moment we cannot answer these questions, but we do at least have some pointers for research to follow up.

Civic Tolerance. Many studies of adult attitudes have confirmed the view that college-educated people are more tolerant than others of social and political diversity and more liberal in their interpretation of the Bill of Rights. Authoritarianism also seems to decline over the college years.[19] A study carried out at Miami University, Ohio, found that toler-

[17] M. Kent Jennings and R. Niemi, "Patterns of Political Learning," op. cit., 453-454.

[18] See studies reviewed in R. Lane, "Political Education in the Midst of Life's Struggles," *Harvard Educational Review*, **XXXVIII** (1968), 468-494.

[19] Cf. R. Alford and H. Scoble, "Leadership, Education, and Political Behavior," *American Sociological Review*, **XXXIII** (1968), 259-272; and N. Sanford, "The Ap-

ance of free speech tended to increase from the freshman to the senior year. Another study, at San Jose State College, California, compared continuing students with dropouts and found that over a period of two years the former became less ethnocentric while the latter did not.[20]

Now, instead of taking college students as a whole, let us consider different kinds of college students. We find that only certain sorts of students are likely to be more tolerant than most people, in particular students majoring in the humanities and social sciences, students who live on campus as opposed to commuters, and students whose attitude towards college is academic or bohemian rather than party-going or careerist.[21] We may also ask in how many cases these attitudes are temporary responses of the student to an academic environment. Some young people who are liberal-minded in college may become more conservative in their views when they enter business or a profession. In general, those attitudes that a person adopts in the course of adjusting to a social group are more short-lived than those that spring from his emotional needs.[22] In order, then, to assess the political influence of the college experience, we need to distinguish temporary changes in attitude from lasting ones.

Liberal and Conservative Views. The classic study of the impact of college experience on political attitudes was carried out by T. Newcomb at Bennington College in the 1930s.[23] Newcomb found that as the girls passed through college, most of them exchanged the conservative attitudes they inherited from their upper-status families for the more liberal attitudes of the college community. The only girls not to change were those who kept close ties with their families and did not form close friendships with other students. When certain women were interviewed again twenty-

proach of the Authoritarian Personality," in J. L. McCary, Ed., *Psychology of Personality*, Grove Press, New York, 1956, pp. 282-315.

20 R. M. Christenson and P. J. Capretta, "The Impact of College on Political Attitudes: A Research Note," *Social Science Quarterly*, **XLIX** (1968), 315-320; W. T. Plant, "Changes in Ethnocentrism Associated with a Two-Year College Experience," *Journal of Genetic Psychology*, **XLIV** (1958), 189-197.

21 R. M. Christenson and P. J. Capretta, loc. cit.; N. Holt and C. E. Tygart, "Political Tolerance and Higher Education," *Pacific Sociological Review*, **XII** (1969), 27-33.

22 Cf. P. Jacob, *Changing Values in College: An Exploratory Study of the Impact of College Teaching*, Harper, New York, 1957. On the different functions which a person's attitudes may fulfill, such as social-orientation or ego-defense, see M. B. Smith, Jerome S. Bruner, and Robert W. White, *Opinions and Personality*, Wiley, New York, 1956, and D. Katz, "Functional Approach to the Study of Attitude," *Public Opinion Quarterly*, **XXIV** (1960), 163-204.

23 T. Newcomb, *Personality and Social Change*, Dryden, New York, 1943.

five years later, it was found that those with liberal husbands or liberal friends retained the liberal outlook of their college days.[24]

However, it has also been found that some students become more conservative at college, particularly those who live in fraternities. Moreover, some students may be conservative one year, liberal the next, and conservative again the year after.[25]

These varied findings yield no firm conclusion, but they do suggest a hypothesis for research to investigate, the hypothesis that a college student tends to change his political attitudes if he encounters attitudes that (a) are different from those to which he is accustomed and (b) are held or adopted by his college friends or acquaintances. Further research is needed if we are to propose general hypotheses about the conditions under which political attitudes adopted at college are retained or abandoned in later life. Even more research must be done if we are to conjecture which aspects of college experience are responsible for such changes. The opinions of friends and acquaintances, of the student's "set," certainly seem to be influential here. If so, however, we must ask where the other members of the set have acquired their attitudes and whether these individuals have come together because they hold similar attitudes already. We may perhaps find that in his freshman year a student associates with students whose precollege attitudes are similar to his own and that in his sophomore year he prefers the company of students whose attitudes have been changed by college life.

Does College Really Change Student Attitudes? What evidence we have suggests that it changes the political attitudes of many students. But the evidence is limited and there are counterarguments to consider. One of these, which we have noted already, is the argument that although lightly held or socially adjustive attitudes may change at college, fundamental or ego-defensive ones do not. The argument is almost a tautology. Fundamental attitudes are not lightly changed or they would not be fundamental. What is more to the point is the consideration of the range of political views that are compatible with a person's ego-defensive attitudes. It seems reasonable to suppose that many people can move from a moderately conservative to a moderately liberal outlook or vice versa without any change in their deep-seated values. The shift in their outlook matters

---

[24] T. Newcomb, K. Koenig, R. Flacks, and D. P. Warwick, *Persistence and Change: Bennington Students after 25 Years*, Wiley, New York, 1967.

[25] R. Goldsen, M. Rosenberg, R. Williams, and E. Suchman, *What College Students Think*, Van Nostrand, New York, 1960.

politically although not necessarily psychologically. The statement that ego-defensive attitudes rarely alter at college is informative about the psychological rather than the political significance of attitude changes.

Rather more persuasive is the argument that changes in political attitudes during the college years may be a result of a general movement in public opinion or the opinion of the young rather than of the college experience itself. Bennington girls may have become liberal in the 1930s not because of Bennington but because of the leftward movement in public opinion generally. However, this argument does not affect the contention that being at Bennington made these students more liberal than they would have been otherwise. Campus opinion responds to public opinion rather than mirrors it. The climate of opinion in most colleges is likely to be somewhat more liberal than the climate of opinion at large. A national movement to the left will probably swing further to the left on campus, while a movement to the right will probably be moderated. In short, while we should avoid confounding the effect of public opinion with the effect of the college experience, we should not rush to the other extreme of treating campus opinion as nothing but public opinion.

There is, however, a third argument. College entrants already possess the political characteristics associated with college graduates. Thus, compared with other seniors, college-bound students are generally better informed about politics and are more politically active, more tolerant of the right of religious dissenters to free speech and of elected communists to hold office, more disposed to read about politics in newspapers and magazines and to discuss politics with their peers, and much more likely to know which of the political parties is liberal and which conservative. Since these characteristics precede the college experience, they should not be attributed to it.[26]

This argument should not be pressed too far. No doubt college-bound seniors are better informed and more tolerant politically than are other seniors. What we want to know is how much more tolerant and how much better informed they become as a result of attending college, and this can be learned only by comparing them, on graduation from college, with those with whom they were compared on graduation from high school. In addition, we need to know more about the content of the political attitudes of both groups at both dates—more, that is, about their opinions on specific issues. We can then tell whether, for this sample at any rate, the

---

26 K. Langton and M. Kent Jennings, "Political Socialization in the High School Civics Course," op. cit.

college experience led young people to adopt political views more liberal or more conservative than those of their noncollege compeers.

What is the Effect of Introductory Courses in Political Science? Two studies have found that introductory courses in political science (principles and processes of American government) have no effect whatever on the political attitudes of those who enroll in them.[27] (Let us recall that high school civics courses had no effect either.) I am inclined to explain these findings by saying that courses in problems of democracy tend to be abstract and therefore neither challenging nor fruitful. The student expects to be bored by them and usually is. Unfortunately, political science tends to be one of those subjects that has to be *made* interesting. It is in fact a challenge to the ingenuity and imagination of the professional educator. Of considerable relevance is the fact that the two studies I have mentioned only compared the responses of students to different sorts of material delivered by lecture. Neither of them sought to assess student response to actual participation in politics (experience in the field) or to presentation of material by film or television. Studies of the effects of such experimental methods are badly needed.[28]

Most of all, we need to know how the student's political attitudes are affected by different aspects of his college experience. What is the influence of his instructors, for example, compared with that of his peers? What is the effect of formal courses compared with private reading? How much is he affected by meetings and rallies on campus and how much by active participation in campus politics? What is the student's response to external events that become symbols on campus of the world at large—events such as race riots, ecological disasters, and foreign wars?

We need, in fact, a survey of the political socialization of the college student to compare with the Hess and Torney survey of political socialization in the elementary school. This survey would examine a cross section of students from many types of colleges, controlled for geographical region, college size, public or private status, and student socioeconomic

27 C. Garrison, "Political Involvement and Political Science," *Social Science Quarterly*, **XLIX** (1968), 305-314; A. Somit et al., "The Effects of the Introductory Political Science Course on Student Attitudes Toward Personal Political Participation," *American Political Science Review*, **LII** (1958), 1129-1132.

28 Cf. F. Newmann, "Discussion of Political Socialization in Schools," *Harvard Educational Review*, **XXXVIII** (1968), 536-545; W. Parente and M. McCleery, "Campus Radicalization and a Contemporary Political Science," *Journal of Higher Education*, **XXXIX** (1968), 316-325; and "The Introduction and Structure of Political Science," *Western Political Quarterly*, **XXII** (1969), 350-364.

background. Either the different samples should be made into a panel study, or repeated cross-sectional studies should be carried out to assess changes over time. By comparing earlier attitudes of students with later ones, and these in turn with adult attitudes and the attitudes of a cross section of noncollege youth, we should be able to judge the independent contribution of the college to political socialization.

Democracy and Political Socialization

My main purpose in this chapter has been to describe the political socialization of the young from kindergarten to college. From time to time, however, I have suggested that this socialization is one-sided—that the young are undereducated politically and that the school is failing in its responsibility to prepare young people for full participation in the political life of democracy. Although it is not incumbent on any critic to propose remedies for shortcomings, I will do so. I propose that instead of teaching the letter of politics we teach the spirit of it.

Political education in a democracy must teach both democratic legitimacy and democratic participation. Legitimacy must be taught (and of course respected), because unless people *believe* that the government is entitled to govern, they will not consent to be governed by it. They may of course be coerced into accepting the government, or they may acquiesce out of apathy or ignorance. But then we no longer have genuine democracy; either tyranny or oligarchic manipulation of the masses prevails under the pretense of democracy. As I indicated in Chapter 6, true democracy rests on the willingness of the people to accept the decisions of their elected government not out of coercion or fear of violence but because they believe that it is morally right to do so. Now we have seen again and again that American schools do indeed convince the young of the legitimacy of the American political system. *Most* American students believe that this system is both just and competent, and therefore deserving of their obedience. Where the school fails is in teaching democratic participation. It fails not so much for want of trying as for want of the right methods. Let us consider three modes: representation, pluralism, and participation. How we choose to teach democracy in our schools will depend in large part on which of these modes we wish most to encourage.

Representative Democracy. Let us suppose we wish to encourage the representative mode of democracy. We believe that the United States is, and should be, primarily a representative democracy, and we wish to teach the sort of participation appropriate in a democracy of this kind. In a representative democracy the work of government, of debating and passing laws, is done by representatives whom the people elect. An elected representative is expected to support those policies he promised to support when he campaigned for election. He is accountable to the constituency he represents, and must submit himself to the public vote at the next election. People participate in the representative mode of democracy mainly at elections, and they do so mainly by voting. How is this sort of participation taught in our schools?

It is taught as an obligation rather than as a right. The child learns that voting is a duty required of him. If he fails to vote, he will not, it is true, be punished, but he will be an unworthy citizen and he will be letting his country down. Moreover, voting is portrayed as an act of citizenship in the abstract rather than as a real choice with real consequences. The young person is not shown that to vote is in effect to support a party with an ideology and the class and local interests that the party defends. Nor is he shown that it is through his vote and the votes of others that alliances of men acquire the right and the power to guide the course of the nation and to influence some conditions of his life.

How can we bring home to him that voting is not a legal formality but a political act? How can we show him the reality of representative democracy? One way, I suggest, is to focus on the heart of the electoral process, the campaign. Let the class analyze and discuss, from start to finish, a particular campaign that interests them—the campaign for the Presidency or the state governorship or a seat in the local assembly, a campaign in swing now, or the campaign before last, or whichever campaign catches their imagination. Let them investigate how candidates are chosen, how they put their case to the public, and how finally one of them is elected. Different groups in the class can each choose a candidate, appraise his program and his record, and plot his campaign strategy move by move. If the campaign is running now, they can attend meetings and rallies and analyze leaflets and handbills. The class should study not only the machinery of electoral politics but also the ideologies that through this machinery find their expression. In this way they will come to realize that there are strong differences of opinion about how this country should run, and that it is the point of democracy to expose these divisions to open debate and to political compromise, so that solutions are found that have the consent—eager or reluctant, but still consent—of those whom the solutions affect. The students will realize that democracy does not (or should not) repress or neutralize conflict but, rather, endeavors to resolve it.

Pluralistic Democracy. But there is more to democratic politics than campaigns and elections. The people's representatives do not make and debate public policy in a vacuum, but are subject to a range of influences. Not only are legislative and executive decisions carried out and interpreted by administrators not directly accountable to the electorate but also Congressmen and Cabinet members alike must conciliate, persuade, or override a variety of powerful private interest groups such as farmers, labor unions, and big corporations. If the student is to understand how democracy really works, he must come to appreciate how these groups exercise their influence.

As we have seen, the school at present pays too little attention to the part played in politics by groups as opposed to individuals. How might a more realistic approach be taken? I suggest two ways. First the class might make a case study of some past law or executive decision that was strongly supported and vigorously opposed by different interest groups, such as Prohibition in the 1920s or unionization in the 1930s. They could identify the groups concerned and see why these groups took the stands they did. They could then examine the different ways in which these groups sought to turn the legislation or the executive decision in their favor. They could also find out which politicians and civil servants were approached by which groups and how they responded to them. Finally, having decided which group appears in the light of history to have had the better case, students might then work out how differently the rights and wrongs might have appeared to them had they lived at the time.

The class might then turn to some present controversy in which contending groups are pressing their interests. They might consider which groups oppose the policy of busing to achieve school integration, which groups support it, and why they do so. Or they might make a study of the relations between the Congress, the Defense Department, and the major arms-producing corporations. The class might divide into sections, each section but one to research the case made by a particular interest group. The last section would act as a review board or advisory commission to whom the other sections would present the cases of their "clients." The review board would weigh the cases put before it and recommend a policy to be followed.

This is the "issue" approach to the study of interest groups. The class examines the political influence wielded by opposing groups in the context of a particular issue. There is also the "historical" approach. The class now considers how a certain social group has organized to publicize, protect, and advance its interests during a period of time. To develop a feeling for the social conflicts expressed in American politics, the class might study how a certain ethnic group, such as the Irish or the Italians, has advanced itself politically in a competitive society. The class should also consider how the struggle for influence takes place not only between but within groups. Here they might examine how such different organizations as the Black Panthers, the Black Muslims, and the NAACP all seek to represent the black American in his quest for political, social, and economic power.

Participatory Democracy. In the representative mode of democracy the individual participates in the electoral process by which his public representative is chosen. In the pluralist mode he participates in various informal processes by which the group to which he feels affiliated organizes itself into a political force. But in neither mode does he take part in the actual making of legislative and administrative decisions. Is this the end of the matter? Is there any room in modern democracy for direct participation in the process of decision making itself? There is. Today there is growing awareness of the need to humanize institutions and to redistribute power among those whom it affects. There is an increasing demand for local control of local affairs. This means that there are various institutions, such as neighborhood school boards and community-development groups, in which direct democracy is possible. Here the individual citizen can take part in the actual process of making decisions. We call this mode of democracy "participatory."

As I have pointed out, studies indicate that participatory democracy does not exist in our schools and barely exists in our colleges. Yet the only effective way to learn participation is to practice it. How might this be done? One way, I suggest, is to allow the individual school much greater opportunity to work out its policies and practices unregimented by higher educational authorities. This principle also applies within the school. Let the teaching faculty have more chance to debate and decide the curricula and textbooks they will use without having to submit to the dictates of outside administrators. Let a distinct sphere of decision be given to the students themselves. Let them form their own library of books and records, run their own coffee house, and hold their own meetings to which they invite outside speakers. Above all, let them organize certain classes of their own, forming as it were a school within a school. Finally, let students, teachers, and administrators cooperate voluntarily. Let teachers invite administrators to attend discussions on curricula and textbooks. Let students invite teachers to the school-within-a-school.

All modes of democracy have their faults. Representative democracy may lead to apathy on the part of the electorate and high-handedness on the part of the government. The participatory mode may even collapse into anarchy. Nevertheless, within the several spheres of the school itself— the principal and his assistants, the faculty, and the students—we have the means of containing anarchy. These spheres are not self-contained but mutually dependent. If we believe in participatory democracy, let us introduce it by degrees into our schools.

References

The *Harvard Educational Review* has a special issue on many phases of political socialization: XXXVIII, 3 (Summer, 1968).

For a valuable resume and systematization of existing data see Byron C. Massialas, *Education and the Political System* (Addison-Wesley, Reading, Mass., 1969, 219 pp.). Massialas is especially good on activism and the socialization of political leaders.

The most comprehensive study of political socialization in the elementary school is Robert D. Hess and Judith V. Torney, *The Development of Political Attitudes in Children* (Aldine, Chicago, 1967). It contains a plethora of tables and data. Using the same samples of children as do Hess and Torney but concentrating on concepts (especially "authority"), David Easton and Jack Dennis have published *Children and the Political System* (McGraw-Hill, New York, 1969). Fred I. Greenstein examines attitudes of children in grades 4 through 8 toward such matters as authority and identification with political parties in his *Children and Politics* (Yale University Press, New Haven, 1970). Greenstein differentiates according to sex and social class.

My choice of more general works would be Kenneth P. Langton's *Political Socialization* (Oxford University Press, New York, 1969, 240 pp.), which is a collection of Langton's own essays, derived from empirical investigations.

19

Economic Factors

Claude W. Fawcett

❖❖

Introduction

Economists generally agree on the following definition of economics:

> Economics is the study of how men and society *choose,* with or without
> the use of money, to employ *scarce* productive resources, which could
> have alternative uses, to produce various commodities over time and
> distribute them for consumption, now and in the future, among various
> people and groups in society.[1]

The educational importance of economic choice is underlined by the
1969 enrollment in public elementary and secondary schools, over 45
million. Support of instruction for this number of pupils required nearly
$40 billion, a sum estimated to be nearly 4 percent of the entire value of
all goods and services produced in the United States (Gross National
Product). Approximately 75 percent of the instruction was carried on in
metropolitan centers that have grown up as a result of economic choices
concerning methods of producing and distributing goods and services.
The schools were asked to cope with a problem of student transiency

---

[1] Paul A. Samuelson, *Economics,* 7th ed., McGraw-Hill Book Company, New York,
1967, p. 5.

402

amounting to nearly 20 percent of the entire student population, which resulted from movements of population to accommodate changes in economic opportunity. They were asked to provide more education over a longer period of years because the economy has been eliminating positions that could be occupied by individuals with limited years of schooling. They were forced to compete in growing metropolitan centers for increasingly scarce tax dollars. Inflationary trends in the economy forced teachers and administrators to develop employee organizations to apply economic force to maintain competitive salaries and wages.

A growing technology has made the production of knowledge a big business. Of the estimated $24 billion spent for research and development and basic research in the United States in 1967, universities and colleges supplied only 3½ percent of the total, and spent approximately 13 percent.[2] The remainder was spent by the Federal government, industry, and nonprofit research organizations. A little more than 69 percent of all funds were spent by industry, usually in large research affiliates working on production problems, new products, and development of established products. A small percentage of the industrial research expenditure was spent on basic or "blue sky" research. This was usually no more than 5 percent of the research budget. The relegation of the discovery of new knowledge, at least certain kinds of new knowledge, to noncollegiate and nonuniversity institutions may very well limit the access of teachers to it. Much of the industrial research is labeled "proprietary" when it is company supported, or "classified" when done with government support. In either event it is often unavailable to teachers until a significant period of time elapses; it is estimated that 7 to 12 years elapse before new discoveries appear as a new product or process.

Nor can the teacher avoid the social philosophers who have at various times developed fables of the inevitability of man's progression from savagery to feudalism, feudalism to capitalism, capitalism to socialism, socialism to communism, and communism to more communism. Legends have a hold on the minds of men. The history of traditional forms of alternative economic systems is of value in itself. It is of particular value when politicians lean heavily on these legends to secure popular support at the polls. The fallout from this activity makes it imperative that teachers be able to cope intellectually with resultant pressures for objectivity in the teaching of controversial issues, for political conformity, and for persistent attention to the demands of the mixed economy system.

Most of all, however, the passage of the Full Employment Act of 1946

---

2 Unpublished data of the *National Science Foundation* used by the *Statistical Abstract of the United States—1969*, 90th ed., U.S. Bureau of the Census, 1969, p. 523.

committed the country to a policy of continuously expanding economic growth. Education is recognized as an important contributor to continued economic growth both in the development of the skills of the labor force, and in the development of creative, inventive persons who provide new inventions, new products, and new processes. Many rough measures of education's contribution to the economy have been developed. Probably the most widely understood is that developed by Theodore W. Schultz of the University of Chicago.[3] He estimates the direct contribution to economic growth of the development of the skills of the labor force to be 21 percent. Others have estimated that about 20 percent is added by invention and innovation. The federal Vocational Education Acts of 1963 and 1968 recognize the responsibility of schools to add to economic growth through development of labor skills. It is recognized that the policy of full employment and the policy concerning vocational education constitute a charter for schools to adopt economic growth as a national purpose.

Public elementary and secondary schools operate in one of the most advanced technological societies the world has ever known. Economic choices concerning the productive and distributive resources of the society affect schools' operations at every significant decision point. They have been designated as an integral part of the operation of a mixed economic system. If they are to contribute maximally to the society, and assist informed citizens to make wise economic decisions, it is incumbent upon personnel working in schools to be cognizant of the elementary methods of economic analysis.

Economic Choices and Public Education

An examination of the effect of past economic choices on public elementary and secondary schools may serve to underscore the extent and quality of the elementary economic analyses required of school personnel.

Metropolitanization

Economic decisions concerning the manner of production and distribution of goods and services have caused massive shifts of population from largely agricultural, rural residences to metropolitan areas. See Table 1.

[3] Theodore W. Schultz, *The Economic Value of Education*, The Columbia University Press, 1963.

Table 1

Metropolitan and Nonmetropolitan Residents, 1950 to 1970 (In Thousands)[a]

Residence	1950	1970 (Estimate)
Total population	150,527	203,388
White population		
Metropolitan	80,288	178,275
Nonmetropolitan	54,201	64,470
Nonwhite population		
Metropolitan	8,934	25,137
Nonmetropolitan	7,164	7,625
Total metropolitan	89,162	131,477
Total nonmetropolitan	61,365	72,169

[a] These figures are taken from the U.S. Department of Commerce, Bureau of the Census, *Current Population Reports,* Series P-20, Nos. 157, 163. The 1970 estimates are made using 1968 figures and the rate of change between 1966 and 1968.

In the twenty years between 1950 and 1970 we have more than doubled the metropolitan white population; we have nearly tripled the nonwhite population. Nonmetropolitan residents have grown in number, but not at the same rate. These trends have placed great responsibility on the public schools.

In five years of the period of 1950 to 1970, the effects of metropolitanism on the size of school systems is dramatically displayed. In 1962 there were 37,019 school systems in the country and 39,719,000 elementary and secondary pupils enrolled. In 1967 there were only 23,390 school systems (a drop of 3629) and a public school enrollment of 43,891,000.[4] The first effect with which the schools were forced to cope was size. Along with size came the necessity of providing large system controls over personnel, curriculum, public relations, purchasing, planning, expenditures, and competition for land on which to build schools. The diversity of populations was caused not only by the large influx of nonwhites, but also by the inevitable in-migrations of all types of economically marginal persons seeking opportunity. This produced a necessity for varied instruction and flexible curricula not known in smaller, rural school districts. These developments necessitated the making of hard economic choices concerning economic uses of resources not only by the districts themselves,

[4] These figures are provided by the Bureau of the Census, *Census of Governments* 1962 and 1967, Vol. 1, *Governmental Organization;* and by the U.S. Office of Education, *Statistics of Public Schools.*

but also by the supporting public beset by demands for welfare, expanding cities, smog controls, ecological demands, freeways, police protection, fire safety, and more efficient local government. It was not only necessary for school personnel to make hard and often discouraging economic choices within school systems, but also essential that they give the public leadership to enable citizens to choose between supporting schools and other very desirable governmental activities.

Transiency

Another inevitable result of economic change is transiency in the population. National business and industrial organizations transfer personnel. People change from one employer to another, seeking economic opportunity. The unemployed move to areas of more favorable economic opportunity. In the period from March 1, 1967 to March 1, 1968, 36,603,000 people (18.8 percent, of a total population of 194,621,000) changed their residence. Of these, 22,960,000 (11.8 percent), changed residence within the county in which they lived and 6,607,000 (3.4 percent), changed residence from one county to another but within the same state. Finally, 7,035,000 (3.6 percent), changed residence from one state to another.[5]

Transiency immediately poses the problem of countywide, statewide, and national goals for education, implying a kind of coordination among school districts that seldom exists. Inevitably, it broadens the geographic area in which economic choices concerning the support of schools must be made. It is unlikely that national, state, and local goals can be made sufficiently alike to handle the problem of transfer from one instructional unit to another unless there is generous support nationally, statewide, and locally to make it possible.

Transiency also poses the problem of transfer of information concerning students. Present practice involves the movement of a transcript of grades, and usually little else. A complete information system will necessitate the use of scarce resources to amplify and modify student records and transfer information so that ready transfers are possible. This may conflict with other choices for the use of school funds.

Labor-Force Changes

Changes in technology are gradually eliminating employment in those occupations that require the least amount of education, thus placing greater pressure on schools and colleges to provide education for longer

---

[5] Bureau of the Census, *Current Population Reports*, Series P-20, 1968.

periods of time. The changes in the employment pattern from 1950 to 1969 are shown in Table 2.

Table 2

Labor-Force Employment, 1950 to 1969 (In Thousands)[a]

Occupation	1950	1969	Percent of Change
Total U.S. employment	59,648	76,520	28%
White-collar occupations Professional, technical, managers, officials, proprietors, clerical, and sales	22,373	36,458	63%
Blue-collar occupations Craftsmen, foremen, operatives, and non-farm laborers.	23,336	27,340	17%
Nonfarm laborers	3,520	3,305	−6%
Service occupations Private household and others	6,535	9,672	48%
Farm workers	7,408	3,050	−51%

[a] Source: 1950 and 1955, Department of Commerce, Bureau of the Census, *Current Population Reports*, Series P-50; beginning in 1960, Department of Labor, Bureau of Labor Statistics, *Employment and Earnings and Monthly Report on the Labor Force.*

Particularly significant is the decrease in employment of nonfarm laborers. At a time when the labor-force employment was rising to 128 percent of its 1950 level, the employment of nonfarm laborers was decreasing in actual numbers. The number of farm workers decreased to almost half that of 1950 at a time of increasing employment.

One result of this decreasing use of persons with lesser education has been the increase in number of years of schooling. In 1940 there were 1,708,000 resident and extension degree-credit college and university enrollments. This represented 15.59 persons per 100 in the 18-21 age group in the population. In 1966 there were 5,526,000 resident and extension degree-credit students in colleges and universities. These were 38.36 per 100 of the 18-21 age group.[6] In 26 years we have more than doubled the proportion of college students among those of college age.

[6] U.S. Office of Education 1940 and 1950, *Biennial Survey of Education in the United States;* in 1960 and thereafter, the annual report, *Digest of Educational Statistics.*

This result of economic change is a two-edged sword for public elementary and secondary schools. First, it places them in direct competition with colleges and universities for scarce public funds. As the public has placed pressures on the legislature for buildings and funds for an expanding public system of higher education, the state support for public elementary and secondary schools has declined.

Second, the most far-reaching effect on public elementary and secondary schools has been the necessity of developing a useful and stimulating program of instruction for those who stay in school because there is no work outside the school. Many schools and districts have been unequal to the task, but the challenge is still there. Many have not succeeded because of the tendency to allocate funds in terms of the number attending, rather than in terms of the difficulty of the educational tasks to be performed. A new way of allocating school resources and skilled teachers may need to be developed if the challenge is to be met.

Competition for Tax Income

The economic choices that most affect public education are those concerning tax income to be devoted to public education. The economic growth of the nation has placed schools in severe competition for the tax dollar. Growing metropolitan areas require vast expenditures for roads, streets, fire protection, police protection, welfare, recreation, and the other services of modern government. Increasing activity of state governments comes with population growth and business and industrial activity. The Federal Government has moved into more and more areas of activity as the result of a continuing nationalization of all types of economic, political, and social action. The competition for tax funds is shown in Table 3.

The extent of the competition is clear when it is noted that Federal taxation has almost quadrupled in the seventeen years between 1950 and 1967. The Federal debt has increased $70 billion although the per capita debt has remained almost constant. Both state and local taxes and state and local expenditures, however, have more than quadrupled in the period. Debts of states have increased six times; debts of local governments have increased $4\frac{1}{2}$ times.

Per capita federal taxes and expenditures, however, have increased about $2\frac{1}{2}$ times from 1950 to 1967. Per capita state and local taxes and expenditures have more than tripled during that period. Although Federal debt has remained substantially the same *per capita,* state and local debts have increased more than $3\frac{1}{2}$ times.

Table 3

Governmental Revenue, Expenditure and Debt, 1950 to 1967 (In Millions of Dollars)[a]

Item and Year	Federal	State	Local	Per Capita (Dollars) Federal	State and Local
Revenue					
1950	$ 43,527	$11,480	$11,673	$ 264	$121
1967	161,351	46,793	44,419	661	383
Expenditures					
1950	42,429	10,864	17,041	250	150
1967	151,821	39,704	66,274	624	472
Debt outstanding					
1950	257,357	5,285	18,830	1,697	159
1970	326,221	32,472	81,185	1,649	574

[a] Source: Department of Commerce, Bureau of the Census, *Historical Statistics on Governmental Finances and Employment*, annual report, *Governmental Finances*, and Census of Governments, 1967, Vol. 4, No. 5, *Compendium of Government Finances*.

The extent of the competition is even clearer when it is noted that in 1967 the Federal Government spent only 4.5 percent of its general expenditure funds for education; the states spent 39.8 percent, and the local governments 48 percent. The greatest burdens for the support of public elementary and secondary education fell on those governments in which taxation and debt have had the greatest proportional increases during the last two decades.

Employee Organizations and Inflation

School employees have organized in an attempt to cause the public to make economic choices that would result in competitive salaries and working benefits. The National Education Association in 1968-1969 had more than a million members among a total of 1,942,785 teaching in public elementary and secondary schools.[7] Affiliated organizations of the American Federation of Teachers now bargain collectively for teachers in

[7] U.S. Office of Education, *Fall 1968 Statistics of Public Schools*.

New York, Chicago, and Detroit. The National Education Association and the American Federation of Teachers are committed to collective bargaining with school boards. Each has approved and supported many strikes of teachers. Each works militantly to secure public support for its policies concerning wages, salaries, and working conditions.

Willingness to join aggressive employee organizations has been the product of constant inflationary trends in the economy. The Consumer Price Index in cities (if 1957-1959 is taken as a base period of 100) has increased from 83.8 in 1950 to 121.2 in 1968.[8] This represents a change of 37.4 points in the Index in a period of 18 years. To translate these Index figures to dollar values, the 1957-1959 dollar would purchase $1.194 worth of consumable goods in 1950; in 1968 the same dollar would purchase only $0.825 worth of consumable goods. In a period of inflation the compensation for inflation is a salary raise.

Pressure for salary compensation for inflation is particularly difficult in public schools because wages and salaries constitute such a large proportion of the entire budget. In 1966, public elementary and secondary schools devoted 55 percent of their entire budgets to instruction.[9] Even though the amounts given included the costs of free textbooks, school library books, and supplies, the salary budget for teachers and clerical assistants was in excess of 50 percent. In that year public elementary and secondary schools devoted 9 percent of their entire budget to plant operation and maintenance. More than half this amount was in the form of salaries. Nearly one fifth of all public school expenditures in 1966 were assigned to capital outlay and interest on debt for capital outlay. All of these items add up to nearly 85 percent of the total outlay for public elementary and secondary schools. There is little leeway in the budget for extensive increases in wages, salaries, and working benefits. Competition within the school systems for allocation of moneys to wages and salaries is as severe as it is among the public for different expenditures of the tax dollar.

The two constraints, competition within the system and external competition for the tax dollar, have normally restrained the advancement of wages and salaries. Almost universally school districts have referenced their wage payments, nonteaching salaries, to the current wage rates paid for similar occupations within the industrial and business community of the school district. Teachers' salaries, on the other hand, have tended to

8 Department of Labor, Bureau of Labor Statistics: *Monthly Labor Review.*

9 U.S. Office of Education, biennial report, *Statistics of State School Systems, 1965-1966.*

bear a relatively constant ratio to the per capita income payments of the population. Lindman has pointed this out in an article appearing in the May 1970 issue of the *Phi Delta Kappan*.[10] Since 1950, the ratio of teachers' salaries to the national average of per capita income payments has varied from 2.09 to 2.54, the latter figure being closest to the median since 1960. Lindman, furthermore, compares the relationships in the United States to those in England and Wales between 1961 and 1967. He finds the range there to be from 2.48 to 2.70, the latter figure being closest to the median.

Production of Knowledge

Economic activity of public school elementary and secondary teachers to maintain equity in salary payments may eventually pale into insignificance when compared with the problem of gaining access to knowledge, particularly scientific and technical knowledge. The production of knowledge has become an industry in itself. In 1958, E. Duerr Reeves, then Executive Vice-President of the Esso Engineering and Research Corporation, estimated that research could bring about an annual increase of 5 percent in industrial plant capacity through the removal of bottlenecks, with research saving 25 percent on plant capacity costs. He estimated that new-product development would have equal value.[11] The year before this statement was made, national expenditures for research were $8.4 billion, or 1.9 percent of the entire gross national product. Expenditures for research in 1967 were $23,770,000,000, or 3 percent of the gross national product.[12]

The manner in which the funds of 1967 were expended may point out the problem of the teacher. Of the nearly $24 billion spent on research nationally in 1967, universities spent a little more than $3 billion, or 12.8 percent. Universities, moreover, provided only $830 million of the money they spent, or 3.6 percent. A little more than two thirds, 67 percent, of the money spent by universities was provided by the federal government. More than two thirds of all research money, nearly $16.5 billion, or 69.9 percent, was expended by industry. The Federal Government pro-

---

[10] Lindman, Erick L., "Are Teachers' Salaries Improving?", *Phi Delta Kappan*, **LI**, 9 (May 1970), pp. 421-423.

[11] E. Duerr Reeves, "Industrial Research," *Stanford Research Institute Journal*, 2(2) (August 1958), 1.

[12] Data provided by the National Science Foundation and published in U.S. Bureau of the Census, *Statistical Abstract of the United States: 1969*, 90th ed., Washington, D.C., 1969, p. 523.

vided a little more than half of the research money spent by industry, $8,390,000,000, or 51 percent. The problem is a little changed if one examines money spent on basic research. Nearly $4 billion, or 10.5 percent of all research money, was spent on basic research. Universities expended almost $2.25 billion, $2,118,000,000, or 69.6 percent of the total spent on basic research. Universities provided 17.2 percent of that money. The conclusion is inescapable, however, that the centers for the production of scientific and technical knowledge in the future are likely to be large research complexes managed by either industry or the government itself.

Much of the government research activity, done in its laboratories or in industrial laboratories at government expense, is devoted to national defense. The product of the research is often labeled "confidential" and is not available to the public. Many industrial laboratories' products are necessarily labeled "proprietary." The time lag between the production of an idea or an invention to public visibility has been estimated to vary from seven to twelve years, depending on its degree of complexity. Even after visibility has been achieved, it may take those who prepare knowledge for consumption by students, such as writers, editors, and curriculum researchers, at least five years to prepare publications. Twelve to seventeen years from time of discovery to utilization in classrooms is hardly likely to promote relevance in the curriculum.

There was a time when the major portion of all new knowledge was produced within university walls. It was a matter of professional ethics for the university researcher to make his knowledge known at once through publication. In a society in which only one seventh of all research in scientific and technical fields is carried on by universities, the campus can no longer be the main source of scientific and technical knowledge. The university, however, is still the chief producer of knowledge of nontechnical problems of mankind. Although industry has poured its money into research activity that is calculated to bring new products, processes, and solutions to technical problems, it has largely ignored the companion research required to assist people in making adaptations to the cultural changes brought about by technical advances. The university has had to assume a constantly growing burden of research in nontechnical problems of mankind. Support for this kind of research has been historically very thin.

Economic choices within the nation have conspired to undersupport research in the social sciences, and to support research in technology and science in such a way that quick access to it is really impossible for teachers to obtain.

Comparative Economic Systems

The social and political implications of economic activity assume greater importance as mechanization proceeds. Governmental activity in a mixed economy implies insightful political choices among the voting public. Responsibility is placed on schools to prepare the citizenry for responsible political, social, and economic activity. At this point, legends concerning the inevitability of the progression of capitalism to communism arouse heated controversy, which makes the normal educational development of capability for intellectual analysis difficult.

Men have always had visions of a more perfect society. Heilbroner, in discussing the leading economists since 1776, characterized them as follows:

> An odder group of men—one less apparently destined to remake the world—could scarcely be imagined.
>
> There were a philosopher among them and a madman, a parson and a stockbroker, a revolutionary and a nobleman, an aesthete, a skeptic, and a tramp. They were of every nationality, of every walk of life, of every turn of temperament. Some were brilliant, some were bores; some ingratiating, some impossible. At least three made their own fortunes, but as many could never master the elementary economics of their personal finances. Two were eminent businessmen, one was never much more than a traveling salesman, another frittered away his fortune.
>
> . . . It was neither their personalities, their careers, their biases, nor even their ideas which bound them together. Their common denominator was something else: a common curiosity. They were all fascinated by the world about them, by its complexity and its seeming disorder, by the cruelty which it so often masked in sanctimony and the successes of which it was so often unaware. They were all of them absorbed in the behavior of their fellow man, first as he created worldly wealth, and then as he trod on the toes of his neighbor to gain a share of it.[13]

Heilbroner thus underlines the almost desperate importance of a system of economic analysis to provide a way not only of assessing the quality of our own economic system, but also of evaluating the many emotional claims for other systems of economic effort. Samuelson provides emphasis to this necessity by pointing out what has transpired since World War II.

> Only the United States and a few other countries [at the end of World War II] remained as islands of declared capitalism in an in-

---

[13] Robert L. Heilbroner, *The Worldly Philosophers*, Simon and Schuster, New York, 1953, pp. 5-6.

creasingly collectivized world. Even here, the scene was drastically changed: ours had become a mixed economy with both private and public initiative and control, and, in those disturbed days, a mixed system of peace and war economy. . . .

Little wonder then that profound social philosophers, like Harvard's Joseph Schumpeter, thought they could foretell the end of capitalism in the years after 1945. Even profound philosophers can turn out to be quite wrong. Following World War II, gradually "New Economics" of the modern mixed economy began to take over. And it actually worked![14]

Samuelson goes on to point out that modern economic analysis is not only useful in providing a method of examining different economic systems analytically, but it is also almost universally used.

In preparing students to develop social, economic, and political responsibility, only the teacher skilled in the use of elementary economic analysis can cope with demands for objectivity and impartial consideration of economic alternatives, and develop the public confidence essential to the consideration of emotionally charged issues.

The Growth Economy

An integral part of the "New Economy" to which Samuelson referred is a commitment to continued growth. Economists have identified education as a major contributor to continued economic growth. The National Defense Education Act and the 1963 and 1968 Vocational Education Acts have recognized education's contribution to it. They have emphasized the development of inventors and innovators and of the skills of members of the work force.

The individual who has a better education has an opportunity to become an inventor and innovator in the economy. As such, he is the agent for technological change. Dow and Monsanto Chemical companies, for example, traced 30 to 40 percent of their 1956 sales volume to research undertaken in the previous decade. The agrichemicals—fungicides, herbicides, and insecticides—became a $400 million business in less than a decade. Westinghouse Electric Corporation reported that 60 percent of its 1956 sales volume was in products introduced since 1946.[15] Among the new product groups of the 1950s, thermoplastics were the most outstanding. Production of polyethylene rose from 20 million pounds in 1948 to

[14] Samuelson, op. cit., pp. 778-779.
[15] American Management Association, *The Commercialization of Research Results,* Special Report No. 20 (1957).

800 million in 1958.[16] Data such as these prompted the passage of the National Defense Education Act. Moneys appropriated under this Act were used to foster instruction in mathematics, science, and languages. It was the beginning of a national policy of utilizing education to produce innovators and inventors capable of keeping the economy growing.

The Vocational Education Acts of 1963 and 1968 also recognized that schools contributed heavily to the expansion of the economy. The typical logic behind these Acts has been proposed by Theodore Schultz of the University of Chicago.[17]

Schultz drew on Bureau of the Census information to determine the average number of years of education possessed by each member of the work force at various times in American economic history. He found, for example, that in 1940 each worker, on the average, had 6.85 years of elementary schooling, 1.71 years of secondary schooling, and 0.46 years of college and university education. Using data from the U.S. Office of Education to calculate the cost per year of education at each of the three levels, he included not only teachers' salaries, administrators' salaries, salaries of classified personnel, consumable supplies, and student transportation, but also the cost of interest on indebtedness and depreciation of capital. By adding the costs of earnings foregone by high school and college students, he was able to produce a figure giving the per year cost for each of elementary, secondary, and collegiate education.

Multiplication of the average number of years of each worker's type of schooling by its average cost per year enabled Schultz to compute the average education cost per member of the work force. From the cost per worker multiplied by the total number of workers, he was able to calculate the value of the total educational investment in the work force. By comparing successive years after 1940, Schultz computed the progression of educational investment. In 1940, for example, total educational investment in the work force was $248 billion; in 1957, it was $535 billion.

Schultz then calculated the lifetime earnings of individuals who had completed elementary, secondary, or collegiate institutions. He developed the ratio between lifetime earnings and educational investments. For example, the 1956 college graduates earned $120,000 more than high school graduates in their lifetimes. The cost of a college education for 1956 college graduates was $13,200. The ratio between added earnings and total cost

---

[16] J. H. Forrester, "A Decade of Progress in Petrochemicals," an address to the American Petroleum Institute (May 1959).

[17] Theodore W. Schultz, *The Economic Value of Education*, Columbia University Press, New York, 1963.

was 9.77. Similar ratios were developed for differentials between high school and elementary school graduates. Ratios were then identified as a "rate of return." Applying them to increases in educational investment, Schultz was able to estimate the proportion of growth in national income attributable to increased education of members of the work force. Using middle ranges, he concluded that 21 percent of the rise in national income during the 1929-1947 period was attributable to education.

The conscious adoption of the public schools as an instrument of national economic policy will have far-reaching effects on them. Consequent evaluations of teaching productivity will certainly necessitate a firming up of educational goals. Since the economy is being treated as a national problem, national goals are imperative. National preoccupation with economic health, both political and social, will necessarily direct greater attention to the activities of education. National support systems will direct attention of educators more intently toward Federal Government activities.

Most significant of all, however, is the effect on the public school teacher. Being a contributor to a nationally recognized desirable economic result will require him to be more sophisticated in his knowledge of the economic system. Being engaged in economic activity, he will be required to possess the tools of economic analysis to direct his own activity.

Economic Analysis

The development of an ability to do elementary economic analysis will necessarily require the teacher to study economic data extensively. It is patently impossible to provide sufficient data within a short essay to make it possible to cover the entire field of economic thought. It is possible, however, to identify economic concepts that need study, to examine briefly their importance within the rationale of economic analysis, and to give direction to further study.

Economic Problems of Every Society

1. Economic Organization. Every society must determine what commodities shall be produced and in what quantities. Each must decide how they shall be produced, that is, by whom, with what resources, and in what technological manner. Each must determine for whom they are to be produced in the sense of who shall share in the benefits of the production.

In a capitalist economy these questions are resolved through a system of prices (markets, profits, and losses).

2. Scarcity. It matters little how "affluent" the society may become in Galbraith's[18] terms; a full-employment economy must always in producing one good be giving up something of another. Any economic analysis must contend with the concept of allocating *scarce* resources of land, labor, capital, and profits.

3. Population. Malthus's *Essay on the Principle of Population* (1798)[19] posed the thought that populations were growing in a geometric projection and would eventually outstrip the ability of the land to produce food for them. He thus underlined the law of diminishing returns, which suggests that as we add more and more input (labor in the case of Malthus) to a fixed input (land) the amount of extra product will fall off because there is less of it for each person. Populations since Malthus have increased enormously. His expected result has not been achieved because technological progress in industry more than offset the effects of the law of diminishing returns.

4. Prices. Adam Smith in his *Wealth of Nations* (1776)[20] was excited by the order in the economic system provided by the "Invisible Hand" of competition. The subsequent years have demonstrated that perfect competition is virtually impossible and that some monopolistic imperfection is inevitable in the market. The capitalistic system compensates for monopoly by government intervention to maintain an equilibrium system of prices and production that make the purchases of the consumer the arbiter of what is produced. It makes the method of production responsive to the market, and regulates the distribution of benefits of production in the form of wage rates, land rents, interest rates, and profits.

5. Capital. The technological advances that obviated the dire predictions of Malthus have been made possible by the use of capital to purchase elaborate machinery, manufacturing plants, big stores, stocks of finished products, and supplies of materials. Private ownership of these items have made us a "capitalistic society." The process of getting people to delay expenditures of income (savings) and invest them in productive enterprise in expectation of greater future rewards has been a major problem in economics.

6. Specialization and Division of Labor. Along with investments in

---

[18] John K. Galbraith, *The Affluent Society*, Houghton Mifflin, Boston, 1958.

[19] Heilbroner, op. cit., pp. 67-95, and George F. Kneller, *Education and Economic Thought*, John Wiley and Sons, New York, 1968, pp. 28-30.

[20] Heilbroner, op. cit., pp. 33-66, and Kneller, op. cit., pp. 24-26.

capital has come a specialization and division of labor. By carefully dividing work into compatible parts, and building as much skill as possible into machines, productive and distributive organizations have been able to utilize individuals with finite abilities by assisting them to concentrate on work that allows concentration on a narrow band of skill development. They were thus enabled to share in a productive enterprise in a way that was impossible if they had to produce the entire product. Thus it was possible to involve almost everyone in the production and distribution of economic products.

7. **Money.** Specialization and division of labor developed an interdependence among producers and distributors that required the development of a flexible medium of exchange. The velocity of its exchange became a classic concern of those studying economics. Money has no value in itself; it is valuable to the extent to which it can be exchanged for goods and services. In a sophisticated economy it consists of coins, paper money, and bank deposits. It is imperative under division of labor and specialization because more than one person contributes to the production of a product. In order to secure that product, no less than products made by other people, it was essential to have a medium of exchange.

8. **Supply and Demand.** The eternal problem of production is to determine the amount of a product to make. The most helpful approach to this question is the observed fact that when the price of a good is raised, the demand for the good is diminished. The equilibrium price, one that may possibly be persistent, is that which causes producers *willingly* to supply an amount of goods that are *willingly* purchased in the marketplace. The willingness of a producer to place a given amount on the market is determined by the price that he expects to receive for it, his costs of production, and the expected profit. The willingness to buy is based on the buyer's observed need of the product, his hierarchy of needs, and the choices between alternative needs as demonstrated in the hierarchy. If the manufacturer provides more goods or services than the public is willing to buy, there is a downward pressure on prices. If he supplies less, then there will be an upward pressure on prices.

9. **Business Organization.** An economic society must decide, in addition to how much shall be made, the size of the unit to be used in the productive or distributive process. Adam Smith in the *Wealth of Nations* envisioned a competitive system derived from multiple small business organizations competing with others. The most numerous business organizations in the American economy are small proprietorships that show an enormous turnover. The American economy, however, has largely avoided partnerships because of unlimited liability. The majority of production

and distribution in America is done by the corporation for reasons suggested by Samuelson as follows:

> Large-scale production is technically efficient, and a large corporation is an advantageous way for investors to pool the irreducible risks of business life. Without limited liability and the corporation, society could simply not reap the benefits that come when large supplies of capital can be attracted to competing corporations that produce a variety of complementary products, pool risks, and best utilize the economies of sizable research units and managerial know-how. That is why the privilege of the corporate form is legalized.[21]

10. Affluence and Poverty. Every economic society is eventually concerned with the distribution of income; poverty; and abundance. While Marx's declaration that an industrial nation fosters increasing poverty for the poor and increasing riches for the rich has proven wrong, there are still great differences in living standards in the United States. As each step forward is made in reducing differences between living standards of different groups, the society sets higher standards.

11. Labor and Industrial Relations. In America unionization has contributed something to a more equitable distribution of income. American labor unions, unlike some foreign unions devoted to political activity, have existed primarily for the economic betterment of their members. They have concentrated on higher wages, shorter working hours, more vacations, easier work rules, fringe benefits in the form of pensions and health plans, democratic rights for men on the job, and participation in the making of corporate policy. Their use of economic power by withdrawal of services and corporate use of the lockout have prompted the public, through the National Labor Management Relations Act of 1946, to set up the conditions under which both employers and unions shall exercise economic power in disputes over wages, salaries, and conditions of work.

12. Government and the Economy. Government, however, has played a larger part in the economy than mere regulation of industrial conflict. It has control over fiscal policy through the Federal Reserve System. Federal expenditures of approximately $200 billion in 1970 will amount to nearly $1 thousand per capita, or a fraction more than one fifth of the 1970 per capita income. Through taxation it will provide extensive welfare income payments to the poor of the country. It is committed to redistribution of the wealth through the graduated income tax and inheritance taxes. It regulates government-allowed monopolies, such as airline

---

[21] Samuelson, op. cit., p. 85.

routes and service, radio and television licenses, interstate gas and oil lines, and interstate telephone and telegraph communications. It controls the quality of production through the setting of government standards. These activities of government have expanded greatly during the past thirty years. Truly it can be said that our economy is "mixed" in the sense that both private and public agencies exercise control over it.

13. Taxation. In taxing themselves people are deciding how resources for social wants will be taken from the various families and the enterprises they own and made available for governmental goods and services. Taxes do redistribute the wealth of a nation to some extent. Justice in taxation means taxing equals equally and unequals unequally. Three fourths of all federal revenue comes from personal and corporation taxes. The principal source of local taxes is the property tax. The principal sources of state taxes are sales and excise taxes. State and local taxes and state and local debt have increased greatly in the past eighteen years.[22] The Federal Government gives grants to states for education, highways, welfare, and other national enterprises. The states assist local governments in the same areas. The incidence of a tax is its ultimate effect on prices and other economic magnitudes.

14. National Income. Eventually every economic society derives a method of examining its successes or failures. The measure used in the United States is the gross national product or the net national product. These are defined as the sum of national personal expenditures on goods and services, government expenditures on goods and services, and investment expenditures. The difference between the two is that the former includes gross expenditures on all new machines and construction and the latter includes only the net national gain by these expenditures.

Macroeconomics

During the Depression of the 1930s it became clear that government should act to maintain appropriate monetary and fiscal policies to ensure an economic environment in which the classical principles of microeconomics can operate for the public good. The Federal Government stated its intention to pursue this policy in the Employment Act of 1946, as follows:

> The Congress hereby declares that it is the continuing policy and responsibility of the federal government to use all practicable means consistent with its needs and obligations and other essential considera-

[22] Supra, p. 9-10.

tions of national policy, with the assistance and cooperation of industry, agriculture, labor and state and local governments, to coordinate and utilize all its plans, functions, and resources for the purpose of creating and maintaining, in a manner calculated to foster and promote free enterprise and the general welfare, conditions under which there will be afforded useful employment opportunities, including self employment, for those able, willing, and seeking to work and to promote employment, production, and purchasing power.

The rationale for Federal Government action in this field was supplied largely by John Maynard Keynes.[23] In *The General Theory of Employment, Interest and Money* published in 1936, he outlined the dimensions of macroeconomics. This is a classic ranking alongside Smith's *Wealth of Nations* and Marx's *Das Kapital*.

Following are some of the basic problem areas of macroeconomics:

1. Savings—Investment. Motivations for saving and investment are different. Historically, there is no automatic tendency for the same number of dollars to be spent at the same rate for each. If governmental fiscal and monetary policies are not designed to stabilize the economy, we would, as a result, be subject to inflationary and depression swings in the economy.

2. National Income. Equilibrium of national income is achieved when the demand for investment equals the savings sufficient to satisfy it. Investment causes income to rise or fall until voluntary, scheduled saving has adjusted itself to the level of maintainable investment. The most important factor in causing income and employment to fluctuate is investment. An increase in net investment will increase the national income by a multiplied amount. Samuelson summarized the problem as follows:

> An increased desire to consume—which is another way of looking at a decreased desire to save—is likely to boost business sales and increase investment. On the other hand, a decreased desire to consume—i.e., an increase in thriftiness—is likely to reduce inflationary pressure in times of booming incomes; but in time of depression, it could make the depression worse and reduce the amount of actual net capital formation in the community. *High consumption and high investment are then hand in hand rather than opposed to each other.*[24]

An increase in taxes, if investment and government expenditures are unchanged, provides less money for consumption, saving, and investment.

---

[23] Heilbroner, op. cit., pp. 236-276; Kneller, op. cit., pp. 53-60.
[24] Samuelson, op. cit., p. 227.

A tax reduction provides more money for these purposes. The government may have to utilize its taxing powers to stabilize the economy in times of both inflation and deflation.

3. Business Cycles. Governmental monetary and fiscal policy can be used to alleviate the great pulses of economic life. Movements of national income, unemployment, production, prices, and profits are not entirely predictable, but expansion, peak, recession, and trough are subject to analysis. The public has grown accustomed to demanding government cooperation in stabilizing the economy. A mixed economy will inevitably be subject to recessions due to inventory fluctuations, government spending, and inflation. The wide swings of the business cycle, however, are subject to control by skillful use of monetary and fiscal policies.

4. Prices and Money. Inflation of prices typically favor debtors, profit-seekers, and risk-taking speculators. Unforeseen inflation hurts creditors, fixed-income classes, pensioners, and conservative investors. Aside from the effects on the latter, mild inflations throughout capitalism's history seem to keep employment high and business brisk. A significant control over inflation-deflation is the regulation of the amount of money in the form of cash, currency, and bank deposits.

5. Federal Monetary Policy. The government regulates the supply of money through the Federal Reserve System consisting of member banks, the 12 regional Federal Reserve Banks, and the Federal Reserve Board. Member banks are required to keep legal reserves on deposit with the regional Federal Reserve Bank or in vault cash equal to about one sixth or less of their demand deposits. By regulating the amount of the required reserves, the Federal Reserve System can expand or contract the money supply by restricting bank credit. In so doing it tends to keep credit conditions conducive to overall spending. It tends to "lean against the wind" of deficient or excessive aggregate spending to promote growth in the economy and price-level stability. The Federal Reserve Board also sells or buys government bonds in the open market to tighten or loosen member bank reserves. In addition, the Federal Reserve Board makes loans to member banks using a market discount rate. All these actions can be used to stabilize inflation-deflation patterns within the economy.

6. Significance of Macroeconomics. Samuelson summarizes the significance of macroeconomics as follows:

> By means of appropriately reinforcing monetary and fiscal policies, our mixed enterprise system can avoid the excesses of boom and slump and can look forward to healthy progressive growth. This fundamental being understood, the paradoxes that robbed the older classical principles dealing with small scale "microeconomics" of much of their relevance

and validity will now lose their sting. In short, mastery of the modern analysis of income determination genuinely validates the basic classical pricing principles; and the economist is now justified in saying that the broad cleavage between microeconomics and macroeconomics has been closed.[25]

Microeconomics

Microeconomics is the classical content of economics study. It deals largely with prices and pricing mechanisms. It typically seeks to ascertain the effect of market supply and market demand on price. It is concerned with monopoly pricing and with the share of price that is distributed in the form of rent, wages, interest, and profits. Some of the key ideas that must be assessed follow.

1. **Price and Demand-Supply.** An increase in demand for a good, if the supply is constant, will raise the price. It will probably also increase the quantity being sold. A decrease in demand will achieve the opposite effect. An increase in supply, if demand is constant, will lower the price and increase the quantity being bought and sold. A decrease in supply will accomplish an opposite effect.

2. **Persistence of Demand.** There is no such thing as an unlimited demand for any good. As each unit is added to the demand there is a declining demand. After all an individual can drink only so much water. The price is, therefore, determined more by the last drink that will be consumed than by anything else.

3. **Persistence of Supply.** Nor is there an unlimited supply of goods. The producer of the good tends to receive less and less for his product as he produces more units. This proceeds until he is unwilling to manufacture more at the price he can get for the last unit he can sell.

4. **Monopoly and Antitrust Action.** It is inevitable that corporations should try to gain as much control as possible over the supply of a good, to keep prices high and profits maximized. Federal and state governments have by law imposed checks and balances by regulation that are not available under automatic competition.

5. **Rent.** One of the factors of cost in the production of a good is rental on the land. This may be land to produce the raw material or land on which the manufacturing plant is located. The returns to the landowner are normally proportional to the price the good secures in the market.

[25] Samuelson, op. cit., p. 352.

6. Wages. Another factor of production cost is wages. Wage differentials between categories of workers tend to remain the same when the supply of each category matches demand. Unions have probably done less to influence wage rates than they wish to claim, but may have done much to influence management styles. If wage costs become excessive in terms of market prices for products, there will be an attempt to substitute mechanical devices for labor.

7. Interest. The market rate of interest on money loaned tends to provide a device for directing investment into enterprises with the greatest profit potential. When interest rates are high, only highly profitable enterprises are supported. When interest rates lower, enterprises with less potential for profit are selected.

8. Profits. Profits accrue to those who have been efficient in making things, creative in selling them, and astute in foreseeing needs. They are rewards for enterprise. They tend to cause the creation of new ventures, reinforce the maintenance or expansion of useful ventures, and maintain organizations that are efficient, creative, and astute.

9. Significance of Microeconomics. Competitive pricing must carry most of the burden of society's decisions concerning what will be produced, how it will be produced, and for whom it will be produced. This is the province of microeconomics. The income-analysis dimension of public policy for keeping the system competitive is found in macroeconomics.

Educators and Economic Analyses

In summary, the educators of the country serve less the function of economic analyzers than of the consumers of economic analysis. As such, they must be thoroughly cognizant of the methods, techniques, and language of economic analysis. If they are not, then they will be unable to respond effectively to the following educational problems that are integral to the economic system.

1. The educational product must be specified clearly if the schools are to compete effectively for tax dollars. Goals of government are usually specific and tangible in the form of sewers, police stations and policemen, fire stations and firemen, streets, welfare, and water supply. Goals of education must be as clearly defined. If it is the intent of the public school system to improve the skills of the work force, then it must specify not only the skills that are to be developed, but also the successive progress goals

essential to achieving their development. If it is the purpose of the public schools to develop the inventor and the innovator, then they must specify skills and knowledge they expect to develop. If it is the purpose of the schools to bring about social change, particularly those changes identified in the Federal Elementary and Secondary Education Act, then they must specify long-range and intermediate goals by which they are to be effected. Competition requires specificity of desirable ends so that rational economic choices can be made.

2. The rational choice cannot be made, however, unless it is possible to relate expenditures to end-product goals. In systems control, this means programmed budgeting. This is the cost-accounting process that assures the ordering of priorities within the schools so that the possibility of maximizing the goal accomplishment is achieved. Programmed budgeting contemplates the examination of alternate uses of the factors of educational production to secure the combination best calculated to reach the desired goal.

3. Educators must develop skills of economic analysis in order to respond quickly and accurately to the changes in the economy that vitally affect the conduct of public education. Large school districts, for example, require organization systems for control of finance, communication, personnel, planning, housing, and transportation. Transiency requires the exchange of information locally, regionally, and nationally concerning students. It may require regional, state, and national goals and cooperation. Lengthening years of education require that we examine carefully the content of instruction not only in public elementary and secondary schools, but also in the college and university. Limited access to knowledge may require exchanges of personnel between industrial and government laboratories and college and university faculties, which are not extraordinarily difficult. Most of these problems are already long overdue for solution primarily because the lack of ability to do economic analysis, or consume economic analyses, has left educators insensitive to the changes in the educational environment. As a result, public elementary and secondary schools are attempting to solve the problems of education in a highly technical industrial society with the tools of the largely rural, agricultural economy of half a century ago.

4. Nor can the public elementary and secondary teacher much longer ignore the necessity for economic education. Macroeconomics has pointed out the economic nature of the political vote. Microeconomics has pointed out the voting character of purchases. Not only must the citizen be an informed purchaser; he must also be an economic voter, putting persons in office who are charged with the maintenance of appropriate fiscal and

monetary policies. Thus the ancient charge to public elementary and secondary schools to develop citizens takes on a broad economic character. Educators can ill afford to ignore the challenge.

References

Benson, Charles S., *The Economics of Public Education*, Houghton Mifflin, Boston, Massachusetts, 1961, 580 pp. Examines public schools as an economic institution and analyzes public school income and expenditures.

Benson, Charles S., *Education is Good Business*, American Association of School Administrators, Association of School Business Officials of the United States and Canada, and the National School Boards Association, Washington, D.C., 1965, 48 pp. Summarizes and updates the 1961 book briefly and gives both Schultz's and Denison's calculations of the economic value of education.

Heilbroner, Robert L., *The Worldly Philosophers*, Simon and Schuster, New York, 1943, 342 pp. Provides brief sketches of the life histories and ideas of noted economists from Adam Smith to Joseph Schumpeter.

Kneller, George F., *Education and Economic Thought*, John Wiley and Sons, Inc., New York, 1968, 139 pp. Contains a history of economic thought and explores current educational problems and their relations to economics.

Samuelson, Paul A., *Economics*, 7th ed., McGraw-Hill Book Company, New York, 1967, 821 pp. One of the most widely used beginning economics texts in the world. Utilizes the rationale of economic analysis to discuss both macro- and microeconomics.

Schultz, Theodore W., *The Economic Value of Education*, Columbia University Press, 1963. Describes a method of determining the economic value of education.

20

Research: Content and Method

George F. Kneller

❖❖❖

Scientific Research in Education

For many centuries the study of education was part of philosophy. Some philosophers, like Plato and Locke, proposed general theories of human nature and man's place in the scheme of things and then recommended appropriate forms of education. Others, such as Pestalozzi and Froebel, put forward philosophies of man and education as a result of their actual experience of teaching. It was not until the end of the nineteenth century, with the rise of the behavioral sciences, that people began to study education scientifically.

The crucial event for the scientific study of education was the invention of the intelligence test, which enabled educators to gain precise, quantitative information about human abilities. In 1905 the French psychologist, Alfred Binet, constructed the first effective psychometric test by putting together a series of tasks of increasing difficulty that he believed to be little affected by any schooling a person might have received. From this beginning there have sprung a host of devices measuring not only intelligence but also attitudes, interests, traits, and performances.

In the United States one of the leaders of the scientific movement in education was the psychologist Edward L. Thorndike, whose aphorism, "Whatever exists at all exists in some amount and can be measured," served as the motto for a generation of researchers.[1] Another influence was that of the philosopher John Dewey, who argued that all problems in life, especially those of education, could *in principle* be solved scientifically by applying the method of "reflective thinking."[2] By 1924 a score of universities and colleges had their own facilities for educational research. A decade later research was underway in a wide range of fields, such as child growth, teaching methods, curriculum studies, and counseling. Today scientific research in education is accepted as essential to national welfare.

Behavioral Sciences and Education

The central purpose of the scientific study of education is to discover knowledge that will help improve the education that is given in our schools. This practical interest affects both the choice of topics to be investigated and the kinds of conclusions that are drawn about them. Most research projects are designed to assess how far certain professional practices, personal qualities, or institutional arrangements either strengthen or weaken the educational process. For example, a study may seek to determine what personal traits make for "good" teaching or "good" supervising, what forms of interview prove most "effective" in counseling, or what classroom atmospheres are most "reassuring" to students.

In each of these cases the conclusions drawn by the researcher from the data he has gathered will incorporate appraisals or evaluations. The researcher will set out the standards guiding his appraisals. He will state, for instance, the criteria by which he is assessing how "good" a teacher's performance is, criteria such as the academic achievement of the children who were taught or the teacher's influence on the children's values. These criteria tend, of course, to reflect the values of the researcher and his cultural milieu. Thus the criterion of academic achievement may presuppose the belief that the school should bring about academic rather than other kinds of achievement. It may also presuppose the superiority of these particular forms of academic achievement over others that might have

[1] Edward L. Thorndike, "The Nature, Purposes and General Methods of Measurements of Educational Products," in *The Measurement of Educational Products,* Seventeenth Yearbook of the National Society for the Study of Education, Part II, University of Chicago, 1918, p. 16.

[2] Dewey spelled out the steps or stages of "reflective thinking" in his *How We Think,* Heath, Boston, 1910. For a resumé, see pp. 268-272 of this text.

been chosen. Similarly, the criterion of teacher influence on student values may imply the judgment that the values figuring in the criterion are worthier of cultivation than others.

To use a distinction I made in Chapter 15, most educational research is "applied" rather than "pure" science. Let me illustrate this point from recent research. During the past few years a number of important studies have been made of the factors influencing student achievement.[3] Nearly all these studies have found that the achievement of students correlates positively with the length of experience of their teachers; in other words, teachers teach better after several years on the job. Some of the studies, notably the Coleman Report, Project Talent, and the Plowden Report (British), also found that student achievement is significantly affected by parental attitudes and behavior. Both these findings have to do with factors influencing the educational process, and both of them incorporate evaluations of teacher and student performance. Both, moreover, are potentially grounds for action. If teachers become effective as a result of extended experience, there is a case for improving preservice, internship, and in-service training programs to see that teachers get practice as quickly as possible. There is also a case for further inquiry to discover whether this experience is gained solely by classroom practice or whether the skills that are the fruit of experience can be communicated formally by training programs or informally by experienced teachers in the novice's school. Again, if a student's performance is likely to be influenced by parental attitudes and behavior, there is a prima facie case for informing parents as to how they can help their children do better in school.

The line between pure and applied science is admittedly hard to draw. Pure science generally seeks knowledge for its own sake, whereas applied

---

[3] These studies include James S. Coleman et al., *Equality of Educational Opportunity*, U.S. Government Printing Office, Washington, D.C., 1966; John C. Flanagan et al., *Studies of the American High School Project TALENT*, Monograph No. 2, University of Pittsburgh, 1962; *Children and their Primary Schools: A Report of the Central Advisory Council for Education*, Her Majesty's Stationery Office, London, 1967, 2 vols.; Torsten Husén, Ed., *International Study of Achievement in Mathematics*, Wiley, New York, 1967, 2 vols.; Jesse Burkhead et al., *Input and Output in Large-City High Schools*, Syracuse University, 1967; Charles Benson's study of pupils' test scores in 392 school districts, conducted for the California Senate Fact-Finding Committee on Revenue and Taxation, and reported by Allen K. Campbell, "The Socio-Economic, Political and Fiscal Environment of Educational Policy-Making in Large Cities," *Ameircan Political Science Association* (1966); and Herbert J. Kiesling, unpublished Harvard Ph.D. thesis (1965), "Measuring a Local Government Service: A Study of School Districts in New York State."

science aims to extend such knowledge so as to satisfy human needs and desires. Although most research in education is of the applied kind, some pure scientific research is also done.[4] An example is Benjamin Bloom's recent analysis of 1000 longitudinal studies of early learning.[5] Bloom found that (1) some of the most important human characteristics develop most rapidly during the first five years of life, (2) changes in the individual are significantly related to changes in his environment, and (3) any change in basic characteristics becomes more difficult to effect as the individual grows older. These findings carry important implications for applied research to investigate. They suggest, for example, that failure to undergo some phase of learning or development in these early years may well cause the child to do poorly throughout the rest of his school career.

For most basic findings about human behavior, however, educators turn to the social sciences and psychology. They do so because education is the behavior of human beings in a certain social setting and is therefore partly to be understood in terms of human regularities that are widely observable. Behavior in school may differ from behavior in the office or in the family, but it does so only in certain respects and not in kind. Consequently, many regularities in the behavior of individuals and groups and in the working of societies are operative also in the behavior and phenomena that go with schooling, although they are modified by educational needs and the educational setting.

Thus educational research is inevitably eclectic. It selects from diverse disciplines whatever knowledge seems likely to aid in understanding and improving the educational process. Some researchers have drawn on the theory of operant conditioning put forward by B. F. Skinner as a result of his experiments with rats and pigeons. Other researchers have learned much from J. P. Guilford's classification of the intellectual abilities. J. S. Getzels and P. W. Jackson used this classification in their studies of creative thinking in gifted children. Guilford in turn was indebted to a hypothesis that has influenced educational research ever since the hypothesis was proposed, Alfred Binet's notion that intelligence is a complex affair of many different abilities. Other basic research of importance to education has been a series of studies in child development performed by the Swiss psychologist Jean Piaget. Piaget has shown that the child grows

---

[4] Cf. John B. Carroll, "Basic and Applied Research in Education: Definitions, Distinctions, and Implications," *Harvard Educational Review*, **XXXVIII**, 2 (Spring 1968), 263-276.

[5] Benjamin S. Bloom, *Stability and Change in Human Characteristics*, Wiley, New York, 1964. (A longitudinal study is one that investigates the development of a phenomenon in time.)

by stages from a state of autism and egocentrism toward one of emotional and intellectual "maturity" (at age 12 or 13) when he is capable of thinking logically and cooperating with other people.[6]

The behavioral sciences not only provide substantive findings which may be used as points of departure for research into education, they also contribute basic concepts or ways of conceiving educational phenomena. Take some concepts that have been borrowed from sociology. Educators have used the notion of a social system to investigate the structure and functioning of the school. They have applied the concept of the social group (a number of persons interacting in a structured situation) to the classroom and the staff room. They have employed the concept of social class to explain the effect of parental attitudes on pupil performance and to account for the presence of middle-class assumptions in intelligence tests. They have also used the notion of social role to gain insights into the behavior of teachers and administrators.

The behavioral sciences also have given educators various techniques for planning investigations and gathering information. Psychology has provided the projective test and the depth interview, both of which lead the respondent to reveal attitudes of which he is not fully aware. Social psychology has furnished the one-way vision room for studying the behavior of small groups, as well as the sociogram for identifying status relations within groups. Sociology has contributed the techniques of the formal interview and the questionnaire.

Nevertheless, the findings of behavioral science, even when they bear on education, do not apply to it directly. An educator cannot use the generalizations of psychology to solve his problems in the way that an engineer uses the laws of physics. An engineer building a bridge can turn to a textbook in physics for information about the elasticity and durability of materials. Given this information, he can be confident that if the bridge is built to certain specifications, it will withstand a predictable amount of wear and tear from traffic, wind, and tide. An educator, however, cannot refer to a book on psychology for information about the

---

[6] B. F. Skinner, "The Science of Learning and the Art of Teaching," *Harvard Educational Review*, **XXIV** (1954), 86-97; J. P. Guilford, *The Nature of Intelligence*, McGraw-Hill, New York, 1967; J. W. Getzels and P. W. Jackson, *Creativity and Intelligence: Explorations with Gifted Children*, Wiley, New York, 1962; Jean Piaget (with B. Inhelder), *The Growth of Logical Thinking from Childhood to Adolescence*, Humanities Press, New York, 1958; *The Moral Judgment of the Child*, Marjorie Gabain, transl., London, Kegan Paul, 1932; *The Psychology of Intelligence*, M. Piercy and D. E. Berlyne, transl., Humanities Press, New York, 1950; *Logic and Psychology*, Basic Books, New York, 1957.

probability with which certain particular experiences at particular ages will produce students who are creative or hard-working. Unfortunately for him, the sciences of man have turned out no theories comparable to those of the natural sciences either in the range of phenomena they explain or in the precision and reliability of the predictions they yield. What they have produced, in addition to a number of controversial theories, are a great many generalizations of limited scope, few of which have won wide acceptance. Both theories and generalizations are of value to the educator, but only if used with due regard for their tentativeness.

Not only are these findings tentative, but they do not as a rule refer to specifically educational phenomena. Take the case of learning theory, which is indirectly relevant to a good deal of educational research. Most learning theorists are concerned with the process of learning in general rather than with the process of teaching particular individuals to learn particular things. Their interest is in learning rather than in education. Educators, on the other hand, are interested in learning from the point of view of instruction. Their concern is less with what happens when learning takes place, particularly when the learning is done by animals, and more with how learning may be made to occur. Their approach is practical, not in the sense of being trivial, but in the sense that its object is to discover how to improve learning of the particular subjects that are taught in schools to pupils of different ages, interests, and aptitudes.[7]

Gathering Data

So far we have considered the nature of educational research as a predominantly applied science. Let us now see how such research is actually carried out. Our first point is the simple but important one that educational research involves making inferences, or coming to conclusions about data. How does the researcher gather these data? He does it by making observations and conducting experiments.

Observational Studies

Large amounts of data about education are acquired by observation alone, without recourse to experimentation. In educational research an

---

[7] Cf. Jerome S. Bruner, "The New Educational Technology," in Alfred de Grazio and David A. Sohn, Eds., *Revolution in Teaching: New Theory, Technology, and Curricula,* Bantam, New York, 1964, p. 5.

"observational study" is generally an attempt to find data characteristic of a group of people who are treated as representative of a more numerous class. For example, an observational study of the recreation habits of California high school girls will seek to ascertain how a sample of high school girls in this state, taken as representative of the entire class of such girls, actually spend their leisure time. Unlike psychologists, educational researchers usually study groups rather than individuals. The reason for this is that most public education in this country is given to groups, and it is therefore the behavior of groups that needs most to be understood.

In education observational studies are of three main kinds: surveys, developmental studies, and differential studies.

Surveys. A survey is the basic form of observational study. Its main purpose is to gather data about a group of people rather than to trace relationships among these data. The data, however, often suggest relationships that can then be traced by developmental or differential studies. In education, surveys are conducted for many purposes. Some gather information about the classroom behavior of teachers, others about children's habits of reading and watching television. Still others collect data about salaries, promotion schedules, and career expectations. The most detailed of all is the school survey, which seeks to put together as much information as possible about every aspect of education in a single school or school system and the community it serves.

In a survey information may be gathered in various ways. One way is by observing people in their natural settings. In a survey of teaching behavior observers visit classrooms and watch teachers in action, recording their characteristics on a checklist and classifying the teachers on a rating form as, perhaps, "above average," "average," or "below average." The researcher may also collect data from observers whom he has not trained himself. For example, he may draw on assessments of teachers made by principals or assessments of principals made by superintendents.

Most surveys make use of a *questionnaire*. This is a set of written questions designed to elicit the information that the survey is seeking. Some questionnaires, consisting of open questions, ask the respondent to answer in his own words. These are a useful way of learning the respondent's opinions but they may produce answers that are irrelevant because unguided. Other questionnaires, made up of closed questions, ask the respondent to choose from a number of answers already listed. Such questionnaires yield data that are easy to tabulate, but they rarely elicit the respondent's deeper feelings and sometimes oversimply his ideas.

The questionnaire saves time and money but it has distinct weaknesses.

For one thing, it does not readily distinguish between snap judgments and well-considered views. Suppose a number of students receive a questionnaire seeking their opinions about different subjects in the curriculum. If they happen to have an unpopular mathematics teacher or if they have just taken a difficult test in French, they may express a dislike for mathematics or French that is merely temporary. Unfortunately the questionnaire will not indicate this unless it is made long and detailed, in which case it is not likely to be answered. Nor does a questionnaire measure at all readily the degree of conviction with which a view is held. Two people answering a questionnaire may both reveal that they are opposed to discussions of drugs and communism in high school, but one of them may easily be persuaded to change his mind whereas the other may be adamant. This difference in conviction will not be registered by an ordinary questionnaire, or at best it will be registered obliquely.

Another means of acquiring information is the *interview*. This has definite advantages over the questionnaire and the written report: the interviewer can persuade the respondent to give his opinions at length, and he can note the significance of tones of voice, gestures, and incidental remarks. Its chief disadvantage is that it is time-consuming.

Interviews may be more or less formal. In some interviews the same questions in the same order are submitted to each respondent, who is asked to answer yes or no or to choose from a set list of alternative answers. Such interviews make for easy tabulation, since they produce limited but comparable data from all subjects. Other interviews begin with a few restricted questions but then allow the respondent to express himself more freely. They therefore provide a modicum of comparable data and a range of less comparable but more illuminating information about people's opinions and the reasons for them.

The researcher will generally use a combination of methods to collect information. Nevertheless, as a rule he can gather data only about a fraction of the total number of people whom he wishes to describe. This fraction is called a *sample* of the population in which he is interested. How then does he ensure that the sample is "representative," that is, that it reproduces accurately the characteristics of the larger population?

One method is that of "random sampling." A random sample is one picked from a hat or read off from a table of random numbers so that each member of the population concerned has an equal chance of being sampled. Actual inclusion may then be regarded as the result of chance rather than of any systematically operating determinant, such as the researcher's preference for certain numbers or letters of the alphabet, which would tend to make the sample less representative.

If the population is large and varied, the researcher will probably use a "stratified sample," or one chosen so as to resemble the larger population in certain important respects. In this case the researcher divides the population into strata according to certain principles and then samples each stratum at random. For example, if he is conducting a survey to predict how people will vote on a school bond issue, he may, before sampling, stratify the population in terms of characteristics known to influence voting, such as age, income, degree of education, and religion. If he uses a "proportionally" stratified sample, he will draw at random from each stratum a number proportional to the actual size of the group in the population. For example, if ten percent of the population are college graduates, he will choose ten percent of his sample from this stratum.

Developmental Studies. A developmental study is more ambitious than a survey. It traces the course of change in a group of people over a period of time. It generally records the maturation of children and adolescents, noting their growth in intelligence, educational achievement, physical characteristics, social maturity, and so forth.

Developmental studies may be *longitudinal* or *cross-sectional*. When carrying out a longitudinal study, the researcher reconstructs the pattern of growth by measuring the same group of children with respect to the same variables at different ages, such as nine, ten, eleven, and twelve. A cross-sectional study is carried out more quickly. Instead of measuring the same group of children at different times, the researcher measures separate groups of children at various ages all at the same time. The average measurement of each group for each variable is then computed and plotted on a curve depicting the course of growth from one age to the next.

Studies of development, like differential studies and experiments, rely heavily on psychometric devices such as tests and inventories. A *test* is a set of standard tasks given to a person so that his performance on them may be appraised in a standard way. The most famous is the intelligence test, which is designed to measure a person's general mental abilities. Alfred Binet devised the prototype of the intelligence test when he was asked by the French Committee on Public Instruction to sit on a committee investigating the problem of "backward" children. In order to distinguish between laziness and real lack of ability, he and his colleague, Simon, constructed a series of graded tests. These tests, which were revised in 1908 and 1911, sought to ascertain a child's "mental age" by measuring his mental performance against the performance fixed as normal for a child of his chronological age. In 1916 Lewis Terman published the Stanford revision of Binet's tests.

Since then the intelligence test has been continuously refined, and many other sorts of test have been developed. *Achievement* tests, for example, are used to measure the proficiency that a person has attained in some subject or skill, such as spelling, arithmetic, or typing. *Aptitude* tests measure his ability to improve his performance in a subject or skill.[8]

Another testlike device is the *projective technique*. This seeks to discover a person's unconscious motivations by requiring him to interpret ambiguous or indefinite materials, such as ink blots, partially obscured pictures, or unfinished sentences, to which he must respond intuitively. His responses are then taken to be a function of his own characteristics rather than of the material itself. The best known projective techniques are the Rorschach Test and the Thematic Apperception Test. For young children similar techniques employ play materials. In the Mosaic Test, for example, the child makes his own designs with small colored tiles, and in the World Test he constructs his own world out of toy objects, animals, and people.

To find out how people interact in groups we use *sociometric techniques,* most of which entail asking each member of a group to name other members whom he prefers most on various criteria. In studies of classroom groups students may be asked to name those pupils with whom they would most like to study, those near whom they would like to sit, and so forth. The answers may be plotted on a *sociogram,* where each person's name is placed in a circle or triangle and the names are connected with lines or arrows (solid for acceptance, broken for rejection) to indicate the interplay of personal relations.

Differential Studies. In educational research differential studies are made more often than any other type of observational study. The aim of a differential study is to find relations between variables as they exist in nature. The study may look for similarities and differences in the characteristics of different groups or in the characteristics of the same group. If the study compares different groups, it is called a "causal comparative" study; if it concentrates on one group, a "correlation" study.

In a causal-comparative study the researcher seeks to find the possible causes of some characteristic by comparing persons who manifest this characteristic with persons who do not. Because the investigation proceeds backward from the characteristic to a range of antecedent circumstances

---

8 Strictly speaking, an inventory is a set of questions about a person's interests or behavior. Many inventories, however, go under the name of tests. Interest tests, for example, are inventories for discovering a person's likes and dislikes, while attitude tests are inventories that elicit his views on various topics.

that may have helped bring it about, the inquiry is said to be made *ex post facto* or after the event. The inquiry moves in the opposite direction, as it were, from an experiment, in which the investigation proceeds forward from some present characteristic (which the researcher manipulates) to its possible effects.[9]

A causal-comparative study enables the researcher to investigate complex states of affairs that contain too many variables (that is, too many varying features) to be handled by present methods of experimentation. A limitation of the causal-comparative study is that it rarely reveals whether a variable that is related to the main characteristic is a cause or a result of that characteristic. For example, when a group of pupils who have been accelerated two grades or more is compared with a group of pupils of matching intelligence who have not been accelerated, the accelerated pupils are usually found to have achieved more. Yet it is impossible to tell by means of a causal-comparative study alone whether the students achieved more because they were accelerated or whether they were accelerated because they had already begun to achieve more.[10]

Whereas causal-comparative studies compare two groups in which the characteristic under investigation (for example, delinquency) is either present or absent, correlational studies compare the members of a single group in which the characteristic is present in varying degrees. They seek to discover whether, and by how much, variations in the main characteristic are associated with variations in one or more other characteristics.

When the characteristics can be measured, the degree to which they are related is represented numerically by a "correlation coefficient." This coefficient always lies between the extremes of $+1$ and -1. If the coefficient is $+1$, the characteristics vary directly; if one increases, so does the other. If it is -1, they vary inversely; if one increases, the other decreases. A coefficient of 0 (zero) indicates that the characteristics are independent of each other, so that one may vary without influencing the other. Thus there are degrees of correlation from perfect positive correlation to no correlation at all and thence to perfect negative correlation.[11]

[9] Sheldon and Eleanor Glueck, *Unraveling Juvenile Delinquency*, Commonwealth Fund, New York, 1950, is a classic causal-comparative study, comparing the behavior of a number of juvenile delinquents with the behavior of some nondelinquents. Characteristics more marked in the delinquents than in the nondelinquents were examined as possible causes of delinquency.

[10] For example, the Gluecks (op. cit.) found that delinquent boys behaved more aggressively than nondelinquent boys, but they could not ascertain whether the former had behaved aggressively before or after becoming delinquent.

[11] An excellent example of a correlational study is James S. Coleman et al.,

Nevertheless, a correlational study does not establish causal connections between the variables it investigates. Two variables may be highly correlated without one being the cause of the other. The correlation may simply reflect the fact that two series of numbers chance to increase or decrease simultaneously. Suppose a high correlation were found between the number of television sets bought in California between 1940 and 1960 and the number of mental defectives certified in the state during the same period. Suppose, that is, that during this time about as many mental defectives were certified as television sets were bought. Not even the most hostile critic of television would claim that either of these variables influenced the other. The correlation between them would almost certainly be a coincidence.[12]

In other cases the nature of the correlation is less easy to determine.[13] Let us take an example. Between 1920 and 1940 the annual increase in the median[14] educational attainment of school leavers was 2.5 percent per year. This was ten times as much as the annual increase between 1875

Equality of Educational Opportunity, U.S. Government Printing Office, Washington, D.C., 1966. This survey collected data at spaced grade levels throughout the nation. The data comprised staff records from some 5000 schools (a sample of five percent), stratified according to geographic region and Standard Metropolitan Statistical Areas, together with about 600,000 student records from grades 1, 3, 6, 9, and 12. The survey found that the student's school achievement was correlated most highly with the group of factors constituting home family background and socioeconomic status. Children of better-educated parents and from better homes achieved more than children from less fortunate families. Parental interest in the child's education also correlated positively with the achievement of students from all socioeconomic levels. Of all school variables (as opposed to student-body variables), the characteristics of the teaching staff were found to correlate most highly with student achievement. These characteristics included years of experience, years of education, socioeconomic background, and whether the teachers originated from or attended school in the school neighborhood.

12 In England and Wales from 1924 to 1937 there was in fact a very high positive correlation of 9.998 between the number of mental defectives certified and the number of radio licenses issued. Cf. G. U. Yule and M. G. Kendall, *An Introduction to the Theory of Statistics,* Griffin, London, 1950, p. 377.

13 Cf. Christopher Jencks, "Social Stratification and Higher Education," *Harvard Educational Review,* **XXXVIII**, 2 (Spring 1968), 274-78.

14 A "median" is an average used in statistics. An ordinary average ("arithmetical mean") is calculated by dividing the sum of a set or "distribution" of numerical data (or "scores") by their number. The median is the middle score of a distribution, the one that has as many scores above it as below it. The mean and the median are equal when the distribution is symmetrical about its middle score and unequal when the distribution is skewed, that is, when it has more extreme scores at one end than at the other.

and 1914. Whereas school leavers during World War I had not as a rule completed the ninth grade, high school leavers at the end of the Depression usually had a diploma. This increase in median educational attainment during the 1920s and 1930s seems to have been followed by a redistribution of income away from the rich during the 1930s and 1940s. The evidence for this is that between 1929 and 1945 the share of national income going to the richest 5 percent of the population fell from about 30 percent to 20 percent. Was the increase in median attainment a factor causing the redistribution of income? It is possible that because children were better educated than before, the children of 95 percent of the country's parents increased their earning power and their share of the national income more than the children of the wealthiest 5 percent. But it is also possible that although better education had *some* effect on income redistribution, the *prime* cause of this redistribution was some further factor not mentioned at all, such as the Depression or World War II.

It also sometimes happens that *both* correlated variables may be correlated positively with a third variable that is the cause of them. To return to our first example, although almost certainly there would be no causal connection between the purchase of television sets and the registration of mental defectives, both these variables *might* be linked causally to a third variable such as increasing industrialization. In any case, a correlational study will rarely settle the matter. The most effective way to verify a causal connection is to conduct an experiment.

Experiments

Causality. To see why this is so we must first understand the scientist's notion of "cause," a notion that does not vary appreciably from that proposed by Galileo in the sixteenth century. According to Galileo, the cause X of an event Y is that state of affairs that is invariably followed by Y and in the absence of which Y does not occur. As Galileo put it, ". . . only that may be properly called a cause which is always followed by the effect, and which when removed takes away the effect."[15] This is sometimes expressed by saying that X is the cause of Y when X is the necessary and sufficient condition for the occurrence of Y. X causes Y in the sense that Y only occurs when X occurs and X never occurs without Y occurring also.

[15] Galileo Galilei, *The Assayer*, **XIV**, in *The Controversy on the Comets of 1618*, Stillman Drake and C. D. O'Malley, transl., University of Pennsylvania, 1960, p. 219.

The causal relation, however, is the only one of temporal conjunction or succession. To say that X causes Y is to claim, not that X *makes* Y happen, but rather that *when* X happens Y also happens. This was shown in the 18th century by the Scottish philosopher David Hume. Most philosophers before Hume had maintained that, if an event X causes another event Y, there must be a *necessary* connection between these events such that if X happens Y must happen also. To this Hume objected that no such connection is discoverable in experience. Take what happens when one billiard ball strikes another and causes it to fall into a pocket. However many instruments we move onto the billiard table, all that we can ever observe is that one ball traveling at a certain speed strikes another and that the other rolls at a certain speed into the pocket. There is an impact and a subsequent movement, but there is no discernible connection between them that would make it self-contradictory to deny that next time an impact of the same force might be followed by no movement at all. In short, when one ball strikes another the latter moves but does not *have* to.

Why, then, do we feel so sure that it *will* move? We feel sure, said Hume, because whenever we have seen one billiard ball strike another at all forcibly in the past, we have always observed that the second ball has moved immediately afterward. Our confidence is a sign of our expectation, repeatedly confirmed before, that when one ball strikes another the latter will move. To say, then, that X is the cause of Y is not to assert that there is any necessary connection between them. It is to state that events of type X have always been observed to precede events of type Y and that events of type Y have always been observed to follow events of type X.

How do we verify that one event is the cause of another? Let us suppose we observe that an event of kind X is regularly preceded by a set of events or conditions of type $A, B, C, D, \ldots$ etc. Let us also suppose we come to suspect that if an event of type A does not occur, an event of kind X does not occur either. To verify that A is the cause of X, or at any rate a causal factor in the production of X, we create a set of events or conditions of type $B, C, D, \ldots$ etc. but excluding an event or condition of kind A. If we find that the set of particular events $b_1, c_1, d_1, \ldots$ is *not* followed by x_1, an event of type X, we infer provisionally that events of type A are causally related to events of kind X. We make this inference because we have found that an event of kind X, which takes place when an event of kind A occurs, fails to take place when an event of kind A does not occur.

Experimentation. What we have just described is the principle of experimentation. In an experiment the researcher actually alters or "manipulates" certain conditions in order to observe whether changes in any of these conditions are accompanied by changes in the phenomenon in which he is interested. He manipulates these conditions by varying one (or more) of them at a time while holding the remainder constant, so as to determine which changed condition is giving rise to changes in the phenomenon itself. This phenomenon, the object of the experiment, is called the "dependent" variable, because the degree to which it is present (or occurs) is, or is thought to be, dependent on the degree to which certain antecedent conditions are present (or occur). These antecedent conditions are known as "independent" variables.

The aim of an experiment, then, is to discover a relationship between the dependent variable and one or more independent variables such that, whenever the independent variable(s) are present to a certain degree (or can be given a certain value), the dependent variable is present to a corresponding degree (or assumes a corresponding value). The experimenter searches for this presumed relationship by manipulating the independent variable(s) and observing the effects on the dependent variable.

Why is such a relationship considered to be a causal one? An event of type X is said to be a cause of an event of type Y if Y occurs when *and only when* X occurs. We can be sure that this is the case if we make X occur and observe that Y occurs and if we make X cease to occur and observe that Y does not occur. More technically, we can ascertain that the relation is a causal one if we impose at will different values on X and then note that Y assumes certain corresponding values. Varying X in order to produce variations in Y is the mode of procedure of an experiment.

Experimental Design. Experiments are of two main kinds: those in which a single independent variable is manipulated at a time, the other independent variables being held constant, and those in which a number of independent variables are manipulated simultaneously. The first sort of experiment is said to have a "single-variable design," the second a "factorial design." Here we will consider the single-variable design.

In educational research most experiments are carried out on the behavior or performance of groups of persons ("subjects"). In a common single-variable experiment, two groups of subjects are used, one—the control group—being employed as a check on the effect exerted on the dependent variable (the performance or behavior being investigated) by conditions not actually manipulated in the experiment. The procedure is to take two equivalent groups of subjects, pretest them on the dependent variable, expose one but not the other to the experimental treatment (the alteration of the independent variable), and test them again on the dependent variable. Any influence exerted on the dependent variable by nonmanipulated (or external) conditions between the pretest and the post-test will be reflected in the scores of the control group. Therefore, the effect brought about by the experimental treatment can be attributed to whatever change takes place in the experimental group *over and above* the change that occurs in the control group.

Let us imagine that an experimenter wishes to test the effectiveness of a new visual aid. Two equivalent groups of students are chosen and pre-tested on the dependent variable, say performance in algebra. The control group is taught in the usual way, while the experimental group is taught by the same teacher using the new aid. After both groups have been taught for the same length of time, they are given the same, or a com-parable, examination in algebra. If the experimental group scores better on the average than the control group, the experimenter may infer tentatively that teaching with the new visual aid is more effective than the conventional method of teaching this subject.

Limits to Experimentation. In educational research, however, as in the behavioral sciences generally, experiments play a smaller role than they do in the natural sciences. There are a number of reasons for this. One is the sheer complexity of human behavior and its setting. In any human act or performance, so many variables are involved that it is hard to guess which of them are causative factors and what relative weight each carries. Consequently it is difficult to set up experiments in which all the relevant variables may be manipulated and controlled exactly.[16]

Another limitation is the difficulty of postulating ideal types of be-havior or setting and approximating them under experimental conditions. The natural scientist can posit ideal entities, such as frictionless surfaces or perfect vacuums, and can then reproduce them closely enough in the laboratory to formulate and test laws that can be applied to the real world, provided that specifiable allowances are made. For example,

[16] Cf. Hendrik D. Gideonse, "The Relative Impact of Instructional Variables: The Policy Implications of Research," *Teachers College Record*, **LXIX**, 7 (April 1968), 628: ". . . recent surveys constituted the best argument for not pursuing the study of experimental research very far. For in choosing the variables they proposed to study, the surveys reveal the rich complexity of factors which are involved in producing student achievement, and because they do, they call into question the validity, for policy purposes, of experimental research on the scale that it has been attempted in the past. Most of that research has manipulated only one, or, at best, a very few variables. Any conclusions derived are thus of limited policy value. There are virtually no experimental efforts which attempt to establish intervention patterns with a large number of variables. Because of this circumstance it is necessary to depend heavily upon the major research surveys which have been undertaken in recent years."

Galileo's law of free fall is formulated for bodies moving in a vacuum, although terrestrial bodies generally move through some resisting medium. When the law is used to compute the speed of an actual body, certain qualifications are made to close the gap between the ideal case and the real one. The educator, on the other hand, even if he can postulate such ideal entities (which is itself doubtful), cannot create ideal laboratory conditions in which he can conduct experiments to verify hypotheses about the behavior of these entities and the allowances to be made when the hypotheses are used to account for actual occurrences. An educator can no more construct, manipulate, and observe an ideal school than an economist can an ideal economy.

There are also strong moral and social constraints on experiments with human beings. One cannot, for example, abandon a child in the wilderness to learn what effect the absence of social contact may have on his personality. Nor can one, for experiment's sake, remove the frontal lobes from a teacher or supervisor in order to investigate the functions of the lobes in guiding intelligent educative behavior. One can compensate in part by conducting experiments on animals, but only in part—for findings about the behavior of rats and pigeons under abnormal laboratory conditions cannot readily be generalized to explain the normal behavior of human beings who talk and live in a social environment.

Educational research, then, makes more use of observational studies than it does of experiments. To say this is not to claim that educational research is unscientific, but rather to point out that here, as in all sciences of human behavior, the opportunity to manipulate suspected causal connections is far more limited than in physics or chemistry.

Understanding the Data

The basic purpose of educational research, however, is not merely to gather data but to understand them. We achieve an understanding of the data of education by describing and explaining them. Description turns raw data into classified facts; explanation tells us why these facts are so and not otherwise. Description, that is, answers the question, "What are the facts?"; explanation, the question, "Why are the facts this way?"

Classifications (Taxonomies)

To turn data into facts, we apply sets of concepts to them. These are known as classification schemes or "taxonomies," and the act of applying them is called "classification."

Since the data about education are numerous and varied, it is important to have terms that describe them accurately and that can figure in testable generalizations. For once we have classified data as facts, we seek to make true statements about classes of facts, that is, we seek to generalize. For example, in order to explain the effects on learning of different styles of teaching, or the effects on pupil motivation of different kinds of teacher personality, we need to know what these teaching styles and personality types are. If our classification scheme picks out facts about teaching and teachers that are superficial, or if its terms are loosely defined, the models and generalizations in which these terms may appear are likely to be superficial or ambiguous too.[17]

No two items of data, in education or elsewhere, are identical, but every datum is like some other datum in certain respects. Classifying data as facts entails ordering them in terms of these common features. For example, a botanist scanning the trees in a park will notice that some of them have similar leaves, bark, and fruit, so he will group them together in a class, that of pine trees perhaps, or oak trees. No two pine trees are identical. They differ in size and shape and in the number of their branches and leaves. But the botanist overlooks these differences and groups the trees together in terms of at least one shared characteristic.

However, pines are only one kind of tree. To classify trees comprehensively, we need a set of concepts that will not only differentiate all things that are trees from all things that are plants or stones but will also identify different species within the class of trees itself. Thus, a taxonomy divides some set or class of things, such as trees, crystals, or teaching practices, into subclasses. The things thus classified are called "members" of the class or subclass. Each subclass is designated by a concept defining the group of characteristics required for membership in that subclass. The more characteristics this concept subsumes, the greater will be the membership of the subclass, and therefore the broader the generalizations into which its members may enter.

Classifying schemes may define, order, or measure facts. A purely definitional scheme categorizes facts in terms of distinct features or attributes but does not arrange them into any significant order. Most schemes in education are definitional. Let me mention three that have been applied to the behavior of teachers.

---

[17] For a technical discussion of the uses of classification schemes in the behavioral sciences, see Richard S. Rudner, *Philosophy of Social Science*, Prentice-Hall, Englewood Cliffs, N.J., 1966, pp. 28-47.

In 1960, after analyzing the data gathered in a survey of teachers across the nation, David Ryans put forward a threefold classification of the personal characteristics exhibited in teaching activities. Teaching, he said, may be classified as (1) warm and friendly, (2) systematic and businesslike, or (3) imaginative. This taxonomy helped him correlate the facts he had described. He found that among primary-school teachers all three characteristics are highly correlated, that is to say, teachers who are friendly are generally businesslike and also imaginative. Among secondary-school teachers, on the other hand, characteristics are more nearly independent, and teachers who are friendly are neither more nor less likely to be businesslike than are those who are aloof.[18] Three years later Ryans proposed a classification of teaching activities. Teaching behavior, he said, may be divided into the following classes: (1) motivating-reinforcing, (2) presenting-explaining-demonstrating, (3) organizing-planning-managing, (4) evaluating, and (5) counseling-advising.[19]

Then in 1964, B. Othanel Smith and his associates at Illinois University proposed a scheme for classifying intellectual operations—such as defining, explaining, and proving—that are involved in dialogues between teachers and pupils. They contended that classroom dialogues are marked by twelve basic forms of verbal exchange, each characterized by a distinct intellectual operation and each possessing its own intellectual structure.[20]

Generalizations

In the long run, however, educational research seeks to do more than classify what happens in and in relation to the school. Research also aims to explain why these things happen by showing that they

[18] David Ryans, *Characteristics of Teachers*, American Council on Education, Washington, D.C., 1960.

[19] David Ryans, "Teacher Behavior Theory and Research: Implications for Teacher Education," *The Journal of Teacher Education*, XIV (September 1963), 275.

[20] B. Othanel Smith and Milton O. Meux, *A study of the Logic of Teaching*, Bureau of Educational Research, College of Education, University of Illinois, Urbana, 1962. This report is summarized by Smith and Meux, "Logical Dimensions of Teaching Behavior," in Bruce J. Biddle and William J. Ellena, Eds., *Contemporary Research on Teacher Effectiveness*, Holt, Rinehart and Winston, New York, 1964, pp. 127-164. A sequel to the first work is B. Othanel Smith, Milton Meux, Jerrold Coombs, and Graham Nuthall, *A Tentative Report on the Strategies of Teaching*, Bureau of Educational Research, College of Education, University of Illinois, Urbana, 1964. This work examines, not the logical operations involved in classroom discourse, but "the larger maneuvers having to do with the control of the subject matter of instruction."

happen regularly when and only when certain other things happen. A statement that something occurs when and only when something else occurs is called an empirical generalization, and it takes the form "If X, then Y," where X is an event of one kind and Y an event of another. An empirical generalization may also state that when X happens, there is a *certain probability* that Y will happen, in which case the generalization is said to be a "statistical" one. Or it may state that, when X happens, Y usually happens or tends to happen, in which case the generalization is called a "tendency" statement.

In educational research it is not easy to make simple and uniform generalizations of any scope. The reason for this is that most generalizations in education are about human beings, who behave, as a rule, neither uniformly nor simply. To appreciate this, let us contrast what happens when a physical object is struck with what happens when a child is struck. When a man strikes a pane of glass, it shatters; when he strikes a steel door, it is unaffected. After observing such facts a number of times a physicist might generalize, "Whenever glass is struck, it shatters" and "Whenever steel is struck, it does not shatter." Now suppose a child is struck by a teacher. If a child were a simple organism, he would probably fight back, stand, or run away. Since he is anything but simple, he may react in these or in many other ways. He may insult the teacher, forgive him, ask for an explanation, plan revenge, cry, blame himself, swagger to the class, or ignore the whole thing. Hence we cannot generalize that "when a child is struck by a teacher, he insults the teacher," or "Children struck by teachers meditate revenge." Each of these generalizations may be true of some children, but none is true of all. Moreover the same child may react differently, depending on which teacher struck him, when he did so, and why.

Thus in the present state of educational research there seem to be two courses open to the investigator who wishes to generalize: to make generalizations that are precise but limited or to make generalizations that are broad but vague. The first course is the one usually followed. It is defended on the grounds that the main purpose of educational research is to produce information that will help educators make particular improvements in the day-to-day enterprise of schooling. Limited generalizations about specific educational problems will help us solve these problems, whereas broad generalizations that must ignore the complex interplay of actual variables will not. Jerome Bruner, for example, has said:

> I would as soon see an end to the conventional educational psychology course and its assertions about learning—so full of broad vacuities. Let

us begin instead with a concrete psychology that occupies itself with wily strategies for learning specific things like mathematics, or geography, or sonnets.[21]

The second course, to make generalizations that are broad but vague, is to put forward "tendency statements." A tendency statement asserts that a given relation holds between certain sorts of events provided that certain other conditions, not all of which can be specified, also hold. It asserts that if X happens, Y *tends* to happen. An isolated tendency statement cannot yield precise predictions, because it does not specify all the conditions under which the event to be predicted takes place; indeed, it may mention very few of them. Consequently, a tendency statement is most useful when it is linked with other tendency statements in a system of deductively related propositions from which predictions can be derived that are confirmable by observation or experimentation. An isolated tendency statement tells us little; a system of tendency statements may tell us a great deal.

Models

A system of tendency statements is sometimes called a *model.*[22] In educational research, however, the term "model" is usually applied more informally to any set of assumptions that provides a rational conception of some area to be investigated. The model consists of a set of statements

[21] Jerome S. Bruner, "On Teaching Teachers," in *Current Issues in Higher Education,* Proceedings of the Nineteenth Annual National Conference on Higher Education, Association for Higher Education, Washington, D.C., 1964, p. 98. Cf. also Michael Scriven, "The Philosophy of Science in Educational Research," *Review of Educational Research,* **XXX,** 5 (December 1960), 424.

[22] In the philosophy of science the term "model" has a number of meanings. We refer here to the sense in which the term is used most often in current educational research. For a general treatment of models in science, see Ernest Nagel, *The Structure of Science,* Harcourt, Brace, and World, New York, 1961, pp. 107-117; R. B. Braithwaite, *Scientific Explanation,* Cambridge University, 1953, Ch. IV; and "Models in the Empirical Sciences," in Ernest Nagel, Patrick Suppes, and Alfred Tarski, Eds., *Logic, Methodology and Philosophy of Science,* Proceedings of the 1960 International Congress, Stanford University, 1962, pp. 224-231. In education the most comprehensive, thoroughgoing treatment of models is Marc Belth's *Education as a Discipline,* Allyn and Bacon, Boston, 1965. Actually, for Belth, p. 60, education itself is a "matter of transmitting the models through which the world is explainable." Models are "windows through which we see the world and our own transactions with the world, and they make the world meaningful to us in their own terms." Newton, Einstein, Freud, Marx all studied aspects of reality as revealed through their own individual conceptual systems, their own theoretical models.

(usually tendency statements, sometimes statistical generalizations), some or none of which may be connected deductively, about the relationships that the researcher hopes to find.

Formulations of this kind are employed in education because, where there are few established laws of any scope and precision, the scientist must necessarily speculate well in advance of the evidence if he is to proceed beyond any but the most limited generalizations. He seeks to reduce the element of speculation and to increase the genuinely explanatory power of his hypotheses by proposing groups of statements. Even if these are only loosely related, they cover more of the field than do statements proposed and tested in isolation. What is more important, since they are related, they generate further statements, either by suggestion or by logical deduction, and so lead to fresh discoveries.

Such a model is valued less for its literal truth than for its capacity to generate useful hypotheses. What matters is not the accuracy of the assumptions made in the propositions of the model but whether making these assumptions enables us to formulate empirical generalizations that can in principle be verified. It is postulated, unlike a theory or a generalization, not as the completed explanation of some class of phenomena but rather as a starting point for investigating these phenomena. Even if the data gathered through an experiment or survey tend to confirm the model, the latter will still be regarded primarily as a tool for further investigation.

Often, however, the researcher must remain content with a limited explanation of the facts he has gathered. Instead of formulating a generalization or tendency statement to explain some kind of behavior, he will state one or more of the factors that *seem* to be responsible for this behavior. These statements will be statements of correlations, or possible causal connections, holding between the behavior itself and various accompanying circumstances. Most surveys in education lead to such statements of possible causality.

Since human behavior is complex and variable, the phenomenon the researcher sets out to explain, such as performance at English composition in high school, may turn out to be the result of many alternative combinations of conditions. Even after exhaustive investigation he may be able to specify neither the sum of possible prior conditions nor any single combination of such conditions, but only certain conditions that he has found.[23] Nevertheless, to point to one possible causal factor, or

---

[23] Cf. C. A. Mace, "Causal Laws in Psychology," in *Politics, Psychology and Art*, Aristotelian Society, Supplementary Vol. **XXIII**, Harrison, London, 1949, pp. 63-66.

set of such factors, responsible for some state of affairs is to move a step nearer to understanding this state of affairs and is a great help to the practicing educator. As we saw earlier, it is of great importance to know that one of the main factors that may influence a student's achievement is the amount of professional experience his teacher has had. Much of our scientific knowledge of education is a product of the gradual accumulation of such correlations.

Summary

We began this chapter by considering the general character of scientific educational research. We saw that educational research is mainly practical in purpose, being concerned with the finding of knowledge that can be used to improve the quality of schooling. We also saw that educational research draws heavily on the behavioral sciences for fundamental knowledge to serve its own purposes.

We looked next at the means by which researchers gather data about education. The most important of these means is the survey, which is an attempt to discover the data characteristic of a representative sample of some wider population. A field survey, using direct observation, interviews, and questionnaires, seeks to collect data without, as a rule, establishing correlations among them. A developmental study, which is more ambitious, seeks to trace the course of change in a group of people over a period of time. It relies more heavily than the field survey on psychometric devices such as tests and inventories. A differential study, still more ambitious, attempts to discover relationships between variables. It may locate these relations in the behavior patterns of contrasted groups or in those of a single group. Nevertheless, the correlations it discovers are only potentially causal connections. To establish genuine causality we usually must conduct an experiment.

In an experiment the researcher actually manipulates the variables that seem to be correlated with the phenomenon he is studying. He does so by varying one or more of them at a time, while holding the remainder constant, in order to find out which of them influences the phenomenon and by how much. Experiments in which one variable is manipulated at a time are said to have a single-variable design. Those in which a number of variables are manipulated simultaneously have a factorial design. In educational research, however, the opportunity to conduct experiments is limited by (a) the large number of variables relevant to most of the phenomena in which we are interested, (b) the difficulty of reproducing ideal states of affairs in laboratories, and (c) moral and social constraints on experimentation with human beings.

Research: Content and Method | 451

We then considered ways in which the data gathered by educators can be described and explained. Describing data scientifically involves classifying them as facts, and explaining facts often involves generalizing about them. Universal laws, however, are rare in educational research, because human beings behave, as a rule, neither uniformly nor simply. Hence, most generalizations in education are tendency statements asserting regularities that hold under unspecified or partly specified conditions. Many inquiries in education, however, do not lead to generalizations at all but rather to statements of correlations that may possibly be causal connections. Another common formulation in educational research is the model, which is a set of assumptions providing a conception of a field and serving as an aid to further investigation.

References

◆◆◆

The best introduction to the subject of educational research is Lee J. Cronbach and Patrick Suppes, Eds., *Research for Tomorrow's Schools: Disciplined Inquiry for Education* (Macmillan, New York, 1969, 281 pp.). This work is the report of the distinguished Committee on Educational Research of the National Academy of Education. A detailed study of the organization and funding of educational research is Robert F. Lazarsfeld and Sam D. Sieber, *Organizing Educational Research: An Exploration* (Prentice-Hall, Englewood Cliffs, N.J., 1964).

Among the best texts on the methods of educational research are David R. Cook, *A Guide to Educational Research* (Allyn and Bacon, Boston, 1965); Robert M. W. Travers, *An Introduction to Educational Research* (Macmillan, New York, 1969); William Wiersma, *Research Methods in Education: An Introduction* (Lippincott, Philadelphia, 1969); and John E. Wise, *Research in Education* (Heath, Boston, 1967).

The outstanding work on most fields of educational research is N. L. Gage, Ed., *Handbook of Research on Teaching* (Rand McNally, Chicago, 1963, 1218 pp.). Among the contributors are Benjamin S. Bloom, May Brodbeck, Harry S. Broudy, Donald T. Campbell, J. W. Getzels, P. W. Jackson, and Julian C. Stanley.

Recent findings in the main branches of educational research are reviewed by specialists in the *Review of Educational Research*, **XXXIX**, 5 (December 1969).

PART FIVE

STRUCTURAL
FOUNDATIONS

21

Organization and Administration

Erick Lindman

❖❖❖

A persistent distrust of centralized authority has always characterized American politics. The framers of the Constitution harbored a deep-seated suspicion of men who wielded political power, especially rulers who were remote and inaccessible. To them a benevolent dictatorship was a contradiction in terms.

The wariness of centralized political authority and concentration of power left its imprint on the organization and control of public education. The omission of any reference to education in the Constitution reflected, in part, the prevailing attitude of the colonial period that education was a proper function of churches and other privately endowed institutions. Those who, at the time of the formation of the Constitution, recognized the need to provide free schools at public expense saw no reason to delegate this function to the Federal Government. Some members of the Constitutional Convention believed that the general welfare clause in the Constitution would permit the Federal Government to enter the field of education to the extent that it might be necessary in the national interest. Thus, primary responsibility for public education was left to the individual states, and the Federal Government has exercised only a supplementary relationship to public education.

The traditional distrust of remote, centralized political authority is also seen in the local school-district system prevalent throughout the United States. State legislatures delegated broad powers to local authorities, and control was usually placed in lay boards of education.

Local School System

The school district and school board symbolize local control of education in America. School districts vary in size from a one-room district employing only a single teacher for a dozen or fewer children to the city school systems in New York, Chicago, or Los Angeles. Efforts have been made in many states to improve the basic character of school districts by reorganizing the smaller ones into larger units. Such reorganization programs have usually sought to preserve local control of schools while creating larger administrative units and consolidating responsibility for both elementary and secondary schools under one school board. But these efforts have often encountered determined political opposition, especially in the rural areas of America. Many rural people firmly believe that the elimination of the one-room school and the transportation of children to larger attendance centers, along with the transfer of control of their schools to a more remote school board, threatens cherished local control. Since school-district reorganization requires approval of state legislatures, which have often been dominated by rural representation, achievement of improved districts has been slow in most states. During the early 1930s there were 125,000 school districts in the United States. By 1970 the number of local school districts operating public schools was reduced to approximately 18,000.

Moreover, the patterns and goals of school-district organization are not the same in all states. In some states, especially in the North and West, the model district is considered to be a large, central high school and its several satellite elementary schools. Such consolidated school districts are usually subject to limitations of size, based on the areas of existing communities and the time required to transport students to the high school. Their boundaries often coincide with small towns and the immediate areas they serve.

In other states, especially in the Southeast, the school districts are often coterminous with the county. In these states each county is a school administrative unit. In a typical county school administrative unit, there are several high schools and, of course, many more elementary schools. This plan of organization is defined by many as more efficient than the school district that approximates a small town in size.

Regional differences in the size and number of school districts are marked. The Southeastern states, in which 22 percent of all public school students are enrolled, have only 10 percent of the total number of school districts. On the other hand, the central plains states, where 8 percent of the public school students are enrolled, have 25 percent of the school districts.

Variations in school-district organizational patterns among individual states are even more striking. For the 1969-70 school year, the Research Division of the National Education Association reported 1600 school districts in Nebraska, 1219 in Texas, and 800 in Minnesota. At the other extreme, fewer than 40 school districts were reported for each of the following states: Rhode Island, Delaware, Maryland, Nevada, and Alaska. One state, Hawaii, has no local school districts; its public schools are administered directly by the state department of education.[1]

These different approaches to school-district organization lead to corresponding differences in the responsibilities that are assigned to county school superintendents. In states that have small school districts, including large numbers of one-room schools, the county superintendent has a full-time job supervising teaching in the rural schools and helping rural, local school boards to select teachers and perform their own duties. Under these conditions the county superintendent of schools is essentially an adviser to the many rural boards, but *authority* in most school matters is vested in the boards.

In a state that has carried school-district organization forward so that all school districts include a large high school and the nearby elementary schools, the county school superintendent may have only two or three school districts under his wing, each employing a full-time school superintendent. Under these conditions the county superintendent spends less time advising local school boards; instead, he serves as an intermediary between the local school districts and the state. He may also be responsible for operating special services, such as audiovisual libraries and special classes for handicapped children, when the independent school districts are not large enough to provide them.

Where a county-unit type of school organization prevails, the county school superintendent administers the school system. Thus, the county school superintendent in American education is an officer whose basic responsibilities and duties differ greatly from state to state. To some extent these differences reflect the nature of county government in the

---

[1] *Estimates of School Statistics,* 1969-70, Research Division, National Education Association (December 1964), p. 26.

different states. In New England, county services are extremely limited, and a supervisory union of several small, independent school systems is sometimes established to perform the functions carried on by the county school superintendent in other states. In the Southeast, historically, the county has been a very active unit of government, and it is not surprising to find in this region that the county has frequently become the administrative unit for the operation of public schools. The number and size of counties in each state also affects their suitability for the administration of public schools. There are 254 counties in Texas, but only three in Delaware and none in Alaska. Under these conditions the relationship between county government and local school districts cannot be uniform.

Local Boards of Education

Even more significant than the number and size of local school districts is the nature of the authority vested in them. In general, state legislatures have placed the governance of school districts under locally chosen boards of education that have been granted broad powers to operate public elementary and secondary schools. These powers are exercised with a high degree of independence from other local governmental agencies. Indeed, one of the significant differences between American school boards and the local education authorities in England is the fiscal and administrative independence of the American school boards. Most American boards of education determine their own local school tax rates under state limitations and procedures, which do not require approval by county or municipal governmental agencies.

The American school board as it is known today developed from the school committees, which, during the early nineteenth century, were appointed to formulate programs of study and to select and evaluate teachers. The competence of an elected board of education or committee of lay citizens to perform these functions has been questioned from time to time throughout our history. Predictions have been made that school boards would be replaced by a more suitable means of controlling public schools.

The American school board, however, has adjusted to changed conditions. In the larger cities and consolidated rural schools, boards of education have delegated responsibility for the administration of the school system to professional school administrators, retaining only policy-making power and general oversight of the educational program. Clarification of the relation between the policy-making responsibility of the school board and the executive responsibility of the school superintendent has helped school boards and school superintendents to work harmoniously.

Because school boards, most of which are elected by the people on a nonpartisan basis, operate under powers granted by the state legislature, their authority is limited. For example, the school board usually has power to employ, assign, and dismiss teachers, but the board can employ only teachers who hold valid, state-issued teaching certificates. Moreover, if a teacher is to be discharged, the procedure is usually spelled out carefully in state law to prevent arbitrary or capricious dismissal.

But more important than the legal responsibilities of a modern school board is its key role as a communication center between the public on the one hand and the professional staff of the school on the other. To do its job effectively, the school board must be able to sense the wishes of the community as a whole and understand the problems and issues that concern the professional staff of the school. In large-city school systems, the problems of school management are so complex and so extensive that no school board could possibly devote sufficient time to familiarize itself with all the important issues. Under these conditions, the school board usually concerns itself with public relations and broad policy matters, leaving the administering of the school system to the school superintendent. This division of responsibility has enabled lay boards of education, with the help of professional superintendents, to manage the vast American public-education enterprise.

Decentralization of School Governance in the Great Cities

While the process of reorganization of rural and suburban school districts moves doggedly ahead, making fewer and bigger school districts, a conviction is growing that some school districts are already too big. In the great cities, large and often cumbersome bureaucracies have been created to cope with the complex school problems. These bureaucracies respond slowly to community pressures and seem insensitive to conflicting demands of school patrons. Stability is a virtue when the public is pleased with school programs; but, during periods of dissatisfaction, stability becomes bureaucratic arrogance.

For these reasons, the demand for decentralization of large-city school systems has been intensified during recent years. As so often happens when administrative reorganization is proposed to change the power structure of an institution, there is more interest in the location of new power centers than in sound management principles. Moreover, words lose their neutrality and become weapons in the struggle.

There are three distinctly different approaches to decentralization of large-city school systems. The first and most drastic is the creation of separate school districts within the city, each with its own board of education and its own school tax. Each such school district would have powers and duties equivalent to those accorded suburban school districts. Under this arrangement, the city school district would cease to exist; its assets and liabilities, as well as its responsibilities, would be transferred to the several, perhaps scores, of newly created school districts located within the city.

Another approach to decentralization requires no change in the legal authority of the city board of education, but involves delegation of more authority to school principals and "advisory committees" for each school or for a group of schools. Under this arrangement, the chain of command is unchanged; the principal is responsible to the superintendent and through him to the city school board. However, he is required to meet and confer with an advisory group representing, for the most part, parents of pupils in his school. He is also given greater freedom to plan and administer his school. Directives issued by the city school board, or by the superintendent, are less confining. The school principal is expected to communicate with his constituents, interpret the school program to them, and modify it in response to their advice. Under this arrangement, the principal's duties and opportunities for leadership are broadened, but his ultimate responsibility and accountability is to the city superintendent and the city board of education.

Between these two extremes—the creation of new school districts and the mere delegation of greater responsibility to school principals—are a number of proposals that would create, under the city school board, several semi-independent school "districts," each with a governing board with limited powers. These proposals usually leave the money-raising responsibility, as well as the responsibility for school-plant maintenance and operation, with the citywide school board, delegating control over instruction to the "subdistrict" boards of education. One of the most controversial issues under such an arrangement relates to the power of hire, fire, or transfer teachers and school principals. If this power is retained by the citywide board of education, the "subdistrict" board has little effective control over the instructional program. On the other hand, if this power is transferred to the "subdistrict" board, teachers may lose their tenure rights and be subject to capricious dismissal by the "subdistrict" board. It was this very issue that lead to a lengthy school strike in New York City in 1968.

Regardless of the type of decentralization proposed, the chief arguments advanced favoring decentralization are:

1. Cooperation between the home and the school, so essential to better education in the ghettos, would be enhanced.

2. Teacher accountability to the community would be more direct, and hence more effective.

3. The community, including parents and students, would take pride in the school. It would become "our school," not "their school." There would be fewer broken windows, more effort to beautify the school, and, in addition, come a greater effort to learn.

Opponents of decentralization usually point out that inequalities in educational programs would be increased. Subdistrict boards would differ greatly in their competence and dedication to school improvement. Some might wish to use the school for personal gain or propaganda purposes.

If separate independent school districts are created, there would be great differences in taxable wealth per student, and the ghetto schools would lack the taxable resources to do their more difficult job. Moreover, the creation of separate districts or subdistricts would probably increase de facto segregation.

Decentralization by itself represents a superficial administrative re-organization that would contribute little to correct a fundamental break-down in the child-rearing process in American cities. The child needs the support of a stable home, the sympathetic understanding of able, dedicated teachers, and the hope that he can earn his way in America. Bringing the home and the school closer together and restoring faith in America as the land of opportunity must be the real target of educational change. Decentralization that fails to make progress in this direction is not worth the time and energy required.

The State Department of Education

The movement to increase the effectiveness of American schools by expanding the size of local school administrative units through unification and consolidation has been accompanied by growing acceptance of responsibility for education by state governments. Every state has a chief state school officer who is responsible for some aspects of elementary and secondary education. In some states the chief state school officer is called the State Commissioner of Education, and in others, the Superintendent of Public Instruction. Chief state school officers in 26 states are appointed by state boards of education; in 20 states they are elected by popular vote; and in 4 states they are appointed by governors. Although in most states a constitutional amendment is required to change the method of selecting chief state school officers, there has been a marked trend since the Second World War toward appointment by state boards of education. In 1940 only eight chief state school officers were appointed by state boards of education.[2]

This trend reflects the changing responsibilities of chief state school officers from political to professional leadership, in addition to an effort to separate education from partisan politics. In many states that continue to choose their chief state school officers by popular vote, the law provides for their election on a nonpartisan ballot.

The chief state school officer, his assistants, and the state board of education, are collectively known as the state department of education. Functions performed by this department are usually classified into three categories. First, there is the regulatory function, including accreditation of schools, certification of teachers, and enforcement of health and safety standards in schools throughout the state. Second is the operational function—maintenance of special schools for the deaf and for the blind, the running of teachers' college, and the administering of state libraries. Finally, there is the leadership function, including research and planning, and the promotion of public interest and support for the improvement of schools. These general functions are typical of most state departments of education, but the specific functions assigned differ from one state to another.

The greater educational responsibilities assumed by state governments have been accompanied by a rapid increase in the duties and activities of state departments of education. An indication of the change is found in the increased number of employees in these departments. In 1900 there was an average of four employees in each state department of education, and most of these were clerks dealing with statistics and school lands. At that time, five chief state school officers had no staff assistants, not even a secretary or a clerk. By 1950, the average number of employees had increased from four to 126, approximately half of whom were professional educators. Thus, in a period of fifty years, the state department of education had grown from a small statistical unit to a major department of state government. The rapid growth of the professional staffs of state departments has continued to the present.

Nowadays, the state department of education occupies a prominent position in the professional leadership of public schools. There are now fifty statewide school systems assuming basic responsibility for public education and sharing with local communities, on a partnership basis, accountability for the operation of schools. The strengthening of state

---

[2] *State Education Structure and Organization,* U.S. Department of Health, Education, and Welfare, Government Printing Office, Washington, D.C., 1964, p. 20.

leadership has done much to compensate for weaknesses inherent in the small school-district system.

Much of the growth of state departments of education is a direct result of increased federal participation in education. Most of the federal programs are administered through such departments, where responsibility for direction and supervision is lodged. Prior to 1950 approximately 50 percent of the work of these departments related directly to federal programs such as vocational education, school lunches, veteran education, disposal of federal surplus property to educational institutions. It is estimated that more than three fourths of the staff added by these departments since 1950 are working on one or more of the new federal programs.

This trend reflects a view that supervision of federal programs directly by the U.S. Office of Education would lead to an excessively large educational bureaucracy in the Federal Government, and would relegate states to a minor role in the field of education. To head off such a development, the National Council of Chief State School Officers has vigorously opposed federal programs that "bypass" state departments of education. Recently, another movement has been started establishing a "compact" among states to formulate common educational policies outside the framework of the Federal Government. Thus, strengthening of state departments of education is a significant by-product of increased federal action in the field of education.

The Federal Government and Public Schools

The Constitution and the Schools

Although the Constitution of the United States contains no direct reference to education, it has a profound impact on the operation of schools and colleges. By implication, the Constitution assigns general responsibility for public education to state governments. It permits federal expenditures for various aspects of education and requires public education to be conducted in a manner that protects the religious and civil liberties of all citizens. This fundamental influence on schooling flows from a few significant provisions of the federal Constitution.

Article I, Section 8, empowered the Congress "to lay and collect taxes, duties, imposts, and excises, to pay the debts and provide for the common defense and general welfare of the United States." This broad language authorizing Congress to provide for the general welfare was adopted by the Constitutional Convention after several more specific proposals had been rejected. The adoption of the general-welfare clause under these conditions, therefore, is open to two contrary interpretations. One is that the framers of the Constitution deliberately rejected proposals to grant responsibility for education to the Federal Government, showing their intent to deny it any authority in this field. The other is that by adopting the broad language, the framers sought to avoid needless listing of details in the Constitution and to authorize the Federal Government to take appropriate action to provide for the general welfare. Subscribing to the second interpretation, no doubt, George Washington and several other members of the Constitutional Convention later advocated the creation of a national university.

Actually the Federal Government has expended funds to supplement and stimulate state action in the provision of public education. Moreover, the Federal Government has operated several educational institutions. In view of these well-established practices, the debate concerning the constitutional authority of the Federal Government to augment state expenditures for education is primarily of historical interest.

The Fourteenth Amendment provided: "No state shall make or enforce any law which shall abridge the privileges of immunities of citizens of the United States . . . nor deny any person within its jurisdiction the equal protection of the laws." This amendment limited the powers of state legislatures and sought to protect individual citizens from abuse at the hands of state and local governments. The Fourteenth Amendment had the effect, among others, of making the First Amendment applicable to the states, since the protection of religious liberty under the First Amendment was deemed to be among the privileges and immunities that could not be abridged by action of state legislatures.

The effect of this amendment on laws establishing separate schools for different races has been more significant for the administration of schools. For many years prior to 1954, the federal courts were called upon from time to time to determine whether separate schools for Negro students were equal in quality to schools maintained for white students of the same school district. These actions were based on the established interpretation that the Fourteenth Amendment was not violated if the separate public schools for children of minority racial groups were equal in quality to those schools provided for other racial groups. Under the 1954 interpretation of the Supreme Court, state legislatures and local school boards were required to end segregation "with all deliberate speed." School boards in the Southern states adopted various plans for gradual desegregation of public schools, and the federal courts were again called on to review these school-board actions to determine whether they complied with the new Supreme Court mandate.

Similar questions arose in connection with de facto segregation in Northern cities where no child was denied admission to a public school solely because of his race, but where segregated residential patterns caused neighborhood schools to be segregated. Here was a different question: Are school boards required by law to change neighborhood school plans, honestly arrived at with no intent to segregate school children, in order to avoid de facto segregation of schools? This issue has not been finally resolved by the courts.

It is apparent that the federal courts, and more recently the executive branch of the Federal Government, exercise some fundamental controls over school board policies.

Federal Educational Activities

Although public education in the United States is recognized as a state responsibility, the national government has participated in its development. The earliest involvement of the Congress in public education came in the form of land grants to the states to help them establish and finance public school systems. The next major congressional action relating to public education occurred in 1862 when the Morrill Act was enacted, providing federal land grants for state colleges of agriculture and mechanical arts. This act, along with eventual additions and amendments, led to the granting of 11 million acres of land in addition to annual appropriations of money to the states to help finance colleges of agriculture and mechanical arts. The federal law included some control over the curriculum, because the land-grant colleges were required to emphasize agriculture and mechanical arts and to offer military instruction. Subsequent federal legislation provided annual appropriations for the support of these institutions and federal funds for agricultural experiment stations and extension services.

A series of acts, beginning with the Smith-Hughes Act in 1917, provided federal funds for vocational education of less than college grade in public high schools.[3] Under this program, each state was required to develop a plan for the administration of federal funds and to supply matching funds from state or local sources. In both the Morrill Act and the Smith-Hughes Act, the Federal Government encouraged emphasis on the practical arts in public education. But the operation and control of the institution were left clearly in the hands of the state or its political subdivisions.

Another step was taken by Congress in 1867 when the U.S. Office of

---

[3] Extended discussions of this matter are found in Chapters 9 and 20.

Education was created. The law establishing the federal education agency stated its purposes as

> . . . collecting such statistics and facts as shall show the condition and progress of education in the several States and Territories, and of diffusing such information respecting the organization and management of schools and school systems, and the methods of teaching, as shall aid the people of the United States in the establishment and maintenance of efficient school systems, and otherwise promote the cause of education throughout the country.

Although the basic purpose of the U.S. Office of Education emphasized the collection of statistics, the office, throughout its history, has performed many other tasks. In recent years much of the energy of the Office of Education has been devoted to the administration of special financial aids to education and to problems relating to education in foreign countries.

Federal Support for Public Schools

The attitude of the American people toward federal participation in education has been ambivalent. On one hand, there has been a national concern for education, an awareness that our effectiveness as a nation depends to a great extent on the effectiveness of our schools. But on the other hand, there has been a fear of federal control and a strong desire to keep the authority over public schools local.

The changing relationship over the years between the Federal Government and the states with respect to education reflects the shifting conditions and problems of the American people. When the first Congress, in 1789, approved federal land grants to endow a common-school system in the Northwest Territory, the action fulfilled the needs of a pioneer people devoted to a free society.

When President Washington urged the creation of a national university so that future leaders from the several states could study together, he recognized a need to build mutual respect and understanding between the North and the South, and between the East and the West. True, Washington's advice was not heeded, and we can only speculate whether the tragic Civil War might have been avoided or lessened in fury if the national university had become a reality.

When the Congress enacted the Morrill Act, it responded to the needs of people struggling to convert the western wilderness into productive farms. The nation's amazingly productive agriculture and much of its engineering skill, to some extent at least, are fruits of this federal intervention in the field of education. Passage of the Smith-Hughes Act reflected the great educational problem of the first quarter of the twentieth century—the influx of more and more American youth into high schools. The high schools, with their classical and college preparatory curricula, were suddenly required to make vocational training available for many students, and the Smith-Hughes Act provided a timely boost for this development.

Education was once primarily a means of self-realization to be purchased and enjoyed by a few. Eventually the advent of self-government and universal suffrage brought the need for an informed electorate. In recent years, the relationship of education to national economic and military strength has been recognized increasingly. Under these conditions, with national survival depending on the effectiveness of education, the Federal Government has developed a new kind of interest in the public school system.

Federal Expenditure for Education

Federal influence on education is exerted primarily by contributing funds for various educational purposes. During the 1969-1970 school year, the U.S. Office of Education administered 108 separate "programs" with appropriations totalling more than $3 billion. In addition to these programs, other departments and agencies of the Federal Government such as the National Science Foundation, the Bureau of Indian Affairs, the Department of Agriculture, and the Department of Defense expended substantial sums for education.

Most of the programs call upon the schools to broaden the scope of their services in order to contribute more effectively to the solution of national problems such as technological unemployment, national defense, and poverty. The purpose of appropriations for vocational education was not so much to support state and local schools as "to deal with the problems of unemployment resulting from automation and technological changes and other types of persistent unemployment."

Such expenditures for education are not intended primarily to upgrade teachers' salaries, equalize educational services among states, or provide financial support for the total school program. This common problem of the fifty states—the provision of sufficient funds to improve the program for all children and youth—is not materially affected by federal contributions designed to broaden the scope of education.

Another quite different category of federal expenditures for education stems directly from the responsibility the Federal Government has accepted for the education of groups of individuals. The large outlays for veterans' education that followed the Second World War, the obligations that the Federal Government has accepted over a long period of time for the education of Indian children, the education of dependents of government workers stationed overseas, the education of Cuban refugees, and the education of children residing on federal reservations in the United States for whom suitable free public education is not available—are all illustrations of federal education programs based on national obligations to individuals. Such programs are not intended to broaden the scope of education, but to provide suitable education to individuals.

Another national interest in education relates directly to the quality of instruction in specific school subjects. International competition for world leadership in military power and industrial efficiency call for more effective education of scientists and engineers. These concerns, along with the growing realization that the cold war would last a long time, led to congressional action in 1950, creating the National Science Foundation and directing it to "develop and encourage the pursuit of a national policy for the promotion of basic research and education in the sciences."

This national concern was even more explicitly stated in the first section of the National Defense Education Act of 1958:

> The Congress hereby finds and declares that the security of the nation requires the fullest development of the mental resources and technical skills of its young men and women. . . . The defense of this nation depends on the mastery of modern techniques developed from complex scientific principles.

Since 1958 Congress has appropriated several million dollars to carry out various sections of the National Defense Education Act, designed primarily to improve the quality of instruction in selected school subjects and to increase the supply of qualified teachers.

Quite different from these national purposes and concerns are federal payments to compensate for deficiencies in the school tax base. Improvements in public schools sought by nearly all Americans are being retarded by inadequacies of the revenue potentials of state and local school tax systems. It is not surprising, then, that much of the discussion concerning the federal role in education relates to general support designed to supplement the public school tax base.

A number of bills providing general federal support to compensate for deficiencies in the public school tax base have been considered by Congress. Under these proposals, the federal funds would not be earmarked for special subjects or groups of children; instead, they would be available for general school purposes. There would be virtually no federal control over the expenditures of such funds. Carefully developed measures of "need," "effort," and "taxable resources" would be used to determine the amount each state was entitled to receive. The purpose would be to supplement the school tax base, not to promote special programs of interest to the Federal Government.

Such general federal aid for public education has not been approved by Congress, primarily because of three basic controversies that inevitably arise.

The "church school" issue is perhaps the most fundamental. Many parents who have elected to send their children to church schools believe that they are penalized for this choice, since they must support the church school and also pay taxes to support the public school. Reflecting this view, some spokesmen for parochial schools oppose general federal aid for public schools unless some federal funds are also made available for children attending church schools.

Equally determined are those who believe that tax support for church schools would violate the Constitution and would promote religious segregation of American schoolchildren.

The second major obstacle to enactment of a general federal school-aid bill is the fear of federal control of school programs. The recent enactment of many "categorical" aids for education, calling for considerable control over the expenditure of these funds, indicates that this obstacle is not insurmountable.

In addition to these two obstacles to enactment of a general federal school-aid law, controversy usually develops concerning the amount to be appropriated and the method for distributing the funds among the states. Some proposals call for relatively small appropriations, concentrating the contributions in states whose per capita income is relatively low. Others would authorize larger appropriations for distribution to all states.

These controversies account for the fact that a general federal school-support law has not been enacted, despite a growing recognition of the need for it. But efforts to provide general support for education from federal sources continue.

Some advocates of general federal aid for education propose four "block grants" as follows:

1. General elementary and secondary education aid amounting to about 25 percent of the total cost.

2. Vocational education aid to enable every student to develop a marketable skill before leaving school.

3. Aid for the education of handicapped and disabled persons, to make them productive citizens.

4. Aid for higher education, with general-support grants replacing existing categorical aids.

State and Local Financing of Public Schools

In the absence of large federal contributions to public schools, which amount to less than 10 percent of their annual operating requirements, the burden of support falls heavily on local property taxes and state sales and income taxes. Moreover, the absence of federal support permits great inequalities among the states in public school expenditure per pupil. For example, during the 1969-1970 school year, the estimated average amount spent per public school pupil in New York was $1134 as compared with $419 in the state of Alabama.[4] These variations in public school support among states are closely related to differences in the per capita income of the people. For example, per capita income is approximately two times greater in New York State than in Alabama.

There are also great ranges in expenditures per pupil among school districts within the same state. These intrastate differences are related closely to the percentage of school funds derived from state tax sources as compared with local tax sources. Estimates for the 1969-1970 school year prepared by the Research Division of the National Education Association show that in three states—Delaware, North Carolina, and Hawaii—more than 60 percent of public school revenues were derived from state sources. In seven states—Nebraska, New Hampshire, South Dakota, Oregon, Colorado, Wyoming, and Massachusetts—the state contribution was less than 25 percent of public school revenues. The percentage of public school funds contributed from state sources ranged from 85 percent in Hawaii to only 9 percent in New Hampshire, and the average for all states was 40 percent.[5]

The proportion of public school funds acquired from state sources has an important effect on the state school system. In states like Nebraska where the state contribution is relatively small, local property-tax rates

---

[4] *Estimates of School Statistics, 1969-70,* Research Division, National Education Association (December 1969), p. 34.
[5] Ibid.

are usually high and inequalities in educational standards among school districts are likely to be great. On the other hand, in those states in which a large percentage of school costs are paid from state sources, local property tax rates are usually lower and school standards more uniform.

Foundation Programs

The effectiveness of state support in equalizing educational opportunities and local school tax rates among school districts within a state is determined largely by the kind of plan used to distribute school funds. During recent years many states have developed *foundation programs,* or equalization formulas, that provide larger amounts of state school funds per pupil to less wealthy school districts.

Under the foundation-program plan, the state, by an objective formula, ascertains how much is needed annually by each school district. The measure of need in some states is a prescribed amount of money for each pupil in average daily attendance. Often greater amounts are allotted for more expensive types of instruction. For example, the per-pupil allotment might be greater for high school students than for elementary pupils. Some school finance plans include, in determination of need, extra funds for pupil transportation and for allowances to meet higher teacher salary costs for better trained and more experienced teachers. Regardless of the elements in the formula, the basic purpose is to calculate, by an *objective formula applied uniformly to all school districts in the state,* the minimum amount of money needed by each school district annually to operate a basic school program.

After the minimal requirement has been computed for each local school district, a second measure is used to determine how much each district should be expected to contribute toward this amount from local tax sources. The local contribution is supposed to represent equal tax efforts by all school districts. Usually this amount is calculated by applying a uniform tax rate to the equalized assessed valuation of all taxable property in the district. The amount so obtained—the local contribution—is then deducted from the total need to determine how much the state contributes to each school district.

The effect of the foundation-program plan is to assure a minimum school budget for each school district in the state and to permit local school systems to supplement this budget by extra local tax efforts. The plan does not assure complete equality of financial support among school districts in the state, since communities may supplement the state-guaranteed foundation program. This explains why, even though there is a state foundation program, the salaries paid to teachers may vary greatly among school districts in the same state.

In the years ahead, the problem of financing public schools is likely to become more difficult. The additional students that have flooded elementary schools since the end of the Second World War have entered high schools and colleges, where costs per pupil generally are greater than in the elementary schools. Substantial increases in school tax rates will be needed to maintain present school standards, and increases in school tax rates usually stir controversy.

The American taxpayer does not enjoy paying high taxes for schools or for any other public service. Understandably he is looking for a bargain; he wants to get the most for his tax dollar. In his search for bargains in the private economy, he holds his own fairly well against the wiles of the American salesman. To do this he judges the relative worth of similar products selling at different prices and he selects the one that he considers the best buy. If he detects no difference in the quality of two products, he selects the one with the lower price.

In judging the quality of education, subtle differences often elude him, and he detects little difference between education that costs $1000 per pupil and education that costs $600 per pupil. If the quality deterioration that tends to accompany low expenditures for education were clearly apparent to the American taxpayer, he would be more inclined to select the higher-priced model. Perhaps the most important problem for school administrators henceforth will be to show more clearly to the American voter and taxpayer the close relationship between the school budget and the quality of education. To do this, more attention must be given to cost-effectiveness studies and to program budgeting.

Administrative Functions

The tasks performed by administrators are essentially the same for schools and colleges as for other institutions and agencies. They are (1) goal setting, (2) planning, (3) budgeting, (4) staffing, (5) directing, (6) evaluating, and (7) reporting. Although these functions are common to many enterprises, the process by which they are performed and the constraints imposed on the administrator are quite different in different settings.

In education, the goal-setting function is jealously guarded by school boards and state legislatures. And teachers, with their professional knowledge, have much to contribute in the goal-setting process. In a very real sense, the goals of a school represent the joint effort of teachers and boards of education, in which the administrator plays a vital, but largely advisory, role. The contrast between this process and the goal-setting process in the military, or in a factory, is obvious.

The planning function involves the development of specific organizational arrangements and administrative procedures for attaining established goals. In the planning process, the administrator normally plays a more prominent role, since he brings to the school system skill in "getting things done." Just as the owners of a ship decide where it is to go and the captain decides how to get there, so the school board determines educational goals and the administrator decides how to attain them—although there is usually much exchange of opinion in both processes.

In the planning process, school administrators are often called upon to present alternate ways to achieve established goals, so that costs and probable side effects can be examined and the best procedure selected.

The budgetary process is essentially an extension of the planning process, in which precise cost estimates are formulated and compared with anticipated income. In this process, the cost of programs and alternate procedures are compared with the expected educational benefits of each, and cost-benefit relationships are explored. But, because of the inherent difficulty in assigning dollar values to educational benefits, such explorations are usually quite subjective.

The budgetary process of any organization is closely related to the nature and sources of its income. Income for public schools comes from three levels of government, and much of it is earmarked for specific purposes. For this reason, the budgetary process for public schools requires school boards to examine various grant-in-aid laws to see whether such funds can be used to meet high-priority local needs.

The staffing process includes the determination of the duties and responsibilities for each position; the negotiation of salary schedules; and the recruiting of new employees and the assigning of employees to appropriate positions. In public schools, until quite recently, there was little variation in teaching assignments. In recent years, however, greater effort has been made to differentiate teaching assignments, to utilize more effectively the special strengths of each teacher. This trend toward team teaching requires administrators to prepare more precise job descriptions for teachers and to search for special strengths in the recruiting process.

One facet of the staffing process, negotiating with teachers' organizations concerning salaries and working conditions, has changed the nature of the administrator's job. Formerly, school principals and superintendents regarded themselves as members of a united profession as well as agents of the board of education. With increasing emphasis on unionization and the gradual imposition of "labor-management" procedures on public schools, school administrators have been compelled to play the management role. They can pretend no longer to be leaders of the teaching corps; that role is being claimed by the paid executive secretaries of teachers' organizations.

The effect of this role change on the overall effectiveness of public schools cannot be assessed at this time, but there is a danger that mutual trust and support between teachers and administrators, so essential for a good school, will be impaired, to the detriment of the effective teaching.

The directing and coordinating process in schools is much less formal than in most other organizations. This is due, in part, to the academic freedom accorded individual teachers and, in part, to the fact that precise coordination is seldom needed. In a military operation, each unit must perform its function at a specific time and place, often with split-second timing. In schools and colleges, the schedule of classes assures a basic coordination of teaching activities, and the course of study indicates what is to be taught. Beyond this, individual teachers are given great freedom to select the methods to be employed.

The evaluation process is receiving greater attention than in the past. If teachers' organizations are going to make demands on school boards, the latter can be expected to make counter "demands." These demands often call for teacher accountability for the performance of students.

Such accountability seems logical enough to parents and to the general public. But teachers point out that a student's performance is the product of his home, his peer group, his former teachers, his health, and his native talents. To hold the present teacher individually accountable for the joint product of our complex child-rearing process makes little sense. Yet, the administrator is expected to devise a plan for evaluating the effectiveness of the educational program. If a sound plan is not devised, heresay and rumor will dominate the evaluation process.

Finally, the school administrator must report to the school board, to the legislature, and to the general public. Some of these reports are routine and technical; others require interpretation and effective communication with various publics. A school administrator's reporting job is similar to that of other administrators, except that he reports to more groups than do most, and the basic difficulty of the evaluation of school programs complicates the reporting procedure.

In performing each of the administrative functions, the administrator is constrained by legal restrictions, by limited resources, and by the need to win public approval of his policies. Moreover, without the enthusiastic cooperation of the teaching staff, little can be accomplished in a school. For these reasons, skill in the art of communication and persuasion is fundamental to effective educational administration.

The School Administrator

Among public servants the school superintendent is unique. No other official in the country inherits so many diverse assignments or so many forces to please. He is, among other things, an executive, an educational leader, a policy adviser, a civic figure, a buffer, a confidant, and a friend. Engaged as an administrative officer, he is thrown at once into the formulation of educational policies and the development of programs, which he submits to his board of education for review. He is thus the board's counselor in the realm of policy. In some states, this function is prescribed by law; in others, it exists as an acknowledged fact. Every local school board relies on its superintendent for policy recommendations.

The superintendent brings to the attention of the school board proposals for the changes he favors, and urges their adoption. As the board's policy adviser, he naturally has its ear, but he must be adept at rounding up support for his proposals. Conversely, unless the superintendent expresses interest in an innovation and becomes an active proponent in its behalf, it normally has slight chance of favorable board consideration.

Having won approval for his recommendations, the superintendent then reverts to his administrative role to carry them out. The delicacy of his position does not ease, for he must administer to the satisfaction of all those around him—his staff, his board of education, and the community itself. His job calls for patience, tact, and action. He must prepare a plan for the operation of the school system and find the money to finance it, the staff to man it, and the facilities to support it. Among these three administrative functions, the most crucial and difficult one is the selection of staff—crucial because the effectiveness of his school program depends largely on the competence of the teachers, and difficult because teaching talent is subtle and difficult to evaluate.

Nor is this the only heavy demand on the superintendent. He is responsible for directing and coordinating the work of his entire school staff. He must cope with needs for supplies, repair of buildings, and internal disputes. He has to build morale and set goals, to listen and encourage, and to give approval as required. Sometimes he has to reprimand and even discipline. And he must accept certain civic obligations, such as participating in Community Chest drives and attending meetings and luncheons of service clubs, the Chamber of Commerce, and the PTA.

As a symbol of the educational system, the superintendent is subject to countless pressures. Parents impose pressures—for lower school taxes, for new courses, and for new methods of classroom procedure. These are instances in which the public *does* attempt to influence policy and school affairs, and swings great weight. Further public pressures stem from diverse sources; among them are the curriculum recommendations from the universities, the new courses and textbooks sponsored by the National Science Foundation, and the studies reported by organizations like the Ford Foundation.

Some school procedures have been subjected to review by the courts, and the superintendent may be ordered to discontinue an ability-grouping program or to institute a busing program to balance the racial composition of schools.

The variety of pressures of the superintendent's job call for an uncommon array of talents. He needs to be a skillful teacher, an efficient business manager, an effective public speaker, an educational philosopher, a man of charm, and a persuasive politician—qualities not often found in equal measure in one individual. Yet he must have enough of all these attributes to be successful.

The demands of the school administrator's job truly point up its complexity. To meet what is asked of him, the superintendent in the larger school systems is usually supported by a corps of assistants. He may have, for instance, one assistant superintendent in charge of curriculum and instruction; another in charge of business affairs; another in charge of personnel or adult education; consultants in guidance; and supervisors of vocational education—all uniquely trained individuals whose special aptitudes help the superintendents to do his job. Under these conditions, the superintendent devotes more time to policy questions, to coordination of staff activities, and to dealing with the public.

Responsibility for the administration of each individual school is usually delegated to a principal who performs many duties similar to those performed by the superintendent. But unlike the superintendent, the school principal, as a rule, does not report to the school board. Instead, he reports directly to the superintendent. Moreover, in most school systems, the employment of teachers and the management of business and fiscal affairs are carried out in the central office under the immediate direction of the superintendent of schools. Although the school principal generally has a voice in selecting teachers for his building, the employment contract between a teacher and a school board is almost always made upon recommendation of the superintendent.

Although the school principal has less responsibility for fiscal affairs and teacher employment, he has correspondingly greater responsibility for the maintenance of discipline in his school, for scheduling classes, for assigning teachers, and for protecting the health and safety of the children in his building. Because the principal is in closer contact with the teachers and pupils than the superintendent is, he is often given broad responsibility for supervising and evaluating the work of his teachers. More than the superintendent, the principal occupies a pivotal position in American education. He is close enough to the teaching process to understand its difficulties and limitations, yet he also has an overall view of educational problems that the individual teacher, busy with his assignment each day, seldom attains.

Educational administration and supervision, notwithstanding their complex nature, offer unusual opportunities for advancement and service for young women and men entering the teaching profession. At no time in the history of our nation has education occupied so prominent a position in the minds of men, and at no time have the problems confronting education been more difficult. The controversies that have raged about it during recent years indicate the growing national awareness of the need for better education, but they also indicate the complexity of the school administrator's job. Polemics may divert the peoples' interest for a while, but soon they will demand a program of action. Despite all the difficulties—the shortage of funds and the misunderstandings about education—the school administrator will be expected to develop a plan to accomplish three things: first, to expand the public school systems to accommodate greatly increased enrollments; second, to improve the quality of education, both academic and vocational, for all children and youth; and, finally, to keep the school program and methodology abreast with the advancement of human knowledge. The nation will owe much to the able, dedicated, and courageous school leaders who perform this service.

References

❖❖

Campbell, Roald F., Luvern L. Cunningham, and Roderick F. McPhee, *The Organization and Control of American Schools,* Merrill, Columbus, Ohio, 1965. The book's special emphasis is on state and federal government roles in education.

Knezevich, Stephen J., *Administration of Public Education,* 2nd ed., Harper & Row, New York, 1969. A brief, well-written comprehensive treatment of public school administration, with special emphasis on local government of education.

Moos, Malcolm, and Francis E. Rourke, *The Campus and the State,* Johns Hopkins, Maryland, 1959. This volume, prepared under the direction of the Committee on Government & Higher Education, contains an analysis of conflict and cooperation between state governments and institutions of higher learning, based on extensive interviews.

Morphet, Edgar L., Roe L. Johns, and Theodore L. Reller, *Educational Organization and Administration,* 2nd ed., Prentice-Hall, New Jersey, 1967. A good comprehensive treatment of the field, with excellent chapters relating to legal structure.

Will, Robert F., "State Education—Structure and Organization," U.S. Department of Health, Education, and Welfare, Misc. 46, Government Printing Office, Washington, D.C., 1964. This report contains charts and descriptions of the structure of educational government for each state.

22

Knowledge and the Curriculum

John D. McNeil

❖❖

There are great difficulties in selecting what schools should teach because as a people we do not have a clear notion about the kinds of lives students should live after instruction. This chapter is designed to support the assumption that the chief sources to use in determining what will be taught are the logical forms, the conceptual structures of the disciplines, with which specialists create knowledge. To this end, definitions are given of (a) curriculum as related to the school, (b) knowledge, and (c) the disciplines of knowledge. Next, there is an account of how the disciplines have most recently influenced the curriculum, followed by a critical analysis of their use in deciding what and how to teach. Finally, a defense is made for keeping knowledge in the school, in the light of the charge that it has not led the student to knowing more about himself, his purpose on earth, and the mystery of life and love.

What is Curriculum?

Curriculum as related to the school is both the process of determining the intents to be sought through instruction and the intents themselves as they appear to guide the planning of programs, courses, activities, and instructional sequences. A governing board at a societal level (such as Congress or the state Board of Education) makes curriculum when it decides on educational aims for given schools, issuing statements such as, "All graduates shall be well informed and possess knowledge about the rights of citizenship." A curriculum committee in the schools, in turn, makes curriculum when it prepares educational objectives that specify what students are to be able to do in order to evidence that they are "informed" and "possess knowledge about civil rights." Individual teachers must then decide on the particular instructional objectives that together promise to produce the desired educational result. An instance of an instructional objective consistent with the above intent might be: "Given reports of current events involving rights of citizenship, the learner will be able to identify those events that have or have not proceeded in accordance with the Bill of Rights."

The central problem of those engaging in curriculum is: How are learners to be different as a result of instruction? Societal planners must decide on the attitudes, skills, and intellectual tools most necessary for life now and in the foreseeable future. Similarly, members of local communities, both parents and nonparents, are sure to want to express their views regarding the kind of human being the schools should shape. The current battle between heads of large corporations and those in "Liberation" movements over the selection of the educational objectives for the school shows the difficulty to be expected in making curricular decisions. Slogans such as "How children feel about themselves is more important than mastering multiplication tables," indicate that many are not yet convinced that the attainment of a feeling of self-worth and the acquisition of intellectual tools are compatible. Unresolved, too, is the question about the degree to which the learner should decide on the changes that he is to exhibit after instruction. What are the objectives that a society has the right to impose on the individual? Many students and parents disregard the fact that laws requiring compulsory attendance at school and taxation for schools came about through arguments that schooling would benefit the community.

What is Knowledge?

A guess is not knowledge, for it is not justified. An opinion has some justification but not enough to make it knowledge. Ideas that are justified are considered "true" or knowledge. As has been shown in Chapter 10,

"Knowledge and Values," in order to be justified, ideas must meet certain criteria. One set of criteria is used by those gaining scientific knowledge. When one can make if-then statements that predict or produce certain observable results, he is said to have scientific knowledge. There are other kinds of knowledge that do not require justification by observation. Mathematical and logical truths are justified by reason. The person who can complete any proposition such as "A is greater than B and B is greater than C, then ___ is greater than ___" demonstrates his knowledge by showing logical consistency, not by observation.

Divine truth is an instance of another kind of knowledge—one that is justified by faith, not to be proven empirically. Also, some hold that there is an intuitive personal kind of knowledge such as is experienced when an individual receives an intense feeling or emotion from a work of art that he says brings him closer to some aspect of reality. This feeling or "insight" is regarded by some as a form of knowledge that requires no public verification. It is the curriculum makers' task to decide on the extent to which the learner should be able to justify ideas, and how many different sets of criteria the learner should use for establishing knowledge.

The world of knowledge is radically plural. Those participating in individual disciplines have their own ways of determining whether knowledge has been won or not, and they have their own methods for winning it. To be either a wise consumer of knowledge or a producer of it, the learner must enter a discipline. There are approximately one thousand separate disciplines, although many of them can be categorized under the headings of the natural sciences, the social sciences, mathematics, and the humanities. Each discipline is composed of an association of researchers who follow common procedures in pursuing an area of inquiry. Disciplines are born and die. They are born when there is a need for the production of knowledge now not available. They die when they can no longer simplify our understanding of life, do not direct attention to factors of importance in resolving problems, do not give ways to relate these factors, and do not generate new questions for investigation.

What is a Discipline?

One way to view a discipline is to regard it as a game in which there is a purpose; objects to which the players attend; rules for playing; and ways for deciding whether a point has been made (a "truth" discovered). A discipline exists only when there are rules of inquiry and when its participants produce new knowledge. Ideally, a discipline has agreement as to (a) the classes of phenomena to which members will attend, (b) the concepts considered relevant, and (c) rules for stating when evidence (proof) has been shown. In practice, the inquirers in any particular discipline are seldom in complete agreement as to what the defining canons are. Most disciplines are in a state of continual change, with new questions being asked, others being extended, and some being abandoned.

Schwab,[1] among others, has posited that all disciplines manifest three kinds of structure:

1. **Organizational Structure.** Organizational structure attempts to define how one discipline differs in a fundamental way from other disciplines. Also, a good organizational structure throws light on the borders of inquiry for that discipline and on how knowledge obtained might be incorporated by those in other disciplines. The fruitful interaction of mathematics and the physical sciences, for instance, illustrates that different kinds of knowledge can be compatible in inquiry.

2. **Substantive Structure.** Substantive structure suggests the kinds of questions to ask in inquiry, the data needed, and ideas to use in interpreting data. Substantive structure includes concepts like velocity, mass, chemical elements, norm, role, and status—the vocabulary that stands for the main ideas used in the discipline. A picture of the importance of substantive concepts in guiding inquiry can be gained by noting how "reinforcement" in experimental psychology directs attention to external stimuli in relation to the individual's own behavior, and "repression" in analytical psychology tends to focus on internal states of the individual. In addition, substantive structure includes verbal statements explaining the relations between concepts. These expressions may be simple descriptions or factual observations of what goes together, or general summaries of facts stated as principles or laws. Laws, too, can sometimes be related to each other by systems.

Much of the tentative nature of scientific truths comes when substantive structures are found inadequate or must be revised in the light of inconsistencies between data collected in subsequent investigation and what the structure predicted.

The revisionary value of knowledge is of curricular significance in that learners who can give examples of it might be better prepared to meet future revisions with understanding. Those who are taught structure as dogma are likely to be bewildered and unaccepting in the face of new truths that depart from older principles.

[1] Joseph J. Schwab, "Structure of the Disciplines: Meanings and Significance," *The Structures of Knowledge and The Curriculum*, 1964, pp. 6-30.

Students completing a school subject that purports to be a faithful representation of a discipline should be able to give examples of how substantive structure in that discipline directs inquiry and to point out the limitations of these structures. It would be desirable for some students to be able to frame new working concepts or principles for generating inquiry. This recommendation is made partly on the assumption that in most disciplines the research with the greatest long-term significance is that which produces new concepts. A prerequisite objective might be that the learner identify disparities in knowledge (show where principles are not working in certain instances). Such identification would also be an indication that the learner regards facts and basic principles as less than perfect, a way to combat the notion that scientific knowledge is not tentative but permanent. To engage a student in the task of trying to develop substantive structures would be helpful in preparing him for a life of change.

3. Syntactical Structures. Different disciplines are characterized by the manner in which members gather data, make interpretations, test assertions, and generalize their findings. The method used in performing these tasks makes up the syntax of a discipline. For example, sociologists generally observe in naturalistic settings, identify indicators believed to correspond to the theoretical framework guiding the inquiry, and often rely on correlational data to show relations between factors observed. The correlations are said to provide support or not for the sociological theory. On the other hand, experimental psychologists manipulate their treatment variables in an effort to produce predicted consequences. Experimentalists make carefully defined events occur rather than depending on a factor presenting itself in the naturalistic setting. The experimentalist believes that he has knowledge when he is able to produce a predicted result. He says that while correlations suggest a connection or association of two or more factors, by manipulating one and thereby producing the other, his evidence makes a strong case for showing the existence of a causal relation.

Those in the arts are divided about their syntax—especially with respect to what is to serve as evidence that knowledge has been produced. In fact, some believe that there is no knowledge in the arts, only affect. Some artists consider art a discipline of feeling, and if a painting, poem, or dance evokes an emotional response, the work is valid. Furthermore, to them, the feeling may be personal and need not generalize to a large public. Others say a "truth" in art has been created if the work meets the standards of connoisseurs. Canons of criticism are available, for instance, to make gross comparisons between good and bad poetry, good and bad books, etc. Agreement about sensory qualities, formal qualities and technical competencies in the arts are not difficult to come by. The problem centers on whether the product must have particular expressive content or "say" something of importance. There are those persons who would determine the validity of an artistic work by asking what it contributes to an understanding of the human condition. Although few expect an art product to be a descriptive statement of reality, many expect a cleverly arranged work to help the beholder make new inferences about the nature of mankind.

Recent Curricular Reform

Prior to about 1958 there were curricular objectives labeled as "subject matter." Illustrative subject-matter objectives from the period are as follows:

1. Given geometric figures on a plane, the student will be able to name them.

2. Given a particular culture, the learner will be able to recall major facts about the culture.

3. Given a number of statements describing biological conditions, the learner will be able to state the principles that best explain the origin of the conditions.

4. Given a paragraph that offers a reasoned argument in economics, the learner will be able to identify the unstated assumptions involved.

Frequently these objectives demand that the learner recall specific information and terminology, and that he categorize instances by classes regarded as fundamental in the subject. Most pre-1960 objectives asked for recall of isolated facts. Some called for applications of what is now termed substantive structure of a discipline to a new situation. None required that the student discover a new fact, a new relationship, or a new technique—something that no one had known before. In short, factual and descriptive content was stressed to the exclusion of the use of basic concepts and methods of scholars in analyzing data and drawing conclusions.

Curriculum reform in American education during the past decade was founded on the desire to equip learners with the means to enter the world of knowledge as opposed to mere recall of a large quantity of information (for example, an objective in social science consistent with the reform movement might be: "the child will read skeptically; he will be able to separate moral precepts from factual ones; and he will be able to state an explanation and to test its adequacy"). The ability to use both the substance and the syntax of a discipline was viewed by many of the scholars preparing the new curriculum as of real and lasting importance to all learners.

The case for reform included these arguments:

1. School subjects should reflect knowledge rather than merely presenting information.

2. Teachers are confused about the nature of the discipline associated with the subject they are teaching (for example, the large majority of elementary and high school teachers of science reject the scholars' view of scientific knowledge that says that "the pronouncements of science are tentative").

3. Because of the phenomenal increase in available information, schools must correspondingly increase the learner's capacity to learn. Economy of learning is thought to occur through transfer, by which something learned can be applied in many other situations. Transfer is more likely to occur when one has practice in using the organizing concepts of a discipline that connect experiences and reveal the regularities in nature. A discipline is held appropriate for teaching because it will help the learner simplify his environment by relating instances to a class of events and gathering a large group of cognitive elements into a common framework—theory, model, or other explanatory scheme.

4. Paradoxically, the best way to prepare for an uncertain future is to master the tools (syntax of discipline) for determining what is certain.

The reform of the sixties was an effort to redefine the role of knowledge in the curriculum by emphasizing structures of knowledge characterizing the various fields of learning. It was not, as some supposed, only a renewed emphasis on subject matter as a correction to a "life adjustment" phase in the school that had given too much attention to the personal interests of learners and the demands of community pressure groups for the dissemination of information on current topics of concern—topics that were not of lasting significance.

It is noteworthy that the reform was chiefly in the hands of academic specialists. Although some professional educators were opposed to this leadership, a few applauded it because they thought that it would overcome narrowness among subject-matter specialists—that scholarship would became more convergent with the interests of the mass of mankind as the specialist attempted to apply his ideas to schools, to adapt content to human nature and to the demands of daily life.

The disciplines approach to curriculum was more than a return to subject matter. Its distinguishing characteristic was that it moved not merely the results of research, but investigators and their methods as well, to the classroom itself. To a limited degree, research was to have been extended from places like industry and the university to the common school. High school students were asked to participate in discovering knowledge. They were asked, for example, to help identify the factors (then unknown) that determine what makes up an adequate bird territory necessary for successful nesting and to develop a method of detecting the heterozygotes (effects of genes). Even pupils in primary levels were to have been started on activities related to ideas on the most advanced plane, with the least to unlearn and correct as regards both particular things and method. Although the learning activities of little children were quite manageable and concrete (except sometimes in math), they were related to sophisticated concepts.

Scholars conducted hundreds of curriculum projects, representing disciplines such as physics, biology, mathematics, history, geography, music, anthropology, and foreign languages. They set new objectives for learners and suggested instructional procedures for reaching these objectives. The planners intended to put learners into the game as players, not as spectators. Learners were to act like physicists, biologists, historians, and the like. The assumption was that after participating, the learner as a citizen would follow developments in the discipline with understanding and support, and those who continued their study of the game could become specialists themselves. The learner was not just to talk about conclusions (facts) produced, but either to produce conclusions himself or to state whether a given conclusion was warranted in accordance with the rules of the discipline.

Illustrative objectives from those available in 1970 show the influence of the concept of structure:

1. Given different kinds of problems, the learner will be able to identify those of concern to particular disciplines.

2. Given a problem in a discipline, the learner will be able to design an appropriate method of attack. (Appropriate is operationally defined.)

3. Given a situation involving photons and matter waves, the learner will be able to suggest new lines of investigation based on his observations.

4. The learner will demonstrate his ability to prepare accurate maps from his own field observations and from other sources. He will be able to identify significant relationships among these maps.

5. The learner will be able to formulate geographic hypotheses and to test them in the light of the data he is able to obtain.

6. Given descriptions of social situations including groups with assumed values, the learner will be able to assess the probability that certain consequences will occur.

Contemporary Concerns

Two kinds of concern have appeared regarding projects attempting to emphasize the structure of knowledge. One kind is a legitimate curricular concern because it treats the validity of the instructional intent (what to teach). The other kind is an instructional concern that deals with the question, "How effective are the procedures, activities, topics, sequences, teaching style and the like that are provided for producing the intended changes in learners (how to teach)?"

It has been charged that those planning the curriculum from the view of the discipline have given insufficient attention to objectives by which the learner can relate one discipline to another. Also, it is said that not enough objectives call for applying the structure of disciplines in the making of choices as individuals, citizens, and workers. Cases in point are questions such as, "What objectives are there to reveal that the learner is able to understand pursuits in disciplines other than those in which he specialized?", "Are there objectives that promise to help the learner to deal with the insistent complex problems of modern life not answerable by a discipline alone?", and "Where are the objectives by which students can see the limitations as well as the uses of a single discipline in interpreting social events as they actually occur?"

Instructional concerns show up in questions about particular teaching strategies, topics, sequences of learning opportunities, and so forth. These questions can be answered empirically by providing evidence that the program did or did not produce the desired results without undesirable by-products. If the objective is that the learner will be able to apply Ohm's law in new situations, there is little need for arguing whether it is helpful for him to first learn how to manipulate electrical circuits. The value of such manipulation in achieving the objective can be demonstrated.

The point I'm trying to make is that criticism can be (a) *curricular,* stating that the objectives selected are or are not appropriate and sufficient, and (b) *instructional,* stating that the programs designed for reaching the objectives are not successful in fulfilling these objectives. It seems to me that if the discipline approach to curriculum has not been satisfactory, most of the fault is an instructional one rather than a curricular one.

Many disagreements about the value of particular objectives can be treated the same way we settle questions about the value of selected topics, activities, and instructional procedures. That is, the objectives are regarded as something to be appraised, not prized. We should look for encompassing objectives, not focus on all objectives as equal and final ends. Considering history, for example, to expect that a learner will be able to recall particular events in black history and the Great Depression can be regarded as an en route objective not of great worth in itself but perhaps able to contribute to an objective of greater importance such as the ability to interpret historical events in terms of economic theory, social movements, personalities, or the hand of God. Consequently, it may be shown experimentally whether the objective calling for recall does indeed enhance achievement in the ability to interpret (or is a factor in the promotion of a positive concept of the self). The particular historical events chosen offer opportunities for practice in recognizing schemes of interpretation, and the events can be selected on the basis of interest to particular learners and pressure groups. The specific events treated in the classroom will always be an inadequate sample of mankind's stories. Objectives that allow students to read and judge history seem more promising than those that restrict him to answering questions about a particular work.

Curriculum may be miseducative when it is assumed that the structure taught has long-term virtues, but no effort is made to demonstrate that these virtues actually follow. An extreme illustration would be teaching mathematics as a formal system and as a consequence expecting the learner to behave more reasonably in his human relations. Without experimental evidence to show that there is a connection, one should not accept the expectation as valid. Long ago, there were those who defended the offering of Latin on the claim that it would contribute to facility in English. Unless the elements in Latin are directly related to one's behavior in English, there is little chance to establish a relationship.

Proponents of the disciplines are not the only ones who are guilty of merely assuming that their objectives transfer to a range of situations outside the school. Recent research reviewing studies on driver education did not produce evidence that driver-education courses reduce accidents or lessen their severity. This is not to say that programs in driver education cannot be changed to include objectives that might be demonstrated to be significant in reducing accidents. Also, it is not meant that all curricular objectives must only be justified by utilitarian criteria.

Specialists within the discipline often find fault with the objectives of popular school programs designed by fellow specialists in the field. These criticisms serve to remind us that there is a lack of agreement by experts at to what makes up the important structures. For example, the objectives of programs in the physical sciences have been found wanting in not equipping learners with a variety of principles of inquiry and not teaching pupils the effect of their choice of principles upon the furtherance of inquiry (for example, The P.S.S.C. Program is said to overemphasize the experimental rather than the theoretical, and in particular, the mathematical, aspects of the structure of physics).

Schoolmen have been cautioned not to prescribe wholesale objectives drawn from the concept of structure in the disciplines, on the grounds that scholars may decide that there is no productive use of the concept in at least some fields. In other words, the concept of structure itself may become suspect. Macdonald,[2] for instance, has associated the word *myth* with the idea that each discipline has a set of fundamental principles about which the fabric of knowledge is woven and from which instruction in schools should proceed. He argues that just because structure is a coherent way of organizing a field of knowledge, it does not necessarily follow that this is the way to organize knowledge in the instructional setting. It might be that the discipline concept of structure is only an after-the-fact description of the way in which knowledge can be organized by mature scholars and not the way in which the knowledge was really won. The intellectual value of a discipline for an individual is not in the fixed inner structure but in its ability to start and direct inquiry for him, to "turn him on." Certainly the scientist who felt the necessity to create knowledge was motivated, but it is another matter to assume that the student who encounters the science already made will be enthusiastic when it is a necessity imposed on him.

Perspectives for the Future

There are signs of disenchantment with the disciplines and with the curriculum. Organized knowledge as the dominating source for instruc-

[2] James B. Macdonald, "Myths About Instruction," *Educational Leadership*, **22**, 7 (1965), 571-576.

tional objectives is being challenged by those reacting to the quantitative revolution that seeks to give a just share of wealth, education, and political freedom to all, and by those in the qualitative social revolution who are searching for ways to achieve meaningness with the goals and leisure that they have. Numbers of professional publications treating the disciplines and the curriculum peaked some time ago. The search for sensation now rivals the quest for reason. Tests of knowledge by fact and logic are being given the back seat to imagination, which can be entertained without proof. Today the schools are asked to look for "humanistic concepts," to find the subject matter that makes one humane.

Educators who seemed to accept the language of the academic specialist when the prestige of those in the disciplines was high are now calling for objectives that reflect moral, ethical, social, and aesthetic values instead of the content of a specific discipline. Most objectives for the new "humanitarian" programs are vague if they exist at all. The response to the idealistic urging that students become "more open, more independent human beings able to function effectively in a world of rapid and social moral change" has not been drawn from the disciplines. Instead we find intents like these:

1. The learner will be able to state the disparity between (a) what he thinks about in school, (b) what he is concerned about in his own life, and (c) the way he acts.

2. The learner will be able to state the masks humans use to hide or express what is human or personal about themselves.

3. Learners will voluntarily form friendships across racial lines.

With the changing objectives have come new instructional means—such as improvisational drama—to develop awareness, "urban affairs" instead of civics, the use of tensions to provide educational stimuli, and the teaching of history as the quest of man to establish identity by religious, territorial, political and educational means. Some curriculum makers are taking advantage of current interests and at the same time are continuing to develop the students' knowledge of structure (for example, teaching rock music as a problem area in aesthetic analysis and as a serious stylistic development in the history of music).

The challenge is how to maintain and achieve valid objectives derived from structures of the disciplines, the concerns of learners, and the problematic situations in human affairs. The structure of certain disciplines may be most helpful in enabling learners to find meaning and love.

Knowledge and imagination must enter the school as partners. If objectives of the discipline approach were not all achieved as desired, it was probably because the objectives were quite appropriate but the instruction inadequate. Revisions in instructional strategies should be attempted before rejecting the objectives. Such revision has been suggested. For example, there is an instance of a teacher who, when confronted with less than satisfactory results (that is, with students turning to an authority figure who served as the criterion for determining what is true, good, and beautiful rather than applying the discipline's syntax) changed his methods to *fallibism*. The fallibist treats a particular body of knowledge as conjectural. He believes that we can grow in knowledge even if we can never *know*—that is, know for certain. He does not try to get his students to justify knowledge. The teacher, for instance, uses laboratory periods not to demonstrate or prove theories of science, but to test those theories by experiments designed to try to refute them. A fallibist wants his students to develop a critical attitude. Students are asked to refute theories by experiment, to criticize historical interpretations, and to replace them with better interpretations.

> Whenever the question "How do you know?" arises, the fallibist replies somewhat in this fashion: I do not know. I have no guarantees. My assertion was only a guess. But if you are interested in the problem which I tried to solve by my tentative assertions, you may help me by criticizing it as severely as you can; perhaps together we can design some test which will refute it. If it can be refuted, this will give us the opportunity to create a new theory that will avoid the errors of the old one, and will therefore be a better theory. In this way we advance knowledge.[3]

One reason for loss of faith in the disciplines is that some have seen the pathetic weakness of the academic specialist when he is confronted with the complexities of making intelligent decisions about social questions as overpowering as "How can a city best improve the quality of life for all citizens?" But he can often make some contribution as an expert with knowledge. The value of knowledge from a specialist is that it enables those studying a problem to take into account more remote consequences, to see more possibilities for dealing with the problem at hand. It may not be in the best interests of society or the specialist to have him become entangled in the overriding social problems beyond his expertise, and it is possible that the scientist's involvement in a particular

[3] Henry J. Perkinson, "Fallibilism As A Theory Of Instruction," *The School Review* (June 1969), 87-93.

immediate social problem may interfere with the production of knowledge. The abstraction of knowledge is sometimes thought to be gained best from observation of a phenomenon in a variety of conditions, not in a single instance. There also may be value in letting a knowledge seeker have time for quietly reflecting on what the data show, something social decisions do not always allow. So too, the current trend to put students in study groups involving action with community groups needs checking out. Combining such action with meetings in seminar format, bringing community experience together with academic pressures and techniques, may succeed in convincing students of the need to command a discipline's structure. They may see how a structure of knowledge can lead to new procedures and make for diversity rather than conformity. However, it would be a mistake to repeat what occurred nearly 40 years ago when social and individual problems were the organizing centers for educational programs labeled *core* and *common learnings*. These early efforts often failed because teachers and students lacked the intellectual tools needed for studying problems selected. Without having had opportunities to learn the structure of a discipline, participants were handicapped in conceptualizing aspects of the problem they faced. Sometimes they could not even identify the disciplines that might be helpful. Sadly, many could not comprehend the knowledge when they tried to "raid" the subject matter or to learn it without instruction.

Curriculum makers have underestimated the instructional requirements for producing citizens who can discover knowledge or even use the knowledge already won. Most students have been exposed to foreign language, music, mathematics, science and a host of other subjects. Few students can do any one of the following: converse like a native in a foreign tongue, play a musical instrument so that others want to listen, continue to learn mathematics after graduation, or identify the framework underlying a scientific problem. Instead of abandoning programs that are aimed at mastery of a discipline, and substituting fragmented activities in response to current interests, elementary and secondary schools should try to strengthen their efforts in the direction of specialization. These efforts can include the linking of individual and social concerns to the structure of knowledge. Specialization might give youth the feeling of personal worth that comes from knowledge that one is reasonably expert in some worthy field of endeavor.

Exploratory functions of the school should be minimized. It is no longer so necessary to merely expose students to a wide range of stimuli, most of which duplicate the environment of the larger society (for example, the irrationality of television, "Hamlet in boxer shorts," the public struggle over war, nature, and technology). Rather, the school should be involved in trying to help the learner use knowledge to clarify what is happening around him and why.

My final argument is that the school should be regarded as an agency for simplifying the environment. It should be a place where pupils pursue a restricted number of studies without the distraction of too many competing demands, and where they can abstract the key ideas with which to interpret life. The school can economically arrange the conditions necessary for the learning of difficult ideas—ideas requiring ordered and prerequisite experience, and the deliberate noting of cause-and-effect relationships. Schools will render a child a unique service by placing him in artificial and simulated situations that are used to create understanding that would not occur by chance or would not be extended in a systematic fashion. It is the business of the school to see that the learner does not form "naturally." That is, the school should not leave certain development of the learner to chance. The ability to read and to apply principles, postulates, theorems, and other abstractions to new situations develops only when the situations, by *prearrangement,* lead to generalization and offer practice in applying the content to new events. It is doubtful that any new knowledge will be gained by those who have not studied to show themselves approved. In brief, nonobvious subject matter—the structure of the disciplines—is especially appropriate for those who desire to know and to find the truth—that dangerous stuff—beautiful and precious.

References

❖❖

Ford, G. W., and Lawrence Pugno, Eds., *The Structure of Knowledge and The Curriculum,* Rand McNally and Company, Chicago 1964, 105 pp. A series of papers reporting examination of disciplines in terms of structure and how these structures relate to curriculum.

Hass, Glen, Kimball Wiles, and Joseph Bondi, Eds., *Readings in Curriculum,* Allyn and Bacon, Inc., Boston, 1970, 544 pp. Cited because one section of the book contains a number of papers treating the nature of knowledge.

King, Arthur, R., Jr., and John A. Brownell, *The Curriculum and The Disciplines of Knowledge,* John Wiley and Sons, Inc., New York, 1966, 213 pp. Has interesting arguments as to why the curriculum should be in the direction of producing an intellectual man working with many realms of knowledge and their structure.

Phenix, Phillip H., *Realms of Meaning,* McGraw-Hill, New York, 1964, 391 pp. A great book for helping one gain a perspective on knowledge treated as a variety of ways of knowing—as opposed to seeing only the values of a single discipline or a single realm of knowledge.

Phi Delta Kappa, *Education And The Structure of Knowledge,* Fifth Annual Phi Delta Kappa Symposium on Educational Research, Rand McNally and Company, Chicago, 1964, 277 pp. A report from members of a symposium who tried to think through the meaning of "knowledge structure" and what bearing the concept has on education and teaching.

23

Elementary Education

John I. Goodlad

❖❖❖

Each September, in the United States, slightly more than half of the nation's five-year-olds enter kindergarten, their first year of school. A year later, they are joined in the first grade by almost all their fellow six-year-olds. Grouped thus by age, these children move together through and out of an educational unit so commonly accepted in this country that it is frequently referred to as "the common school."

This mass system of acculturation is taken for granted, likewise, in such developed countries as Canada, Japan, Australia, Israel, Sweden, and England. In dozens of underdeveloped countries, however, no parallel herding of the young occurs; for them, universal schooling is still a far-off dream. These tend to be the countries with the highest birth rates, and so the effects of efforts to build schools and train teachers for them are frequently offset by increasing numbers of children to be accommodated. While getting children into schools is a major problem for these nations, keeping them there often is an equally formidable one. In some countries, for example, only fifteen percent of those who begin secure the four successive years of schooling usually regarded as necessary for the attainment of functional literacy.

It becomes apparent, then, that the priority problems of elementary schooling are not everywhere the same. The problems perceived as most significant for Japan are not those perceived to be most critical for Pakistan. In underdeveloped countries, the overriding problem is getting children into school and keeping them there. In developed countries, it is providing education at a *quality* level for all children. The fact that children are in school is no guarantee that their education there is meaningful and well-suited to the development of individual potential.

Worldwide, "primary education" is the term most frequently used to designate this first stage of formal schooling. Primary or elementary education embraces a unit of schooling commencing at age five or six and concluding between the ages of eleven and fourteen, depending on the country and its organization for education. In the United States, the 6-3-3 plan (six years of elementary, three years of junior high, and three years of high school), or 7-3-3 when kindergarten is available, is increasingly becoming the most common pattern of organization. The 8-4 plan still remains in sections of the country, as does the 7-5. Some recent interest in a new "middle school," resulting in 4-4-4 and 5-3-4 plans of organization, has tended to blur the termination point of the elementary school. And non-graded plans, eliminating grade levels completely, have blurred organizational distinctions within the structure of elementary schooling.

There has been an unfortunate tendency, in this country and elsewhere, to equate education and schooling so that elementary education and the elementary school are, in the minds of most people, virtually synonymous. It is a mistake to assume that school is the only or even the major influence on human behavior during childhood. A child views television during the formative years preceding entry into school. By the time of graduation from high school, he has attended for approximately 12,000 hours and watched television for about 15,000. The latter may very well be the more powerful educative force, for good or ill. Home and peer group likewise contribute significantly to formation of the boy who will become the man. In his controversial and provocative report on equality of educational opportunity in the nation's schools, Coleman posed the intriguing hypothesis that, more compellingly than what the school puts in by way of process and substance, what the child brings from his own home and encounters in school from other homes contributes significantly to educational performance.[1] The Coleman Report, probably more than any document since the 1954 Supreme Court ruling, has served

---

[1] James S. Coleman, *Equality of Educational Opportunity,* United States Department of Health, Education, and Welfare, Washington, D.C., 1966.

as a basis for legal decisions pertaining to integration of the races in schools.

The dominant issue of elementary schooling in the United States carried from the 1960s into the 1970s is that of providing equal educational opportunity for all children regardless of the economic conditions surrounding their birth, their race, or their place of abode. Full implementation of this principle will not be attained easily. It has been and will be accompanied by strife, hardship, and injustice. But another issue of even more formidable dimensions lies just behind this one: the provision of educational opportunities, whether in school or out of it, of a kind most likely to assure maximum development of those talents leading to both individual and societal self-renewal.[2] This issue encompasses our present scars from social injustice and carries us into profound questions pertaining to the nature of man, his freedom, and his learning.

These have been classic areas of inquiry for philosophers and educators. Recently, however, they have been most visibly preempted by a group of neohumanists (Edgar Friedenberg, Paul Goodman, John Holt, Jonathan Kozol, and others) of amateur philosophical standing, on one hand, and the neobehaviorists (most notably represented by B. F. Skinner) of psychological orientation, on the other. Many of the questions involved are dealt with elsewhere in this volume. But they are of profound concern in this chapter, since the dialogue—a generous word, given the polarization of viewpoints—swirling about the elementary school proposes at one extreme the elimination of the entire system and at the other the precise delineation of each step in a programmed sequence of learning leading to mastery of predetermined educational objectives.

The balance of this chapter attempts to do three things. First, it sketches broadly the development of elementary education in this country, with only brief mention of the years before 1900, greater attention to this century, and some lingering over events since 1950. This section is followed by a longer one dealing with the current scene, with special attention to the major ideologies seeking to influence the schools. The chapter concludes with a brief look into the future. Throughout, the focus is on the United States and on issues rather than on details of curriculum, instruction, and classroom organization. It is assumed that future teachers will become involved in the specifics elsewhere in their teacher-education programs and that those students with other career goals in mind will have little need for them.

[2] John Gardner, *Self-Renewal: The Individual and the Innovative Society*, Harper and Row, New York, 1965.

The Development of Elementary Education

The form of the elementary school we know today was molded largely during the second half of the 19th century. The graded Quincy Grammar School, opening in 1848, quickly became the pattern for the cities along the eastern seaboard and westward. It was, in fact, the parallel growth of cities and industrialization that institutionalized elementary education.

The Massachusetts Laws of 1642 and 1647 had laid a basis for tax-supported schools two hundred years earlier. The Dame School—the primary school of colonial New England—assembled children between the ages of three and ten in a kitchen, living room, attic, or barn. The Dame was more a governess than a teacher, teaching what little she knew in letters, knitting, sewing, and good manners. The "district" school of a century later was more formal but still casual in regard to definition of curriculum. The circuit teacher moved across the district in a series of "removes," each stop lasting several months. When he returned a year or more later, he endeavored to pick up with the pupils more or less where he had left off. Throughout these years, the requirements for admission to the Academy or grammar school were reading, writing, and spelling, conditions that were met by tutoring in well-to-do families, the only ones that could aspire to higher learning. Elementary education, in modern parlance, was not, then, a unit or set of grades preceding a secondary school, but a minimal set of literacy skills. What became the secondary school and the elementary school grew up apart, in a kind of nonsequence that explains at least some of the problems of articulating the two today.

The reader is referred to Chapter 1 for an analysis of the factors in the first half of the 19th century that combined to produce the common school of the second. Among these, increasing population and its constellation in the cities, industrialization and its fresh demands on literacy, and new motivations for schooling as a vehicle for upward mobility were powerful. By the mid-1860s, city schools and attendance at them were regarded as essentials. Pupils were classified by grade; each grade was defined by work to be covered; the work was spelled out in textbooks; and teachers began to identify themselves with the age group and work requirements of a grade. The modern, graded school was born and thriving.[3]

---

[3] Henry C. Morrison, *The Evolving Common School,* Harvard University Press, Cambridge, 1933, p. 10: "By the turn of the new century, the process had become complete and you could write the table of educational denominate numbers: eight years make one elementary education; fifteen Carnegie units make one secondary education; one hundred-twenty semester hours or thirty-six majors make one college education."

The elementary schools have never been as polarized in practice as the debate surrounding their function and character. Rather, they have tended to represent a blending of two major threads of thought ably represented during the early decades of this century by John Dewey, a psychologist-turned philosopher, and E. L. Thorndike, a psychologist. Many of the ideas developed by Dewey in "his school" during a brief period of years spanning the end of the nineteenth century and the beginning of the twentieth infused the laboratory schools of the University of Chicago and are found there today.[4] These had to do with the importance of children's interests in the selection of learning fare, the use of activities connected with the home as a medium for learning, and the importance of a process of inquiry through which learners reconstructed knowledge (and, ultimately, society itself) in a "scientific" process of problem-solving. Like Alfred North Whitehead, Dewey eschewed the limp passage of inert knowledge into an uncomprehending vessel, the child. Contrary to the interpretations of many critics and followers, Dewey did not reject the importance of organized knowledge in the problem-solving process.

Interestingly, even schools heavily influenced by Dewey's views have incorporated a strong subject-matter orientation into both the curriculum and teaching. Dewey may have captured and held the attention of educators, particularly those of a philosophical bent, but Thorndike influenced the textbooks. He sought, for example, to break down mathematical operations into small, manageable components and order them into hierarchies and sequences. More than the shades of Thorndike are still in the schools today. Textbooks are the prime medium of instruction; they depend on the precise ordering of "arithmetic combinations," for example. Around them, a major industry has developed, an industry that responds readily to the reordering of subject matter but apathetically to proposals for reconstructing the schools. This industry, in turn, is tuned closely to the political structure. As astute curriculum reformers well know, for ideas to make a difference soon they must find their way through the political structure. Curriculum materials, particularly textbooks, constitute one of the most effective means of influencing the schools.

Although the ideas of progressive education, espousing the central role of the child's own interests and motivations (a movement attributed to Dewey and which he found necessary to repudiate in part), dominated elementary education for a quarter of a century (from the late 1920s into the early 1950s), grade-by-grade coverage of subject-matter was both the

[4] Ida B. De Pencier, *The History of the Laboratory Schools,* Quadrangle Books, Chicago, 1967.

primary expectation for and the major preoccupation of the schools. There are several explanations for this. One is that the ideas of the progressives could not be readily packaged. In fact, textbooks were antithetical to the views on teaching promulgated by leaders such as Kilpatrick. One could sit at his feet and be intrigued by the prospect of organizing "activity" projects around the interests of children and problems of the community, but implementation was a quite different matter, especially when neither exemplar models of such enterprises nor appropriate materials for them were readily available. How much easier to hand out the textbook!

Without having established many beachheads (but after having significantly influenced educational thought), the faltering progressive-education movement was finished off by a deadly salvo of attack early in the 1950s.[5] Although the progressives influenced elementary more than secondary education, it is of interest to note that the secondary school—notably its so-called life-adjustment programs—received the brunt of this attack. We tend to be lenient toward our children, wanting for them a happy and carefree period before the burdens of adulthood descend on them. But we are far less tolerant of our adolescents, fearing with each passing year that they are to be not better than we are or—perish the thought—like us.

Change, by definition, is away from what exists or existed. The spokesmen for change during a decade or so following World War II were *against* what was perceived to have existed before. They were largely *for* what progressive education had eschewed. Academicians in the universities began to take an interest in the high school curriculum, an interest shared and supported by the National Science Foundation. A handful interested themselves in the science and mathematics deficiencies of the elementary school. There was more talk and analysis than action. Suddenly, in 1957, a man-made satellite was circling the earth.

Sputnik was catalytic. Here in the United States, the instant orgy of condemnation of the schools and of self-condemnation by educators was followed by a decade of educational reform, with reconstruction of the subject-fields at the core. This education decade outdid the optimism of progressive education for what the schools should and could do. Education and the schools became linked with integration of the races, the

---

[5] The Progressive Education Association closed its doors in 1955. But 1953 witnessed the bumper crop of critics: for example, Arthur Lynd, *Quackery in the Public Schools*, Little, Brown and Co., 1953; Arthur E. Bestor, *Educational Wastelands*, University of Illinois Press, 1953; Robert M. Hutchins, *The Conflict in Education in a Democratic Society*, Harper and Bros., 1953.

eradication of crime and poverty, health, prosperity, and peace for all mankind.

Impetus and direction for change came from both within and without. Federal leadership in Washington viewed rapid improvements in the teaching of mathematics, science, and foreign languages as essential to the nation's ultimate strength and status in world affairs. The National Science Foundation (which had been established in 1950) financed large-scale curriculum-reform projects in these fields. Subsequently, the United States Office of Education extended support to English and the social studies. Education in the nation's interest became the name of the game.

The flow of money into education tended to attract a flow of men, and the field suddenly became more vigorous than it had been in decades. The decade from 1957 to 1967 was rich in proposals for reform in the curriculum, school organization, and instruction. A book by the psychologist Jerome Bruner significantly influenced the new breed of curriculum reformers in the academic disciplines. Two of the terms that he legitimatized, "structure" (of the disciplines) and "intuition" (in learning), became as central to the new era as "the whole child" and "life adjustment" had been to the progressive era. A sentence from Bruner's book was one of the most quoted of the decade, being used commonly to justify both early schooling and solid fare in the young child's curriculum: ". . . any subject can be taught effectively in some intellectually honest form to any child at any stage of development."[6]

A substantial body of data on individual differences in human development and learning was available and expanding. To some educators, these data appeared to suggest certain rather fundamental reforms in school practices. It was clear by now, for example, that the mean achievement of pupils in a fourth-grade class spreads across at least four grade levels, and that reading achievement often extends from the second to the seventh or eighth. The nongraded plan of school organization was proposed to replace the graded organization, which had prevailed for more than a century. The nongraded plan seeks to abolish grade-level designations such as two, four, or six; to raise the ceilings and lower the floors of expectancy in a class group to correspond more precisely with the realities of children's attainments and potentialities; to adjust subject matter and materials to these pupil realities; to substitute continuous progress for the stops, starts, and repetitions of the graded plan; to replace mass procedures of instruction and evaluation with more individualized techniques

---

[6] Jerome S. Bruner, *The Process of Education*, Harvard University Press, Cambridge, Mass., 1960, p. 33.

—in effect, to adjust the system to what we know about individuality and individual differences.[7]

Just as nongrading was designed as an alternative to the rigidity of the graded structure, a second proposal for reorganization of the elementary school, team teaching, was designed as an alternative to the traditional self-contained classroom. It is difficult for teachers to keep up-to-date with advancements in one field. Traditionally, the elementary-school teacher has taught many. The complex problems of teaching all subjects were compounded during the curriculum-reform movement of the late 1950s and early 1960s. Advocates of team teaching proposed that, instead of one teacher supervising a group of thirty, a team of specialists and aides be responsible for instructing a group of 75, 100, or 150. Such a team deploys teachers and pupils into instructional groups of various sizes according to the purposes to be accomplished, the learning needs of pupils, the abilities of teachers, and so on.[8] A team may be as simple as a combination of two classes or as complex as human ingenuity permits, with team leaders, master teachers, apprentices, aides, and parent helpers. Some are teams in name only, with teachers exchanging classes in a form of organization known as departmentalization. Some stay together long enough to become adept at team planning, teaching, and evaluating, and include extensive provision for diagnosing pupils' learning needs and providing for the remediation of learning disabilities.

Not surprisingly, many of the changes proposed were in the realm of instruction. Some psychologists believe that learning is enhanced and learning disabilities avoided when what is to be mastered is "programmed" into carefully sequenced sets, each set leading naturally from the preceding one into the one to follow.[9] Difficulties encountered by students in a sequence suggest imperfections in the program or unwise choice of an entry point for beginning the sequence. Out of such thinking and such work the term "programmed instruction" has emerged. Programmed lessons become the fodder for teaching machines designed to assist and reinforce the learner in progressing at his own rate of speed through the lessons.[10] The computer is regarded as the master teaching

---

[7] See John I. Goodlad and Robert H. Anderson, *The Nongraded Elementary School,* rev. ed., Harcourt, Brace and World, Inc., New York, 1963.

[8] See Judson T. Shaplin and H. F. Olds (Eds.), *Team Teaching,* Harper and Row, New York, 1964.

[9] See Robert Glaser, "The Design of Instruction," in John I. Goodlad, Ed., *The Changing American School,* Sixty-fifth Yearbook (Part II) of the National Society for the Study of Education, University of Chicago Press, Chicago, 1966, pp. 215-242.

[10] See Robert M. Gagné (Ed.), *Learning and Individual Differences,* Charles E. Merrill Books, Columbus, Ohio, 1967.

machine, and much experimental work designed to individualize instruction, using the principles of programming, now centers on it. But the era of computerized instruction still lies ahead.

By 1967, the heady postsputnik decade of school reform was about over. A certain disenchantment was setting in. In preparing Congress to consider precedent-setting legislation for education, President Johnson had said that, if one looks deeply enough, one finds education at the heart of every problem. The subsequent Elementary and Secondary Education Act of 1965 provided for education as no piece of legislation before it had done. It was couched in the language of great expectations: education, as the President had implied, would overcome disadvantage, disability, and impoverishment and would create employment, clean up the slums, and ultimately bring peace.

President Johnson was both right and wrong. For the long run, education is probably the answer to man's problems. For the short haul, however, social engineering is the more likely answer to overpopulation, hunger, joblessness, war, and human misery. Most of us, particularly the young, have rather short-term goals. We want action and results now. Legislators must show the voters within a year or two the results of their legislation. Within a year or two of the passage of the ESEA of 1965, they were unable to do so. It was not education as a process that was at fault. Rather, it was our grandiose, short-run expectations for what can only produce significant change over the long haul. We became disillusioned with education without realizing that we were only beginning to try it.

Elementary Education Today

There is a significant difference between the context producing the educational priorities of the sixties and that influencing those of the seventies. The response to Sputnik was to do better (and, in general, this meant more rigorously) in the schools what we had been trying to do before. The schools had responded rather well, we believed, to previous challenges and could do so again. They had simply gone soft under the influence of the progressives. The concern of the late sixties and early seventies has been more disturbing. It not only includes dissatisfaction with the school's performance but also runs deeply down into a more basic questioning of the school as a viable social institution.

The doubt is not a new one; insightful critics have spoken out about it for some time. It is only now reaching the dimensions of a general concern in our society. James B. Conant (for some years a self-appointed constructive critic of American education) effectively pointed out in 1961 that our inner-city schools were in dire trouble.[11] As the decade moved along, the shocking data of urban neglect became ever more apparent. But we still tended to regard the solutions in somewhat conventional terms: more and better materials, inner-city experiences for future teachers, remedial teachers, and Head Start programs to prepare the disadvantaged for more favorable entry into the educational system. A growing group of neohumanists saw the problems differently. They questioned the school itself.

The names and even the faces of several in this group are familiar to college audiences, in particular: Edgar Friedenberg, Paul Goodman, John Holt, Jonathan Kozol, and George Leonard.[12] The message throughout has been rather consistent: the schools enforce conformity at the expense of creativity, stultifying the personality to the point of dehumanizing it. The harshest critics accuse the schools of fostering prejudice, racism and, ultimately, individual and social malfunctioning with attendant mental illness, crime, and violence. In effect, they say, the schools are promoting the very ills they are designed to eradicate.

A larger group of psychologists, sociologists, educationists, and lay critics assumes a much less harsh position but, nonetheless, they are dubious of the school's influence on childhood learning. Some in this group have studied the school in depth.[13] There is overwhelming agreement that, although the school in some places and at some times has a very negative impact on the child, the appropriate charges to lay against it pertain to its general lack of effectiveness as an educational institution. In brief, they say, the school is not "gripping" its students in powerful, productive ways. One finding, in particular, of the Coleman Report adds credence to such a claim: namely, that what a child gets from his own home and encounters at school from other homes affects his learning more than what the school itself puts in.[14] Concern for the school's effectiveness

11 James B. Conant, *Slums and Suburbs*, McGraw-Hill Book Co., Inc., New York, 1961.

12 Influential books include Jane Bergen et al., *Robots in the Classroom*, Exposition Press, New York, 1965; Paul Goodman, *Compulsory Mis-Education*, Horizon Press, New York, 1964; Nat Henthoff, *Our Children are Dying*, The Viking Press, New York, 1966; and George Leonard, *Education and Ecstacy*, Delacorte Press, New York, 1968.

13 See, for example, Leslie A. Hart, *The Classroom Disaster*, Teachers College Press, Columbia University, New York, 1969; Philip W. Jackson, *Life in Classrooms*, Holt, Rinehart and Winston, New York, 1968; Martin Mayer, *The Schools*, Harper and Bros., New York, 1961; and Louis M. Smith and William Geoffrey, *The Complexities of an Urban Classroom*, Holt, Rinehart and Winston, New York, 1968.

14 James S. Coleman, op. cit.

focused first on the inner city but, increasingly, it has expanded to include schooling in most places.

Several of the harshest critics believe that the school is beyond repair and that the system of public education we have known must be abolished. In its place is to be a loosely organized "open" and informal approach to education, involving home, television, private schools, and storefront learning centers of many kinds. The cures for our present educational follies and fallacies are much less clear than the criticisms. Given the complexities of urban life and culture, the number of broken homes, and the present fare of television and movies, it is difficult to envision how more than 30,000,000 boys and girls now in elementary schools are to be protected, let alone educated, under such a plan. At the same time, however, the prospect of unleashing education from the present restraints of a nine-to-three place called school has many enticing possibilities to which we shall return in the concluding section of this chapter.

In my judgment, we are not yet ready to give up the schools. Nor can we afford to give up *on* them. The schools must be reconstructed, there is no doubt of that, and their reconstruction constitutes the educational agenda of the seventies. In seeking direction for this reconstruction, one hears at least four sets of drummers, two of whom rise more stridently above the others. All four have been with us for some time, in various guises.

The most strident and the most in conflict might be termed the neohumanists and the neobehaviorists. A superficial analysis would align the former with Dewey and the latter with Thorndike. There are some comparisons, to be sure, but one dares not push them very far. One is on sounder ground to leave out such individual comparisons but to note the fact that the present dichotomy represented by the two groups is one that has marked American education in various ways throughout the century. On one hand, we have passionate concern for self-fulfillment of the individual in an environment of minimal adult prescription and control. Adherents of this view frequently cite Maslow,[15] Rogers,[16] and, less frequently, Erikson[17] and Fromm,[18] for conceptual and theoretical support. Some of these see no hope for the schools and urge their abolition. Others

[15] Abraham H. Maslow, *Toward a Psychology of Being,* Van Nostrand and Company, Inc., Princeton, N.J., 1962.

[16] Carl R. Rogers, *Freedom to Learn,* Charles E. Merrill, Columbus, Ohio, 1969.

[17] Erik Erikson, *Childhood and Society,* second ed., W. W. Norton & Company, Inc., New York, 1963.

[18] Erick Fromm, *The Art of Loving,* Harper & Row, New York, 1956.

look to the British Infant Schools[19] or Neill's Summerhill[20] for guidance and concepts and urge "open structure" schools that provide open-space buildings rather than classroom boxes, much self-selection of learning activities, extensive use of the outdoors, and very permissive adult guidance.

Diverging sharply from this group are those who wish to assure the formulation of certain behaviors in the child and see the construction of carefully planned learning environments as the key. They draw heavily on Skinner[21] in proposing the precise delineation of behavioral objectives for the learning process and the careful selection of learning activities and instructional procedures in order to achieve these objectives in economical fashion.[22] Precision in instruction (and, presumably, learning) is achieved through systematic reinforcement (by human or machine teacher) of the behaviors selected for modification or attainment and equally systematic extinction (through withholding rewards, ignoring certain behaviors, and so on) of unwanted or interfering behaviors.[23]

Somewhat less visible these days are those academicians and subject-matter specialists who may agree with some aspects of what the neo-humanists and neobehaviorists are saying but who espouse their own particular route to educational salvation. They view the schools as needing intensified attention to organized subject-matter, either as separate disciplines or as various combinations of disciplines.[24] The separate subject-approach to curriculum organization and teaching returned to favor following Sputnik. Currently, however, there is increasing concern for combining and interrelating fields into what are sometimes known as broad fields (for example, social studies rather than history, geography, and civics) and core curricula (the intermeshing of two or more subjects through the selection of cross-cutting problems). Such approaches were common during the 1930s and 1940s but dropped several rungs down the ladder of academic respectability during the 1950s and 1960s.

[19] Institute for Development of Educational Activities, Inc., *The British Infant School*, |I|D|E|A|, P. O. Box 446, Melbourne, Fla., 1970.

[20] A. S. Neill, *Summerhill*, Hart Publishing Company, Inc., New York, 1960.

[21] Skinner has applied his ideas to shaping an entire fictitous community. See B. F. Skinner, *Walden Two*, The Macmillan Co., New York, 1948.

[22] For curricular and instructional applications, the reader is referred especially to three little volumes by W. James Popham and Eva L. Baker, *Establishing Instructional Goals, Planning an Instructional Sequence*, and *Systematic Instruction*, Prentice-Hall, Inc., New York, 1970.

[23] Madeline H. Hunter, *Reinforcement Theory for Teachers*, TIP Publications, P. O. Box 514, El Segundo, Calif. 90245, 1967.

[24] See John I. Goodlad, *The Changing School Curriculum*, Fund for the Advancement of Education, New York, 1966, for an analysis of this approach.

This last segment of those oriented to the preeminence of subject matter comes rather close to what is essentially a fourth position. This group, too, is somewhat eclectic in borrowing from all of the other positions, but its central concerns are with what might be termed societal or, in the broadest sense, mankind problems.[25] Usually, adherents are deeply concerned about the individual but see his freedom and potentiality as being sharply restrained by problems of such dimensions that they can be resolved successfully only by cooperation and, indeed, the subjugation of nationalistic preoccupations to imperatives of mankind. There is nothing new about this position, either, so far as school curricula and instruction are concerned. It is receiving fresh impetus from our growing anxiety over the possibility that we may be buried in our own garbage and poisoned by our own gases. "Ecology" and "our ravished environment" are key words. Publishing houses and the elementary-school curriculum are responding to them.

It is recognized, of course, that neither educational activity in general nor the schools in particular can be compartmentalized into such discrete categories. In fact, even conceptually and theoretically, the several positions are fuzzy around the edges, overlapping, blending, and fusing. Furthermore, even those distinctions among them that can be rather sharply made become blurred in translation and blunted in implementation. It is a long way from Maslow or Skinner to Miss Thompson or Miss Ludlow, first-grade teachers. The ideas of the former do, indeed, influence the latter but, usually, not in the form of a consistent philosophy or a comprehensive theory. Some applicable concepts are sifted out, popularized, and used, often without insight into or even reference to the larger conceptual framework. These concepts, in turn, are combined with others into the conventional wisdom of the teacher, wisdom that must then be accommodated to the varied demands of classroom teaching.

At any given time in the conduct of schooling, there are prevailing ideologies and their exponents who, for periods of time ranging from several years to a decade or more, are regarded as fashion-setters. They and their ideas are highly visible at educational conventions and in certain journals and popular magazines. These ideologies and their high priests come and go, but those that stay around the longest and have the greatest impact tend to be those best grounded in knowledge and most clearly focused on central, persistent problems of learning and teaching. Taken together, the

---

[25] See, in particular, publications of the Council for the Study of Mankind, such as Robert Ulich Ed., *Education and the Idea of Mankind*, Harcourt, Brace and World, Inc., New York, 1964; and Bert F. Hoselitz, Ed., *Economics and the Idea of Mankind*, Columbia University Press, New York, 1965.

prevailing ideologies provide the practitioner with a backdrop as to "what is good," a level of wisdom to which he sometimes seeks to raise his own.

The four sets of drummers referred to earlier, in spite of the philosophical differences among them, currently provide this multihued backdrop. Elements of it have been around long enough and have been endorsed often enough to provide virtually a set of expectations for the elementary schools. One of these, going back to Dewey and beyond, is that the subject matter of instruction should be selected so as to have intrinsic appeal for children. A second is that there should be agreement on what the school is for. From this agreement, teachers should specify rather clear-cut objectives and select both learning activities and evaluation procedures in the light of these objectives. Third, rather than emphasize the coverage of facts, the school should focus on teaching children *how* to learn, using inductive, discovery methods for a major part of instruction. Fourth, such an approach to learning calls for the use of a wide range of instructional materials, not dependence on textbooks and workbooks. Fifth, school organization and teaching should be guided by and make extensive provision for individual differences among students. Sixth, teachers should bring to bear in their instruction those principles of motivation, transfer of training, extinction, reinforcement and all the rest that are central to educational psychology courses in teacher-preparation programs. Seventh, a substantial portion of classroom activity should be characterized by small-group interaction over topics selected by the pupils themselves. Eighth, classroom organization should be flexible, marked by little attention to grade levels and extensive use of parent aides, outside resources, and team teaching. Ninth, the curriculum should represent a balance among the language arts, fine arts, mathematics, and the natural and social sciences.

One could add extensively to this list, but it is long and varied enough to provide a kind of checklist of expectations for today's elementary school. One must not assume, however, that it accurately reflects reality. To determine this, one must look at the schools themselves. With the thought in mind that prevailing ideology and practice might not coincide, several colleagues and I took a look at 185 classrooms of 79 elementary schools located in 33 school districts of 17 states and the District of Columbia. We had anticipated a discrepancy between the two, but the gap far exceeded our anticipations.[26]

From our observations, it proved to be exceedingly difficult to deter-

---

[26] John I. Goodlad, M. Frances Klein, and Associates, *Behind the Classroom Door*, Charles A. Jones Publishing Co., Worthington, Ohio, 1970.

mine what teachers were endeavoring to accomplish at any time or in any segment of the program under way. Even in subsequent conversations, the teachers were unable to be explicit about what any lesson or any part of a lesson was designed to do. Conversations with principals did not clarify a set of priorities for the schools. Principals were simply unable to identify a sense of direction, to be explict about changes under way, or to suggest what they would like to do if given the freedom and resources to push toward preferred ends. Neither in schools nor in classrooms were we able to find a set of functions or objectives agreed on by the staff.

Not "how" but "what" to learn dominated consistently. Teachers and children were busy "covering" what was set forth in textbooks and workbooks. Children, either as individuals or in groups, were not seeking solutions to problems identified by them as important and meaningful. Instead, they were moderately busy on assignments predetermined by teachers.

In general, the subject matter studied appeared to be remote from the daily concerns and interests of the children. The topics were academic in character; most of the activity pertaining to them consisted of responding to teachers' questions, reading, or completing workbooks. While the children were not bubbling with enthusiasm, they appeared not to be completely bored either. Rather, they went about their business in a somewhat dutiful fashion, appearing to us to be more involved than the subject matter deserved.

The textbook predominated throughout as the medium of instruction, except in the kindergarten. With each advance in grade level, dependence on the textbook increased. Even when pupils shifted from the regular lesson to supplementary activities, textbooks still prevailed, sometimes with a different series being introduced. Rarely were the children using primary materials; rarely were films, filmstrips, record players, tape recorders, and so on in use either as instructional or learning tools. As other studies have documented, the textbook was the dominant instructional medium.

Given such enormous recent interest in individuality and individual differences, we were surprised to find so little provision for either. The bulk of instruction was of the total group variety, with children responding to teachers' questions. Classes were, indeed, divided into groups— usually three—for reading and language activities. But the slower children simply took longer to get to the material that the faster children had covered previously. Thus, such individualization as was provided sought to make minor provisions for differing rates of speed rather than for differing kinds of learner needs.

Learning principles, such as motivation, reinforcement, transfer of training, and goal setting were not clearly in use in the classrooms we visited. We found very few instances in which teachers were identifying the behavior sought, reinforcing pupil responses related to such behaviors, extinguishing irrelevant responses, and the like. In brief, there was a lack of precision in guiding the learning process, suggesting either inadequate understanding or inability to use pedagogical tools.

As suggested in the findings summarized above, there were few instances of children working productively in small groups on problems of mutual interest or concern. Instead, classroom interaction was almost entirely teacher to child, child to teacher, teacher to child, child to teacher, and on and on. Occasionally, children raised unique questions, whether or not relevant, but discussion seldom moved beyond to a child-to-child interaction pattern.

Rather than finding flexibility in the selection of learning activities and in standards of evaluation, we found rather strict adherence to grade levels and group norms. Most classes were operated as though all the children were, indeed, in first or second or third grade, and not widely varying in all aspects of endeavor. The tests used—except for those prepared by the teachers themselves—were of the standardized, norm-based variety. Teachers' tests covered the work laid out for a segment of the grade. The standard of comparison was the grade or group, not some identifiable criterion of performance by means of which pupil progress could be diagnosed. There were very few signs of pupil diagnosis being a factor in selecting learning activites or in evaluating.

The classrooms were largely self-contained. Children sometimes went to classes taught by specialists and specialists sometimes came into regular classrooms, but specialists rarely joined teaching teams. Some of the schools claimed to be team taught, but most of these smacked more of departmentalization, with teachers taking over from each other at various times in the instructional day. We could find little evidence of clusters of teachers coming together to plan for the studies of an identifiable group of students. There was a paucity of teacher aids and of special resource personnel actually used in classrooms. Groups seldom went out into the community to extend the learning environment from confined class cells to a larger world of fields, ponds, museums, and zoos. Almost all the instruction was carried on by a teacher identified as responsible for an entire class at a specific grade level.

It would appear that there is an enormous slippage from educational ideas to implementation in schools and classrooms. The expectations that we had set forth did not include the most dramatic proposals for reform suggested during the sixties. Rather, these were ideas that have been with us for some time, ideas discussed frequently in teacher-education classes, institutes, and workshops. There appears to be a level of dialogue about what is desirable for our schools, and a second level of implementation that is far removed from this one. Getting change from conceptualization into schools and classrooms appears to be a formidable problem.

Elementary Education Tomorrow

Our findings appear to support the Coleman conclusion that the school does not provide a very intensive learning environment, and to add fuel to the fires of those who would abolish it. Before taking such radical steps, however, replacing an inadequate known with what could be a disastrous unknown, we must assure ourselves that the school is beyond redemption and incapable of reconstruction. Several other findings in the study reported above, coupled with additional knowledge about the schools, suggest that we may not have given them an adequate chance, just as we have not yet given education an adequate chance to achieve the high expectations we had had for it.

One interesting finding coming out of our interviews and discussions with teachers and principals was the discrepancy between the observations of our staff and their self-perceptions of practices and programs. They *thought* they were using a wide range of instructional materials, individualizing instruction, using inductive procedures, and the rest. It began to dawn on us that few of them had ever seen schools redesigned along such lines or had been exposed to such practices in their preparation to teach. They had heard about them, read about them, and talked about them, but had not been exposed to or involved in working models. Further reflection brings the realization that very few redesigned models of schools exist. There is much talk of educational change and innovation in the United States, but little effort to move all the way from rigorous conceptualization to simulation, and finally to implementation of models for observation, analysis, and research.

In our interviews, we were also struck by the apparent discrepancy between the in-service education activities of the staffs and what appeared to be the ongoing, persistent problems of the schools. Teachers and principals went off in all directions after school: to attend a university class, to meet with colleagues from other schools, to a community affair, and to their homes. But in only four of the schools we visited did there appear to be a core of teachers working under the leadership of principals in sustained efforts to grapple with the school problems that teachers and principals identified as most troublesome. It should not come as a surprise, therefore, that almost all the schools we visited lacked the character and vitality that come from sustained, cooperative effort on the part of those in them to hammer out a purpose.

Further reflection reveals that schooling is probably the largest enterprise in the United States that does not provide for the systematic updating of its personnel at the cost of that enterprise. Industry teaches new techniques on the job, bringing in task forces to do the teaching or to relieve regular workers while they are paid to learn. But school teachers are expected to keep school and to change it simultaneously. It is not at all surprising, then, that the changes effected are usually peripheral rather than fundamental.

Increasingly, we hear the word "accountability" in reference to teachers' responsibility for teaching children to read, write, and spell. With accountability, however, must go both the opportunity to learn what new demands require and the authority to exercise judgment according to the demands of the instructional situation. The opportunity is not systematically assured and provided and, ironically, the authority is systematically eroded by state laws, the education code, district regulations, central-office administrators, and community pressure groups. To be held accountable under such conditions is both ludicrous and tragic.

A beginning point in the necessary reconstruction of schooling is to regard the individual school, with its principal, teachers, pupils, and parents as the key unit for educational change. The larger system takes on meaning from the individual school units comprising it and exists only to support them. The responsibility of the central office shifts from maintaining district uniformity to creating conditions conducive to effective local school attack on its own problems. The use of time, personnel, and money are directed to this end.

It would be foolhardy to believe that the decentralization of authority and responsibility to local schools simultaneously removes the need for any outside coordination and stimulation and produces an effective reconstructed school. A large-scale research study on a strategy for change involving considerable decentralization and relaxation of district requirements suggests otherwise. The new freedoms and their accompanying expectations create frustrations for principals and teachers alike; new skills and techniques are required; and there appears to be more rather than less demand for ideas, recognition, and approval.[27] It is clear, how-

27 Institute for Development of Educational Activities, Inc., *Change*, |I|D|E|A|, P. O. Box 446, Melbourne, Fla., 1969.

ever, that enormous creative power is unleashed. The schools do become more attractive, exciting, enjoyable places for children and, given the opportunity to communicate, begin to exchange ideas and techniques in a process of helping each other. Alternative models begin to emerge.

We do not yet know what makes a good school. We will never know so long as a monolithic system prevails. To destroy the school along with the system in order to begin all over again is to create far more disequilibrium than is desirable or necessary. The trick, rather, is to create a situation of planned and controlled disequilibrium, a situation that appears possible within a system of authority and responsibility decentralized to the local school. Coordination of the whole should be designed, not to secure uniformity, but to secure the collaboration of other educational agencies: colleges and universities, various education industries, and the communications media. Until recently, educators were almost completely unaware of the advent and power of radio and television as educational forces in our lives. The computer, still in the experimental stage so far as instruction is concerned, is about to follow.

One of the greatest errors of educators throughout all time has been the equating of education and schooling. The error was not so serious when the school was doing its clearly defined job. But that job is no longer clear. Should school continue to be an enterprise taking up 1000 hours or less of a child's life each year, during which certain minimum essentials of linguistic, quantitative, and social literacy are taught? If so, we probably need to add the machine teacher to the human teacher and pay strict attention to the efficient relationship between input and output factors, with output measured in terms of achieving these minimum essentials. Through rigorous application of behavioristic principles, we may be able to shorten the 1000 hours to 700, 500, or 300 with an accompanying gain in achievement and reduce the cost by increased use of electronic rather than human teachers. As a corollary, of course, we will want to turn more of our attention to educational agencies other than the schools to be sure that our more humanistic concerns are being taken care of through radio, television, theater, and museums and through self-selective classes in the arts, individual sports, and sensitivity training.

Or perhaps the school should be a concept rather than a place, encompassing the whole rather than a segment of human experience. Rather than becoming narrow in focus, perhaps the school should be as broad as life itself, drawing from all of society's educational institutions and agencies in the provision of a 24-hour-a-day diet for the whole person. The child would then plan his particular diet with the aid of a teacher-counselor who, in turn, would have access by way of a computer to the full educational smorgasbord currently available. He would spend all or part of some days in places not unlike today's schools, with access to books and people. He would spend part of his time at home, studying by means of individual cassette videotapes played and viewed through his own television set. And he would learn to paint from an artist and to play the violin from a musician. School and education, for the first time, would be virtually synonymous.

These are neither wild dreams nor visions of an unattainable future. They are, rather, predictions of what will probably come to pass and, in fact, descriptions of what is already on the drawing boards. How soon they will come to pass and how effective the elementary school of tomorrow will be depends on human engineering. The place to begin is with the reconstruction of the schools we now have.

References

❖❖

Anderson, Robert H., *Teaching in a World of Change*, Harcourt, Brace & World, New York, 1966. Anderson analyzes both the nature of teaching and the context within which teaching occurs. He gives special attention to the organization of the school and the use of instructional resources.

Committee for Economic Development, *The Schools and the Challenge of Innovation*, The Committee, 477 Madison Avenue, New York, 1969. This volume contains the background papers for the report on educational change and innovation released in 1968 by the influential Committee for Economic Development.

Cremin, Lawrence A., *The Genius of American Education*, University of Pittsburgh, Pittsburgh, 1965. In this Horace Mann lecture, Cremin points out that many agencies, radio, and television are now contributing to the child's education. This necessitates our raising basic questions about the function of the school.

Goodlad, John I., Ed., *The Changing American School*, National Society for the Study of Education, University of Chicago, 1966. This is a critical analysis of both recent forces affecting American education and many of the changes effected in response to these forces.

Goodlad, John I., *School, Curriculum, and the Individual*, Blaisdell Publishing Company, Waltham, Mass., 1966. One of several themes running through this volume is the need for decisions pertaining to the curriculum and to school organization to reflect our knowledge of learners, particularly that pertaining to individual differences.

Joyce, Bruce, *Alternative Models of Elementary Education*, Blaisdell, 1969. Joyce argues impressively that the character of local schools should be determined, not by external prescription, but by critical self-selection, under the guidance of responsible parties representing the school board, local citizens, the district office, the principal, and the teachers.

515

Michaelis, John U., *New Designs for the Elementary School Curriculum*, McGraw-Hill, New York, 1967. Michaelis describes recent developments in the elementary school curriculum, with special reference to materials of instruction.

24

Secondary Education

Lawrence E. Vredevoe

❖❖

The term "secondary education" may mean many things to different individuals in different parts of the world. To some it begins with the fourth grade, with others the sixth, eighth, or ninth, and it may extend through the twelfth or fourteenth year. Recently, some have attempted to associate the thirteenth and fourteenth years with higher education, although the basic financial educational programs of some states classify these grades with the secondary schools. Then too, in the past in some countries, the term could apply to many different types of grade organizations. Secondary education for this discussion will refer to the grades from six or seven through the twelfth grade and will also include the programs of the continuation schools and adult-education programs designed for the completion of the work leading to the certificate or diploma of graduation. Biologically it covers primarily the period from puberty to adulthood. Chronologically it covers the years from eleven or twelve to eighteen or twenty. Secondary schools refer to the public or private schools accredited by the state authorities or a regional accrediting agency. The program of the schools for this discussion includes all the courses and activities under the supervision and responsibility of the school.

Before considering the structure, program, and other aspects of secondary education it is important to consider its goals and objectives through the years and primarily the last three decades during which it has experienced its greatest expansion in this and other countries. Originally the primary objectives were vocational and in some countries military or defense. Those attending secondary schools were in general preparing for the professions such as medicine, law, teaching, or religious work. Later, as education became compulsory, the vocational and industrial aspects were added. In recent years the need for a comprehensive program became imperative because of the extension of the compulsory school-attendance age. The requirement that youths attend school was instituted because of the recognition of a need for more education to enable one to succeed as both a citizen and a worker. However, many question how well secondary schools have measured up to the claims of its leaders and proponents as meeting the needs for all students. In the first decade of this century the secondary schools in most countries confined their goals and programs to those preparing to go to college or into business. In the last three decades, the emphasis has been on a program for all youth. Although separate schools had developed, such as the commercial school, industrial and trade schools, and technical schools in addition to the traditional secondary school, the theory that predominated in both the program and organization of our schools since the 1940s is that of the comprehensive school. Primarily the objective was to meet the needs of all students and it was believed that this could be done best by bringing all schools together. The comprehensive secondary school was an American innovation for compulsory secondary education. It has been copied by other countries and leaders and in theory is recognized as sound. It enables the school authorities to tailor the program to the needs of the individual student rather than the student to the program of the specialized school in which he is placed. However, practice has not always demonstrated that the theory has been identified with the program. As a result many district, state, and national leaders are challenging both the theory and the practice today. Too many schools give lip service to the theory but in practice give emphasis to the college-preparatory program.

What really determines the programs of our secondary schools? The programs of most public schools and some of the others are directly related to the following.

State and local district laws and policies
College and university requirements
Federal grants and subsidies for secondary schools and students
Criteria and standards of regional accrediting associations

State, regional, and national testing programs
Technological and social changes and pressures
International involvement and commitment

Some of the programs remind me of one of the instant-food manias of recent years. Boards of education and administrators seemed to be most eager to come up with an instant program or change of policies and requirements to meet one or all of the demands of some of the above agencies of pressures. Federal grants and subsidies seemed to have brought about the most rapid changes. The smell of money had greater impact than did educational philosophy and goals. Some schools and districts appointed or hired full-time administrators to keep them abreast of all the possible grants and subsidies for which their schools might qualify. National and state programs quickly designed and adopted by the legislators to appease the pressures of their constituents and social groups indicated that the programs of secondary schools were most susceptible to monetary and political influence. As a result, too many schools sold their birthright for a mess of pottage. Now that the period is past when it appeared that we could afford the waste of time, money, and human resources, our secondary schools are found wanting. Accountability for what the program is and does for those enrolled appears to be the demands of both parents and constitutents in this decade. Then, too, as the secondary-school students become more militant, it is already clear that their greatest revolt will be against the inadequate programs in their schools. Perhaps the shortage of money, the inability to continue wastefulness, and the demand for accountability will prove to be a blessing in disguise. They may force school administrators, teachers, and board-of-education members to go back to where they have detoured and begin once again to look to the philosophy and goals of secondary education in a country that demands compulsory attendance by all and a society that makes the high school diploma a must for employment and social acceptance. It might be profitable for us at this time to review briefly the development of the objectives and goals as they have dominated secondary schools.

Purposes and Objectives of Secondary Education

The development of secondary education is directly related to the purposes and objectives of those in control of the education of the adolescent in the different cultures, countries, or locale. In some cultures, programs were designed only for boys. The American Indian boy was given the experience and knowledge to serve as hunter and warrior for his tribe, the Spartan boy was trained as warrior and citizen, and the Hebrew boy was prepared for religious, social, and economic leadership. Time, culture, geography, economic or political atmosphere, and other influences determined the objectives and purposes of education for the adolescent.

Fundamental to all these purposes and objectives was the basic concept of the role of education. If this concept was primarily concerned with perpetuation of the status quo or the traditions and beliefs of a political, social, or religious group, the value of a static program of education was recognized. If the development of creativeness and the pioneering spirit of investigation into the political, social, and religious thought of the period was of major concern, the need for a dynamic program of education for youth was encouraged and supported. The ability to think quickly, logically, and clearly has been one of the objectives of education for adolescents through the ages, and efforts to control this thinking become evident as one studies the methods and content of different educational programs, especially the static programs designed to preserve tradition. What, how, when, and where certain concepts and ideas are introduced are directly related to the controls that the system seeks to place on the thought processes of youth.

The objectives and purposes of secondary education within a country are affected by the stage of development. A young, pioneering government or culture first concerns itself with the practical aspect of secondary education and later with cultural and leisure-time instruction. The early settlers of this country were primarily concerned with maintaining the development of agriculture, commerce, and industry. Formal education was considered necessary only to provide religious leaders and professional men who were trained either in Europe or at Harvard. Therefore, the purpose of the first secondary programs was to train for the clergy and prepare students for entrance to Harvard or European universities. The program, designed for the few, reflected the European pattern.

Before turning to the present purposes and objectives of secondary education in this country, it pays to review the individuals and groups that are trying to influence and determine them. Consider the secondary school as standing in the center of a number of agents and agencies concerned with what takes place within the school program. The taxpayer is concerned because whatever happens affects him. Parents are vitally interested in what happens to their children. This group should be divided into the preschool, in-school, and postschool parents because the age and place of a person's children has an affect on that person's interest in the school. Place of residence may affect parental attitude. Those parents living in the developing suburbs usually take a more active part in school affairs than do those in the urban centers. Rural residents tend to be conservative and more traditional than are those in the suburbs. These differences are not as sharp in some localities any longer because of the disappearance of the purely rural communities in some parts of the country. The age group, work interest, and location of the residential area are often reflected in the purposes and objectives of the secondary-school program (Figure 1).

Occupational groups have an interest in the program for the education

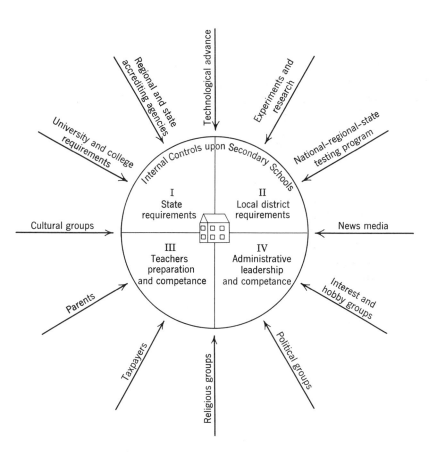

Figure 1. External and internal control on secondary schools in the United States.

of youth. Labor, management, professional, and other groups concern themselves with how the secondary-school program interprets their place in the life and function of the citizen. Furthermore, special-interest groups such as conservationist, social, political, religious, and economic groups have a real concern in what is taught or experienced by students in the secondary school. All these groups and others seek to influence the program and materials to which the adolescent will be exposed in the school. Nevertheless, there appears to be more agreement than disagreement as to the basic objectives of an educational program. The groups may differ in degree or scope, but essentially all of them seem to recognize the part that the school plays in developing citizenship, health habits and physical fitness, language arts, vocational competence, and cultural interests.

A summary of the objectives of different groups and committees since 1900 identifies the areas of agreement among these basic goals. Although certain groups have divided their objectives into specifics, all fall under the general headings of citizenship, language arts, vocational competence, and physical fitness. A definition of these four basic objectives might help us to detect them in the purposes and objectives of the different groups.

Citizenship in its broader sense includes the knowledge and skills to live successfully as an individual and a member of the group. The individual must be able to get along with his fellow citizens, recognize the need for group action to bring about the greatest good for the greatest number while protecting the rights and privileges of the individual, participate intelligently in civic duties, develop a true sense of the moral and spiritual values in group and personal decisions, understand the basic principles of our economy and way of life, and appreciate the need for conservation of human and natural resources.

Language arts include the skills and knowledge needed by the individual to comprehend and communicate thoughts and ideas. He should be able to read, write, listen, think logically, observe, and speak effectively. These skills should be developed to the highest possible degree according to the individual's ability. No society or group can perpetuate its culture or ideals unless language arts are developed by its members.

Vocational competence includes the knowledge and skills to successfully carry on the trades, professions, and work of society. The efforts of the individual should be rewarding both to himself and to the society of which he is a member. The objectives of vocational competence should emphasize the creative, inventive, and service aspects of each man's work, as well as the development of marketable skills.

Health and physical fitness include health mental as well as the health of the body. The individual should be encouraged to develop physical fitness for work, play, and service of society. Conservation of human resources as they relate to health and safety should be stressed in this phase of the education of the adolescent.

With these four definitions in mind, examine Table 1 for a summary of objectives and purposes and note how many are directly or indirectly related to citizenship, vocational competence, health and physical fitness, or the language arts in their broader concepts.

Notwithstanding the efforts of different groups and organizations to write or rewrite the goals and objectives of secondary education, fundamentally the needs of the secondary-school student can be stated as follows.

Language arts—ability to read, write, observe, think logically, listen, and communicate ideas.

Health and physical fitness—mental and body health.

Vocational correctness—proper attitudes, craftsmanship, creativeness, and adjustability.

Table 1

Objectives of Education as Developed by the Major Committees and Commissions

Commission on the Reorganization of Secondary Education 1918 *Seven cardinal principles:*	Committee on Standards for Use in the Reorganization of Secondary School Curricula 1920 *Ultimate objectives:*	American Youth Commission *(Secondary Eduction for Youth in Modern America)* 1937 *Objectives:*
1. Health	1. To maintain health and physical fitness	1. Citizenship
2. Command of fundamental processes	2. To use leisure in right ways	2. Home membership
3. Worthy home membership	3. To sustain successfully certain definite social relationships: civic, domestic, community, etc.	3. Leisure life
4. Vocation		4. Physical and mental health
5. Citizenship		5. Vocational efficiency
6. Worthy use of leisure	4. To engage in exploratory vocational and vocational activities	6. Preparation for continued learning
7. Ethical character		

Progressive Education Association (The Eight-Year Study) 1938	Education Policies Commission (*Purposes of Education in American Democracy*) 1938	White House Conference on Education Nov. 28–Dec. 1, 1955 *Objectives which will develop:*
Needs of youth:	*Objectives:*	

1. Physical and mental health	1. Self-realization	1. Fundamental skills of communication, arithmetic, and mathematics
2. Self-assurance	2. Human relationships	
3. Assurance of growth toward adult status	3. Economic efficiency	2. Appreciation for our democratic heritage
4. Philosophy of life	4. Civic responsibility	
5. Wide range of personal interests	*Education for All American Youth* 1952	3. Civic rights and responsibilities
6. Aesthetic appreciations	*Objectives which will equip youth to:*	4. Respect and appreciation for human values
7. Intelligent self-direction	1. Enter an occupation suited to his abilities	5. Ability to think and evaluate constructively
8. Progress toward maturity in social relations with age mates and with adults	2. Assume responsibilities of American citizenship	6. Effective work habits and self-discipline
	3. Attain and preserve mental and physical health	7. Social competency
9. Wise use of goods and services	4. Stimulate intellectual curiosity	8. Ethical behavior
10. Vocational orientation	5. Think rationally	9. Intellectual curiosity
11. Vocational competence	6. Develop an appreciation of ethical values	10. Aesthetic appreciation
		11. Physical and mental health
		12. Wise use of time
		13. Understanding of the physical world
		14. Awareness of our relationship with the world community

Domestic competence—ability to live successfully as a member of a family group or as a leader.

Social confidence—appreciation and understanding of man's progress and potential in solving political, social, and economic problems.

Moral and spiritual depth—value judgment and recognition of need for self-discipline and service to others.

The better these objectives are attained, the more certain the individual and society can be of secondary-school graduates' succeeding as individuals, citizens, and workers in the years ahead. This is especially true as one considers the type of student we find in our secondary schools in this decade.

The Administrative Organization of Secondary Education

The administrative type of secondary districts varies widely throughout the country. Some secondary-school districts are concerned only with administration of the secondary programs; others include the elementary or college program, and some cover all three levels. Many urban centers have a unified type of district that has jurisdiction over the educational program from nursery schools through college, and the number of union secondary districts that include continuation and adult-education programs is increasing. Each district, after complying with state requirements, establishes its own type of programs and standards within the framework of powers delegated to it by the state authorities (Figure 2).

The control of secondary education by the people within the states has resulted in different standards and programs and in social lag in the curriculum of many schools. Those who seek efficiency, uniformity, and change are disturbed by the slowness with which change takes place under our system. It is important, however, to recognize that any national system of secondary education would require a constitutional amendment and a change in the philosophy of our American concept of control and administration. An understanding of the basic legal structure and concept of education in America is essential for anyone entering the teaching profession. Schools in our country represent the social view that the state is subservient to the individual and not the individual to the state. Schools are, therefore, established to serve the individual and, through his improvement, to enhance the state. This accepted principle will be likely in the foreseeable future to make any attempt to give control to the Federal Government, in order to bring about greater efficiency or uniform standards, unattractive to the citizens of this country.

Organizational Patterns

The composition of the political units within the different states has resulted in a variety of types of secondary schools. Certain generally accepted descriptive names of the schools should be understood by those interested in secondary education. The following types of schools are the

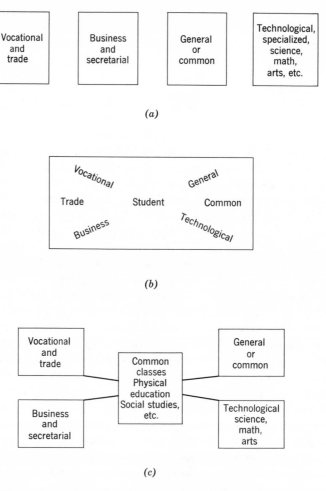

Figure 2. Types of secondary-school organization. (a) Specialized secondary schools—student must adjust to program of the school. (b) Comprehensive secondary school—program is tailored to the needs of the student. (c) Schools within a school—common administration and certain common courses and activities.

most common in the present administrative organization of individual schools:

High School. A school including grades nine through twelve (9-12).

Senior High School. A school including grades ten through twelve (10-12).

Junior High School or Intermediate School. A school including grades six or seven through nine, or seven through eight (6-9, 7-9, or 7-8).

Continuation School. A school or program within a school system, catering to youths who are of legal age for work but who are required to attend school on a part-time basis.

Comprehensive High School. A school that combines the special programs formerly provided by trade, commercial, general, and academic high schools and that offers both general and special training.

Vocational or Trade High School. A school providing specialized programs for trade and industry plus apprenticeship training.

Junior College. A school including grades thirteen and fourteen (13-14). It generally affords the opportunity to complete work leading to the associate in arts degree.

Community or City College. An institution that includes grades thirteen and fourteen and in addition offers special courses and programs to meet individual needs and interests for which credit may or may not be given. It sometimes includes the junior college, adult education, secondary-school program for those beyond high school age, and special courses for interest groups and in-service training programs. The academic program may be two or four years in length.

The traditional high school (9-12) predominates, although the junior-senior (7-9 or 7-8, and 10-12) types are increasing in many parts of the country. Most states have some of these different types, and many reflect new experiments in secondary-school administration.

Recent national enrollment reports show that, although the traditional type of high school (9-12) is still most numerous in many states, the junior and senior or junior-senior secondary schools enroll more than half the secondary students attending grades seven through twelve. This is due to the fact that these schools are larger and are found in the more populated urban centers or reorganized districts, which cover wider areas.

Private Secondary Education

Private schools have contributed much to public education in the development of new types of schools and experimentation. All public schools, with the exception of the junior high school, can trace their origin to private sources. The nursery school, elementary school, high school, junior college, four-year college, and university were first established as private schools, independent or parochial, and later adopted as types of public institutions by states or school districts. Private laboratory schools have carried on experiments that later influenced public school methods and procedures. They were better able to do this than public schools because they could select and reject for experimental purposes in order to establish control groups. Then, too, the public has not been too eager to give to local schools the right, time, money, or equipment to carry on experiments. Not until recently have school districts been interested in supporting experimentation in their public schools. Most of the experimentation now being carried on in public schools results from gifts from private funds and from grants. It is not to be concluded that all private schools have availed themselves of the opportunity to experiment. Some have been rigidly controlled and held to a traditional pattern. Nevertheless, several of the most daring experiments in education have been carried on in private laboratory schools where the staff, facilities, and student body have made experimentation possible.

This leads to the recurring question, "Which is superior, the public or the private secondary school?" The author has visited over seventeen hundred secondary schools throughout the country and others, including large and small; rural and urban; boys, girls, and coeducational; segregated and mixed (with respect to race and creed); and all types of parochial schools. It is safe to conclude from this background that neither all public nor all private schools should be placed into one group, and further, that neither type has a monopoly on what is good or bad in secondary education. The bad and undesirable as well as the good can be found in both public and private schools. Private schools have a greater opportunity to obtain their objectives because they can select and reject. Public schools must take and keep all those of compulsory school age and, in some districts, accept the mentally deficient, which includes the slow learner as well as the belligerent student. Other districts permit the dismissal or rejection of these by public school authority. It is unfair to generalize relative to good or bad standards of education. Each school should be judged individually or in comparable groupings.

The growth of private education is influenced by four major factors: legal interpretations of laws and statutes affecting segregation and the like, desire by certain groups to provide their own programs for the adolescents, general prosperity, and new federal grants to provide secondary-school enterprises. The right of schools to exist as private institutions and the right of parents and guardians to send their children to private secondary schools does not imply that a state does not have power to regulate and supervise private schools. The degree and extent of regulatory and supervisory powers differ according to state constitutions, but the right to establish and maintain private schools exists in all states.

The desire of certain groups to provide a program of education for adolescents apart from the public schools has emerged from the criticisms of public education, religious objectives, and belief in select grouping and segregation. Whenever public education has been under severe attack for failure to meet the needs of certain adolescents, schools have been established to provide for those preparing for college, or for the retarded, or for some other group. Parochial secondary schools increase as church leaders and parents seek to include indoctrination of a religious creed or faith as part of the daily instructional program. Private schools also receive greater enrollment where social and racial tensions develop.

A factor aiding the development of private education is general prosperity. Parents and groups are more inclined to support private enterprises in addition to their support of public schools when their incomes permit it. Increased costs of education and the expanded curriculum make private-school enterprises more and more dependent on endowments and contributions. These usually reflect the economic status of the community or country.

Many districts are eager to cooperate with private and parochial schools in providing part-time programs in such subjects as industrial and homemaking arts as well as in certain specialized classes. The basic reason for such cooperation is the recognition of the increased burden on public secondary schools in districts where private institutions would close and transfer their enrollment to state schools. However, any significant change in our economic pattern may halt or witness a retrenchment of private secondary schools.

Accreditation of Secondary Schools

Accreditation of secondary schools was first practiced by the University of Michigan in 1871. The University had previously recognized certain courses in a selected group of schools, which excused students from examinations in these subjects. The new program excused students who graduated from the accredited high schools from all entrance examinations. It provided schools with a set of criteria that were to be met and maintained for the period of accreditation. Periodic inspections were made by faculty members and accreditation would be extended for one, two, or three years. Other universities soon followed and by 1900 not only was accreditation recognized as a convenience for graduates of those schools but also certain prestige was enjoyed by those on the accredited list. Some states developed a program of approval or accreditation of schools in cooperation with the state universities. Thus we find two basic programs within the states—accreditation by the university or by the department of public instruction. Recently, most of the universities have withdrawn from the program, and the University of Michigan remains as the only institution that accredits all qualified schools within the state. However, the state department of public instruction approves schools for eligibility for state funds. As a result there are two lists, the one of schools approved by the state, and the one of schools accredited by the university. Most secondary schools are on both lists.

Two major influences have brought about the change from university to state-department accreditation. The first is the increase in the number of universities within some states and the question of control of accreditation by one institution. The second is the expense and personnel needed to carry on such a program. It has become increasingly difficult to use regular qualified university staff members for visits to schools, and the proliferation of secondary schools has made it almost impossible for the university to undertake the task. Since state departments of public instruction must approve schools for distribution of state funds, establish minimum standards, and visit schools to check on these standards, it seems logical that approval of schools within a state should be the function of a state department of public instruction with the assistance of a competent staff.

Approval does not automatically grant admission of high school graduates to universities and colleges. In some states admission to community colleges, state universities, and colleges is assured by law to all graduates of all approved high schools within the state. But the law does not give the graduate the right to select his course. It only says that he must be accepted upon graduation irrespective of grades or courses. Some states assures admission where facilities permit to all state colleges and branches of the university upon achievement of a certain grade-point average and completion of certain subjects. Thus, approval of secondary school may or may not automatically assure the graduate admission to college without examination.

Many secondary schools enjoy the accreditation of a regional association of secondary schools and colleges. These are nonlegal, voluntary groups, and schools must measure up to their regulations and standards in order to qualify for or maintain membership. Secondary schools in all fifty states have the opportunity to affiliate with such an association. All six associations cut across state lines. The six, in order of their organization dates, are the New England Association of Colleges and Secondary Schools, 1885 the Middle States Association of Colleges and Secondary Schools, 1892; the North Central Association of Colleges and Secondary Schools, 1895; the Southern Association of Colleges and Schools, 1895;

the Northwest Association of Secondary and Higher Schools, 1917 and the Western Association of Schools and Colleges, 1962.

At first, the New England and Middle States Associations did not accredit secondary schools, choosing instead to bring about improvements in them through conferences that stressed the importance of standards. Both of these now follow the procedures of the other regional groups in publishing lists of the accredited schools or those schools maintaining membership.

The criteria and regulations for accreditation in the six regional associations have several similar provisions and requirements. They stress the qualifications of administrators and teachers, the comprehensiveness and quality of programs, the library and laboratory facilities, the guidance program, requirements for graduation, the teacher's load, the administrative and supervisory procedures, and other aspects of the school that the associations regard as essential for a good secondary-school program. All criteria and regulations are developed and adopted at the annual meetings of the associations.

Although accreditation or approval of secondary schools is primarily a function of the department of public instruction or a corresponding agency in the different states, and approval is a legal requirement to qualify for state support, regional associations also accredit schools. They do so through voluntary membership which is granted upon satisfying the established policies, criteria, and regulations, and such approval gives their graduates college admission without entrance examinations and acceptance of high school credits. An increasing number of colleges and universities are requiring all candidates to take national entrance examinations. If this trend continues, the original purpose of accreditation may no longer matter because all students will be taking entrance or qualifying examinations.

Students of the Secondary School

Almost one out of every four persons in the American population is enrolled in some form of day or evening secondary-school education. Those who teach in the secondary schools should be familiar with some of the characteristics of those in their classes.

Biological

The majority of the students are passing from childhood through pubescence and adolescence into adulthood. The individual student represents a package of forty-six chromosomes, twenty-three from the father and twenty-three from the mother. This package contains many items that affect his physical makeup, mental potential, and other factors. Although genetic composition may impose certain limitations, nobody has yet defined what they are. We do know that more change takes place biologically during pubescence and adolescence than during any other period of development. It is a period in which imbalances and stresses cause concern and misunderstandings. Voice, heart, the arterial system, glands, and the neurological system affect coordination, complexion, growth, appearance, and general physical characteristics just when the individual is more conscious of them. The adolescent's shuffle and imbalances sometimes change the gracious, well-coordinated individual into a person of physical stress and strain, and clumsiness. He often fails to understand the changes himself, and those with whom he is associated also lack appreciation of his problems. This, in turn, produces more conflicts in both his home and his school.

Social

This secondary-school period is characterized by the desire of the individual to grow up and to show it. A wish to escape the controls of adults at home often causes strange behavior. Physically and at heart, he may still be a young boy (or girl), yet he seeks to emulate the adult. The approval of his parents and teachers may be desired, but that of his peers takes on greater prominence and importance. His desire to be identified with a peer group often leads to a sacrifice of standards and principles in order to belong.

The secondary-school student is attracted by the protest movements, riots, and demonstrations. To some students these represent real commitment and leadership. Many are eager to take an active part in social reform and even revolution. The leaders of these demonstrations are nearer to the students' ages than are their parents or adults who now appear to belong to a bygone period.

Moral standards and ethics in society raise many questions about what course of action really pays off in the end. The student sees many in high office and in local community leadership prosper with a new code of morals and ethics (or lack of them). The end seems to justify the means. This is a period of reevaluation and assessment of religious, family, or group mores and beliefs. Dope, drinking, sex and dishonesty are part of his school environment if not participation. All of his value judgements are challenged.

As a secondary-school student, he is exposed to crowded schools and then moves into a crowded labor market, college, or professional activity. More and more of his decisions must relate to the programs of state and federal agencies. At the same time, less and less independence of choice and activity confronts him. He seeks and desires a feeling of value in the scheme of things, a sense of achieving and belonging that brings identification with those movements, activities, and individuals that seem to give these to him. The secondary school has the opportunity to provide the positive leadership and guidance so critically needed at this period.

Other Characteristics

The secondary-school student of the next decade will represent an important segment of our population. Student styles, diet, recreation, music, and culture will be the concern of those in the fields of sales and marketing. This group will represent one of the greatest potential markets.

This student will live in a large megalopolis or strip-city center in which his home is likely to be a unit in a housing project or an apartment house. The identity of home as a house and lot or small acreage will typify only the minority. The student will have accepted the crowded neighborhood, recreation centers, and social groups.

He will never have experienced a period of peace; or of the absence of a hot or cold war, of the shadow of the draft, or of a budget slanted toward paying for a war or preparing for a new one. His freedom to choose a vocation, domestic plans, or activities will be affected by these. His major objective in education will seem to be to pass tests and compete in oral examinations for college admission, employment, and status. Competence will be measured by the computer and what it can measure or test. Dependence on state and federal agencies for scholarships, employment, and security will be greatly increased. His society will appear to be in a state of confusion relative to moral and spiritual values. The end will seem to justify the means. Laws and their enforcement will become more complex and more difficult.

The student's family life will experience more stress and strain, and his home will reflect more mobility and lack of privacy. His greatest needs will be for privacy, a sense of social security, value judgment, and direction. His teachers and administrators will represent a wide area of competence, philosophy, interests, and professional objectives.

Predictions as to Behavior Problems in Secondary Schools

Student behavior will become of more and more vital concern both within and without the school. The restlessness and disturbing influences will be felt to a greater degree in the school than in previous times. Outside leaders and pressure groups will be of increasing importance. Leadership, understanding, and gentle firmness will be of greater importance than supervision, rules, regulations, and adult autocracy.

The majority (95 percent of the students) will desire a well-disciplined school in which the basic principles of the greatest good for the greatest number will be implemented. Between 90 and 95 percent can be depended on to exercise self-discipline. The remaining 5 percent will become more violent and disturbing.

Segregation, desegregation, or the social composition of the school will not be as important as the competence and attitude of staff members. The emerging concept of second-class teachers on the basis of what they teach will create new problems in our larger schools. New problems of discipline will result from the awareness on the part of students of poor teaching, programs, and guidance. Students will be more motivated and excited than ever for both good and bad behavior.

Students will be more critical of social mores, standards, and beliefs and in more need of better interpretation and demonstration of those values society wishes to maintain. The schools and their programs will be one of the major hopes for perpetuation of the good and elimination of the bad. Moral and spiritual values will be the only basis for establishing personal and group controls and implanting the ability to live in a congested, confused community of nationalities, cultures, religions, and political beliefs.

Causes of Good and Bad Behavior

Most of the students identify with one of two classes: the deviates and the conformists. Interviews with deviates reveal the following basic reasons why they want to be different.

To attract attention.

To rebel against patterns of which they do not feel a part or in which they have been rejected.

To gain identity with a particular group or person.

A weariness over conforming and an attempt to escape.

To annoy or disturb certain individuals: parents, teachers, fellow students, or other groups.

A sense of achieving or a feeling of frustration and hopelessness is often reflected in the student's behavior. Personality factors of superiors that range all the way from the inspiring, motivating, and positive to the repelling, annoying, and negative do indeed affect student behavior. Sometimes behavior may be a result of a combination of more than one person's effect.

The very nature, characteristic, or atmosphere of the school influences positive and negative behavior. So does cultural or ethnic-group attitudes toward education, society, and superiors, which tend to influence positive and negative response toward rules and regulations. Economic or social status may also affect behavior positively or negatively. Furthermore, stature, appearance, complexion, or other physical characteristics; home and parental attitude toward education or school; and society, intellectual challenge, and respect for rules and regulations and their enforcement all are likely to influence the student's behavior pattern.

Toward Better Secondary-School Behavior

Clearly defined goals and objectives and an understanding of these by both staff and student body lead to better behavior in the secondary school. This is likewise true of an appreciation of the value of the imagery of the school to both staff members and students and of an understanding of the need for rules, regulations, and their enforcement in a democratic society. Liberty lies in law, not in the lack of it. There must be a respect for private and public property and a recognition that we all suffer where it does not exist.

The respect for the other fellow and his work is basic in developing the ability to get along with people. Also needed are the development of rules and regulations through the coordinated efforts of all and their enforcement until changed by due process of law; pride and interest in high standards and good workmanship; identification with a small group and a carefully selected competent adviser or counselor; reasonable standards relative to dress and grooming; and finally, moral and spiritual emphasis in the classroom, assemblies, activities, and personal relations with fellow students and peers. The secondary-school student presents not only a real challenge to teachers and administrators but also one of the greatest opportunities to help develop effective and creative leaders for the dynamic social and political world of tomorrow.

Teachers of the Secondary School

Uniform certification of teachers in the secondary school did not occur in the early American schools, because teaching was not a regular, but rather a part-time, position. In New England, approval by the local minister, Bishop of London, or colonial governor was the usual requirement of the common schools. Religious rather than academic qualifications were the chief concern. In many districts, the ability to discipline and control students received greater weight in the selection of teachers than their educational backgrounds. At first, the pressures to remove the right to license teachers from local to state authorities received great resistance. Licensing became a state function in the last century, and now all public school teachers are certificated by state standards.

Today all states require graduation from an accredited college for certification, and a number of states have extended this requirement to include the fifth year of professional or academic work. The uniformity we find in the requirements for teaching in the secondary schools can be attributed, in a large part, to the regional and national accrediting agencies. The trend in certification is to certify not only the basic qualifications to teach, but also the subjects and areas of supervision in which the individual is permitted to perform.

Recently the general characteristics of secondary-school teachers have changed. The average age has dropped, and men teachers outnumber the women teachers in many states. The master's degree is generally considered necessary for anyone who desires to continue teaching and to advance in both salary and position. In many districts, the doctorate is mandatory for chief administrators and directors. The master's degree is the one mostly found in the larger schools at this time.

Secondary-school teaching candidates have been on the increase for several years, and now there is a surplus in some areas of instruction. Part of this surplus is due to the greater number of candidates for secondary schools than for elementary grades. It is also a result of a stepping up of requirements for elementary-school teachers and of emphasis on academic preparation. Quite likely a surplus of candidates will develop in most areas of instruction in many districts before long. This will be beneficial, because school authorities will have a greater opportunity to select better-qualified candidates. Too many districts have had to accept what was available rather than being in a position to select those best qualified for the job.

Teaching in the secondary school is becoming more and more attractive. In some districts the salary schedule is better than is found in institutions of higher learning and is comparable with many scales in the commercial and industrial world. The trend to make classroom teaching attractive as a lifelong career rather than one from which an individual must advance to make a suitable income is evident in many districts. The former practice of a successful classroom teacher's becoming an administrator for economic reasons rather than professional interest or desire is disappearing. Districts are now making it possible to become a master teacher and make both professional and economic progress without leaving the classroom.

The greatest need is for better evaluation of the secondary-school teacher. Periodic examinations and evaluations are needed to insure the teacher's remaining competent in this age of technological and social change. It will become more and more apparent that the need for competence in secondary-school classrooms and administrative offices is of concern to all society. Better evaluation of teaching personnel is needed if students are to be protected against those who attain tenure and then retire intellectually or professionally, and if the secondary schools are to develop and maintain a high-quality program of instruction.

The Program of the Secondary School

The program of the secondary school depends on the level of instruction and the type of students enrolled as well as the factors discussed under the goals and objectives of secondary education. The intermediate or junior high school, which includes grades seven through nine or seven through eight, and sometimes six through eight, is usually considered a transitional school from the child-centered elementary grades to the subject- or vocational-centered senior high school. Recent pressures for college preparation and the changing technological demands by industry have resulted in emphasis on subject matter in the high schools. This emphasis has carried over into the adult-education program and continuation school.

A significant change has come over the program of the secondary schools in the United States since the First World War. Until then, secondary schools, particularly in the urban centers, were specialized to a large degree. Some remnants of the trade and industrial; commercial or business; and technical schools are to be found in different parts of our country. Schools provided specialized programs to meet the needs of both the individual and the employer or institution of higher learning. An attempt was made to determine the ability and interests of the individual and then assign him to the proper type of school. Eventually, it was recognized that no single school met all the needs of the individual and that specialized schools did not always offer the best educational climate and stimulation for motivation and learning. Therefore, the comprehensive secondary school emerged and has now become the type of public school found in most districts.

Sound as the comprehensive secondary school may be in theory, its soundness is not always reflected in practice. Many districts, in reorganizing their secondary schools, have given preferential treatment to the college-preparatory or general-education courses. As a result, some secondary schools provide only a token program for the practical arts. Indeed, some educators are now urging a return to the specialized type of school. In the comprehensive schools, the opportunity to provide a more democratic environment has often degenerated into a social classification of teachers and students within the school, depending on which courses they teach or take. It is not surprising to find some students in these schools taking courses for which they are not qualified or that do not suit their needs in order to maintain social status. Although sound in democratic and educational theory, the comprehensive secondary school needs better implementation in practice.

The grouping of students for guidance in secondary schools reflects four major practices. The first is the homeroom, in which the students are assigned by grade to a group of 25 to 35 with an advisor who meets with them briefly every day and usually stays with the group until graduation or transfer to the next school. The second practice is the assignment of two to four hundred students to a counselor or administrator who is responsible for the guidance of those within his group. A third is the use of a certain class, which may be social studies or English, and a period such as the third period, irrespective of subject matter, as the basic guidance unit; thus the student may have a different advisor every semester or at least every year. The fourth is the organization of each grade or class level into a guidance unit; the individual in charge may or may not have assistants, depending on the size of the group.

A common criticism today is that our secondary schools are becoming too impersonal and are organized for administrative convenience rather than for the student's need. If the student's need is of primary concern, then it is obvious that a small group and advisor who has the opportunity to get to know and understand the individual is most needed. Too many of the larger guidance units provide recognition only for those who are outstanding either through achievement or through poor conduct. The average individual received only the counseling necessary to develop a program, assign classes, and check on requirements.

The organization of administrative units for instruction in the secondary schools presents a mosaic pattern throughout the country. Basically, the need is being more widely recognized for the intermediate school as a transitional one from the elementary to senior high school. As a result, the three-year or two-year school for this purpose is burgeoning. Another factor in its increase is that more and more communities are becoming urbanized and population is becoming concentrated. The basic problem facing those responsible for these intermediate schools is to keep them transitional and not subject-centered institutions.

The continuation school for those who drop out and are required to continue their education on a part-time basis because of the compulsory school age laws is becoming part of the adult-education program in the community college or evening school. This is also true of those over eighteen years of age who fail to complete the requirements for a high school diploma. The adult-education program, which was originally designed for teaching elementary school subjects to immigrants and laborers, is now primarily secondary in its offerings. Many of those enrolled are completing high school requirements or taking high school subjects for personal or vocational improvement.

The need for continuing education for all those who wish to remain vocationally or socially competent suggests a different type of administration and organization for instruction in our secondary schools. This organization would provide for an intermediate school, senior high school, and community-college unit better suited to the needs of our time.

The grouping of students for instructional classes and activities in most schools is based on ability, which is determined by past achievement or testing. This results in many disadvantages for the student in that he becomes identified with a group or program based on a test that classifies him for all parts of his program. Careful analysis of this practice shows that it is based on administrative convenience rather than on psychological principles. A student is neither bright nor dull in all things, but rather bright in some and dull in others. It is, therefore, more logical to classify him for each class and activity according to his ability and interests. This seems almost impossible, but may be nearer to becoming a reality through the use of some of the new automated aids. The secondary school of the future must be more accurate and sound in its grouping practices for instructional purposes.

Attempts to provide better instructional programs for students in the comprehensive secondary schools can be identified as schools within the school, multiphasic or tract plans, team-teaching, and the traditional subject-centered programs. Although there are many experimental and combination types, these are the ones usually found in the secondary schools of this country. Some of these may or may not turn up under the titles that appear here, but will essentially be identified with one of them.

The school-within-a-school provides some basic core classes with all students involved, such as physical education and driver education. The students and their classes and activities are grouped according to abilities and vocational plans. Each group has its own faculty and often its own buildings and laboratories. Instruction is designed to meet the needs of those enrolled in the different schools—namely, college preparatory, practical arts, business and distributive-education arts, fine arts, and general or basic school programs. The school-within-a-school plan really brings to one campus and under one central administration the programs formerly found in the separate or specialized schools. At the same time, it gives cohesiveness to those interested in certain types of programs, and also through the general classes affords contact with those in the other groups (see Figures 3, 4, and 5).

The multiphasic or tract plan has many variations. Basically, it keeps the entire student body together but provides an opportunity for each student to select an individually constructed program to meet his needs. He is required to include the basic requirements for graduation, but is given a wide range of possible combinations of subjects and activities to

The Math/Science Center

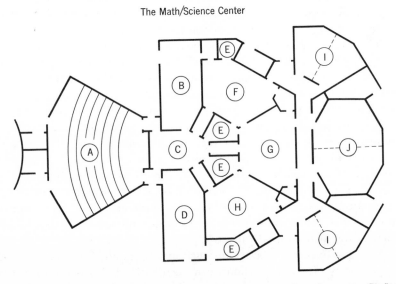

Figure 3. Instructional-area design. (A) Large group presentation classroom. (B) Storage. (C) Teacher-preparation area. (D) Teacher offices. (E) Individual research areas. (F) Chemistry laboratory. (G) Physics laboratory. (H) Biology laboratory. (I) Classroom—divisible into small group spaces. (J) Regular classrooms which can be combined.

A New Shape for Our Schools

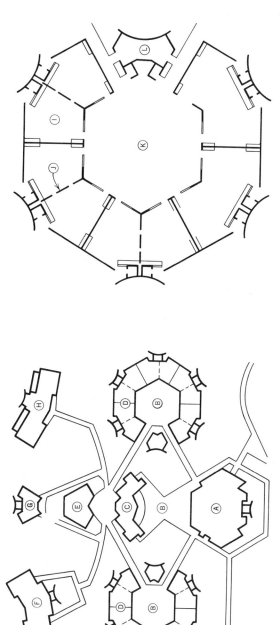

Figure 4. Changes in secondary-school design and construction. (A) Administration, kitchen, and cafeteria. (B) Outdoor assembly areas. (C) Library. (D) Classroom pods (20 classrooms). (E) Unscheduled multiuse room. (F) Homemaking—art—industrial arts. (G) Music. (H) Physical education. (I) Single classroom. (J) Movable wall—converts two classrooms into one. (K) Outdoor assembly—instruction area. (L) Teacher and teacher-aide work space.

The Instructional Resource Center

Figure 5. Design for secondary-school instructional-materials center. (A) Library. (B) Teacher workroom. (C) Electronic distribution center. (D) Audiovisual library and individual viewing center. (E) Professional library. (F) Offices.

suit his needs and interests. This plan requires more personal guidance and continual checking than do other plans. Unless adequate supervision is provided, the student might end up with a hodgepodge of subjects and credits. However, the plan does provide for more individualization than do other programs.

The traditional subject-centered programs are built around majors and minors in subjects—for example, mathematics, foreign language, homemaking, business education, science, or some other area. The student selects the subject or area of concentration and is then obliged to meet the requirements of the program. Although there is some opportunity to elect certain subjects, the major part of the student's program is determined by the course in which he is enrolled. The majority of the secondary schools follow this type of program.

The team-teaching organization is characterized by a group of teachers representing the different subject areas, who are assigned to a group of students. The teachers are given freedom in scheduling and class arrangements to meet the needs of both the students and the subject. Proponents of the plan point to the advantage of group planning and better correlation of the instructional activities as well as to more flexibility in classes and laboratories. Students are grouped in large-lecture, small-discussion, and different-size laboratory classes for instructional purposes and the opportunity for individual study and laboratory work. The library, in addition to providing the usual services, also contains an instructional-materials center to which groups or individual students may go for assistance with their projects and personal studies. One of the impediments to the adoption of this program by some schools is the traditional type of building, which has been primarily designed for the traditional type of classes and laboratories. In addition, many point to the lack of properly trained teachers for participation in such an organization.

The increase of knowledge, the profusion of materials and methods, and the impact of technology on our society and court decisions, demand that secondary schools give more attention to the organization and supervision of the instructional program. By a valid evaluation, the school's efficiency and effectiveness need to be determined more accurately than they were in the past. There is more than ever to teach and less uninterrupted time in which to teach it. The importance of the instructional program must be kept in proper focus at all times.

A Suggestion for the Administration Reorganization of Public Education and a Program for Youth

The need for the improvement of our educational program to meet the demands of the age of research and our changed social, economic, and political position is evident. Any changes should provide for both immediate and long-range requirements. Suggestion for a change does not imply a condemnation of the present program but recognition of need for adjustment to the changing pattern of the world in which we live.

Changes in the administrative organization are basic to any improvement that will make it possible to enrich, improve, and develop a quality program of instruction. Recommendations for the reorganization of our administrative units are based on these beliefs:

1. That children are maturing sociologically at an earlier age as the result of improved methods of communication, travel, private and public nursery schools, mobility of population, methods of instruction, and training.

2. That time is important in bringing about any improvement because we need all of our talents and human resources since we must now compete as a minority in world affairs. We can no longer afford to be wasteful of human or natural resources.

3. That the legal basis and authority of education in the United States will remain with the individual state, and the basic political unit of the state will continue to be the school district.

4. That the type of organization of the school district by and large will continue to be elementary and secondary. This gives administration of grades kindergarten through eight to an elementary district and nine through twelve or fourteen to a secondary district. The ideal of some to unify all under one district comprising grades kindergarten through fourteen cannot be brought about in time to face present needs. Then, too, some districts in reorganization have become unwieldy and too large. It is also true that the inability of districts that are too small to provide adequate programs has been clearly demonstrated. There are, however, thousands of districts that could bring about the suggested improvement under their present political structure.

5. That pupils should be introduced to laboratory experiences in science, industrial arts, homemaking, fine arts, modern languages, physical education, and advanced mathematics at an earlier age.

6. That the kind of program needed to meet the needs of all pupils requires more specialized teachers, classes, shops, and laboratories than are now possible under present school organizations in certain grades.

7. That certain pupils are required to remain in our secondary schools too long and would benefit from a work experience with continuation in an adult-education program.

8. That in this age of research, education for all is a continuing process and is not completed upon graduation from high school.

9. That experiments in the United States that permitted pupils to begin their college program at the end of the eleventh grade, either at college or in their secondary schools, have indicated certain values.

10. That the opportunity to complete the high school requirements earlier would give a better opportunity for the provision of more specialized programs through city college and adult-education schools.

11. That an increasing number of individuals will find it necessary to extend their formal education programs through the fourteenth year, thus making more education and training opportunities necessary.

12. That the opportunity to reorganize and improve our educational programs under existing conditions and school-district organizations is a better solution than waiting for the reorganization of districts.

13. That the need of education in this age of research is to provide laboratory and specialized work in comprehensive intermediate and senior school divisions. The present elementary program gives the responsibility for too many pupils and too much work to the limited number of teachers who cannot be expected to be trained for competent teaching in all the special fields.

14. That many sixth graders would be better motivated to read and use mathematics, languages, art, music, and other skills if they had better opportunity to apply them in properly constructed and supervised laboratories.

15. That a reorganization of our administrative units would make it more inviting for men teachers to participate in the teaching and guidance of our present sixth graders. Many pupils would have an opportunity for a better-adapted physical education program.

Recommended Reorganization of our Administrative Units

The author first proposed the following reorganization to the National Association of Secondary School Principals in 1956. Since that time other leaders have endorsed or implemented parts of the recommendations. Certain school districts have now organized their elementary and intermediate grades on the K-5, 6-8 type of administrative units.

The educational organization for a local district or area would be on a six-three-three-three (6-3-3-3) basis (see Figure 6):

Primary and Elementary unit would include kindergarten and grade five (K-5).

Intermediate unit would include grades six, seven, and eight (6-8).

High School unit would include grades nine, ten, and eleven (9-11).

Community or Junior College would include grades twelve, thirteen, and fourteen (12-14).

Primary-Elementary Unit (Grades K-5). This unit would deal with the basic social and educational skills similar to the present program. Nursery schools for four-year-olds should be encouraged to carry on much of the kindergarten program and extend into the kindergarten, but ad-

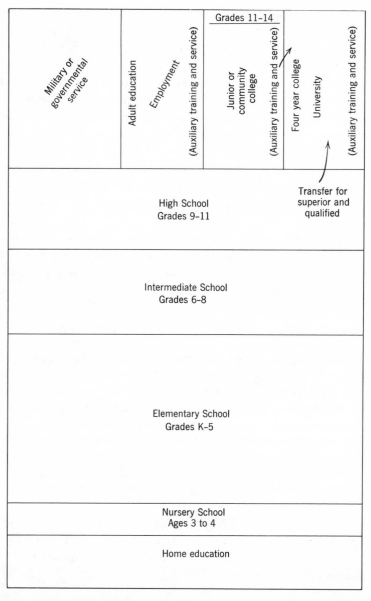

Figure 6. Plan for reorganization of education. All youth would be required to serve their government in armed service or auxiliary units after graduation from high school.

vanced pupils would be introduced to some skills now assigned to the first grade. Classes would be of a size that would permit the individualization of instruction.

Kindergarten may be a bore for those who have had nursery school experience. Sufficient evidence is available to recognize nursery-school programs as valuable for most four-year-olds. Opportunity should be available for all and not for only those whose parents are economically able or for those whose mothers are working.

Intermediate Unit (Grades 6-8). Pupils would be introduced to laboratory experiences in such areas as science, homemaking, industrial arts, art, music, and physical education. This would require schools similar to the junior high schools found in certain states at present. Qualified pupils would have the opportunity to begin modern languages and special mathematics courses when ready. Junior high or intermediate schools would include grades six, seven, and eight instead of seven, eight, and nine or seven and eight as found in some states at present.

The intermediate unit would provide more opportunity for the gifted, average, and slow learners because they would have more chance to have their programs tailored to their abilities and talents rather than to limited facilities, staff, and teaching opportunities.

More specialized teachers and laboratories as now provided in our junior high schools would make a wider range of offerings possible. This does not imply, nor would it need to encourage, departmentalization.

High School Unit (Grades 9-11). Pupils would participate in a general-education and a special-education program. Those who desired to begin their language courses at this time would not find the break that now comes between junior and senior high schools. Most pupils taking language and special mathematics begin at the ninth-grade level under our present program. Those attending junior high schools change schools and sometimes teaching methods between their first and second years. The ninth-, tenth-, and eleventh-grade unit would enable the pupil to complete language, three units of advanced mathematics, and science under one administrative unit without the need for an adjustment to a new administrative organization, staff, and program.

Graduation at the end of the eleventh grade would free many pupils, who would profit more from work in industrial and commercial positions than from present twelfth-grade work. Recognition for the need of more school work for self-improvement and job upgrading would witness a return to the community-college or adult-education programs. The present twelfth-grade work would have more meaning for these pupils because it would be related to recognized values by the individual. Districts could continue their efforts in offering these community college programs. Those going on to college and professional work could begin a more specialized program in either the local community college or other institutions of higher learning.

The three-year high school would make it possible to keep our units smaller and prevent the development of some of our secondary school monstrosities that are neither efficient nor personal in dealing with all those enrolled. Emphasis should be on keeping these units to 1500 pupils or fewer.

Community or Junior College (Grades 12-14). This unit would include grades twelve, thirteen, and fourteen. Provision would be made for general and special education with adequate shops, laboratories, and clinics to provide a program of challenge to all. Terminal as well as parallel courses would be offered. A degree would be given to those completing a three-year program, but students would be encouraged to take special courses for on-the-job training as well as for personal improvement.

Through cooperation with institutions of higher learning, the new organization would provide studies that would give full credit on a transfer basis.

This organization would enable larger areas to unite in providing such institutions where individual districts would find it financially impossible.

The community college would provide the individual the chance to try college work before enrolling in a college and discovering that he is not interested in paying the price of what it takes to succeed in professional work. The community college would provide some students with the opportunity to pursue college work near home and be able to pursue graduate work when limited space might rule out many.

It is not the purpose of this proposal to explain in detail all the advantages of the reorganization of the administrative units. There are some programs that have already attempted to do some of these things. Their experiences seem to substantiate the success of such a change. The present emphasis on discovering the gifted, average, and exceptional pupils is of little value unless our schools are organized to take them in their logical social groups and provide the quality program needed.

The suggested program would enable districts now organized on elementary basis K-8, and unified districts K-12 or K-14, to develop the units as outlined. This would make the transition of pupils easier, as they are increasingly being forced to move from one district or city to another. The high school districts would find it possible, where a community college exists, and possibly where it does not exist, to hasten to provide opportunity that will be needed in the near future. In some cases present school plants could be used as they now exist. In others, some building and adjustment would need to be made. School-district reorganization, where needed, could continue.

The reorganization of our educational administrative units with graduation from the high school at the end of the eleventh grade should also be accompanied by a new program for youth, before it is too late. Here is a suggested program for youth:

1. Students will not be classified as bright or dull. Every individual is bright and dull in some things. It depends on the type of test, examination, or measurement being used.

2. Schools will be required to develop a program of testing and an examination for guidance purposes in order that the abilities and potentials of each individual can be developed.

3. A coordinated local, state, and national program of defense and offense will be developed, in which every boy and girl will be required to serve according to his ability, interest, leadership, and the need of society. This program would include the training of auxiliary policemen, firemen, forest rangers, observers, traffic guides, and all necessary workers and supervisors for emergencies in the community, state, or nation. Work programs would be developed to give youth a chance to participate in a meaningful way in the activities of democracy. Selection would be on the basis of ability and competence. Such a program would provide a reservoir of trained personnel for any emergency or need. It would also give our youth a feeling of responsibility and importance. The program should be broad enough to provide opportunity to train recreational leaders, directors, and assistants among our youth, for younger groups. Young people would assist in solving the growing problems of youth and adult delinquency. We cannot afford the present situation of uncertainty relative to service to the country, or idleness among youth. A program designed to require all to serve in civilian or armed forces training or work projects, at a time that will help them complete their formal education, begin their vocation, and establish their families, would be fair and beneficial to all.

4. Upon graduation from high school, every youth will have one of three opportunities from which to select:

(a) Enlistment into the above program of service to his country for a limited period of time not exceeding one year, after which he will be placed on a reserve status.

   (b) Continuation of formal schooling, after which some service to his country will be required.

   (c) Employment in industry, agriculture, business, or other work, and the opportunity to continue his formal education on a part-time basis in the community college or adult education program, and service to his country in a reserve program.

   5. The elimination of the uncertainty of the present draft program, which makes it difficult for young people to plan with any assurance as to when their services will be required.

   6. The right to vote as well as the obligation to register at their eighteenth birthday.

Investing more money into some of the antiquated educational units and programs is not the solution. If we want improvement it must begin with our basic administrative units. The reorganization of these basic units must take place within the present political framework of the state and district unit. If teachers and administrators are given a chance to provide the type of programs needed, in administrative units that make such a program possible, there is no need to worry about the future. Our educational system can then be geared to new geography, new economy, new social order, and the age of research.

Conclusion

The program of the secondary school, both in organization and in quality, is to a great extent influenced by the competence of the administrators and teachers, demands of the colleges and universities, criteria of the accrediting agencies, federal and state grants and subsidies, political and social pressure groups, and the willingness of citizens to supply the finances necessary to provide the secondary-school program needed by youth and society.

Secondary education is one of the most vital areas or levels of all educational systems. The majority of the students attend under compulsory school-attendance laws of the states and a need for the high school diploma. The wide range of interests and abilities, the democratic composition of the student body, and the cross currents of political and social movements that affect the attitudes and actions of these youths make the secondary school most inviting to competent, sincere, and dedicated teachers. It is no place for the faint of heart or the individual who seeks a quiet and peaceful professional career. The rewards a teacher gets from contributing to the molding and guiding of future workers, homemakers, leaders, and citizens during this most critical period far outweigh the salary and fringe benefits of the position.

References

Barnett, L. L., G. Handel, and H. Weser, Eds., "The School in The Middle," Center for Urban Education, New York, 1968, 311 pp. A compilation of significant articles dealing with the organization and programs of the intermediate school but also valuable for a ready reference of articles dealing with secondary education.

Clark, Leonard H., *Strategies and Tactics in Secondary School Teaching*, Macmillan Co., New York, 1968, pp. 451. A book of readings that brings together the theoretical basis and some examples of the various teaching techniques and methods incorporated in most of the textbooks relating to secondary schools.

Conant, James B., *The Comprehensive High School*, McGraw-Hill Book Company, New York, 1967, 95 pp. A case for the comprehensive secondary school with suggestions relative to the program and discussion of the inherent problems.

Evaluative Criteria—1970. The National Study of Secondary School Evaluation, Washington, D.C. This edition of the evaluative criteria will likely dominate the procedures and methods for evaluating and accrediting secondary schools for all regional accrediting agencies during this decade.

Hahn, R. O., and D. B. Bidna, *Secondary Education, Origins and Directions*, Macmillan Co., New York, 1970, 448 pp. This collection emphasizes the origins of secondary education as they relate to current educational problems in the secondary school.

Unruh, G. G., and W. M. Alexander, *Innovations in Secondary Education*, Holt, Rinehart and Winston, New York, 1970, 245 pp. A good summary of the innovations in secondary education during the past decade.

25

The University

George F. Kneller

❖❖❖

During the academic year 1968-69, I was invited by the editors of UCLA's student newspaper, *The Daily Bruin*, to write a series of articles on the history of the idea of the university. What follows is a revision of some of these articles, together with certain thoughts that have occurred to me since.

I decided to discuss the university in history because I believe that many of today's problems, however novel they may seem, are really very similar to problems that have troubled institutions of higher education ever since they were founded. I realize that none of us approaches history with an open mind. We are all inclined to gild or blacken the past according to our beliefs about the present. I will do my best, however, to distinguish between historical evidence and the lessons I draw from it, so that those who disagree with me will have the facts with which to do so.

Because I am writing mainly for students, I will say little about technicalities of organization, administration, finance, and personnel. My concern is with principles. My themes are academic freedom, student demands, and courses of study.

The First "Universities"

In the Western world the idea of the university sprang from the circumstances in which the first universities were founded. These institutions were in fact corporations (*universitates*) chartered by popes and emperors. Unlike other schools they were virtually independent of outside control. Many privileges previously limited to the clergy were written into the contracts of all corporation members. As a result students and masters alike enjoyed exemption from taxation, military service, arrest by civil authority, and trial by civil court. The rector (president or chancellor) was elected by both masters and students, and in some Italian universities he was a student himself. A number of universities were run almost entirely by students. The professors were obliged to swear an oath of allegiance to the student rector and to abide by student regulations about the content of lectures, the length of the academic term, and so forth. However, let me remind those who would like to set the clock back that students had to finance the universities. There were no government subventions, no philanthropic endowments, and no revolving scholarship funds, all of which today absorb more than 90 percent of the costs of America's public universities.

There is some argument about which European university appeared first, but most historians have settled on Bologna, which was founded late in the eleventh century. At that time popes and emperors were on fairly good terms and both vied for the allegiance of students and masters, who naturally exploited this rivalry to the full.

In fact, these early universities badly needed the support of the mighty. Being voluntary associations of students and masters, they carried little official weight and were regarded as fair game by local authorities and townees. At Bologna the students, mostly foreign and lacking citizens' rights, received no protection from the city police. They therefore banded together to outwit profiteers and outpunch local toughs. In Paris during the twelfth century students and teachers used the boycott and the strike to bring local tyrants to heel. If such actions were ineffective, scholars and masters would "disperse" (leave town), taking their purchasing power with them.

From the very first, students wanted to learn how to acquire the good things of life, and they chose their masters accordingly. Masters in turn collected fees directly from their students and found it advisable to please them in order to be assured of a livelihood. In Italy and the French provinces especially, masters touted courses that were short, snappy, and immediately applicable.

Higher Education and the Modern University

Although the word "university" was first used in the eleventh century, it did not acquire its modern meaning until six centuries later. Some say that Halle (Germany, 1694) was the first modern university; but Göttingen, established fifty years later, and Berlin, founded shortly thereafter, are probably better candidates for this title. I realize that normally not much is gained by knowing which university came before which. But in this case it is important to know that many American universities were modeled on their German predecessors, as I shall show. True, Harvard was established fifty years before Halle, and Yale several decades before Göttingen. Harvard and Yale, however, were not universities in the modern sense but "colleges," for they did not offer graduate studies. And this is putting things charitably, for at early Harvard the average student was 16 years old and the curriculum was roughly equivalent to that of a modern high school.

Having spoken of universities and colleges, I had better say something about higher education, of which universities are only one institution. Higher education comprises all procedures for conserving, transmitting, and increasing the more complex kinds of knowledge that many people in a society have neither the inclination nor the ability to master. In all but the most primitive societies the sum of knowledge is too much for any one person to use or remember. Consequently specialists arise— potters, weavers, canoe-builders, navigators, traders, priests, sages, artists, story-tellers. The systematic mastering of such special skills foreshadows the higher education that sustains and advances the most highly developed societies.

Even societies ignorant of writing developed forms of higher education. The Incas of Peru required the children of the nobility to reside in the capital, where they learned not only the more exacting handicrafts and special skills, such as weaving and warfare, but also the art of government and the keeping of accounts by means of knotted cords. In New Zealand select young Maoris had to memorize a massive body of genealogy, theology, philosophy, poetry, ritual, strategy, and mental telepathy.

Thus higher education begins whenever a select group is instructed in branches of knowledge that are acquired only by concentrated effort. The palace sages of China, the wandering gurus of ancient India, the industrious scribes of Sumeria, and the pious theocrats of the Middle East all devoted themselves to the increase and transmission of higher learning, whether under the open sky, in temples, among guilds of architects or navigators, in secret societies, or in organized schools.

Today higher education is offered to many people and one day it may be offered to all. But the university, an institution that educates both graduates and undergraduates, is by definition selective and will always remain so. I realize that some may object to this principle. They will say that in a democracy everyone is equal and so everyone is entitled to all the education he wants. This might be true in the perfect society where scarcity is abolished and the resources for education are infinite. But in our present society we cannot afford, in the name of equality, to educate obviously incompetent people to be nuclear physicists or experimental sociologists. Moreover, it is inconceivable that in any society all men should desire to be educated to the same degree. No doubt we all wish we were more talented, but who wants to study what he cannot understand?

American Colleges and Universities

The history of American higher education makes a fascinating study. Harvard, founded in the early 1630s, was for nearly a decade virtually a one-teacher college. History was taught there as an extracurricular subject, and students had to have their parents' permission to study French. A seven-year-old once passed the entrance examinations to Yale. For half a century students at William and Mary learned no more than eighth-graders do today. They were taught the meaning of the Gospel and also how to spread it among the Indians.

Princeton grew out of a different tradition. Old Nassau was founded in 1764 by the colonial government of New Jersey. It was then called the College of New Jersey and only acquired its present name when it moved to the town of Princeton twenty years later. Princeton adopted the European tradition of classical learning. In Pennsylvania, on the other hand, Benjamin Franklin saw to it that higher education paid more attention to the technical and scientific needs of a developing nation. It was in Pennsylvania that the country's first medical school was founded (1765).

American higher education eventually became a synthesis of classical humanism, French romanticism, German scholarship, British paternalism, and native egalitarianism. If anyone doubts that German scholarship and American equality were at the heart of the early American university, let him examine the 1859 catalog of the University of Michigan. There it says: "The general organization of the University . . . conforms to the Prussian system in those liberal and benign points which have made this system to be regarded as the most perfect in the world." Liberal, benign, perfect! Again: "All the colleges of the University shall . . . correspond in general to the course in the *Gymnasia* [classical secondary schools] of Germany. In the University of Michigan it is a cardinal object to make this correspondence as complete as possible." Nothing half-hearted about that! The catalog also declares that university courses should be as "ample and rich as possible" and "adaptable to the wants of all classes of students. . . ." An institution "cannot deserve the name of a University which does not aim . . . to make it possible for every student to study what he pleases and to the extent that he pleases." This, remember, was in 1859. Even before the Civil War a rising state university had a free elective system of the kind that many students are demanding today.

Moreover, the doors of the University were open "freely to all the people, without distinction." (I like that word "distinction"; it has more class than "discrimination".) Indeed, "there is no man so poor that industry, diligence, and perseverance will not enable him to get an education here. . . ." What kind of education? "The University meets the wants of the people in all the higher degrees of education": classics, liberal arts, sciences, mechanical arts, manufacturing, commerce, agriculture, civil engineering, and a variety of other subjects.

Here is a clear example from early in our history of the characteristic American synthesis of the Prussian tradition of academic freedom for the scholar with the American tradition of educational opportunity for the many. However, this synthesis was to have its problems, some of which we will now examine.

Academic Freedom

Supported by popes and kings, the early universities were well able to guarantee to all their members the right to pursue the truth. Frederick Barbarossa's *Habita* (1158) set out the provisions of the guarantee, and Pope Alexander III accepted and applied them.

The guarantee was not unconditional. Having the sole right to charter universities, the Holy See also had the power to expel atheists and heretics. But since most students were Christians anyway, little conflict of conscience arose. Academic freedom also depended on good behavior. Emperor Frederick let it be known in his *Habita* that "only those should enjoy Our approval and protection who by their learning enlighten the world and mold the life of Our subjects to the obedience of God and of Us, His Minister." Although students could not be tried by civil authorities, they still had to face their professors or the Bishop, "to whom We have given jurisdiction in these circumstances."

The modern student may well envy the right of his predecessor to move from one university to the other without fear of losing credits. The student had this right because the early universities were not confined to certain buildings. There were no campuses as such. Also when the scholars decided to move, so literally did the university or at least a good part of it. Cambridge was organized when students and masters left Oxford in 1209, and some twenty years later Oxford was reorganized when scholars from Paris joined like-minded colleagues there.

Today students are again on the move, although the destination is different. They are moving out of the classroom and into academic senates and presidential offices, demanding a greater share of academic freedom. Does not the freedom to learn, they ask, imply a voice in determining what shall be taught? Why should students not participate in the policy formation and governance of the institutions of which they are members?

Until recently students limited their demands to such matters as fraternity welfare, student housing, and personal conduct. Today they seek to have a share in deciding most if not all institutional matters that concern them. Like their medieval predecessors, many students now want to exercise what they believe is their right to decide (a) programs of studies, (b) the appointment, tenure, and promotion of teachers and administrators, and (c) the place of their institution in the life of the community.

However, in attempting to increase their own freedom, some students have often attacked the freedom of others. They have (a) assaulted teachers, administrators, and fellow students, (b) interfered physically with normal school routine, (c) presented "nonnegotiable" demands together with threats of violence, (d) destroyed valuable scholarly materials, and (e) disregarded that respect for the rights of others on which the life of Western democracy depends.

I do not deny the justice of many student complaints. Too many administrators have assumed that the limits of academic freedom are theirs to define. They have treated students as children too young to choose the conditions under which they will live and as transients with no stake in the university. Many teachers have acted like autocrats, expecting students to receive with gratitude whatever knowledge has been handed to them.

Nevertheless, as I have stated previously, a university is not a political entity any more than a business corporation, or a labor union, or a church is. The public function of a university is not to legislate but to educate. It is right that each man should have an equal voice in the election of those by whom he is to be represented, but it is doubtful that each student should have an equal say in the choice of those by whom he is to be taught. Since teachers do not represent students, there is no reason why they should be chosen by them. In the classroom the teacher represents his department and the branch of learning that it cultivates. It is his department, therefore, that has the final right to judge him.

This does not rule out student participation in the general governance of a university. But here the role of students will depend on their capacity to assume personal or corporate responsibility for the decisions they help to make. In academia especially freedom entails *accountability*. Even as professors themselves are limited to certain roles in the governance of a university, and as boards of regents and trustees are likewise restricted, so too students, through their elected representatives, may participate only within the limits of their competence.

The student has an inalienable right to acquire knowledge, which includes the right to criticize and even reject it. But with this right goes the responsibility to make the effort of learning. The student must accept the rigors of studying just as the teacher accepts the demands of teaching. A student is entitled to have the finest teachers that can be hired, but how much he learns from them depends on him. A student learns best if he asks questions, challenges views, and *commits himself* to learning. The right to learn involves the responsibility to learn; it calls for hard work and genuine commitment.

Again, student rights cannot exceed university rights. The university has no right to break the laws of the land. Nor has the student. If students wish to protest against those they consider intruders on the campus, such as the Dow Chemical Corporation or the Marine Corps, they must do so peacefully. If they use violence, they break the law and are liable to its penalties. Similarly, attempts to disrupt the operation of the university by force must be met by whatever means the university judges fit. If some students deny some teachers the right to teach, other students are denied the right to learn from them. That right must be restored—if possible, by persuasion, and if necessary, by force.

Finally, academic freedom presupposes a deep sense of responsibility toward the society that makes that freedom possible. Students, faculty, and administrators have every right to criticize society for its faults and to recommend gradual or radical reforms. They may demonstrate, remonstrate, confront, and peacefully disobey. But they may do so only as individuals. They may not criticize society in the name of the university as such. For society has given the university a special function, that of seeking knowledge and disseminating it. It is in virtue of this function that the university possesses the academic freedom that it does. If the university seeks to turn itself into an agency for social reform, it becomes a political force and invites the application of all those political pressures from which it is now relatively exempt. To these and related matters I will shortly return.[1]

Student Demonstrations

I have spoken of student demonstrations. As a matter of fact, students have always demonstrated.[2] Nine hundred years ago the wilder element shaved their heads instead of cultivating them and took to the streets to bait authority. They did so the more readily because the police could not arrest them. Rowdyism and even thuggery flourished for more than a century. At last residence halls were built and students were compelled to live in university confines according to university discipline. Unfortunately the authorities overreacted, and students did not take kindly to the new rules. They were forbidden to lie, steal, swear, use obscene language, play at cards or dice, get drunk, frequent inns, associate with persons of bad reputation, fornicate, fight cocks, use nicknames, buy, sell or exchange anything, or be disrespectful, tardy, or disorderly at public worship. They were punished by public confessions, reprimands, whippings, expulsions, suspensions, and fines.

In the United States the first big student protest took place in 1716 at Saybrook, Connecticut, two years before the college moved to New Haven to be called Yale. The students claimed that they were poorly taught, demanded a full-time rector (president), and refused to be housed more than a mile from the school. The trustees promised to build a new residence hall and provide a resident rector—eventually. But the students wanted them at once and went on strike to get them. The trustees held firm, however, and the strike collapsed. In victory the trustees were magnanimous, allowing dissident students to return for the September commencement.

---

[1] The traditional approach to academic freedom and responsibility is ably defended by Sidney Hook, *Academic Freedom and Academic Anarchy,* Cowles, New York, 1970. Tom Hayden's *Rebellion and Repression,* World, Cleveland, 1969. presents the student activist point of view.

[2] For a brief, objective history of student revolts, see Elvin Abeles, *The Student and the University,* Parents' Magazine Press, New York, 1969. Also recommended are two anthologies: Julian Foster and Durwood Long, Eds., *Protest! Student Activism in America,* Morrow, New York, 1969; and Seymour M. Lipset and Philip G. Altbach, Eds., *Students in Revolt,* Houghton Mifflin, Boston, 1969.

Harvard, too, had its confrontations. In 1766 there was a rebellion over "bad" butter in the Commons dining hall. The authorities cracked down hard. Students were forbidden to use gunpowder, swords, stilettos, canes, or other offensive weapons; to strike a college president or faculty member; or to insult a villager. But faculty and students remained at loggerheads. In 1805, after another "bread-and-butter rebellion," the authorities suspended half the college. The students hit back vigorously. They lit bonfires, set off explosions, dropped cannonballs from upper windows, and dowsed tutors with buckets of ink. In general, students treated their professors as natural enemies and no self-respecting undergraduate would ever be seen in "kindly discourse" with his teacher. Often the entire faculty would chase offending students amid hoots of laughter and rounds of applause. After a riot in 1834 all Harvard sophomores were ordered to leave town.

Students were restless everywhere. At Princeton the Riot of 1807 led to the suspension or expulsion of more than half the student body. In 1842 at the University of Virginia an undergraduate gunned down his professor. At Oakland College, Mississippi, the president was murdered for refusing to yield to a crowd of students. At Yale in the 1880s, writes William Lyon Phelps in his autobiography, "Every instructor's first duty was to maintain order." Teachers were often chosen for their abilities as policemen. "In those days," according to Phelps, "it was so customary to throw coal through a tutor's window that the usual saying was, 'My salary is a thousand dollars, and the coal thrown in'!"

Toward the end of the nineteenth century, however, it became clear that university students had to be treated with more respect. The old belief in the sanctity of authority gave way to a new notion that students should by and large discipline themselves. In the 1860s Oberlin College substituted friendly counseling for corporal punishment and arbitrary dismissal. In 1869 Swarthmore hired a matron to look after the health and conduct of coeds. Next year Harvard appointed its first dean of the faculty, whose main duty was to "administer the discipline of the college." In 1880 Amherst College adopted what became known as "the Amherst System," under which the entering student actually signed a contract to observe certain regulations and principles of conduct. If he violated them, he broke the contract and was considered no longer to be a student.[3]

---

[3] There was a very pleasant incident at Wellesley. In 1882, at 26, Alice Palmer (then Miss Freeman) was offered the presidency of the College. Summoning the members of the senior class, she asked them for their advice. She pointed out that she was too young for the office and that in any case the job was too taxing for one person. She would accept the post, she said, only if the students would consent to discipline themselves and

Early this century university authorities embraced the new science of experimental psychology. Whatever the student's problem, they thought, psychology would solve it. Psychology didn't of course, but the belief that it would proved on balance beneficial. Student revolts did not end but at least they mellowed. As late as 1961 one reliable commentator wrote that "never before in history of colleges and universities have students and faculty enjoyed such amiable relationships as they do today."

In the early 1960s minor demonstrations occurred, mainly in response to civil rights violations, but in the fall of 1964 at the University of California, Berkeley, the lid blew off. The campus was rocked by a series of protest demonstrations, culminating in a large-scale sit-in at the adminstration building, mass arrests, and, in reponse to them, a major strike. Calling themselves the Free Speech Movement, hundreds of students demanded the right to speak out on vital social and political issues. They bitterly criticized the procrastination and paternalism of an administrative machine that refused to treat them as persons.

They won their case. More than any other event, the victory of the FSM inspired a new spirit of realism, courage, and resolution. Ultimately this victory was to cause many an institution of higher education throughout the world to examine its conscience and to institute much-needed reforms. At Berkeley itself the faculty made an exhaustive study of conditions and submitted a long list of recommendations for reform and development. The Muscatine Report, named after the chairman of the committee that wrote it, provided a model for other universities to follow.

But American students not only criticized their universities, they also called into question many assumptions of American foreign policy and social practice. In Washington, D.C., during April 1965, some 20,000 students marched in protest against the Vietnam War, the draft, the foreign policy, the educational system, and social injustice everywhere. The following year at the University of Chicago 500 students seized the administration building and held it for three days as a demonstration of dissatisfaction not only with internal policies but also with university support of government activities that students regarded as immoral. Similar seizures took place at the University of Wisconsin, the City College of New York, and even normally staid Oberlin. In every case the students involved demanded that university authorities should make no contracts with government departments, corporations, or other agencies

leave her free for general administration. The students leaped at the opportunity, Miss Freeman took the position, and serious indiscipline disappeared.

without first consulting student representatives. Small but strong groups of student activists refused to allow their campuses to serve as bases for military recruitment or for interviewing by companies engaged in armaments production. Berkeley activists celebrated the first anniversary of the 1965 sit-in by bringing Navy recruiting to a halt. At Brown, Columbia, and elsewhere activists prevented the Dow Chemical Company from holding interviews and even forced a strategic retreat on the U. S. Marine Corps.

The rebellion at Columbia in 1967 was important for a number of reasons. First, the faculty joined in, adding their own demands to some of those of the students. Second, white students protested against the Vietnam War, while black students protested against racism (in this case the construction of a gymnasium against the wishes of the black community). Third, white "conservative" students, among whom varsity athletes were prominent, for the first time went into battle against activists who were interfering with the normal routine of the University.[4] The uprising led to the resignation of President Kirk.

The siege at Cornell was laid initially by white students protesting a range of abuses: large lecture classes, inflated prices for necessary perquisites, a mismanaged bookstore and cafeteria, an unfair grading system, lack of contact with faculty, and the frequent absence of President Perkins. (Even freshmen got into the act, submitting as their special grievance the excessive cost of laundering their shirts, and a poor job of it at that!) But the black students were far more aroused. They demanded an autonomous black study program and seized the building in which they wanted it housed. They banished the professors, refurnished the place, and proceeded to reorganize facilities in the building (such as library stacks) to accord with their own views. To the accompaniment of the University's bongo drums they hauled President Perkins from a speaker's platform at a conference on South Africa, attacked job recruiters from the Chase Manhattan Bank (for allegedly practicing racial discrimination), and declared guerilla warfare on the opposition.

The most surprising revolt took place at San Francisco State, surprising because this institution had long enjoyed a worldwide reputation for liberalism. Its administrators and teachers had been unusually sensitive to community needs and had fostered a great variety of educational experiments. Here black militants, "chicanos" (Mexican-Americans), and other

---

4 In the minds of many there was a fourth factor: the excessive force used by the police, which caused many moderates to side with the radicals. See Roger Kahn, *The Battle for Morningside Heights: Why Students Rebel,* Morrow, New York, 1970.

minorities joined to form a "Third World Liberation Front," demanding greater recognition of minority needs, admission of more minority students, autonomous study programs, better facilities, and a greater effort to find minority graduates more rewarding jobs.

The struggle at San Franciso State was a bitter one. On several occasions the College was shut down for days at a time. But the appointment of President Hayakawa proved to be a turning point. A member of a minority group himself, the famous language scholar stood his ground and called on police, state troopers, and undercover men to remove the "gangsters" who, he claimed, were forcibly preventing 95 percent of the student body from pursuing their studies. The rank and file of Americans immediately proclaimed Hayakawa the hero of the hour (in 1969 a Gallup poll named him the country's most valuable educator), and his example was followed elsewhere. At the University of Wisconsin authorities refused to give in to students and called on the police and national guard to back them up. At Berkeley, California's Governor Reagan declared a state of "extreme emergency" when students marched through the streets to occupy a park that had been reclaimed by the Board of Regents. The National Guard were quartered in Berkeley for several days.

Student protests will undoubtedly continue, but from now on they will be handled more firmly and (hopefully) more intelligently. State and federal legislators are passing preventative statutes, and faculty and administrators will yield less readily to violence and unreason. School officials will do what they can to settle differences internally, but when students and their supporters turn to vandalism and bodily harm, officials will not hesitate, as they have in the past, to counter violence appropriately.

This being said, how do student grievances today differ from those of the past? First, they are more extensive and also more ideological; they concern the ills of society as well as the shortcomings of the university; and they constitute a criticism of life. Students today call for an end to such evils as imperialism, racism, environmental pollution, and poverty.[5]

Second, the university is asked to define its central mission. Is it to become a "multiversity," a "megaloversity," a "cosmoversity," or what? How long can a university afford to remain adrift in a society that is

---

[5] Some students would like to make the university a crusading agency for social reform. But as I already have pointed out, the university cannot as a body prosecute a social cause and at the same time pursue truth as such. Commitment to a social cause presupposes commitment to a point of view; dedication to the quest for truth presupposes a readiness to submit all points of view at all times to rational debate. Individuals and groups within the university may, and should, mobilize for social reform. But they should not be allowed to speak for the university itself.

itself off course? Although students themselves are not agreed on the purposes a university should fulfill, they are deeply concerned about them.

Third, students are greatly disturbed about the increasing dehumanization of higher education. Universities are growing so huge that they can no longer treat students as individual persons. How much more, students ask, are they and their studies to be computerized? When will professors give priority to teaching rather than to research? How much longer must students remain "pawns" of the university, campus "niggers" as Jerry Farber has put it? When will universities realize that the average age of their students is at least 21?

Fourth, many demonstrations are held by minority groups demanding fairer treatment. The university has a dual responsibility here: to foster the values of minority cultures for their special contribution to American life and at the same time to help launch minority students into the mainstream of American society. As a result of these demands, programs of ethnic studies are being designed with two ends in view: (1) to help minorities understand their own history and present potential, and (2) to give minority students the skills and confidence they need to profit from all the opportunities American society has to offer. Minority students are also demanding more places at the university and a voice in the appointment of faculty members and administrators. They are asking to be represented at the university in proportion to their numbers in the population at large.

Finally, students are in revolt against (a) what they are required to study, (b) methods of teaching, and (c) methods of evaluation. Students have protested against these matters ever since education began, but their recent criticisms have been powerful enough to effect some quite radical reforms. Let us see what has happened to courses of study.

Courses of Study

In the early universities courses of study were heavily professional. Their main purpose was to prepare candidates for offices of church or state—"that there may never be wanting a supply of persons duly qualified to serve God both in church and state," as the Oxford prayer book put it. The curriculum was rigid, courses were long, and the examinations were grueling. Students began by studying grammar (for language), logic (for argument), and rhetoric (for oratory). They then elected their major subjects, generally law (Bologna), medicine (Salerno), or theology (Paris). Grammar consisted mainly of Latin, logic of the syllogism, and rhetoric of traditional themes and commonplaces. Final examinations often lasted an entire week, and most candidates failed.[6]

From the very first, neither content nor method escaped criticism. John of Salisbury called logic a "polite term for frivolous, subtile, and sophistical disputation." Roger Bacon complained that his colleagues ignored the evidence of their senses. He refuted arguments based on the Greek classics by quoting such "modern" men of wisdom as Seneca, Cicero, Avicenna, and St. Jerome. Even so, it would be hard indeed to find a trusted scholar who questioned the assumptions that guided the social order: that Christianity should inform all men's thoughts and activities; that the human race had been divided by God into classes; and that political and economic interests should remain subordinate to the salvation of souls.

Although universities have evolved slowly in many respects, their curriculums in recent years have changed radically. Courses of study have multiplied in accordance with the growth of knowledge and the demands of an increasingly complex society. They have also been profoundly affected by the so-called "free-elective" system, which is hardly more than a century old.

I say "so-called" because there was never one system of free electives, but many. By the end of the 19th century five such systems were in use in American universities: (1) a choice of one or two electives per term from a set list of perhaps fifty traditional courses; (2) a selection from among established disciplines up to about half a student's load: (3) a choice among majors and minors; (4) an option among groupings of subjects such as science, a language, and a literature; and (5) more or less total free choice from a set list. Most colleges preferred the third and fourth systems. Yale and Wellesley adopted the first; Brown and Amherst, the second; and Cornell and Harvard, the fifth.[7]

Now Harvard and Yale had students from similar backgrounds and

---

[6] Other studies in the curriculum—mathematics, astronomy, music, and (later) philosophy—were more professionally slanted than was the *trivium* (grammar, logic, and rhetoric) to which they were added. However, professional studies were less specialized than they are now. Laboratory methods and learning by experience were the essence of education, and it was therefore easier than it is today to reconcile a liberal or general education with the study of law or medicine. Furthermore, the printed word had not yet achieved its present power, so that the student read less about a subject and practiced it more.

[7] At Harvard, under President Charles Eliot, the senior year became "totally elective" in 1872; the junior year in 1878, "except for themes"; the sophomore year in 1884, "except for themes and rhetoric"; and the entire college in 1894, except for a freshman course in literature and "bonehead" English. So it took Harvard 22 years to create a comprehensive free-elective system.

faculty and administrators of equal caliber. Yet Harvard gave each student almost complete freedom of choice, whereas Yale restricted him. Why? Because course election is not a single procedure but an ideal that can be realized in many ways. There is no evidence whatever that students who follow one system of electives are better educated than those who follow another. A university should choose the elective system that is most in harmony with its own clearly specified objectives. Unfortunately, the elective systems of most American universities today are petty compromises arranged by committees whose members believe that no one is properly educated unless he has studied *their* particular subjects.

I will now mention four changes that are occurring in university curriculums today. First, curriculum policies everywhere are becoming more liberal. The fourth of the elective systems I mentioned above is being adopted by more and more universities. It allows the student to make his own choice from a group of subjects, such as a science, a language, and an art or literature. He is thus able to specialize at the same time that he acquaints himself with the main ways of acquiring knowledge.

Second, as supplements to the main curriculum, "experimental" courses are being created by students themselves, usually in cooperation with certain faculty members. Some courses are for credit, and others for free. Some give grades and some do not. Faculty members may or may not consider them part of their teaching load. These courses are usually thought up by students and individual faculty members and do not need the sanction of faculty committees, although universities generally encourage them on the grounds that they are a fertile source of new ideas for the standard curriculum. Like contemporary rock groups, they are splendidly named: "20th Century Mysticism," "Intermediate Sidereal Astrology," "Dianetics-Scientology," "Creative Fulfillment," and "Shivers Down My Backbone: Rock and Roll and Its Consequences."

Third, and perhaps most important, are the ethnic studies I have mentioned. These studies generally provide (a) political as well as educational enlightenment, (b) training for leadership within ethnic subcultures, and (c) general education of all students interested in the actual and potential contributions of ethnic groups to American life. A small number of activists would like to use these studies not only to create a new political and cultural awareness among minority groups but also to teach specific tactics for the attainment of sweeping social reforms.

Finally, steps are being taken to make courses contribute to the personal growth of the student and to the life of the local community. It is argued that, in the social sciences especially, study on location—study that involves or follows from social activity—not only gives the student a deeper insight into the life-relevance of his subject but also benefits the community itself. Students majoring in the social sciences or preparing for entry into the professions are now being allowed to observe and participate in the practice of their professions much earlier than before. This innovation not only lightens the load on the working profession but also enables the student to discover how genuine his own commitment is. Service courses and field practice thus become a means of filtering out unsuitable candidates as well as of challenging able ones.

My Own View

From time to time in this chapter I have given my opinion on various controversies dividing the university today. I wish to close by offering a few more thoughts on what I believe to be the true nature of the university.

First, as regards the purposes of a university, I endorse the statement adopted by the Faculty Assembly of the University of Wisconsin in 1969:

> The primary purpose of the University [of Wisconsin] is to provide an environment in which faculty and students can discover, examine critically, preserve, and transmit the knowledge, wisdom, and values that will help to ensure the survival of the present and future generations with improvement in the quality of life.

Given this fundamental purpose, the university has three main functions to fulfill:

> (1) To provide students with optimum opportunity for learning from the heritage of the past, for gaining experience in the use of their intellectual and creative capacities, and for developing themselves as concerned, responsible, humane citizens; (2) to extend the frontiers of knowledge through research; (3) to provide society with objective information and with imaginative approaches to the solution of problems which can serve as a basis for sound decision-making in all areas.[8]

What about the proper place and function of the university in community life? Because the university has admitted teachers and students from all social groups and classes, and because it has increased its services to the community and nation, many people have argued that the university is no different from any other civic institution and must respond sensitively to popular and sectional demands. It is also said that, since the university is just another civic institution, it is a suitable forum for

8 Reported in *Science,* **167** (March 20, 1970), 1953.

conventional political tactics such as demonstrations, strikes, and disruptions. To these arguments I reply that, although the public university is publicly founded and publicly funded, it is also by right and constitution self-governing, and is therefore entitled to resist whatever political pressures are brought to bear on it. These pressures come from within and without. They come from campus groups that seek to use the university as an instrument of political power for transforming society, and from external groups that would compel the university to adopt policies favored by powerful interests or by what is loosely called "public opinion." But the university does not exist to pass laws, curb crime, reform abuses, or promote the public interest. It exists to seek and to transmit knowledge. The truth or cogency of claims to scientific, historical, or philosophical knowledge are decided not by public opinion or political parties but by scientists, historians, and philosophers. The university, then, must defend its right to seek truth above all things and to resist subversion by political interests.

Next, although I believe that students and teachers should participate in politics and in community activities, I do not believe that the university as such should advocate particular social and political reforms. The university should neither be a political party nor act as the arm of one. Of course, studies undertaken by members of the university may well provide information that is used by social groups that are proposing or implementing changes in society. Members of the university—students and faculty—must surely study and debate the social and political issues of the moment. But they must not expect the university *as an institution* to endorse or advocate any of the views they propose. The university is a forum for debate, not an instrument for political action.

Finally, let me offer some concrete suggestions for bringing the practice of our universities closer to the ideals I have mentioned.

1. Eliminate the freshman and sophomore years. This will (a) limit enrollment to students who are more academically and professionally minded than the present rank and file, and (b) make the university essentially a graduate institution as opposed to a state college for undergraduates.

2. Let the state colleges be responsible for the bachelor's degree and the university for the master's and doctor's degrees. This not only corresponds with university practice abroad, but also responds to rising graduate enrollments in upper-division and graduate courses. The university would in effect become a graduate institution and would be released from the need to "make up for high school deficiencies" and "establish basic course requirements" (beyond those of the student's major subject).

3. Create better and closer relations between students and teachers by (a) keeping the student-teacher ratio at twelve to one, (b) substituting individual tutorials and group seminars for lectures, and (c) giving the student more responsibility for his own learning.

4. When appointing or promoting faculty, allow the candidate to state the special achievement for which he wishes to be judged, whether teaching, research, or service. Let him be known in the university for the special contribution he can make.

5. In judging research, value most highly that which contributes directly to a professor's teaching or to social-service functions unique to the university.

6. Encourage teachers and students to (a) consider the social applications of knowledge and (b) study and practice on location.

7. For the M.A. degree in particular, take the interdisciplinary approach to learning, emphasizing the unity of knowledge.

8. As regards student schedules, aim for quality of work rather than quantity. (Twelve class hours a week are enough for any student.)

9. Allow graduate students, as part of their education, to take responsibility for the tutoring of two or three undergraduates.

10. Create an environment in which students and teachers dedicate themselves to the life of the mind and to the fulfillment through hard work of their special talents.[9]

None of these ideas is original. All have their historical precedents. But I wish to reaffirm them for our time, for they express my faith in the abiding idealism of the university and of the youth who attend it.

I believe that in the young of each generation mankind renews itself, setting out on its never-ending quest for the ideals of justice, beauty, and truth.The university must forever remember that for the young all things seem possible, because for them all things are untried. Uncorroded by failure and unclouded by disillusion, the young are the bearers of life's everlasting promise—that the race will never grow old and that there are no limits to what men will achieve.

9 For further information on these and other recommendations, see the "Kneller Report," published in 1968 in mimeograph by the Academic Senate Office, University of California, Los Angeles 90024. The Report, available only while present supplies last, contains 52 recommendations for development and innovation at UCLA put forward by a select committee of which I was chairman.

References

❖❖❖

For a select bibliography see Philip G. Altbach, *Student Politics and Higher Education in the USA* (United Ministries in Higher Education, St. Louis, 1968, 86 pp.).

The "conservative" case is argued effectively by Jacques Barzun, *The American University* (Harper & Row, 1968) and Robert Goheen, *The Human Nature of a University* (Princeton University Press, 1969, 116 pp.). The "progressive" view is presented convincingly by Harold Taylor, *Students without Teachers: The Crisis in the University* (McGraw-Hill, 1969). In *The Uses of the University* (Harvard University Press, 1963), Clark Kerr, a moderate, discusses the idea of the "multiversity".

For a balanced anthology of manageable length I recommend John Lawlor, Ed., *The New University* (Columbia University Press, 1968, 200 pp.). More historically oriented, *The Campus in the Modern World*, John Margolis, Ed. (Macmillan, 1968, 381 pp.), has challenging essays by T. S. Eliot, R. M. Hutchins, Mark Van Doren, Paul Goodman, Jacques Barzun, John W. Gardner, Theodore Roszak, Richard Lichtman, and others. Theodore Roszak, Ed., *The Dissenting Academy* (Pantheon, 1968, 304 pp.), is a collection of essays by radical faculty members such as Louis Kampf, Sumner Rosen, Staughton Lynd, and Noam Chomsky. For an exercise in futurology, see Alvin C. Eurich, Ed., *Campus 1980* (Delacorte, 1968, 327 pp.) with contributions by J. W. Gardner, Logan Wilson, William Birenbaum, Christopher Jencks, David Riesman, Nevitt Sanford, Clark Kerr, and others.

Stephen Spender's *The Year of the Rebels* (Random House, 1969) is an eyewitness account of student protests throughout Europe and America. Spender shows how bystanders are led to become activists. Charles Frankl's *Education and the Barricades* (Norton, 1968, 90 pp.) is an acute analysis of the claims of student protesters. In *The Ideal of the University* (Beacon, 1969, 161 pp.), Robert Paul Wolff incisively defines the limits of the university as (a) a sanctuary of scholarship, (b) a training ground for professionals, (c) a social service station, and (d) an assembly line for future members of the Establishment.

571

26

Vocational Education

Melvin L. Barlow

❖❖

Vocational education is concerned with people and work. Its scope is broad in terms of both the people to be served and the range of occupations involved.

In general terms, a person's vocation is what he does to earn a living; hence "vocational" applies to all people and all occupations. The term "vocational" (of late Middle English origin) was first related to ecclesiastical affairs, but for more than 400 years has referred to a person's ordinary occupation, business, or profession. Acts of Congress related to vocational education have focused attention on educational preparation for work. At first, the educational effort was concentrated at the high school level; subsequently the range was extended to include two years of postsecondary education. Current definitions of the term "vocational education" include all occupations except those identified as professional and that require a baccalaureate degree. Thus vocational education is concerned with 80 percent, or more, of the jobs in the world of work.

Contemporary influences on education such as welfare, unemployment, disadvantaged and handicapped persons, and technology have focused attention on vocational education. Learning to work and learning to live are not separate entities, and yet education has given only scant attention to the problem of education for work. Thousands of youths, high school dropouts, high school graduates, college dropouts, and college graduates are seeking admission to the world of work. By many standards some of these youth are well educated, but they can't answer employment's fundamental question—what can you do? Providing the educational experience to answer the question is the task of vocational education.

The Structure of Vocational Education

Vocational education is a social process. It was designed as a benefit to society and is self-adjusting to the needs of society. Inherent in the structure of vocational education are three primary elements, (1) principles, (2) interpretation, and (3) implementation.

Principles. The principles of vocational education are sound, and relate to the structure of vocational education as the Bill of Rights relates to Government, or the Ten Commandments to moral conduct. These principles are fundamental and do not change with time. Many are expressions of other accepted truths. For example, a person is not to be eliminated from a vocational-education program on the basis of sex, creed, color, or nationality. Other principles reflect an emphasis of program content and relationships to education in general. For instance, a vocational-education program must provide for both practical experience and theoretical instruction, but these must be accomplished as a part of the total educational environment. There is no dichotomy between the principles of vocational education and those of education in general.

The fact that the principles of vocational education are basic does not insure that all persons will recognize, honor, or use them appropriately. Despite the soundness of the theoretical structure of vocational education, many violations of principles exist. Such violations may be due, in part, to improper interpretation.

Interpretation. The second primary element in the theoretical structure of vocational education is concerned with interpretation of the principles in the light of social, economic, and technological need. Society and the work that society needs done change continuously. The population grows, new jobs are invented, old jobs go out of existence, attention is focused on the large cities with its ghettos and unemployment, ad infinitum. It is necessary, therefore, to review the principles of vocational education from time to time in order to maximize the contributions of this education to social and economic needs.

Because the development of vocational education is tied directly to Congressional action, the basis for interpretation of principles stems largely from various acts of Congress. The vocationally related acts of 1917, 1929, 1934, 1936, 1946, 1963, and 1968 did in fact provide an interpretation of vocational education in the light of the social and economic needs of the times. It is reasonable to expect that other acts of Congress will be forthcoming.

Implementation. The third element in the general scheme of vocational education is concerned with planning, organizing, and conducting the program. It is at this point that courses are planned, teachers are hired, and students receive instruction. Courses are planned that represent an area of actual or anticipated employment opportunities. The course content includes the practical experience and related technical knowledge required by a beginning worker. In general, such courses lead to a grouping of jobs known as "families" or "clusters." For example, the vocational part of an allied health curriculum in the high school would provide instruction in the skills and related science common to about a dozen different jobs. The student, upon graduation, can actually go to work in one of these jobs.

Implementation includes a number of key points. (1) Instructional content is kept relevant to the occupational area concerned by the use of advisory committees and through knowledge of trends in the occupational structure—national, state, and local. (2) The vocational instructor is a competent practitioner of the subject matter involved. The idea here is that it is as impossible to teach something that you have not experienced as it is to return from someplace you have never been. (3) Instruction is carried out in an educational setting representative of the occupation(s) for which training is provided. For example, practical-nursing students receive part of their instruction in the hospital or in a real-life medical setting. Automechanics students work on modern, up-to-date automobiles. A cooperative work-experience program in merchandising involves student experience in the day-to-day world of work. A petroleum-technology course operates as a miniature oil company, with the actual oil field as a laboratory for the course. (4) Full-time students complete their vocational preparation with opportunities to study in other disciplines.

The three basic elements in the structure of vocational education—principles, interpretation, and implementation—keep the program sound and on a even keel, relevant to the educational and occupational environment.

Vocational Education and Change

Vocational education has been stimulated from federal sources. In 1862, the Land Grant College Act, known more popularly as the Morrill

Act, established vocational education at the college level. This act embodied the dream of Senator Justin Morrill (Vermont) to establish a college of agriculture and mechanics (A&M) in each of the states. Neither Morrill nor his supporters were very definite about the kind of an institution which was to be established, and the actual act itself is somewhat vague on this point. From the rationale about the need for the A&M Colleges, as expressed in the *Congressional Record,* one gets the distinct impression that such colleges were to become practical colleges and that their educational thrust would be aimed at study of direct benefit to the farmer and the mechanic.

Some of the A&M Colleges did in fact carry out this tradition, but many became large universities and in time lost, or forgot, their original commitment and stimulated the development of the liberal arts. However, the success of the vocational-education movement at the college level created interest and concern about the development of a similar program at the high school level.

The legislative movement for vocational education at the high school actually began about 1906, but received major emphasis beginning in 1910, with final legislative action in 1917. For many years the vocational-education movement was championed in Congress by Senator Carroll S. Page, also of Vermont, who wanted to do for high school students what his predecessor had done for college students a half century earlier.

By 1917, the term "vocational education" was applied almost exclusively to the high school program, and vocational education at that period included instruction for in-school high school students in agriculture, home economics, and trade and industrial education. Instruction was also provided for employed workers in the same occupational areas. Some change occurred in 1936 and 1946, but the large changes in the scope and direction of vocational education did not actually take place until the 1960s.

The Vocational Education Act of 1963. The extraordinary technological gains of the 1950s produced significant changes in the occupational structure, particularly in the number of new kinds of technological occupations. Such gains made new kinds of technical instruction necessary and brought to light an imperative need for retraining and updating of employees in many other occupations. In adjusting to these changes, vocational education was restructured, for the most part, by the nature of the vocational-education laws. In 1961, President John F. Kennedy appointed a Panel of Consultants on Vocational Education to investigate needed changes in vocational-education legislation.

Late in 1961, and throughout 1962, the panel studied the nation's system of vocational education and reported its findings to the President and the Congress. The panel found a growing need for expansion in vocational education in both the number and the kinds of persons to be involved and in the scope of occupations to be served. The focus, prior to 1963, had been on the occupational structure. However, the panel stressed the traditional principle of vocational education by emphasizing the people to be served. In brief, the emphasis was placed on (1) youth in high school, (2) youth in high school who have special educational needs, (3) students in postsecondary institutions (generally not exceeding two years of postsecondary instruction), and (4) the vast group of employed and unemployed youth and adults in the nation's labor force.

The report of the panel, *Education for a Changing World of Work,* was used by Congress to formulate a new vocational education law, the Vocational Education Act of 1963 (Public Law 88-210). Financial support was substantially increased, and within a period of five years enrollment in vocational education doubled.

Vocational education had been frequently criticized for failing to react promptly to social and labor-force needs. Although such accusations were largely unfounded, it was true that previous federal laws included certain restrictions that did impede change. Accordingly, Congress provided in the act of 1963 that vocational education have a formal review every five years. The act specifically indicated that an Advisory Council on Vocational Education be appointed in 1966 and that the council report its findings no later than January 1, 1968.

The Vocational Educational Amendments of 1968. The Advisory Council on Vocational Education was appointed late in 1966 and studied the problems of vocational education throughout 1967. Between 1962, when the panel had studied vocational education, and 1967, when the council studied it, a startling change had taken place in the social structure of the nation. In 1962 few people had ever heard of Watts; and Cleveland, Detroit, and Trenton were just names of cities. Marches, confrontations, and student revolts were rare. However, when the council undertook its task in 1967, it did so in an emotion-charged atmosphere, deeply concerned with social values.

Throughout the council's deliberations, attention was directed towards expansions in vocational education that would have a positive impact on a large "forgotten" group of people—those who had been allowed to fall through the cracks in both the educational structure and the social structure. Consequently, the council's reviews of the needs for vocational education were expressed in terms that were on every tongue during the late years of the 1960s—disadvantaged, handicapped, unemployed, ethnic groups, welfare, and poverty.

The council's report, *Vocational Education, the Bridge Between Man and His Work,* was used by the Congress as the basis for the Vocational Education Amendments of 1968 (Public Law 90-576). The Act, which was passed unanimously by Congress, provided for a significant increase in federal funding, and for extreme flexibility and broad coverage of individual and occupational needs.

The general tenor of the Vocational Education Amendments of 1968 is expressed succinctly in the declaration of the purpose of the act.

> It is the purpose of this title to authorize Federal grants to States to assist them to maintain, extend, and improve existing programs of vocational education, to develop new programs of vocational education, and to provide part-time employment for youths who need the earnings from such employment to continue their vocational training on a full-time basis, so that persons of all ages in all communities of the State—those in high school, those who have already entered the labor market but need to upgrade their skills or learn new ones, those with special educational handicaps, and those in postsecondary schools—will have ready access to vocational training or retraining which is of high quality, which is realistic in the light of actual or anticipated opportunities for gainful employment, and which is suited to their needs, interests, and ability to benefit from such training.[1]

This declaration of purpose is a far cry from the general purposes of the Vocational Education Act of 1917, but it is representative of the contemporary program of vocational education in the United States.

The Major Issue

When the Smith-Hughes Act became effective in 1917, its passage was hailed by many as the great "democratizer" of secondary education. Here at last was a realistic subject-matter component of education directly representative of American life. The introduction of vocational education into the secondary-school curriculum was calculated to add a new dimension of attractiveness toward schooling for many students. The tragedy of the eighth-grade dropout was frequently used as a target for vocational education. The proponents of vocational education felt strongly that it would in fact make education more palatable and interesting.

[1] *Public Law,* 90-576, October 16, 1968.

For more than a half century the major statements of the purposes and goals of education have made reference to "vocational efficiency," or the development of "saleable skills," as an integral part of the total education of the individual. This was precisely the intent of the vocational-education movement. Vocational education was not to be "added on" or "attached to" education, but to become a "part of" the educational process. A major problem confronting vocational education today is that its integration with education in general has not been achieved. In a large part the failure to achieve this integration of subject matter has been caused by a lack of commitment to do so.

Educational commitment for vocational education is the major issue, but whose commitment? Obviously, those persons directly in charge of the educational process must hold deep concerns for the vocational development of students. But such commitment must be backed up by an equally strong commitment from parents and the community at large, and in particular from boards of education. What vocational education is now, and what it becomes in the future are dependent in a very large measure on the policy of school boards concerning the matter of vocational preparation. These boards are presumably representative of the people and are responsible for providing the policy upon which educational programs are planned, conducted, and administered. The following theoretical statement of policy is an example of the kind of commitment that appears to be necessary.

> It is the policy of this district to provide occupational education for all youth and adults of the district to the end that no student drops out of school who is not prepared to enter the world of work; that no student graduates who does not have saleable skills; and that no adult is denied an educational opportunity to become properly employable.[2]

A commitment of this nature has measurable dimensions, and educational programs can be designed for students to implement the commitment. Such a commitment indicates that the student's vocational future is a concern of the school, and the school intends to provide instruction geared to the interests, abilities, and vocational goals of its students.

A theoretical commitment is one thing, but actual practice by school boards may be something else. It is not known how many school boards have a positive policy related to occupational preparation, but it is known that many such boards throughout the nation are concerned about the vocational phase of education. An example may show the kinds of com-

[2] James A. Rhodes, *Alternative to a Decadent Society*, Howard W. Sams & Co., Inc., Indianapolis, 1969, p. 16.

mitment one school board adopted. On August 26, 1969, the Board of Education, Long Beach Unified School District, Long Beach, California, adopted the following resolution.

> WHEREAS, Common labor is no longer common in the changing nature of the American economy; and
>
> WHEREAS, In this period of rapid technological change, thousands of good paying jobs for skilled workers are unfilled; and
>
> WHEREAS, A recent state-wide study disclosed that only 15 persons out of every 100 entering the fifth grade in California graduate from a four-year college; and
>
> WHEREAS, More than half of all persons who enter the American colleges drop out by the end of their freshman year and seek entrance into the workaday world without a marketable skill; and
>
> WHEREAS, The unemployment level for unskilled teenagers is from three to five times higher than for adults throughout the United States; and
>
> WHEREAS, It has been clearly demonstrated that teenagers without skills have the poorest chance of obtaining employment at other than poverty level wage rates:
>
> THEREFORE BE IT RESOLVED, That members of the Board of Education strongly urge the restructuring of a more effective educational program for the Long Beach Unified School District along the lines of the changes being considered as a result of the George Miller, Jr. Education Act (S.B. 1); and
>
> BE IT RESOLVED FURTHER, That more of our youth be encouraged to take advantage of the opportunity to master marketable occupational skills while enrolled in local high schools and the City College.[3]

Thus far in the discussion commitment has been cast in a frame of reference relating to what a local school board can, and must, do concerning vocational education. But the major issue of commitment is far more complex than a simple declaration of a policy statement. The policy statement is exceedingly important because it states as a matter of educational policy that vocational, or occupational, preparation is a major goal of education. Coupled with the declaration of policy is a clear understanding of the implications of implementing such a policy.

Vocational-education theory visualizes a pattern of relevant vocationally oriented subject matter supplemented generously by other studies calculated to provide breadth and foundation support for the vocational goals of youth. Rousseau wanted Emile to become a carpenter—not to be a carpenter in the ordinary sense, but to rise to the state of being a car-

[3] Reprinted by permission of the Long Beach Board of Education.

penter. Rousseau suggests that Emile's occupational future be cast in a degree of understanding and reward a cut above the simple mechanics of being a carpenter. In short, all that vocational education requires is a place in the total environment of education where it can influence, and be influenced by, other disciplines of education. This calls for a new juxtaposition of the subject matter areas and new understandings about a variety of educational values.

> What is obviously needed is a truly liberal academic community in which the study of art and typewriting, of philosophy and accounting, of theology and medicine, of pure and applied science are, though admittedly very different, judged to be equally honorable and valuable in their several ways. In such a community the so-called liberal disciplines would indeed be liberal because they would be studied and taught with an eye to the total enrichment of the life of responsible members of a free society; and in such a community the acquisition of the vocational skills, from the simplest to the most complex, would be equally liberal because they would be taught, not in a spirit of predatory egoism, but in a spirit of deep social concern for the needs of others and for the common good.[4]

Achieving a relationship among subject-matter areas as described above, and giving to vocational preparation a place of greater centrality in the scheme of education, requires school-board policy as a starting point, but it also requires the will of the faculty and the adminstration. Because a person's occupation is the principal determinant of his social and economic future, it is imperative that education recognize its obligation to help the individual shape his occupational direction. The old idea that a person "gets his education" and then "gets his job" is not a tenable position in the educational structure of the 1970s. These two equally important facets of a person's preparation for the adult world are not separate entities. The baby left on education's doorstep, more than a half century ago, must be admitted to family membership. The school board can knock on the door, but the school faculty and administration must open the door and take the baby in.

Faculty commitment represents the major portion of the problem confronting American education. Age-old ideas of subject-matter superiority and subject-matter compartmentalization have clouded the purposes of education in relation to individual development and preparation for adult life. The school has made education harder, thereby separating

---

[4] Theodore M. Greene, "A Liberal Christian Idealist's Philosophy of Education," *Modern Philosophies and Education,* National Society for the Study of Education, Chicago, 1955, p. 119.

out a large number of students, instead of using its talents to provide an educational environment where students—all students—can learn.

One of the deterrents to faculty commitment is a misunderstanding of the role and function of vocational education as a part of the educational enterprise. Vocational education is intended for all students—not just for those who have failed in the academic studies. For the most part, vocational education has dealt with the rejects of the academic curriculum —students for whom liberal education provided no basis for liberation and who have had to make up for their failures by turning to the vocational-education program. The principles of vocational education exceed by far the mere mechanics of learning job skills.

Although vocational education has done a creditable job in relation to the total individual in the world of work, it has become increasingly evident that this task has grown to gigantic proportions. The vocational education of youth in school is now a responsibility of the total faculty of the school—not the responsibility of the vocational educator alone. The school and the faculty have become increasingly dedicated to the vocational education of only one out of five students; the requirements of the 1970s demand that they be concerned with the vocational education of all students. What is needed in the future is a better mix of the educational experiences provided by the school, and this requires the talents of all of the members of the faculty.

The major issue confronting vocational education has been identified as a commitment by school boards and school faculty. Inevitably the purposes of education must enter the discussion. It is not enough to describe these purposes in terms of citizenship, human relations, and so on unless it is understood that inherent in these goals is preparation for the world of work. Vocational preparation must become a concern of all school boards and all faculties. The educational mix must be redesigned to provide one track that provides (1) a good basic education with no rejects; (2) preparation to perform some of the work society wants done— at the secondary school, preferably in relation to "families" or "clusters" of occupations; and (3) opportunity for the individual to continue his education if he desires to do so. The present idea of treating all students as if they were going to occupy 15 to 20 percent of the jobs in the world of work is not compatible with the needs of the 1970s.

Problems and Myths

Vocational education is an essential element in maintaining a healthy national economy. In a sense it is a safety valve in relation to many social and economic problems. In its basic purpose vocational education acts to prevent unemployment and poverty, but in no sense is it solely devoted to remedial measures. In many respects the existence of unemployment, welfare, and a variety of associated cultural and ethnic problems represent failures of society. Vocational education seeks to prevent these accidents of social development by attacking the problem at its source—the education of people. Education has been criticized severely for its persistent lack of attention to education for work, but it is only through education that hope exists for a brighter future. In order to achieve national goals and a better outlook for the future, the structure of education must change. Within the new structure vocational education must figure prominently. The question is not a clash between liberal education and vocational education; it is essential that the new structure include both.

The focusing of attention on the development of vocational education brings to light a number of problems and myths that must be considered. Much of what people "know" about education and vocational education is wrong and outdated. Fantastic claims are made for and against vocational education with few facts to back them up. Although many problems and myths about education and vocational education can be considered, only a few of the most significant will be reviewed.

The Go-to-College Myth. One of the great tragedies of American education has been an almost complete preoccupation with college preparation as the ultimate goal. Few people bother to ask why, or for what purpose, and yet educators and parents alike appear to be bent on forcing all students into the same mold. The national facts about youth in school follows a pattern somewhat as follows:

Pupils in the 5th Grade, 1959-60	100
Entered the 9th Grade, 1963-64	97
Entered the 11th Grade, 1965-66	85
Graduated from High School in 1967	72
Entered College in Fall, 1967	40
Likely to earn a 4-Year Degree, 1971	20

The main thrust of the secondary school has been based on a premise that all youth will go to college. But, what happened to the 28 students who didn't finish high school, or the 32 high school graduates who did not continue their education, or the 20 who failed to complete the 4-year postsecondary-school program?

Only about 25 percent of the youth in high school are enrolled in a program having vocational objectives; 75 percent are following the college-preparatory route, and yet less than half of this group will continue their education. Assuming that the 20 percent of the students who complete a vocational program at the 4-year college level are in fact prepared to enter the world of work, then vocational education is concerned with the occupational preparation of the other 80 percent. It is clear that education has a problem crying for a solution, and it is doubtful that the "college for everyone" route contains the answers.

The College-Preparatory Curriculum. The college-preparatory curriculum in the high school enrolls 70 to 80 percent of the students. It represents the royal road through high school education and is based on a premise that a certain body of subject matter represents the best preparation for continued education. In general, this body of subject matter consists of courses in English, mathematics, languages, science, and social science—other subjects such as home economics, industrial arts, and vocational courses do not count.

Experimental studies have challenged the assumption that a fixed pattern of courses must be completed in order to succeed in college. Studies during the past 40 years have shown that colleges place too much emphasis on a certain group of high school subjects for college admission. The "Eight-Year Study" concluded:

> The results of this study seem to indicate that the pattern of preparatory school program which concentrated on a preparation for a fixed set of entrance examinations is not the only satisfactory means of fitting a boy or girl for making the most out of the college experience.[5]

The thesis that the so-called "academic" subjects provides a better preparation for college entrance than the nonacademic subjects is not supported by research data. More than 20 years ago the abolition of subject requirements for college admission was advocated.

> Our system of public secondary schools, therefore, is in the grip of a standard curriculum which is based on the fundamental premise that the pursuit of certain prescribed studies is essential to success in college. It has been proved, as completely as anything in life is ever proved, that this premise is false.[6]

Despite the evidence against the college-preparatory curriculum as a predictor of future educational success, students are herded into the college track, losing interests and motivation to be gained from other fields. Excellence is where you find it; excessive emphasis on the college-

[5] Wilford M. Aiken, *The Story of the Eight-Year Study*, New York: Harper & Brothers, 1942, p. 150.

[6] Paul B. Diederich, "The Abolition of Subject Requirements for Admission to College," *School Review* (September 1949), p. 369.

preparatory curriculum reduces the number of subject-matter choices for the high school student.

Teach Them How to Think, Industry Will Do the Rest. This frequently expressed view represents a vague understanding of the problem of subject matter as it is related to vocational education. During the formative years of the vocational-education movement, the relative responsibilities of industry and education were thoroughly discussed. The conclusion was that neither industry nor education alone could do the job of preparing people for work; both were necessary. It was further concluded that the beginnings of education for work should be conducted in an educational environment. Students can be taught to think, solve problems, analyze circumstances, and reach conclusions in the subject-matter environment of vocational education. These essential aspects of life and work are not the special province of any particular subject or group of subjects.

Educators frequently rationalize their failure to provide vocational instruction by calling attention to the fact that many large industries have extensive educational facilities. These facilities are in fact excellent, but unfortunately all people do not work for these organizations. Furthermore, the educational programs of business and industry are primarily devoted to their corporate interests, and the organizations do not generally relish the idea of making up for the failures of education.

A properly organized vocational-education program uses generously the advisory services of business and industry. Meetings of advisory committees composed of representatives of business, industry, and education are able to make recommendations to the school concerning course content (keeping the course up to date), employment of instructors, placement of students, and the need for new courses or the replacement of old ones.

Obviously the mores of a particular business and industry must be taught largely on the job. Such indoctrination programs are not the province of the school; however, vocational education can provide the background on which industry-based programs can build. Now, as it was 50 years ago, the problem of vocational education is a joint responsibility of education and industry. The strongest support for vocational education comes from Congress, business, industry, and labor, and this support is based on the belief that education has a fundamental responsibility to prepare youth for the world of work.

Outdated Vocational Programs? Vocational education values its constructive critics and listens carefully when the voices of experience and considered judgment make observations and suggestions about the needs of vocational education. But criticism arising out of ignorance about vocational education, and vicious and vague in its intent, has little value.

From time to time professional journals and the public press contain statements such as the following: "vocational education is for outdated programs that have small relevance today," "technical competence . . . where it is required, will have to be obtained on the job, due to rapidity of technological change," and "the vocational education program . . . consists largely of the purchase of shop equipment and the training of students for long-vanished jobs." Such criticism is not factually correct, and never has been. None of the critics, as indicated above has ever been able to identify specifically an out-of-date vocational-education program.

The hard-core part of vocational education—the part where the actual salable skills and knowledges are developed—compares favorably with employment needs. It is true that there are not enough students enrolled in vocational-education programs to meet employment demands, but there are no students enrolled in any program for which there are no employment demands. The nature (program content) of vocational education changes with occupational needs. Instruction in vulcanizing went out of existence when there were no longer occupational demands. New programs—aerospace and oceanographic technology, for example— are added to the vocational-education program when such needs appear in the occupational structure. Instruction is given in more than 250 different occupations.

The rapidity of technological change leads some educators to the view that nothing can be done—you can't prepare for today's jobs because they will not be available tomorrow. The scare that automation will render preparation for work useless is a dead issue. Technological change, including automation, does require that vocational education programs be planned with more than usual care, but the time when work will go out of style is not just around the corner.

A Rationale for the 1970s

Among the expectations that society has for its members is that they will become economically stable and will not be a burden on society. This means that every person must either be a wage-earning member of the social structure or be dependent on someone who provides an income in which they share. This theoretical goal is never quite reached, and society must take measure to look out for some of its members. During the colonial period, the children of paupers, homeless children, and the children of reasonably well-to-do parents were apprenticed, voluntarily or involuntarily, until they reached an age and a competence to earn their own living. Colonial apprenticeship practices applied to both boys and girls. Forms of education have been used over the years as a means of achieving economic independence—not so much for the primary purpose of individual benefit, but because the state would suffer if education were not provided. Vocational education is the modern means of accomplishing economic independence.

For more than 250 years a common-school education provided the basic ingredients for economic independence, and until comparatively recently a high school diploma (regardless of the nature of the studies) represented a passport to occupational security. But now the upsurge of technology and new levels of social conscience have changed the picture completely.

Vocational education, an invention of this century, was introduced into the educational structure in order to provide more youth and adults an opportunity to successfully enter the world of work. Changing social mores and rapidly advancing technology make the problem of occupational preparation a central theme of education for the 1970s.

For Whom is Vocational Education Intended? In terms of educational goals, youths are sometimes classified into two groups—the college-bound, and the noncollege-bound. Such classification is meaningless in terms of vocational education because the college goal is not the issue. It is to be hoped that persons who attend college also become vocationally prepared for the world of work.

The program of vocational education for in-school youth is concentrated in high schools and in postsecondary institutions—junior colleges, community colleges, area vocational schools, technical institutes, and the like. During the past decade the fastest-growing segment of vocational education has been in the postsecondary-school area. It is at this point that instruction for highly skilled technicians is largely concentrated. However, the postsecondary school cannot limit its instruction to technical education, because it must also accommodate the vast group of young adults who were not prepared for a career in the secondary school.

About 25 to 30 percent of the high school youth of the nation were enrolled in vocational education programs in the secondary school in 1970. Considering the number of students who elect to enter the world of work without further educational experience, this percentage should increase to a range of 50 to 70 percent of the youth in secondary schools. A similar percentage increase—double or more—can be anticipated in the postsecondary school as such schools recognize their responsibility for vocational preparation.

The rationale for the 1970s includes a new point of view about the availability of vocational instruction. Whereas the previous disposition of school officials was "here it is, come and get it," a new attitude of "we will bring it to you" should prevail. Such a point of view, converted into action, will provide vocational instruction for youth and young adults who are not in school. Special classes of all kinds may be set up in any location convenient for the students concerned. This "outreach" characteristic of the expanded vocational education program is an imperative aspect of the future. The social and economic values of such an expansion are obvious. The rigid college-preparatory program has not reached this group of youth and there is little evidence to believe that it will do so in the future.

The program of vocational education for out-of-school youth and adults is intended to be conducted by high schools, adult schools, occupational centers, and posthigh-school institutions. Such programs for the 1970s must include an opportunity to prepare for and enter upon a career, to change occupational goals, and to update and upgrade occupational skills and knowledge. Occupational-education problems of the unemployed must be recognized and programs provided that will in fact make the unemployed employable. This is one of the major challenges of the 1970s for vocational education, and the burden to provide appropriate programs rests with the schools.

Vocational education is a primary responsibility of the establishment of education and not of labor, business, agriculture, or industry. Recognition of this primary responsibility by action programs in the schools should become increasingly characteristic of education.

Occupational Status. We still find people who measure a man by the kind of work he does rather than by the quality of his performance, whatever his work may be. What is needed in the rationale is a new system of educational values based on individual goals and preferences, and not on predetermined standards of achievement related to a very limited subject-matter area. This system of educational values should recognize achievement along a broad subject-matter base, and would consider such achievement to be as honorable as achievement in any other area of subject matter. To paraphrase John Gardner, excellence in plumbing is as honorable as excellence in philosophy.

A decadent system of ideas about occupational status still pervades education. We have entered on an era in which our future is vitally connected to high-level performance along a vast continuum of occupational preparation. Education must face the issue that it cannot place value on the name of the occupation. There is no way to determine that engineering is more valuable than carpentry—both are essential in the economy of the future. What counts is the quality of performance.

The school can change ideas about occupational status and it must do so. The concept of the primacy of the person keeps getting lost amid extreme occupational prejudice. The irony of the situation is that youth are directed occupationally in an educational environment of ignorance about the vast number of occupational opportunities available, and of predetermined attitudes about occupational value. The rationale of the 1970s requires complete elimination of the concepts of occupational status in the education of youth.

Dichotomy of Educational Goals? The literature of education, over the years, has contained a dialogue about liberal education and vocational education that dichotomizes these two areas. The values of liberal education are extolled over the values of vocational education, or vice versa depending on the writer. Liberal education has been cast as the ultimate goal despite the fact that the area has yet to liberate anyone.

Among educational theorists, who focus their attention on the role of vocational education in the educational structure, no dichotomy of values is suggested. Vocational education was presented in its original context as a part of the total education of the individual, and this included areas of education loosely identified as liberal or academic. From the beginning the point of view was advanced that education devoid of vocational education is in fact illiberal—a point of view still sound in the 1970s. Both areas are in fact essential, and with increasing social complexity they are becoming more so. At no time has vocational education denied the values of cultural heritage.

But some strange things happen in education. Some students in elementary and secondary schools do not get the attention they need in order to succeed. We permit students to fail in the subject matter thought to be essential for their general success as persons in the social structure. Many of these students become the dropouts and pushouts and are turned over to vocational education to be made into instant workers. This has not been an easy task because subjects such as they have failed are in fact an essential background for a successful occupational future. Society cannot tolerate an educational system that rejects students. The commitment for the future must honor the individuality of the student and not measure him against predetermined standards of achievement related to a limited subject-matter area.

The multitrack system of education encourages a basis for a dichotomy. A single-track system, in which a student can more successfully complete the general subjects, begin preparation for an occupational future, and continue his education beyond high school, is an attractive goal for the 1970s.

References

American Vocational Association, *Vocational Education and Manpower Training,* American Vocational Association, Washington, 1969, 32 pp. A report of a national seminar, summarizing the major issues confronting federal legislation for vocational education, with particular reference to responsibilities of federal and state agencies to provide vocational education.

Barlow, Melvin L., Ed., The Sixty-Fourth Yearbook of the National Society for the Study of Education, Part I, *Vocational Education,* The University of Chicago Press, Chicago, 1965, 301 pp. A rich source of ideas concerning change in education and vocational education with reference to social, economic, and educational issues.

Barlow, Melvin L., *History of Industrial Education in the United States,* Chas. A. Bennett Co., Inc., Peoria, 1967, 512 pp. Contains a comprehensive documentation of the historical background of industrial and vocational education.

Department of Health, Education, and Welfare, Office of Education, *Education for a Changing World of Work,* OE-80021, U.S. Government Printing Office, Washington, 1963, 296 pp. Report of the Panel of Consultants on Vocational Education appointed by President John F. Kennedy. Represents the rationale to support a change of emphasis in vocational education. Principal source document for the Vocational Education Act of 1963.

Department of Health, Education, and Welfare, Office of Education, *Vocational Education the Bridge Between Man and His Work,* OE-80052, U.S. Government Printing Office, Washington, 1968, 220 pp. Report of the Advisory Council on Vocational Education appointed by President Lyndon B. Johnson. A rationale for vocational education in an era of extreme social consciousness. Principal source document for the Vocational Education Amendments of 1968.

Roberts, Roy W., *Vocational and Practical Arts Education,* Second Edition, Harper & Row, New York, 1965, 596 pp. A general text in vocational education. Contains

589

historical background, the general themes for the development of vocational education, and discussions of principles of vocational education.

Rhodes, James A., *Alternative to a Decadent Society*, Howard W. Sams & Co., Inc., Indianapolis, 1969, 108 pp. A critical review of education by the Governor of Ohio (1962-1970), with an emphasis on the need for expanded programs of vocational education.

27

The Learning Society

Paul and June Dow Sheats

❖❖

The Climate of Adult Education

There are at least two approaches to an understanding of the field of adult and continuing education in 20th-century America.[1] The one most frequently employed is a quantitative overview, an analysis of the agencies and institutions that provide adult-education programs, and a description of methods of financing, staffing, and recruiting professional staff and clientele. Readers of this chapter will find in the *1970 Handbook of Adult Education in the U.S.* extensive coverage of these and other aspects of the field.

The approach *least* often employed to explain this amorphous field may be called "contextual." It considers the field in relation to other levels and types of American education and also relative to the overall determinants and trends in American society. Because of the unique situation confronting adult educators in the U.S. in the 1970s, we choose to take the contextual approach.

[1] The terms "adult education" and "continuing education" are used interchangeably in this chapter.

Social Determinants

The context can best be understood if we consider (1) the social determinants that historically mark adult education in America from its early beginnings to the present; and (2) those social determinants that contemporaneously confront this nation in the 1970s. Before describing both sets of determinants, it should be noted that the current forces, while they have been gathering impetus during the preceding decade, have now reached proportions that mandate action. The thrust must come from federal, state, and local jurisdictions, and from professional bodies, the academe, the industrial establishment, and concerned influentials in each community. In short, what has long been the cry of adult educators becomes now a major national goal that cannot be ignored or shunted elsewhere. To do so is to invite further social malaise, economic disaster, and negative political consequences of considerable magnitude.

The Historical Context

It has been pointed out by C. Hartley Grattan that

> The American people have been peculiarly successful in the diffusion of knowledge, as many witnesses have testified . . . even before the Revolution, observers were noting that the wide diffusion of knowledge was an outstanding characteristic of the country.[2]

He stresses, however, that the education of adults in this country has occurred in a broad range of ways and means, of which adult education, as defined later in this chapter, is but one.

If Benjamin Franklin can be called the patron saint of adult education in America, we must also add Cotton Mather, Thomas Jefferson, Abraham Lincoln, and a spate of other early leaders. Both Franklin and Lincoln were self-educated, but it is more significant that these and other great men in our early history used their learning as leaders and problem-solvers. The so-called Renaissance Man has appeared only spottily in U.S. society, and he always has been overshadowed by the pragmatist, the doer, and the change agents of his time. Thus, it is consistent that the image of adult education has strong connotations of utility and of im-

---

[2] C. Hartley Grattan, *In Quest of Knowledge,* Association Press, New York, 1955, p. 136. A historical perspective on adult education.

provement of the self and the social scene. This historical social determinant explains, at least in part, the tendency to regard adult education in a cost-effectiveness context, rather than perceiving it as a function of value *for its own sake*. It is easy to understand why subsidy has been largely lacking for adult education unless the programs possessed practical objectives, despite the fact that their very practicality was redefined by each generation of Americans.[3]

Adult Education, Handmaiden of Necessity

Despite the specific barriers to educating various categories of American youth and adults, certain programs for the latter emerged historically when societal needs were pressing. In the late eighteenth century, the Mechanics' Institute idea was borrowed from England to render the working classes more godly, self-improved, and vocationally better equipped to do their jobs. The Lyceum of 1826-39 and the Chautauqua (1874 to, roughly, the turn of the century) were phenomena of our rural past, when the small town flourished and before mass media existed to link the then-scattered population. Americanization courses remained a major thrust of the late 19th and early 20th centuries as a means of enculturating and assimilating vast numbers of immigrants, attracted to this country as cheap industrial labor.

Some indication of the cultural lag in meeting the educational needs of adults is evidenced by the Smith-Lever Act of 1914 for agricultural extension. It was on the books, but was shunted aside until 1917 when the Smith-Hughes Act added vocational education and home economics to the legislation. Only then did the nation create a scientific basis for agriculture (which had begun in colonial days), and by 1920 the urban population of the U.S. had already exceeded the rural. It is noteworthy that for the last fifty years the overwhelming trend has been toward urbanization, yet only in the 1960s did we look inward at the educational wasteland of our ghettos, barrios, and other impoverished inner-city communities. Indeed, future historians may question why it took until

3 Indeed, every generation of adult educators has defined its own horizons. Thomas Pole's 1816 printed polemic in England argued for schools for adults by insisting that subsequently neither such schools nor schools for children would be needed. Every adult would know how to read and would teach his reading skills to his progeny, thus eliminating the need for both types of educational institutions! See Coolie Verner, *Pole's History of Adult Schools,* A Facsimile of the 1816 Edition, Adult Education Association of the U.S.A., Washington, D.C., 1967, p. 18; and Grattan op. cit., p. 76.

1963 for Michael Harrington (or any other observer of the American scene) to write *The Other America*.

There are repeated examples in the wake of the first and second world wars and the Great Depression of the 1930s that adult education served as a handmaiden to major crises—economic, social, and political. These historical determinants tended to shape the field, giving it the present image of a problem-solving, grittily oriented, short-term type of education to meet a given need. Until now at least, the climate has not been conducive to long-range planning, stable fiscal undergirding, or professional parity with the other three levels of American education. Predictably, in the 1970s these inequities will change. What is not yet clear is how much—and what share—of the total adult and continuing education job will be performed by the practitioners in the field, and how much will be assumed by those in higher education, industry, government, and health and welfare agencies.

The Contemporary Context

There are four social determinants extant that will undoubtedly make the 1970s a crucial time of change for the field of adult and continuing education. Although they relate to one another, they are, in a contextual sense, discrete; that is, four separate influences are operating to force an expansion and growing professionalization within the field. Hopefully, they will also allow for more long-range planning rather than the fight-the-current-fire role that has marked so much of American adult education in previous decades and centuries.

The current social determinants are (1) the population explosion, (2) the knowledge explosion, (3) the increase in leisure time, and (4) the changing nature of the work force. Any one of these would be a powerful force in reshaping adult education and, taken in consort, they constitute a battering ram of pressure. Indeed, it might be hypothesized that if adult educators do not capitalize on these current influences within the coming decade, their potential leadership role will pass to other specialists and they will miss their greatest chance to figure prominently in American history.

There will be 230 million people in the U.S. by 1975, and 250 million by 1980. The greatest increase will be of young and old people: by 1980, fifty percent of the population will be under 21 or over 65. Because most members of these two groups of citizens will not be working, their need for educational, cultural, and recreational opportunities will be far greater than those of citizens between 21 and 65.

The growth in sheer numbers, coupled with the particular age brackets affected, is the most salient demographic trend affecting the adult-education field. But there are other peripheral trends.

> People will move more frequently. Some 20 per cent of the U.S. population moves every year. This mobility has increased greatly during the past few decades and will probably continue at an accelerated rate. . . . People will continue to move to metropolitan areas.[4]

The knowledge explosion has been variously documented, and the news of its scope has been widely disseminated.

> The engineer who graduated today has half-life of only about ten years; half of what he learned at the point of graduation will be obsolete in a decade.[5]

Not only will he be professionally obsolescent without constant retraining and upgrading of his education, but most of the engineering knowledge that he will need to learn ten years hence has not even been produced as he marches off the stage with his college diploma today. Medicine, another field that is turning out research and development apace, would force doctors to read an average of one new book a day were they to keep up with all new medical techniques and findings. Business administration, architecture, law, the sciences—all are turning out new knowledge faster than curriculum specialists can design new educational programs. When, exactly, did this explosion begin?

> We are all aware that we live in what has sometimes been called "the age of change." It is difficult to determine when this era began, but it probably was with the years of recovery after the end of World War II . . . education, technology, and science are all rapidly accelerating. The information suggests that the rate of change has become approximately geometrical. Perhaps the general rate of change is paralleling the present exponential rate of growth of our country's population—despite a present short-term decline.[6]

4 A. A. Liveright, *A Study of Adult Education in the United States,* Center for the Study of Liberal Education for Adults, Boston University, 1968, pp. 7-8.

5 Paul H. Sheats, *The Case Against the Adult Dropout,* Occasional Papers No. 11, Center for the Study of Liberal Education for Adults, Boston University, 1965, p. 5.

6 Robert I. Johnson, *The Magic Society: A Look into the 21st Century,* The 11th Annual Seminar on Leadership in Continuing Education, Proceedings, Kellogg Center for Continuing Education, Michigan State University, April 8-11, 1968, published by The Continuing Education Service, Michigan State University.

The field of adult education received unsolicited kudos (or, at least, its practitioners interpreted them thusly) when the president of IBM allegedly told the president of the Massachusetts Institute of Technology: "Give me your leading graduate and in five years I shall have to retire him as obsolescent unless he continues his education."

In point of fact, the knowledge explosion cannot really be slotted into one particular year, decade, or generation in the way that we can date man's first steps on the moon. (Even this type of dating is spurious, of course, because the first steps were taken on Earth some time before 1969.) The electron microscope, used to see minuscule living bits of energy, opened up the huge scientific world of nucleic acids in the 1950s and 1960s, and this created a whole explosion of microscopic energy. Although the electron microscope can be *said* to have been perfected in 1931 or 1932, in Germany, its origin can be traced back 300 years to Holland, where a merchant named Leeuwenhoek first experimented with lenses and communicated his findings over almost fifty years to the Royal Society of London.

Just as the knowledge explosion is a social determinant for continuing education, so there exists a combination of forces that feed into the phenomenon of rapidly multiplying knowledge:

> . . . the world before us is very different from the experience of the past . . . [today we see] . . . large increases in per capita wealth, an increase in technological innovation and diffusion, exponential growth in the stock of knowledge, a decrease in the proportions of unskilled workers accompanied by large increases in professional, technical, and managerial personnel, a growth in leisure time with the opportunity for either earlier retirement or successive participation in a number of careers during the span of a single lifetime, the increasing importance of service industries, a more rapid rate of occupational obsolescence. . . .[7]

In sum, we see that the social determinants affecting the field of adult education are also affecting each other, and the result is a vast and rapid economic and social change unprecedented in man's total experience.

Growth in Leisure Time

This trend has been evidenced for many years, and all indications point to its acceleration. Workers will work fewer hours, have longer vacations, and retire at an earlier age. The implications of this social

[7] Stanley Moses, *Excerpts from The Learning Force: An Approach to the Politics of Education,* Educational Policy Research Center, Syracuse University, 1969.

determinant pose a special challenge for adult educators, because all the data demonstrate that lower-class persons have the most difficulty in coping with their free time, and they do not react positively to the prospect of more leisure.

Despite this, some of the nation's largest unions, such as the United Automobile Workers, are working to achieve earlier retirement with larger pensions. Already, a clause guaranteeing thirteen weeks' vacation with full pay every five years, for senior employees, has been negotiated by the Steelworkers Union in contracts covering the steel, tin, and aluminum industries. Moreover, it is unlikely that blue-collar workers will change their orientation and welcome the notion of more free time with the concomitant opportunities for education. Rather, the changing will have to be done by adult educators in motivating these potential clients and designing programs to attract them.

Research shows that the tendency to use leisure passively (for example, by watching television) is evidenced more by lower-class persons than by the middle or upper classes, even at the sixth-grade level. In 1968-69, Bradley S. Greenberg of the School of Communications, Michigan State University, did a study on communication among the poor, comparing media use of poor whites and poor blacks. Even his children's group showed an inordinately high use of media among poor white elementary school students and even the viewing of television among their poor black peers.

Changing Nature of the Work Force

Almost half a million women are joining the work force in the United States yearly, and, by 1975, it is estimated that 25 million American women will be employed. Clerical and sales jobs, along with the service industries, absorb most of this increase, but management and the professions are also employing more women. Some unions are already at work to build into their contracts a provision for nurseries, day care, and after-school centers for children of working mothers. As these and other conditions compatible with family responsibilities develop, even more women will join the work force. Adult educators must meet this societal need by providing special occupational and related programs for women of all ages wishing to enter or reenter the labor market. Many of the new offerings developed in the late 1960s uncovered a need by this clientele for more than job training and skills. The need was related to self-confidence. Women who have never worked, or who have performed a domestic role for many years, need to gain poise and inner assurance that they *can* do a paid job. Courses that offer human-relations training, or that provide opportunity for women to get a sense of identity, will be needed increasingly. Other changes in the work force also are predicted:

> . . . there will be a continuing decline in the percentage of white-collar jobs and a continuing decline in the percentage of farm and blue-collar workers. The number of jobs requiring unskilled or semi-skilled members of the labor force will continue to decline, and more highly trained individuals will be required in the service, governmental, technical, and professional categories. . . . The implications for continuing education are staggering.[8]

Definition and Scope

The United States today, as this volume makes clear, has acquired a massive and complex educational establishment. Adult education is both part of and part from the core institutions that have traditionally been identified with the educational process. The typical image of what we call education in the United States is that of a ladder with children and youth advancing vertically from one rung to another—kindergarten, elementary school, junior high, senior high, and, for some, on up to the rungs of higher education and even graduate school. Central to the prevailing image is the element of preparation for life and, more particularly, for entrance into the work force. By contrast,

> Adult Education is a process through which persons no longer attending school on a regular, full-time basis undertake activities with the conscious intention of bringing about changes in information, knowledge, understanding, skills, appreciation, and attitudes; or to identify and solve personal or community problems.[9]

As we shall see, the major units of the formal educational structure do provide, in varying degrees, learning opportunities for adults, but such services are peripheral to more central functions of providing education for children and youth. Moreover, of the total number of adults currently estimated to be engaged in some kind of organized educational activity, more than half of this learning force participates in programs sponsored by agencies outside the "core." Education for adults is provided in proprietary institutions (private business and trade schools, for

[8] Paul H. and June Dow Sheats, "Continuing Education," *Encyclopedia of Education,* Macmillan Publishing Company, 1971 (no page reference available yet).

[9] A. A. Liveright, *A Study of Adult Education in the United States,* Center for the Study of Liberal Education for Adults, Boston University, 1968, pp. 3-4.

example), in business and industry in antipoverty programs, by way of educational television, and in programs sponsored by religious groups and community agencies. The participation study by the National Opinion Research Center estimates that some twenty-five million adults participated in adult-education programs during 1962, and that, of all courses taken, 21 percent were sponsored by churches and synagogues, 15 percent by community organizations, 12 percent by business and industry, and 7 percent by private schools.[10]

Moreover, the number of adults in "the learning force"[11] is growing rapidly. Wilbur J. Cohen, former Under-Secretary and later Secretary of the Department of Health, Education and Welfare, with the assistance of a group of staff colleagues, undertook projections of general adult education and vocational, technical and professional enrollments to 1974.[12]

These projections were further studied and adjusted by Stanley Moses of the Educational Policy Research Center at Syracuse University. His findings and deductions therefrom were reported in a paper, "The Learning Force: A New Concept for Education," presented September 5, 1969 at the Annual Meeting of the American Political Science Association. The paper contained a table reproduced here as Table 1:

Table 1

The Educational Periphery: Enrollments (in Millions)[13]

The Educational Periphery	1940	1950	1955	1960	1965	1970	1975
1. Organizational	8.2	10.2	10.9	13.0	14.5	21.7	27.4
2. Proprietary	2.5	3.5	3.5	4.0	7.8	9.6	18.1
3. Antipoverty	—	—	—	—	2.8	5.1	7.0
4. Correspondence	2.7	3.4	3.5	4.5	5.0	5.7	6.7
5. TV	—	—	—	.01	5.0	7.5	10.0
6. Other adult	3.9	4.8	5.1	6.6	9.1	10.7	13.2
Total	17.3	21.9	23.0	28.3	44.2	60.3	82.4

[10] John W. C. Johnstone and Ramon J. Rivera, *Volunteers for Learning*, Aldine Publishing Co., Chicago, 1965, p. 61.

[11] This term was coined and defined by Bertram M. Gross, Professor of Political Science at Syracuse University, in 1965-66, as follows: "The total number of people developing their capacities through systematic education—that is, where learning is aided by teaching and there are formal, organized efforts to impart knowledge through instruction." See Wilbur J. Cohen, "Education and Learning," *The Annals of the American Academy of Political and Social Science*, 373 (Sept. 1967), p. 83.

[12] Ibid., pp. 84-85.

[13] Since the proceedings are available only on microfilm from University Microfilms, Ann Arbor, Michigan 48106, we are giving as our source an abridged working

Note that in 1965 more than 44 million participants were part of the learning force. Of these, 25 million were engaged in vocational, technical, and professional training outside the formal structure, and 19 million were engaged in more general educational activities. But the projections for 1975 dramatize the extent to which the educational periphery has become the dominant feature of the total educational enterprise. With 82.4 million participants in the learning force by 1975, we shall, by that date, have more adults engaged in vocational and adult education than children and youth attending the formal units in the traditional ladder system.

It would seem reasonable to expect that educational planning for the 1970s will include both an assessment of national needs for adult education and the establishment of realistic national educational goals that will recognize the special claims and characteristics of adult education as differentiated from youth education. Professor Malcolm S. Knowles of Boston University has explained these differences by identifying the study of adult learning and teaching as *"andragogy,"* a term derived from the stem of the Greek word for a mature male, *Aner (Andros)*. By the use of this term we can more accurately differentiate adult education from *pedagogy* and the study of youth learning and teaching.[14]

Knowles then describes the "four main sets of assumptions on which andragogical theory is based. . . ." These are:

1. The adult's *"self-concept,"* his self-directedness and willingness to build a student-teacher relationship of mutual responsibility.

2. *Experience*—"The adult has a broader foundation on which to build, and he is himself a richer resource for learning than when he was younger."

3. *Readiness to Learn*—"The adult's developmental tasks concern performance in the changing roles of worker, spouse, parent, and responsible citizen."

4. *Orientation to learning*—"The mature person approaches learning with a time perspective different from that of youth. The adult intends to apply immediately what he learns . . . and brings to learning a problem-centered frame of mind."[15]

paper prepared for use in connection with the Galaxy Conference on Adult Education described later in this chapter.

[14] Malcolm S. Knowles, *Higher Adult Education in the United States,* American Council on Education, Washington, D.C., 1969, pp. 28-29.

[15] Ibid., pp. 29-30.

The growing recognition that lifelong learning is indispensable to a free society should lead to some adjustments in the list of national educational priorities. We have become so accustomed to equating education with formal schooling that we have overlooked some glaring weaknesses in the present system. It may well be that some of what we now try to teach in school could be taught with more success in the adult years. This could materially lighten our overcrowded school curriculum. This view is supported by what we know about learning, as is argued cogently by Sir Richard Livingstone in the following passage:

> [We know] that almost any subject is studied with much more interest and intelligence by those who know something of its subject matter than by those who do not; and conversely that it is not profitable to study theory without some practical experience of the facts to which it relates. We act like people who should try to give their children in a week all the food they require for a year. . . . Someday, no doubt, we shall abandon this practice and give everyone a chance of thinking about life when he is facing it and about its problems when he has to solve them. When that day comes, we shall stop one of the chief sources of educational waste and inefficiency, and make the greatest advance in our history towards the creation of an educated democracy.[16]

Or, to quote a more recent analysis,

> We must free ourselves from seeing education, work, and leisure-retirement as three separate periods of life. We must begin thinking of these activities as running concurrently and continuously throughout life. Existing financial supports—private and public funds for education, unemployment insurance, in-service training funds, social security, pensions, etc.—would, of course, have to be reallocated to support such a basic reshuffling of life-cycle activities. Youth could then feel free to work or loaf as well as to attend college. The 35-year-old would be encouraged to take time off to study, change directions, or relax. The 70-year-old . . . would be as prepared for work and study as he would be for a true enjoyment of leisure.[17]

Institutional Response

The first truly comprehensive study of the Federal Government's involvement with adult and continuing education was issued in 1966, and contained the following statement:

[16] Sir Richard Livingstone, *On Education*, Macmillan, New York, N.Y., 1944, pp. 6, 143-144.

[17] Robert N. Butler, M.D., *The Burnt-Out and the Bored*, as excerpted in *Current*, 114 (January 1970), pp. 63-64.

This volume attempts to paint a broad picture, describing briefly the chief agencies that support adult education programs in any significant way. It is conservatively estimated that this support amounts to more than one billion dollars per year, expended through more than one hundred different agencies and offices of the Federal Government.[18]

Adult educators examining this study were filled alternately with elation and despair. Clearly, the federal agencies had finally accepted continuing education as a prime need and were backing its programs and practices with substantial dollars. Just as clearly, they were proliferating and fragmenting the total adult education expenditure and responsibility for its administration and execution until no cohesive image emerged of the vast involvement with adult learning.

In the study, 22 programs were found under the Office of Education, and 19 others under other branches of the Department of Health, Education, and Welfare. Liveright points out that HEW allocations do not include National Institute of Health Research grants. Nor is the number of programs necessarily a proper yardstick. The Department of Agriculture, for instance, involves 16 million participants through its one program of Cooperative Extension Service, although it ranks fourth behind other departments for annual expenditures, and receives matching funds from both state and county budgets.

Other adult-education programs come under the Departments of Commerce, Defense, Housing and Urban Development, Interior, Justice, Labor, and State, and the Peace Corps and the Office of Economic Opportunity are under the Executive Office of the President. This does not include programs under independent executive agencies or independent agencies of the legislative branch. Even then, the difficulty of choosing a yardstick impinges: both the Atomic Energy Commission and the National Science Foundation, with one program each, spend inordinately higher amounts per participant than do the other agencies. In short, the picture of adult education at the federal level in the U.S. is every bit as chaotic, paradoxical, and incomprehensible as is the general practice of adult education on the local level and in the various agencies and institutions that offer continuing education.

Higher Adult Education

The concept of university extension was imported from England in the 1870s and introduced in American universities. When it jumped the

---

[18] *A Directory of Federal Aid to Adult Education*, Adult Education Association of the U.S.A., Washington, D.C., 1966, p. iii.

ocean, however, extension underwent certain modifications that made this form of education for adults more pragmatic and less classical than that offered by Oxford and Cambridge in the 19th century. About 1906-07, extension in the U.S. was retooled under the leadership of the University of Wisconsin to make it a service agency responsible to the local economy and government. Essentially, its boundaries were defined as coterminous with those of the state. Again, adult education had found a foster home—this time within an institution, the main function of which was to provide learning for youth and degree-credit programs for full-time students.

Higher adult education is carried on in all land-grant universities and in some comprehensive state universities, sectional state institutions, many religious private universities, and many specialized institutions such as theological seminaries and technical institutes. In the 1960s, also, the number of public community colleges (2-year institutions of higher education, also called junior colleges) grew dramatically in number (refer to Chapter 24) and these are open to adults desiring to enroll in either a regular curriculum or "Extended day" classes. Once again, however, the core purpose of the community college is to educate youth, and the adult educational function is secondary.

Both the number and the type of adult-education activities offered by higher educational institutions vary greatly. Correspondence study, radio and television programs, short courses, the cooperative extension program, and dozens of other learning models are provided. Knowles states, "The number of registrations in higher adult education activities in the mid-1960s was estimated variously at from 2,500,000 to 4,354,000, reflecting both the problem of definitions and the inadequacy of data-collection machinery in the field."[19]

One example will suffice. When the U.S. Office of Education began to record university extension offerings many years ago, it categorized them by format. Thus, correspondence study was in one category, courses in another, and lectures were reported separately, along with other types of educational programs for adults. This codification is no longer workable, either to define or to measure activity in continuing education. The proliferation of offerings and the interdisciplinary design of many programs, coupled with the combining of various formats, has rendered these hard-and-fast yardsticks inadequate. Moreover, the vast and burgeoning growth of the field still lacks any mechanism for coordination of the adult-educational activities of all these institutions at any level.

Success in the form of increased demand and income (whether from

---

[19] Malcolm S. Knowles, *Higher Adult Education in the U.S.*, op. cit., p. 13.

fees, grants and contracts, or institutional subsidy) only compounds the confusion. Unlike the parent institutions of higher education, the policies and practices concerning faculty, financing, and organization and administration of adult education vary enormously. Two key organizations serve the professional personnel in this field nationally. They are the National University Extension Association and the Association of University Evening Colleges. The latter combines member organizations that evolved from this nation's urbanization movement in the early twentieth century. University evening colleges, for the most part, are designed to provide degree-credit programs in the evening for men and women who initially dropped out of college for financial or familial reasons.

Certain forces, both within and outside the institutions of higher adult education, are pushing toward an academic revolution in the field of continuing learning for men and women whose years of formal schooling are ended. Some adult educators believe it is unlikely that these institutions of higher learning can change sufficiently to adequately meet the need for socially relevant programs in the short time available. There are many reasons for this belief, but two are salient. Firstly, the colleges and universities have their own list of priorities, of which extension is only one and of peripheral significance. Rarely, if ever, in American history have campuses been so beleaguered by budgetary problems, and never have they been so maligned and misunderstood by the public and certain politicians. Secondly, the sheer force of numbers—the full-to-bursting ranks of adult enrollees—makes the pressure for change extremely critical and immensurable. Although research in the field of adult education is less, relative to other levels of education, one fact has been theoretically known and demonstrated empirically for a long time: The more education an adult has, the more he seeks. Johnstone further states:

> Even very conservative projections suggest that within two decades the population will contain as many as 64 percent more adults who have been to college, 59 percent more who have attended high school, and by contrast, some 15 percent fewer with only a grade school education. . . . It should be abundantly clear, then, that the potential audience for adult education is increasing at a much faster rate than the population as a whole. Just as in the fifties and sixties the regular school system had to tool up rapidly to accommodate the greatly increased numbers of young persons in the population, so too in the seventies and eighties adult education will be subject to greatly increased demands as this group moves into the social categories where greatest uses are made of adult education.[20]

[20] Johnstone and Rivera, op. cit., p. 27.

In short, the irony is inescapable. If adult and continuing education is an "idea whose time has come," it has arrived on the U.S. scene almost tragically late, in incredibly large numbers with unprecedentedly pressing needs to confront and confound a disjunctive array of miscellaneous agencies and institutions whose reason for being and number-one mandates are *not* the continuing education of adults. Rarely, if ever, has history played such a grotesque trick on a national culture at a time when, competitively speaking, the chips are down and world leadership and the democratic process are at stake. Readers grasping the full dimension and complexity of this problem need only ask themselves how rapidly and easily it might be solved in a country where motivating the individual was not essential and recruiting the physical and human resources did not require getting consensus. Increasingly, the trend is for higher adult education to serve agencies and institutions as well as individual enrollees. A corollary to this is the focus on urban problem solving. The latter, in turn, involves the educational institution with controversial issues such as environmental pollution control, interracial strife, drug use and abuse, and the whole gamut of stressful crises that plague our cities.

Public Schools

At present the State of California Board of Education is working diligently with a Statewide Advisory Committee on Adult Education to assess the new role of California's public adult schools in the 1970s.

One of the top priorities in California as well as in the nation is recognized to be the achievement of functional literacy for every adult. One of the major thrusts in the whole adult-education field is the Federal Government's current expenditure on Adult Basic Education classes. Formerly called literacy training and given short shrift at both the national and local levels, this new crusade is a direct result of the anti-poverty program and related causes. America was supremely embarrassed to discover how many festering areas of illiteracy were harbored within her affluent ranks. The self-perpetuating nature of poverty became a widely known fact—no longer one to which only sociologists and welfare workers were privy. The ABE program had begun to gather momentum in 1965, and although by 1967 it spent only $26.28 million on this instruction, $70 million was authorized for fiscal year 1969 and $80 million for fiscal year 1970. Private nonprofit agencies were permitted to participate in the program if included in the state plan. The 90 percent federal and 10 percent state-local funding ratio was continued through fiscal year 1970. Also, a minimum allotment of $100,000 was granted to each state, regardless of population, and in addition to the regular grant formula amount it had received in the past. Although the recruitment and counseling of clientele and the administering of these programs poses certain unique problems, it seems likely that ABE efforts will be undergirded until a drastic reduction of the number of functional illiterates in the U.S. has taken place.

The goal of most public adult-school educators is now an educational attainment level of a high school education for every adult. "Today, a high school education plus a marketable skill have become the minimum job requirement, but two-thirds of the youth who center the ninth grade in the typical metropolitan high school will not meet this minimum requirement."[21]

In general, the stress in public adult schools is on greater identification with the total community—including the disadvantaged minorities and unmotivated dropouts of every age. The curriculum is coming in for close scrutiny and revision. Teaching methodology and credentialing of teachers are the foci of increased professionalization, and considerable attention is being paid to physical facilities. For instance, the segment of the population that resists attending classes in a school can often be reached in storefront locations, community centers, and "backyard" sites. Most important is the accessibility of the classes to the public, and in one Florida county even empty apartments in housing developments are used for classes. Also, the scheduling of adult programs is becoming more flexible. The decade of the 1970s will find increasing interaction between the state university, the state department of education, and such national organizations as the U.S. Office of Education and the National Association for Public Continuing and Adult Education.[22]

In sum, public adult-school leadership is acutely aware that it must remodel its thinking and *doing* to accommodate the two largest, growing segments of the population: persons age 65 and older, and teenagers and young adults, many of whom need a second chance at education. Still another recent development in adult classes nationally is the growing use of teacher aides. The latter are employed mainly in two ways: (1) to do clerical work with some instructional responsibility under the teacher's supervision, and (2) to bridge the social gap between teacher and class. In the second example, aides would be drawn from the same population as the class members and chosen for leadership qualities.

---

[21] Robert E. Finch, *Administration of Continuing Education,* National Association for Public School Adult Education, Washington, D.C. 1969, p. 2.

[22] Ibid., Chapter 6.

Business and Industry

Carl Rogers has said that "of all the institutions of present-day American life, industry is perhaps best prepared to meet the year 2000. I am not speaking of its technical ability. I am speaking of the vision it is acquiring in regard to the importance of persons, of interpersonal relationships, and of open communication." Rogers also states that in view of his partial prejudice he "found it somewhat difficult but necessary" to make this prediction. In the same article, he asserted that "educators are showing greater resistance to change than any other institutional group." Further, he identified as the greatest problem which man faces in the year to come:

> . . . not the hydrogen bomb . . . not the population explosion . . . but the question of how much change the human being can accept, absorb, and assimilate, and the rate at which he can take it . . . can he adopt . . . the continual changingness which must be his if he is to survive?[23]

Certainly, the growth of company schools from 7.2 million in 1965 to a projected 17.5 million in 1974 indicates that business and industry recognize adult education as a necessary investment. The 1960s saw a dramatic rise in the number of corporate educational directors at the vice-presidential level, apart from in-service training directors. There will be more changes in the 1970s regarding business and industry's formats and their media approach to educating personnel. Seminars held in headquarter cities or in residential conference centers are already being replaced by telecasts from educational stations in Iowa, Minnesota and Nebraska. These combine in-plant discussion and video-tape viewing with assigned reading.

> The big advantage lies in the organization of common-interest programs for wide usage and low unit-cost; a cost comparison of $30 per participant versus perhaps $300, plus travel and accommodation and time away from work, for a seminar held in another city.[24]

In many businesses today, training is almost continuous for those who remain within that particular company. Thus, we note the paradoxical situation that the very institution once considered the most conservative part of the American establishment, at least in this respect, is behaving more progressively than the country as a whole and the educational

[23] Carl R. Rogers, "Interpersonal Relationships: USA, 2000," *The Journal of Applied Behavioral Science*, **4** (3), July, August, Sept., 1968, p. 266.

[24] John Ohliger, Ed., *Mass Media/Adult Education*, No. 23 (November-December, 1969), p. 11.

establishment in particular. Indeed, it is estimated that American business and industy now spends more than $17 billion yearly on adult-education activity.

Finally, it is not surprising that business and industry is hyperactive in adult education. This nation early learned that vast enterprises require management training. Rapid assimilation of new knowledge led to our present high state of technology. Now that same technology requires that the work force continue its education throughout each person's lifetime—and the pace continues to accelerate.

Prospects for the Seventies

In the closing days of 1969, some twenty national and international adult-education organizations jointly sponsored, in Washington, D.C., a Galaxy Conference on Adult Education. Among the sponsors were many organizations designed to strengthen and promote the adult-education programs of core institutions in the formal educational structure. The National University Extension Association, the Association of University Evening Colleges, and the National Association for Public Continuing and Adult Education are examples. More broadly representative of non-establishment agencies were the Adult Education Association of the U.S.A. and the Council of National Organizations, the latter being a weak but needed voice for the common interests of voluntary and community organizations, such as the National Conference of Christians and Jews, the National Council of Churches, and the Chamber of Commerce of the U.S.

Submitted to the assembled delegates was a document entitled "Imperatives for Action,"[25] the draft of which was prepared by a group of distinguished citizens meeting under the chairmanship of Dr. Arthur S. Flemming, President of Macalester College. The statement was approved unanimously by the more than three thousand delegates in attendance.

The central tasks of and challenges to adult education, as defined in this document, constitute a benchmark against which can be measured progress in the 1970s. The nine major tasks are as follows:

1. To eliminate educational deficiencies of American adults.

2. To strengthen adult and continuing education and community-service efforts of community colleges, colleges, and universities.

---

[25] Reproduced in its complete form in the National University Extension Association's "The Spectator," **XXXV**, 2 (Dec. 1969-Jan. 1970), pp. 4-8.

3. To provide adult and continuing education in the arts and humanities, public affairs, and in the democratic process.

4. To improve financial support for adult and continuing education.

5. To provide adequate and appropriate opportunities in adult and continuing education for persons in low-income groups.

6. To strengthen within our educational institutions the supporting structures for adult and continuing education.

7. To urge national nongovernmental organizations to strengthen their role.

8. To increase public awareness.

9. To achieve higher levels of federal support and coordination.

It was further proposed that the informal coalition of adult-education organizations that sponsored the Galaxy Conference be formalized and strengthened, and that funds be raised to create a political-action unit with responsibility for influencing legislation at state and federal levels.

It is quite apparent from the nature of the tasks defined that a major effort will be made to reduce the marginality of adult education within the educational establishment. It could be argued that, in view of the projected growth in the numbers of adult participants, some new institutional structures exclusively concerned with the provision of adult-education services will be needed. It is also quite clear that professionally trained adult-education administrators, teachers, and counselors are in much too short supply to staff the expansion of facilities that will be required. Graduate programs in adult education will have to be multiplied rapidly if manpower needs are to be met.

Task 5 would require major changes in the traditional approaches to adult education. The Johnstone and Rivera study makes it quite clear that the agencies of adult education in the United States have been notably unsuccessful in reaching the undereducated and the socially deprived.[26] Nor has the record to date demonstrated that traditional adult-education agencies have the outreach and know-how to develop increased citizen skills in decision making and community problem solving. This weakness is especially apparent in the urban effort to involve the uninvolved in our ghettos and barrios. The war on poverty, the federal programs aimed at improvement of housing for the poor, the struggle to teach adult basic education to the illiterate, the efforts at dissemination of health information and expansion of clinical facilities—

[26] Johnstone and Rivera, op. cit., pp. 95-107.

all these and other programs underscore the ineffectuality of traditional forms of recruitment and instruction.[27]

The U.S. Commissioner of Education, Dr. James E. Allen, Jr., speaking at the Galaxy Conference referred to above, discussed the creation of a National Center for Lifelong Learning, which would undertake research and experimentation in the extension of adult education to segments of the population not now being reached.[28] It is not difficult to expand this idea to include the establishment of similar centers within the states.

To satisfy projected consumer demand, however, new neighborhood learning centers will have to be created, with counseling staffs, programmed learning sequences, and referral services. A major thrust will be needed in the area of education for public responsibility. It is estimated that only 7 percent of those currently enrolled participate in programs of civic education. No real effort has yet been made to provide learning opportunities for the acquisition of citizen skills needed for effective participation in community-action and development programs.

The concept of neighborhood learning centers, sensitive to changing social needs, alert to the educational requirements of a free society, and serving as a resource for the whole community as it searches for the answers to the complex problems of our times, may require institutional reorganization and the redefinition of traditional responsibilities. But the dimensions of the educational task now before us require no less.

---

[27] Hans B. C. Spiegel, Ed., *Citizen Participation in Urban Development,* NTL Institute for Applied Behavioral Science, Washington, D.C., 1968 (2 vols.). See especially Vol. 1, on *Concepts and Issues,* Sec. V, "Implications for Community Decision Making," pp. 209-270.

[28] James E. Allen, Jr., *The Educational Third Dimension,* The NUEA Spectator, **XXXV,** 2 (Dec. 1969-Jan.-1970), pp. 9-12.

References

❖❖

Jensen, Gale, et al., *Adult Education—Outline of an Emerging Field of University Study*, Adult Education Association of the U.S.A., Washington, D.C., 1964, 334 pp. Written by a team of professors of adult education. Gives primary attention to the conceptual foundations of the field.

Johnstone, John W. C. and Ramon J. Rivera, *Volunteers for Learning*, Aldine Publishing Co., Chicago, 1965, 624 pp. The most extensive study available on the educational pursuits of adults in the U.S. Conducted by the National Opinion Research Center.

Knowles, Malcolm S., *The Adult Education Movement in the U.S.*, Holt, Rinehart and Winston, Inc., New York, N.Y., 1962, 335 pp. Review of historical foundations of adult education, the growth of the movement, and the outlook for the future.

Knowles, Malcolm S., *Higher Adult Education in the United States*, American Council on Education, Washington, D.C., 1969, 105 pp. A special report on trends and issues prepared for the Committee on Higher Adult Education of the American Council. Excellent introduction by Paul A. Miller, President of the Rochester Institute of Technology.

Liveright, A. A., *A Study of Adult Education in the United States*, Syracuse University Press, Syracuse, N.Y., a Center for the Study of Liberal Education for Adults Research Report, 1968, 138 pp. Commissioned by the U.S. Office of Education, this report gives the best brief overview of the field of adult education, with problem areas identified and recommendations for action.

Smith, Robert M. et al. Eds., *Handbook of Adult Education*, Macmillan, 1970, 594 pp. The most complete source book available on the field of adult education. Agency programs ranging from the cooperative extension service to religious institutions are described. Chapter I on the "Social Setting of Adult Education" is particularly recommended.

611

Spiegel, Hans B. C., Ed., *Citizen Participation in Urban Development*, 2 Vols., NTL Institute for Applied Behavioral Science, Washington, D. C. Vol. I, 1968, 291 pp. Vol. II, 1969, 348 pp. Vol. I deals with concepts and issues; Vol. II with cases and programs. See especially Vol. II, Chapters VIII and IX on "The Community Development Catalyst" and "Training for Participation."

28

Education in International Perspective: Focus on Change and Modernization

Andreas M. Kazamias

❖❖

A major concern of policy-makers and students of education, as shown in the present volume, has been with innovation, reform, and more broadly, change and modernization. It would seem, therefore, that the concluding chapter might best serve its purpose if it provided an international or comparative perspective on this practical and intellectual interest. Such a focus also allows us to go beyond descriptive accounts of educational systems; and it suggests a framework by which education in one nation or cross-nationally may be examined.

In scope, intensity, and magnitude educational change has perhaps never engulfed the world as much as it did in the decades following the Second World War. Nor has so much faith been placed on schools and other educational institutions to improve society and the condition of man as in recent years. The new states that were carved out of colonial territories have envisaged education as the means to create self-identity, dignity, and national awareness as well as to spur economic and social development—in short, to shake the shackles of colonialism and to build independent nations. Older nations, industrially advanced or not, have

613

sought to transform prewar educational structures and orientations in order to adapt them to the demands of rapid economic political and intellectual changes. At the same time, education was to contribute to development in all its aspects, namely, to economic growth, social equality, and greater political cohesion. In most societies, the postwar and contemporary educational scene have been marked by continuing efforts to modernize the educational system. This chapter will focus on this process of educational modernization in selected societies of Europe (including the Soviet Union) and Africa.

Educational Change in Western Europe

While the war was still going on many European governments were discussing the new society they hoped to create when victory or liberation was attained. Education was believed to be a key factor in the postwar social reconstruction. In England, for example, Sir Winston Churchill proclaimed in 1941 that "When the day is won, it must be one of our aims to work to establish a state of society where the advantages and privileges which hitherto have been enjoyed by the few shall be more widely shared by the men and youth of the nation," and in 1944, a famous Education Act was passed. Soon after the Free French Government was established in 1943, the Algiers Commission was set up to examine radical reforms of the French educational system; and in 1944, the Algiers Commission was merged into a *Commission d'études* with M. Paul Langevin as president and MM. Henri Piéron and Henri Wallon as vice presidents. During the war years also, the "governments in exile" of Denmark, Norway, the Netherlands, Poland, Belgium, Greece and others set up study groups and discussed plans for educational reconstruction while England and the United States were planning the educational policies of Germany, Italy, and Japan after these countries were defeated and occupied.

The ferment for educational reform was heightened in the years of peace that followed. Generally speaking, educational plans sought to broaden opportunities for secondary and higher education, to bridge the gaps between elementary and secondary schools, to strengthen and elevate the status of technical and vocational education, to reorganize the governmental machinery, and to modernize the curriculum. This was particularly true of England and France, which will be taken here as representative cases and examined in greater detail.

Gentlemanly Culture in a Welfare Case

The Education Act of 1944 and the measures covering several other social services, such as health, social security, children's welfare, and family allowances, enacted between 1946 and 1948 provided the basic structure of what has often been referred to as the British welfare state.

In its ideal form, the welfare state implied a new and different conception of society, government, knowledge, education, freedom, and the individual, from what had been characteristic of the English tradition. Set against this tradition, here called "gentlemanly culture," the welfare state, in theory and in practice, provides a useful conceptual framework to interpret and assess educational change for most of the postwar period.

Gentlemanly Culture. In its broad aspects, gentlemanly culture was based on authority, discipline, diligence, compliance, a Platonic epistemological model, and a binary system of thought, institution, and practice. Thus there were sharp distinctions drawn between the gentleman and the outsider or "cad"; between the selected and the rejected; between those who pass and those who fail; between a superior, character-forming liberal education or culture and an inferior, utilitarian and banausic one. Gentlemanly culture was elitist and deferential; it viewed human beings in unequal terms and society in stratified, compartmentalized, or "class" units; it emphasized freedom rather than equality, and it assumed that "a natural hierarchy characterized society and the universe alike."[1] The educated gentleman was a generalist rather than a specialist (except perhaps a specialist in the art of ruling). Among other things, he had breadth of vision, intolerance of falsehood, clarity of thought, and above all else, "character."

The schools for gentlemen were the public schools, but the values associated with gentlemanly culture pervaded other educational establishments, such as the grammar schools and the universities; indeed, they filtered into the government, the civil service, and even business. Education for "nongentlemen," mostly "the people," was provided in terminal elementary schools with a leaving age of 14, and in higher or upper elementary schools, central schools, and later "modern" and technical

---

[1] For excellent commentaries on the "gentleman ideal," see Rupert H. Wilkinson, "The Gentleman Ideal and the Maintenance of a Political Elite," reprinted in A. M. Kazamias and E. H. Epstein, Eds., *Schools in Transition: Essays in Comparative Education*, Allyn and Bacon, Boston, 1968, pp. 94-110. Also see E. J. King, *World Perspectives in Education*, Methuen & Co., London, 1962, pp. 360-368.

schools. The prestige of these schools was lower and so were their rewards. The gentlemanly class had a certain absorptive capacity, and a degree of social mobility through education and other means was present. But the aggregate rates of mobility were low, class demarcations remained clear and distinct, the elitism of the public schools persisted, and so did the aura of the type of education they provided and the type of individual they fashioned.

The Welfare State Conception of Education: The 1944 Act. The welfare state, on the other hand, rejected the laissez-faire, liberal, capitalist doctrines of voluntarism and unfettered freedom; instead it signified a system in which organized power or State action should be deliberately used to regulate the market forces, and to ensure the well-being of all citizens by guaranteeing certain basic social services, including education. It implied a more positive view of freedom, in the sense that government power must be used to create conditions for the enhancement of the liberty of the greatest number, even if this meant the curtailment of the freedom of some. A hallmark of the welfare-state conception of society was the principle of universalism in welfare, considered essential (a) "to reduce and remove barriers of social and economic discrimination," (b) to break down "distinctions and discriminatory tests between first and second-class citizens," and (c) to promote "social integration."[2] Related to the above, the welfare-state ideology emphasized the principle of equality, often clarified by the term "opportunity."[3]

The educational innovations embodied in the 1944 act and in the subsequent institutional arrangements may be viewed as one of the elements of the new society based on the aforementioned principles. Government authority over education was consolidated and extended through the appointment of a Minister of Education, rather than the previous President of the Board of Education. It was the duty of the minister to promote national education and to see that local authorities, "under his direction and control," carried out national policy. Local education authorities, in turn, were made responsible for the spiritual, moral, mental, and physical development of all children, and were compelled to provide adequate education (primary, secondary, and further), according to the children's ages, aptitudes and abilities. Another innovation pertained to parental rights and responsibilities. Prior to 1944, a parent was obligated

[2] See Perry Anderson, Ed., *Toward Socialism*, The Fontana Library, London, 1965, pp. 355-356.

[3] See David C. Marsh, *The Future of the Welfare State*, Penguin Books, Baltimore, 1964, pp. 79-80.

to "cause his child between the ages of 5 and 14 to receive efficient elementary instruction in reading, writing, and arithmetic." This allowed for considerable latitude in "parental choice," for there was no obligation on the parent to know, or care, anything about the child's capacity or inclinations. Although the 1944 act stated that "pupils are to be educated in accordance with the wishes of the parents," it also stipulated that a parent was obligated "to cause him [that is, the child] to receive efficient, full-time education suitable to his age, ability and aptitude, either by regular attendance at school or other wise." Thus parental responsibility became more onerous and complex. In actual fact the State henceforth controlled a child's education, and parental choice was extremely limited.

The welfare-state conception of education implicit in the above (for example, more purposeful use of public power to make education "national"; and schooling for all at least through the secondary level, which further implied that everyone has a right to an education) was also in part evident in the arrangements concerning the so-called religious question. Although the old "church-state" conflict was evident in the 1940s, it was quite clear that the churches could not meet their statutory obligations in supporting the voluntary schools, and the State was determined to "nationalize" the system for purposes of socioeconomic development and political integration. One could also view the new trend as a further push toward "secularization," a characteristic of educational modernization in other countries. Unlike the United States, however, there was no complete separation of church and state, and the associated policies of proscription of religious instruction in public schools and nonpublic support of denominational schools. A delicate religious concordat was reached entailing a rather cumbersome set of arrangements whereby (a) religious instruction, subject to certain restrictions, continued to be taught in the state "controlled" schools, and (b) voluntary schools continued to function and were eligible for public funds but at the same time were subject to degrees of public control and supervision. The general framework of the Concordat of 1944 is in force today.[4]

Tripartitism and Eleven-Plus. In 1947 the Ministry of Education gave its official blessing to the tripartite organization of secondary schools (grammar, technical, and modern) and indirectly to selection by examination at the age of 11-plus. It was argued that since the tastes, aptitudes and

---

[4] For more details on the religious question in England and America, see Kazamias and Epstein, op. cit., pp. 308-326. On the same issue in England, the Netherlands, Sweden and the United States, see A. Stafford Clayton, *Religion and Schooling: A Comparative Study*, Blaisdell Publishing Co., Boston, 1969.

abilities of pupils are different, that is, unequal, equality of opportunity implied that such pupils should be carefully selected and allocated to separate schools with different aims, functions and curriculum emphasis.[5] "Equal educational opportunity", R. A. Butler, the architect of the 1944 act later stated, "is not identical educational opportunity." Referring to the American experience, he argued that nonselectivity and nondiversity would stunt and retard the growth of the "uncommon child."[6]

At that time, the institutional arrangements, the selection procedures, the curriculum, and the socioeducational values underlying them were perceived to be consonant with the new social and cultural ideal inherent in the welfare state. And this was true even of the Labourites, the future champions of such an alternative arrangement as the comprehensive schools. It was clear, however, that the new conception was not devoid of the traditional elements inherent in the gentlemanly culture. The three-fold typology of pupils—bookish intellectual, technical-scientific, and practical—that went with the grammar, the technical, and the modern schools respectively, and the differential status attached to each, was but a pale modification of the traditional gentlemanly view of the innate abilities of particular groups of people. Similarly, one sees an elitist view of society and education with its emphasis on the selection of the best, "the uncommon children" as Butler called them, and the elimination of the worst. (The best would go to the grammar schools and thence to the universities and to high-status positions, while the worst would go to the modern schools, terminate their education at the age of 15, and enter the "business of life.") Added to this was the fact that not much was done to eliminate or minimize the elitism of the public schools. Although they educated about 3 to 5 percent of the relevant age groups, they provided a disproportionately high number of entries into the prestigious universities and positions of influence and leadership in the society. Further, under-lying the content prescribed for each type of school, one sees the per-vasiveness of the intellectualist, literary-scientific, and generalist elements of the traditional gentlemanly view of liberal education. Although science had been accepted as an ingredient of liberal education, technical, voca-tional, or other "practical" subjects still continued to be regarded as inferior and "illiberal"; and it is interesting to point out that Latin, the staple of gentlemanly culture, continued to occupy a preeminent posi-

---

[5] See Ministry of Education, *The New Secondary Education,* His Majesty's Stationery Office, London, 1947, Pamphlet 9, p. 22.

[6] R. A. Butler, "Education: The View of a Conservative," *The Year Book of Education,* Evans Brothers, London, 1952, pp. 35-36.

tion in the curriculum of the grammar schools, and to be required for entrance into the universities. A relatively low value, still the case today, was given to the social sciences. Finally, human beings were still viewed in unequal terms and society in "class" units.

Equality of Opportunity, Social Citizenship, and Comprehensive Education. From our orientation, the most noteworthy characteristics of British educational thinking and policy in the 1950s and 1960s were the movements toward equality of opportunity, comprehensive reorganization, and the social and cultural implications of them. The optimism of the welfare-state legislation of the 1940s evaporated, at least so far as the Labour Socialists were concerned. It was felt that "social citizenship," to use T. H. Marshall's concept, had not developed as anticipated, and the rights entailed by it were not enjoyed by all the people.[7] Education was one of those basic rights. Contrary to expectations, the educational system, as it took shape after the war, contributed to social division, inequality, economic disparities, "competitive antagonism," and human alienation. Further, it did not eliminate the educational disadvantages of certain groups, particularly the working classes. The existing system prevented them from full participation in the society and from sharing fully "in the social heritage." The cultural ideals fostered by the system were still dominated by the upper classes. In 1966, when Anthony Crosland, a leading Socialist spokesman, was Secretary of State for Education and Science, he indicted the system (tripartitism, selection at 11-plus, private schools) as "educationally and socially unjust, inefficient, wasteful and divisive."[8] Similar criticisms were made throughout the 1950s and 1960s by others (Labour politicians, educationalists, and social critics). Such critics adduced research evidence showing the bearings of environmental, cultural, or societal factors on education in general (for example, performance at 11-plus, access to schools and universities, performance, and wastage); some argued that the "meritocratic" principle underlying the system intended to create a different class structure, was no less inhumane and unjust than the previous, and no less politically and socially divisive.[9]

7 On social citizenship, Marshall wrote: "By the social element I mean the whole range from the right to a modicum of economic welfare and security to the right to share to the full in the social heritage and to live the life of a civilized being according to the standards prevailing in the society." See T. H. Marshall, *Class, Citizenship and Social Development,* Doubleday & Co., Garden City, N.Y., 1965, pp. 78-79.

8 *Comprehensive Education,* Speech by Anthony Crosland, Secretary of State for Education and Science, at the North of England Education Conference, January 7, 1966, pp. 1-2.

9 See John Vaizey, *Britain in the Sixties: Education for Tomorrow,* Penguin

As an alternative to the existing arrangements, reformers called for the elimination of the 11-plus and the reorganization of the secondary system along comprehensive lines. "Comprehensivisation" dominated political and educational thinking in the 1960s and continues to be a burning issue today. The Labourites saw it as an integral part of their welfare-state socialist conception of society with its emphasis on fairness or, as Crosland put it, a more equitable "distribution of privileges and rewards"; on the natural right of every individual to "an equal opportunity for wealth, advancement, and renown"; and on an increase in "social contentment."[10] So in 1965, shortly after they were returned to office following a long period of Conservative rule (1951-1964), they issued the famous Circular 10/65 requesting local authorities to prepare and submit plans for comprehensive reorganization and suggesting different ways to do so.[11]

Since the name "comprehensive" has mostly been applied to the American secondary education, it would be helpful to clarify the English use of the term. Before Circular 10/65, there were generally two types of comprehensive schools: the rural and the urban. Rural comprehensives were merely enlarged grammar schools in terms of numbers, range of courses, and educational opportunities.[12] Comprehensive schools in the cities included "all-through" comprehensives (notably those of London and Coventry) and the "two-tier" system (the Leicestershire plan). The former have generally been large, serving all children of the area between the ages of 11 and 18, except the subnormal and the financially privileged, who went to special or independent schools. The Leicestershire system provided for "junior high schools" (ages 11 to 15) for all pupils and "senior high schools" (ages 15-plus). When a child reached the age of 14, parents were given the option of keeping him in the junior school for one more year or transferring him to a senior high school (still retaining the name of grammar school) until at least the age of 16.[13]

In addition to the above, the new policy recommended other two-tier

Books, Baltimore, 1962, and Michael Young, *The Rise of the Meritocracy*, Random House, New York, 1959.

[10] See, for example, C. A. R. Crosland, *The Future of Socialism*, Jonathan Cape, London, 1964, pp. 140-147, and Labour Party, *Fair Deal for Kids: Why Labour Believes in Comprehensive Schools*, Talking Points, No. 5, April 1965.

[11] Department of Education and Science, *The Organization of Secondary Education*, Circular 10/65, July 12, 1965.

[12] See Robin Pedley, *The Comprehensive School*, Penguin Books, Baltimore, Md., 1963, p. 49.

[13] See A. D. C. Peterson, "Secondary Reorganization in England and Wales," *Comparative Education*, I, 3 (June 1965), pp. 164-168.

variations, with transfers from lower to upper levels of schools at the ages of 12, 13, 14, or 16. The emphasis was on variation rather than uniformity, and the particular pattern to be developed was left to the local education authorities. The main intent of the new policy was to eliminate the 11-plus examination and the allocation of the students into different types of schools. Streaming would still take place within the comprehensive school, especially after the first year, and there would be "ability grouping" in certain subjects. But it was felt that the rigidity that existed under the tripartite system would be eliminated (students would be able to move from one stream to another more easily).

Most local education authorities submitted plans for comprehensive reorganization, modified their selection procedures, and started recasting curricula and methods of teaching. Comprehensive schools "were beginning to come into their own as educational institutions," as one source put it, and offered signs of "the growth of a genuine popular philosophy of education."[14] But criticisms, doubts, dilemmas, and ambivalences persisted. Some local education authorities refused to comply with the Ministry's circular. Others drew up hasty plans to satisfy the Ministry's flexible requirements, without really making any substantive changes. Selective grammar schools continued to function side by side with comprehensives, a situation that was not conducive to elevating the latter's status. Wealthy parents could still buy the more privileged education of the public schools. Increased competition for entrance to universities, which still required the passing of rigorous examinations, made demands on comprehensive schools to develop "sixth forms" and to offer an education not dissimilar from that of the grammar schools. Segments of public and educational opinion as well as Conservative politicians were still uncomfortable about the size of comprehensive schools, something that they felt could not but result in miseducation or educational mediocrity. In the first of the two much publicized "black papers," Angus Maude wrote:

> . . . the most serious danger facing Britain is the threat to the *quality* of education at all levels. The motive force behind this threat is the ideology of egalitarianism. . . . In the name of "equality of opportunity," the egalitarian seeks to destroy or transmogrify those schools which make special efforts to bring out the best in talented children . . . in his impatience, the egalitarian takes the alternative course of leveling down the higher standards towards a uniform mediocrity.[15]

[14] David Rubinstein and Brian Simon, *The Evolution of the Comprehensive School, 1926-1966*, Routledge and Kegan Paul, London, 1969, p. 101.

[15] Angus Maude, "The Egalitarian Threat," in C. B. Cox and A. E. Dyson, Eds., *Fight for Education*, The Critical Quarterly Society, London, n.d., p. 7.

In the same publication, which was sent to every member of Parliament, R. R. Pedley, one of the closest students of comprehensive education, echoed a similar idea that "standards of quality" were being threatened by what he called the "comprehensive disaster."[16]

At this time the fate of comprehensive reorganization as a national policy is unclear, especially with the defeat of the Labourites, who were planning to introduce a bill to force comprehensivization. The Conservatives have always been opposed to such uniformity, preferring a variety of arrangements, which included comprehensives but also selective grammar schools and the public schools. But the recent "black papers," as well as numerous other utterances, indicate that while England has gone a long way to modify its system along the principles of the welfare state, there is still a strong carry-over of the ideas, values, and assumptions of what we have called "gentlemanly culture."

Culture Générale and the Democratization of Education in France

There are some striking similarities between French and English education, as discussed above. *La culture française* or *culture générale,* the essence of French educational tradition, may be viewed as analogous to the English "gentlemanly culture." It was elitist and nonutilitarian; it was based on discipline, authority, and a Platonic concept of knowledge; and it emphasized generalism and man's nonmaterial, spiritual existence. More than its English counterpart, *culture générale* signified a rigorous mode of intellectual discipline, and it stressed the grasp of basic "principles," as well as encyclopedic knowledge.

The French analogue to the English public school was the *lycée.* Established by Napoleon, the *lycée* defined secondary education, which in turn was often used synonymously with *culture générale.* Traditionally the *lycées* educated a bourgeois minority or, as Ardagh stated, ". . . they have moulded a cultured elite where technocrats can turn to any problem with the same clarity they were taught to apply to Racine, and where literature and the arts have flowered naturally in a society indoctrinated with belief in their supremacy."[17] Like the English public schools, the *lycées* moulded a colonial officialdom and, along with higher institutions, prided themselves in turning out "aristocracies of mind," so necessary, according to the French, for a well-governed democracy. French democ-

---

[16] R. R. Pedley, "Comprehensive Disaster," Ibid., p. 47.

[17] John Ardagh, *The New French Revolution: A Social and Economic Study of France,* 1945-1968, Harper Colophon Books, New York, 1968, p. 307.

racy, not unlike the English, has stressed the significance of the "guiding role of the elite," thoroughly grounded in *culture générale*.[18]

The movement for reform was intensified after the war. In 1947 the Langevin-Wallon Commission issued its report, which stressed the principles of justice, "equality and diversity," the maximum development of the individual personality, and the "equal dignity of all social tasks." In line with its highly democratic tenor, the report stressed that education "must open the way to culture for everybody, must become more democratic, not by means of a selection which removes the most gifted from the people, but by a continuing process of raising the cultural level of the mass of the nation." It further called for the "reclassification of real values," meaning recognition of the dignity of manual activities, "practical intelligence," and "technical worth." And it sought to broaden the definition of *culture générale*.

> We conceive of general culture as an initiation into the various forms of human activity, not only to determine the aptitudes of the individual and to allow him to choose from his own knowledge before embarking upon an occupation, but also to allow him to remain in contact with other men, to understand the value and appreciate the results of activities other than his own, and to fix his own activity in relation to the whole . . . . General culture represents what draws men together and unites them . . . .[19]

The changes in the educational system recommended by the Langevin-Wallon Commission encountered strong resistance and were not even discussed by the French Parliament. Yet the Commission's report acted as a seminal document for the reforms that followed De Gaulle's return to power in 1958. In the meantime, however, it should be noted that several bills were formulated and some changes, such as the establishment of the *collèges modernes*, the *classes nouvelles*, and their successor, the *lycées pilotes*, were made.

The urgency for reform, which was initiated under the ministry of M. Jean Berthoin in 1959, was dictated by several factors. Among these were "a new cultural consciousness" concerning the role of the individual

---

18 For more information on the meaning of "culture générale," see W. D. Halls, *Educational Innovation in France: A Study of French Secondary Education*, Oxford University, manuscript; Laurence Wylie, "An American Looks at a French School," in A. Carr and W. Steinhoff, Eds., *Points of Departure*, Harper and Bros., New York 1960, p. 184; and J. E. Talbot, *The Politics of Educational Reform in France, 1918-1940*, Princeton University Press, Princeton, N.J., 1969, pp. 12-14.

19 Quoted from Halls, op. cit., pp. 82-83.

in the emerging social order, demography, and what may be called the "democratization of education." There were sharp increases in the over-all population, in the school-age population, and in the number of people moving from rural to urban areas. At the same time there was a greater demand for education. These conditions, together with the "new cultural consciousness," meant not only that the existing system must expand and be attuned to changing needs; it also meant that concerted efforts had to be made to alleviate the anxieties of youth as revealed by the changes in the relationship between the individual and the masses. But the French analogue to the English welfare state and its essential elements of universalism and equality was "democratization."

More Educational Opportunities. One of the educational imperatives of democratization was to put more children into the schools and to open up opportunities for the underprivileged, viz., the children of the agricultural and industrial workers. Between 1953 and 1962 the class chances of children of agricultural and industrial workers, artisans, and small tradesmen for the selected and prestigious *lycées* and the universities improved. But, compared to the chances of the children of those in the liberal professions, they were still limited. Halls estimated that in 1962 "one in five of all children left in the *lycée* comes from a liberal professional background, which nevertheless furnishes only 4 per cent of the total labour force."[20] Comparing England and France, one writer generalized that "there has been far less democratization than in postwar Britain, where at least the grammar schools are now full of workers' children," and that "higher education remains a middle-class or near monopoly too, and only 12 per cent of French university students are from workers' families against 30 per cent in Britain." The same writer also noted that in some *lycées* the teachers maintained a snobbish attitude and were biased against admitting working-class children, but more often the workers excluded themselves for social, cultural, and financial reasons. "A worker," according to him, "may feel . . . that his son will lack the right kind of cultured home background to be at ease in the rarefied lycée atmosphere, and even though tuition is free, there are always extras such as books, meals, and transport, and the loss of a valued bread-winner for the family."[21] It would appear, therefore, that the perceptions and expectations of certain groups of teachers and parents reinforce the system of social stratification.

A Different Model of Man and a Different Concept of Culture. Democratization also meant that the traditional interpretation of *culture*

[20] Ibid., p. 113.
[21] Ardagh, op. cit., p. 309.

générale was too restrictive for the increased school population and the demands made by the economy for new skills. The overemphasis on Latin and on the immersion of the individual in the classical tradition tended to atrophy the development of the scientific and technical aspects of education.[22] This, in turn, necessitated that expressions of intelligence other than verbal reasoning should be included; and in view of the fact that *culture générale* was based on certain assumptions about the nature of man, an alteration in its meaning and scope implied a change in the model of the educated individual.

Toward a "Democratic" School System. As in most European countries, including England, a dual system (*dualisme scolaire*) existed in France: one for the majority of students who received the legal minimum of schooling and another for the very few who went to the secondary schools (*lycées* and *collèges*). Then a five-year common school was created, followed by a diversified secondary school system. But those who did not gain admission into the *lycées* or *collèges* terminated their education at fourteen—this constituted the majority of students—or continued into the upper cycle (*cours complementaires*), which administratively was classified as elementary education. As it should be clear by now, this pattern was in line with the elitist conception of education discussed above.

One of the most significant aspects of the Berthoin reforms of 1959 was the establishment of a two-year observation and guidance stage (*cycle d'observation*) that would continue the general training of the five-year elementary schools. The aptitudes, abilities, tastes, and interests of the pupils would be studied for purposes of allocation into different educational paths (practical, technical, and academic). Other features of the Berthoin Law included the differentiation of the postobservation stage of education into a three-year final stage (*cycle terminal*) providing a general education with a practical bias; a five-year stage comprising various academic streams—classical, modern, and technical; and a vocational stage comprising various streams and lasting for three, four, five, or six years.[23]

The pressure to democratize the system continued. In 1963 the observation stage was lengthened to four years; the school-leaving age was to be raised to sixteen by 1967 (more recently it was announced that this could not be done until 1972); and the hitherto separate administrative branches—for primary, secondary, and technical education—were to be

[22] W.R. Fraser, "Reform in France," *Comparative Education Review*, 11, 3 (October 1967), 302.

[23] For the full text of the Act, see Cultural Services of the French Embassy, *Education in France*, No. 5 (February 1959), pp. 16-32.

merged within the central Ministry of Education. The evolving plans for the reorganization of the French school system envisage a four-year "middle" stage (ages eleven to fifteen) with relatively little differentiation and a common curriculum (a sort of middle comprehensive school similar to the American junior high school) and a diversified upper secondary stage (ages 15-plus) providing a number of options (such as preparation for the university, specialized technical education, or apprenticeship).[24]

The Modernization of the Curriculum. The French concept of culture referred to above went with an authoritarian, deductive, rhetorical and formal sort of pedagogy, and a rigid, uniform curriculum that emphasized more the classical-literary tradition and a Platonic-Cartesian form of rationality and intellectualism. The Langevin-Wallon Commission of 1947 criticized the schools in general as being "an enclosed environment, impermeable to the experiences of the world." Children have a right to "complete development," the commission stressed; and education must "be carried out with respect for the personality of children in order to discern and develop in each one his original aptitudes."[25] Features of "progressive pedagogy" could be observed in such new ventures as the *école nouvelle* or the *classes nouvelles*—new classes—the precursors, one might say of the *cycle d'observation*. These experiments, however, should not be construed as reflecting a widespread and complete acceptance on the part of the French of what in America and elsewhere has been associated with "modern pedagogy." A noted French scholar[26] and an American anthropologist[27] both commented on the heavy demands made on the pupils to follow a rather stringent code of social conduct and a rather uniform curriculum. The degree of freedom in the classroom is still limited; there is less opportunity for self-discipline and free debate, and more emphasis on intellectual development than on the total personality development of the child.[28]

---

[24] For more details, see W. D. Halls, *Society, Schools and Progress in France,* Pergamon Press, Oxford, 1965.

[25] Ibid., pp. 182-185.

[26] Jean Boorsch, "Primary Education," in K. Douglas, Ed., *Yale French Studies,* No. 22 (1959), pp. 17-46.

[27] Laurence Wylie, *Village in the Vaucluse,* Harvard University Press, Cambridge, Mass., 1957, Chapter 4.

[28] This does not mean that there is in France a military type of school atmosphere with martinet-type teachers and cowishly obedient students, or that the stress is on learning for the sake of learning. There are stringent expectations, on the one hand, but benevolence, affection, friendliness, and fairness on the other. Moreover, the methods of instruction, with their emphasis on basic principles, help the students "solve the problems which they will be confronted with after they leave school." Ibid., pp. 73-94; also see Boorsch, op. cit., p. 27.

Rigidity, uniformity, formality and a heavy academic burden have been especially strong characteristics of secondary and higher education.[29] The academic burden in the *lycées* has been made heavier, intolerably so according to some, by the *baccalauréat,* a rigorous and brain-searching examination that has signified successful completion of secondary education and acquisition of *culture générale* as well as the right to qualify for admission to the university. Authoritarianism, formalism, elitism, centralization, academic isolation, professorial aloofness, nonutilitarianism, and overclassicism have created a major crisis in the universities and largely accounted for student unrest and the events of May 1968.[30]

Attempts to change the old system culminated in the reforms under the Ministry of Christian Fouchet in 1965-66. One of the areas affected was the *baccalauréat,* the syllabus and options of which were rearranged and modernized. Subjects such as sociology, economics, and statistics would be included in the "modern" option; there would be more literature, less philosophy, and more modern subjects in the philological option; less philosophy and arts would be included in the science and math options; and it would not be possible any longer for any option to grant entry to any faculty of the university. Ardagh summarized the aims and reactions of these changes as follows:

> The aim of the reform is not solely to lessen the range of encyclopedic study and bring the *bac* closer to modern life: it is also frankly utilitarian, to force scientists to get down to their own subjects earlier, and to oblige students to be less dilettante about their choice of university work. It is a step towards the English model and away from the tradition of "culture générale". . . .[31]

Attempts have also been made to modernize the general atmosphere of schools: to break down the rigidity, the distance between teachers and pupils, to introduce more cultural and other activities, such as music and visual arts, and to provide more opportunities to practice some sort of democratic or parliamentary government.

The reforms mentioned above were partly aimed at making French education more "humane," but they were also dictated by the utilitarian demands of the postwar economy. This was also reflected in the development of the colleges of technical education (*colleges d'eseignement tech-*

---

[29] See, for example, Jean Cocteau's portrayal of education in the *lycée,* in K. Douglas, op. cit., p. 47.

[30] For a vivid description of these events, see Stephen Spender, *The Year of the Young Rebels,* Vintage Books, New York, pp. 39-58. Also see Raymond Aron, *The Elusive Revolution: Anatomy of a Student Revolt,* Praeger Publishers, New York, 1969.

[31] Ardagh, op. cit., p. 314.

nique) and the technical *lycée* (*lycée technique*), in the institution of the technical *baccalauréat,* and in the emphasis on planning. More than ever before, studies are made and plans are formulated to adapt the various types and methods of education (both general and technical) to the industrial and commercial needs of an expanding economy.

Educational Change in the Soviet Union

Following the Bolshevik Revolution of 1917, the Soviet government embarked on the gigantic undertaking "to organize free, compulsory general polytechnical education for both sexes up to 17 years of age" along Marxist-Leninist principles.[32] The Bolsheviks repudiated the major features of traditional Tsarist education, which in many respects were similar to those of Western European countries. They sought to destroy its selective and class orientation; schools were to be completely secularized; classical languages were declared nonobligatory; the mastery of academic subjects was relegated to a subordinate position; and teaching was to be closely connected with socially useful labor and to prepare members of a communist society. For a time also (1919-1929), the Soviets introduced a permissive and *laissez faire* type of pedagogy; children openly defied teachers, who were relegated to the back of the classroom to be consulted by the pupils when they needed help.

A. V. Lunacharsky, the first Soviet Commissar of Education, expressed the paradoxical Soviet policy as one aimed at creating a classless educational system dominated by the proletarian class, and constructing a new type of school oriented toward productivity. Under the slogan of "socially useful labor," a Unified Workers' School, or Unified Labor School, was established. In addition, special institutions like the *Rabfacs* were set up to recruit people from the working classes for high positions in the society; and such organizations as the *Young Pioneers* and the *Komsomol* were instituted to capture the youth and socialize them according to the Communist ideology.

The Ideology of Communal Culture

There were several intellectual strands that went into the making of the Soviet Communist conception of education. In the 1920s important Soviet educators such as Krupskaya, Lenin's wife, were attracted by John

---

[32] See Deana Levin, *Soviet Education Today,* John deGraff, New York, 1959, p. 3.

Dewey's ideas, particularly his activity school, which prompted her to say that "new Russia needs American-type schools where the children work while they learn."[33] But as is generally known, a major intellectual afflatus was Marx, whose theory of society, knowledge, and the individual was used by Lenin, Krupskaya, Stalin, and other Soviet leaders and pedagogues to justify the new policy.

The social ideas of Marx and Lenin and some of their educational components are examined elsewhere in this volume.[34] It would help, however, to restate Marx's collectivist view of society in contrast to the individualistic, capitalist, liberal view that Marx criticized as being exploitative, materialistic, atomistic, and destructive of the "essence" of man. Man, according to Marx, is not only an individual; he is a social being as well. Hence his education cannot be understood apart from his social existence. Marx's ideal society, the classless communist utopia, would overcome the "contradiction between the interest of the separate individual or the individual family and the communal interest of all individuals who have intercourse with one another."[35] In addition, one should bear in mind Lenin's revisions of Marxism, and the differences between Soviet socialism, and other types, as in the already discussed English welfare-state socialism.[36]

In addition to Marx, Lenin, and Krupskaya, the emerging Soviet conception of education was forged by Anton Semyonovitch Makarenko in the Gorky and Dzerzhinsky communes for homeless children, orphans, delinquents, and criminals. Makarenko has been described as "the creator of perhaps the most impressive demonstration of the Marxist view of human nature."[37] The main concepts of Makarenko's collectivist philosophy have been aptly summarized as follows:

1. Education *in and for the collective* . . . and organization of mutual responsibility, self-governing and self-determining, within which the individual first learns the meaning of moral principles and in their observance finds the security he needs to mature.

[33] Quoted by Lajos Biro, *Paradoxical Influences on Soviet Education: Krupskaya and Makarenko Compared*, manuscript, p. 5.

[34] See Chapter 6.

[35] Quoted by Paul Nyberg, "The Communal Man: Marx," in P. Nash, A. M. Kazamias, and H. J. Perkinson, Eds., *The Educated Man: Studies in the History of Educational Thought*, John Wiley & Sons, Inc., New York, 1965, p. 283.

[36] See G. F. Kneller's discussion in Chapter 6.

[37] See Frederick Lilge, *Anton Semyonovitch Makarenko: An Analysis of his Ideas in the Context of Soviet Society*, University of California Press, Berkeley and Los Angeles, Calif., 1958.

2. Education in the collective is *planned moral growth* . . . a good teacher expresses his respect for the personality of the student by convincing him that difficult things are expected of him.

3. The successful guidance of moral growth requires teachers who have learned how to use education as a *practical science* . . . what he really hoped to establish were techniques of personality-engineering.

4. *Sense of the mean* . . . children should neither be recipients of blind affection nor the objects of harsh oppression, but should learn to feel the firmness of reasonable authority. Discipline is preferable to mere obedience because it is capable of becoming self-discipline conscious of its own ability and meaning.[38]

Thus Makarenko reconciled the conflicting claims of society and the individual by equating "the discipline of the collective with the freedom of the individual," which clearly differentiated his views from those of Western societies. In Makarenko's words the solution to the problem of the individual versus the society was "to incorporate the individual into the collective in such a way that he believes himself to belong to it freely and without compulsion."[39]

Universalism and Polytechnism in Education

The Unified Labor School, already mentioned, was an attempt to eliminate social class divisions and to give labor a dignified place in the society. It was based on Marx and Lenin, both of whom advocated the combination of "productive labor" with book knowledge and instruction, and on the contemporary progressive ideas and practices, such as Dewey's activity school, with its emphasis on what Krupskaya called the "close articulation of the entire school program with practical life."[40]

The experiment in "universalism" and "polytechnism" inherent in the Unified Labor School did not measure up to the expectations of Soviet theoreticians and politicians. With the initiation of the first five-year plan in 1928, industrialization became the key element in the building of Soviet socialism and this required engineers, technicians, scientists, and efficient administrators. In 1931 the Communist Party declared the Unified Labor School to be inadequate, and it was soon replaced by the ten-year school in which knowledge of academic subjects, particularly the sciences, was

[38] Ibid., pp. 2-3.

[39] Ibid., p. 20.

[40] On Lenin's views, see G. S. Counts, *The Challenge of Soviet Education*, McGraw-Hill Book Company, Inc., New York, 1957, p. 63. On Krupskaya, see A. Pinkevitch, *The New Education in the Soviet Republic*, John Day Co., New York, p. 276.

reasserted. At the same time, the permissive type of progressive pedagogy was discarded and firm discipline and the authority of the teacher were reestablished.

In the postwar period, particularly the 1950s, a movement for change was initiated by Stalin, mainly for the purpose of meeting the great need for specialized jobs created by the ever-accelerated pace of technological and industrial development. With this the concept of "polytechnism" revived, but its aims were redefined as the mastery of scientific principles of modern production, the teaching of certain skills and working habits, and the preparation for choosing a profession. A new program of polytechnic instruction was introduced in 1955, but the situation remained unsatisfactory. In 1956 Khrushchev criticized the system as being too far removed from the orthodox Marxist-Leninist principles. Education, according to him, was becoming too intellectual, bookish, abstract and the like, and both students and parents shunned work with their hands. In an effort, therefore, to relate "instruction to life and work," new reforms were made in 1958. The reforms provided, *inter alia,* for a compulsory eight-year school (in Soviet terms, "the first stage of secondary education" or "incomplete general education"), and for "complete secondary education" (generally a three-year course in addition to the eight-year "incomplete" stage). This complete secondary education could be given in "schools for working or rural youth," in "general labor polytechnical schools," or in *technicums,*[41] which would combine production training with academic work. (Students would spend two days of the week working at a plant.) In addition, secondary-school graduates were to have a two-year work experience before being admitted to institutions of higher education.

In 1961 the Communist Party decreed that by 1971 "compulsory secondary general and polytechnical 11-year education" would be provided. Secondary education, according to the new directive, must provide "a solid knowledge of the fundamentals of the basic sciences, an understanding of the principles of the Communist world outlook, and a labor and polytechnical training in accordance with the rising level of science and engineering."[42]

The study-cum-work arrangements of the 1958 reforms did not bring

[41] For more details on the changes during this period, see G. S. Counts, *Khrushchev and the Central Committee Speak on Education,* University of Pittsburgh Press, Pa., 1959, pp. 41-44.

[42] Jaan Penner, "Five Years After Khrushchev's School Reform," *Comparative Education Review,* 8 (1) (June 1964), 73.

about the anticipated results. Moreover, the pressures of international competition called for greater emphasis on "skilled hands" rather than "dirty hands." Hence in the 1960s several modifications were made: the amount of manual work forced on general-education students was cut; the percentage of young people holding jobs or serving in the army, who were given priority to enter universities, dropped from 80 to 30 percent; 20 percent of those admitted to higher institutions would come directly after finishing a secondary school, thus modifying the compulsory two-year working requirement for secondary-school graduates; and plans were laid for the increase of highly selective secondary schools that would concentrate on single subjects, such as physics, that would be useful to the nation.[43]

The developments in the 1960s highlight the problems as well as the conflicts and dilemmas of "universalism" and "polytechnism," two basic principles underlying Soviet educational change and modernization. In some respects the Soviet experience is but a variation of the same phenomenon observed in other societies, despite differences in political ideologies. In a rather short period illiteracy has been wiped out (it has been estimated that in the immediate prerevolutionary period 76 percent of the entire population was illiterate); over 90 percent of the 6-13 age group are attending school; and there are more people enrolled in institutions of higher learning than in any other country except the United States. Yet the Soviet Union has not attained the classless society of Karl Marx, nor indeed has it established a universal educational system free from any "class" encumbrances. The available research, although limited, points to a high correlation between occupational and educational background of parents and opportunities for education. In addition, while the school representation of the rural population has increased considerably, it is still lower than the urban population, especially in the secondary schools. Moreover, it would appear that the demands of accelerated industrialization and technological development have created in the Soviet Union a dilemma similar to that in other countries, namely, the extent to which the schools should emphasize economic and social efficiency more than equality and social justice.

How to "learn the love of manual labor" has eluded the Soviets as much as it has most other nations of the world—and this despite the element of compulsion. Moreover, the various changes in polytechnism

---

[43] Ibid., p. 74. Also see "Russia's New Elite," *Wall Street Journal*, October 14, 1969, and Abraham Kreusler, "U.S.S.R.," in C. E. Carlton, Ed., *Perspectives on World Education*, Wm. C. Brown, Dubuque, Iowa, 1970, pp. 118-120, 125-126.

have not raised the worker above the level of the other social classes, as Marx and Lenin theorized.

Decolonization and Education in Africa

Among the most significant events of the postwar era has been the dissolution of European-centered empires and the emergence of new states, often the result of violent struggles for independence. This process of "decolonization," still going on, has itself been marked by ambivalences, contradictions, social and economic problems, and, in some instances, by political unrest and violence. It has also been the subject of impassioned controversy, as was demonstrated quite clearly in the area of education and social modernization in general. The new African states that were created from British colonial territories furnish challenging case studies for the analysis of the complex processes of decolonization and nation building. Here we shall first make some general statements about education as it relates to these processes, and then examine in greater detail educational change in Tanzania, one of the most interesting and publicized postcolonial African nations.

Colonial Education and Independence

The British colonial educational policy did not mature until the 1920s, when the Advisory Committee for Education in Africa was established and the famous Phelps-Stokes Commission issued its reports. However, colonial education and the reactions to it cannot be understood apart from the educational activities of the missionaries. Christian mission societies preceded the British imperial governments, and when the latter assumed more responsibility in education, mission schools continued to provide much of what is often subsumed under "colonial education."

The educational activities of the missionaries varied according to the nature of the mission and the local conditions. Typically the missionaries set up stations, with schools, for the avowed purpose of spreading the word of God, saving the souls of the "heathen" by converting them to the true religion, and spreading Western Christian culture and civilization. Schools were necessary to accomplish these goals and hence missions, Christianity, and education became inextricably intertwined. In many parts missionaries also developed trade activities.

Missionary education was essentially similar to the education provided by the churches at home for the lower social orders. It consisted of the basic rudiments of knowledge and included heavy doses of religious instruction.

When, in the latter decades of the 19th century and the opening decades of the 20th, British imperialism was firmly established in Africa, the colonial governments supported, among other things, the educational role of the missions. This relieved them of a great deal of financial and administrative responsibility and, in any case, the cultural and "civilizing" goals of the missions coincided with those of the colonial governments. Thus it was not surprising that British colonial educational policy in the 1920s and after was in large part congruent with the ideas and principles of the famous reports of the Phelps-Stokes Commission (1922 and 1925).[44]

Drawing from the American experience in Negro education and the contemporary educational climate, the Phelps-Stokes reports recommended, *inter alia,* that the education of the African should be adapted to the agricultural, vocational, and other utilitarian aspects of the African environment. Furthermore, African education should be different from that of "civilized" Western societies, but similar to that of the American Negro; it should be such that it does not create political "poison centers;" and it should stress character development and the religious life of the pupils (according, of course, to the moral and religious principles of the colonial powers, the U.S., and generally the West).[45] These principles, particularly what has come to be known the principle of "adaptation," were reiterated in successive policy statements by the British colonial government. In addition, they have been the subject of debate not only among scholars but also among African political leaders.

According to the critics, colonial education, provided by missionaries, traders, or administrators, sought to impose the values of the colonizers and destroy those of the colonized. The motive was to exploit the African and use him for the colonizer's benefit. This cultural imperialism in time undermined the indigenous culture, created a feeling of inferiority among Africans, and destroyed their sense of dignity and self-respect. In the course of time the transferred foreign schools created a local elite in the image of the colonizers but different from the indigenous elites, thus

---

[44] These reports, entitled *Education in Africa* (1922) and *Education in East Africa* (1925), were the result of a commission appointed by the American Phelps-Stokes Fund at the request of English and other missionary groups and apparently with the encouragement of the colonial authorities.

[45] See David G. Scanlon, Ed., *Traditions of African Education*, Bureau of Publications, Teachers College, Columbia University, New York, 1964, pp. 51-89.

altering the traditional social structure. Under these circumstances, educational adaptation, meaning vocationalism, agricultural training, and the like, was construed as inferior education, one that would adapt the African to traditional roles and hence perpetuate his inferior colonial status. European-oriented schools led to high-status jobs in the society, particularly white-collar jobs in the civil service. African educational expectations, and hence "needs," shifted in favor of an education that led to such occupations, not the dreary existence of working on the farms or in some low-level trade.

With independence, the new states sought to build up simultaneously viable polities, from diverse and disparate local units lacking "national" cohesiveness, and viable economies. The catchall became one of decolonization—all the evils of the society, such as illiteracy, disease, poverty, hunger, malnutrition, and economic underdevelopment, were blamed on the British colonists—and general modernization based in part on the technology of the West but also on traditional local values. In education, development plans were designed to train the manpower needed to fill the gaps created by decolonization, to put more children into the schools and increase literacy, to Africanize the curriculum, and to establish a sense of identity among the people. To accomplish the goals of nation-building and modernization, the governments of the new states assumed considerable control. Strong centralized governments, in the hands of either the military or individuals; one-party political systems; and guided socialist planning have been commonplace. But the avowed policy of creating something different from that bequeathed by the colonialists has been difficult to accomplish. In most excolonial new nations, the educational systems have preserved many characteristics of the colonial structures (the organization of schools, the system of examinations, the training of teachers, the universities, and the curriculum). In the immediate post-independence years, in fact, deviations from the colonial past were regarded with suspicion. As regards Africanization, educational developments were marked by ambivalences. As Foster points out in the case of Ghana and the Ivory Coast, "At one level, political leadership has stressed the necessity for an educational system which would reflect 'African nature and substance,' while at the same time there has been some reluctance to allow either the structure or content of the educational program to deviate markedly from that prevailing in England."[46]

[46] Philip Foster, *Education and Social Change in Ghana,* The University of Chicago Press, Chicago, 1965, p. 186.

Tanzania and Education for Self-Reliance

In recent years Tanzania, under the leadership of Julius Nyerere, has sought to break away from the heritage of colonialism, and to build a socialist state that would modernize the country along different lines from those encountered in Western or Western-influenced societies. As in other new nations, Nyerere assigned a major task to education, the goals and means of which he himself stated in a provocative document that has already attracted world attention, called "Education for Self-Reliance."

Compared to other areas in Central and West Africa, Tanzania's contact with the West, especially Britain, has been relatively brief. In 1884 it was brought under German influence; and in 1920, the United Kingdom, under a mandate from the League of Nations, assumed the administration of the territory, then known as Tanganyika. In 1946, Tanganyika became a United Nations Trust Territory under British administration and remained so until the fall of 1960, when it emerged as a self-governing territory. Finally, in December 1961, it attained complete independence, and in 1964 it merged with Zanzibar to form the United Republic of Tanganyika and Zanzibar.

Like most other African countries, Tanzania is predominantly agricultural (agriculture together with forestry, livestock, and fishing accounts for about 60 percent of the gross national product), with the large majority of the population engaged in subsistence activities. Racially, its population, estimated at over 10 million (1965), consists of three major groups: Africans, comprising about 98.5 percent of the population; Asians —Indians, Pakistanis and Arabs; and a few thousand Europeans of several nationalities. The African population itself is culturally diverse; there are about 120 different tribes varying in size, social structure, language, and religion. Compared to many other African countries, however, Tanzania is fortunate in that Swahili, a local language, is spoken by most people; hence, the problem of establishing a national medium of linguistic communication is not acute.

The educational system of Tanzania is organized as follows: a seven-year primary stage (Standards I-VII), a four-year secondary stage (Forms I-IV), and a two-year upper secondary stage. The function of primary education has been to provide basic skills of literacy and citizenship, and to prepare for the secondary schools. The secondary schools have been selective institutions; admission to them depends on competitive examinations. They prepare for further education in the upper secondary "forms" (V and VI) and for paid employment. The upper secondary forms provide highly specialized courses in the natural sciences or the humanities leading to the advanced level (A level) Cambridge Overseas School Certificate examinations.

In the past there was limited provision for vocational and technical education; there were two secondary technical schools that prepared students for various trades and for the Technical College in Dar es Salaam.

As in other African countries, the postindependence period in Tanzania has been characterized by concerted efforts to plan the educational system in accordance with the goals of national development, particularly those of economic development. The inherited system, it was argued, left much to be desired. Educational diffusion and opportunities were limited; technical, vocational, and practical education were neglected; wastage was high; the quality of teacher training was poor; and generally education served the interests of the colonial power rather than the local population. The British avowedly espoused a policy of a fairly uniform spread of education. But what actually developed was an imbalanced system: there were few educated and skilled Africans, and these were sharply divided in terms of income, status, and aspirations from their more numerous uneducated tribal brothers; there were more opportunities in areas where cash crops and wage employment were prevalent; and the British relied heavily on expatriates for high-level manpower.

Various studies were carried out after independence, and the Five-Year Plan (1964-1969) followed a method and general orientation that has been typical of educational planning in the 1960s. Estimates of manpower requirements were made in the various occupational categories over a period of time and, on the basis of such estimates, the educational needs of the country were assessed. This approach assumes, of course, that the educational system is a major supplier of the estimated skills and that there is a correspondence between occupational categories and types of education, a point that has been subjected to criticism. Be that as it may, educational plans have come up with recommendations for major adjustments in the Tanzanian educational system, such as (a) increases in enrollments, particularly at the secondary level (general and technical) commensurate with projections of needed skills in such areas as industry, commerce, agriculture, and the civil service; (b) the introduction of some "practical" or technical elements into the secondary school curricula; (c) some provision of vocational counseling and assistance to secondary school pupils; (d) a revision of the curriculum of the trade schools and the introduction of evening courses, sandwich courses, and the like to meet lower-level manpower requirements; and (e) better adaptation of courses to the economic needs of the country and the aptitudes of the pupils.[47]

In introducing the Five-Year Plan in 1964, President Nyerere underscored the economic aspect of educational planning and policy when he said:

> . . . one of the major long-term objectives of our planning is to be self-sufficient in trained manpower by 1980 . . . the purpose of Government expenditure on education in the coming years must be to equip Tanganyikans with the skills and the knowledge which is needed if the Development of this country is to be achieved. It is this fact which has determined educational policy.[48]

Three years later (1967), Nyerere's conception of educational modernization for Tanzania was substantially broadened. In his much-publicized "Education for Self-Reliance," he went beyond the definition of education as production of manpower and training of skills for the modern sector of the economy to stress the importance of formal instruction in the formation of citizens in a socialist and democratic state. The principles of the new society were "equality and respect for human dignity; sharing of the resources which are produced by our efforts" and "work by everyone and exploitation by none."[49]

Progress towards these goals, according to Nyerere, rests on accepting the reality that Tanzania is a "poor, underdeveloped, and agricultural economy" and hence giving top priority to agricultural development rather than to urbanization and industrialization. Agricultural development would entail "improvement in village life," which could be accomplished if people worked "hard, intelligently, and together; in other words, . . . in co-operation." In this task education must play a central part, and it must stress values different from those of the colonial system. Colonial education emphasized and encouraged "intense individualism," inequality, and "intellectual arrogance"; it was elitist, bookish, and racist;

---

[47] See, for example, George Skorov, *Integration of Educational and Economic Planning in Tanzania*, Unesco, International Institute for Educational Planning, Paris, 1966. Also see The United Republic of Tanganyika and Zanzibar, *Tanganyika Five-Year Plan for Economic and Social Development*, Vol. I., *General Analysis*, Government Printer, Dar es Salaam, 1964, and The International Bank for Reconstruction and Development, *The Economic Development of Tanganyika*, The Johns Hopkins Press, Baltimore, Md., 1961.

[48] The United Republic of Tanganyika and Zanzibar, op. cit., p. xi.

[49] Julius K. Nyerere, "Education for Self-Reliance," reprinted in Idrian N. Resnick, Ed., *Tanzania: Revolution by Education*, Longmans of Tanzania Ltd., Arusha, 1968, p. 53.

it was unadapted to the Tanzanian society; and "it led to the possession of individual material wealth being the major criterion of social merit and worth." The new education should foster such social goals as "living together," "working together for the common good," and "co-operative endeavour," and it must "inculcate a sense of commitment to the whole community." Furthermore, it should produce "good farmers," and individuals who will learn "both a practical respect for the knowledge of the old 'uneducated' farmer, and an understanding of new methods and the reason for them."[50]

In order to correct the "colonial faults" and to accomplish the new goals, Nyerere recommended that (a) primary schools provide a "complete education in itself" that would prepare "for the life which the majority of the children will lead," rather than simply prepare for secondary schools; (b) secondary schools not solely select children for higher institutions, but "prepare people for life and service in the villages and rural areas of the country"; (c) examinations "be down-graded in government and public esteem," and (d) the curriculum of the schools be adapted to the type of life that the child will live in a "socialist and predominantly rural society." But by far the most important recommendation was that "schools must—become communities—and communities which practice the precept of self-reliance."

All schools, according to the concept of "self-reliance," must be "economic communities as well as social and educational communities." They should maintain farms and workshops that will produce food and contribute to the total national income. "Every school," Nyerere argued, "should also be a farm," and the school community "should consist of people who are both teachers and farmers, and pupils and farmers." Education, in short, should be integrated with national life and the schools with their environment.

"Education for Self-Reliance" has provided a rationale for an educational policy that would be based not merely on economic considerations but on social and political ones as well. It is an attempt to create, among other things, what students of politics call a new "political culture," a task defined by Apter and Coleman as the creation of a "sense of common citizenship in which there are shared political values, a measure of common purpose and a respect for institutions and established authority."[51]

---

[50] Ibid., 51-59.
[51] David E. Apter and James S. Coleman, "Pan-Africanism or Nationalism in Africa," in American Society of African Culture, *Pan-Africanism Reconsidered,* University of California Press, Berkeley, 1962, p. 96.

In Tanzania the new political culture is what may be called "guided socialism," which, according to Nyerere, represents a natural evolution of an autochthonous system of social obligations clustered under the kinship concept of *ujamaa*. The schools are called on to develop socialist national values and attitudes and thus create the new political culture. In addition, they are expected to contribute to economic development. Whether indeed the schools can accomplish these tasks remains to be seen.

Nyerere's view of making education more practical or more "adapted" to African needs is not very different from the British policy, which failed. Further, Nyerere, like the British, assumes that by manipulating the schools and the curriculum, the vocational aspirations of students will change, meaning that students will shift their interests away from white-collar jobs—one of the evils of colonial education—and will be more positively inclined towards manual or technical occupations. But evidence from other societies suggests that the curriculum may not play as critical a part in occupational attitudes as educational planners and policy makers often assume.[52] It would appear that it may be wishful thinking or mere political propaganda to suppose that educational change by itself can bring about social improvement or that it can be a panacea for all social evils. Despite these strictures, however, Nyerere's views as expressed in "Education for Self-Reliance," which are congruent with his socialist political ideology, represent an alternative and in certain respects a challenging path to educational modernization in Africa and, one might say, in other developing societies.

Conclusion

An important characteristic of the postwar educational systems in the societies examined above, and in most other countries, has been changes in "educational structures." Among the propelling forces behind this phenomenon have been the ever increasing expansion and growth at all educational levels and branches, and the socioeconomic and political objectives of equality of opportunity, democratization, nation building, development of human resources, and regional or rural modernization.

---

[52] See, for example, Foster, op. cit., pp. 135-136, and by the same author, "The Vocational School Fallacy in Development Planning," in John W. Hanson and Cole S. Brembeck, Eds., *Education and the Development of Nations*, Holt, Rinehart and Winston, New York, 1966, pp. 168-174.

Examples of structural changes have been (a) the merging of primary education, until recently separate and terminal in character, with lower secondary education, until recently selective; (b) the growth of the "comprehensive school," the "middle school," the "community school," the "farm school," or the "polytechnical school"; (c) postponement of selection; (d) the coordination of general and technical branches of schooling and training; and (e) a greater flexibility, allowing for more mobility within the system. Such developments reflect a greater concern for the socioeconomic and political functions of education; the educational system is ever becoming an instrument of national policy, manipulated to subserve societal needs. Often it is difficult to disentangle the *educational* from the political or economic aspects of school systems. More significantly, perhaps, in the interests of social or economic efficiency and national development, the education of the individual *qua* individual is being neglected.

Equalization and democratization have implied greater concern for the individual, particularly of the underprivileged or lower classes. Despite considerable advances in eliminating social elitism and injustices, socioeconomic and other factors continue to influence access into secondary schools and higher institutions. Moreover, the structural changes made to equalize opportunities or democratize education have usually denoted the lessening of the influence of noneducational factors such as income, place of residence, race, religion, and the like. A problem that now looms larger than ever is the *pedagogical* or intraeducational adjustments that must be made to make equalization and democratization a reality. Structural changes by themselves, without concomitant pedagogical changes, can be but mere labels. In Western European societies, in particular, the persistence of such elements as the prestige of the arts and the humanities, the low esteem in which vocational and technical education are held, the higher value attached to literary skills, and in general the traditional attitudes toward knowledge and the educated man, have been serious obstacles in accomplishing the aforementioned objectives at the individual or pedagogical level.

References

❖❖

General

Adams, Don, and Robert M. Bjork, *Education in Developing Areas*, David McKay, New York, 1969.

Kazamias, A. M., and B. G. Massialas, *Tradition and Change in Education: A Comparative Study*, Prentice-Hall, Englewood Cliffs, N.J., 1965.

Kazamias, A. M., and E. H. Epstein, Eds., *Schools in Transition: Essays in Comparative Education*, Allyn and Bacon, Boston, 1968.

King, E. J., *Education and Development in Western Europe*, Addison-Wesley, Reading, Mass., 1969.

Specific Countries

England

Baron, G., *Society, Schools and Progress in England*, Pergamon Press, Oxford, 1965.

Rubinstein, D., and B. Simon, *The Evolution of the Comprehensive School, 1926-1966*, Routledge & Kegan Paul, London, and Humanities Press, New York, 1969.

France

Capelle, Jean, *Tomorrow's Education: The French Experience* (translated and edited with an introduction and notes by W. D. Halls), Pergamon Press, Oxford, 1967.

Halls, W. D., *Society, Schools and Progress in France*, Pergamon Press, Oxford, 1965.

Wylie, Laurence, *Village in the Vaucluse*, Harvard University Press, Cambridge, Mass., 1957.

Soviet Union

Counts, G. S., *Khrushchev and the Central Committee Speak on Education*, University of Pittsburgh Press, Pittsburgh, Pa., 1959.

DeWitt, Nicholas, "Polytechnical Education and the Soviet School Reform," *Harvard Educational Review,* **30**, 2 (Spring 1960), 95-117.

Grant, Nigel, *Soviet Education,* Penguin Books, Baltimore, Md., 1964.

Tanzania

Resnick, Idrian N., Ed., *Tanzania: Revolution by Education,* Longmans of Tanzania, Nairobi, 1968.

Index

Abeles, Elvin, 560n
Abington versus Schempp, 160-161, 182n;
  see also Supreme Court, United
  States, decisions on education
Abrams, Morris H., 295-296, 306n
Absolute values, 220; *see also* Values
Academy, the, 9-10
Academic freedom, 92, 557-560
Accreditation, secondary schools and, 529-
  531
Acculturation, 101, 495
  enculturation and education, 50-51
  Mexican-Americans and, 103-105
Achievement test, 437; *see also* Tests
Adams, Don, 642
Adams, John Couch, 325
Addams, Jane, 29, 32
Adler, L., 364n
Adler, Mortimer, 232, 234
Administration, educational, 472-478
  secondary schools and, 525-527
Administrators, school, 106, 475-477
  Mexican-American, 110
  Negro, 125
Adolescents, 84; *see also* Youth
Adult Basic Education, 605
Adult Education Association, 608
Adult education, 539, 591-612
  business and industry and, 607-608
  definition and scope of, 598-601

federal government and, 601-602
higher, 602-605
public schools and, 605-606
social determinants of, 594-598
  changing nature of work force, 597-598
  growth in leisure time, 596-597
  knowledge explosion, 595-596
  population explosion, 594-595
Adulthood, childhood versus, 62-64
Aesthetics, education and, 223-225, 289-
  311
  expressivist theory of, 299-301
  formalist or objectivist theory, 301-307
  imitative theory of, 296-298
  realist theory of, 298-299
  significant form and, 303
  see also Values
Affluence and poverty, 419
Africa, 120
African education, 633-640
  colonialism, independence and, 633-636
  Tanzania and education for self-reliance,
  636-640
Afro-American, 122; *see also* Black; and
  Negro
Agriculture, United States Department of,
  467, 602
Aiken, Henry D., 304, 307-308
Aiken, Wilford M., 242n, 583n
Alabama, 118-119, 470